THE COLLEGE PRESS NIV COMMENTARY

MATTHEW

THE COLLEGE PRESS NIV COMMENTARY

MATTHEW

LARRY CHOUINARD

New Testament Series Co-Editors:

Jack Cottrell, Ph.D.
Cincinnati Bible Seminary

Tony Ash, Ph.D.
Abilene Christian University

COLLEGE PRESS
PUBLISHING COMPANY
Joplin, Missouri

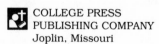

Printed and Bound in the United States of America

Library of Congress Cataloging-in-Publication Data
Chouinard, Larry, 1948–
Matthew / Larry Chouinard.
p. cm. – (The College Press NIV commentary)
Includes bibliographical references.
ISBN 0-89900-628-0
1. Bible. N.T. Matthew–Commentaries. I. Title. II. Series.
BS2575.3.C465 1997
226.2'077–dc21 97-43055
CIP

A WORD FROM THE PUBLISHER

Years ago a movement was begun with the dream of uniting all Christians on the basis of a common purpose (world evangelism) under a common authority (the Word of God). The College Press NIV Commentary Series is a serious effort to join the scholarship of two branches of this unity movement so as to speak with one voice concerning the Word of God. Our desire is to provide a resource for your study of the New Testament that will benefit you whether you are preparing a Bible School lesson, a sermon, a college course, or your own personal devotions. Today as we survey the wreckage of a broken world, we must turn again to the Lord and his Word, unite under his banner and communicate the life-giving message to those who are in desperate need. This is our purpose.

ABBREVIATIONS

ABD . . . . *Anchor Bible Dictionary*
AnBib . . . . . . *Analecta Biblica*
ANTJ . . . . . . *Arbeiten zum Neuen Testament und zum Judentum*
BAGD. . . . . . *A Greek-English Lexicon of the New Testament by Bauer, Arndt, Gingrich, and Danker*
BETL . . . . . . *Bibliotheca ephemeridum theologicarum lovaniensium*
Bib . . . . *Biblica*
BibRev . . . . . *Bible Review*
BSac . . . . *Bibliotheca Sacra*
BZNW . . . . . *Beheifte zur ZNW*
CBQ . . . . *Catholic Biblical Quarterly*
ConBNT. . . . *Coniectanea biblica, New Testament*
ConNT . . . . . *Coniectanea neotestamentica*
DJG . . . . *Dictionary of Jesus and the Gospels*
ETL . . . . *Ephemerides theologicai lovanienses*
ExpTim. . . . . *The Expository Times*
HTR. . . . . . . *Harvard Theological Review*
ICC. . . . . *International Critical Commentary*
IDB. . . . . *Interpreter's Dictionary of the Bible*
Int . . . . *Interpretation*
ISBE. . . . . . . *International Standard Bible Encyclopedia*
JBL. . . . . *Journal of Biblical Literature*
JETS. . . . . . . *Journal of the Evangelical Theological Society*
JSNT. . . . . . . *Journal for the Study of New Testament Theology*
LXX . . . . *Septuagint*
NIDNTT . . . *New International Dictionary of New Testament Theology*
NIGTC. . . . . *New International Greek Testament Commentary*
NIV . . . . *New International Version*
NovT . . . . . . *Novum Testamentum*
NT . . . . *New Testament*

NTM . . . . . . *New Testament Message*
NTS . . . . *New Testament Studies*
OT . . . . *Old Testament*
RevQ. . . . . . . *Revue de Qumran*
RQ . . . . *Restoration Quarterly*
SBLASP . . . . *Society of Biblical Literature Abstracts and Seminar Papers*
SBLDS . . . . . *SBL Dissertation Series*
SBLMS. . . . . *SBL Monograph Series*
SJT . . . . *Scottish Journal of Theology*
SNTSMS. . . . *Society for New Testament Studies Monograph Series*
Str-B . . . . *Kommentar zum Neuen Testament by Strack and Billerbeck*
TDNT. . . . . . *Theological Dictionary of the New Testament by Kittel and Friedrich*
TIM . . . . *Tradition and Interpretation in Matthew by Bornkamm, Barth, and Held*
TrinJ. . . . . . . *Trinity Journal*
TynBul . . . . . *Tyndale Bulletin*
UBSGNT . . . *United Bible Society Greek New Testament*
USQR. . . . . . *Union Seminary Quarterly Review*
WUNT . . . . . *Wissenschaftliche untersuchungen zum Neuen Testament*
ZNW . . . . . . *Zeitschrift für die neutestamentliche Wissenschaft*

INTRODUCTION

HISTORY OF INTERPRETATION

It may surprise the modern reader to realize that for the first two centuries of the Christian era, Matthew's Gospel prevailed as the most popular of the Gospel accounts. Not only was Matthew's text the most frequently quoted NT book among second century Christians,[1] in virtually all textual witnesses and canonical lists Matthew is placed first.

Several factors may have contributed to the premier position assigned Matthew's Gospel. Certainly its comprehensive detail and the systematic structuring of ethical and pastoral material contributed to the Gospel's favored place in the church. In addition, the Gospel's popularity was undoubtedly based upon its explicit Jewish tendencies that enabled the church to affirm its Jewish roots while at the same time distancing the Christian movement from the synagogue. In short, both in form and content, Matthew's Gospel provided second century Christianity with an eminently practical and useful compendium of what was foundational to the Christian faith.

The priority and dominance extended Matthew's Gospel prevailed as the consensus for roughly 1700 years, until the early decades of the nineteenth century. With the development of an historical consciousness, and the refinement of literary methodology, questions of historical reliability and Synoptic relationships dominated post-Enlightenment Gospel research. While the chronological priority of Matthew was not immediately challenged, the

[1]See the comprehensive survey of Edouard Massaux, *The Influence of the Gospel of Saint Matthew on Christian Literature before Saint Irenaeus*, trans. Norman J. Belval and Suzanne Heche (Macon, GA: University Press, 1990).

privileged position given Matthew began to erode as scholarship presupposed that Gospel composition demanded a movement from the "more primitive" to the "more advanced." Mark's size, inferior quality, and seemingly "primitive theology," suggested to many that it was Mark not Matthew that should be regarded as the oldest Gospel, and hence the most reliable for a reconstruction of the life and teachings of Jesus.[2] As a result, Matthew was gradually dismissed by many (esp. German scholarship), as a secondary development, being permeated by late and legendary additions (e.g., birth and infancy stories), representing more church tradition than a factual record of the life and teachings of Jesus.

The emerging nineteenth century consensus of the secondary character of Matthew received its most substantial endorsement in 1863 from H.J. Holtzmann, who argued that Mark wrote first and was used independently by Matthew and Luke. While subsequent defenders of Marcan priority have supplemented the theory with additional sources (e.g., Q, L, and M) to explain Synoptic relationships, the hypothesis that Mark is the earliest of the Gospel narratives has remained the dominant scholarly opinion for the past 100 years.[3]

The initial result of the emergence of Mark as the pivotal document to explain Synoptic relationships was a decline of interest in Matthew in the early decades of this century. It was to Mark, rather than Matthew that scholarship turned either to find raw materials from which to reconstruct the life and teachings of Jesus, or to penetrate to the earliest form of the tradition in order to elucidate the possible factors within the Christian communities that generated the rise and preservation of certain text-forms (Form Criticism). As long as the scholarly agenda was preoccupied with penetrating behind the Gospels to isolate sources or to reconstruct early Christian communities, Matthew's Gospel would remain only of secondary interest.

---

[2]As noted by W.R. Farmer, *The Synoptic Problem* (Dillsboro, NC: Western North Carolina Press, 1976), p. 1, the central issue in the eighteenth century was to establish a true chronology of Gospel materials to assure their historical accuracy.

[3]See Farmer, *The Synoptic Problem*; and H.H. Stoldt, *History and Criticism of the Marcan Hypothesis*, trans. D.L. Niewyk (Macon, GA: Mercer University, 1980).

Graham Stanton singles out the date of 1945 as marking a new phase in Matthean studies.[4] The first two decades after 1945 witness a number of studies addressing Matthean themes or sections of the Gospel that begin to call attention to the editorial skills and theological concerns of the Gospel's author. The shift to an emphasis on the role of the evangelist in his selection, arrangement, and modification of the material he received, brought renewed interest in Matthew as an effective communicator and sophisticated theologian (Redaction Criticism). However, such an assessment was ultimately grounded in the hypothesis of Marcan priority and the subsequent evaluation of how Matthew used Mark as his primary literary source. The result has been an exegetical method overly preoccupied with slight literary deviations from Mark, with little sensitivity to the interconnected sequence of events, and their contribution to the whole Gospel.

Recent years have witnessed a resurgence of studies on Matthew, with many books and articles concerned to elucidate Matthew's Gospel as a "unified narrative" or "story" told by a competent story-teller who organizes his thought into a coherent sequence of events. The new concern for the Gospels as literary masterpieces demands that the reader be attentive to how Matthew develops his themes and focuses his account on a retelling of the story of Jesus in a way that does not merely rehearse the past, but speaks meaningfully as a guide for Christian discipleship.

Rather than reading Matthew through the lens of other Gospels or a hypothetical reconstruction of the evangelist's sources, priority has shifted to the whole Gospel as a unified coherent narrative. It follows that whatever written or oral sources the evangelist may have had access to, the writer has so shaped his composition that it has a life of its own, discernable only by attention to the structure of the parts and their contribution to the whole.

In order to read and appreciate Matthew's story of Jesus one must be attentive to the codes and conventions that govern the

---

[4]Graham Stanton, "The Origin and Purpose of Matthew's Gospel: Matthean Scholarship from 1945 to 1980," *Aufstieg und Niedergang der romischen Welt* II.25.3., ed. H. Temporini and W. Haase (Berlin: Walter de Gruyter, 1983), p. 1893.

literary and social context of the first century. A coherent reading of any document demands an awareness of the literary rules that govern the various types of literature. Knowing the general category of literary genre of a text enables the reader to know what types of questions can legitimately be asked of the material. For example, if one is reading poetry, questions of factual accuracy or scientific precision may not be the most relevant inquiry for ascertaining a text's meaning. Knowing the genre of a writing enables one's understanding to be informed by the features and intentions that characterize the writing, and not by our modern expectations and concerns we may impose upon the text.

While Matthew's Gospel has certain affinities with the literary genres of biography and historiography, the Gospel is not strictly an historical biography. No Gospel writer was driven by an impulse simply to record the facts of what happened with strict chronological precision. In fact, one need only to read the Gospels side by side to see the freedom and creative manner with which each writer communicated his message. The authors have selected, arranged, and interpreted events, characters, and settings in the best way to communicate with their respective audiences. The result is four unique accounts of Jesus' life and teachings told from a particular "point of view," informed both by the primary events and the theological concerns and needs of the expanding church.

Matthew's Gospel builds reflectively upon the primary events to capture the significance of what happened in story form. An appreciation of the literary and communicative skills of the author enables one to recognize in the dramatic sequence of events a carefully constructed "plot." In this way the storyteller communicates his values and theological commitment and seeks to persuade the reader to accept his perspective.

COMPOSITION OF THE GOSPEL

Some issues and questions that may be extremely important for understanding one category of literature may contribute little to the understanding of another. For example, an informed interpretation of Paul's letters necessitates a reconstruction of the world that produced the text. The modern reader would need to know as much as possible about the author, destination of the letter, and the factors that gave rise to the text. The letter itself will constitute a prime source for acquiring such information.

However, when one approaches Gospel narratives with the same concerns the matter is complicated by the lack of information afforded by the text. The anonymity of the Gospels, alongside their silence concerning the place, time, and circumstances that may have generated their writings, necessitates that such historical inquiries be answered in terms of probability. What this means is that there is no direct access, via the text, to the historical author or primary recipients of his document. The difficulty is centered in the fact that the text is not primarily designed to function as a "window" through which to gain access into the mind and environment of the author and original readers. The author does not purport to tell his own story or that of his readers, but the story of Jesus of Nazareth. Fortunately, following the sequential development and sense of Matthew's story of Jesus does not depend on identifying with certainty the author or the historical and social matrix that may have prompted his writing.

In what follows, traditional introductory questions will be briefly discussed, alongside important insights afforded by literary theorists who focus on the Gospels as narratives.

A. AUTHORSHIP

The anonymity of the canonical Gospels necessitates heavy reliance on external evidence as a point of departure to establish Gospel authorship. The external testimony from the second century is virtually unanimous that Matthew the tax collector authored the Gospel attributed to him. Even before explicit patristic testimony regarding Gospel authorship there is convincing evidence that no Gospel ever circulated without an appropriate heading or title (e.g., ΚΑΤΑ ΜΑΘΘΑΙΟΝ, "according to Matthew"), identifying the person thought to be the author. The common assumption that the Gospels circulated anonymously until the mid-second century when titles were finally affixed to them has been seriously challenged by Martin Hengel.[5] While certain details of Hengel's theory regarding the origins of Gospel headings have been challenged, the lack of variation in the second-century tradition regarding Matthean authorship could well owe its origin to the time when the Gospels first began to circulate among the Christian communities.

The earliest patristic source addressing Gospel authorship comes from Papias, the Bishop of Hierapolis (ca. 60-130), whose comments are available only in quotations preserved by Eusebius, Bishop of Caesarea (ca. 260-340, *H.E.* 3.39.14-16). Eusebius' citation of Papias regarding Matthean authorship has been subject to various interpretations dependent upon the translation of key terms. The citation reads:

> Matthew collected (συνετάξατο, *synetaxato*, "composed," "compiled," "arranged") the oracles (τὰ λόγια, *ta logia*, "sayings," "gospel") in the Hebrew language (διαλέκτῳ, *dialektō*, "Hebrew or Aramaic language," "Semitic style") and each interpreted (ἡρμήνευσεν, *hērmēneusen*, "interpreted," "translated," "transmitted") them as best he could (Eusebius, *H.E.* 3.39.16).

It appears that patristic testimony subsequent to Papias was dependent upon his testimony and thus perpetuated the tradition of Matthean authorship alongside the notion of an original Semitic version. The testimonies of Irenaeus (*Adv. Haer.* 3.1.1), Pantaenus (quoted in *H.E.* 5.10.3), Origen (quoted in *H.E.* 6.25.4), Eusebius himself (*H.E.* 3.24.6), Epiphanius (quoted in *Adv. Haer.* 29.19.4; 30.3.7), Cyril of Jerusalem (*Catecheses* 14.15), Jerome (*DeVir.* III.3), as well as Gregory of Nazianzus (329-389), Chrysostom (347-407), Augustine (354-430), and Syrian and Coptic authorities are all unanimous in affirming that Matthew authored the first Gospel originally in a Semitic language.[6] However, since the tradition seems ultimately to rest upon the view of Papias, as cited by

---

[5]See Martin Hengel, *Studies in the Gospel of Mark* (ET, London: SCM, 1985), pp. 64-84.

[6]For a convenient summary see John Wenham, *Redating Matthew, Mark and Luke* (Downers Grove, IL: InterVarsity Press, 1992), pp. 116-135.

Eusebius, the accumulated evidence of patristic testimony, in the view of some, has very little independent worth. Especially since the idea of an original Semitic Matthew, from which our Greek Matthew has been translated has been challenged on textual and linguistic grounds. Matthew simply does not read like translated Greek. These and other difficulties with the view of Papias[7] have resulted in many dismissing all patristic testimony concerning Matthean authorship.

While much critical opinion has assumed that Papias' errant view of an original Semitic Matthew discounts his testimony about Matthew being the author, in recent times the evidence afforded by the testimony of Papias has been reassessed. On the one hand, some scholars have argued that the terms Εβραΐδι διαλέκτῳ (*Ebraidi dialektō*), do not refer to the Hebrew or Aramaic language, but rather to a Jewish style or literary form. In this view, Papias would be referring to Matthew's penchant for Semitic themes and devices, not an original Semitic Gospel. Others have rejected such an interpretation as an unnatural way to read the passage from Papias, and prefer to acknowledge that Papias was simply wrong when he claimed that Matthew was originally written in a Semitic language. However, such an admission does not warrant the complete dismissal of the testimony of Papias concerning the authorship of Matthew. One must still explain how Matthew's name became attached to the first Gospel. The obscurity and relative lack of prominence of the Apostle Matthew argues against the view that the early church would pseudonymously attribute the Gospel to Matthew. Surely, patristic tradition had some basis for attributing the Gospel to Matthew. Therefore, as noted by Davies and Allison, "the simplistic understanding of Papias which dismisses him out of hand must be questioned if not abandoned."[8]

There is nothing inherent in the Gospel itself that convincingly argues against Matthean authorship. Contrary to the view of a few, the decided Jewish flavor of the Gospel argues decisively for the

[7]For a full discussion see R.T. France, *Matthew: Evangelist and Teacher* (Grand Rapids: Zondervan, 1984), pp. 53-66.

[8]W.D. Davies and Dale C. Allison, *The Gospel According to Saint Matthew,* ICC (Edinburgh: T&T Clark, 1988), 1:16.

author of the first Gospel being a Jew.[9] Other scholars have noted that Matthew's background and training as a "tax collector" along with other professional skills offers a plausible explanation for the Gospel's sophisticated literary form and attention to detail. Certainly the combined weight of external and internal considerations make the traditional view of Matthean authorship a reasonable, if not a most plausible position. However, in the words of R.T. France there is "an inevitable element of subjectivity in such judgments."[10] Not only is hard data difficult to come by to establish the authorship of any of the Gospels, what is available is often subject to diverse but equally credible explanations. It follows that while the issue of authorship is an intriguing historical problem, it is extremely doubtful that any consensus will ever emerge given the nature of the available evidence.

The question must be raised whether the veracity of the first Gospel or its interpretation are ultimately dependent upon one's verdict concerning authorship. While one's theological bias concerning authorship may influence how the text is evaluated, the two issues are not integrally connected. Since the first Gospel offers very little (if any) insight into the identity of its historical author, recreating the figure behind the Gospel is neither relevant or particularly important for understanding Matthew's story of Jesus. Thus, while I see no compelling reason to abandon the traditional attribution of Matthean authorship to the first Gospel, no significant exegetical or theological concern hangs on the issue.

B. NARRATION OF THE STORY

Of much greater importance than deciding the identity of the author, is an evaluation of the way the author has decided to present his story of Jesus. In literary terms the way a story gets told is called "point of view."[11] A storyteller may tell his story in the first

---

[9]See extensive treatment by Davies and Allison, *Matthew,* 1:17-33.

[10]France, *Matthew*, p. 77.

[11]For detailed discussion see Jack D. Kingsbury, *Matthew as Story*, 2nd ed. (Philadelphia: Fortress Press, 1989), pp. 1-42.

person (i.e., "I"), and portray himself as one of the characters in the story. From a first person point of view the storyteller would necessarily be limited to what he personally has experienced or learned from other characters. Matthew's story is told in a third person narration, wherein the storyteller is not a participant in the story, but refers to characters within the story as "he," "she," or "they." From such a vantage point the Matthean narrator provides the reader with an informational advantage over story characters, and thereby, situates the reader in an advantageous position for evaluating events and characters in the story.

Perhaps the most prominent characteristic of a third person narration is the storyteller's ability to provide the reader with insights which are not normally available to one in real life. His ability to move inside his characters to reveal their innermost thoughts, feelings, emotions, and motivations, enables the reader to use these insights to form evaluations and opinions about characters and events within the story. For example, the narrator reveals when the disciples are amazed (8:29; 21:20), fearful (14:30; 17:6), sorrowful (26:22), filled with grief (17:23), and indignant (26:8). He knows when they understand (16:12; 17:13), and when they doubt (28:17). The overall impact of these insights enables the reader to better evaluate the traits exhibited by the disciples.

Similar insights are provided into the thoughts, emotions, and motivations of minor characters in the story. The inner thoughts of Joseph (1:19), Herod (2:3), the crowds (7:28; 22:33; 9:8; 12:13; 15:31), the woman (9:21), Herod the tetrarch (14:59), Judas (27:3), Pilate (27:14,18), the centurion (27:54), and the reaction of the women at the tomb (28:4,8) are all accessible to the Matthean narrator. The narrator even supplies the reader with inside information about the thoughts and motivations of the Jewish leaders (2:3; 9:3; 12:14; 21:45-46; 26:3-5; 12:10; 16:1; 19:3; 22:15). These insights function to establish in the mind of the reader the antagonist of the story.

The Matthean narrator is also not bound by time or space in his coverage of the story. Matthew provides the reader access to private conversations between Herod and the Magi (2:3-8), John and Jesus (3:13-15), Jesus and Satan (4:1-11), the disciples (16:7), Peter and Jesus (16:23), Judas and the chief priest (26:14-16; 26:40), and Pilate and the chief priest (27:62-64). He makes known to the reader the private decisions made by the chief priest and the Sanhedrin (26:59-60), and the plan of the chief priest and elders concerning the disappearance of the body (28:12-15). The narrator is present when Jesus prays alone, while at the same time he knows the difficulties of the disciples on the sea (14:22-24). He easily takes the reader from the courtroom of Pilate to the courtyard of Peter's denial (26:70f.), and eventually to the scene at the cross (27:45). For the most part, the narrator in Matthew's story stays close to Jesus, and views events and characters in terms of how they affect his main character.

Whoever the actual historical author may be, it is clear that the Matthean storyteller narrates his Gospel in a way to reliably guide his readers through the story so as to properly evaluate events and characters. On occasion the narrator will interrupt the flow of the story in order to provide the reader with an explicit comment or explanation. These intrusions may take the form of various types of descriptions (e.g., 3:4; 17:2; 28:3-4; 27:28-31), summaries (e.g., 4:23-25; 9:35-38; 12:15-16; 14:14; 15:29-31), or explicit interpretive commentary (1:22-23, 2:15, 17-18, 23; 4:15-16; 8:17; 12:17-21; 13:35; 21:4-5; 27:9-10). Detecting the narrator's voice in the story enables the reader to be sensitive to the manner in which Matthew instructs, leads, and encourages the reader to adopt a particular point of view.

SETTING OF THE GOSPEL

Traditional approaches to Gospel introduction usually treat under the heading of "setting" such issues as the date and place of the Gospel's writing, alongside the identity and problems confronting the community addressed. It is important to remember that practically speaking our exclusive source for information about the time and circumstantial factors generating the Gospel's production come only from the Gospel itself. No explicit outside information speaks directly to the issue of the social and historical conditions of the Gospel's primary readers. Essentially, scholarly efforts to establish a life-setting for the writing of the Gospel must search the Gospel for possible clues that hint at the time and circumstances of the writing. The fact that, although reading the same evidence, scholarly proposals for the setting of Matthew's Gospel have resulted in reconstructions that are opposed to one another should give one caution about dogmatic claims in such areas.[12]

A. DATE

Efforts to recover the environmental setting that best explains the form and content of Matthew's Gospel have not resulted in a scholarly consensus. Concerning the date of the Gospel's composition scholars are divided into two broad proposals. The majority view is that Matthew was written after Mark sometime between the dates of A.D. 80-100. However, the arguments adduced to establish such a dating scheme are largely based upon prior judgments concerning the order of Gospel composition or hypothetical reconstructions of developments in the first century. Pivotal to the post-70 dating of Matthew is the contention that Matthew knew and used Mark as a major source for the writing of his Gospel. Since the consensus of scholarly judgment dates Mark in the 60s, it is therefore likely that Matthew composed his Gospel sometime after A.D. 70. Of course, if one rejects Marcan priority or the suggested date for Marcan composition, the argument fails to be convincing.

A post-70 date has also been assumed based upon Matthew's explicit language concerning the destruction of Jerusalem and his references to the "church" (16:18; 18:17). Such language is thought to be anachronistic and therefore indicative of a post-70 composition. The reference to a "king" in the parable of the wedding feast who "sent his army and destroyed those murderers and burned their city" (22:7), appears to reflect historical knowledge of Jerusalem's destruction retrojected into Jesus' ministry as prophecy. However, apart from the fact of whether Jesus could predict Jerusalem's fall, the wording of 22:7, as France observes, "is precisely the sort of language one might expect in a genuine prediction of

[12]For a convenient list of proposals see Davies and Allison, *Matthew*, 1:138-139.

political annihilation in the Jewish context, and does not depend on a specific knowledge of how things in fact turned out in A.D. 70."[13] There also is no need to read a developed ecclesiology into Jesus' references to the "church." The term ἐκκλησία (*ekklēsia*) in Matthew says nothing about church order, and with the communal imagery attached to the term in Jewish circles (cf. Qumran), it becomes entirely credible that Jesus could speak of his disciples as constituting an *ekklēsia*.

Perhaps the most heavily relied upon argument for dating Matthew in the last decades of the first century is the decided Jewish polemic that seemingly dominates the first Gospel. It is thought that formative Judaism in the post-70 period provides the most suitable background for Matthew's portrayal of the Jewish leaders and his underlying view of Israel. After the destruction of the temple in A.D. 70 it was the Pharisaic movement that emerged as the normative form of Judaism. Pharisaism was particularly suited to bring stability and a renewed sense of Jewish identity after the tragedy of A.D. 70. The Pharisees saw themselves as "the most accurate interpreters of the law" (see Josephus, *JW* 1.5.1; 2.8.14; *Life* 38.191), and definers of both the social and cultic boundaries delimiting the covenanted people of God. The community addressed by Matthew's Gospel is thought to be a rival to a post-70 formative Judaism, having endured severe hostility and rejection by official Judaism.

However, the evidence does not warrant the supposition that Matthew's community has severed all contact with the Jewish community. Furthermore, not enough is known about pre-70 Pharisaism to emphatically deny a setting for Matthew's Gospel before Jerusalem's destruction. Indeed, an impressive list of scholars have cogently argued for a pre-70 dating of Matthew.[14] Not only does such a view have solid patristic evidence, some passages in Matthew may be intended to imply that the temple was still standing at the

---

[13]See France, *Matthew*, p. 84.

[14]For example see Robert H. Gundry, *Matthew: A Commentary on His Literary and Theological Art* (Grand Rapids: Eerdmans, 1982), pp. 602-606; France, *Matthew*, pp. 88-91; D.A. Carson, "Matthew," in *Expositor's Bible Commentary*, vol. 8 (Grand Rapids: Zondervan, 1984), p. 21; Leon Morris, *The Gospel According to Matthew* (Grand Rapids: Eerdmans, 1992), pp. 8-11.

time of the Gospel's writing (cf. 5:23-29; 12:5-7; 17:23; 16:22; 26:60-61). It appears that the evidence is not sufficiently decisive so as to completely discredit all competitive views. Fortunately, understanding Matthew's story of Jesus is not dependent upon reconstructing the historical context from which the Gospel emerged.

B. PLACE OF ORIGIN

Even less important for a competent reading of the first Gospel involves the effort to decide the Gospel's precise place of origin. Because of its large Jewish community and strategic role in the Gentile mission most Matthean scholars have opted for Antioch of Syria as the Gospel's place of origin. Other proposals have included Jerusalem, Alexandria, Caesarea, Phoenicia, and simply "east of the Jordan." While certain evidence may tend to weigh in favor of one provenance over another, in the final analysis we cannot be certain where Matthew's Gospel was composed. Nevertheless, as observed by France, deciding "the geographical location in which the Gospel originated is probably the least significant for a sound understanding of the text."[15] Much more relevant to the interpretation of the gospel is the dimension given the discussion of "setting" by a literary reading of the first Gospel.

C. NARRATIVE WORLD

In literary terms the discussion of "setting" does not involve the delineation of factors generating the text, but rather the descriptive context or background in which the action of the story transpires. Settings, as described by the narrator, are like stage props in a theatrical production. Oftentimes, the narrator's description of the place, time, or social conditions in which action takes place is charged with subtle nuances that may generate a certain atmosphere with important symbolic significance. For example, early in Matthew's story the narrator relates places and events to create a distinct atmosphere from which to evaluate his central character,

[15]France, *Matthew*, p. 95.

Jesus. The story opens with a series of events that are calculated to evoke memories of Israel's past, and thereby to highlight the significance of the times inaugurated by Jesus. By means of a genealogy, cosmic signs, dream-revelations, the appearance of the "angel of the Lord," and the repeated reference to prophetic fulfillment, the narrator highlights God's renewed involvement with his people and the climactic nature of the times realized in Jesus. The locations of Jerusalem, Bethlehem, and Egypt evoke feelings of continuity between Jesus' history and that of Israel's. Other locations such as the "desert" and "mountain" function to create a certain aura around events and characters in the story. Later in the story specific locations such as "synagogue," the "sea," and the "temple" all contribute to a distinct atmosphere from which to evaluate the course of events. While real-life settings of the author and his readers can only be reproduced in terms of probability, the temporal and spatial settings established in the story provide an integral context for interpreting Matthew's story.

THE LITERARY CHARACTER OF MATTHEW

A. LITERARY AND RHETORICAL SKILL

Since Matthew's text would have been handwritten without systematic punctuation or modern techniques for delineating structural features such as bold print, underlining, paragraph indention, or chapter headings, any clues for discerning the structure and nature of the composition is dependent upon "verbal clues" within the narrative itself. Within both Hebrew and classical traditions communication on a literary level assumed a level of competency in conventional communicative techniques. While NT authors may not have been formally trained in rhetoric, an effective exchange of ideas demands some awareness of conventional patterns for communication. A study of Matthew's literary style puts emphasis on the literary devices he employs to lead the reader to experience his story in a certain way.

Reading Matthew's story (whether orally before an audience, or in private), would have demanded that the reader attend to the various structural features which might illumine the meaning and flow of the narrative. Some of these literary strategies function on a broader structural level providing the text with a sense of progression and cohesion (e.g., see the formulaic phrases in 7:28; 11:1; 13:53; 19:1; 26:1; and 4:17; 16:21). However, most structural features primarily contribute to a sense of cohesion within smaller textual units. These features may highlight or bracket unifying themes by opening and closing distinct units with similar words or phrases (see, e.g., 4:23-24 and 9:35); build anticipation by foreshadowing subsequent events (e.g., ch. 2 foreshadows the passion narrative); or stimulate reflection and a sense of development in the story by verbal repetition and episodic similarities (cf. 8:23-27/14:22-33; 9:27-31/20:29-34; 9:32-34/12:22-34; 14:13-21/15:32-38). These elements along with Matthew's fondness for grouping materials according to a thematic or even numerical scheme,[16] are indicative of an environment largely educated through oral proclamation not the written word.[17] Matthew's compositional scheme greatly facilitated learning by providing the listener (or reader) with a coherent and orderly presentation that aided comprehension and memorization.

The meticulous structural concerns, both in the whole and the smaller details of Matthew, have been widely recognized by scholarship. However, as we shall see in the next section, there is great diversity with respect to the overall structural pattern of the first Gospel. The difficulty lies with going from clearly delineated structural features in the smaller units of text, to the use of the same devices to explain the total composition. Often the analysis seems forced and unable to fit the details into a single coherent pattern. It may not always be easy to identify the precise contribution that a particular literary device makes to the overall composition of a literary work, and certainly there always exists the danger of reading too much into a text by artificially imposing symmetrical patterns where none exist. However, these problems are overcome by a

---

[16]See especially his fondness for threes and sevens; as documented by Davies and Allison, *Matthew*, 1:85-87.

[17]See Paul J. Achtemeier, "Omne verbum sonat: The New Testament and the Oral Environment of Late Western Antiquity," *JBL* 109 (Spring 1990), 3-27.

greater sensitivity to the nature and function of literary devices, and not by ignoring these features of a text. The question remains concerning what features might provide clues to the overall structure of Matthew's Gospel.

B. STRUCTURAL-PLOT

Consideration of Matthew's skill in the smaller portions of his text has stimulated numerous efforts to locate structural indications that may provide the organizing pattern for the entire Gospel. Structural appraisals of Matthew's Gospel usually begin with the discovery of a literary device or formulaic expression that appears to be unique to the evangelist. However, while scholars may agree on the existence of a literary device or formula, they may diverge widely concerning the function or theological significance of a literary feature. For example, although the expressions καὶ ἐγένετο ὅτε ἐτέλεσεν ὁ Ἰησοῦς (*kai egeneto hote etelesen ho Iēsous*, "and when Jesus had finished;" 7:28; 11:1; 13:53; 19:1; 26:1), and ἀπὸ τότε ἤρξατο ὁ Ἰησοῦς (*apo tote erxato ho Iēsous*, "from that time Jesus began," 4:17; 16:21) are recognized to be structurally significant, it is difficult to establish that Matthew consciously adopted these expressions as the organizational key to his entire Gospel. As helpful as these phrases are for marking off the major discourses of Jesus or highlighting major new developments in the story, neat structural schemes based upon repeated formulae cannot do justice to the subtle twists and turns of the dramatic flow of Matthew's story.

Several scholars have centered on Matthew's use of Mark to determine the structure of his Gospel. Attention has been called to the peculiar Matthean organization of 4:12-13:58 in contrast to the faithful following of Marcan order in 14:1-28:20. Certainly a source-critical study of Matthew must account for the seemingly independent structural form and sequence in the first half of the Gospel as opposed to the latter half. However, it is doubtful that Matthew intended his readers to compare his Gospel with Mark in order to understand his structural scheme. If Matthew could clearly structure patterns on a smaller scale, independent of Mark, why not on a larger scale? Furthermore, there are too many structural peculiarities even in the second half of the Gospel to assume that Matthew merely succumbed to a slavish reproduction of Mark in the second half of his Gospel.

More recent investigations have delineated the Gospel's structure in terms of how the individual events or episodes connect sequentially to form a discernable plot.[18] It is the organizing principle of plot which determines the incidents selected, their arrangement, and how the sequence of events or episodes are to impact the reader. Given the episodic and thematic flavor of Matthew's narrative, his plot development does not exhibit a linear tightness or the flair for the dramatic found in other narratives (cf. Mark). Nevertheless, Matthew does tell a story, and thus the various episodes are carefully interrelated by causal and thematic developments. There are definite major and minor story lines and character development, with certain episodes marking key turning points in the unfolding drama. An analysis of plot has the advantage of moving the discussion away from isolated literary devices or contrived symmetrical patterns, to a consideration of how the sequence of events and portrayal of characters connect meaningfully to tell a continuous and coherent story.

Matthew's story is organized around several narrative blocks comprised of events that are interconnected according to a particular emphasis or theme. The unifying factor giving coherence to the overall sequence of events is the explicit and implicit presence of the central character Jesus in virtually every episode. Within this story-form events of similar nature are often clustered or repeated for their accumulative impact, as various themes are reinforced and developed. An analysis of the sequence and function of Matthew's major narrative blocks enables the reader to discern an overall progression of events according to a consciously constructed plot. The following seven narrative blocks provide the story with a clear sense of dramatic progression:

---

[18]For discussions on "plot" consult the following essays: Frank Matera, "The Plot of Matthew's Gospel," *CBQ* 49 (April 1987), 233-253; H.J.B. Combrink, "The Structure of Matthew's Gospel as Narrative," *TynBul* 34 (1983), 61-90; M.A. Powell, "The Plot and Subplots of Matthew's Gospel," *NTS* 38 (1992), 187-204; Warren Carter, "Kernels and Narrative Blocks: The Structure of Matthew's Gospel," *CBQ* 54 (July 1992), 463-481; J.D. Kingsbury, "The Plot of Matthew's Story," *Int* 46 (October 1992), 347-356.

1:1–4:16	Establishing the identity and role of Jesus, the protagonist of the story.
4:17–11:1	Jesus embarks upon a ministry of teaching and healing to manifest God's saving presence in Israel.
11:2–16:20	While faulty interpretations of Jesus' ministry lead to misunderstanding and repudiation, the disciples, through divine revelation, are provided special insight into Jesus' person and mission.
16:21–20:34	During Jesus' journey to Jerusalem he engages his disciples in explicit discussion concerning the ultimate values, priorities, and intentions of his messianic mission.
21:1–25:46	Upon entering Jerusalem Jesus' actions and teachings lead to conflict and rejection by the Jewish authorities.
26:1–27:50	While hostility and misunderstanding coalesce in betrayal, desertion, and death, Jesus is resolved to consciously and voluntarily fulfill the divine plan.
27:51–28:20	God ultimately vindicates his Son as evidenced by cosmic signs and by raising him from the dead and giving him authority to commission his disciples to a worldwide mission.

OUTLINE

I. ESTABLISHING THE IDENTITY AND ROLE OF JESUS THE CHRIST – 1:1–4:16

- **A. Genealogy of Jesus** – 1:1-17
- **B. The Annunciation to Joseph** – 1:18-25
- **C. The Infancy of Jesus** – 2:1-23
  1. The Gentile Pilgrimage – 2:1-12
  2. The Messiah's Exile and Exodus – 2:13-23
- **D. The Mission and Message of John the Baptist** – 3:1-12
- **E. The Baptism and Commission of Jesus** – 3:13-17
- **F. The Testing of the Son** – 4:1-11
- **G. Introducing the Ministry of Jesus** – 4:12-16

II. GOD'S SAVING PRESENCE IN THE MIDST OF HIS PEOPLE – 4:17–10:42

- **A. Programmatic Heading: Proclamation of the Kingdom** – 4:17
- **B. Call of the Disciples** – 4:18-22
- **C. Programmatic Summary** – 4:23-25
- **D. Sermon on the Mount: Ministry in Word** – 5:1–7:29
  1. The Setting – 5:1-2
  2. The Beatitudes – 5:3-12
  3. Salt and Light – 5:13-16
  4. Jesus and the Law – 5:17-20
  5. Practicing Greater Righteousness Toward One's Neighbor – 5:21-48
     - a. Murder – 5:21-26
     - b. Adultery – 5:27-30
     - c. Divorce – 5:31-32
     - d. Oaths – 5:33-37
     - e. An Eye for an Eye – 5:38-42
     - f. Love Your Enemies – 5:43-48

6. Practicing Greater Righteousness Before God – 6:1-18
   a. Summary – 6:1
   b. Giving to the Needy – 6:2-4
   c. Prayer – 6:5-15
   d. Fasting – 6:16-18
7. The Priorities and Values of the Greater Righteousness – 6:19-34
   a. Treasures in Heaven – 6:19-24
   b. Worry – 6:25-34
8. The Conduct of Greater Righteousness – 7:1-12
   a. Judging Others – 7:1-5
   b. Honor What Is Valuable – 7:6
   c. Ask, Seek, Knock – 7:7-11
   d. The Golden Rule – 7:12
9. The Call for Decision – 7:13-27
   a. The Narrow and Wide Gates – 7:13-14
   b. A Tree and Its Fruit – 7:15-23
   c. The Wise and Foolish Builders – 7:24-27
10. Conclusion – 7:28-29

E. Ministry in Deed – 8:1–9:34
1. Cleansing of a Leper – 8:1-4
2. Request of a Gentile Centurion – 8:5-13
3. Peter's Mother-in-Law – 8:14-15
4. Summary and Fulfillment Citation – 8:16-17
5. Two Would-Be Followers – 8:18-22
6. Stilling of the Storm – 8:23-27
7. The Gadarene Demoniacs – 8:28-34
8. Healing of the Paralytic – 9:1-8
9. Jesus' Association with Tax Collectors and Sinners – 9:9-13
10. Question on Fasting – 9:14-17
11. Raising the Ruler's Daughter and Cleansing the Unclean Woman – 9:18-26
12. Healing Two Blind Men – 9:27-31
13. Healing of a Deaf Mute – 9:32-34

F. A Call to Mission – 9:35–10:4

G. The Missionary Discourse – 10:5-42
1. Instructions for Mission – 10:5-15

B. Walking on the Water – 14:22-33
C. Summary: Healings at Gennesaret – 14:34-36
D. Jesus and the Teachings of the Pharisees – 15:1-20
E. The Canaanite Woman – 15:21-28
F. Feeding of the Four Thousand – 15:29-39
G. Request for a Sign – 16:1-4
H. The Leaven of the Pharisees and Saducees – 16:5-12
I. Confession at Caesarea Philippi – 16:13-20

V. THE WAY OF THE CROSS – 16:21–20:34
A. The Things of God Versus the Things of Men – 16:21-28
B. Transfiguration – 17:1-8
C. The Coming Elijah – 17:9-13
D. The Power of Faith – 17:14-21
E. The Second Passion Prediction – 17:22-23
F. Jesus and the Temple Tax – 17:24-27
G. Fourth Discourse: Life in the Christian Community – 18:1-35
1. Becoming Like a Child – 18:1-5
2. Avoiding Offense – 18:6-9
3. Value of the "Little Ones" – 18:10-14
4. Reconciling an Offending Brother – 18:15-20
5. Importance of Forgiveness – 18:21-35

H. Transition from Galilee to Judea – 19:1-2
I. Marriage and Divorce – 19:3-9
J. The Bewildered Response of the Disciples – 19:10-12
K. The Little Children – 19:13-15
L. The Rich Young Man – 19:16-22
M. Wealth, Reward and Discipleship – 19:23-30
N. The Generous Landowner – 20:1-16
O. Third Passion Prediction – 20:17-19
P. Requests on Behalf of the Sons of Zebedee – 20:20-28
Q. Two Blind Men Receive Sight – 20:29-34

VI. CONFLICT IN JERUSALEM – 21:1–25:46
A. Jesus' Entry into Jerusalem – 21:1-11
B. Demonstration in the Temple – 21:12-17
C. The Fig Tree – 21:18-22
D. The Authority Question – 21:23-27

BIBLIOGRAPHY

SELECTED COMMENTARIES:

Albright, W.F. and C.S. Mann. *Matthew*. AB. Garden City: Doubleday, 1971.

Beare, Francis Wright. *The Gospel According to Matthew*. San Francisco: Harper and Row, 1981.

Blomberg, Craig L. *Matthew*. New American Commentary 22. Nashville: Broadman, 1992.

Carson, D.A. "Matthew." In *The Expositor's Bible Commentary*, 8:3-599. Edited by Frank Gaebelein. 12 vols. Grand Rapids: Zondervan, 1984.

Davies, Margaret. *Matthew Readings: A New Biblical Commentary*. Sheffield, U.K.: JSOT Press/Sheffield Academic Press, 1993.

Davies, W.D. and Dale C. Allison. *Introduction and Commentary on the Gospel According to Saint Matthew I-VII*. Vol. 1 of *A Critical and Exegetical Commentary on the Gospel According to Saint Matthew*. International Critical Commentaries. 3 vols. Edinburgh: T&T Clark, 1988.

__________. *Introduction and Commentary on Matthew VIII-XVIII*. Vol. 2 of *A Critical and Exegetical Commentary on the Gospel According to Saint Matthew*. International Critical Commentaries. 3 vols. Edinburgh: T&T Clark, 1991.

France, R.T. *Matthew*. Tyndale New Testament Commentaries. Grand Rapids: Eerdmans, 1985.

Gardner, Richard B. *Matthew.* Believers Church Bible Commentary. Scottdale, PA: Herald Press, 1991.

Garland, David. *Reading Matthew: A Literary and Theological Commentary on the First Gospel.* New York: Crossroad, 1993.

Gundry, Robert. *Matthew: A Commentary on His Literary and Theological Art.* Grand Rapids: Eerdmans, 1982.

Hagner, Donald. *Matthew 1-13.* Word Biblical Commentary 33A. Dallas: Word, 1993.

____________. *Matthew 14-28.* Word Biblical Commentary 33B. Dallas: Word, 1995.

Harrington, D.J. *The Gospel of Matthew.* Sacra Pagina 1. Collegeville, MN: Liturgical, 1991.

Hill, David. *The Gospel of Matthew.* New Century Bible. Grand Rapids: Eerdmans, 1972.

Keener, Craig S. *Matthew.* The IVP New Testament Commentary Series. Ed. Grant R. Osborne. Downers Grove, IL: InterVarsity Press, 1997.

Luz, U. *Matthew 1-7.* Minneapolis: Fortress, 1989.

Malina, Bruce J. and Richard L. Rohrbaugh. *Social Science Commentary on the Synoptic Gospels.* Minneapolis: Augsburg Fortress, 1992.

Meier, J.P. *The Vision of Matthew.* New York: Crossroad, 1979, 1991.

Morris, Leon. *The Gospel According to Matthew.* Grand Rapids: Eerdmans, 1992.

Patte, Daniel. *The Gospel According to Matthew: A Structural Commentary on Matthew's Faith.* Philadelphia: Fortress, 1987.

Schweizer, Eduard. *The Good News According to Matthew.* Translated by David E. Green. Atlanta: John Knox Press, 1975.

SELECTED STUDIES:

Allison, Dale C. *The New Moses: A Matthean Typology*. Minneapolis: Fortress, 1993.

Bauer, D.R. *The Structure of Matthew's Gospel: A Study in Literary Design*. JSNTSup 31. Sheffield: Almond, 1988.

Borg, Marcus. *Conflict, Holiness, and Politics in the Teachings of Jesus*. New York: Edwin Mellen Press, 1984.

France, R.T. *Matthew: Evangelist and Teacher*. Grand Rapids: Zondervan, 1989.

Hill, David. "Son and Servant: An Essay on Matthean Christology." *JSNT* 6 (1980) 2-16.

Kingsbury, Jack D. *Matthew As Story*. 2d ed. Philadelphia: Fortress, 1988.

Lohr, C. "Oral Techniques in the Gospel of Matthew." *CBQ* 23 (1961): 339-352.

Luz, U. *The Theology of the Gospel of Matthew*. Translated by J. Bradford Robinson. Cambridge: Cambridge University Press, 1995.

Matera, Frank. "The Plot of Matthew's Gospel." *CBQ* 49 (1987): 233-253.

____________. *Passion Narratives and Gospel Theologies*. New York: Paulist, 1986.

Powell, M.A. *God With Us: A Pastoral Theology of Matthew's Gospel*. Minneapolis: Fortress, 1995.

Senior, D. *The Passion of Jesus in the Gospel of Matthew*. Wilmington: Michael Glazier, 1985.

____________. *What Are They Saying About Matthew?* Revised and Expanded Edition. New York: Paulist Press, 1996.

Stanton, Graham. *A Gospel For a New People: Studies in Matthew.* Edinburgh: T&T Clark, 1992.

__________. "The Origin and Purpose of Matthew's Gospel: Matthean Scholarship from 1945 to 1980." In *ANRW* II.25.3. Edited by W.Haase. Pages 1889-1895. Berlin and New York: Walter de Gruyter, 1985.

Verseput, Donald J. "The Title Son of God in Matthew's Gospel." *NTS* 33 (1987): 532-556.

Westerholm, Stephen. *Jesus and Scribal Authority.* ConNT 10. Lund, Sweden: CWK Gleerup, 1978.

Wilkens, M.J. *The Concept of Discipleship in Matthew's Gsopel as Reflected in the Use of the Term Mathētēs.* Leiden: E.J. Brill, 1988.

Witherup, Ronald D. "The Death of Jesus and the Rising of the Saints: Matthew 27:51-54 in Context." *SBLASP.* Pages 574-585. Atlanta: Scholars Press, 1987.

Wright, N.T. *Jesus and the Victory of God.* Minneapolis: Fortress Press, 1996.

__________. *The New Testament and the People of God.* Minneapolis: Fortress Press, 1992.

MATTHEW 1

I. ESTABLISHING THE IDENTITY AND ROLE OF JESUS THE CHRIST (1:1–4:16)

The opening scenes of Matthew's Gospel are fundamental for molding first impressions, creating certain moods and expectations, establishing thematic concerns, and foreshadowing the course of subsequent events. Matthew has chosen to open his story by disclosing to the reader explicit information concerning the origin, nature, and role of his central character, Jesus. It is therefore no accident that at the beginning of the story the reader encounters the greatest concentration of normative affirmations concerning Jesus' identity and mission.

On the one hand, explicit names and titles cast Jesus as Israel's long awaited Messiah: Son of David (1:1); Son of Abraham (1:1); Christ (1:1,16,17,18; 2:4); King of the Jews (2:2); Ruler (2:6); and Coming One (3:11). However, the force of these expressions is tied directly to Jesus' messianic mission: "he will save his people from their sins" (1:21); "shepherd of my people Israel" (2:6); "baptize in the Holy Spirit and fire" (3:11); bring "light" to the people "living in darkness" (4:16). As the Davidic Messiah, Jesus comes to deliver his people from "sin" and "darkness," and to bring restoration to Israel by being their Shepherd King.

The spiritual dimensions of Jesus' messianic mission also point to his transcendent status. Indeed, explicit normative affirmations concerning Jesus indicate that he is much more than an earthly Messiah: He is "conceived by the Holy Spirit" (1:18,20), and called Immanuel (i.e., "God with us," 1:23), Lord (3:3), and Son of God (2:5; 3:17; 4:3,6). Matthew is concerned to give content to Jesus' Sonship by developing the concept against the background of Israel's covenantal story (cf. 1:1-17; 2:15; 4:3-6), and in terms of royalty (3:17; cf. Ps 2:7), and the Suffering Servant theme (3:17; cf. Isa 42:1).

Hence, Matthew's initial strategy is to impress the reader with both a sense of Jesus' uniqueness as God's Son, alongside his fundamental continuity with Israel's past. His strategy necessarily assumes that his readers possess a competency to appreciate both his explicit citations of the OT (1:22-23; 2:6,15,18,23; 3:1; 4:15-16), and his subtle allusions to OT characters, events, institutions, and theological themes. By opening his narrative with a genealogy (1:1-17), Matthew deliberately links his story of Jesus with Israel's sacred past, and thus creates a sense of expectation of God's renewed involvement with his people in the person of Jesus.

A. GENEALOGY OF JESUS (1:1-17)

Modern readers may find the opening portion of Matthew's Gospel (i.e., 1:1-17) both puzzling and wearisome. Often modern readers approach biblical genealogies with questions pertaining to chronological precision or historical accuracy. However, biblical genealogies were not so much concerned with one's strict biological history as they were with establishing a person's corporate and tribal identity in order to bolster one's own status. Genealogies also provided a means to ground one's personal identity in the collective community of one's ancestors.[1] As such, they can function as direct characterization in which a storyteller foreshadows events or traits in the life of the descendant. Rather than a mere litany of names, biblical genealogies provide valuable information to prepare the reader for the narrative that follows.

By means of a symmetrical numerical structure Matthew's genealogy highlights the time inaugurated by the birth of Jesus (1:1-

---

[1]See D.S. Huffman, "Genealogy," in *Dictionary of Christ and the Gospels*, eds. Joel B. Green and Scot McKnight (Downers Grove, IL: InterVarsity, 1992), pp. 253-259; David R. Bauer, "The Literary Function of the Genealogy in Matthew's Gospel," *SBL Seminar Papers* (Atlanta, GA: Scholars Press, 1990), 451-468; and the earlier, M.D. Marshall, *The Purpose of Biblical Genealogies* (SNTSMS 8, 3rd ed.; Cambridge: University Press, 1988).

17). Israelite history is compressed to accentuate various phases, and to accent its culmination in Jesus. In the pre-monarchical period, from Abraham to David (1:2-6), the reader is reminded of the diverse selective process that culminated in the Davidic monarchy. In the second period, Matthew reminds his readers of both the glory of the Davidic reign and the steady decline of Israel's fortunes, culminating in Israel's darkest period, the Babylonian captivity (1:7-11). By initiating the third period (1:12-16) with the Babylonian exile and portraying Israel as without a king, subject to foreign powers, Matthew skillfully rekindles basic hopes and expectations associated with the Davidic throne. By culminating the third period with the arrival of Jesus (1:16), Matthew has constructed a solid bridge of continuity, linking Israel's sacred past to the story of Jesus. In addition, by the numerical symmetry summarized in verse 17, Matthew has underscored the sovereign hand of God who brings all history to its culmination and promised goal.

1A record of the genealogy of Jesus Christ the son of David, the son of Abraham:

2Abraham was the father of Isaac,
Isaac the father of Jacob,
Jacob the father of Judah and his brothers,
3Judah the father of Perez and Zerah, whose mother was Tamar,
Perez the father of Hezron,
Hezron the father of Ram,
4Ram the father of Amminadab,
Amminadab the father of Nahshon,
Nahshon the father of Salmon,
5Salmon the father of Boaz, whose mother was Rahab,
Boaz the father of Obed, whose mother was Ruth,
Obed the father of Jesse,
6and Jesse the father of King David.
David was the father of Solomon, whose mother had been Uriah's wife,
7Solomon the father of Rehoboam,
Rehoboam the father of Abijah,

Abijah the father of Asa,
8Asa the father of Jehoshaphat,
Jehoshaphat the father of Jehoram,
Jehoram the father of Uzziah,
9Uzziah the father of Jotham,
Jotham the father of Ahaz,
Ahaz the father of Hezekiah,
10Hezekiah the father of Manasseh,
Manasseh the father of Amon,
Amon the father of Josiah,
11and Josiah the father of Jeconiah[a] and his brothers at the time of the exile to Babylon.
12After the exile to Babylon:
Jeconiah was the father of Shealtiel,
Shealtiel the father of Zerubbabel,
13Zerubbabel the father of Abiud,
Abiud the father of Eliakim,
Eliakim the father of Azor,
14Azor the father of Zadok,
Zadok the father of Akim,
Akim the father of Eliud,
15Eliud the father of Eleazar,
Eleazar the father of Matthan,
Matthan the father of Jacob,
16and Jacob the father of Joseph, the husband of Mary, of whom was born Jesus, who is called Christ.

17Thus there were fourteen generations in all from Abraham to David, fourteen from David to the exile to Babylon, and fourteen from the exile to the Christ.[b]

[a]*11* That is, Jehoiachin; also in verse 12 [b]*17* Or *Messiah*. "The Christ" (Greek) and "the Messiah" (Hebrew) both mean "the Anointed One."

1:1. Matthew's opening line clearly intends to link his story of Jesus to the broader story of the descendants of Abraham. The words **record of the genealogy** (Βίβλος γενέσεως, *Biblos geneseōs*) allude to the LXX of Gen 2:4 and 5:1, while the names David and Abraham evoke memories of two of Israel's most illustrious characters. Matthew may intend the words *Biblos geneseōs* to be taken literally as a reference to the "book of Genesis," thus suggesting that his story be read as a "new genesis," a new beginning of God's redemptive involvement with his people. Or, as is more likely, *geneseōs* is intended to refer directly to Jesus' "origins," and thus the heading should be read as introducing both the genealogical list of 1:2-17 and the story of Jesus' birth in 1:18-25.

Usually, OT genealogies are concerned to document the offspring of the forefather (first entry), rather than the ancestry of the final descendant (cf. Gen 10:1). Matthew departs from OT usage and instead of recording a genealogy of Abraham, he begins with the name of the last descendant, i.e., Jesus Christ. By closing his genealogy with the birth of Jesus, "who is called the Christ" (v. 16), Jesus' uniqueness and superiority are highlighted in terms of fulfillment. Instead of Jesus' identity and character being defined by his forefathers, the forefathers are subordinated to their last descendant, who gives meaning and significance to Israelite history.

The designation **Jesus Christ** combines the personal name with an explicit reference to Jesus' messianic status (cf. 2:4; 16:16,20; 22:42; 24:5,23; 26:63,68). While pre-Christian Jewish messianic hopes were diverse and ultimately tied to a cluster of nationalistic concerns, Matthew intends the title to highlight God's anointing of Jesus to bring the history and religious hopes of Israel to its intended fulfillment.

By the expression **son of David**, the evangelist evokes memories of the famed king and the divine promises associated with his royal offspring (e.g., 2 Sam 7:12-14a; cf. Ps 2:8; 89:24-29; 110:6; Gen 49:10; Isa 9:6-7). Several factors suggest that David is the pivotal figure in the genealogy. His name occurs most frequently (5×; 1:1,6,17), and the added epithet "king" singles him out among the monarchs of Israel (1:6a). In addition, a number of scholars have explained Matthew's numerical scheme of three sets of fourteen generations (see v. 17) by observing that the numerical value of the Hebrew consonants comprising David's name (דוד) adds up to fourteen (d=4, w=6, d=4). While the expression "son of David" evokes messianic expectations, the "how" of Jesus' descent from David and his role as the Davidic Messiah will be developed in subsequent narrative scenes.

Jesus' Abrahamic sonship connects him to the covenantal

people of God as the one through whom God promised to bring blessings to all the nations (Gen 12:1-3; 18:18; 22:15-18). As the fulfiller of the Abrahamic covenant Jesus' messianic role promises to have a universal emphasis. Jesus, as a descendant of Abraham, is therefore God's chief agent for bringing salvation to the Gentiles. Indeed, subsequent story scenes where Abraham is mentioned (3:9; 8:11), and Gentile respondents are portrayed (e.g., 2:1-12; 8:5-11; 15:21-28) do clearly highlight the universal overtones of Jesus' messianic mission (cf. 28:19).

Beginning with **Abraham**, Matthew highlights the contours of Israelite history by a series of thirty-nine stereotyped expressions involving a rhythmic pattern in which a father begets (ἐγέννησεν, *eggenēsen*) a son, whose name enters the next line as the father of a new son and a subsequent generation (i.e., A begets B; B begets C). The list does not strive for completeness by documenting in every instance a father's immediate offspring. The verb translated **the father of** (γεννάω, *gennaō*) does not demand immediate relationship, but may only mean "was the ancestor of" or "became the progenitor of."[2] It is therefore not surprising to find hundreds of years accounted for by only a few generations (cf. vv. 12-16).

1:2-6a. The first section of the genealogy from Abraham to David underscores the privileged status of Israel by drawing attention to God's selectivity and providential choice standing behind Israel's election. Judah, the fourth born son of Jacob, was selected over his brothers (cf. Gen 49:10); and of the twin sons of Judah and Tamar, the royal line is sustained through Perez (Gen 38:29-30; cf. Ruth 4:12,18ff). Matthew's ongoing story will repeatedly place emphasis on Israel's privilege and potential associated with the nation's elected role (8:11; 10:5; 15:24).

The consistent pattern of the genealogy is occasionally broken by explicit notations which provide the reader with insight into Matthew's reading of Israelite history. Most intriguing is the inclusion of four women in an otherwise male genealogy (i.e., Tamar, v. 3; Rahab, v. 5; Ruth, v. 5; and Bathsheba, v. 6). While women are occasionally listed in genealogies (cf. Gen 11:29; 22:20-24; 35:22-26;

---

[2]Donald Carson, *Matthew*, Expositor's Bible Commentary vol. 8 (Grand Rapids: Zondervan, 1984), p. 65.

1 Chr 2:18-21,24,34,46-49), the oddity of Matthew's genealogy is the mention of these four particular women.

Their precise role in the genealogy has been the subject of much discussion, and consequently space will not allow a full investigation of the proposals offered.[3] Certainly, their Gentile status alongside their gender limitations are common denominators linking their stories with crucial themes in Matthew's story. The presence of four Gentile women in the genealogy foreshadows Matthew's pronounced interest in Jesus' role as the Abrahamic Messiah who undermines ethnic boundaries by including Gentiles in the new community of faith (8:5-13; 15:21-28; 28:18-20). Prominent also in Matthew's story is his emphasis upon the positive response of social outcasts to Jesus' announcement of God's reign. Thus early in Matthew's story we learn that neither one's ethnic origin nor one's social status proves to be an obstacle to full participation in the blessings of God.

1:6b-11. While the first fourteen names (1:2-6a) culminate in the rise of the monarchy, documented by the reference to King David (1:6a), the second series of fourteen names highlights the failure of the Davidic kings leading to the nations deportation to Babylon (v. 11). The historical note of Israel's exile in Babylon underscores the failure of the covenantal people of Abraham and the lack of fulfillment associated with the Davidic throne. Matthew's reading of Israelite history documents a pattern of election and privilege followed by obstinate rebellion and rejection of God's will. For Matthew, the climax of this pattern of rebellion and judgment comes in Israel's repudiation of Jesus, which results in the loss of the kingdom (21:33-22:10), the destruction of the nation (21:41; 22:18; 23:29–24:3), and eschatological judgment (8:10-11; 22:11-14).[4]

1:12-17. For the most part, the names of the first two-thirds of the genealogy can be accounted for by consulting the LXX of 1 Chronicles 1-3 and Ruth 4:12-22. However, the nine names between Zerubbabel and Joseph (1:13-15) follow no known OT genealogy. Furthermore, while Matthew employs only nine names

---

[3]For the various proposals see the discussion in Raymond Brown, *The Birth of the Messiah: A Commentary on the Infancy Narratives in Matthew and Luke* (New York: Doubleday, 1979), pp. 71-74.

[4]Bauer, "Genealogy in Matthew's Gospel," p. 460.

to cover around five hundred years, Luke uses eighteen (Luke 3:27-37), with the Matthean list agreeing with the Lukan list in only four names (i.e., Shealtiel, Zerubbabel, Joseph, and Jesus). However, omissions in genealogies are common, and since neither evangelist sought strict biological accuracy or completeness, it is not impossible for genealogies of the same person to differ, especially if they differ in function.[5] As evidenced from 1:17, Matthew constructs his genealogy based upon a numerical scheme involving a pattern of 3 × 14 generations; perhaps, as noted earlier, alluding to the numerical value of David's name (ד + ו + ד = 14). It appears that Matthew's numerical scheme is indicative of theological interests rather than statistical accuracy.

The rhythmic pattern of thirty-nine names in which a father begets a son is shattered in 1:16 by the fact that there is no immediate link between Jesus and Joseph. The feminine pronoun ("of whom," ἧς, *hēs*) shifts the reader's attention from Joseph to Mary, while the passive ἐγεννήθη (*egennēthē*) deliberately leaves open the question of who begat Jesus. The climactic nature of 1:16 not only points to a new beginning inaugurated by the coming of Jesus the Messiah, the language also indicates that Jesus cannot ultimately be understood in terms of physical descent. The unexpected way that Matthew concludes his genealogy surfaces questions that beg for an answer: e.g., Who is the subject of the passive verb *egennēthē*? and, How can Jesus be the son of David if Joseph is not his natural father? In Matthew's story, the questions stimulated by the ambiguity of 1:16 are immediately addressed in the next scene, although the implications of the answers encompass the entire story.

B. THE ANNUNCIATION TO JOSEPH (1:18-25)

18This is how the birth of Jesus Christ came about: His mother Mary was pledged to be married to Joseph, but before they came together, she was found to be with child through the Holy Spirit.

---

[5]As observed by Brown, *Birth of the Messiah*, p. 85, while the genealogies may pose historical difficulties, they are "accurate in terms of the function they serve."

[19]Because Joseph her husband was a righteous man and did not want to expose her to public disgrace, he had in mind to divorce her quietly.

[20]But after he had considered this, an angel of the Lord appeared to him in a dream and said, "Joseph son of David, do not be afraid to take Mary home as your wife, because what is conceived in her is from the Holy Spirit. [21]She will give birth to a son, and you are to give him the name Jesus,[a] because he will save his people from their sins."

[22]All this took place to fulfill what the Lord had said through the prophet: [23]"The virgin will be with child and will give birth to a son, and they will call him Immanuel"[b] – which means, "God with us."

[24]When Joseph woke up, he did what the angel of the Lord had commanded him and took Mary home as his wife. [25]But he had no union with her until she gave birth to a son. And he gave him the name Jesus.

[a]*21 Jesus* **is the Greek form of** ***Joshua*****, which means** ***the Lord saves*****.**
[b]*23* **Isaiah 7:14**

Strictly speaking, it is probably more accurate to speak of Jesus' "virginal conception" than it is to speak of his "virgin birth." While both Matthew and Luke are discreetly reserved regarding the details of Jesus' birth, they both affirm that Jesus' conception took place without a human father, i.e., while Mary was a virgin. Even in their respective genealogies the anomaly of Jesus' origin is clearly alluded to by the awkward references to his relationship to Joseph (Matt 1:16; Luke 3:23).

In part, Matthew intended 1:18-25 to form an explanation to the problems associated with the suggestive language of 1:16. The passive *egennēthē* (v. 16) associated with Mary receives its interpretation in the phrase "she was found to be with child through the Holy Spirit" (1:18). While Joseph has no direct paternal role with respect to the "child," angelic revelation instructs him to receive the child as his own by giving him the divinely appointed name (1:21). The reader now learns that Jesus' Davidic descendancy is to be realized not through paternal descent but through legal adoption.

For Matthew these features are designed to underscore the

composite nature of Jesus' person and role. In Joseph, Matthew upholds Jesus' continuity with Israel's history and his fulfillment of the Davidic promises, while in Mary the evangelist lays the groundwork for Jesus' exalted status (cf. Matt 22:41-46) by portraying the child as a new creation generated by the power of God.

1:18. Matthew's opening line functions as a transitional statement to inform the reader of his intent to relate the "origin" of Jesus the Messiah.[6] The Greek word for "birth" (i.e., γένεσις, *genesis,* best translated "origin") is the same as 1:1, and the repetition of Χριστός (*Christos*) links the events described in 1:18-25 to the previous genealogy (1:1, 16-17). Thus, by relating the "origins of the Messiah" Matthew continues his emphasis on Jesus as the culmination of Israel's messianic hopes.

However, the unusual circumstances surrounding the conception of Jesus highlight the transcendent dimensions of Jesus' person. Mary's pregnancy occurs during the engagement period (μνηστευθείσης, *mnēsteutheisēs*), before any sexual contact with Joseph (πρὶν ἤ συνελθεῖν, *prin ē synelthein*). According to Jewish marriage customs the betrothal or engagement period lasted about one year (see m. Ketub 5:2), during which time the woman usually remained in the house of her parents. The marriage was officially consummated by the woman's move from her parents house to that of her husband. It should be observed that betrothal or engagement constituted a binding legal contract which could be terminated only by the death of one's spouse or by formal divorce proceedings. Thus betrothal was the legal equivalent of marriage and any sexual impropriety constituted adultery (see Deut 22:23-28).[7] This explains the situation of Joseph, who, although his marriage to

---

[6]While the textual support for the reading "Jesus Christ" is very strong, the awkward presence of the article before the expression "Jesus Christ," and scribal tendency to add the personal name "Jesus," weighs in favor of the original reading being a reference to the "origins of the Christ"; see discussion in B.M. Metzger, *A Textual Commentary on the Greek New Testament.* (New York: United Bible Societies, 1971), pp. 7-8.

[7]For a discussion of marriage contracts in the first-century Mediterranean world see, Bruce Malina and Richard L. Rohrbaugh, *Social-Science Commentary on the Synoptic Gospels* (Minneapolis: Augsburg Fortress, 1992), pp. 26-31.

Mary had not been formally consummated, seriously contemplated divorce proceedings in response to Mary's condition (1:19).

Matthew's emphatic explanation of the cause of Mary's pregnancy (i.e., **through the Holy Spirit**) assures that the suspicions of Joseph (v. 19) are not entertained by the reader. Jesus' conception is attributed to the creative empowering of God's Spirit (cf. Luke 1:35), who is traditionally associated both with the creation of life (Gen 6:3; Job 27:3; 33:4; Ps 33:6; Isa 32:15; Ezek 37:9-10, 14), and the messianic age (Isa 11:2; 42:1; 61:1; Joel 2:28-29; Ezek 37:1-14). Given the decided Old Testament background which deeply informs Matthew's narrative, it is futile to search for pagan parallels to the extraordinary conception of Jesus.[8] Matthew clearly intends his readers to understand that the mystery of Mary's pregnancy can only be attributed to a miraculous conception generated by a divine causation. As such, the narrative underscores Jesus' divine origin and thereby heightens his messianic status by implicitly pointing to his unique filial relationship with God.

1:19. Compared to the reader, Joseph is initially at an informational disadvantage concerning the source of Mary's pregnancy. Accordingly, Joseph interprets Mary's condition as evidence of sexual impropriety, demanding some sort of legal action.[9] Joseph is described as a **righteous man** (δίκαιος, *dikaios*), meaning that he took seriously the legal procedure for addressing a suspected adulteress. In view of the Mosaic injunction concerning the unfaithfulness of "a virgin pledged to be married" (Deut 22:23-27; cf. m. Sota 1:1, 5), Joseph could not in good conscience fulfill his marital obligations with Mary.[10] The only options apparent to Joseph were either to

---

[8]See the review by N.T. Wright, *Who is Jesus?* (Grand Rapids: Eerdmans, 1992), pp. 65-92, of John Spong's, *Born of a Woman: A Bishop Rethinks the Birth of Jesus* (San Francisco: Harper, 1992).

[9]Robert H. Gundry, *Matthew: A Commentary on His Literary and Theological Art* (Grand Rapids: Eerdmans, 1982), p. 21-22, suggests that the language of v. 18 ("she was found to be pregnant through the Holy Spirit") is a reference to Joseph learning early in the episode both the fact and cause of Mary's pregnancy. His resolve to divorce her is not therefore motivated out of a "suspicion of unfaithfulness," but rather out of "reverential hesitation to intrude." But such a view is difficult to square with the apparent nature of the angel's disclosure to Joseph in vv. 21-22.

expose Mary to public shame by initiating legal proceedings (perhaps the procedure outlined in Deut 22:23-27), or to pursue a private settlement by simply handing her a bill of divorce in the presence of two witnesses (cf. Deut 24:1-4; m. Sota 1:1-5; m. Git. 9:3-5). Joseph's decision to pursue the latter course of action is reflective of his effort to fuse his sense of legal obligation with his compassionate regard for Mary. Not only does Joseph exhibit the qualities of a true Israelite, his blending of righteousness with compassion foreshadow important aspects of Jesus' own character (e.g., see 12:7, 12).

1:20-21. Joseph's evaluation of Mary's condition and subsequent resolve (ἐβουλήθη, *eboulēthē* = "made up his mind") to divorce her are dramatically altered by divine intervention. This is the first of several scenes, early in Matthew's story, where the reader is drawn into "the world of Old Testament piety,"[11] as human decisions and actions are determined by means of a **dream** (1:20; 2:12, 13, 19, 22),[12] usually marked by the appearance of the **angel of the Lord** (1:20; 2:13, 19; 27:19; cf. Gen 16:7, 13; 22:11, 14; Exod 3:2; Judg 6:12). In this instance, Joseph, who is explicitly identified as a legal heir of David (i.e., "son of David") is provided a true assessment of Mary's condition and explicitly instructed concerning the proper course of action. No longer should Joseph be hesitant to complete the matrimonial process, but he is to take Mary into his home, thus consummating the marriage. Now Joseph learns what the reader already knows, that Mary's condition, rather than being shameful, is the direct result of the empowering of God's Holy Spirit.

The angel continues to assimilate traditional Old Testament phraseology by addressing Joseph in a form common to Old Testament birth announcements (cf. Gen 16:11; 17:19; 1 Kgs 13:2; Luke 1:31). The name which the angel commanded Joseph to give to Mary's child becomes indicative of his messianic mission, i.e., **save his people from their sins**. Although to save from sin is a

---

[10]Jewish tradition typically required a man to divorce an adulterous wife (see m. Sota 1:5).

[11]R.T. France, *Matthew,* Tyndale (Grand Rapids: Eerdmans, 1985), p. 78.

[12]On the importance of dreams as a form of divine communication, see R. Gnuse, "Dream Genre in the Matthean Infancy Narratives," *NovT* 32 (1990), 97-120.

work of God (Ps 130:8) and was not a major focus of Israelite messianic expectations, by popular etymology of the personal name **Jesus** (Heb., *Yeshua* meaning "the Lord saves," NIV margin), the angel highlights the spiritual dimensions of Jesus' messianic work. He will liberate his people not from political oppression, but from the tyrannical hold of sin, the ultimate oppressor of the people of God. For Matthew, Jesus' identity cannot be separated from his mission. Even his personal name becomes indicative of "the single most fundamental character trait ascribed to Jesus,"[13] i.e., his role as savior of the people. With the personal name "Jesus" occurring no less than 150 times in Matthew's story, it becomes an important rhetorical device to continually reinforce the message associated with the name.[14]

1:22-23. Abruptly the story flow is interrupted with an intrusive comment by Matthew designed to interpret Mary's pregnancy in terms of prophetic fulfillment. This is the first of several fulfillment citations (2:15, 17-18, 23; 4:15-16; 8:17; 12:17-21; 13:35; 21:4-5; 27:9-10) which interpret and illuminate almost every aspect of Jesus' life and ministry in terms of the fulfillment of God's promises to his people. This concurs with Matthew's interest in establishing a clear line of continuity between the history and promises associated with Israel and their ultimate realization in the person and mission of Jesus.

While Matthew's citation of Isaiah 7:14 appears straightforward, the preponderance of literature written on this one OT citation have surfaced several complex issues associated with Matthew's use of the OT in general, and specifically his reading of Isaiah 7:14. Essentially, the major difficulties associated with the Matthean use of Isaiah 7:14 have been prompted by detailed linguistic studies involving key Hebrew and Greek terms (e.g., παρθένος [*parthenos*] and עלמה [*'almâh*]), and by contextual historical factors that seem to cast suspicion on an exclusively messianic reading of Isaiah. (See Supplemental Study on p. 51 for a brief overview of some of the issues involved.)

The text cited by Matthew agrees with the LXX, with the excep-

---

[13]J.D. Kingsbury, *Matthew as Story*, 2nd ed. (Philadelphia: Fortress, 1988), p. 12.

[14]See the study of Fred Burnett, "The Undecidability of the Proper Name Jesus' in Matthew," *Semeia* 54 (1991), 123-144.

tion that the plural **they will call** replaces the LXX singular "you will call." By the use of the third person Matthew turns the quotation into a confession made by the "people," who have benefitted from Jesus' saving action of verse 21. Those who are the Messiah's people recognize in Jesus' saving work that God has drawn near to dwell with his people. It may appear that the designation **Immanuel** is in conflict with the angel's instruction to give the child the personal name "Jesus." However, Matthew intends his readers to understand that while "Jesus" is his personal name, the designation "Immanuel" emphasizes that in Jesus "God is present to bring salvation to his people."[15] It follows that Matthew's interest in "Immanuel" is not as a personal name, but as descriptive of Jesus' role to mediate the presence of God. Given the recurring Matthean theme of the presence of Jesus in the midst of his people (1:23; 18:20; 26:29; cf. 11:25-30) the implications are obvious: "where Jesus is, there God is."[16] In fact, the climactic declaration of the risen Lord: "I am with you always, to the very end of the age" (28:20), serves to enclose the entire Gospel with the theme of God's presence in Jesus.

1:24. Not only is Matthew careful to document that the course of events involving Jesus fulfills God's sovereign plan, he is also concerned to highlight the role of human volition in accepting and carrying out divine instructions. Joseph, in the spirit of a true patriarch, is obedient to God's demand, first by consummating his marriage to Mary, and secondly by giving the child the divinely appointed name. By so doing, Joseph accepts Jesus as his own, thus legally adopting him into the Davidic line. For Matthew there is no conflict between Jesus' divine origin and his Davidic descent. As son of David he has come to liberate his people from the bondage of sin, and in so doing mediates the divine presence as God's unique Son.

1:25. Matthew is emphatic that Joseph abstains from sexual contact with Mary **until** the birth of Jesus. Such an expression may imply that after Jesus' birth Joseph and Mary proceeded with

[15] As noted by Murray Harris, *Jesus as God: The New Testament Use of Theios in Reference to Jesus* (Grand Rapids: Baker, 1992), pp. 256-258.

[16] Paul S. Minear, *Matthew: The Teacher's Gospel* (New York: Pilgrim Press, 1982), p. 33.

normal sexual relations, thus resulting in Jesus having brothers and sisters (see Matt 12:46, 47; 13:55-56; cf. Mark 6:3). While the Greek term does not demand such a conclusion, the dogma of Mary's perpetual virginity has absolutely no biblical basis.

Matthew's opening chapter has provided the reader with foundational insights concerning Jesus' origin and identity. The coming of Jesus the Christ is the culmination of God's dealings with Israel (1:1-17). As the long awaited Davidic Messiah Jesus is commissioned with the task of "saving" his people (1:21). While legally, Jesus qualifies as an heir to the Abrahamic and Davidic promises, the anomaly of his origin ("from the Holy Spirit," 1:20), and the spiritual dimensions of his work, (i.e., to manifest God's saving presence), alert the reader to the uniqueness of Jesus' status. The focus on Jesus' Davidic royalty alongside his divine Sonship will continue to dominate the infancy narrative of chapter 2.

SUPPLEMENTAL STUDY

MATTHEW'S USE OF ISAIAH 7:14

While Matthew clearly teaches the virginal conception of Jesus, his use of Isaiah 7:14 has been the subject of extensive discussion.[17] The apparent absence of a pre-Christian Jewish messianic interpretation of Isaiah 7:14 has led some to suggest that Matthew either misunderstood Isaiah or falsified the text to fit his Christian presuppositions. After all, as many have observed, one may understand the Isaiah prediction to refer to a "young girl," presently a virgin, who would at some later time conceive and give birth, without any miraculous overtones.

Neither is the linguistic evidence conclusively in support of a strictly messianic prediction of Jesus' virginal conception. The LXX *parthenos* translates the Hebrew term *ʿalmâh* which is not a technical term demanding the translation "virgin" (cf. Prov 30:19); although

---

[17] John T. Willis, *Isaiah*, Living Word Commentary (Austin: Sweet Publishing, 1980), pp. 165-167, list eight different proposals for understanding how Matthew may have used Isaiah 7:14.

contextually its usage in the OT seems to accent both a young girl's marriageable age as well as her virginity. It may be argued that the LXX's rendering of ʿ*almâh* with *parthenos* conclusively demonstrates that at least some Jewish translators understood ʿ*almâh* as referring to a "virgin" and not merely a "young woman." Although virginity is ordinarily implied by *parthenos* some have pointed to Gen 34:3 as an exception. Even if Isaiah had in mind a conception by a virgin, it is still possible to understand the fulfillment as a purely natural conception of a young woman who at the time of Isaiah's prediction to Ahaz was a virgin. Therefore, notwithstanding the extensive linguistic discussions that the term "virgin" has stirred, a more convincing line of argument detailing Matthew's use of Isaiah lies elsewhere.

Rather than arbitrary "proof-texting," Matthew's use of the OT is driven by a profound Christological commitment which finds in the OT not only predictions, but also events and persons which lend themselves to secondary applications in Christ. Texts that may originally have addressed a specific individual or even a nation "were often *idealized* in anticipation of God's end-time deliverer who would fill the categories as no one else had."[18] Climactic events in Israel's history often became paradigmatic to explain new situations and to establish a "pattern of divine activity," thus linking the past with the present. While such an approach to Scripture may go beyond the original intention of the human author, it does serve to highlight that "the same God who acted in the story of Israel and who spoke through the prophets now brings his redemptive scheme to fruition."[19]

Those who view Isaiah 7:14 as solely a messianic prediction of Jesus' miraculous conception often fail to adequately relate the text to its primary context. In fact, the historical context out of which the Isaianic prediction arose is quite clear. According to Isaiah 7:1-2, Rezin of Syria and Pekah of Israel wage war against Jerusalem,

---

[18]K. Snodgrass, "The Use of the Old Testament in the New," in *New Testament Criticism and Interpretation*, eds. D.A. Black and D.S. Dockery (Grand Rapids: Zondervan, 1991), p. 418. As Snodgrass rightly observes, the NT writers "did not find texts and then find Jesus.They found Jesus and then saw how the Scriptures fit with him."

[19]France, *Matthew*, p. 184.

seemingly because Ahaz of Judah refuses to join their league of western states to rebel against Tiglath-pileser II of Assyria (745-727 B.C.). The Syrians and the Israelites reacted to the refusal of Judah to join their league by marching to Jerusalem in order to dethrone Ahaz and put "the son of Ta'be-el" on the Davidic throne in Jerusalem (7:6). In 7:3-9 God instructs Isaiah to go to Ahaz with the assurance that their mission will fail if only Ahaz will believe (7:9). It soon becomes clear that Ahaz was not going to follow this advice. As a matter of fact, it appears that he toyed with the idea of sending to Assyria for help (cf. 2 Kgs 16:5,7; Isa 7:17). Consequently, the Lord sends Isaiah a second time to persuade him to believe. He offers Ahaz the opportunity to request a sign from the Lord to confirm the validity of the promise (7:10-11). Ahaz refuses the sign (7:12), therefore the Lord, through Isaiah, chooses his own sign: "The virgin will be with child and will give birth to a son" (7:14). The "sign" is explained in verse 16: "But before the boy knows enough to reject the wrong and choose the right the land of the two kings you dread will be laid waste." The words call attention to the speedy deliverance of Judah. In view of the fact that Isaiah bases his timetable for the downfall of Rezin and Pekah on a relatively short period of time in the life of the promised child (i.e., Immanuel), it would seem that the prophecy had at least a partial fulfillment in Isaiah's day.

Nevertheless, given the principles discussed above it would not be unusual for Matthew to see an extended, more complete fulfillment in the person of Jesus. Clearly the broader context (i.e., Isa 7-11) is permeated with the threat of exile (7:18-25; 8:1-10, 19-22), alongside the theme of God's presence (Immanuel, 8:8, 10), and the explicit promise of the birth of a great and mighty Davidic son (9:6-7; 11:1). Thus while Isaiah may have expected and hoped for an immediate fulfillment, such an expectation by no means exhausts the implications or applications of his prophecy. It follows that Matthew's understanding of prophetic fulfillment need not rule out a partial and typical fulfillment in Isaiah's own time, and thereby foreshadow a more complete and glorious fulfillment of a different order in the time of Jesus.

MATTHEW 2

C. THE INFANCY OF JESUS (2:1-23)

Matthew tells his story of Jesus in terms that resonate with OT imagery and the sacred stories of Israel's past. These elements in the story signal God's renewed involvement with his people. On five occasions in the first two chapters, human decisions and actions are determined by means of a dream (1:20; 2:12, 13, 19, 22), usually marked by the appearance of the "angel of the Lord." In four instances, Matthew concludes a descriptive scene with a fulfillment citation (2:6, 15, 18, 23), thus creating the impression that the events that transpire are an expression of God's sovereign will. By highlighting the significance of the times in terms of prophetic fulfillment, cosmic signs, and divine disclosures in dreams, Matthew constructs solid lines of continuity linking Jesus' story to Israel's past. Clearly, the scenes of chapter two provide greater depth and new dimensions to Jesus' messianic character.

Chapter two naturally divides into two sections comprising 2:1-12 and 2:13-23.

1. The Gentile Pilgrimage (2:1-12)

**1After Jesus was born in Bethlehem in Judea, during the time
of King Herod, Magi[a] from the east came to Jerusalem 2and
asked, "Where is the one who has been born king of the Jews? We
saw his star in the east[b] and have come to worship him."**

**3When King Herod heard this he was disturbed, and all
Jerusalem with him. 4When he had called together all the people's
chief priests and teachers of the law, he asked them where the
Christ[c] was to be born. 5"In Bethlehem in Judea," they replied,
"for this is what the prophet has written:**

6 "'But you, Bethlehem, in the land of Judah,
are by no means least among the rulers of Judah;
for out of you will come a ruler
who will be the shepherd of my people Israel.'[d]"

7 Then Herod called the Magi secretly and found out from them the exact time the star had appeared. 8 He sent them to Bethlehem and said, "Go and make a careful search for the child. As soon as you find him, report to me, so that I too may go and worship him."

9 After they had heard the king, they went on their way, and the star they had seen in the east[e] went ahead of them until it stopped over the place where the child was. 10 When they saw the star, they were overjoyed. 11 On coming to the house, they saw the child with his mother Mary, and they bowed down and worshiped him. Then they opened their treasures and presented him with gifts of gold and of incense and of myrrh. 12 And having been warned in a dream not to go back to Herod, they returned to their country by another route.

[a] *1* Traditionally *Wise Men* [b] *2* Or *star when it rose* [c] *4* Or *Messiah* [d] *6* Micah 5:2 [e] *9* Or *seen when it rose*

2:1-2. Matthew opens his second chapter by providing the reader with spatial and temporal references thus setting the stage for the narration that follows. Although the exact date of Jesus' birth is unknown,[1] the use of the aorist participle ´ (*gennēthentos*) indicates that Jesus' birth had occurred sometime before the arrival of the **Magi**.

The geographical reference to the place of Jesus' birth (**Bethlehem**) reinforces Jesus' Davidic roots by aligning Jesus' birth place with the hometown of Israel's famed monarch (see 1 Sam 16:1-13;

[1] Efforts to date with precision the birth of Jesus are complicated both by calendrical changes (e.g., Julian to Gregorian calendar) and the failure of sixth century scholarship (notably Dionysius Exiguus) to accurately date the time of Herod's death (4 B.C.). Thus traditional dating of Jesus' birth must be pushed back sometime between 7 and 4 B.C. Certainly the date of December 25 owes its origin more to accommodation to Roman holidays than any biblical or historical evidence.

17:12, 15, 58; 20:6, 28). The added phrase **of Judea** provides additional emphasis that Jesus "came from the tribe and territory that produced the Davidic kings (cf. 1:2; Gen 49:10)."[2] The general temporal reference **during the days of King Herod** documents that the events of chapter two transpire during the reign of Herod, a half Jew, half Idumean who through shrewd political moves gained the favor of Rome and was named King of Judea in 40 B.C. Although Herod made every effort to legitimize himself as a genuine king, he never won Jewish favor and was regarded by many as a usurper of the throne. His later years were characterized by fits of rage stimulated largely by an increasing paranoia concerning possible threats to his person and throne.[3] When Matthew highlights that the events of chapter two take place during the time of King Herod, the reader is led to expect a crisis to ensue with the birth of Israel's true Davidic King.

The **Magi from the east** were probably astrologers from Persia or Arabia "who gained special insight into world affairs from their observations of the planets and stars."[4] Matthew's description of the Magi is wholly positive, as their inquiry and actions are calculated to present them as ideal Gentile respondents. In true prophetic spirit (cf. Ps 72:10-11; Isa 2:1-4, 43:5-10, 60:3-6; Micah 4:1) the Magi mark the beginning of the eschatological pilgrimage of the Gentiles to Jerusalem and its Davidic ruler.[5] Their inquiry in Jerusalem constitutes an announcement to all Jews that their King has been born and is worthy of worship. There is something ironic about a situation where Gentile foreigners bring news to Jerusalem that the **king of the Jews** has been born. Not only does Matthew intend the assessment and worship of the Magi to function as a dramatic contrast to the indifference and unbelief of Jerusalem, the pilgrimage and testimony of the Magi highlight their awareness that the birth of Israel's King has universal significance, thus foreshad-

---

[2]Gundry, *Matthew*, p. 26.

[3]We learn the most about the character of Herod the Great from Josephus' *Jewish Antiquities*, sections 14-18.

[4]Donald Hagner, *Matthew 1-13*, Word Biblical Commentary, vol. 33a (Dallas: Word Books, 1993), 1:26.

[5]Brian Nolan, *The Royal Son of God: The Christology of Matthew 1-2 in the Setting of the Gospel* (Göttingen: Vandenhoeck and Ruprecht, 1979), p. 44.

owing a major theme in Matthew's Gospel (cf. 8:5-13; 15:21-28; 28:18-20).

2:3. While one might have expected Jerusalem to be filled with joy and great anticipation at the prospects of a Jewish deliverer, ironically, both Jerusalem and Herod experience the same emotional reaction, i.e., extreme agitation and fearfulness (ἐταράχθη, *etarachthē*). Although historically such reactions are probably stimulated by diverse concerns, by linking an obdurate Jewish leadership with the paranoid Herod, Matthew portrays in vivid terms the forces of opposition aligned against the Davidic child. Not only does Matthew's account stimulate memories of another time in Israel's history when evil forces, personified in a political leader, were set against God's chosen one (cf. Exod 4:19-20), his account also constitutes an ominous foreshadowing of the rejection of Jesus by a city later "shaken" (σείω, *seiō*, 21:10) by his triumphant arrival.

2:4. To discover the exact location where the Christ child would be born Herod summons representatives from the religious authorities in Jerusalem. The term translated **called together** (συναγαγὼν, *synagagōn*) is a favorite Matthean term usually found in contexts signifying the sinister gatherings of Jewish leaders who plot the demise of Jesus (see 26:3,57; 27:17,27,62; 28:12). Rather than being an innocent theological inquiry, such a gathering is intended to foreshadow "ominous gatherings yet to come."[6] In addition, the natural interchange of messiahship (Christ) with kingship finds its culmination and significance in the passion narrative (26:63,68; 27:11,17,22,29,37).

2:5-6. The religious leaders are portrayed as knowledgeable of popular messianic expectations that the Christ would be born in **Bethlehem in Judea** (cf. John 7:40-44). However, although they correctly identify the Messiah's birthplace, Israel's leaders exhibit no interest in proceeding to Bethlehem to welcome their King.

By recording the Scriptural citation as the direct speech of the Jewish leaders Matthew underscores the obduracy of Israel's leaders. In addition, his independent interpretative translation of Micah 5:2 clearly highlights his own convictions concerning Christ's

---

[6]See Richard B. Gardner, *Matthew*, Believers Church Bible Commentary (Scottdale, PA: Herald Press, 1991), p. 47. Contra Hagner, *Matthew*, p. 28.

person. First, by changing the reference from the "house of Ephrathah" to the **land of Judah**, Matthew reaffirms Jesus' Davidic roots by recalling his descent from Judah. Second, rather than Bethlehem being considered "small among the clans of Judah," Matthew gives Bethlehem special status (**by no means least**) in view of its messianic significance. Finally, Matthew supplements his citation from Micah by including a line, evidently dependent upon 2 Samuel 5:2, where the Lord says to David that he "will shepherd my people Israel." Not only does this final phrase initiate an important contrast between Israel's leaders and the true Shepherd-King Jesus, Jesus' messianic task of "saving his people" (1:21) is now supplemented by seeing Jesus as a compassionate Shepherd-King who seeks the welfare of his people (cf. 9:36).[7]

2:7-8. While Herod's duplicity is calculated to deceive the Magi, the reader suspects that Herod's motives are less than honorable. Assuming that the birth of the newborn King coincided with the appearance of the star, Herod seeks from the Magi a temporal precision that will enable him to fix the approximate date of the child's birth. Once having secured sufficient information detailing the place and time of Jesus' birth, Herod seeks to win the favor of the Magi by disguising his true intent behind a pretense of intended worship (cf. 2:2). The Magi are then sent to Bethlehem to **search carefully** for the child while Herod awaits their return to fulfill his sinister plans.

2:9-10. The Magi now proceed to Bethlehem, their destination given precision by divine guidance in the form of an astronomical sign. The language of the text describing the movement of the star seems to negate all efforts to explain the appearance of the star in terms of a natural astronomical phenomenon. Even though the event may defy exact scientific description, the star's appearance before the Magi "brought not critical embarrassment but great joy."[8]

---

[7]For shepherd theme in Matthew, see Francis Martin, "Image of Shepherd in the Gospel of Matthew," *Science Et Esprit* 27 (1975), 261-301; and more recently John Paul Heil, "Ezekiel 34 and the Narrative Strategy of the Shepherd and Sheep Metaphor in Matthew," *CBQ* 55 (October 1993), 698-708.

[8]France, *Matthew*, p. 84.

2:11. Finally, the intention of the Magi to worship the newborn King (2:2) is realized when they discover Jesus in a **house** in Bethlehem. Evidently some time had elapsed since the birth of the child (cf. Luke 2:16), as the family now resides in a house. The focus of the text is upon **the child** and **his mother Mary**, perhaps to reinforce Jesus' supernatural origins as described in 1:16-25. Upon seeing the child the Magi respond with homage befitting the child's royal dignity.[9] It has been observed that the scene is reminiscent of the language of Ps 72:10f. wherein representative kings from all the nations bestow gifts upon God's endowed King, who will ultimately become a blessing to all the nations (cf. Isa 60:1-3). Indeed, the Magi, although not kings, may be intended to represent the first of the Gentile pilgrimage who will honor a Jewish King having universal significance (cf. Isa 2:1-4; Matt 28:18-20).

2:12. The scene closes with the observation that divine instruction, by means of a **dream**, effectively countered Herod's effort to use the Magi to accomplish his treacherous scheme. Instead of returning to Herod, the Magi in response to the dream, return to their homeland by a different route. Their obedient spirit, alongside the offer of true worship, form a striking contrast to the religious leaders in Jerusalem.

2. The Messiah's Exile and Exodus (2:13-23)

[13]When they had gone, an angel of the Lord appeared to Joseph in a dream. "Get up," he said, "take the child and his mother and escape to Egypt. Stay there until I tell you, for Herod is going to search for the child to kill him."

[14]So he got up, took the child and his mother during the night and left for Egypt, [15]where he stayed until the death of Herod. And so was fulfilled what the Lord had said through the prophet: "Out of Egypt I called my son."[a]

---

[9]While the specific gifts of gold, myrrh, and frankincense are reminiscent of gifts offered to King Solomon (David's son) by a foreign delegation, homiletical efforts to find symbolic significance to the gifts are purely speculative.

16When Herod realized that he had been outwitted by the Magi, he was furious, and he gave orders to kill all the boys in Bethlehem and its vicinity who were two years old and under, in accordance with the time he had learned from the Magi. 17Then what was said through the prophet Jeremiah was fulfilled:

18"A voice is heard in Ramah,
weeping and great mourning,
Rachel weeping for her children
and refusing to be comforted,
because they are no more."[b]

19After Herod died, an angel of the Lord appeared in a dream to Joseph in Egypt 20and said, "Get up, take the child and his mother and go to the land of Israel, for those who were trying to take the child's life are dead."

21So he got up, took the child and his mother and went to the land of Israel. 22But when he heard that Archelaus was reigning in Judea in place of his father Herod, he was afraid to go there. Having been warned in a dream, he withdrew to the district of Galilee, 23and he went and lived in a town called Nazareth. So was fulfilled what was said through the prophets: "He will be called a Nazarene."

[a]*15* **Hosea 11:1** [b]*18* **Jer. 31:15**

2:13-14. Earlier suspicions concerning Herod's evil intentions are now confirmed by angelic forewarnings of his malicious scheme. Once again, the **angel of the Lord**, by means of a **dream**, communicates critical information to Joseph designed to counter the imminent danger posed by Herod's threat. Although seemingly vulnerable and powerless, the infant Jesus is nevertheless continually protected by means of divine intervention (cf. 2:12, 13-15, 19-22).

Angelic instructions call for an immediate move of the family to **Egypt**, a traditional place of refuge for Israelites facing political hostility in Palestine (1 Kgs 11:40; 2 Kgs 25:26; Jer 41:16-18; 26:21; 41:17; 43:1-7). In this instance the angel's explanation for the urgency of departure is based upon Herod's murderous intention. With the barest of details Matthew simply notes that Joseph departs, evidently the same night, for Egypt and remains there until the death of Herod (vv. 14-15). The evangelist seems much more interested in documenting Joseph's explicit obedience than he is in detailing the family's journey and stay in Egypt (cf. second-century Apocryphal Gospels).

2:15. It is Matthean reflection on Joseph's exile to Egypt and eventual return that perceives a typological parallel in Israel's sacred history. Perhaps drawing on the "son" imagery used of Israel in Exod 4:22-23, Matthew is able to see in the words of Hosea: "out of Egypt have I called my Son," the emergence of God's true son who relives Israel's sacred past, but in a manner pleasing to God (see 3:17; 4:3, 6). Accordingly, as representative of true Israel, Jesus as God's ideal son initiates an exodus which will bring both a new covenant and the messianic blessings associated with true liberation (see 26:27-29).

2:16. After assuring the reader of Jesus' safety and eventual return to Judea (vv. 14-15), Matthew returns to Herod and Jerusalem to report his **furious** response at being foiled (ἐνεπαίχθη, *enepaichthē*) by the Magi. However, Herod formulates an alternative plan to assure that any potential rival coming from Bethlehem would be eliminated. Giving himself a geographical and temporal margin for error, Herod orders the massacre of all male infants **two years old and under**, in and around Bethlehem. The scene is reminiscent of another crisis in Israelite history, when another paranoid King ordered that "every boy that is born you must throw into the Nile" (Exod 1:22).

While the historicity of this event has been disputed by some,[10] R.T. France has provided compelling evidence giving credibility to the Matthean account.[11] Not only is the slaughter of the infants consistent with what is known about Herod, population estimates in and around Bethlehem, coupled with probable birth and infant mortality rates, have led to estimates of around twenty infants being slain by Herod. While not diminishing the tragedy of the situation, such a crime in the light of Herod's other atrocities may very

---

[10]Notably, Brown, *Birth of the Messiah*, p. 227; and D.C. Allison and W.D. Davies, *A Critical and Exegetical Commentary on the Gospel according to Saint Matthew*, ICC, vol. 1 (Edinburgh: T & T Clark, 1988) 1:265.

[11]See R.T. France, "Herod and the Children of Bethlehem," *NovT* 21 (1979), 98-120.

well have gone unnoticed by contemporary historical sources.[12]

2:17-18. Even in the midst of such tragedy Matthew is careful to document God's providential hand in terms of Scripture's fulfillment. While God is not responsible for Herod's evil actions, the citation from Jeremiah 31:15 is intended to generate hope in the face of such tragedy. Originally, 31:15 alludes to the lament of Rachel (representative of all Jewish mothers), who mourns the exile of her children, probably to Babylon. The connection to the Bethlehem episode seems to be based upon the tradition that **Rachel** was buried near **Ramah**, in the vicinity of Bethlehem, where also the people gathered for their march into exile (cf. Gen 35:19; 1 Sam 10:2; Jer 40:1-2). Hence, Matthew's point may be, that just as the tragedy of the exile was ultimately overcome by God's providential restoration of his people (cf. Jer 31:16-22), so the sorrow accompanying Jesus' exile to Egypt will be turned to joy by his return to inaugurate the blessings of God.

2:19-20. Matthew now returns the reader to Jesus' exile in Egypt (cf. v. 15) as the family awaits divine confirmation that the threat to Jesus' life is now past. While the length of their stay in Egypt is unknown, the angel's revelatory disclosure concerning the death of Herod signals that it is now safe to return to the **land of Israel**. Although angelic instructions will become more specific ("land of Israel" – "district of Galilee" – "Nazareth"), initial instructions are careful to link Jesus' return with the Exodus story (cf. Exod 2:15; 4:19).

2:21-22. Once again Joseph complies precisely with angelic instructions (cf. v. 14), returning to the "land of Israel." However, the presence of Archelaus, Herod's son, as ruler over Judea gives Joseph some cause for concern. With the death of Herod his kingdom was divided between his three sons (Herod Antipas, Archelaus, and Philip), with Archelaus granted rule over Judea, Samaria, and Idumea. Archelaus seems to have inherited his

---

[12]Herod's brutality knew no bounds when it came to protecting his throne as evidenced by the execution of his wife Marianne and three of his sons (Josephus, *Ant.* 16.11.7; 17:7). With his death Josephus describes him in the following words: "a man he was of great barbarity towards all men equally, and a slave to his passions; but above the consideration of what was right," (*Ant.* 17.8.1).

father's brutal tendencies as evidenced by his slaughter of 3000 Jewish protestors who brought economic and political grievances before him (Josephus, *Ant.* 17.213-218). Eventually, Jewish outrage managed to bring about his banishment to Gaul in A.D. 6.

2:23. The journey of the family is altered accordingly by divine guidance, taking them north into the **district of Galilee** (cf. 4:15-16), specifically to a small village called **Nazareth**. This obscure village, not mentioned in the OT, was little more than an agricultural settlement, with a population of maybe 200 people.[13] Here the family settles, thus providing the background for Jesus being called **the Nazarene**.

The legitimacy of the move is Scripturally defended by citing prophetic fulfillment. However, instead of citing a specific prophet (1:22; 2:5, 15, 17), Matthew indicates that his quotation "rests upon or alludes to more than one OT text"[14] (pl. **prophets**). Since neither Nazareth or Nazarene occur in the OT, scholarly efforts have looked for possible phonetic word plays connecting the Greek terms with some Hebrew term. Of the options proposed, the similarity between the Hebrew term for "branch" (נֵצֶר, *nēṣer*) (see Isa 4:2; 11:1) and Nazarene seems best to explain the wordplay that Matthew had in mind. The "branch" language in the OT is clearly messianic (cf. Isa 4:2; 11:1; Jer 23:5; 33:15; Zech 3:8; 6:12), thus enabling Matthew to stress Jesus' Davidic roots, while at the same time the obscured and despised Nazareth is perhaps prophetic of a ministry despised and rejected by men.

Throughout the infancy stage of Jesus' life Matthew works with traditional messianic terminology to stress both God's favor upon the infant and his universal saving significance. Everything happens by divine design as God draws near to his people to inaugurate the promised messianic blessings. Clearly, the reader anticipates a messianic vocation quite unlike traditional expectations. Indeed, as the narrative proceeds traditional categories of messianism are either shattered by Jesus or redefined in terms shocking to the status quo.

---

[13]R. Riesner, "Archeology and Geography," in *DJG*, p. 36.

[14]Davies and Allison, *Matthew*, 1:275.

MATTHEW 3

D. THE MISSION AND MESSAGE OF JOHN THE BAPTIST (3:1-12)

Although a temporal gap of roughly thirty years exists between the events of chapter 2 and the appearance of John the Baptist (3:1), Matthew makes very little of it since he is more concerned with the significance of John than in detailing the chronological sequence of events leading to his appearance. One particular form of Jewish messianic hope anticipated the return of Elijah as a precursor to the messianic age (cf. Matt 11:14; 17:10-13; Mal 3:23,24; 4:5-6; Sir 48:9-10; I Enoch 90:31). Matthew takes great care in describing the character and role of John, ultimately to mark his presence and action as a decisive turning point in the unfolding of God's redemptive scheme. John appears in the Davidic territory (3:1), in the spirit of Elijah (cf. 3:4; 2 Kgs 1:8), preaching a message of reform (3:2, 7-10; cf. Mal 3:1-5; 4:5-6), in view of the nearness of the Kingdom (3:2), and the eschatological judgment brought by a "mightier one" to come (3:11-12). In subsequent episodes of Matthew's story the person and work of John function to highlight the messianic contours of Jesus' character and mission (cf. 3:14; 11:1-19; 14:1-12; 16:14-20; 17:9-13; 21:23-27).[1]

While 3:1 does signal a new phase in the pre-ministry stage of the story, the material comprising 3:1–4:16 still anticipates Jesus' public ministry (4:17). The preparatory work of John consists of two sections highlighting his ministry (3:1-6) and his message (3:7-12).

---

[1]For detailed discussions on the significance of John the Baptist see R.L. Webb, *John the Baptizer: A Socio-Historical Study* (Sheffield: JSOT, 1991); R.T. France, "John the Baptist?," in *Jesus of Nazareth: Lord and Christ,* eds. Joel B. Green and Max Turner (Grand Rapids: Eerdmans, 1994), pp. 94-111; and J.P. Meier, "John the Baptist in Matthew's Gospel," *JBL* 99 (1980), 383-405.

[1]In those days John the Baptist came, preaching in the Desert of Judea [2]and saying, "Repent, for the kingdom of heaven is near." [3]This is he who was spoken of through the prophet Isaiah:

"A voice of one calling in the desert,
'Prepare the way for the Lord,
make straight paths for him.'"[a]

[4]John's clothes were made of camel's hair, and he had a leather belt around his waist. His food was locusts and wild honey. [5]People went out to him from Jerusalem and all Judea and the whole region of the Jordan. [6]Confessing their sins, they were baptized by him in the Jordan River.

[7]But when he saw many of the Pharisees and Sadducees coming to where he was baptizing, he said to them: "You brood of vipers! Who warned you to flee from the coming wrath? [8]Produce fruit in keeping with repentance. [9]And do not think you can say to yourselves, 'We have Abraham as our father.' I tell you that out of these stones God can raise up children for Abraham. [10]The ax is already at the root of the trees, and every tree that does not produce good fruit will be cut down and thrown into the fire.

[11]"I baptize you with[b] water for repentance. But after me will come one who is more powerful than I, whose sandals I am not fit to carry. He will baptize you with the Holy Spirit and with fire. [12]His winnowing fork is in his hand, and he will clear his threshing floor, gathering his wheat into the barn and burning up the chaff with unquenchable fire."

[a]*3* Isaiah 40:3 [b]*11* Or *in*

3:1. The phrase **in those days** draws from an OT precedent designed to draw the reader's attention "to a period of historical interest" (cf. Gen 38:1; Exod 20:11; Jer 3:16, 18; 50:4; Dan 10:2; Joel 3:1; Zech 8:23; also I Enoch 99:10).[2] Rather than accenting chronological or temporal elements Matthew is more concerned to highlight the uniqueness of the times now dawning with the arrival of John. His presence in the **Desert of Judea** conforms to the widely held belief that a return to the desert followed by a second

---

[2]David Hill, *The Gospel of Matthew* (Grand Rapids: Eerdmans, 1979), p. 89.

exodus would herald the messianic age (see Isa 40:3-4; 42:14–55:13; Ezek 20:33-44; Hos 2:14-15; 1 Macc 2:29-30; 1 QS 8:12-18). Thus, Matthew continues to draw extensive correlations between the story of Jesus and the story of Moses and the Exodus. The reference to John's geographical location also anticipates the language of Isa. 40:3 subsequently cited by Matthew (v. 3).

3:2. John's prophetic call for reform (μετανοεῖτε, *metanoeite*) demands both a change of attitude and conduct (see v. 8). The appeal for the renewal of all Israel is motivated (γάρ, *gar*) by the drawing near of God's sovereign reign (βασιλεία τῶν οὐρανῶν, *basileia tōn ouranōn*). The perfect tense verb translated **is near** (ἤγγικεν, *ēngiken*) conveys the nuance of "having drawn near and remaining near."[3] With respect to the present and futurity of the kingdom the comment of Davies and Allison best resolves the tension: "When Jesus announces that the Kingdom of God has come and is coming, this means that the last act has begun but not yet reached its climax: The last things have come and will come."[4]

While Matthew favors the expression **kingdom of heaven** (33×) over the terminology "kingdom of God," the latter form is not entirely absent from Matthean diction (see 12:28; 19:24; 21:34, 43). Most scholars view the expressions as equivalent (cf. 19:23-24), with the variations explained as either typical Jewish avoidance of the divine name or as reflecting nothing more than stylistic diversity. However, it is important to understand that the primary focus of the term "kingdom" is not territorial, but rather the accent is upon God's very presence that has drawn near to his people with saving power. While Jesus will echo the same proclamation of God's dynamic reign (see 4:17), his ministry will transcend John's by both inaugurating and mediating the saving presence of God's reign.[5]

3:3. Matthew continues his penchant for interpreting events in terms of OT fulfillment by illuminating John's ministry in terms of Isa 40:3. Originally, Isa 40:1-5 functioned to highlight the consolation of God as he draws near to assure his people of their eventual

[3]Hagner, *Matthew*, 1:47.

[4]Davies and Allison, *Matthew*, 1:390.

[5]See discussion in G.R. Beasley-Murray, *Jesus and the Kingdom of God* (Grand Rapids: Eerdmans, 1986); and his "The Kingdom of God and Christology in the Gospels," in *Jesus of Nazareth*, p. 25.

return to their homeland following the Babylonian captivity.[6] However, by following the LXX reading (cf. Hebrew text), Matthew places the emphasis upon what was said rather than the place where it was said.[7] A distinctly messianic reading is made possible by following **Lord** with the personal pronoun **him** rather than the LXX rendering "of our God." Thereby, "Lord" refers to Jesus rather than in the original instance to God. Clearly, Matthew has no hesitation to alter the wording of an OT text in light of his sense of a deeper christological significance. John's mission is anchored in the imperatives of Isa 40:3: **prepare the way**, **make straight his paths**. His message of reform becomes the means whereby the people were "prepared" for the arrival of the Lord.

3:4. John's prophetic role is further confirmed by his appearance and dietary habits. Matthew's description of John's appearance has strong verbal parallels with the prophet Elijah (see 2 Kgs 1:8; cf. Zech 13:4). Indeed, implicit identification with Elijah becomes explicit later in Matthew's story (11:14; 17:12-13). His diet of **locusts and wild honey** points to an ascetic lifestyle characteristic of a holy man fully consecrated to God.[8] Efforts to link John with the Qumran community usually fail to give adequate attention to major differences between the message and mission of John and the ideology characterizing Qumran.[9]

3:5-6. John's message of reform was met by a favorable response among the Jews throughout **Judea**, even impacting the capital city, **Jerusalem**. John's success is highlighted by the imperfect verb ἐβαπτίζοντο (*ebaptizonto*) which matches the continual "coming out" (ἐξεπορεύετο, *exeporeueto*) of the previous verse. The present participle (ἐξομολογούμενοι, *exomologoumenoi*, **confessing**) calls attention to the penitent spirit of those participating in John's baptism. Matthew does not explicitly link John's baptism to "forgiveness of sins" (cf. Mark 1:4; Luke 3:3), perhaps because cleansing from sin is so emphatically tied to Jesus' messianic task (1:21; 9:2-5; 26:28).

---

[6]For a survey tracing the use and interpretation of Isa 40:1-5 see Klyne R. Snodgrass, "Streams of Tradition Emerging From Isaiah 40:1-5 and their Adaptation in the New Testament," *JSNT* 8 (1980), 24-45.

[7]Cf. Dead Sea Scrolls, 1QS8:12-16; 1QS9:17-20.

[8]Davies and Allison, *Matthew*, 1:297.

[9]See discussion by B. Witherington, "John the Baptist," in *DJG*, p. 384.

The question concerning the background of John's baptism has been much discussed.[10] While John's baptism has certain similarities with OT ablutions, Jewish proselyte baptisms, and even the multiple washings at Qumran, distinctive features associated with John's baptism establish his unique contribution: not the least of which is the fact that "his baptism was directed towards the nation as a whole (*contra* Qumran), administered once and for all (*contra* OT ablutions), and was for Jews only (*contra* proselyte baptism).[11] Those participating in John's baptism in effect became a remnant within Israel, actually constituting "true Israel," the beginning of the new community of God.

3:7. Major antagonists of Matthew's story make their debut with the appearance of the Pharisees and Sadducees. While the two groups represent diverse and even competitive sects within Judaism (see Josephus, *Ant.* 17:42), in Matthew they function as a "monolithic front,"[12] sharing a common hostility toward both John and Jesus. Historically, the Pharisees were advocates of a righteousness grounded in the precision of law-keeping based upon the interpretation and application of both the written and oral Torah.[13] Practically, Pharisees were concerned with ritual purity and its implications for defining and defending the boundaries of true Israel. The result was a holiness code which sought to extend priestly purity regulations to all Israel. Loyalty to the covenant and God's election demanded a strict observance of purity ordinances, which in effect produced a factional separatism and a self-righteous

---

[10]For a survey of options see G.R. Beasley-Murray, *Baptism in the New Testament* (Grand Rapids: Eerdmans, 1962), pp. 31-44.

[11]See discussion by Davies and Allison, *Matthew*, 1:294.

[12]The words of J.D. Kingsbury, "The Developing Conflict between Jesus and the Jewish Leaders in Matthew's Gospel: A Literary-Critical Study," *CBQ* 49 (January, 1987) 58; see also his *Matthew as Story*, pp. 115-127.

[13]For studies on Pharisaism see J.D.G. Dunn, *The Partings of the Ways: Between Christianity and Judaism and Their Significance for the Character of Christianity* (Philadelphia: Trinity Press, 1991); Jacob Neusner, *From Politics to Piety: The Emergence of Pharisaic Judaism* (Englewood Cliffs, NJ: Prentice-Hall, 1973); also his response to E.P. Sanders, "Mr. Sanders' Pharisees and Mine," *SJT* 44 (1991), 73-95; A.J. Saldarini, *Pharisees, Scribes and Sadducees in Palestinian Society* (Wilmington, DE: Michael Glazier, 1988); E.P. Sanders, *Jewish Law from Jesus to the Mishna* (Philadelphia: Trinity Press, 1990).

condemnation of all others not embracing their agenda. Their ongoing conflict with Jesus throughout Matthew's story is largely driven by his refusal to give credence to a righteousness based solely upon observing legal requirements.

While the Pharisees function in Matthew as the dominant opponents of Jesus, it is the political influence of the Sadducees that ultimately orchestrates the death of Jesus (see 26:57-65; 27:1, 20). Although their leverage with the populace is minimal, in comparison with the Pharisees, their priestly and aristocratic clout controlled cultic life associated with the temple. Their religious and political conservatism resulted in their rejection of Pharisaic oral tradition, along with any movement that tended to subvert the established order. Although perhaps motivated for different reasons, it is not at all surprising for a delegation composed of both Pharisees and Sadducees to be concerned with the implications of John's activities in the Judean desert (cf. John 1:19-25).

The NIV is probably correct in translating ἐπι τὸ βάπτισμα (*epi to baptisma*) as **coming to where he was baptizing**, rather than "coming for baptism" (cf. NRSV; see Luke 3:7). John's assessment of their character (lit. "offspring of vipers") as both detestable and a danger to others (cf. 16:6), followed by his sarcastic question, **who warned you to flee . . . ?**, indicates that John is not fooled by their hypocritical front. They, in fact, do not feel themselves to be in any danger of God's eschatological wrath, after all they are the offspring of Abraham, children of the covenant.

3:8-9. John challenges such thinking with a demand for concrete evidence of a penitent spirit. They cannot entertain the idea that mere physical descent from Abraham assures their immunity from God's eschatological wrath. John emphatically repudiates their contention that ethnic Israel and the covenantal people of God are one and the same. Neither is salvation guaranteed to Jews as such, but only to those who undergo a radical change of conduct.

3:10. The language of John bristles with a note of urgency in view of the imminent ushering in of the end-times: **the ax is already at the root of the tree**. Having earlier called for **fruit in keeping with repentance** (v. 8), John now elucidates the consequences of failure to bear fruit. In the spirit of a true prophet (cf. Isa 8:6-8; 66:24; Jer 7:16-20; Micah 2:1-3), John envisions a fiery judgment upon those who fail to heed his warnings. The demise of fruitless Israel and a redefining of the true people of God constitutes a major theme in Matthew's story (see 7:21-23; 8:10-13; 21:43-44).

3:11-12. John's message now turns to explicit comments about the nature and role of the expected Messiah.[14] John frankly acknowledges the superior status and mission of the one who comes after him. He readily confesses himself to be unworthy to perform even the most menial task of a slave on behalf of the "mightier one" to come.[15] While John's baptism in water both presupposed and brought to expression the act of repentance, it functioned only as a "prophetic symbol"[16] of a future Spirit-fire baptism producing inward cleansing and genuine renewal. The contrast reinforces John's preparatory function with a greater ministry to be realized in Jesus.

The meaning of the words **baptize you with the Holy Spirit and with fire** has been the source of some dispute. Some clarity is brought to the discussion with the observation that the two nouns "Spirit" and "fire" are governed by the single preposition ἐν (*en*, in/with/by), thus most naturally indicating one baptism composed of two elements. In addition, it seems clear by the personal pronoun ὑμᾶς (*hymas*), that those baptized in water by John can ultimately expect a baptism composed of both Spirit and fire.[17] It therefore appears that John did not envision a twofold baptism wherein some are "baptized in the Holy Spirit," while others receive a fiery baptism resulting in their destruction. It may be that

[14]The reference to the "Coming One" (ὁ . . . ἐρχόμενος, *ho . . . erchomenos*) has definite messianic connotations in Matthew's Gospel (cf. 11:3; 21:9; 23:39), and perhaps reflecting the language of Ps 118:26. For alternative views see Davies and Allison, *Matthew*, 1:313-314.

[15]F.W. Beare, *The Gospel According to Matthew* (Oxford: Blackwell, 1981), p. 96, observes that "the full force of such words is felt when we learn that the disciple of a rabbi ought to do anything for his master that a slave would do except take off his shoes. John confesses himself unworthy to perform even this servile task for the 'mightier one.'"

[16]See discussion by J.D.G. Dunn, *Baptism in the Spirit* (Philadelphia: Westminster Press, 1970), pp. 8-22.

[17]It should be observed that there is only one "you" in the text; see Davies and Allison, *Matthew*, 1:317.

John had in mind a single baptism experienced both as a cleansing (cf. Ezek 36:25-27; 39:29), and as a means of refinery (cf. Isa 1:25; Zech 13:9; Mal 3:2-3). By extension the Spirit-fire baptism, received as a blessing by the penitent, spells judgment and destruction upon all who reject the message of God's coming reign (cf. Isa 4:2-4).

John's message concludes with an ominous warning of impending separation to be executed by the *Mightier One*. The final separation is likened to the final phase of the harvesting process wherein wheat is separated from the chaff by tossing both elements into the air and allowing the wind to blow away the chaff while the heavier wheat falls to the floor. The wheat is then gathered for storage, while the worthless chaff is destroyed by fire. Like the unfruitful trees of 3:10 (cf. 13:42,49) the metaphoric use of fire is employed to describe the finality of the wicked's irreversible condition.[18] While John's perception of the Messiah as eschatological judge and dispenser of the Holy Spirit is accurate, it will become apparent that he does not, as yet, possess the depth of insight to understand how the Messiah will fulfill his role. Later in the story there develops a seeming conflict between John's "christological expectations" and Jesus' messianic performance (11:2-6).

E. THE BAPTISM AND COMMISSION OF JESUS (3:13-17)

[13]Then Jesus came from Galilee to the Jordan to be baptized by John. [14]But John tried to deter him, saying, "I need to be baptized by you, and do you come to me?"

[15]Jesus replied, "Let it be so now; it is proper for us to do this to fulfill all righteousness." Then John consented.

[16]As soon as Jesus was baptized, he went up out of the water. At that moment heaven was opened, and he saw the Spirit of God descending like a dove and lighting on him. [17]And a voice from

[18]See R.K. Harrison, "Asbestos," in *The New International Dictionary of New Testament Theology*, vol. 3, ed. Colin Brown (Grand Rapids: Zondervan, 1978), p. 111: "Fire was the most powerful destructive force known in the ancient world, and the NT use of asbestos implies utter and complete destruction of whatever is rejected by God as unsuitable or unworthy" (cf. Mark 9:43 and Luke 3:17).

heaven said, "This is my Son, whom I love; with him I am well pleased."

3:13. By the use of τότε (*tote,* then) and the historical present παραγίνεται (*paraginetai*) (cf. 3:1), Matthew vividly connects the appearance of Jesus to the mission of John. Jesus comes **from Galilee** (cf. 2:22) to John for the express purpose of being baptized by him (τοῦ [*tou*] + infinitive = purpose).

3:14-15. Thus far in the story Matthew has stressed Jesus' kingly-messianic dignity, as well as his unique transcendent status. Yet, the first independent act of Jesus is submission to John's baptism. Even from John's limited perspective, Jesus' submission to his baptism seemed incongruent with their respective roles. Why would the "mightier one" who will administer a "Spirit-fire baptism" submit to his preparatory baptism? Apparently, John even made several unsuccessful attempts **to deter him** (διεκώλυεν, *diekōlyen,* conative imperfect), insisting on his own need for the greater messianic baptism (3:11). However, the first words spoken by Jesus clarify his purpose in submitting to John's baptism. He affirms that it is the "proper and right" (πρέπον, *prepon,* BAGD, p. 699) thing to do for the "time being" (ἄφες ἄρτι, *aphes arti*), given their appointed roles to **fulfill all righteousness**. Jesus understands that the time of fulfillment has arrived and submission to John's baptism functions to usher in God's salvific plan. The two key terms "fulfill" (πληρῶσαι, *plērōsai*) and "righteousness" (δικαιοσύνην, *dikaiosynēn*) are best understood not in terms of conformity to legal or moral requirements, but rather to highlight his submission as an important step in the realization of God's saving presence.[19] John participates (ἡμῖν, *hēmin*) in initiating the age of fulfillment by yielding to the authoritative request of Jesus. The brief exchange sets the stage for God's positive assessment and commission of Jesus to his messianic mission.

---

[19]See the discussion by J.P. Meier, *Law and History in Matthew's Gospel* (Rome: Biblical Institute Press, 1976), pp. 76-80; and Donald Hagner, "Righteousness in Matthew's Theology," in *Worship, Theology, and Ministry in the Early Church,* eds. Michael J. Wilkins and Terence Paige (Sheffield: JSOT Press, 1992), pp. 101-120.

3:16. Immediately following the immersion of Jesus he receives divine confirmation by being empowered by the Holy Spirit and receiving God's revelatory approval. Jesus' emergence from the water has been linked to both creation (cf. Gen 1:1-2) and Exodus motifs (cf. Exod 4:22; 14:29-30). Certainly, the story of Israel is never far below the surface of Matthew's plot and structure. It should be observed that the baptismal scene also has certain verbal affinities with Ezekiel 1-2, wherein Ezekiel is commissioned by God to his prophetic task (see Ezek 1:1,28; 2:2-3).

The expression **heaven was opened** was commonly used to signal some form of divine disclosure or revelation (cf. Ezek 1:1; Isa 63:19; Acts 7:56; Rev 4:1). In this instance, Jesus is the recipient of God's anointing Spirit which empowers him for his messianic ministry (cf. Acts 10:38). Although the symbolism conveyed by the Spirit as a dove is unclear,[20] the image of a bird alongside references to water and the Holy Spirit may be intended to recall creation imagery (see Gen 1:1-2), thus suggesting in Jesus the beginning of a new creation. Be that as it may, it should be observed that the Spirit's anointing is not to be construed as a form of adoption wherein Jesus only now becomes God's Son. The role of the Holy Spirit in his birth (1:18-25), and the earlier recognition of his Sonship (2:15) rule out such an interpretation. The anointing of the Spirit is in conjunction with his commissioning to his messianic mission, not to make him something he was not before.[21]

3:17. The coming of God's Spirit is accompanied by the revelatory announcement of God who speaks explicitly both to approve and to commission his Son to his messianic task. It is obvious by the use of the third person (**this is**), rather than the second person ("you are," cf. Mark 1:11; Luke 3:22), that the announcement was not intended as a direct address to Jesus. Hence, the words of God in 3:17 (cf. 17:5) function either as a "narrative aside directed to

---

[20]For a survey of proposals see Davies and Allison, *Matthew*, 1:331-334.

[21]As Dunn, *Baptism in the Holy Spirit*, p. 28 observes: "The descent of the Spirit on Jesus reflects not so much a change in Jesus, his person or his status, as the beginning of a new stage in salvation-history. The thought is not so much of Jesus becoming what he was not before, but of Jesus entering where he was not before – a new epoch in God's plan of redemption . . . ."

the reader,"[22] or in view of the subsequent temptation scene (4:3,6), the announcement may constitute a challenge to Satan reminiscent of his challenge with respect to his servant Job (see Job 1:8).[23] Whatever may be the significance of Matthew's form of God's announcement, the divine assessment certainly provides significant insights into the nature and role of Jesus' Sonship by linking it to key OT texts.

While disputed by some, it appears that the three significant terms of 3:17 (i.e., **son**, **beloved**, **pleased**) have been influenced primarily by the language of Ps 2 and Isa 42 (and possibly, Gen 22:1). Specifically, in Ps 2 the Anointed King (2:2), who represents both the nation and the Lord (2:4), is designated by God as his "son" on the day of his coronation to his throne (2:7). In Isa 42:1-5 God puts his Spirit upon his "chosen one," in whom he "delights" and commissions his "servant" to lowly paths of service (cf. Matt 12:18-21). In this way Matthew gives content to Jesus' Sonship and messianic mission by linking it to the themes of Davidic royalty and suffering service. The prophetic influence of Ps 2 and Isa 42 also emphasize that the basic thrust of God's announcement is to be viewed as a commission of Jesus to his messianic task. Subsequent narrative scenes will show how Jesus fulfills his role as God's Son and servant.

---

[22]As contended by David E. Garland, *Reading Matthew* (New York: Crossroad, 1993), p. 37.

[23]Kingsbury, *Matthew as Story*, p. 58, observes that God's assessment was directed to the "world of transcendent beings."

MATTHEW 4

F. THE TESTING OF THE SON (4:1-11)

[1]Then Jesus was led by the Spirit into the desert to be tempted by the devil. [2]After fasting forty days and forty nights, he was hungry. [3]The tempter came to him and said, "If you are the Son of God, tell these stones to become bread."

[4]Jesus answered, "It is written: 'Man does not live on bread alone, but on every word that comes from the mouth of God.'[a]"

[5]Then the devil took him to the holy city and had him stand on the highest point of the temple. [6]"If you are the Son of God," he said, "throw yourself down. For it is written:

"'He will command his angels concerning you,
and they will lift you up in their hands,
so that you will not strike your foot against a stone.'[b]"

[7]Jesus answered him, "It is also written: 'Do not put the Lord your God to the test.'[c]"

[8]Again, the devil took him to a very high mountain and showed him all the kingdoms of the world and their splendor. [9]"All this I will give you," he said, "if you will bow down and worship me."

[10]Jesus said to him, "Away from me, Satan! For it is written: 'Worship the Lord your God, and serve him only.'[d]"

[11]Then the devil left him, and angels came and attended him.

[a]*4* Deut. 8:3 [b]*6* Psalm 91:11,12 [c]*7* Deut. 6:16 [d]*10* Deut. 6:13

4:1-2. Following Jesus' emergence from the water the ensuing temptation narrative is perhaps the clearest expression of Matthew's fondness for linking his story of Jesus with the experiences of the Israelite nation. The same Spirit of God who is "particularly active among the Israelites during the exodus and wilderness wanderings" (cf. Num 11:17,25,29; Neh 9:20; Ps 106:33; Isa 63:10-14)[1] now leads Jesus into the desert "to humble [him] and to test [him] in order to know what was in [his] heart, whether or not [he] would keep his commands" (see Deut. 8:21). The "testing" (πειράζω, *peirazō*)[2] of Jesus is therefore not a fortuitous event, but is staged by God to demonstrate his strength of character and depth of devotion (cf. Gen 22; Job 1:6-8). Essentially, Satan's efforts are calculated to encourage Jesus to exercise his divine prerogatives and supernatural power in a way that would belie the lowly path of service and obedience suggested by the commission of 3:17. The fast, lasting **forty days and forty nights**, most probably is intended to recall the forty year experience of Israel in the desert (Deut 8:2).

4:3-4. The words of Satan in the first temptation (**If you are the Son of God**) should not be construed as expressing some doubt on the part of the Tempter. In fact, the statement assumes the validity of Jesus' Sonship (first class condition), but raises significant questions concerning what it means to be God's Son. For Satan, Sonship certainly assumes the right to exercise divine power in order to sustain one's life (cf. 16:22-23; 27:42-43). Jesus appropriately responds by citing Deut 8:3, thus demonstrating that he has learned the lesson that Israel failed to perceive, i.e., he will trust his God to be the giver and sustainer of life and will not break faith by yielding to Satan's suggestion to satisfy his physical need by the exercise of divine power. True Sonship finds sustenance in compliance to the Father's will which takes priority over even the preservation of one's own life (cf. 16:25-26).

---

[1]Davies and Allison, *Matthew*, 1:355.

[2]The notion expressed by the verb is theologically ambiguous. In the OT, as B. Gerhardsson, *The Temptation of Jesus: The Testing of God's Son (Matt. 4:11 & Par.)*, ConBNT 2.1 (Lund, Sweden: Gleerup, 1966), p. 31, has shown, the term often has the more positive "to test," where God "tests" his people for the purpose of developing character (see Lev 22:1-2; Exod 20:20; Deut 13:3; Judg 2:22; Ps 26:2). Gundry, *Matthew*, p. 55, observes that "πειράζω refers to testing when God stands in the forefront, to temptation when an evil force such as the Devil stands in the forefront. The leading of the Spirit and the enticement of the Devil give the verb a double connotation here."

4:5-7. Next, Satan seeks to persuade Jesus to test God's protective care by leaping from the pinnacle [3] of the temple. The change of sites from the desert to the temple is most likely a visionary experience designed to set the stage for Satan's response to Jesus' absolute trust in God's care. The temple represented the very presence of God, the place where divine protection was certainly most assured.[4] By citing Psalm 91 Satan invites Jesus to test God's promise that he will "rescue" and "protect" the one who "dwells in the shelter of the Most High" (see vv. 1,14). Essentially, Satan would have Jesus condition his loyalty to God upon God acting in certain ways. Like Israel at Massah (Exod 17), who made their faithfulness contingent upon God meeting their physical needs (cf. Num 14:22; Ps 78; 1 Cor. 10:9; Heb 3:7–4:13), Satan suggests that Jesus test his Father's concern by staging an event to make God demonstrate his power or faithfulness. Jesus avoids the sin of Israel by citing Deut 6:16, thus emphasizing that his fidelity is not dependent upon manipulating God to protect him from all harm. As God's ideal Son, Jesus is resolved to be faithful and trust even if it means a path of suffering and death (cf. 16:21f.; 26:53-54; 27:40).

4:8-11. Jesus' visionary experiences take him from the desert to the temple and finally to **a very high mountain**,[5] where Satan offers him world sovereignty in exchange for his worship.[6] Although sovereignty over the nations is promised the Son (see Ps 2:6-8), it will only be realized by a lowly path of service leading to the cross (cf. 28:18-20), not by shifting allegiance to Satan. Jesus repudiates Satan's proposal by citing Deut 6:13, thus indicating that he understood submission to Satan as tantamount to idolatry, the ultimate

---

[3]The exact meaning of the term "pinnacle" (πτερύγιον, *pterygion*) remains unclear: "it serves to designate the tip or extremity of anything" (*BAGD*, p. 727). Suffice it to observe that Jesus found himself on a very high portion of the temple.

[4]The temple was viewed as the place where Yahweh had put his name, where God's presence was manifested in Israel (see, e.g., 1 Kgs 8:48; 9:3; Ps 76:1-2; 87:1-3; Isa 49:14-16; Ezek 43:6-7).

[5]On the importance of the "mountain" theme in Matthew see T.L. Donaldson, *Jesus on the Mountain: A Study in Matthean Theology*, (JSNTSup 8; Sheffield: *JSOT*, 1985).

[6]On Satan as the "god" or "ruler" of this world see 2 Cor 4:4; John 12:31; 14:30; 16:11.

renunciation of one's loyalty to God. For the sake of political advantage or momentary prosperity Israel repeatedly renounced loyalty to God in favor of foreign gods. Jesus refuses to compromise his devotion to God for the ease of an alternative path that would avoid the path of suffering and service. The Devil is therefore forcefully dismissed (ὕπαγε, *hypage*, cf. Luke 4:13) and is replaced by **angels** who minister to his need (cf. Matt 26:53), thus signifying both the victory of God's obedient Son (cf. Heb 1:6), and the ultimate faithfulness of God toward the obedient (cf. 1 Kgs. 19:5-8).[7]

The temptation narrative succinctly maps out the path that Jesus, as the lowly servant, will take. The episode provides the reader with significant character insights that help to explain the actions and words of Jesus in subsequent scenes. The will of God and his devotion to fulfill it will take precedent over everything else, including sustaining his own life (cf. 16:20-21; 26:36-46). The mission of Jesus embodies and concretizes what it means to say: that in Jesus God is with his people (1:23). Jesus refuses to carry out his divine mission according to the principles of the world. Hence, the exercise of his divine power and the accomplishment of God's will are not determined by popular expectations or human ambitions (cf. 16:1-4; 27:40). The extraordinary power and transcendent status belonging to Jesus as God's Son is necessarily tied to his submission to God's will and the lowly path of service marked out for him by the Father. The temptation narrative constitutes Jesus' response to the heavenly voice in 3:17, as the Son resolves to walk the path of total devotion to God's sovereign will. The Son conquers where Israel failed (Deut 6:10-19; 8:1-10; cf. Exod 4:22-23) because he is the obedient Son who loves God with his whole heart.

G. INTRODUCING THE MINISTRY OF JESUS (4:12-16)

12When Jesus heard that John had been put in prison, he returned to Galilee. 13Leaving Nazareth, he went and lived in Capernaum, which was by the lake in the area of Zebulun and

---

[7]Hagner, *Matthew*, 1:69.

Naphtali — [14]to fulfill what was said through the prophet Isaiah:

> **[15]"Land of Zebulun and land of Naphtali,**
> **the way to the sea, along the Jordan,**
> **Galilee of the Gentiles —**
> **[16]the people living in darkness**
> **have seen a great light;**
> **on those living in the land of the shadow of death**
> **a light has dawned."[a]**

[a]*16* Isaiah 9:1,2

The language of 4:12-16 provides a fitting closure to the preministry phase of Jesus' life by drawing together several themes dominant in 1:1–4:11. The continued emphasis on geographical fulfillment citations serves to alert the reader that God's providential direction of events is not complete until Jesus arrives in Galilee (cf. 2:6,15,22-23).[8] By recalling the tribes of Zebulun and Naphtali Matthew continues to correlate significant experiences in Israelite history with events in the life of Jesus. The universal significance of Jesus' messianic mission is once again reinforced by defining Galilee as Galilee of the Gentiles (v. 15). The Son's mission in Galilee is dominated by a salvific emphasis, wherein God's people are rescued from darkness by the dawning light in their midst (v. 16). While the texts comprising 4:12-16 do bring together key themes and emphases from earlier sections in the story, they also advance the story by setting the stage for Jesus' public ministry and his calling of people to experience God's rule and presence (4:17ff.).

4:12. Matthew is careful to document that Jesus' departure **to Galilee** is motivated by his having **heard** (ἀκούσας, *akousas*) concerning John's arrest (cf. 14:13; Mark 1:12). A strong case can be made for seeing Jesus' departure not as a flight from danger, but as Matthew's way to connect the mission of Jesus to that of John as part of a "providentially guided sacred history" whereby "the cessation of

[8]Note especially the verbal parallels with the early travels of Joseph (2:22-23). For a detailed treatment of the function of 4:12-16 in the broader structure of the first Gospel see Warren Carter, "Kernels and Narrative Blocks: The Structure of Matthew's Gospel," *CBQ* 54 (July, 1992), 463-481.

one becomes the divinely appointed sign of the commencement of the other."[9] Nevertheless, the reader must wait until 14:3-11 to learn the basis of John's arrest and the eventual outcome.

4:13-14. The geographical references in 4:13 prepare the reader for the fulfillment citation (4:15-16), as Jesus takes up residence on the northwest shore of the Sea of Galilee, specifically in a relatively large village known as **Capernaum.**[10] The language **by the lake**, and the identification of the territory as once belonging to the tribes of **Zebulun and . . . Naphtali**, anticipate the Isaianic citation to follow (i.e., Isa 8:23–9:2, in the Hebrew text).

4:15-16. It should be observed that Matthew's citation of Isaiah does not slavishly follow either the LXX or the Hebrew text, but probably represents an "independent rendering of the Hebrew."[11] Originally, Isaiah's oracle was intended to contrast the tragic devastation of the regions of Zebulun and Naphtali by the Assyrians[12] (see 1 Kgs. 17:1-6) with a promise of a reversal of fortunes to be realized in the indeterminate future. However, Matthew shifts the emphasis away from the political plight of the people to their desperate moral and spiritual condition, as a people "living in darkness," under the very "shadow of death" (cf. Ps 107:14; Luke 1:79).[13] Clearly, Matthew sees the **darkness** about to be dispelled

---

[9]See G.M. Soares Prabhu, *The Formula Quotations in the Infancy Narrative of Matthew: An Inquiry into the Tradition History of Mt. 1-2* (AnBib 63; Rome: Biblical Institute, 1976), p. 126.

[10]R. Riesner, "Archaeology and Geography," in *DJG*, p. 39, estimates the population at 1,500. However, Davies and Allison, *Matthew*, 1:378 contend that the population may have been as high as 12,000.

[11]See R.H. Gundry, *The Use of the Old Testament in St. Matthew's Gospel* (Leiden: E.J. Brill, 1967), p. 108.

[12]The language "way to the sea" and "along the Jordan" (πέραν, *peran*, lit., "on the other side") may reflect the Assyrian invasion coming from the east of the Jordan progressing to the Mediterranean Sea.

[13]It may be that Matthew intends to highlight the living conditions of Jews who are despondent and frustrated by life among pagan Gentiles (so Hagner, *Matthew*, p. 74 and Carson, *Matthew*, p. 117). It should be observed, however, that the language "Galilee of the Gentiles" is not intended to imply that Galilee was comprised mostly of Gentiles. In fact, "in NT times Jews comprised the vast majority of the Galilean population" (Reisner, "Galilee," in *DJG*, p. 252); *contra* Blomberg, *Matthew*, p. 88.

with the "dawn" (ἀνέτειλεν [*aneteilen*], cf. LXX λάμψει [*lampsei*]) of a **great light** which will shine upon them in the person and ministry of Jesus. It is significant that the first blessings of the messianic age come to those people in Northern Palestine who first went into exile (see 1 Kgs 15:29). However, Jesus' ministry will ultimately transcend both political and ethnic boundaries (cf. "Galilee of the Gentiles") by heralding a kingdom with universal significance (4:17ff.). Thus, with Jesus situated in the "divinely ordained" locality, poised to begin his messianic mission, Matthew brings the introductory phase of his story to a close.

II. GOD'S SAVING PRESENCE IN THE MIDST OF HIS PEOPLE (4:17–10:42)

As noted earlier, attempts to delineate structural patterns and themes linking the parts of Matthew's story immediately confronts a composition so complex and intricately woven that a clear and uncomplicated structural scheme seems difficult to discern. Nevertheless, it does appear that the language of 4:17 is intended to formally signal to the reader the beginning of Jesus' public ministry. Earlier role descriptions, and the explicit commissioning of Jesus to his assigned task (see 1:21, "save his people from sins;" 2:6, "shepherd the people of Israel;" 3:17, commissioned to the role of God's Son and Servant; 4:15, a "light" to "Galilee of the Gentiles"), anticipate the performance, and raise questions concerning how (or if) Jesus will carry out the mission given him.

Clearly, the language of 4:17 is parallel in form to 16:21: "From that time on Jesus began to explain to his disciples that he must go to Jerusalem . . ." Both statements serve as general headings marking major transitions in Matthew's story of Jesus. The transitional heading of 4:17 makes it clear that the material comprising 4:17–16:20 is predominantly concerned to highlight Jesus' public announcement that God's sovereign reign has drawn near, thus necessitating a radical reformation (cf. 3:1). As indicated by three summary statements, the narrative block of 4:17–11:1 underscore the manner in which Jesus discharged his ministry and revealed his person in Israel:

> Jesus went throughout Galilee, teaching in their synagogues, preaching the good news of the kingdom, and healing every disease and sickness among the people (4:23).

> Jesus went through all the towns and villages, teaching in their synagogues, preaching the good news of the kingdom and healing every disease and sickness (9:35).

> After Jesus had finished instructing his twelve disciples, he went on from there to teach and preach in the towns of Galilee (11:1).

It is significant, as Kingsbury has observed, that these summaries "occur solely in the block of material 4:17–11:1," wherein Jesus is portrayed as "proffering salvation to Israel in word and deed."[14] In the first phase of his public ministry (i.e., 4:17–11:1), Jesus emerges as a man endowed with divine authority in the midst of his people (ἐν τῷ λαῷ, *en tō laō*, 4:23). The reader knows that Jesus' authority is ultimately grounded in the status of his person as God's Son (1:23; 2:15; 3:17; 4:3,6), his reception of the Spirit (3:16), and the divine mission conferred upon him (1:21,23; 2:5-6; 3:17; 4:12-16). Jesus thus embarks upon his public ministry with both the right and the power to be God's messenger and inaugurator of the time of salvation. The events recorded exhibit the following structural pattern:

- Call of the Disciples 4:18-22
  - Summary 4:23-25
    - Ministry in Word 5:1-7:28
    - Ministry in Deed 8:1-9:24
  - Summary 9:35
- Mission of the Disciples 9:36-11:1

A. PROGRAMMATIC HEADING: PROCLAMATION OF THE KINGDOM (4:17)

17 From that time on Jesus began to preach, "Repent, for the kingdom of heaven is near."

---

[14]Kingsbury, *Matthew: Structure and Christology*, p. 20.

As noted earlier, the phrase **from that time on . . .** (ἀπό τότε, *apo tote*) marks the beginning of a new phase of Matthew's story of Jesus. Even before Jesus, John had made the coming Kingdom central to his own proclamation (3:1). Ultimately, even the disciples will embark upon a mission heralding the "nearness of the kingdom of heaven" (10:2). However, in contrast to John and the disciples, Jesus is portrayed not as a mere announcer of God's imminent reign, but as the primary agent through which the reign of God would be realized.[15] In Jesus, God's kingly power and authority come to expression in a ministry marked by healing, restoration, and true liberation. Thus, Jesus is not merely a proclaimer of some distant future hope, but he uniquely exhibits the reality and implications of the message he proclaims. The reality now coming to expression in Jesus' ministry calls for a radical reformation (*metanoeite*) affecting the very course and direction one's life.

As noted earlier (see 3:2), the idea behind repentance involves the alteration of basic values, attitudes, and aspirations; essentially, a conversion that results in yielding one's entire life to the rule of God. Basically, Jesus' entire ministry is concerned to spell out the dimensions and practical implications of a life lived in submission to the kingly authority of God.

B. CALL OF THE DISCIPLES (4:18-22)

18As Jesus was walking beside the Sea of Galilee, he saw two brothers, Simon called Peter and his brother Andrew. They were casting a net into the lake, for they were fishermen. 19"Come, follow me," Jesus said, "and I will make you fishers of men." 20At once they left their nets and followed him.

21Going on from there, he saw two other brothers, James son of Zebedee and his brother John. They were in a boat with their father Zebedee, preparing their nets. Jesus called them, 22and immediately they left the boat and their father and followed him.

15Joachim Jeremias, *New Testament Theology: The Proclamation of Jesus* (New York: Charles Scribner's Sons, 1971), p. 49.

4:18-19. Jesus' sense of the critical times now dawning with his presence in Galilee is graphically illustrated by this vocational calling of the disciples. In the first episode following Matthew's summary of Jesus' proclamation (4:17), four fishermen are confronted by his authoritative summons to **follow** (lit., "come after") him. Although Matthew's account of the call of these early disciples is less informative than we might wish (cf. Luke 5:1-11; John 1:35-51), their response to Jesus' call is illustrative both of true discipleship and the compelling character of Jesus' person.

4:20-22. Two sets of brothers, called fishermen, are confronted by Jesus' authoritative call while they are engaged in their occupational livelihood (vv. 18,21). Unlike typical rabbinic practice, Jesus takes the initiative to select his own followers by confronting them with an unconditional demand to join him in ministry. It is clear, in Matthew's story, that discipleship, in the sense of accompanying Jesus, arose primarily through his authoritative call (cf. 8:19-22; 9:9).

Jesus promises that he will exercise a creative influence in their lives by transforming them into "fishers of men" (cf. Jer. 16:16). The metaphor builds on their occupational skills, and promises their eventual involvement in gathering people under the reign of God (cf. 4:19 with the parallel imagery of "harvesters," 9:37-38). As such, their call to service has a sense of urgency that supersedes both livelihood and personal family relations (cf. 8:22).

Matthew is careful to document the willingness of these early disciples to forsake the security of home and vocation (cf. 19:27), thus establishing early in his story the necessary elements of true discipleship (cf. 8:18-22; 19:27-29). Jesus' authoritative call must take precedence over all family ties (cf. 10:34-36) and concern for physical well-being (cf. 6:25-33). It demands nothing less than a decisive break from old loyalties and a radical reorientation of one's values and priorities.[16]

As Matthew's story continues, the disciples will often fluctuate between faith and understanding (14:33; 16:16-18; 26:16-17) on the

---

[16]See the discussion by James D.G. Dunn, *Jesus' Call to Discipleship* (Cambridge: Cambridge University Press, 1992); also M.J. Wilkins, *The Concept of Disciple in Matthew's Gospel* (Leiden: Brill, 1988).

one hand, to failure and "little faith" (14:31; 16:8; 17:20; 21:20; 28:17) on the other. However, their initial response to Jesus establishes an important role relationship which will become an important story-line in Matthew's overall narrative.

C. PROGRAMMATIC SUMMARY (4:23-25)

[23]Jesus went throughout Galilee, teaching in their synagogues, preaching the good news of the kingdom, and healing every disease and sickness among the people. [24]News about him spread all over Syria, and people brought to him all who were ill with various diseases, those suffering severe pain, the demon-possessed, those having seizures, and the paralyzed, and he healed them. [25]Large crowds from Galilee, the Decapolis,[a] Jerusalem, Judea and the region across the Jordan followed him.

[a]*25* That is, the Ten Cities

4:23. The summary that follows the call of the disciples serves primarily as a programmatic transition between scenes, succinctly highlighting the contours of Jesus' public ministry and the extent of his initial success. Summaries in Matthew (cf. 8:16; 9:35; 12:15; 14:35-36; 15:30-31; 19:1-2) are characterized by generalizations that underscore recurrent acts of ministry and the response to them. As such, they indicate that the specific events narrated are only representative of what was generally characteristic of Jesus' ministry. The activities described in 4:23-25 provide the reader with an overview of the scope and impact of Jesus' messianic activity.

The language of verse 23, alongside the parallel statement in 9:35 outlines the ministry of Jesus in terms of three activities: ***teaching* in their synagogues, *preaching* the good news of the kingdom, and *healing* every disease and sickness among the people** (italics added). There is probably no clear distinction to be made between teaching (διδάσκων, *didaskōn*) and preaching (κηρύσσων, *kēryssōn*) since both are ultimately concerned with the advancement of the kingdom. The content of Jesus' proclamation is **the good news of the kingdom**. While βασιλεία (*basileia*, kingdom) focuses one's attention on God's sovereign presence, the "good news" is that

God's presence and reign are actualized and revealed in the person of Jesus (cf. 1:23; 12:28). Hence when Jesus preaches the kingdom he is in effect saying that God's saving presence must be understood in terms of his own ministry and proclamation. The practical implications of a life lived in submission to God's reign are spelled out in the discourse to follow (chs. 5-7).

As many have noted, 4:23 and 9:35 function as literary brackets (*inclusio*), enclosing prime examples of Jesus' teaching (chs. 5-7), and his healing ministry (chs. 8-9). The effect is to cluster major themes and to give the narrative a coherent focus, as Matthew provides concrete examples of Jesus' preaching and teaching, alongside his healing ministry (θεραπεύω, *therapeuō*).

4:24-25. The geographical influence of Jesus' ministry extends to the whole of Israel,[17] even impacting predominantly non-Jewish areas (Syria). "Large crowds" follow him and bring their sick seeking relief from their afflictions.[18] Jesus' *therapeutic* activity involves the healing of diseases and various sorts of painful conditions. Restoration to health and the liberation of those possessed by demons graphically demonstrate that God's powerful reign has drawn near in the person of Jesus. His healing ministry is also illustrative of Jesus' willingness to assume the role as Israel's compassionate Shepherd-King, who truly cares for his people and delivers them from their afflictions (cf. 1:21; 2:6). The miracles recorded in chapters 8 and 9 provide concrete examples of Jesus' healing ministry.

---

[17]As several have noted, the list of geographical places is comprehensive: NW Galilee, NE Decapolis, SW Judea, SE Perea.

[18]The function of the "crowds" in Matthew has been the subject of much discussion; for a recent proposal see Warren Carter, "The Crowds in Matthew's Gospel," *CBQ* 55 (January 1993), 54-67.

MATTHEW 5

D. SERMON ON THE MOUNT: MINISTRY IN WORD (5:1–7:29)

The *Sermon on the Mount* (=*SM*) is the first of five major discourses in Matthew, each concluding with a similar formulaic statement marking the end of the discourse (cf. 7:20; 11:1; 15:53; 19:1; 26:1). The wealth of literature addressing these three chapters (i.e., 5-7), testifies to their enduring appeal and profundity of content.[1] Surveys detailing the history of the *SM's* interpretation reveal that often questions of practicality and applicability determine exegetical conclusions.[2] It is critical that the meaning of the *SM* emerges from its function in the narrative sequence, and not in some modern agenda or social concern. The *SM* is not a manual for universal ethics or a blueprint for social and political utopianism. But, neither is there anything in the *SM* to suggest that Jesus' words may be dismissed as unrealistic or wholly assigned to some future realization. The message and the *SM's* application are best understood contextually, as the discourse is fully integrated into the surrounding narrative.

Critical scholarship has often been preoccupied not with the finished form of Matthew's *Sermon on the Mount*, but with the origin of various sayings comprising the *SM* and how the evangelist shaped and interpreted his pre-existing sources. Clearly, a study of the relationship between Matthew's *Sermon on the Mount* and Luke's so-called *Sermon on the Plain* (see Luke 6:20-49) argues conclusively

---

[1]For an overview of material on the Sermon on the Mount since 1960 see Warren Carter, *What are They Saying About Matthew's Sermon on the Mount* (New York: Paulist Press, 1994). Earlier bibliographical material can be found in W.S. Kissinger, *The Sermon on the Mount: A History of Interpretation and Bibliography* (Metuchen, NJ: Scarecrow, 1975).

[2]See the survey of approaches in H.K. McArthur, *Understanding the Sermon on the Mount* (New York: Harper, 1960).

for the *SM* being a composite product and not the verbatim record of a single sermon. However, efforts to sort out with any degree of precision the literary and historical origins of a saying, and then to determine Matthew's intention and meaning, is at best only hypothetical. Furthermore, such a proposal tends to attribute the bulk of the *SM* to the creativity of the early church rather than the historical Jesus. While the sermon comprising Matthew 5-7 may not have been a single sermon preached on one occasion by Jesus, its essential content and function owe their origin to Jesus. The general observation by France on Matthew's discourses is worth noting:

> . . . Matthew's discourses are not single sermons delivered all together on one occasion, but careful compilations of sayings of Jesus which Matthew has brought together into 'anthologies' to illustrate Jesus' teaching on particular themes . . . In other words, the teaching is that of Jesus, but the arrangement is that of Matthew."[3]

Although the organizing genius of the evangelist is widely recognized, there is no scholarly consensus concerning the overall structural form of the *SM*. It is generally agreed that key texts do highlight smaller structural units (e.g., 5:17, 20; 6:1; 7:12), but efforts to delineate a consistent pattern connecting all the parts into a coherent whole has not found scholarly unanimity.[4] While the *SM* is not a random collection of sayings without structural concerns, it is probably best to see theological themes as the dominating factor controlling the shape of the *SM*, and not symmetrical patterns.

The *SM* is framed by an introduction and conclusion (5:12 and 7:28-8:1) with clear verbal parallels: crowds (5:1 and 7:28); mountain (5:1 and 8:1); "he went up" and "he came down" (5:1 and 8:1); teaching (5:2 and 7:28); and "open his mouth" has the corresponding "when Jesus finished these words" (5:2 and 7:28). The discourse formally begins with a description of the character and mission of those who take seriously God's reign (5:3-16). The blessings of the New Age have come near for the poor in spirit, those who mourn, the lowly, hungry, and the persecuted (5:3-12). These disciples are

---

[3]France, *Matthew,* pp.159-160.

[4]See the various proposals in Carter, *What Are They Saying*, pp. 35-55.

destined for a positive vocation in the world, thereby bringing glory to the Father (5:13-16).

Even the interpretation and practice of the Law is now conditioned by the new state of affairs introduced by the time of fulfilment (5:17-20). Those who live under the reign of God practice a "greater righteousness" (5:20), both toward one's neighbor (5:21-48), and before the Father (6:1-18).

Although the unifying theme(s) of 6:19-7:12 is in much dispute, Davies and Allison's proposal that the section addresses "life in the temporal secular world," by instructing the disciple "how to behave in the world at large" does give the *SM* a comprehensive focus. Thus, 6:19-34 addresses the question "What should I do with and about wealth," and 7:1-12 focuses on the issue "How should I treat my neighbor."[5]

The *SM* concludes with a series of warnings and alternatives designed to confront the hearers with a crisis of decision. Eternal consequences are attached to one's choice between a broad and narrow way (7:13-14). Distinguishing between true and false prophets cannot be based upon external credentials or confessionary claims (7:15-23). The metaphor of good and bad trees and the production of fruit places the emphasis upon one's internal character that manifests itself in compliance to the will of God. The importance of both "hearing and doing" is continued in a final parable depicting two builders who construct houses on very different foundations (7:24-27). The wise builder is distinguished from the foolish one because the words of Jesus are not only heard but put into practice. It is clear that Jesus' teaching is to be taken with all seriousness since it is the determinative factor in one's eternal destiny.

From the above overview it appears that the unifying theme of the *SM* is the Kingdom of God. Even before the discourse the dynamic presence of the kingdom is realized in acts of healing, by which people are made whole (4:23-25). As observed by Allison, the sequence of the narrative has important theological implications:

> Before the crowds hear the Messiah's word they are the object of his compassion and healing. Having done nothing, nothing at all, they are benefitted. So grace comes before task, succor before

[5]Davies and Allison, *Matthew*, 1:627.

> demand, healing before imperative. The first act of the Messiah is not the imposition of his commandments but the giving of himself. Today's command presupposes yesterday's gift.[6]

The *SM's* ethical idealism assumes that the presence of God's reign requires a radical transformation of values and ambitions. The beatitudes are framed by the promise that "theirs is the kingdom of heaven" (5:3,10), thus highlighting qualities peculiar to the kingdom. Experiencing the blessings of God's kingdom demands a qualitatively different form of righteousness than that practiced by the "Pharisees and teachers of the law" (5:20). The heart of the Lord's Prayer is concerned that God's reign be fully realized upon "the earth as it is in heaven" (6:10). The petition echoes the continual tension between the present experience of the kingdom and the future consummation of God's redemptive scheme. Meanwhile, disciples must make the kingdom and the righteousness commensurate with the rule of God, the very center of their lives (6:33). The realization and full experience of God's kingdom demands that the will of God, as interpreted by Jesus, be fundamental to one's life (7:21-23).

Since the entirety of the *SM* assumes the presence of God's gracious presence, it cannot be reduced to a legal code requiring a certain performance to earn divine favor. Instead the *SM* should be read as an expression of the visible fruit and character development that comes when God's sovereign reign is taken seriously. The imperatives assume that God's grace has first drawn near bringing transforming power. The ethic of the *SM* is not unlike NT ethics in general, wherein "being" always precedes "doing" (cf. Eph 4:1–5:2; Col 3:1-17).

With this orientation to the *SM* we will now examine in more detail the contents of Jesus' first discourse.

1. The Setting (5:1-2)

[1]Now when he saw the crowds, he went up on a mountainside and sat down. His disciples came to him, [2]and he began to teach them, saying:

---

[6]D.C. Allison, "The Structure of the Sermon on the Mount," *JBL* 106 (1987), 441.

5:1-2. Matthew describes the setting of Jesus' first discourse in terms that connect the *SM* to the previous narrative. The "crowds" that prompt Jesus' move to the mountain setting are those who have benefitted from Jesus' healing ministry and continue to follow him (4:23-25). They however, are distinguished from the "disciples" who have already made a commitment to live under the reign of God as proclaimed by Jesus (4:17-22). It is these disciples who come to Jesus and he teaches "them" (5:2). While the "crowds" hear the *SM* as "outsiders" (cf. 7:28–8:1), the primary recipients of Jesus' teachings are those who have embarked upon a life of discipleship. For those committed to the reign of God the *SM* describes what it means to lead a life in which God's kingdom is taken seriously. For the "crowds" who hear the *SM* as "outsiders" Jesus' words constitute an implicit invitation to become disciples.

Although the exact physical location where Jesus delivered his discourse is unknown, it is possible that Matthew intends his readers to see typological or theological significance in Jesus' ascent to the mountain. The phrase "he went up on a mountainside" has been linked to Sinai typology, associated with the Mosaic giving of the Law (cf. Exod 19-20, 34) and the eschatological gathering of the people of God before Mt. Zion to receive a new Torah (cf. Isa 2:2-4; Jer 31).[7] While the Mosaic overtones seem stronger, one should not press the notion that Jesus is portrayed as a new Moses introducing a new Law. In reality, Matthew portrays Jesus as the medium through which God speaks to disclose the true intent and interpretation of the Law given at Mt. Sinai. Ultimately, the revelation given by Jesus is based upon his unique intuitive awareness of the mind of his Father. Thus, Jesus assumes the authoritative role of God's spokesman, who sets forth the nature and demands of God's kingdom.

2. The Beatitudes (5:3-12)

[3]"Blessed are the poor in spirit,
for theirs is the kingdom of heaven.

[7]These themes are developed by Terence L. Donaldson, *Jesus on the Mountain: A Study of Matthean Theology* (JSNTSup 8; Sheffield: JSOT, 1985).

[4]Blessed are those who mourn,
for they will be comforted.
[5]Blessed are the meek,
for they will inherit the earth.
[6]Blessed are those who hunger and thirst for righteousness,
for they will be filled.
[7]Blessed are the merciful,
for they will be shown mercy.
[8]Blessed are the pure in heart,
for they will see God.
[9]Blessed are the peacemakers,
for they will be called sons of God.
[10]Blessed are those who are persecuted because of righteousness,
for theirs is the kingdom of heaven.
[11]"Blessed are you when people insult you, persecute you and falsely say all kinds of evil against you because of me. [12]Rejoice and be glad, because great is your reward in heaven, for in the same way they persecuted the prophets who were before you.

Jesus' first discourse begins with a series of nine beatitudes describing in ideal terms the character and lifestyle of those who experience God's saving presence. The inbreaking of God's dynamic reign means a radical reversal of fortunes where the poor, the hungry, and the persecuted are called "blessed" (μακάριοι, *makarioi*).[8] They are "blessed" because the presence of the kingdom initiates a new era conferring both present and end-time blessings. The beatitudes are not "entrance requirements" in order to get into the kingdom, but are descriptive of the character and blessings of those in the kingdom.[9] The character traits described are gracious gifts resulting from God's saving presence and modeled in the person of

---

[8]Davies and Allison, *Matthew,* 1:431-434, provides a good overview of the use of beatitudes in the OT and Hellenistic literature; see also D.E. Garland, "Blessing and Woe," *DJG,* pp. 77-81.

[9]Argued convincingly by R.A. Guelich, "The Matthean Beatitudes: 'Entrance Requirements' or Eschatological Blessings?" *JBL* 95 (1976), 415-434.

Jesus. As a fitting introduction to the *SM*, the beatitudes remind the disciple that God's gift always precedes the demand.

Each beatitude is composed of a statement identifying the character blessed by God (e.g., "blessed are the poor in spirit"), followed by a clause explaining the basis of their blessed state (e.g., "theirs is the kingdom of heaven"). The collection neatly divides into two sets of fours (i.e., 5:3-6 and 5:7-10), with the ninth beatitude (5:11-12) expanding on the theme of the eighth. The first group of four (5:3-6) focus attention on one's relationship to God, while the second group (5:7-10) highlight horizontal relationships. The collection is bracketed by a literary device known as *inclusio*, where an identical line begins and ends a section (i.e., "for theirs is the kingdom of heaven," 5:3, 10). It is the present reality of the kingdom that assures future blessings of those deemed "blessed."

5:3. The term translated "blessed" (*makarioi*) is descriptive of the present state of those who have received God's favor and thus are to be "congratulated." The disciple's deep joy and happiness is predicated upon God's gracious response to their condition, not upon favorable external conditions. They are "blessed" because they now experience the long-awaited saving presence of God.

The first beatitude identifies the **poor in spirit** as the subject of this blessed state. Divine approval rests with those who acknowledge their impoverished condition and desperate dependency upon God. Too much has been made of the distinction between Luke's simple "the poor" (Luke 6:20), and Matthew's addition "in spirit." There is no reason to assume that Matthew spiritualizes Luke's explicit socioeconomic reference. In fact, as noted by Hagner Matthew "too means the literally poor, but he focuses on their psychological condition or frame of mind."[10] While the term translated "poor" (πτωχοί, *ptōchoi*; sing., *ptōchos*) does primarily refer to unfavorable economic conditions, in the OT *ptōchos* and its Hebrew equivalents draw special attention to one's lack of status and social rights, thus highlighting one's utter dependency upon God (see Ps 40:17; 86:1; 113:7). Since Jewish piety often attached a religious significance to poverty, Matthew's "in spirit" simply highlights the internal disposition resulting from oppression and economic deprivation.

---

[10]Hagner, *Matthew*, 1:91.

The force of the present tense (ἔστιν, *estin*) indicates that the disciples experience the kingdom as a present reality. As observed earlier, in Jesus' proclamation (4:17) and ministry (4:21-24) the kingdom is already in some sense present, and thus the disciples have begun to realize its saving and transforming power. However, subsequent future tenses (vv. 4-9) indicate that the experience of the kingdom has both a present and future orientation. While the consummation and ultimate expression of God's reign lie in the future, those who stand before God without pretense, stripped of any claim of self-righteousness and self-sufficiency even now experience the blessings of God's rule. Truly, Jesus has come "to preach good news to the poor" (Isa 61:1).

5:4. The term **mourn** (πενθέω, *pentheō*) recalls the language of Isaiah 61:2: "to comfort all who mourn." In the context of Isaiah 61 mourning is based on the fact that "the righteous suffer, because the wicked prosper, and because God has not yet acted to reverse the situation."[11] It follows that the grief experienced by the disciples should not be limited to sorrow over personal sin. Participants in the kingdom of God are genuinely grieved by the general tyranny of sin characteristic of this present evil age. **Blessed** is the disciple who can be truly saddened by the world's hostility and rebellion against the realization of God's will. In an expression of intense despair and sorrow the sensitive disciple yearns "for God to act to make things right (cf. Isa 66:2, 13: Rev 21:4)."[12]

The mourners are blessed because they will ultimately experience God's deliverance and consolation. The future passive (παρακληθήσονται, *paraklēthēsontai*) points to God's direct involvement in bringing comfort to his afflicted people. Even now the blessed state of those in the kingdom rests on the realization that in Jesus the consolation of God has already drawn near (cf. Luke. 2:25), bringing inner joy and resolve in spite of one's external conditions. Ultimately, the mighty reign of God will bring an everlasting **comfort** befitting the eternal age to come.

5:5. The term translated **meek** (πραΰς, *praüs*) is essentially parallel in thought to the first beatitude's "poor in spirit" (cf. Ps 37; Isa

[11]Davies and Allison, *Matthew*, 1:448.

[12]Garland, *Reading Matthew*, p. 56.

61:7). Both ideas highlight the powerless condition of those who stand without this world's resources, utterly dependent upon God. The "meek" are not weak, cowardly, or passively resigned to oppression. The strength of these powerless ones derives from their dependency upon God, and thus they repudiate worldly ambitions and methods for achieving better conditions. The "meek" are blessed because their ultimate vindication comes from God, not a shortsighted attempt through the use of force or violence to break the grip of oppression. Jesus is the example *par excellence* of meekness in Matthew's story (11:29; 12:15-21; 21:5).

The promise of inheriting the earth has its roots in the Abrahamic covenant (cf. Gen 12:7; 22:17), and originally referred to the land of Palestine. Jewish eschatological hopes ultimately expanded the promise to envision a radically renewed earth where God would reign over all the nations (Isa 57:13; 60:21; 65:17; 66:22; cf. Matt 8:11; 19:28). Jesus' words move beyond territorial or geographical bounds by paralleling the promise of 5:3: "Theirs is the kingdom of heaven." As Guelich observes, the only difference between "inheriting the earth" and possessing the kingdom is "the temporal perspective of the promise" (i.e., 5:3 present; 5:5 future).[13] Ultimately, the meek receive the long awaited inheritance not by military conquest, but by the gracious gift of God (see Isa 61:7).

5:6. As with previous beatitudes (cf. 5:3-4), the language of this one seems also to be drawn from Isaiah 61, where "righteousness" is described as God's eschatological gift: God will clothe his people with a "robe of righteousness" (61:10); he will cause "righteousness and praise to spring up before all nations" (61:11); and those whom God comforts will be called "oaks of righteousness" (61:3; cf. 49:8-10; 61:7). Fundamental human needs such as **hunger and thirst** are often used in the OT to describe the desperate conditions of those who seek divine intervention (Ps 42:2; 63:1; 107:5-7; 143:6; Isa 55:1-2; Amos 8:11). Therefore, those who "hunger and thirst" are the same group of destitute people who are earlier described as the "poor" and those who "grieve."

The object of their yearning is **righteousness** (δικαιοσύνη, *dikaiosynē*). The term is an important concept in Matthew's Gospel

[13]Guelich, *Sermon*, p. 101.

especially as it is developed in the *SM* (see 5:20; 6:1; 6:33). However, the precise connotation suggested by the word has been the subject of some dispute. Does the term in 5:6 suggest a personal pursuit of conduct in keeping with the will of God,[14] or as proposed by others, does it express the deep longing of the downtrodden and oppressed for the manifestation of God's eschatological justice.[15] Given the immediate context and the apparent background of Isaiah 61 it seems that greater weight should be given to the latter. Nevertheless, the desire for personal righteousness is never far removed from genuine eschatological hope (cf. 5:20; 6:33).

Those who "hunger" for God's saving presence are blessed because they will ultimately be **filled** or "satisfied" (χορτασθή-σονται, *chortasthēsontai*). Such language reflects OT expectations associated with the triumph of God's cause (Ps 17:15; 107:9; 132:15; 146:7; Isa 49:10; 65:21-22). The consummation of God's reign means that one's deepest needs will be met.

5:7. The next four beatitudes (vv. 7-10) move from social or physical conditions underlying spiritual attitudes, to fundamental virtues reflective of Christian character. "Blessedness" is reserved for those who relate to others according to the values of the kingdom. Extending **mercy** to others simply models God's compassionate and forgiving response to our unworthy condition (cf. Exod 34:6; Matt 18:23-35). The importance of "mercy" in Matthew's Gospel is demonstrated by the fact that Jesus identifies merciful action as the most basic expression of one's relationship to God (9:13; 12:7; 23:23; 25:31-46).[16] The merciful are those who reflect God's acceptance of the unworthy, the guilty, and the ones in the wrong, based upon the premise that God's forgiving and restoring acceptance has been manifested in the message and person of Jesus. They are blessed because in the last day **they will be shown mercy**.

---

[14]As argued by Davies and Allison, *Matthew*, 1:452-53; and Georg Strecker, *Sermon*, p. 37.

[15]As proposed by Guelich, *Sermon*, pp.102-103; and Hagner, "Righteousness in Matthew's Theology," in *Worship, Theology, and Ministry in the Early Church: Essays in Honor of Ralph Martin*, eds. Michael Wilkins and Terence Page (Sheffield: JSOT, 1992) pp. 112-113.

[16]Davies and Allison, *Matthew*, 1:455.

5:8. The language here may have its roots in Ps 24:3-4: "Who may ascend the hill of the Lord? Who may stand in his holy place? He who has clean hands and a pure heart, who does not lift up his soul to an idol or swear by what is false." The Psalmist understands that drawing near to God in worship is conditioned upon the integrity of one's character, not mere ritual. A **pure heart** is descriptive of one's innermost being and motivations. Those who are blessed to **see God** are those with individual loyalty and sincerity of purpose, who act with absolute integrity and transparent honesty.[17] Like the Psalmist who experiences God's presence in the context of temple worship, those who act before God with single-minded devotion and a genuine spirit, will, in the end experience God's presence in a most intimate way.

5:9. Those living under the reign of God actively pursue restoration of wholeness and well-being in a world shattered by hostility. A premium is placed on the restoration of relationships (5:22-24; 18:10ff.) including those identified as enemies (5:38-47). The disciples will soon learn that the message of peace does not always meet with positive acceptance (10:34). Nevertheless, the active pursuit of peace models the very character of God, and these **peacemakers** are identified by God as beloved children.

5:10. The final beatitude (vv. 10-12) rounds off the series (cf. v. 3) with the assurance that like the "poor," those **persecuted** are also blessed because they participate in **the kingdom of God**. Those experiencing persecution have evoked hostility not because of misconduct or selfish ambitions, but because of their devotion to God's will (cf. 1 Pet 3:14; 4:12-14). In this text **righteousness** is best understood as emphasizing a behavior or ethical stance in keeping with the will of God (cf. v. 6). However, it should be observed that the beatitude (v. 10) is followed by another (v. 11), now in the second person (**blessed are you**), which pronounces a "blessed" state upon those persecuted for Jesus' sake. The conduct which is described as "righteous" behavior is therefore defined as that which identifies with Jesus and his mission. For Matthew, Jesus is both the standard and source of true righteousness (cf. Phil. 3:9).

---

[17]*Contra* Strecker, *Sermon*, p. 39, who interprets the "pure in heart" as those who stand before God "spotless, without sin."

5:11-12. Those enduring the world's hostilities and insults can even now rejoice because the hope of future reward makes bearable present suffering. While Matthew's Gospel speaks much of "reward" (5:46; 6:1-6; 6:18; 10:41; 16:27; 19:27-30), the ultimate blessing of the faithful should not be construed as some meritorious claim upon God.[18] The righteous simply stand in a noble succession of true servants (i.e., **the prophets**) who endure opposition and hostility for the sake of God's redemptive plan. They are under no illusion that such conduct places God in their debt. In fact, their **reward in heaven** is vastly out of proportion to their earthly accomplishment (19:29–20:16; 25:2, 23). Future hopes should not obscure the fact that the presence of the kingdom brings transforming power and salvation even in the present.

Jesus pronounces his beatitudes upon those who constitute the new people of God, who are resolved to live in submission to God's sovereign reign. They are descriptive (and implicitly prescriptive) of the attitudes and character of those who participate in God's kingdom. By God's grace these virtues reflect the transforming power of God's reign over his people. However, the character traits of the kingdom also challenge the people of God to truly cultivate the counter-cultural qualities reflected in the beatitude.

3. Salt and Light (5:13-16)

13"You are the salt of the earth. But if the salt loses its saltiness, how can it be made salty again? It is no longer good for anything, except to be thrown out and trampled by men. 14"You are the light of the world. A city on a hill cannot be hidden. 15Neither do people light a lamp and put it under a bowl. Instead they put it on its stand, and it gives light to everyone in the house. 16In the same way, let your light shine before men, that they may see your good deeds and praise your Father in heaven.

Those who exhibit the character traits developed in the beatitudes are now described as exerting a positive influence in the

[18]Davies and Allison, *Matthew*, 1:633-634, have an excellent discussion on the concept of "reward" in Matthew.

world. The disciple's vocation in the world is patterned after Jesus' ministry which is described as the promised "light" for "Galilee of the Gentiles" (4:15-16), and whose activity results in people giving glory to God (see 9:7; 15:31; cf. 6:2). Jesus' descriptive language would probably have struck most Jewish ears as most presumptuous:

> For it is not Torah or the Temple or Jerusalem or Israel or some group within Israel (such as the Pharisees) that is the salt or light of the world (see Isa 60:1-3; Bar 4:2; Liv. Pro. Hab. 10; Sop. 15:8; Pesiq. Rab Kah. 21:5; Str-B 1:237), but Jesus' followers (the 'you' is emphatic).[19]

5:13. In the ancient world, **salt** had a variety of purposes,[20] therefore the precise significance of the metaphor is difficult to determine. Probably Jesus meant to highlight the indispensable role the disciples will have in the world, and their obligation to use their unique qualities to make a positive contribution. The imagery of salt that has lost its taste (lit. "to become foolish") envisions a scenario where the essential components of salt have become so diluted or adulterated that it no longer has a useful function.[21] In the same way, if the disciples fail to fulfill their role by diluting the values and priorities of the kingdom, they become useless as agents of renewal and redemption. Like salt that has become worthless, disciples who fail in mission are discarded as useless for kingdom purposes.

5:14. The positive influence of Jesus' followers is next described as the **light of the world**. The metaphorical imagery of "light" is a rich Old Testament symbol associated with Israel (cf. Isa 42:6; 51:4-5), or elements connected to Israel's historical and religious experience (e.g., Torah, Temple, or Jerusalem). It appears then that a role once fundamental to the identity of Israel has been transferred to Jesus' disciples. Furthermore, the global scope of the mission anticipates the worldwide commission to "disciple all the nations" (28:19).

---

[19]Allison, "The Structure of the Sermon on the Mount," 431, n.22.

[20]E.g., as seasoning for tasteless food, preservative, and even in small portions as a fertilizer; see N. Hillyer, "Salt" in *NIDNTT* 3:443-449.

[21]It should be noted that while sodium chloride as a chemical cannot lose its chemical properties, Palestinian salt came from the Dead Sea, and could lose its savor due to either chemical impurities or physical disintegration.

5:15-16. The significance of the "light" metaphor is further clarified by reference to a **city on a hill** and a **lamp** placed upon a **stand** (vv. 14-15). Both illustrations emphasize that it is the nature of light to shine and be seen. It is significant that before the imperative (**let your light shine**), the indicative (**you are**) provides the incentive for witness: "The disciples are not admonished to accomplish a task which will bring them into a desired state, but rather to be or become what they already are."[22]

Disciples "let their light shine" by modeling the values and priorities of the kingdom, as taught by Jesus. In contrast to those who do good works "before people" to call attention to themselves (cf. 6:1, 16, 18; 23:5, 28), Jesus' followers see their "good works" as a means to glorify God as Father. In this way they become a witness to God's transforming presence in the world.

4. Jesus and the Law (5:17-20)

Having identified the character of the new people of God (5:3-12) and their worldwide mission (5:13-16), the question inevitably arises: What role does the Law play within the life of the new people of God? The response first comes in the form of a brief paragraph setting forth the relationship of Jesus to the Law (5:17-20). Actually, the real question addressed is not to what extent does Jesus square with the Mosaic Law, but rather what are his followers to do with the Law in light of the fulfillment realized in Jesus? The so-called "antitheses" to follow (5:21-48) spell out in a practical manner the implications of Jesus' fulfillment of the "Law and the Prophets."

It is not my purpose to provide a detailed account of all the exegetical difficulties associated with 5:17-20.[23] My concern is to

---

[22]Herman Hendrickx, *The Sermon on the Mount: Studies in the Synoptic Gospels* (London: Geoffrey Chapman, 1979), p. 42.

[23]Some of the more helpful studies include Robert Banks, *Jesus and the Law in the Synoptic Tradition* (Cambridge: Cambridge University Press, 1975); J.P. Meier, *Law and History in Matthew's Gospel* (AnBib 71; Rome: Biblical Institute, 1976); D.J. Moo, "Jesus and the Authority of the Mosaic Law," *JSNT* 20 (1984) 3-49; K. Snodgrass, "Matthew and the Law," *SBLASP* (1988), 536-554.

highlight the salient features illustrating Jesus' relationship to the Mosaic Law.

[17]"Do not think that I have come to abolish the Law or the Prophets; I have not come to abolish them but to fulfill them. [18]I tell you the truth, until heaven and earth disappear, not the smallest letter, not the least stroke of a pen, will by any means disappear from the Law until everything is accomplished. [19]Anyone who breaks one of the least of these commandments and teaches others to do the same will be called least in the kingdom of heaven, but whoever practices and teaches these commands will be called great in the kingdom of heaven. [20]For I tell you that unless your righteousness surpasses that of the Pharisees and the teachers of the law, you will certainly not enter the kingdom of heaven.

5:17. The paragraph opens with an imperatival statement (μὴ νομίσητε, *mē nomisēte*) negating a faulty assessment of Jesus' vocation, i.e., "He came to destroy the Law and the Prophets." On the contrary, Jesus' coming (ἦλθον, *ēlthon*) signals the Law's fulfillment (πληρῶσαι, *plērōsai*) not its abolishment or annulment (καταλῦσαι, *katalysai*). It is significant that the first reference of Jesus to the **Law and the Prophets** is introduced with an expression **I have come** (*ēlthon*), thus highlighting his intent to define and establish his own vocation in terms of fulfilling God's will as expressed in Scripture (=Law and Prophets). The effect is to set the Law question within the context of a new state of affairs initiated by the coming of Jesus (cf. 10:24). Jesus' statement of purpose (*ēlthon* and infinitive) implies that the function of the Law can only be determined in the light of his messianic mission. A critical moment in history has dawned with the coming of Jesus, therefore the Law must be interpreted accordingly.

The positive purpose of the *ēlthon*-saying is defined in terms of Jesus' intent to introduce the moment of fulfillment. The exact meaning of **fulfill** (πληρόω, *plēroō*) in 5:17 has been the subject of much dispute.[24] Since throughout Matthew's story Jesus is portrayed as the true interpreter of God's will as expressed in

[24]For a discussion see Davis and Allison, *Matthew*, 1:485-486.

Scripture (cf. 12:13, 5, 7; 15:13-14;16:6, 12; 19:3-9; 22:23-46; 23:10), it would appear that "fulfilling" the "Law and the Prophets" necessarily includes revealing in word and deed the true intention of God's will as preserved in Scripture. Fulfillment is therefore not to be seen in terms of a Pharisaic legalistic adhesion to the minutia of law keeping. In fact, Jesus' interpretative agenda shifts the focus from the letter of the Law to the heart of the Lawgiver.

5:18. With Jesus as the definitive interpreter of the Law it continues to have validity **until** (ἕως, *heōs*): (1) **heaven and earth disappear** and (2) **everything is accomplished** (cf. 24:35). As indicated by the figurative expression **smallest letter . . . least stroke of a pen** (ἰῶτα . . . κεραία, *iōta . . . keraia*) the enduring validity of the law extends to the slightest detail.[25] The significance of the temporal limitations suggested by the *heōs* clauses has been much debated. Are the two clauses to be taken synonymously, both highlighting the permanent validity of the Law? It may be that the second *heōs* clause (until everything is accomplished) is added to clarify the former clause (until heaven and earth disappear), thus limiting the Law's validity until all God's purposes on earth are accomplished.[26] The view is in harmony with Matthew's "fulfillment" theme where the intended purpose of the Law is realized in the words and deeds of Jesus. It follows then that πάντα γένηται (*panta genētai*, "everything is [fulfilled]") parallels *plērōsai* in v. 17, and qualifies the normative character of the Law in terms of its accomplishment in Jesus.

5:19. The legalistic tone at 5:19 has resulted in many scholars attributing the saying to a strict Jewish-Christian element in the church which Matthew clumsily included in Jesus' discourse. In fact, the language at verse 19 continues the theme of verses 17-18 by affirming the importance of the Law in the life of Jesus' followers. Just as Jesus did not come to "abolish" the Law so his disciples are prohibited from "setting aside" even the **least of the commandments**. Like Jesus, the disciples should exhibit a high regard for

---

[25]As noted by Guelich, *Sermon*, p. 144; "The iota, representing the smallest Hebrew letter yod, and hook, representing the ornamental touches added to some Hebrew consonants . . . represent the indestructible character of even the smallest detail of the written Law."

[26]Proposal of Hagner, *Matthew*, 1:107.

faithfully practicing and teaching God's will as expressed in the Mosaic Law (cf. vv. 17-18). However, as noted earlier, the actual interpretation and application of the "least of these commandments" is now conditioned by a new state of affairs introduced by Jesus. He is the definitive interpreter of Scripture who ultimately defines faithfulness to God's will.

It has been observed that Matthew's Gospel places a great deal of emphasis on the role of teaching.[27] It is imperative that "every teacher of the Law who has been instructed in the kingdom of heaven" (13:52), learn how to read and interpret Scripture like Jesus. Indeed, it can be said that Matthew presents Jesus as providing a foundational hermeneutic for reading Scripture.[28]

The metaphorical language of **least** and **great** in the kingdom is reflective of the Matthean interest in rank and degrees of reward in heaven (cf. 11:1; 6:1; 10:41-42; 19:29; 25:21, 23). While such may seem to run counter to 20:1-16, the language may simply be intended to highlight figuratively the conduct pleasing to God in contrast to that which is displeasing.[29] Whatever the precise significance, it is crucial that Jesus' followers exhibit the spirit of the Lord toward the Law, both in conduct and teaching.

5:20. The **righteousness** exceeding the **Pharisees and the teachers of the Law** is anchored in the revelation of God's will as revealed in Jesus. It is both qualitatively and quantitatively different from a "righteousness" grounded in the minutia of Law keeping. Because the "greater righteousness" is patterned after God's own character (cf. 5:45), not legal niceties, its practice can truly extend to every aspect of one's life. The Pharisaic model of legal observance only results in a superficial righteousness oriented toward human recognition (cf. 6:1-4), thus leading to hypocritical pride (23:10). Entry into God's eschatological reign depends upon the practice of "righteousness" as taught by Jesus. What it means to exhibit such a "righteousness" is forcefully illustrated by the examples to follow (5:21-48).

---

[27]See, e.g., Paul S. Minear, *Matthew: The Teacher's Gospel* (New York: Pilgrim Press, 1982).

[28]The thesis of Gary D. Collier, *The Forgotten Treasure: Reading the Bible Like Jesus* (West Monroe, LA: Howard Publishing, 1993).

[29]See Snodgrass, "Matthew and the Law," 548.

5. Practicing Greater Righteousness Toward One's Neighbor[30] (5:21-48)

At the heart of Jesus' discourse is the elucidation of what it means to exhibit a "righteousness" surpassing that of the Pharisees (5:20). The greater righteousness which Jesus will illustrate with six examples (5:21-47), moves beyond the surface level of Law keeping to a life reflecting the very character of God (5:48; cf. 19:20-21). The point in each case is to move beyond the letter of the Law to an authoritative pronouncement of God's intention underlying the Law. In this way, Jesus exhibits his profound respect for the Law (cf. 5:18-19), while at the same time demonstrating the full extent of God's will for our lives. Legalism alone cannot possibly bring wholeness (τελείος, *teleios*, 5:48) to one's relationship with God and others.

Although 5:21-48 is typically labeled the "antitheses" it should not be concluded that all six paragraphs are intended to place Jesus' teaching in direct opposition to the Law of Moses. Such a notion is difficult to square with 5:17-20. While the adversative δέ (*de*, "but . . .") does establish a mild antithetical structure (cf. ἀλλὰ, *alla*)[31] between the internal application of the Law and Jesus' words, Jesus' application seems more concerned with God's intended will than the propagation of mere external observance. It appears that Jesus' words are intended to bring to full realization the "deeper principles of the will of God which underlie the specific laws of the OT."[32] Being driven by the disclosure of God's ultimate will necessarily entails countering both a literal and superficial understanding of the Law's specific commandments. On occasion, Jesus' teaching deepens the commandments by stressing the internal dimensions of God's will (5:21-22, 27-28; cf. 12:7; 15:10-20). Sometimes Jesus' interpretation counters contemporary practice by highlighting deeper principles in line with God's will and the ethics

---

[30]The titles are dependent upon Kingsbury, *Matthew as Story*, p. 112.

[31]See Jack Levison, "A Better Righteousness: The Character and Purpose of Matthew 5:21- 48," *Studia Biblica et Theologica* 12 (October 1982), 174-175.

[32]France, *Matthew: Evangelist and Teacher*, p. 193.

of the kingdom (5:33-37, 38-42). On other occasions certain implications drawn by contemporary interpreters are clearly set aside as not in harmony with God's ideal will (5:31-32, 43-44). It is apparent that Jesus' interpretation and application of the Law assumes an independent authority and insight into God's will not explicitly apparent in a literal reading of the Law.

Before examining the individual sections comprising 5:21-48 a word should be said about the introductory formula which, with slight variations, all six sections have in common: "You have heard that it was said to people long ago. . . but I tell you" (5:21, 27, 31, 33, 38, 43). While the phrase has a technical rabbinic usage[33] it is probably best to understand the phrase in this context as a reference to the general Jewish experience of hearing the OT read and interpreted in the synagogue.[34] The use of the passive ἐρρέθη (*errethē*, **it was said**) refers explicitly to what God said to **people long ago**. It seems apparent that "the people long ago" (τοῖς ἀρχαιοις, *tois archaiois*) refers to the original recipients of God's Law at Mt. Sinai. It follows that Jesus' words introduced with the phrase **but I tell you** are intended to take its point of reference from the words of Torah, not mere scribal interpretation. While there is an element of continuity between the words spoken at Sinai through Moses and Jesus' authoritative words, it is clear that Jesus understands himself to be the definitive interpreter of the Law who operates on a level above the mere external observance of a legal code. Although Jesus starts with a familiar passage from the OT, his teaching shows how God's true intent leads to a "righteousness" surpassing the scribes and Pharisees (v. 20).

Murder (5:21-26)

21"You have heard that it was said to the people long ago, 'Do not murder,[a] and anyone who murders will be subject to judgment.' 22But I tell you that anyone who is angry with his brother[b] will be subject to judgment. Again, anyone who says to his brother, 'Raca,[c]' is answerable to the Sanhedrin. But anyone who says, 'You fool!' will be in danger of the fire of hell.

---

[33]See discussion in Guelich, *Sermon*, p. 181f.; and Davies and Allison, *Matthew* 1:510-511.

[34]Guelich, *Sermon*, p.182.

[23]"Therefore, if you are offering your gift at the altar and there remember that your brother has something against you, [24]leave your gift there in front of the altar. First go and be reconciled to your brother; then come and offer your gift.

[25]"Settle matters quickly with your adversary who is taking you to court. Do it while you are still with him on the way, or he may hand you over to the judge, and the judge may hand you over to the officer, and you may be thrown into prison. [26]I tell you the truth, you will not get out until you have paid the last penny.[d]

[a]*21* Exodus 20:13 [b]*22* Some manuscripts *brother without cause* [c]*22* An Aramaic term of contempt [d]*26* Greek *kodrantes*

5:21-22. Jesus first cites the prohibition of murder from the sixth commandment of the decalogue (Exod 20:13), along with an allusion to the legal proceedings leading to punishment for its violation (see Exod 21:12; Num 35:12; Deut 17:8-13). Although the letter of the Law may appear clear, Jesus extends the grounds for "judgment" to include "anger" and demeaning and insulting language directed at one's brother (Raca ="empty-headed," "good for nothing," and the synonymous term "fool").[35] While the prohibition **Do not murder** may have originally been concerned to regulate acts of violence within the covenant community of Israel, the intent underlying the command was to cultivate a deepened sense of the worth and sanctity of human life and the preservation of community. Jesus' words, in fact, address fundamental attitudes and practices that reflect the devaluing of others which is the source and root of a wanton disregard for human life. Whereas the Law prohibited "murder" Jesus envisions a scenario where the factors that lead to hostility and broken relationships are no longer present.

The ascending order of judicial procedure (**judgment**, **Sanhedrin, hell**)[36] is probably intended to counter (ironically) the Jewish understanding that one's standing before God can be determined

[35]For discussion see Davies and Allison, *Matthew,* 1:513f.

[36]The "fire of hell" (γέεννα, geënna) originally referred to the Valley of Hinnom where Ahaz sacrificed his sons and burned incense to idols. The location later became a place for dumping garbage that was consumed by a perpetual fire. It was a familiar Jewish symbol for the final destruction of the wicked.

by one's legal standing. The irony of Jesus' words is that while human courts may declare one guiltless of the external act of murder, who would be declared innocent if the criteria of judgment was every angry thought or demeaning insult that undermined true brotherhood? The surpassing righteousness which Jesus upholds extends to every thought and action that is destructive of the bond that unites people under the reign of God.

5:23-24. Jesus draws out the practical implications of his teachings with two illustrations designed to impress the hearer (and reader!) with the importance of pursuing the restoration of broken relationships (5:23-26). First, cultic piety in the form of **offering your gift at the altar** is to be interrupted in the pursuit of seeking reconciliation with a brother **who has something against you**. Observe that Jesus expects the offender to pursue the offended in an effort to restore relationships. In the kingdom one's relationship to God is intimately related and practically exhibited by the willingness to take the initiative to be reconciled with an offended brother or sister (cf. 18:15-18). Jesus' form of righteousness places a high priority on restoring broken relationships (cf. 5:9).

5:25-26. The second illustration depicts a legal scene where broken relationships result in a judicial proceeding leading to the possibility of imprisonment. Jesus' point seems to be that the only way to avoid the escalation of legal action (**way**, **judge**, **officer**, **prison**) is to seek reconciliation early in the process. In the face of grievous consequences, Jesus enjoins his followers with a sense of urgency in seeking reconciliation.

Both examples place the initiative upon the one who becomes aware of a severed relationship to pursue with diligence all efforts to overcome the alienation with a spirit amenable to reconciliation. Truly the depth of God's demand, as disclosed in Jesus, reveals a standard of righteousness far surpassing all legal maneuvering and external forms often characteristic of the Pharisaic tradition.

Adultery (5:27-30)

27"You have heard that it was said, 'Do not commit adultery.'[a] 28But I tell you that anyone who looks at a woman lustfully has already committed adultery with her in his heart. 29If your right eye causes you to sin, gouge it out and throw it away. It is better

for you to lose one part of your body than for your whole body to be thrown into hell. [30]And if your right hand causes you to sin, cut it off and throw it away. It is better for you to lose one part of your body than for your whole body to go into hell.

[a]*27* Exodus 20:14

5:27. Jesus once again goes to the core of Jewish Law, this time citing the seventh commandment of the Decalogue: **Do not commit adultery** (Exod 20:14; Deut 5:18). In the OT adultery was understood to involve sexual relations between a man (married or single) and another man's wife, or a virgin betrothed to be married to someone else (Lev 18:20; 20:10; Deut 22:22). The primary concern in the injunction against adultery was the violation or defiling of another man's wife. Hence, the seventh commandment ("you shall not covet your neighbor's wife"). The excessive desire for the wife of one's neighbor (along with anything else that belonged to the man, v. 12, "house," "manservant," "maid servant," "ox," "donkey," Exod 20:17; Deut 5:21), is viewed as a serious breach of a covenantal relationship and the "gateway to the violation of every other principle in the Decalogue."[37]

5:28. Jesus radically internalizes the concept of adultery by tracing its root to a lustful look. The phrase, **looks at a woman lustfully** (πρός τὸ [*pros to*] + infinitive) describes a look that results in another's spouse becoming the object of one's sexual desire (cf. 2 Pet 2:14). Since Jesus intends the whole person to be captivated by the will of God, he places emphasis upon the inner disposition of the heart, not just the overt physical act. God would rule over his people from the inside out.

It should be observed that unlike some Jewish thinking, Jesus does not regard women as the sole or primary causal factor of male involvement in sexual sins.[38] According to certain rabbis, men do

---

[37]See discussion by John I. Durham, *Exodus*, Word Biblical Commentary, vol. 3 (Waco, TX: Word Books, 1987), p. 298.

[38]Cf. T. Reub. 5:1–6:2; T. Jud. 15:5f; T. Issa. 4:4; ben Sirach 25:23-26; 26:10-12. It appears that some tendencies toward sequestering women in the home (Philo, Spec. Leg. 169) and rabbinic attempts to reduce contact between the sexes (b. Kidd. 70a; b. Erub. 536; b. Ber. 61a; b. Ned. 20a) were motivated by the prevailing notion of female seductiveness.

not initiate a lustful look or an adulterous act but are merely enticed by the alluring look of a woman.[39] Rather than demanding the seclusion of women, Jesus places the responsibility upon the male to exercise sexual restraint.

5:29-30. Two hyperbolic illustrations now follow to dramatically reinforce the radical measures one must take to avoid succumbing to illicit desire. If the **eye** or **hand** cause one to sin, drastic action must be taken (**gouge it out**, **cut it off**) to avoid the snare of sin. Of course, the language is not to be taken literally, since lust cannot ultimately be controlled by maiming the body. The "eye" and "right hand" metaphorically illustrate valued possessions or desires that must be sacrificed for the sake of the kingdom of God. The alternative is the loss of the **whole body** in *gehenna*.

Obviously, such a standard of righteousness cannot be measured by a mere legal criteria. The entire person, including inner motivations must be radically transformed to reflect a righteousness commensurate with the very character of God. It should also be observed, as noted by Levison,

> As in 5:21-26, the hearer must take initiative: there, to effect reconciliation, and here, to keep oneself from stumbling. Jesus makes no concession for various inner motivations or external causes. He calls his hearers to radical, responsible initiative, particularly in the light of the inevitable judgment of sin (cf. 7:24-27).[40]

Divorce (5:31-32)

31"It has been said, 'Anyone who divorces his wife must give her a certificate of divorce.'[a] 32But I tell you that anyone who divorces his wife, except for marital unfaithfulness, causes her to become an adulteress, and anyone who marries the divorced woman commits adultery.

[a]***31* Deut. 24:1**

[39]As noted by E. Schweizer, *The Good News According to Matthew*, trans. David E. Green (Atlanta: John Knox Press, 1975), p. 121.

[40]Levison, "Better Righteousness," 182.

5:31. Jesus now counters popular Jewish notions concerning divorce which were based on a faulty reading of Deut 24:1-4. Jewish divorce laws grounded the authorization of a husband's right to divorce his wife in Deut 24 by reading the language "he writes her a certificate of divorce" (24:1) as a legitimation of divorce. Since it was assumed that only the husband could initiate a divorce, rabbinic debate shifted to the precise meaning of the vague phrase, "he finds something indecent about her" (24:1). On the one hand, the rabbinic tradition represented by the school of Shammai interpreted the phrase as some form of immorality, while the school of Hillel understood the phrase to include virtually anything that her husband found displeasing (which could include something as trivial as burning his food). Later Rabbi Akiba emphasized the phrase "she finds no favor in his eyes," and concluded that divorce was permitted when the husband was attracted to someone more beautiful than his wife (m. Gitten 9:10). It should be noted that originally Deut 24:1-4 was not intended to provide divine sanction for divorce, but was intended as a legal provision to protect the woman from a potentially abusive situation.[41] Later Jesus will interpret the Mosaic legislation not as a command, but as a concession to the hardness of heart characterizing Jewish males (see 19:8-9).

5:32. While the Mosaic Law implicitly upheld the sanctity of marriage, Jesus explicitly held males accountable for propagating adulterous unions if women are persistently discarded because of a husband's frivolous displeasure. Jesus' radical limitation on the right of divorce is later explained as an expression of God's ideal will who places value and sanctity upon the marital state (cf. 19:3-9).

Jesus' words are intended to drive home, especially to Jewish males (cf. Mark 10:11-12), the seriousness of initiating divorce proceedings against one's wife. The husband, in effect, cannot divorce his wife, unless the "certificate of divorce" is intended to publicly announce that the wife has already severed the relationship through some form of illicit sexual activity (πορνεία, *porneia*, cf. 1:18-19). In that case the formal act of divorce is simply the legal ratification that the wife has dissolved the union by her infidelity. It

[41]See Carson, *Matthew*, p. 152; and the discussion in William F. Luck, *Divorce and Remarriage: Recovering the Biblical View* (San Francisco: Harper, 1987), pp. 57-67.

follows that Matthew's unique exception clause (cf. Mark 10:11; Luke 16:18) is not intended to introduce a new provision for divorce, but simply makes explicit what any Jewish reader would have taken for granted.[42]

Precisely what is meant by the "exception clause" (**except for marital unfaithfulness**, παρεκτὸς λόγου πορνείας, *parektos logou porneias*) has not found unanimity of opinion. In general, proposals tend to gravitate either to a specifically restrictive meaning of *porneia* (e.g., premarital sex, incest, adultery), or to a much more inclusive meaning, referring to any form of illicit sexual conduct. Since there is no contextual reason in 5:32 (or 19:9) to limit *porneia* to some specific form of sexual immorality, it appears that the NIV rendering of "marital unfaithfulness" adequately communicates the broad range of sexual misconduct inherent in the term. While adultery (μοιχεία, *moicheia*) is not to be equated with *porneia*, it certainly falls within the broad semantic domain suggested by *porneia*. However, by the use of *porneia* rather than *moicheia* the Matthean "exception clause" would probably be understood by Jewish readers to include any form of indiscretion or illicit conduct undermining the marital covenant.[43]

The husband who divorces his wife for reasons other than *porneia* is guilty of promoting subsequent adulterous unions. Two unstated assumptions seem to undergird Jesus' perspective. First, the saying assumes a first century culture where a divorced woman would naturally remarry. Second, any remarriage of the divorced woman is viewed as adulterous because she is still the wife of her first husband. Hence, implicitly Jesus upholds the permanence of marriage in contrast to the legal maneuvering of Jewish males based on Deut 24. Certainly, calling a man who legally marries a divorced woman (not guilty of immorality) an adulterer would have struck Jewish hearers as overly rigid (cf. 19:10). However, the idealism of kingdom righteousness demands a return to God's original intent for marriage.

---

[42]France, *Matthew*, p. 123. There is evidence that the death penalty, originally mandated for adultery was replaced by compulsory divorce (see 19:7).

[43]See discussion of Craig S. Keener, *And Marries Another* (Peabody, MA: Hendrickson, 1991), pp. 31-33. Πορνεία might be used to mean sexual passion of any sort, since degrees of sexual activity were recognized by Roman society.

It is doubtful that Jesus intended his words to be construed as case law demanding legal extrapolation to cover all circumstances leading to divorce. In fact, a survey of the divorce sayings within the Synoptic tradition (i.e., 5:31-32; 19:3-12; Mark 10:2-12; Luke 16:18), reveals a fluidity of interpretation and application of Jesus' words. By far the clearest emendation of Jesus' words is the notorious "Pauline privilege" (1 Cor 7:12-15) which seems to permit divorce and remarriage for reasons not explicitly stated in the Gospel tradition. It appears that the disconcerting realities of our fallen condition, to some extent, determine the application of God's ideal will.

While Jesus assumes a prophetic spirit by articulating the timeless truth that God "hates divorce" (Mal 2:16), his disclosure of the heart of God also reveals a compassionate response to the particulars of the human condition (cf. 9:13; 12:7). It would seem that while we should never compromise our pursuit of the ideal, the hard reality of our persistent failures demands a redemptive response to those who fail. After all, the radical demands of the kingdom include statements about anger, lust, revenge, and loving our enemies, along with the prohibition of divorce. Interpreting Jesus' words legalistically always fails to take seriously both the depth of God's demand and the extent of human failure.

Oaths (5:33-37)

33"Again, you have heard that it was said to the people long ago, 'Do not break your oath, but keep the oaths you have made to the Lord.' 34But I tell you, Do not swear at all: either by heaven, for it is God's throne; 35or by the earth, for it is his footstool; or by Jerusalem, for it is the city of the Great King. 36And do not swear by your head, for you cannot make even one hair white or black. 37Simply let your 'Yes' be 'Yes,' and your 'No,' 'No'; anything beyond this comes from the evil one.

5:33. Jesus' reference to oaths has no explicit OT parallels, but reflects a summary of OT texts that call for the faithful performance of one's oaths or vows (cf. Lev 19:12; Num 30:2; Deut 23:33). The Law's prohibition of false oaths and unfulfilled vows was intended to create a community where one's word, strengthened by an oath, was a guarantee of performance or truthfulness. However, the mere need for oaths and vows is a concession (cf. divorce, Deut 24:1-4) to the reality of our fallen state. An oath assumes that the reliability of one's word is suspect unless accompanied by some external confirmation. Ultimately, scribal tradition developed a hierarchal system whereby the relative value and binding force of various oaths and vows could be distinguished.[44] Such efforts contributed to much abuse, since one's veracity or performance of a vow was predicated upon legal niceties not personal integrity.

5:34-36. Jesus counters such practice by an absolute prohibition of all oath taking. He totally rejects the subtle distinctions often used to distinguish between binding oaths and those less binding (cf. 23:16-22). It was common within some Jewish circles to view swearing by "heaven," "earth," "Jerusalem," and "one's head" as less binding than an oath that evoked the name of God. Jesus repudiates such notions by contending that **heaven**, **earth**, **Jerusalem**, and one's own **head** are inseparably linked to God, and that all oaths are equally binding. Jesus calls his disciples to a new realization of the presence of God in every aspect of life.

Jesus expects that among his followers the veracity of a **"yes"** or **"no"** will be grounded in one's personal integrity, not the appeal to some external confirmation. In effect, "Jesus raises every spoken word to the level of an oath."[45] Consequently, all appeals to external oaths amount to a concession to the ongoing power of the "evil one" over our lives. But in the new state of affairs introduced by Jesus, a person's word can be relied upon without need for confirmation by an oath. In the kingdom a simple "yes" or "no" is raised to the status of a sacred oath.

An Eye for an Eye (5:38-42)

[38]"You have heard that it was said, 'Eye for eye, and tooth for tooth.'[a] [39]But I tell you, Do not resist an evil person. If someone

---

[44]See the preponderance of legislation concerning vows and oaths in the Mishna: Shebuoth 3:1,5,7, 4:1-3; 5:1, 6:1; 7:1; Nedarim 3:4; Kelim 17:16; Shebiith 4:3; Taanith 1:7; Berakhoth 1:3; 2:1; 3:5; 4:5; et al. Levison, "Better Righteousness," 187.

[45]Levison, "Better Righteousness," 187.

strikes you on the right cheek, turn to him the other also. [40]And if someone wants to sue you and take your tunic, let him have your cloak as well. [41]If someone forces you to go one mile, go with him two miles. [42]Give to the one who asks you, and do not turn away from the one who wants to borrow from you.

[a]*38* **Exodus 21:24; Lev. 24:30; Deut. 19:21**

5:38. Following the call for personal integrity in every aspect of life (vv. 33-37), Jesus now spells out the proper response to injury, insults, and those who make unjust demands upon us. As usual, Jesus begins with a familiar portion of OT texts, from which he draws radical conclusions more in keeping with the mind of the Father than conclusions drawn by rabbinic leaders. In this instance, Jesus cites verbatim a legal precept fundamental to the social order of the Jewish nation: **Eye for eye, and tooth for tooth** (Exod 21:24; Lev 24:20; Deut 19:21). In these texts the *lex talionis* (=law of retribution) was intended to establish a legal basis for assuring that injured parties received just compensation or retribution, while at the same time, limiting punishment to what was commensurate with the crime. It appears that the *lex talionis* was not always practiced literally in ancient Israel, and by the time of Jesus, physical penalties were largely replaced by monetary fines.[46] Nevertheless, the precept presupposes a world where violence and injustice are taken for granted.

5:39. Jesus radically undercuts the need for such legislation among his followers by prohibiting all retaliation and personal vengeance. Jesus' prohibition not to **resist** (ἀντιστῆναι, *antistēnai*) **an evil person** probably includes both physical and legal retaliation. However, Jesus' words are not intended to produce a passive disregard for injustice or to reduce his followers to doormats in a hostile world. Jesus calls his followers to a radical self-denial that refuses to insist on personal rights over the well-being of others. In the face of evil, we pattern our lives after him, whom "when they hurled their insults at him he did not retaliate; when he suffered, he made no threats. Instead he entrusted himself to him who judges justly" (1 Pet 2:23).

---

[46]H.B. Huffmon, "Lex Talionis," *ABD* 4:321-322.

The four graphic examples that follow (i.e., personal insult, taken to court, forced labor, and requests for assistance) demonstrate that Jesus' words should not be interpreted to imply a passive resignation to the reality of evil. In each instance the disciple is to respond to the situation with an active concern to overcome evil with good (cf. Rom 12:17-21).

To be slapped on the **right cheek** would be interpreted more as an insulting act of contempt than a violent physical attack (cf. 26:67).[47] The tendency would be to respond to such demeaning and abusive behavior by striking back. Remarkably, the course of action Jesus demands is one that exposes the disciple to even further abuse. Jesus' words are illustrative of the extreme measures to which one would go not to respond to hurting insults with a vindictive and vengeful spirit. While "turning the other cheek" stands in deliberate tension with the way one normally thinks and lives, it illustrates a powerful principle that must be taken seriously when we encounter similar situations. Even when wrongfully abused, our course of action must always be governed by the higher principles of the kingdom, not the mere satisfaction of personal rights.

5:40. Next, Jesus envisions a scenario where legal action has resulted in the loss of one's inner garment (χιτών, *chitōn*, "tunic, shirt, a garment worn next to the skin," *BAGD,* p. 882). Rather than taking action to recover the garment, Jesus instructs his disciples to be willing to give up the outer, more important garment (ἱμάτιον, *himation*, cf. Luke 6:29). Legally, one was required to return another's outer garment by sunset since it was necessary to protect one from the cold of the night (Exod 22:26-27; Deut 24:12-13). However, in the kingdom, higher principles sometimes supersede our personal and legal rights. Paul seems to allude to this principle in his effort to preserve Christian community and witness among the Corinthian Christians (1 Cor 6:7).

5:41. The Roman practice of commandeering civilians to carry military equipment or a soldier's personal items was especially infuriating to the Jewish population of Palestine. Jesus alludes to this practice, but rather than excite outrage or resentment he charges his fol-

---

[47]Assuming the blow to be a backhanded strike to the cheek (cf. Job 16:10; Ps 3:7; 1 Esdr. 4:30).

lowers to volunteer for extended service. Once again Jesus assumes a new starting point for human relationships based upon kingdom principles that even responds to humiliating situations by doing good.

5:42. The final illustration calls for a charitable response to all who ask for assistance. Several OT texts encourage a sensitive regard for the plight of the poor and those in need (Exod 22:25; Lev 25:36-37; Deut 15:7-11). Almsgiving and interest-free loans were grounded in the "care for the community which God had liberated from slavery."[48] Jesus' words call for a generous spirit that refuses to put one's personal possessions or needs above the needs of others. While the specific response given to a request will vary according to genuine needs, the presence of God's kingdom, not one's personal interest, will be the primary factor shaping our response.

In each of Jesus' illustrative statements he proposes a course of action that runs counter to conventional thinking and behavior. Such texts should not be read legalistically, as if Jesus had in mind a new law legislating behavior along literalistic lines. In reality, these illustrations are intended to radically challenge how we think and respond to all instances of abuse, insult, and injustice. In an unredeemed world the radical selflessness of genuine discipleship constitutes a powerful witness to the presence of the kingdom and a new way of righteousness.

Love Your Enemies (5:43-48)

[43]"You have heard that it was said, 'Love your neighbor[a] and hate your enemy.' [44]But I tell you: Love your enemies[b] and pray for those who persecute you, [45]that you may be sons of your Father in heaven. He causes his sun to rise on the evil and the good, and sends rain on the righteous and the unrighteous. [46]If you love those who love you, what reward will you get? Are not even the tax collectors doing that? [47]And if you greet only your brothers, what are you doing more than others? Do not even pagans do that? [48]Be perfect, therefore, as your heavenly Father is perfect.

[a]*43* Lev. 19:18 [b]*44* Some late manuscripts *enemies, bless those who curse you, do good to those who hate you*

---

[48]B. Chilton, "Debts," *ABD* 2:114.

The concluding paragraph brings to a fitting conclusion a major theme implicit in the previous five sayings. Critical in Jesus' effort to distinguish the righteousness of the kingdom from that practiced by the scribes and Pharisees is his concern to reveal the ultimate intention of God's Law. Jesus' description of a superior righteousness challenges a Pharisaic reading of the text which minimalizes the Law through legal loopholes and natural tendencies. He reveals the depth of God's demand, which in this section involves nothing less than unrestricted love toward all and the active pursuit of the perfection of the Father.

5:43-44. Jesus cites the language of Lev 19:18 (**love your neighbor**) and follows with a popular deduction based on a narrow definition of "neighbor," therefore **hate your enemy**. Since "neighbor" was understood to refer only to a fellow Israelite, it follows that love was restricted by ethnic boundaries. After all, are not the enemies of Israel also the enemies of God (see Deut 7:2; 30:7; Psa 139:21-22; 26:5)? And, at Qumran the truly pious Jew was explicitly instructed to hate his enemy (1QS 1:4,10-11; 9:21-26). It is this popular interpretation of the love command that Jesus counters with the words: **love your enemies and pray for those who persecute you**. Contemporary Jewish literature has no parallel to the nondiscriminatory, all-embracing love demanded by Jesus. It is a love that knows no class or ethnic boundary, but actively seeks the eternal well-being of others, regardless of the harm they seek to inflict upon you.

5:45-47. For the first time Jesus' ethical instructions are supported by explicit statements setting forth a basis and goal for his demand. Jesus' command for unrestricted love is grounded in one's relationship to the Father, which necessarily demands a love surpassing conventional standards or expectations. The Father's indiscriminate love and goodness results in natural blessings being poured out upon all alike. God's children will emulate his benevolent compassion by exhibiting the same unrestricted love for all humanity. Such love is not conditioned upon reciprocity. As Jesus illustrates: to love in response to love is natural; to be favorably disposed to those whom we like is a common everyday occurrence. Even those considered outsiders and undesirables respond favorably when it is reciprocated. Jesus calls his followers to an uncommon love grounded in the very character of God. It is this distinctive feature that separates Jesus' form of righteousness from that of the Pharisees.

5:48. The resumptive **therefore** followed by the emphatic **you** (cf. 7:12) introduces "one all-embracing demand"[49] that aptly concludes and summarizes the basis for the "greater righteousness" (5:20), which has been illustrated in 5:21-47. The "righteousness" Jesus demands is not to be confused with mere external conformity to the letter of the Law. Such godly behavior cannot be comprehensively legislated by a legal code. The "righteousness" that goes beyond the scribes and Pharisees finds its "completeness" or "wholeness" (τελείος, *teleios*)[50] in conformity to the character of God. The realization of the qualities discussed in 5:21-47 came only by the creation of a new heart (cf. Ezek 36:26; Jer 31:33) and a new starting point for human relationships. As Israel was set apart and challenged with the words, "You shall be holy, for I am holy" (Deut 18:13; Lev 11:44-45; 19:2; 20:26), so the new people of God are called to a life wholly consumed by and integrated with the character of the God who calls them into the kingdom.

The true intent of God's will is nothing less than a "perfection" conforming to the perfection of the Father. Jesus refuses to compromise God's ideal will either by a casuistic reading of texts or by sifting God's demand through natural or conventional tendencies. He upholds the integrity of the Law by unfolding its full and intended meaning. While the ethics of the kingdom may appear extreme or hopelessly unattainable, they are fundamental to our identity as children of God. The practicality and applicability of Jesus' words become clearer if they are not read as case law demanding literal observance. The concluding words of Davies and Allison are helpful on this point:

> The text [i.e., 5:21-48] functions more like a story than a legal code. its primary character is to instill principles and qualities through a vivid inspiration of the moral imagination. What one should come away with is not a grossly incomplete set of irrevocable statutes or bloodless abstractions but an unjaded

---

[49]France, *Matthew*, p. 129.

[50]See the discussion of τελείος in Guelich, *Sermon*, pp. 234-236.

impression of what is right and wrong, a challenging moral ideal. That ideal may, in truth, forever exceed human grasp. Yet it is precisely because it is always before us and never within reach that our gospel's window on the ideal, like a guiding star, ever beckons the faithful to move forward.[51]

[51]Davies and Allison, *Matthew*, 1:566; for other practical treatments of the Sermon see, J.R.W. Stott, *Christian Counter-Culture* (Downers Grove, IL: InterVarsity Press, 1978); D.A. Carson, *The Sermon on the Mount* (Grand Rapids: Baker, 1978); and D.S. Dockery and D.E. Garland, *Seeking the Kingdom: The Sermon on the Mount Made Practical* (Wheaton: Harold Shaw, 1992).

MATTHEW 6

6. Practicing Greater Righteousness Before God (6:1-18)

Jesus now moves from a "greater righteousness" expressed in relationship to others (5:21-48), to the exhibition of a "greater righteousness" in one's relationship to God. Accordingly, contemporary forms of religious piety (e.g., almsgiving vv. 1-4; prayer vv. 5-15; fasting vv. 16-18) are evaluated in terms of one's relationship to the "Father who sees what is done in secret" (6:4, 6, 18), and not in order to win the praise of men. As in the previous section (5:21-48), Jesus expands a "righteousness" concerned with the intentions and motivations of one's inner being. True piety stems from a heart singularly devoted to God as Father, and thus all pious acts should be a positive expression of that relationship. Such religious devotion stands in stark contrast to the "hypocrite" who tailors every act of piety to maximize public recognition. Once again, Jesus' discussion assumes a new ideal state of affairs where his disciples practice a selfless righteousness and live only for God's reward.

Summary (6:1)

1"Be careful not to do your 'acts of righteousness' before men, to be seen by them. If you do, you will have no reward from your Father in heaven.

6:1. The opening line succinctly summarizes the central theme governing the paragraphs to follow (6:2-18). Jesus warns his followers not to do their **acts of righteousness** for the purpose (πρός + infinitive) of being seen by others. The use of the term "righteousness" clearly indicates that what follows is still concerned to expand the theme of "greater righteousness" (5:20). In this context, "acts of righteousness" are defined as pious acts motivated by one's devotion and relationship with God. Jesus has no quarrel with the traditional forms of religious piety, but calls his followers to be truly God-centered in their performance, not oriented toward self-glorification. Elsewhere in Matthew, Jesus specifically identifies the Pharisees as those who seek public recognition for their religious observances (23:5). If performance of religious devotion is motivated by public acclaim one's reward is limited to mere earthly applause (6:2, 4, 5, 6, 16, 18). Jesus recognizes that there are proper rewards that are intrinsic to the performance of various activities. However, God's reward of true piety is always "disproportionately greater than one's effort,"[1] and qualitatively superior to mere human recognition. The illustrations that follow demonstrate the selfless devotion of true piety.

Giving to the Needy (6:2-4)

[2]"So when you give to the needy, do not announce it with trumpets, as the hypocrites do in the synagogues and on the streets, to be honored by men. I tell you the truth, they have received their reward in full. [3]But when you give to the needy, do not let your left hand know what your right hand is doing, [4]so that your giving may be in secret. Then your Father, who sees what is done in secret, will reward you.

6:2. A fundamental expression of Jewish piety involved a charitable and benevolent response to the poor and needy.[2] In fact, in rabbinic Judaism almsgiving was seen as more important than all the commandments, only being outranked by meditation on the Torah. Even within the Intertestamental period, the term "righteousness" became a technical expression meaning the "giving of alms" (cf. Tob 1:3, 16; 4:7-8; Sir 5:10). It should also be observed that Jesus' warnings against the ostentatious practice of charity has many parallels in Jewish literature.[3]

Although Jesus assumes an ongoing benevolent concern for the needy he is emphatic that his followers are to refrain from actions

---

[1]Guelich, *Sermon,* p. 277.

[2]See J. Jeremias, *Jerusalem in the Time of Jesus* (Philadelphia: Fortress, 1969), pp. 126-134; P.H. Davids, "Rich and Poor," *DJG*, 701-710.

[3]See Davis and Allison, *Matthew*, 1:579 for examples.

calculated to shift attention to oneself. While we are called to let our "light shine before men" (5:16), the intention is to bring praise to God, not to call attention to ourselves. To announce benevolent deeds with a "trumpet" is illustrative of the extreme measures to which some will go in pursuit of public acclaim. Therefore, if charitable acts are performed for worldly acclaim the performer will be well compensated by the world's temporary applause.

It is the "hypocrite" who offers his or her gift with much fanfare, designed to get as much public attention as possible. Early usage of the term **hypocrite** (ὑποκριταί, *hypokritai*) stemmed from the world of the theater and simply described an "actor" who played a role in some theatrical production.[4] By the time of the NT the term came to have a metaphorical usage describing one who through pretense, either consciously or unconsciously, assumes a role that conceals an inner reality. It appears that the inherent duplicity attached to the term made it a fitting caricature of Israel's religious leaders (15:7; 23:13, 15, 23, 25, 27, 29).

6:3-4. The figurative expression of not letting **your left hand know what your right hand is doing** graphically illustrates the unpretentious and unassuming manner of true piety. Charitable acts are so fundamentally inherent to the character of those in the kingdom that they are performed even without self-conscious recognition or appraisal. They are therefore performed in **secret**, and only the **Father, who sees what is done in secret, will reward** accordingly (v. 4). We serve a God who looks upon the heart, not mere outward appearance (cf. 1 Sam 16:7), therefore religious devotion begins with the heart and the inner motivations behind the external act.

Prayer (6:5-15)

[5]"And when you pray, do not be like the hypocrites, for they love to pray standing in the synagogues and on the street corners to be seen by men. I tell you the truth, they have received their reward in full. [6]But when you pray, go into your room, close the door and pray to your Father, who is unseen. Then your Father, who sees what is done in secret, will reward you. [7]And when you

[4]W. Gunther, "Hypocrite," *NIDNTT*, 2:467-470.

pray, do not keep on babbling like pagans, for they think they will be heard because of their many words. [8]Do not be like them, for your Father knows what you need before you ask him.

[9]"This, then, is how you should pray:

"'Our Father in heaven, hallowed be your name,
[10]your kingdom come, your will be done
on earth as it is in heaven.
[11]Give us today our daily bread.
[12]Forgive us our debts,
as we also have forgiven our debtors.
[13]And lead us not into temptation,
but deliver us from the evil one.[a]'

[14]For if you forgive men when they sin against you, your heavenly Father will also forgive you. [15]But if you do not forgive men their sins, your Father will not forgive your sins.

[a]*13* **Or** ***from evil*****; some late manuscripts** ***one, / for yours is the kingdom and the power and the glory forever. Amen.***

6:5. The second illustration of the general principle stated in 6:1 focuses on prayer. Like almsgiving, prayer was intricately woven into the fabric of Jewish religious life. Besides one's personal prayer life, certain prayers were committed to memory and regularly recited at fixed times during the day. It appears that Jesus' quarrel is not with traditional fixed times for prayer, or even the public location where prayers were offered. Jesus' words are concerned with the tendency to use public prayer as a means to enhance one's personal reputation for devoutness. The **hypocrites** position themselves for prayer in the most public place so that their pious expressions will get maximum attention. As with almsgiving, prayer motivated by such worldly aspirations can only look forward to a reward of momentary fame and admiration.

6:6. In contrast to the hypocrites, the truly devout seek an environment where one's prayers can be truly focused upon God. The proverbial locked inner room (ταμεῖον, *tameion*) graphically conveys the extreme measures one should go to seek God's presence, rather than the admiration of others. Prayer should stem from an undivided heart wholly focused on the "unseen God," not an audience of would-be admirers. God acknowledges such prayers and is faithful to bless such petitioners.

6:7. The emphasis on the manner and setting for prayer (vv. 5-6) is followed by material setting forth the nature and content of true prayer (vv. 7-13). First, Jesus encourages his followers not to pattern their language of prayer according to the prayer habits of the Gentiles. They have a tendency to resort to meaningless repetitive babble (βατταλογήσητε, *battalogēsēte*), and endless verbosity (πολυλογίᾳ, *polylogia*) in an attempt to be heard by God. Jesus probably alludes to the use of magical formulas or incantations within various forms of Gentile religions, whereby the god is compelled or enticed to act by the sheer tenacity and manipulative skill of the petitioner. Even the Stoic philosopher Seneca ridiculed such efforts as merely "fatiguing the gods" (*Epistulae Morales* 31.5).

6:8. In contrast to the Gentile's fear of not being heard, Jesus assures his followers that God as Father is fully aware of the needs of his children. Prayer, then, is not so much an effort to inform God on matters of which he is ignorant, as it is an expression of our confidence in God. It is an act of worship whereby we acknowledge his presence, and in intimate familiarity and trust we lift our petitions to a loving Father. The efficacy of prayer is therefore not grounded in technique or formulas but in a relationship with God as Father.

6:9. Jesus now illustrates the proper elements and attitude of true prayer by giving his hearers a positive model (vv. 9-13). Tradition has designated the prayer as the Lord's Prayer, even though Jesus' words are primarily intended to shape the prayer-life of the disciple. In addition, in light of verses 7 and 8 it certainly was not intended to be repeated mechanically, as if the "frequent repetition develops spirituality."[5] However, the sentiment and theological focus of the prayer does provide key components that every disciple should incorporate into his/her prayer-life.

While some understand the prayer to be totally oriented toward an end-time realization, it appears that the language of the prayer lends itself to both a *now* and *not yet* perspective. In other words, each petition has both a present and end-time perspective. The first three petitions focus on God and the realization of his sovereign will on earth ("you petition," vv. 9-10). The final three petitions

[5]As noted by Blomberg, *Matthew,* p. 118.

("we petitions," vv. 11-13) focus on human need and call upon God to care for us both physically and spiritually.

The prayer opens with an invocation reminding the disciples that all prayer is grounded in a relationship to God as **Father**. The designation **in heaven** reminds the hearers of God's transcendent power and distinct sovereignty. Intimacy must always be properly balanced with a sense of reverential awe.

6:10. As noted earlier, the first three petitions (vv. 9b-10) focus exclusively on God and the accomplishment of his ultimate purpose in the world. First, the petitioner requests that God's name be **hallowed** (ἁγιασθήτω, *hagiasthētō*). In Hebraic thought the very person and character of Yahweh is suggested by the term **name**. Hence, the first petition asks God to act in such a way so as to reveal his holy presence in the world, thus silencing his opponents and creating a renewed sense of reverential awe among his people. In a similar view, the second petition asks that God's sovereign presence and reign be fully realized in every way. While the reality of the kingdom age has dawned with the coming of Jesus (cf. 4:17), this petition calls for the full realization and experience of all that God purposes for his people. The third petition (**your will be done . . .**) synonymously parallels the preceding petition by envisioning God's will as fully established in the world, so that the present evil order has been completely and utterly vanquished by God's sovereign will. There is thus envisioned a new reality where all creation ("heaven and earth") is united under the Rule of God.

While these petitions call upon God to act, they all assume a human willingness to participate in their realization. By reflecting the character of God (5:47), and letting our light shine so as to glorify God (5:14-16), we play a vital part in the accomplishment of God's purpose in the world. Inherent in a request for God's purposes to be realized in the world is the commitment to become an instrument through which God can work and manifest his presence.

6:11. The next three petitions (vv. 11-13) focus on fundamental human needs. Each of them express a request that looks both to present daily needs as well as ultimate end-time concerns. The first petition (v. 11) looks to God for the very basic provisions of life: **daily bread**. The exact meaning of the adjective modifying bread ("daily," ἐπιούσιον, *epiousion*) has been the subject of much dispute.

The term is found only here and in Luke's parallel reference (11:3), and is rarely if ever found in noncanonical sources. Several proposals have been suggested: A "bread" that is (1) necessary for existence; (2) for today; (3) for the "coming day"; (4) for the future. Colin Hemer has made a convincing case for the translation "give us today the bread for our coming day's need."[6] Thus, the petition is a morning prayer which looks to God for the basics to sustain one's life in the upcoming day. However, the request may legitimately be understood secondarily to refer to the ultimate spiritual nourishment to be realized in the end time messianic banquet (cf. 8:11).

6:12. The second petition reflects an awareness of one's personal failures and sin and thus beseeches God for forgiveness. The term translated "debts" (ὀφειλήματα, *opheilēmata*) is usually used as a commercial term describing financial debt not personal sin (cf. Luke 11:4, ἁμαρτία). However, the term may have an Aramaic background which does understand sin as a "debt owed to God."[7] The point is that true prayer is motivated by a humble spirit ever cognizant of personal failures and inadequacies. Expectation of God's forgiveness is predicated upon a forgiving spirit extended to those who have sinned against us. Erecting barriers and continually harboring resentment toward others will have a corresponding negative impact on our relationship to God (cf. vv. 14-15; 18:21-35). In fact it is a betrayal of our identity as God's children to maintain a spirit of animosity and bitterness toward others.

6:13. The final petition has two parts (**lead us not into temptation** and **deliver us from the evil one**), both seeking divine protection from factors having the potential to destroy one spiritually. The term translated **temptation** (πειρασμόν, *peirasmon*) can have, depending on the context, either a negative connotation meaning "to entice to sin," or a positive sense "to test" in order to prove one's character. Since God does not tempt one to sin (Jas 1:13), many have understood the petition to be a request that one not be led into circumstances unduly risky to one's spiritual survival. It has elsewhere been noted that the parallel thought "deliver us from the evil one," assumes that Satan is ultimately behind the trial, hence

---

[6]C. Hemer, "ἐπιούσιος," *JSNT* 22 (1984), 81-94.

[7]As suggested by Hagner, *Matthew,* 1:250.

"temptation," in the sense of "enticement to sin" may be a legitimate rendering in this text. The idea behind the petition then asks God to empower us so that we do not succumb to the continual enticement of Satan. It is an acknowledgment of our desperate dependency upon God to lead us in victory over the forces seeking our spiritual demise.

6:14-15. The extended treatment on the matter of "forgiveness" (vv. 14-15) reinforces the thought of 6:12 by linking the experience of God's forgiveness to a reciprocal exhibition of forgiveness toward others. The sentiment expressed is a reminder that there must be a direct correspondence between the way God has responded to our sin and the way we respond to those who sin against us. Extending forgiveness to others takes its incentive and distinctive qualities from the way that God, in Christ, has responded to our condition.

Fasting (6:16-18)

16"When you fast, do not look somber as the hypocrites do, for they disfigure their faces to show men they are fasting. I tell you the truth, they have received their reward in full. 17But when you fast, put oil on your head and wash your face, 18so that it will not be obvious to men that you are fasting, but only to your Father, who is unseen; and your Father, who sees what is done in secret, will reward you.

6:16. The third expression of Jewish piety used to illustrate the principle in 6:1 involved the common practice of fasting. Fasting as an act of religious devotion was highly valued, not only among Jewish sectarian groups, but also in popular piety.[8] Not only was fasting observed by the entire community during major festivals (e.g., Day of Atonement), voluntary individual fasting was widely approved of as a vital mark of religious devotion. The pious Pharisee fasted twice a week (cf. Luke 18:12), usually on Monday and Thursday. Jesus has no problem with fasting as a spiritual discipline, but as in previous expressions of piety, it is the ostentatious use of fasting as a means to display one's religious devotion for public approval that he takes issue with.

---

[8]John Muddiman, "Fasting," *ABD* 2:773-776.

The **hypocrites** go out of their way to play their pious roles by **disfiguring their faces** (ἀφανίζουσιν, *aphanizousin*, lit. "to make invisible"), probably by a disheveled and dirty appearance. By an ironical use of the word "play" Jesus describes their efforts as an attempt to be unrecognized, so that they can be recognized (φαν–ῶσιν, *phanōsin*) as engaging in the pious act of fasting.

6:17-18. While Jesus assumes that his disciples will fast (9:15), he is explicit on the external demeanor and appearance of his disciples. Rather than resorting to extravagant means to appear mournful or remorseful, Jesus instructs his followers to comb their hair and wash their faces so as to provide no external indication of their fasting. Like prayer and almsgiving, fasting should be an expression of a heart totally focused upon God, not a religious gimmick designed to produce accolades for oneself.

7. The Priorities and Values of the Greater Righteousness (6:19-34)

This section continues the theme of "greater righteousness" by sharply defining the implications of a wholehearted devotion to God and his kingdom. Building on the earlier theme contrasting "earthly reward" with an "eternal reward" (6:1, 2, 4, 5, 6, 16, 18), 6:19-24 challenges the disciple to a radical transformation of values and priorities. The section is composed of three distinct units each containing contrasting perspectives and pursuits in life: "treasures on earth" contrast with "treasures in heaven," (vv. 19-21); "light" produced by "good eyes" are contrasted with "darkness" the result of "bad eyes" (vv. 22-23); and in verse 24 two "masters" are contrasted. The common theme uniting all three units is the call to a singularity of devotion to divine rather than worldly priorities.[9]

The reduction of anxiety and a sense of security can never by fully realized by investing in earthly treasures or by depending on wealth. If, on the other hand, we give priority to the pursuit of God's kingdom and righteousness we can be confident that God will provide the basic necessities of life (6:25-34). Anxious concerns

[9]See Craig L. Blomberg, "On Wealth and Worry: Matt 6:19-34 – Meaning and Significance," *Criswell Theological Review* 6 (Fall 1992), 75.

about daily needs are therefore resolved by trusting in God's sovereign presence and his fatherly care for his people.

Treasures in Heaven (6:19-24)

[19]"Do not store up for yourselves treasures on earth, where moth and rust destroy, and where thieves break in and steal. [20]But store up for yourselves treasures in heaven, where moth and rust do not destroy, and where thieves do not break in and steal. [21]For where your treasure is, there your heart will be also.

[22]"The eye is the lamp of the body. If your eyes are good, your whole body will be full of light. [23]But if your eyes are bad, your whole body will be full of darkness. If then the light within you is darkness, how great is that darkness!

[24]"No one can serve two masters. Either he will hate the one and love the other, or he will be devoted to the one and despise the other. You cannot serve both God and Money.

6:19. The present prohibition (μή θησαυρίζετε, *mē thēsaurizete,* **stop storing up**) calls for one to cease putting emphasis on the accumulation of worldly wealth. Hendrickx observes that in the ancient Near East possessions such as clothing, grain, gold, and precious stones were invested in as a source of security to minimize anxiety about the future.[10] Jesus demonstrates that these earthly possessions offer no security, since they are subject to elements bringing about their destruction and loss: Beautiful clothes become "moth-eaten," and expensive stones either corrode or are stolen by thieves who can easily penetrate the typical mud or adobe-brick Palestinian house. Thus, "far from minimizing anxiety, the possession of material wealth becomes a source of anxiety, since it is constantly subject to decay and loss."[11]

6:20-21. In contrast, Jesus exhorts his followers to continually **store up** (θησαυρίζετε, *thēsaurizete*) heavenly treasures that are not subject to the transient liability of earthly possessions. To be focused on **treasures in heaven** is to pursue those goals and activities that have eternal significance and that have a relationship to God as the ultimate concern. Since one's treasure is indicative of a person's

[10]Hendrickx, *Sermon*, pp. 129-130.

[11]Ibid.

loyalty and inner commitment, one's ultimate pursuit and interests provide a window to the true self (**heart**).

6:22-23. The language of 6:22-23 continues the theme of verses 19-21 but shifts the imagery from treasure/heart to eye/body. Although the particulars of verses 22-23 are somewhat ambiguous in meaning, the overall emphasis reinforces the thought of verses 19-21, and the concluding point of verse 24 (i.e., the call to single minded devotion and allegiance before God). The **eye** is viewed as a medium through which light enters the body and gives it direction. The language reflects a popular perspective and is not intended to provide physiological precision. If one has clarity and unimpeded vision, that is, a worldview and ethical perspective grounded in undivided loyalty to God, then one can avoid the obstacles and pitfalls that lead to spiritual destruction. On the other hand, an "evil eye" is reflective of a life distracted by worldly factors, resulting in an inner darkness or blindness to true spiritual realities. This saying spells out in a practical manner the delimiting consequences of a life devoted to material pursuits.

6:24. The final saying rounds out the section (vv. 19-23) by delineating the incompatibility of attempting to serve both God and money. Since both God and the pursuit of this world's resources make absolute demands, the commitment to the one necessarily means the diminishing of the other. God calls for exclusive devotion and self-sacrifice which diminishes significantly the importance placed on the accumulation of this world's goods. The fact of the matter is, "the marching orders of God and of mammon are in entirely different directions."[12]

Worry (6:25-34)

25"Therefore I tell you, do not worry about your life, what you will eat or drink; or about your body, what you will wear. Is not life more important than food, and the body more important than clothes? 26Look at the birds of the air; they do not sow or reap or store away in barns, and yet your heavenly Father feeds them. Are you not much more valuable than they? 27Who of you by worrying can add a single hour to his life[a]?

---

[12]Davies and Allison, *Matthew*, 1:642.

[28]"And why do you worry about clothes? See how the lilies of the field grow. They do not labor or spin. [29]Yet I tell you that not even Solomon in all his splendor was dressed like one of these. [30]If that is how God clothes the grass of the field, which is here today and tomorrow is thrown into the fire, will he not much more clothe you, O you of little faith? [31]So do not worry, saying, 'What shall we eat?' or 'What shall we drink?' or 'What shall we wear?' [32]For the pagans run after all these things, and your heavenly Father knows that you need them. [33]But seek first his kingdom and his righteousness, and all these things will be given to you as well. [34]Therefore do not worry about tomorrow, for tomorrow will worry about itself. Each day has enough trouble of its own.

[a]*27* **Or** ***single cubit to his height***

6:25. Jesus is emphatic that his disciples need not be overly concerned (μὴ μεριμνᾶτε, *mē merimnate*) with the basics of life, such as food, drink, or clothing. The intent is not to cultivate a carefree irresponsible attitude that refuses to work or plan for the future. The rhetorical question, **Is not life more important than food, and the body more important than clothes?** indicates that Jesus intends his hearers to cultivate a sense of priorities where even the essentials of life are not given ultimate concern. After all, a life consumed by the concern for material needs will of necessity lack commitment and devotion to that which is of ultimate value.

6:26. Jesus then uses a series of illustrations to drive home the absurdity of being anxious about the basic elements of life. First, Jesus calls attention to the birds who, although they do not labor in the typically human sense (**sow**, **reap**, **gather into barns**), are nevertheless sustained by a concerned Creator. The rhetorical question **Are you not much more valuable than they?** assumes that the hearer (and reader) will agree and draw the proper conclusion. If disciples are of more value than birds they then can live confidently in God's providential care. However, the promise should not be construed as a guarantee of health, wealth, or the absence of trial and suffering. This text promises that God will provide the sustenance needed to do his will and to be active in service.

6:27. The futility of worry is demonstrated by its inability to add anything to one's life span (ἡλικίαν, *hēlikian*).[13] In fact, medical evidence points to the damaging effects of anxiety, possibly resulting in an actual shortening of one's life. Jesus' rhetorical question is therefore calculated to remind the hearer that anxiety makes no positive contribution to the quantity or quality of life.

6:28-30. Anxiety concerning clothing is countered by another example from nature, i.e., the **lilies of the field**. Once again Jesus argues from the "lesser to the greater" to emphasize God's fatherly concern for his children. The hearer is to take note that "flowers" merely grow, they are not involved in the process of preparing clothing (**labor** or **spin**). Yet, God in his providential care suitably adorns each flower for its natural environment. The splendor of God's creative clothing of flowers surpasses even what Solomon, with all his wealth (cf. 1 Kgs 3:13; 10:14-27) could provide for himself. Although the imagery shifts from "lilies" to **grass** in verse 30 the point is the same: if God exhibits such care for the temporal existence of a flower or grass, he will certainly be responsive to the needs of his children. Therefore, anxiety must be replaced by a faith that trusts in God's protection and care. Faith, in Matthew's Gospel, always demands a committed trust that overcomes anxiety and doubt (8:26; 14:31; 16:8; 17:20; 18:8-10; 19:2, 11-22, 28-29).

6:31-32. In what follows (6:31-34) Jesus summarizes (v. 31) and draws out the implications of 6:25-30. Gentiles are representative of those who do not know God and thus are consumed by the pursuit of earthly needs. But those who know God as Father find confidence that he knows their needs (cf. 6:8), and thus they can give priority to the pursuit of the kingdom (v. 33).

6:33. The climactic exhortation to **seek first his kingdom and his righteousness** sets forth the dominant concern and highest priority of the disciple. Since the presence of the kingdom is already dynamically present in Jesus (4:17f.), the imperative "seek" (ζητεῖτε, *zēteite*) calls for a persistent wholehearted devotion to the realization of God's reign in one's life. Giving the kingdom our highest priority necessarily demands a commitment to a new form of righteousness (5:20) as defined by Jesus (5:21-48). When his "kingdom

---

[13]The reference refers to length of life, not one's body size; see, *BAGD*, p. 345.

and his righteousness" are given ultimate priority, the disciple can be assured that God will provide the necessities of life (i.e., food, drink, clothing). Anxiety is therefore incompatible with a life devoted to the pursuit of God's kingdom.

6:34. The final words extend the prohibition of anxiety to include all possible concerns, even about the future. Jesus' confident assurance should calm all fears concerning what tomorrow may bring. Since God's faithful presence can be trusted for daily needs it is foolish to be fearful about tomorrow or the distant future. The proverbial saying about tomorrow's troubles and worries is intended to reinforce the need for living in the present, fully aware of the Father's care and concern for our well being. It surely is the case that while Christians may not know what the future holds, we live in confidence in the One who holds the future.

MATTHEW 7

8. The Conduct of Greater Righteousness (7:1-12)

The next section is composed of a series of exhortations with accompanying illustrations. Efforts to link 7:1-12 thematically or structurally with the previous sections have not found a scholarly consensus. Few have followed Bornkamm's proposal that the entire second half of the Sermon (6:19–7:12) forms an elaborate commentary on the Lord's Prayer (6:9-13).[1] While certain sections may square with such a proposal (e.g., 6:25-34 interprets "give us today our daily bread," 6:11), it is not immediately apparent how 7:1-5 constitutes a commentary on the Prayer's concern with forgiveness. Other efforts to link the petitions of the Lord's Prayer to specific sayings comprising 6:19–7:12 are equally unpersuasive.

Much more plausible is the contention of Davies and Allison that 7:1-12 should be viewed as a "structural twin" with 6:19-34.[2] They observe that both sections open with exhortations (7:1-2 and 6:21-23), continue with the use of the eye as a parabolic illustration (6:22 and 7:3-5), and share a common interest in the care of the Father (7:7-11 and 6:25-34). In addition, both sections employ similar argumentation that reasons from the "least to the greatest." The two sections are thematically linked by a concern to instruct disciples "how to behave in the world at large." While the former section (6:19-34) deals with the issue of earthly possessions, the latter (7:1-12) is instructive of "how to treat one's neighbor." Although this proposal is not without difficulties,[3] it does offer a

---

[1]G. Bornkamm, "Der Aufbau der Bergpredigt," *NTS* 24 (1977), 419-432; however, see Guelich, *Sermon*, pp. 324-325; and U. Luz, *Matthew 1-7* (Minneapolis: Augsburg, 1989), p. 203.

[2]Davies and Allison, *Matthew*, 1:627.

[3]Not the least of which is how 7:6 fits into their structural scheme.

coherent reading that thematically connects 6:19–7:12 to the rest of the *SM*.

Most scholars are agreed that 7:12 constitutes both a summary and a conclusion to the body of the *SM*, beginning with 5:17. Hence this section (i.e., 7:1-12) concludes the theme of "greater righteousness" by summarizing in a concrete manner the essence of God's will as expressed in the "Law and the Prophets."

Judging Others (7:1-5)

[1]"Do not judge, or you too will be judged. [2]For in the same way you judge others, you will be judged, and with the measure you use, it will be measured to you.

[3]"Why do you look at the speck of sawdust in your brother's eye and pay no attention to the plank in your own eye? [4]How can you say to your brother, 'Let me take the speck out of your eye,' when all the time there is a plank in your own eye? [5]You hypocrite, first take the plank out of your own eye, and then you will see clearly to remove the speck from your brother's eye.

7:1-2. The present imperative (κρίνετε, *krinete*) preceded by μή (*mē*) suggests a general rule of conduct best understood as "Don't get into the habit of being judgmental" or "Don't make judgmentalism a part of your lifestyle."[4] The reason (γάρ, *gar*, v. 2) that a judgmental spirit is to be avoided is that such an attitude directly impacts how others, including God, respond to our deficiencies. It should be observed that the principle suggested in verses 1-2 anticipates the wider premise of verse 12.

7:3-5. It becomes apparent in verses 3-5 that Jesus was not issuing an ultimatum against all critical thought or assessment of others. In fact, Jesus expects his followers to be sensitive and responsive to the failures of others (18:15-18), and to be critically discerning toward those who lack receptivity (7:6). What Jesus condemns is a censorious judgmentalism which is preoccupied with faultfinding in others while refusing to honestly assess the enormity of one's own failures. The graphic illustration contrasting a **speck**

---

[4]See Richard Young, *Intermediate New Testament Greek: A Linguistic and Exegetical Approach* (Nashville: Broadman, 1994), p. 143.

of sawdust with a **plank** (δοκός, *dokos*, "beam of wood" *BAGD*, p. 203) intentionally exaggerates the absurdity of pointing out the minor flaws of another, while at the same time ignoring the far more serious shortcomings in one's own life. Furthermore, Jesus insists that only by an awareness of personal failures can one adequately assess and properly treat the spiritual wounds of others. Jesus calls his followers to a scrupulous self-judgment as a prerequisite to the unimpaired vision necessary for helping others.

Honor What Is Valuable (7:6)

6"Do not give dogs what is sacred; do not throw your pearls to pigs. If you do, they may trample them under their feet, and then turn and tear you to pieces.

7:6. Although this text appears to be a detached saying, unrelated to the immediate context, it does qualify the prohibition of verse 1 by calling for a discerning spirit toward those unreceptive to the gospel. The terms **dogs** and **pigs** are among the most derogatory in Jewish vocabulary. Although the terms can be used for "Gentiles" (cf. 15:26), it is improbable that the saying was meant to be restrictive to any individuals or groups. Most likely the dangers envisioned refer to the possibility of resistance or hostility coming from anyone who lacks receptivity (cf. 10:13-14). Those who lack the capacity for appreciating the intrinsic worth and value of the gospel often respond with vicious scorn and hardened contempt. Although no one knows in advance what the response of others will be, the disciple must be keenly sensitive to when it is appropriate to move to a more receptive environment (cf. 10:16; Acts 13:46-48).

Ask, Seek, Knock (7:7-11)

7"Ask and it will be given to you; seek and you will find; knock and the door will be opened to you. 8For everyone who asks receives; he who seeks finds; and to him who knocks, the door will be opened.

9"Which of you, if his son asks for bread, will give him a stone? 10Or if he asks for a fish, will give him a snake? 11If you, then, though you are evil, know how to give good gifts to your

children, how much more will your Father in heaven give good gifts to those who ask him!

Once again it appears that these verses constitute a self-contained unit with no connection to what precedes or follows. However, the emphasis on prayer does provide a fitting conclusion to the imperatival thrust of preceding sections by reminding the hearers of their need for divine resources and assistance in the "doing" of the Lord's will. Furthermore, after being told how to treat others (7:1-6), it is most appropriate to detail how God treats those who seek him in prayer. Finally, it should also be noted that the depiction of God as a caring Father (vv. 9-11) anticipates the general principle enunciated in verse 12: "disciples are to do unto others as they would ask, seek, and knock for God to do for them."[5]

7:7-8. The three present imperatives (**ask**, **seek**, **knock**, v. 7) demand a persistency that refuses to give up. The passives (**will be given**, **will be opened**) anticipate God's response to our continual "asking," "seeking," and "knocking." Verse 8 balances the present imperatives of verse 7 with three present participles (**asks**, **seeks**, **knocks**), followed by three verbs (**receives**, **finds**, **opened**) emphasizing God's unfailing response to those who seek his presence. The text is not intended as a magical formula for manipulating God through sheer tenacity in prayer (cf. 6:7-8). The object of our "asking" and "seeking" is best understood in light of the petitions outlined earlier in the Lord's Prayer (6:9-13).

7:9-10. The rhetorical questions of verses 9-10 anticipate a negative response: No parents when asked by their children for bread or fish (typical daily food, cf. 14:17) would give them a stone or snake (i.e., that which is useless or even harmful, cf. Luke 11:13). Jesus then reasons from the "lesser to the greater" to demonstrate God's unfailing care for his own children. In contrast to God, humanity can only be assessed as fundamentally evil or sinful (cf. 19:17). Yet, earthly parents respond to their children's requests by providing that which would be beneficial (ἀγαθά, *agatha*, cf. 5:45). Thus, *a fortiori*, God's fatherly care can be relied upon to provide what is best for his children. Hence, the stress on the persistency in prayer in verse 7 should not be construed as suggesting God's

---

[5]Garland, *Reading Matthew*, p. 88.

unwillingness or reluctance to provide for his own. In fact, it is our relationship to God as Father that gives confidence in his benevolent care and goodness.

The Golden Rule (7:12)

[12]So in everything, do to others what you would have them do to you, for this sums up the Law and the Prophets.

7:12. The main body of Jesus' sermon (5:17–7:11) closes with what has traditionally been called the Golden Rule (7:12).[6] Jesus summarizes the essence of God's will as expressed in the **Law and the Prophets** by giving his hearers a general principle designed to govern human relationships in all circumstances. Probably Jesus' words are intended as a commentary on Leviticus 19:18: "You shall love your neighbor as yourself" (cf. 22:34-40).[7] While other Jewish sources have expressed similar sentiments in a negative form (e.g., Hillel's saying, "What is hateful to you, do not do to your neighbor: this is the whole Torah while the rest is commentary on it," *Babylon Talmud Sabbat* 31a), Jesus' emphatic insistence on pursuing the good of others, is at the least, extremely rare in ancient sources. Nevertheless, the truly unique aspect of Jesus' words is his contention that such unbounded love constitutes the interpretive key for correctly understanding God's will in the "Law and Prophets." In Matthew's presentation of Jesus' teaching concerning the Law one learns that the Law must be read in light of the greater principles expressed in the love command (22:34-40), the "golden rule" (7:12), and God's desire for mercy not sacrifice (9:13; 12:7).[8]

The contextual significance of the "golden rule" is aptly summarized by Hendrickx:

> In this context the 'golden rule' is not so much a summation of Jesus' ethical demands, as a bridge which leads men to turn

---

[6]Hendrickx, *Sermon*, p. 158, observes that 7:12 has been called the "golden rule" since the sixteenth century; however, cf. Stanton, *A Gospel for a New People*, p. 303.

[7]So Hagner, *Matthew*, 1:176.

[8]This point is developed by Snodgrass, "Matthew and the Law," pp. 541-545.

> themselves radically toward their fellow-men, as this demand results from the message of God's eschatological action and expresses itself in practice in the love of enemy and the waiving of one's own rights. This means then that the good of one's fellow-man is not an autonomous principle of action within Jesus' ethics. The radical concern for one's fellow-man is rather a principle derived from the eschatological proclamation of the kingdom which constitutes the decisive principle of action and bestows on the concern for one's fellow-man its radical dimension which receives its orientation from God's concern for men. Only in this context can the 'law and the prophets' be fulfilled.[9]

9. The Call for Decision (7:13-27)

The Sermon concludes with a series of illustrations stressing the importance of faithful obedience to the words of Jesus. Jesus' followers must make the choice between a "broad road" and "wide gate" that leads to destruction, and a "small gate" and "narrow road" that leads to life (7:13-14). They must avoid the hypocrisy of the "false prophets," who fail to bear "good fruit," by truly obeying the will of the Father (7:15-23). Finally, Jesus' disciples must build on the solid rock of Jesus' teaching and not on the shifting sand of this world (7:24-27). In each instance the choice has eternal consequences, with salvation granted to those who both "hear and obey" the words of the Lord.

The Narrow and Wide Gates (7:13-14)

[13]"Enter through the narrow gate. For wide is the gate and broad is the road that leads to destruction, and many enter through it. [14]But small is the gate and narrow the road that leads to life, and only a few find it.

7:13. The opening exhortation to **enter through the narrow gate** places before the disciples the difficulties and rigors of discipleship. The imagery of a "narrow gate" signifies that the "doing"

[9]Hendrickx, *Sermon*, p. 159.

of Jesus' commands necessitates a focused and disciplined pursuit. The **many**, however, prefer to travel a spacious and popular road that demands little conscientious effort. Although the **broad road** leading to a **wide gate** is the popular choice, it ultimately leads to one's destruction. The **life** Jesus offers cannot be realized by mindlessly following the crowds.

7:14. Although the "narrow gate" and the "road less traveled" are not a popular option, they constitute the way that leads to "life." There are **few** that travel this path because its value is not readily perceived nor its demands easily endured. Jesus' words are not intended to generate speculation about the numbers to be saved or lost (cf. 8:11; 20:28). Rather they are intended to encourage disciples not to compromise their commitment by pursuing the popular path of least resistance.

A Tree and Its Fruit (7:15-23)

15"Watch out for false prophets. They come to you in sheep's clothing, but inwardly they are ferocious wolves. 16By their fruit you will recognize them. Do people pick grapes from thornbushes, or figs from thistles? 17Likewise every good tree bears good fruit, but a bad tree bears bad fruit. 18A good tree cannot bear bad fruit, and a bad tree cannot bear good fruit. 19Every tree that does not bear good fruit is cut down and thrown into the fire. 20Thus, by their fruit you will recognize them.

21"Not everyone who says to me, 'Lord, Lord,' will enter the kingdom of heaven, but only he who does the will of my Father who is in heaven. 22Many will say to me on that day, 'Lord, Lord, did we not prophesy in your name, and in your name drive out demons and perform many miracles?' 23Then I will tell them plainly, 'I never knew you. Away from me, you evildoers!'

7:15. Jesus now warns his followers against false teachers and their deceptive and hollow claims. The connection to 7:13-14 may be that Jesus envisions false teachers like those condemned in the OT who counter the rigors of God's command with an easier, more convenient alternative (cf. Jer 8:11; Ezek 13).[10] While precise

---

[10]See France, *Matthew*, p. 147.

identification of the false teachers is not possible, it does seem that their confession "Lord, Lord," and the claim of miracles performed "in his name" clearly indicate that they profess discipleship and pose a threat not in Jesus' day but to the later Christian community.

The call to "beware" (προσέχετε, *prosechete,* cf. 6:1; 10:17; 16:6) of false prophets demands a keen awareness of their deceptive tactics. Their true character and intent are disguised behind a deceptive facade, giving the appearance that they belong to the "flock." It appears that Jesus is describing those with well-defined sinister motives and strategies for undermining the community of God. It is critical that God's people have some criteria whereby to discern those who are **wolves** at heart and not really part of the flock.

7:16-17. The phrase **By their fruit you will recognize them** brackets vv. 16-20, thus highlighting the central theme. The criteria for identifying the false teacher is behavioral not doctrinal. "Fruit" is a common metaphor used to describe human conduct (3:8; 21:43; Gal 5:22; John 15:2-8). False teachers are discernible by the ethical inconsistency between their profession and their performance. They may claim to have the welfare of the sheep at heart, but their true character is discernible by good deeds, not mere claims or pretensions. While judgmentalism is prohibited (7:1-5), the welfare of the church depends on the ability to critically assess the fruits of another's stance or practice.

7:18-20. By a series of metaphors (**grapes/thornbushes**; **figs/thistles**, **good** and **bad trees**) Jesus makes it clear that bearing fruit is integrally related to one's basic inner nature. Fruit is naturally exhibited in those plants whose nature is to bear fruit. Hence one would not expect to find fruit associated with **thornbushes** and **thistles**. Even so, false teachers lack the basic inner nature to exhibit the fruits of righteousness. Furthermore, both the quality and worth of all fruit must be assessed in terms of the health and quality of the tree from which it comes. It is the ethical and behavioral stance of the false teachers that provides the most penetrating insight into their basic character.

7:21-22. It appears that the language of 7:21-23 continues the focus on the false teachers by demonstrating that their sham religious pretensions will not be persuasive before the Lord at judgment day (=**on that day**). Mere confession of Jesus' Lordship or impressive exhibitions of divine power (cf. 1 Cor 12-14) are by no means sufficient for assuring one's participation in God's eternal kingdom. What is of ultimate concern is obedience to the will of God as spelled out in the teaching of Jesus. In the final analysis, Jesus refuses to recognize those as his own who substitute obedience for mere confession and supernatural exhibitions performed "in his name." Jesus demands a "righteousness" that encompasses the whole person and that results in doing the will of God.

7:23. It should be observed that Jesus defines "doing the will of God" (7:21) in terms of one's relationship to himself (**I never knew you**, 7:23). Jesus is thus ascribing to himself a decisive role in determining one's eternal welfare. As the proclaimer and doer of the perfect will of God Jesus exemplifies both the demand and promise of God's covenant with his people.

The Wise and Foolish Builders (7:24-27)

24"Therefore everyone who hears these words of mine and puts them into practice is like a wise man who built his house on the rock. 25The rain came down, the streams rose, and the winds blew and beat against that house; yet it did not fall, because it had its foundation on the rock. 26But everyone who hears these words of mine and does not put them into practice is like a foolish man who built his house on sand. 27The rain came down, the streams rose, and the winds blew and beat against that house, and it fell with a great crash."

7:24-27. The *SM* concludes with a simple yet powerful parable emphasizing the importance of "putting into practice" (ποιέω, *poieō*) the words of Jesus. The **wise [person]** is the one who builds upon a solid foundation by obeying Jesus' teachings as delineated in the *SM*. Various forms of calamities and afflictions, depicted as violent storms, fail to bring about its downfall, because it has sufficient foundation to withstand them. Thus, the ultimate test of a house's solidity is depended upon the nature of the foundation on which it is built. The **foolish** builder who builds his house upon the **sand**, cannot possibly hope that the structure will survive the heavy winds and rain characteristic of seasonal Palestinian storms.

It follows that Jesus expects his disciples to take his teaching with the utmost seriousness by translating his commands into action. However, the "practice" of Jesus' demands should not be reduced to a new form of legalism. The commands of Jesus presuppose God's grace and dynamic presence to enable the disciple to become "doers of the word" (cf. Phil 1:6; 2:13). Nevertheless, the parable of the two builders effectively brings the *SM* to a close by putting the hearer/reader into a crisis of decision concerning one's ultimate allegiance. Will God be allowed to reign (=rock) in our lives, or will we ground our existence in the futility of this world (=sand)?

10. Conclusion (7:28-29)

28When Jesus had finished saying these things, the crowds were amazed at his teaching, 29because he taught as one who had authority, and not as their teachers of the law.

7:28. Matthew marks the conclusion of the first discourse with words similar to the closing words of each of Jesus' major discourses (cf. 11:1; 13:53; 19:1; 26:1). Typically, the saying marks the end of a discourse and provides a transition to a series of episodes highlighting Jesus in action. Before resuming the narrative flow of his story, Matthew in 7:28-29 emphasizes the immediate response of the "crowds," and what prompted their reaction.

Although the disciples appear to be the primary hearers of the *SM* (5:2), it is the "crowd" who reacts with "amazement." Though the **crowds** are open to Jesus' ministry (4:25), they are not disciples, and thus the *SM* constitutes a challenge to accept the reign of God in their lives.

7:29. The crowd's amazement with Jesus' teaching is grounded in their ability to discern a clear distinction between Jesus' authoritative teaching and that characterizing "their scribes." Essentially, Jesus' teaching is unlike the "scribes" because it depends neither on OT citations or Jewish tradition, but in his intuitive awareness of the will of God. The implications of Jesus' authoritative claims and absolute demands are perceptively elucidated by W.D. Davies: "Thus the expression of the absolute demand of God in the *SM*, as elsewhere in the New Testament, drives us back to the mystery of the person of Jesus himself."[11] His authority will next be demonstrated in mighty deeds of compassion.

[11]Davies, *Setting of the Sermon*, p. 432.

MATTHEW 8

E. MINISTRY IN DEED (8:1–9:35)

While it has been recognized that chapters 8 and 9 comprise a distinct section within the first Gospel, there is no consensus concerning the themes developed by the arrangement of episodes.[1] Patte's observation is certainly correct: "The unity [of these chapters] is clearly not found in a narrative progression, in the sense that one event would need to take place before the next one can unfold."[2] While it is difficult to neatly isolate sections of these chapters around distinguishing themes,[3] it is clear that the collection was intended to have an accumulative impact (cf. 9:33-34), with the unifying factor being the dominating presence of Jesus in every episode.

It would seem that Matthew collected ten miracle scenes (nine healings), quite similar in form,[4] in order to give specificity to the programmatic summaries of 4:23-25, 9:35 and 11:3-5. Jesus' proclamation of God's reign (chs 5-7) is therefore accompanied by "mighty deeds" that verify that in Jesus God has drawn near to his people.

Unlike Mt. Sinai where God's holiness was protected through rigorous separation, Jesus descends from the mountain and manifests

---

[1]For detailed discussions of 8:1–9:34 see W.G. Thompson, "Reflections on the Composition of Mt. 8:1–9:34," *CBQ* 33 (1971) 368-387; J.D. Kingsbury, "Observations on the Miracle Chapters in Matthew 8-9," *CBQ* 40 (1978) 559-573; and J.P. Heil, "Significant Aspects of the Healing Miracles in Matthew," *CBQ* 41 (1979) 274-287.

[2]Patte, *Matthew*, p. 109.

[3]See Davies and Allison, *Matthew*, 2:1-4 for a survey of proposals.

[4]For discussion on the structural form of the miracle stories see G. Theissen, *The Miracle Stories of the Early Christian Tradition* (Philadelphia: Fortress, 1983).

God's presence as fundamentally merciful and transforming.[5] In order to illustrate the redemptive significance of Jesus' *therapeutic* activity Matthew describes Jesus' activity in terms that point beyond the mere restoration of physical health. Recall that in the beginning of the story the spiritual dimensions of Jesus' messianic role were clearly delineated with the words, "he will save his people from their sins" (1:21). Healing and forgiveness are tied together in 9:1-8, as the healing of the paralytic's infirmity becomes conclusive proof of Jesus' authority to forgive sin (9:5-6; cf. 26:28). The cleansing (ἐκαθαρίσθη, *ekatharisthē*) of the leper (8:1-4) not only relates the healing of the disease, but also symbolizes the removal of "the social rupture caused by the illness."[6] Jesus' positive response and assessment of a Gentile centurion (8:5-11) is anticipatory of the removal of ethnic boundaries and Gentile inclusion in the blessings of the kingdom (cf. 10:5; 15:24; 28:18-20). Jesus' powerful presence overcomes all barriers of ritual impurity that prohibited full participation with the people of God. According to the Law (i.e., Lev 15:25-27), Jesus becomes ritually unclean by his contact with a "woman subject to bleeding" (9:20). However, the woman's touch of faith resulted not in Jesus' defilement, but in her salvation (9:22). This scene is bracketed by an episode in which Jesus is on his way to an even more serious defilement, i.e., physical contact with a corpse (9:18-19, 23-25; cf. Num 19:14). Yet the powerful touch of Jesus overcomes the barrier of impurity by restoring the girl to life (9:25-26). The incident highlights the fact that no obstacle is too great (not even death) that his redemptive powers cannot overcome and dramatically transform. Indeed, Jesus' authoritative powers indicate that "the healer of Israel is [also] the Savior of Israel."[7]

---

[5]This theme is developed in Marcus Borg, *Conflict, Holiness and Politics in the Teaching of Jesus* (New York: Edwin Mellen Press, 1984).

[6]See H.J. Held, "Matthew an Interpreter of the Miracle Stories," in *Tradition and Interpretation in Matthew*, trans. Percy Scott, New Testament Library (Philadelphia: Westminster, 1963), p. 281.

[7]B. Gerhardsson, *The Mighty Acts of Jesus According To Matthew* (Lund, Sweden: CWK Gleerup, 1979), p. 51.

1. Cleansing of a Leper (8:1-4)

[1]When he came down from the mountainside, large crowds followed him. [2]A man with leprosy[a] came and knelt before him and said, "Lord, if you are willing, you can make me clean."

[3]Jesus reached out his hand and touched the man. "I am willing," he said. "Be clean!" Immediately he was cured[b] of his leprosy. [4]Then Jesus said to him, "See that you don't tell anyone. But go, show yourself to the priest and offer the gift Moses commanded, as a testimony to them."

[a]*2* The Greek word was used for various diseases affecting the skin—not necessarily leprosy. [b]*3* Greek *made clean*

8:1. It is clear that the words of verse 1 are intended to form a closure to the previous discourse. Reference to the **mountainside** and the **crowds** refer back to 5:1, and function to help the reader see that the authoritative teacher now enters the realm of everyday life by descending from the mountain (cf. 5:1; 14:13; 15:29; 17:1; 28:16).[8] The "crowds" who hear his powerful discourse are now privileged to see his powerful deeds. Much like the conclusion of the discourse (7:28-29), this section (8:1–9:34) also closes with an assessment of Jesus offered by the "crowds" (9:33).

8:2-3. The next sentence (v. 2) focuses the reader's attention upon a petitioner who steps forth to make a request of Jesus. The suppliant is identified as a "leper,"[9] thus indicating both his social and religious status. According to the OT law the leper's uncleanness compelled him to avoid all social contact (Lev 13:46; cf. Num 5:2f; 12:14f). Any contact with a leper resulted in ritual defilement and necessitated specific steps for purification. But Jesus is recognized by the leper as having authority to effect his healing. The cluster of words describing the leper's approach to Jesus (προσελθών, *proselthōn*, προσεκύνει, *prosekynei*, κύριε, *kyrie*) forms a positive

[8]The Mosaic overtones between Mt. Sinai and the mount of Jesus' discourse have been developed by D.C. Allison, *The New Moses: A Matthew Typology* (Minneapolis: Augsburg Fortress, 1993).

[9]See P. Ellingworth, "Leprosy," *DJG*, pp. 463-464; the term is used to cover a variety of skin disorders.

picture of genuine faith and a confession of Jesus' majesty.[10] The tension between the faith of the leper and his unclean status mounts, as with "modesty and restraint"[11] he announces his confidence in Jesus' ability to "cleanse him." Unlike on Mt. Sinai, the holy presence of God, now active in Jesus (1:23), does not call for the avoidance of those deemed "untouchable," but engages human affliction and overcomes its debilitating consequences with his powerful touch. Not only is Jesus totally indifferent to OT regulations concerning contact with a leper (Lev 5:3), but his "touch" results not in his defilement, but in the cleansing of the leper's contaminating condition. The imagery of "extending the hand" (cf. 8:12, 13; 12:49; 14:31; 26:51) to a leper graphically illustrates Jesus' willingness to "take up our afflictions and carry away our diseases" (8:17).

8:4. Instead of narrating the leper's response to his cleansing (cf. Mark 1:45), Matthew focuses on the authority of Jesus by following the cleansing with four imperatives. The first imperative (**see that you don't tell anyone**) is intended to counter any notion that Jesus is to be understood as a mere wonder-worker. The instructions to present himself before the priests in Jerusalem and to comply with the Mosaic legislation regarding the sacrificial offering (Lev 14:10-11; 21-22), indicate Jesus' respect for the provisions of the Law (cf. 5:17-19). The procedure also assured that the one formerly excluded from society could now be restored to full communal and spiritual life. The actions of the leper are also interpreted **as a testimony to them**. Probably the pronoun "them" refers to the Jewish leadership in Jerusalem, and the leper's sacrifice is intended as a witness to Jesus' restorative powers, and a challenge to Israel's leadership to acknowledge his authoritative status. Indeed, in Jesus, God has drawn near to bring his cleansing power, thus removing all contamination that results in alienation.

---

[10]Although the address "Lord" (κύριος, *kyrios*) can be used simply as a polite address, meaning "sir," the leper's confidence in Jesus' healing powers seems to point to a deeper regard for Jesus as "Lord."

[11]As noted by M. Zerwick, *Biblical Greek Illustrated by Examples*, trans. J. Smith (Rome: Pontifical Biblical Institute, 1963), p. 105, ἐάν θέλῃς (*ean thelēs*) is accounted for by the speaker's "modesty and restraint."

2. Request of a Gentile Centurion (8:5-13)

[5]When Jesus had entered Capernaum, a centurion came to him, asking for help. [6]"Lord," he said, "my servant lies at home paralyzed and in terrible suffering."

[7]Jesus said to him, "I will go and heal him."

[8]The centurion replied, "Lord, I do not deserve to have you come under my roof. But just say the word, and my servant will be healed. [9]For I myself am a man under authority, with soldiers under me. I tell this one, 'Go,' and he goes; and that one, 'Come,' and he comes. I say to my servant, 'Do this,' and he does it."

[10]When Jesus heard this, he was astonished and said to those following him, "I tell you the truth, I have not found anyone in Israel with such great faith. [11]I say to you that many will come from the east and the west, and will take their places at the feast with Abraham, Isaac and Jacob in the kingdom of heaven. [12]But the subjects of the kingdom will be thrown outside, into the darkness, where there will be weeping and gnashing of teeth."

[13]Then Jesus said to the centurion, "Go! It will be done just as you believed it would." And his servant was healed at that very hour.

8:5. The second respondent following Jesus' discourse (chs. 5-7) would be viewed by Jewish observers as equally offensive and unclean, being a Gentile centurion. While the leper's physical state excluded him from participation with the covenanted people of God, the centurion was excluded because of his ethnic background. However, the episode foreshadows the universal appeal of the gospel (28:18-20), and shows how faith in the authoritative status of Jesus shatters sociocultural boundaries.

The reader was earlier informed that Jesus selected Capernaum as his base of operations after leaving Nazareth (4:13; cf. Mark 1:21; Luke 4:31). Consequently, the city has become a center for the teaching and healing of Jesus over an extended period of time. Later, Jesus will denounce Capernaum for its lack of faith (11:23).

8:6-7. In Matthew's accounting of this episode only one individual approaches Jesus, i.e., a Gentile soldier (cf. Luke 7:1-10).[12] The

---

[12]For a plausible explanation to reconcile the accounts see Carson, *Matthew*, p. 200.

cluster of verbs describing the centurion's approach (προσῆλθεν, *prosēlthen*, παρακαλῶν, *parakalōn*, κύριε, *kyrie*) is reminiscent of the leper's appeal, and serves to highlight the centurion's reverent confidence in Jesus' power to meet his request. However, unlike the leper's request, the centurion does not make a formal request, but simply lays before Jesus the distress of his **servant** (παῖς, *pais*, 8:6).[13] Although the NIV translates Jesus' response (v. 7) as compliance to the centurion's request, there are grounds for understanding Jesus' words as a question: "Shall I come and heal him?"[14] This translation explains the emphatic "I" and perhaps best explains the centurion's protest that follows (vv. 8-9). It might also be compared with the way Jesus responds to the request of a Gentile woman in 15:21-28. Be that as it may, Jesus' response does not deter the centurion, but rather provides an opportunity for an expression of faith unlike anything Jesus had found within Israel.

8:8-9. The centurion both acknowledges his unworthiness and recognizes in Jesus' words God's authoritative healing power. He reasons from the "lesser to the greater" by comparing the invested authority he has as a military leader[15] to evoke obedience, to the view that the mere authoritative command of Jesus will result in the healing of his "servant." The restrained confidence of the leper's faith in Jesus' powerful "touch" (8:1-4) is surpassed by the centurion's confidence in Jesus' powerful **word** to heal.

8:10-11. Even Jesus is **astonished** at the level of perception and faith characteristic of this Gentile soldier (cf. 15:28). Indeed, Jesus acknowledges to those **following him** that such faith has not been found among any within Israel. Although later Jesus will acknowledge that his mission is primarily to "the lost sheep of Israel" (cf. 10:5-6; 15:24), such faith, even though manifested by those outside ethnic Israel, will be privileged to the blessings of God's kingdom.

---

[13]The term can be translated either "son" or "servant." Hagner, *Matthew*, 1:204 prefers "son," while Davies and Allison, *Matthew*, 2:24 prefer "house slave."

[14]So Davies and Allison, *Matthew*, 2:21-22; Morris, *Matthew*, p. 193; Carson, *Matthew*, p. 201; *Contra*, Hagner, *Matthew*, 1:204; Blomberg, *Matthew*, p. 141; (cf. John 18:28; Acts 10:28; m. Ohol. 18.7).

[15]As the name implies, a centurion was an officer in charge of one hundred soldiers.

The imagery of the **many . . . from the east and west** reclining with **Abraham, Isaac, and Jacob in the kingdom** recalls a common Jewish eschatological idea built on passages from the OT (e.g., Isa 25:6; 65:13), highlighting Jewish hopes in the blessings and celebration to come with the consummation of the victory of God. However, Jewish expectation never envisioned the end-time "messianic banquet" as being anything other than the exclusive privilege of Israel, with some Gentiles being only fringe benefactors. Remarkably Jesus envisions a scenario where Gentiles, not Jews, come "from the east and west" (cf. Baruch 5:5), and are extended places of honor beside Israel's famed patriarchs. Such a picture appears to be "without analogy in the whole of Jewish apocalyptic"[16] expectations.

8:12. The reversal of Jewish expectations is further delineated by the description of the fate of those who should have been major participants in the festive occasion. The **subjects of the kingdom** (lit., **sons of the kingdom**) are the literal offspring of Abraham, i.e., ethnic Israel, who suffer the fate traditionally reserved for Israel's enemies. Obviously, the exclusion is not to be understood as involving all Jews (see Rom 9-11), but only those who obstinately reject Jesus as God's final agent of salvation (cf. 22:1-14). The figurative expressions of **darkness** and **weeping** and **gnashing of teeth** communicate their ultimate expulsion from God and the redeemed, and their sense of terror and rage with the inevitability of God's final judgment.

8:13. The scene closes with Jesus accenting the importance of the centurion's faith in the accomplishment of the healing. Faith was the catalyst that activated the divine and authoritative healing power of Jesus. The link between faith and healing in Matthew's Gospel is an important theme (cf. 9:29; 15:28), because it is representative of a deeper dimension, i.e., the bringing of salvation whereby people are truly made whole. Matthew is especially fond of bringing out the remarkable results when faith comes into contact with the ἐξουσία (*exousia*) of Jesus.

---

[16]See J. Jeremias, *New Testament Theology: The Proclamation of Jesus*, trans. John Bowden (New York: Charles Scribner's Sons, 1971), p. 246; *Contra* Davies and Allison, *Matthew*, 2:21-28, who dispute that Gentiles are intended as those who come "from east and west."

3. Peter's Mother-in-Law (8:14-15)

[14]When Jesus came into Peter's house, he saw Peter's mother-in-law lying in bed with a fever. [15]He touched her hand and the fever left her, and she got up and began to wait on him.

8:14. In this scene Matthew keeps the focus on Jesus by specifically mentioning his name (cf. 1:23; Mark 1:29), and by including as participants in the episode only Jesus and the sick woman (cf. Mark 1:30). Gerhardsson has noted the "unbelievable degree of consciousness and care"[17] with which the Evangelist has narrated this brief scene. The episode falls into two halves with three main verbs highlighting the actions of Jesus (**came**, **saw**, and **touched**), and three verbs associated with the woman and her healing (**fever left**, **got up**, and **wait on**). The scene begins with Jesus and ends with him (αὐτῷ, *autō*, v. 15; cf. Mark 1:33-34). Jesus comes to a sick person and by contact with him healing occurs and the healed becomes a servant.

8:15. This is the only episode in the Synoptic tradition where Jesus takes the initiative in a miracle of healing.[18] Thus far in chapter eight we have seen Jesus' willingness to be responsive to requests for healing, thus performing the messianic tasks associated with his ministry. In this account, as noted by Held, Jesus is portrayed "as answering of his own accord this call laid upon him by God."[19] It may also be that Matthew intends his readers to see another social boundary crossed by Jesus in his willingness to touch a sick woman.[20] Certainly, the **touch** highlights his authoritative power and willingness to relieve the distress of physical affliction. The action of Peter's mother-in-law models a fundamental aspect of discipleship by responding to her healing with grateful service.

4. Summary and Fulfillment Citation (8:16-17)

[16]When evening came, many who were demon-possessed were

---

[17]Gerhardsson, *Mighty Acts*, p. 40.

[18]Held, "Matthew as Interpreter," p. 169.

[19]Ibid., p. 170.

[20]See J. Jeremias, *Jerusalem in the Time of Jesus* (Philadelphia: Fortress, 1969), p. 377ff.; Carson, *Matthew*, p. 204.

brought to him, and he drove out the spirits with a word and healed all the sick. [17]This was to fulfill what was spoken through the prophet Isaiah:

"He took up our infirmities
and carried our diseases."[a]

[a]*17* Isaiah 53:4

8:16. By means of a brief summary Matthew highlights Jesus' messianic deeds in terms of exorcisms and healings. Summaries have the effect of reminding the reader that the variation of specific examples of exorcisms or healings are only isolated incidents among the many performed by Jesus. Matthew never includes in his summaries healing references that are not documented by specific examples.

The verb translated **brought** (προσήνεγκαν, *prosēnenkan*) is characteristic of Matthew's description of the sick being brought to Jesus (cf. 4:24; 9:2, 32; 12:22; 14:35). The verb almost takes on sacrificial connotations as the distressed are offered to Jesus.[21] The reference to exorcisms with a mere word highlights his authoritative power over the forces of evil which plague humankind (cf. 8:8). Not only were the **many who were demon possessed** cured, but **all** (cf. Mark 1:34) who came with various forms of sickness were healed. The effect is to indicate that no human need went unmet when Jesus was encountered. The summary prepares the reader for the following fulfillment citation that highlights the way Jesus' miracles are to be viewed.

8:17. With a fulfillment citation Matthew indicates that Jesus' healings are to be understood as the fulfillment of Isaiah 53:4. In order to highlight Jesus' activity in terms of the Servant Songs of Isaiah (cf. 12:1-21; Isa 42:1-4), Matthew's rendering of Isaiah 53:4 does not follow the spiritualizing tendency of the LXX ("bore our sins"), but translates literally the Hebrew חֳלָיֵנוּ *ḥŏlāyēnu* (=sickness) as ἀσθενείας (*astheneias*, weakness) and νόσους (*nosous*, diseases). The effect is to highlight Jesus' total life and ministry in terms of God's suffering servant. J.P. Meier has best captured the significance of Matthew's use of Isaiah 53:

[21]See J.R. Edwards, "The Use of προσέρχεσθαι in the Gospel of Matthew," *JBL*, 106 (March 1987), 65-74.

Jesus' servanthood is not to be restricted to his death, it stretches throughout his ministry. Throughout that ministry he freely chooses to be a lowly servant among his people, associating with sinners, showing mercy to the outcasts or mistreated (notice that the three miracles are performed for a leper, the servant of a Gentile, and a woman). In short, from his baptism onward Jesus the servant embraces a sinful, suffering, sick humanity, in order to save his people from their sin (1:21) and bear their illnesses.[22]

5. Two Would-Be Followers (8:18-22)

18When Jesus saw the crowd around him, he gave orders to cross to the other side of the lake. 19Then a teacher of the law came to him and said, "Teacher, I will follow you wherever you go."

20Jesus replied, "Foxes have holes and birds of the air have nests, but the Son of Man has no place to lay his head."

21Another disciple said to him, "Lord, first let me go and bury my father."

22But Jesus told him, "Follow me, and let the dead bury their own dead."

8:18. The presence of the **crowds** prompts Jesus to give command, apparently to his disciples, to withdraw to the other side of the lake (cf. 5:1). Before they embark on the journey, they are approached by two potential followers who both express an interest in accompanying Jesus in his travels. It may be that these brief encounters are included at this point in the narrative to highlight basic tenets of discipleship. Certainly, features of discipleship dominate Jesus' conversations both in 8:18-22 and in the following episode of stilling the storm (8:23-27).

8:19. The first respondent is described as a **teacher of the law**, and appears to think highly of Jesus as a **teacher**. This "student of the Torah" evidently recognizes Jesus as an authoritative teacher, and expresses his willingness to follow him, with the obvious intention of learning from him. In terms of Jewish custom, the request of

---

[22]Meier, *Vision of Matthew*, p. 69.

the "scribe" is in accord with the rabbinic practice of a student petitioning a teacher or rabbi with the intent of being trained by him. There is no reason to suspect anything but the best of intentions from this scribe.[23] However, it does appear from Jesus' response that he had not fully thought through the implications of his request.

8:20. Jesus' reply is calculated to dispel all faulty notions that following him means a leisurely involvement with little or no personal hardship or self-denial. Jesus makes it clear that association with him means embarking on the rigors of an itinerant ministry marked by the deprivation of basic securities and comforts. Such an assessment must have surprised the scribe who was probably used to seeing rabbinic teachers greatly benefit and even prosper form their teaching skills. Yet, Jesus claims that the relative security of a "resting place" enjoyed by even lowly creatures, such as **foxes** and **birds** is denied Jesus and his followers (cf. 10:24ff.). The force of Jesus' illustration is realized when the relative security of foxes and birds is contrasted with the deprived existence of the one identified as the **Son of Man**.[24]

Here, for the first time the designation "Son of Man" is used by Jesus as his own self-reference to highlight certain features of his ministry. In this instance the reference underscores Jesus' itinerant ministry as one characterized by a lack of a permanent dwelling place. Jesus is unlike any rabbi in that he invites his followers to share in his repudiation and hardship. Indeed, a striking feature about the reference "Son of Man" is that the work and destiny of the Son of Man is also said about the disciples (cf. ch 10).

8:21-22. The second inquirer is described as "another disciple" (ἕτερος, *heteros*),[25] a term appropriate for one who had made a prior

---

[23]*Contra* J.D. Kingsbury, "On Following Jesus: The 'Eager' Scribe and the 'Reluctant' Disciple (Matthew 8:18-22)," *NTS* 34 (1988), 49-52.

[24]Matthew is united with the Synoptic tradition which limits the use of "Son of Man" solely to Jesus' own self-designation. It is customary to group the Son of Man-sayings into three distinct categories according to their reference: (1) to Jesus' earthly ministry (8:20; 9:6; 11:19; 12:8, 32; 13:37(?); 16:13); (2) suffering and resurrection of Jesus (12:40; 17:9, 12,22; 20:18-19, 28; 26:2,24); (3) and the glorification and parousia of Jesus (10:23; 13:41; 16:27-28; 19:28; 24:27, 30, 37, 39, 44; 25:31; 26:64).

[25]While ἕτερος can mean another of a different kind, it is probably used here in the same sense as ἄλλος (*allos*).

commitment to Jesus. Rather than immediately obey Jesus' orders to cross the lake (v. 18), the disciple requests a leave of absence in order to attend to his father's burial. Certainly, by ancient standards, a reasonable request. Based on the Law (Exod 20:12; cf. Deut 27:16) Jewish tradition considered the burial of one's parents a sacred duty (cf. Tob 4:3; Sir 38:16; m. Ber. 3:1; see also Gen 25:9; 35:29; 50:13). There is no indication of insincere motives in the disciple's request.[26] Neither should the request be construed as either an attempt to secure an indefinite period of time in order to look after his elderly father until he dies,[27] or to be involved in the traditional seven days of mourning following his father's death.[28] While these interpretations may soften the shocking response of Jesus (v. 22), there is really no way to know with certainty what possible provisions the disciple had in mind. However, there appears to be no reason not to accept at face value the urgency and priority of following Jesus over even the duty of burying one's parents (cf. 10:37). The disciple is told to leave the business of physically burying the dead to those who are "spiritually dead" (cf. Luke 15:24, 32; John 3:13; Eph 2:1; 1 Tim 5:6; Rev 3:1). While the saying may appear unduly harsh, the language is intended to reinforce the absolute priority and uncompromising demands of discipleship. Any postponement, even for the noblest of purposes, cannot take precedence over the urgency of following Jesus. Such a radical challenge to discipleship can only be grounded in an astonishing conception of one's own person and mission.[29]

---

[26]*Contra* Carson, *Matthew*, p. 209.

[27]So Morris, *Matthew*, p. 203, who follows the suggestion by K.E. Bailey, *Through Peasant Eyes* (Grand Rapids: Eerdmans, 1983), p. 26, that the Jewish idiom "to bury one's father" refers to the duty of a son to remain at home to care for his elderly parents until they are laid to rest.

[28]Jeremias, *Theology*, p. 132.

[29]Even E.P. Sanders, *Jesus and Judaism* (Philadelphia: Fortress, 1985), p. 255, is forced to acknowledge that at least this one incident indicates that Jesus "was willing to say that following him superseded the requirements of piety and the Torah."

6. Stilling of the Storm (8:23-27)

[23]Then he got into the boat and his disciples followed him. [24]Without warning, a furious storm came up on the lake, so that the waves swept over the boat. But Jesus was sleeping. [25]The disciples went and woke him, saying, "Lord, save us! We're going to drown!"

[26]He replied, "You of little faith, why are you so afraid?" Then he got up and rebuked the winds and the waves, and it was completely calm.

[27]The men were amazed and asked, "What kind of man is this? Even the winds and the waves obey him!"

8:23. Matthew is careful to link this scene with the previous episode by resuming the story line of v. 18, and by his reference to the *disciples* who *follow* Jesus (cf. vv. 19, 21, 22). The overall structure is typical of Matthew's depiction of Jesus' supernatural activity: vv. 23-25 dire conditions described; v. 26 Jesus' response; v. 28 human amazement. The dual themes of discipleship and Christology are prominent in the episode. Gerhardsson observes that only in the nontherapeutic miracles in Matthew do the disciples play a prominent role.[30] In this episode a dimension of Jesus' majesty is revealed that shows Jesus to be capable of handling any crisis. On the other hand, the disciples suffer a "crisis of trust,"[31] and must learn that the one who called them can sustain them no matter what the crisis.

8:24. Matthew describes the stormy condition of the sea with a term rarely used to describe a storm at sea (σεισμός, *seismos*; cf. Mark 4:37). In Matthew the term is translated "earthquake" in the depiction of Jerusalem's downfall (24:7), at the crucifixion of Jesus (27:54), and at the resurrection account (28:2). By the use of the term the storm takes on catastrophic proportions (as further indicated by the fearful response of these seasoned fishermen). Even though the rough seas threaten to swamp the boat, Jesus continued to sleep. While it may be true that the demands of Jesus' ministry

[30]Gerhardsson, *Mighty Acts*, p. 54.

[31]Words of Kingsbury, *Matthew As Story*, p. 135.

left him exhausted, it is doubtful that the depiction of a sleeping Jesus is intended to suggest that he was worn out from the day's activities. More likely is the suggestion that Jesus' sleep in the midst of such chaos is indicative of his trusting confidence in God's protective care. Perhaps the background of Isaiah 51:9-10 is in mind: "Awake, awake! Clothe yourself with strength, O arm of the LORD; awake, as in days gone by, as in generations of old. . . . Was it not you who dried up the sea, the waters of the great deep, who made a road in the depths of the sea so that the redeemed might cross over?" (cf. Lev 26:6; Job 11:18-19; Ps 3:5; 4:8; Prov 3:23-24) It should also be observed that the scene has many similarities with the experience of Jonah (cf. 1:5; 12:41).

8:25-26. The address and petition of the disciples take on prayer-like qualities: **"Lord, save us! We're going to drown!"** Unlike the frightened sailors who arouse Jonah to call upon his God for deliverance (Jonah 1:6), the disciples petition Jesus directly to exercise his saving power. Nevertheless, Jesus' question, **"why are you so afraid?"** and his characterization of them as men of **little faith** indicates that he expected a greater level of trust and understanding. They thought the storm to be a danger as long as Jesus remained asleep. In Jesus' estimation they should have had confidence in his mere presence to assure their safety.

The terrifying power of the raging sea is calmed with Jesus' authoritative demand. Power over the sea in the OT is often associated with Yahweh's victory over chaotic forces (cf. Ps 29:3; 65:7; 89:9, 93:4; 107:25-32; 124:4-5; Isa 51:9-10). Like his healings and exorcisms, Jesus' power over the sea testifies to God's sovereign presence in him. No obstacle, including natural forces, can in any way inhibit the accomplishment of his mission.

8:27. The disciples are described as **amazed** because Jesus has completely shattered all their limited expectations of his sovereign power. It may be that they are described as **men** because they continue to "think the things of men" not "the things of God" (16:23). At least they are on the right track by asking the question, **what kind of man** could exercise such authority over the elements? This question indicates their realization that such power could not come from an ordinary man. In a later boat scene they will come to the proper evaluation of Jesus' person (14:33). Howbeit, the reader of the Gospel already knows the answer and finds in this scene a timeless message of faith and courage.

7. The Gadarene Demoniacs (8:28-34)

[28]When he arrived at the other side in the region of the Gadarenes,[a] two demon-possessed men coming from the tombs met him. They were so violent that no one could pass that way. [29]"What do you want with us, Son of God?" they shouted. "Have you come here to torture us before the appointed time?"

[30]Some distance from them a large herd of pigs was feeding. [31]The demons begged Jesus, "If you drive us out, send us into the herd of pigs."

[32]He said to them, "Go!" So they came out and went into the pigs, and the whole herd rushed down the steep bank into the lake and died in the water. [33]Those tending the pigs ran off, went into the town and reported all this, including what had happened to the demon-possessed men. [34]Then the whole town went out to meet Jesus. And when they saw him, they pleaded with him to leave their region.

[a]*28* Some manuscripts *Gergesenes*; others *Gerasenes*

8:28. With this scene we arrive at **the other side** of the lake, a destination already mentioned in verse 18. The exact location is complicated by three variant readings characterizing the manuscript tradition: Gadarenes, Gerasenes, or Gergesenes. Based on superior external evidence it appears that Gadarenes is to be preferred.[32] Thus the "region of the Gadarenes" (cf. Mark 5:1; Luke 8:26) refers to a district controlled by the city of Gadara, located midpoint on the eastern side of the Sea of Galilee. The territory was predominantly a Gentile region, as indicated by the presence of a "large herd of pigs" (v. 30), which would be strictly forbidden in Jewish territory.

Upon arrival Jesus is met by two demoniacs (cf. Mark 5:2; Luke 8:27) who are described as extremely violent and reclusive, hiding

[32]For discussion see B.M. Metzger, *A Textual Commentary on the Greek New Testament* (New York: United Bible Societies, 1971) pp. 23-24.

out in the cave-like tombs in the adjacent hills. Certainly, Jewish sensitivities would quickly evaluate such a setting as extremely unclean: a possessed man living among the tombs, in Gentile territory, in close proximity to a large herd of pigs!

8:29. The demons immediately recognize the identity of Jesus and address him as **Son of God**. The same perception was articulated by Satan, the chief of demons earlier in the temptation scene (4:1-11). While the demons know Jesus' identity, the implications are understood in terms of their inevitable destruction. This is suggested by the two rhetorical questions posed by the demons. The first question, **"What do you want with us"** (lit., "what to us and to you") is an idiom that acknowledges that they have nothing in common with the divine status of Jesus. By the second question, **"Have you come here to torture us before the appointed time?"** they concede their eschatological fate, but perceive Jesus as exercising his judicial power before the "appointed time." However, the presence of God's reign even in the here and now spells the overthrow of Satan and the destruction of his agents. There is no hint, even given the fierceness of these demons, that they pose any great obstacle to Jesus. On the contrary, they know they are clearly "outmatched and faced with the mighty ἐξουσία [=authority] of Jesus, they immediately prepare for flight."[33]

8:30-31. The presence of a **large herd of pigs** prompt the demons to request that their expulsion from the men result in their being sent into the pigs. It is difficult to know why the demons make such a request. It may be that unclean pigs provide a suitable habitat for unclean spirits. Whatever the reason, their request certainly acknowledges Jesus' sovereign power to do with them what he wills.

8:32. With a mere one word command (ὑπάγετε, *hypagete*) the demons take their flight to enter the pigs. However, the result is a stampede that leads to the entire herd (cf. Mark 5:13, "two thousand in number") plunging to their death by drowning in the sea. Essentially, unclean spirits that seek "waterless" places (12:43) are brought to their destruction by water. Earlier Jesus calmed the raging seas of a watery chaos, now he cleanses the land of evil

---

[33]Gerhardsson, *Mighty Acts*, p. 49.

unclean forces. Indeed, the time has come for the tyrannical hold of Satan to be broken.

8:33-34. The scene closes by noting human reaction to the exhibition of Jesus' awesome power. The pig-keepers rush to town (possibly Gadara) to report the loss of their pigs and what had happened to the demoniacs. While one might expect the inhabitants of the town to be positively disposed toward Jesus, the whole city comes out to meet Jesus (ὑπαντᾶν, *hypantan,* the same verb used by the demons in v. 28), and eventually plead with him to **leave their region**. It may be fear of Jesus' supernatural power, or fear of further economic loss (or both), that prompts their rejection of Jesus. Whatever the reason, they show themselves to be without faith and understanding in the significance of Jesus' power and authority.

MATTHEW 9

8. Healing of the Paralytic (9:1-8)

[1]Jesus stepped into a boat, crossed over and came to his own town. [2]Some men brought to him a paralytic, lying on a mat. When Jesus saw their faith, he said to the paralytic, "Take heart, son; your sins are forgiven."

[3]At this, some of the teachers of the law said to themselves, "This fellow is blaspheming!"

[4]Knowing their thoughts, Jesus said, "Why do you entertain evil thoughts in your hearts? [5]Which is easier: to say, 'Your sins are forgiven,' or to say, 'Get up and walk'? [6]But so that you may know that the Son of Man has authority on earth to forgive sins . . . ." Then he said to the paralytic, "Get up, take your mat and go home." [7]And the man got up and went home. [8]When the crowd saw this, they were filled with awe; and they praised God, who had given such authority to men.

9:1. The participle (ἐμβάς, *embas*) followed by two prepositional phrases and two aorist verbs establish the geographical transition of Jesus to the other side of the Sea of Galilee (v. 1, cf. 8:23). The specific destination is described as **his own town**, by which is clearly meant Capernaum (4:13; 8:5; cf. Mark 2:1-12). In typical fashion, Matthew's straightforward narration of this scene leaves out many of the lively details found in the Markan account (cf. Mark 2:1-12). The result is to focus more on Jesus' authoritative power to forgive sins rather than on the actual details of the healing.

9:2. With the imperfect verb (προσέφερον, *prosepheron*) Matthew vividly captures the manner of the coming as a kind of sacrificial gift which these men lay before the feet of Jesus (cf. Matt 2:11; 5:23; 8:4; 9:32; 12:22; 14:35; 19:13). Jesus is fully aware of their faith without the elaboration of all the details concerning their efforts to come before him, as in Mark 2:1-4. Probably the plural **their faith** included the paralyzed man. At least he is the benefactor of the rather startling announcement that his **sins are forgiven**. Jesus' words should not be construed as a mere announcement that God has forgiven his sins,[1] but in effect, Jesus is at that very moment, forgiving the man's sins. The man's physical condition was only symptomatic of a greater spiritual need. While there is no attempt to draw a causal connection between sin and sickness, Jesus' healings are intended to be signs of the ultimate overcoming of evil and cleansing from sin. As Hagner has noted:

> If the healings done by Jesus presuppose the invasion of the kingdom of God into the realm of suffering caused by evil (as can graphically be seen in the demon exorcism of the preceding passage), then the healing of diseases is only a part of a much larger picture, wherein sin itself, and not just its symptoms, is dealt a final blow. The primary mission of Jesus is the overcoming of sin through the cross (cf. 1:21; 20:28; 26:28); the healings are only a secondary indication of that fact. This connection, indeed, has already been seen in the citation of Isa 53:4 in 8:17. In Isa 53 the sin-bearer is also the disease-curer . . ."[2]

9:3-4. Some "teachers of the law" found Jesus' words offensive and charged him with blasphemy. According to the law, blasphemy consisted of "cursing" or "slandering" the name of God (Exod 21:18; Lev 24:25-26), and was punishable by being stoned. Evidently, these "scribes" think Jesus has assumed a prerogative reserved for God alone (cf. Mark 2:7), hence defaming the divine name. Although such thoughts are not vocalized (ἐν ἑαυτοῖς, *en heautois*), Jesus knows their inner thoughts (v. 4) and responds accordingly. They are the ones who harbor evil, blasphemous thoughts as demonstrated by their malicious and slanderous thoughts concerning Jesus (cf. 12:33-37). Eventually, their thoughts will turn to public accusations and a hostile rejection of Jesus (chs. 11-12).

---

[1]*Contra* Sanders, *Jesus and Judaism*, p. 273.
[2]Hagner, *Matthew*, 1:232.

9:5-6. Jesus is willing to accommodate their skeptical suspicions by providing objective verification to validate his claim to forgive sins (vv. 5-6). Jesus' argument is in accord with basic rabbinic reasoning, where what applies to the easy or light will surely apply to the more difficult or heavy.[3] Since a miraculous healing would be considered the more difficult, its performance will confirm the reality of what is considered easy, i.e., the claim to forgive sins. Thus, Jesus intends to offer concrete evidence that he truly has been given authority on earth to forgive sins. The second **Son of Man** reference clearly alludes to Daniel's "Son of Man" who receives from the "Ancient of Days" "authority, glory, and sovereign power" (Dan 7:14). The one who has no place to "lay his head" (8:20) has been invested with transcendent authority to effect cleansing from sin.

9:7-8. The authoritative orders for the paralytic to **Get up, take your mat and go home** (v. 6), amounts to orders to do that which appears impossible. The paralytic's response (v. 7) corresponds precisely to the command, and is obviously an expression of great faith in Jesus' healing powers. The scene closes with the **crowds** suddenly being introduced as a kind of chorus responding to the series of events. Two verbs are behind the NIV translation, **they were filled with awe** (ἐφοβήθησαν, *ephobēthēsan*, cf. 1:20; 2:22; 17:6; 27:54; and δοξάζω, *doxazō*, cf. 5:16). While the "scribes" think evil in their hearts, the crowds "glorify God," and thus recognize Jesus' authority both in his teaching (7:28-29), and his works. Nevertheless, their limited perspective of Jesus' person may be hinted at by the fact that they were surprised that such authority had been granted to mere "mortal men." However, the reader knows that Jesus is much more than an endowed human being sent to exercise divine authority. He is God's unique Son, Immanuel, who in himself manifests God and his powerful reign.

9. Jesus' Association With Tax Collectors and Sinners (9:9-13)

[9]As Jesus went on from there, he saw a man named Matthew

---

[3]See R. Longenecker, *Biblical Exegesis in the Apostolic Period* (Grand Rapids: Eerdmans, 1975), p. 34.

sitting at the tax collector's booth. "Follow me," he told him, and Matthew got up and followed him.

[10]While Jesus was having dinner at Matthew's house, many tax collectors and "sinners" came and ate with him and his disciples. [11]When the Pharisees saw this, they asked his disciples, "Why does your teacher eat with tax collectors and 'sinners'?"

[12]On hearing this, Jesus said, "It is not the healthy who need a doctor, but the sick. [13]But go and learn what this means: 'I desire mercy, not sacrifice.'[a] For I have not come to call the righteous, but sinners."

[a]*13* Hosea 6:6

9:9. Jesus' call of Matthew and association with sinners in table-fellowship (vv. 10-13) continues the themes of discipleship and forgiveness of sins. The dinner scene may also function to foreshadow the messianic banquet (8:11), where "outsiders" enjoy the festive occasion, while the Jewish leadership looks on in anger.

The call of Matthew (called Levi in Mark 2:14) follows essentially the same pattern as noted in the call of the four in 4:18-22: (1) Jesus is walking along; (2) he sees an individual whose name is given; (3) he invites the individual to "follow him"; and (4) he immediately follows.[4] The unusual feature of Matthew's call is his occupational background: tax collector.[5] Few were despised more among the Jews than tax collectors. Not only were they considered national traitors, they were deemed unclean by their association with Gentiles; and they were notorious for their greedy exploitation of their own countrymen. Nevertheless, Matthew's immediate response is illustrative of the compelling force of Jesus' presence.

9:10-11. The scene abruptly changes from the "tax collector's booth," located probably on the outskirts of Capernaum, to a dinner party at Matthew's house (cf. Luke 5:29). It appears that Jesus is the guest of honor, and Matthew invited some of his tax-collecting friends, along with others viewed by Jewish standards as "sinners." The term was a popular derogatory reference to all those who did

---

[4]Davies and Allison, *Matthew*, 2:96.

[5]See J.R. Donahue, "Tax Collector," *ABD*, 6:337-338.

not ascribe to their understanding of *halakah*.[6] Jesus' willingness to have table fellowship with such a sordid group undermined basic Pharisaic standards of acceptable behavior. The ancient world found a great symbolic value in sharing a meal. Not only were ritual factors to be considered, eating meals together also symbolized the most solemn and intimate of social relationships.[7] Jesus' willingness to eat with such people not only undermined Pharisaic purity codes, but made a powerful prophetic statement about the extent of God's mercy. Rather than confront Jesus directly concerning his actions, the Pharisees question the disciples about their teacher's conduct. The underlying assumption is that Jesus cannot be a reliable teacher since he violates the traditions concerning table fellowship.

9:12-13. Although the Pharisees' question is directed to the disciples, Jesus offers his own defense of his actions. First, by the use of a proverbial saying Jesus highlights the contours of his mission: **It is not the healthy who need a doctor but the sick**. The significance of the saying is clearly delineated in the closing line: **For I have not come to call the righteous, but sinners**. Therefore, Jesus' defense of his association with sinners (=sick) is grounded in his conscious fidelity to his divinely appointed mission. Once again Jesus' therapeutic activity is tied to concepts of sin and sickness. Jesus is the great physician who has come to make the sick healthy and the sinner righteous.

Jesus also challenges his accusers to go and learn the meaning of his citation of Hosea 6:6: **I desire mercy, not sacrifice**. A fundamental difference between Jesus and his opponents relates to how one interprets Scripture. Ultimately, for Jesus, the law must be understood in terms of its disclosure of the character of God. Mere external adherence to the letter of the law may in fact fail to achieve God's ultimate intention. While Jesus has no objection to cultic observances (cf. 1 Sam 15:22; Ps 51:15-17; Isa 1:12-17; Amos 5:21-24; Micah 6:6-8), he is emphatic that all law keeping be subsumed

---

[6]See G.G. Porton, "Halakah," *ABD*, 3:26-27, the term "focuses on activity, specifically that activity in which primarily Jews should be engaged in personal, social, national and international relationships, as well as in all other practices and observances of Judaism." M.J. Wilkins, "Sinner," *DJG*, pp. 257-260.

[7]D.E. Smith, "Table Fellowship," *ABD*, 6:302-304.

and conditioned by the "weightier matters of the law" (23:23), such as "love" (22:36-40), the "golden rule" (7:12), and God's desire for "mercy" (cf. 12:7). Mercy is an important theme in Matthew, inasmuch as Jesus twice cites Hosea 6:6 to counter a faulty understanding of law keeping (cf. 9:13; 12:7; 18:33; 23:23). Whereas the Pharisees tended to sift the OT Scriptures through a holiness grid that focused on separation and purity, Jesus read and applied the law through the prism of God's character. Therefore, his association with "tax collectors and sinners" is mandated by his awareness of God's merciful character.

10. Question on Fasting (9:14-17)

14Then John's disciples came and asked him, "How is it that we and the Pharisees fast, but your disciples do not fast?"

15Jesus answered, "How can the guests of the bridegroom mourn while he is with them? The time will come when the bridegroom will be taken from them; then they will fast.

16"No one sews a patch of unshrunk cloth on an old garment, for the patch will pull away from the garment, making the tear worse. 17Neither do men pour new wine into old wineskins. If they do, the skins will burst, the wine will run out and the wineskins will be ruined. No, they pour new wine into new wineskins, and both are preserved."

9:14. It is difficult to know with certainty if Matthew intended the reader to understand that John's disciples pose their question during the dinner occasion of 9:10f.[8] If that is the case then the dinner scene would not end until verse 19 when Jesus gets up and leaves with a "ruler" to see about his daughter. Remember, however, that Matthew is not particularly interested in developing a chronology, detailing the sequence of events.

In this scene some of the disciples of John question the rigors of his devotion and pious observance, since fasting was not an important expression of his, or his disciples' form of righteousness. As

[8]See R.A. Edwards, *Matthew's Story of Jesus* (Philadelphia: Fortress, 1985), p. 30, "the dinner conversation continues . . ."

was noted earlier (see 6:16-18) the practice of fasting twice a week was typical of Pharisees, and voluntary, self-imposed fasts were considered a fundamental expression of Jewish piety. While Jesus certainly fasted on occasion (see 4:1-2; and Day of Atonement, Lev 16:29-31), his sense of mission necessitated a new response to the traditional mores and rituals of Judaism. Jesus uses a series of analogies to defend his willingness to forego certain elements of the law and Jewish tradition.

9:15. First, Jesus' messianic mission and presence of the kingdom is comparable to the joyous celebration of a wedding feast. When the **bridegroom** is present and the festivities of the wedding are taking place, fasting is certainly not the appropriate response. However, there will come a time **when the bridegroom will be taken from them**. At such a time of mourning and loss fasting is the appropriate response. Jesus no doubt is alluding to his eventual suffering and death, of which the current opposition in this chapter is a mere foreshadow. It is remarkable that it is his presence or absence that determines when fasting ought to be observed. Fasting also contributes to one's spiritual discipline, and Jesus seems to assume the ongoing practice among his followers.

9:16-17. The next two illustrations basically affirm the same general truth: what is new cannot be superimposed or restricted by the forms of the old. In order for the reader to appreciate the force of Jesus' comparisons, one must understand the common elements between **unshrunk cloth** and **an old garment**, and **new wine** and **old wineskins**. Essentially, the elements are incompatible, and any attempt to unite them results in disastrous consequences: **the patch will pull away from the garment making the tear worse**; and **the skins will burst, the wine will run out and the wineskins will be ruined**. Certain adjustments must be made in order to make the "new" compatible with the "old." Jesus' point is that the old forms of Judaism cannot possibly be used to defend or legislate how life in the kingdom is to be manifested. While there is certainly some continuity with the "old," the age of fulfillment has introduced a new way of understanding the will of God. For the disciples it is the authoritative presence and teaching of Jesus that are definitive for understanding and doing the will of God. While fasting may have its place among Jesus' followers it should not be viewed as a prime expression of religious devotion; neither should it be made a matter of coercion.

11. Raising the Ruler's Daughter and Cleansing the Unclean Woman (9:18-26)

[18]While he was saying this, a ruler came and knelt before him and said, "My daughter has just died. But come and put your hand on her, and she will live." [19]Jesus got up and went with him, and so did his disciples.

[20]Just then a woman who had been subject to bleeding for twelve years came up behind him and touched the edge of his cloak. [21]She said to herself, "If I only touch his cloak, I will be healed."

[22]Jesus turned and saw her. "Take heart, daughter," he said, "your faith has healed you." And the woman was healed from that moment.

[23]When Jesus entered the ruler's house and saw the flute players and the noisy crowd, [24]he said, "Go away. The girl is not dead but asleep." But they laughed at him. [25]After the crowd had been put outside, he went in and took the girl by the hand, and she got up. [26]News of this spread through all that region.

9:18-19. It may be that Jesus is still at the home of Matthew when an unnamed "ruler" (cf. Mark 5:22; Luke 8:41: Jairus) appears to request his presence on behalf of his daughter. What is, of course, structurally significant about this episode is that between the ruler's request (vv. 18-19) and Jesus' raising of his daughter (vv. 23-26), there is injected a scene involving the healing of a hemorrhaging woman (vv. 20-22). The placement of the story encourages the reader to read each episode in the light of the other, and to compare the approach and petitions of each suppliant. While the socially acceptable "ruler" publicly approaches, does obeisance to Jesus, and makes his request, the ritually unclean woman approaches Jesus from behind, hoping only to touch the fringe of his garments.[9] Although the two are not equal in social or religious

[9]See J.C. Anderson, "Matthew: Gender and Reading," *Semeia* 28 (1983), 21.

status, they are equal in the exhibition of exemplary faith and trust in Jesus' power to resolve their situation.

Much like the centurion (8:5f.), the reverent approach of the **ruler** is highlighted by a request (προσεκύνει, *prosekynai*) that takes the form of a report concerning the physical condition of his daughter. In Matthew's account the daughter has just died (cf. Mark 5:23) and yet the "ruler" is confident that Jesus has the power to restore his daughter's life. The effect is to draw attention to the ruler's faith, that even with his daughter's death he is confident that Jesus' presence can reverse the situation by giving life to the dead. Jesus is immediately responsive to such faith and arises from the dinner to follow the "ruler" to his house. Jewish readers may be somewhat surprised that Jesus appears unconcerned about the ritual implications of entering a home where a young girl lay dead (cf. Lev 21:11; Num 5:2; 6:6; 9:6-10; 19:11-13).

9:20-22. On the way to the location of the dead girl his progress is momentarily impeded by a woman, driven by desperation to perform a bold and presumptuous act. The woman had suffered from some form of bleeding disorder for the past twelve years. Although Matthew describes her condition with a bare three words (αἱμορροοῦσα δώδεκα ἔτη, *haimorrousa dōdeka etē*), details from Mark's account (5:16) indicate that her condition was medically incurable. In addition, according to the law, such regular loss of blood rendered her perpetually unclean (Lev 15:19-30), and anyone she touched would be unclean until evening. Once the seriousness of her condition is known, Matthew provides the reader with an insight into her inner thoughts and motivations. Although she is resolved to be inconspicuous, she nevertheless manifests great faith and boldness in her conviction that the mere "touch" of his cloak will result in her healing (σωθήσομαι, *sōthēsomai*; cf. 1:21; 10:22; 16:25; 18:11; 19:25). In terms of endearment (**daughter**) Jesus congratulates her faith and grants that which her faith desired. Moreover, the woman's impediment or lack of wholeness, that rendered her ritually unclean has been removed, thus liberating her from cultic and social restrictions.[10]

---

[10]See the discussion of Marla J. Selvidge, "Mark 5:25-34 and Leviticus 15:19-20," *JBL* 103 (1984), 619-623, who argues that Jesus' healing had cultic significance as well as physical benefits.

9:23-26. Matthew now returns to the plight of the ruler and his daughter by observing that when Jesus arrives at the ruler's home funeral proceedings had already begun. The presence of the **flute players** and **noisy crowd** contrast dramatically with the faith of the unpretentious woman in vv. 20-21. The woman believes and is saved (ἐσώθη, *esōthē*), whereas the mourners laugh in disbelief and are cast out. With Jesus' presence funeral proceedings are inappropriate since the girl's life is about to be restored. Without much fanfare (cf. Mark 5:37-42) Matthew indicates that Jesus took the girl by the hand and her life was restored. The scene closes with the observation that the deed become well known **throughout all the region**.

While both these miracle scenes characterize Jesus as an object of faith, the depth of insight surpasses previous episodes, as the ruler sees Jesus as a restorer of life, and the woman is persuaded that her salvation depends on making contact with Jesus, even if it be only the edges of his garment. Jesus knows the hearts of those he comes into contact with and exhibits a compassionate willingness to restore and bring wholeness to their lives.

12. Healing to Two Blind Men (9:27-31)

27As Jesus went on from there, two blind men followed him, calling out, "Have mercy on us, Son of David!"

28When he had gone indoors, the blind men came to him, and he asked them, "Do you believe that I am able to do this?"

"Yes, Lord," they replied.

29Then he touched their eyes and said, "According to your faith will it be done to you"; 30and their sight was restored. Jesus warned them sternly, "See that no one knows about this." 31But they went out and spread the news about him all over that region.

9:27. The rather vague transitional phrase (**Jesus went on from there**) could describe movement either from the ruler's house (v. 23), or possibly implying a departure from Capernaum. Jesus' departure was accompanied by two blind men who implore him as the **Son of David** to have mercy upon them (cf. the episode in 20:29-34). Blindness was not only a physical handicap reducing one to utter dependency upon others, but like most physical defects in the ancient world, it also had religious and social connotations (Lev 21:20).

The verb translated "have mercy" (ἐλέησον, *eleēson*) is found four times with the title Son of David (9:27-31; 15:21-28; 20:29-34), and only once elsewhere (17:15). Although the reader knows from the infancy narratives that Jesus is indeed a Son of David (1:20-21; 2:1-12; 2:23), this is the first time it is used as a form of address. However, throughout Matthew's story Jesus' royal Davidic messiahship continues to crop up in key places. Kingsbury argues that the title functions "theologically . . . to portray Jesus as Israel's royal messiah in which OT prophecy concerning David is fulfilled," and "apologetically . . . to underline the guilt that devolves around Israel for not receiving its messiah."[11] It is interesting that it is the so-called outcasts of the Jewish society who repeatedly acknowledge Jesus as the Son of David (=Messiah). In this scene two blind men *see* what Israel's leadership failed to see.

9:28-30. Perhaps because of the political ambitions and nationalistic hopes associated with the title Son of David, Jesus waits until he is in the house to respond. When the two blind men come to him, Jesus' question is calculated to elicit an emphatic expression of faith. The blind men express their absolute confidence in Jesus' healing powers, even addressing him as **Lord**. Their faith is rewarded by Jesus' healing touch. The giving of sight to the blind is a distinctly messianic blessing heralding the arrival of God's kingdom (see Isa 29:18; 35:5; 42:7).

9:31. It is difficult to know precisely what Matthew intended to convey by recording the failure of the blind men to obey Jesus' orders not to tell anyone about their healing. It may be that his readers are to sense the incongruity between the faith they express

---

[11]See J.D. Kingsbury, *Matthew: Structure, Christology, Kingdom* (Philadelphia: Fortress, 1975), p. 103; see also his "The Title 'Son of David' in Matthew's Gospel," *JBL* 95 (1976), 591-602. The proposal by D.C. Duling "Solomon, Exorcism, and the Son of David," *HTR* 68 (1975), 235-252, that Matthew expands on the tradition of Solomon as an exorcist to a therapeutic Son of David has not found much favor; see Ulrich Luz, *The Theology of the Gospel of Matthew* trans. J.B. Robinson (Cambridge: Cambridge University Press, 1995), pp. 70-75.

and the disobedience they exhibit.[12] Or it could be that Matthew intends to convey the idea that the joy of the blind men simply could not be contained,[13] albeit their limited perspective, knowing Jesus only as a powerful healer, was not sufficient to qualify them to give reliable testimony to the significance of Jesus' identity and mission.

13. Healing of a Deaf Mute (9:32-34)

[32]While they were going out, a man who was demon-possessed and could not talk was brought to Jesus. [33]And when the demon was driven out, the man who had been mute spoke. The crowd was amazed and said, "Nothing like this has ever been seen in Israel."

[34]But the Pharisees said, "It is by the prince of demons that he drives out demons."

9:32. With this brief miracle scene Matthew closes his collection of the mighty acts of Jesus recorded in chapters eight and nine. Like the previous episode (9:27-31), the inclusion of the healing of the deaf mute anticipates the later summary of Jesus' messianic activity (11:3-5). In addition, the response of the crowds, "Nothing like this has ever been seen in Israel" (v. 33) forms a fitting summary of Jesus' unprecedented work; while the negative assessment of the Pharisees, "It is by the prince of demons that he drives out demons," foreshadows a growing hostility toward Jesus, and eventually his disciples (10:25f; chs 11-12).

It appears that Jesus had no sooner healed the two blind men (9:27-31), and was just proceeding out of the house (v. 28), when "they brought to him" (προσήνεγκαν αὐτῷ, *prosēnengkan autō*; cf. 8:16; 9:2; 12:22; 14:35) a deaf mute (κωφός, *kōphos*, the term can refer to one who is deaf, mute, or both, *BAGD*, p. 463), who was demon possessed. In this case, the man's disability was caused by

---

[12]J.M. Gibbs, "Purpose and Pattern in Matthew's Use of the Title 'Son of David'," *NTS* 10 (1963/64), 457, 459; Gibbs sees Matthew portraying the blind men negatively by his concluding lines.

[13]See Hagner, *Matthew*, 1:254.

the demon possession (cf. 8:16). However, Matthew often links physical infirmities to deeper spiritual causes.

9:33-34. Given his passion for brevity, Matthew says nothing about the man's faith, Jesus' words, or his method of procedure. The expulsion of the demon becomes known by the simple affirmation, **the man who had been mute spoke**. While sixteen words are used to describe the healing of the man, twenty-three words narrate the twofold reaction to Jesus' exhibition of authority. The **crowd is amazed** (ἐθαύμασαν, *ethaumasan*; cf. 7:28; 9:8) and expresses awareness that something out the ordinary is taking place in Jesus. Their open-ended assessment is quickly countered by the Pharisees who attribute Jesus' power to the **prince of demons**. For the first time the Pharisees appear in the story as a clearly defined group in opposition to Jesus. Later in the story Jesus will demonstrate both the absurdity of their charge, and the eternal consequences of their evaluation (12:24-28). It is interesting that with each positive acknowledgment of Jesus by the crowds or various supplicants there is also a Pharisaic objection or protest that attempts to detract from the confession (9:34; 12:34; 15:23; 21:15). Thus Jesus' enabling the blind to see and the deaf to hear underscores that by Israel's rejection of Jesus they remain "blind" and "deaf" (cf. 13:13-15).[14]

F. A CALL TO MISSION (9:35–10:4)

[35]Jesus went through all the towns and villages, teaching in their synagogues, preaching the good news of the kingdom and healing every disease and sickness. [36]When he saw the crowds, he had compassion on them, because they were harassed and helpless, like sheep without a shepherd. [37]Then he said to his disciples, "The harvest is plentiful but the workers are few. [38]Ask the Lord of the harvest, therefore, to send out workers into his harvest field."

[1]He called his twelve disciples to him and gave them authority to drive out evil[a] spirits and to heal every disease and sickness.

---

[14]See W.R.G. Loader, "Son of David, Blindness, Possession, and Duality on Matthew," *CBQ* 44 (1982), 248.

[2]These are the names of the twelve apostles: first, Simon (who is called Peter) and his brother Andrew; James son of Zebedee, and his brother John; [3]Philip and Bartholomew; Thomas and Matthew the tax collector; James son of Alphaeus, and Thaddaeus; [4]Simon the Zealot and Judas Iscariot, who betrayed him.

[a]***10:1* Greek *unclean***

9:35. By means of repetitive summaries (4:23-25 and 9:35), Matthew constructs a literary bracket setting off the previous section by emphasizing the major contour of Jesus' Galilean ministry, i.e. preaching the kingdom and healing illnesses. It has also been observed that "both 4:24–5:2 and 9:35–10:4 consist of two major parts, the first having to do with Jesus and the Jewish multitudes (4:23-25; 9:35-38), and the second with Jesus and his disciples (5:1-2; 10:1-4)."[15] It follows that 9:35–10:4 functions both as a concluding summary and an introductory transition to the discourse to follow. The events recorded exhibit the following structural pattern:

Call of the Disciples	4:18-22
Summary	4:23-25
Ministry in Word	5:1–7:29
Ministry in Deed	8:1–9:34
Summary	9:35
Mission of the Disciples	9:36–11:1

The verbatim summary (9:35; cf. 4:23) highlights Jesus' itinerant ministry throughout Galilee. The summary also indicates that Matthew has only provided "a representative sampling of the words and deeds of Jesus."[16] Thus far in the story the disciples have been only observers as Jesus' teachings and healings announce the presence of God's reign. However, if they are to be "fishers of men" (4:19), they too must embark on a ministry of healing and announcing the kingdom (10:5ff.).

9:36. The response that best captures Jesus' attitude and emotional identification with the crowds is his deep compassion

[15]Davies and Allison, *Matthew*, 2:143.

[16]Hagner, *Matthew*, 1:259.

(ἐσπλαγχνίσθη, *esplangchnisthē*; cf. 10:34: 14:14; 15:32). It is the plight of the crowds that evoke his compassionate concern: **they were harassed and helpless like sheep without a shepherd**. The two verbs (ἐσκυλμένοι, *eskylmenoi*, and ἐρριμμένοι, *errimmenoi*) are used metaphorically to depict the crowds as vulnerable and without resources to offset their brutal attackers. Their condition is likened unto a defenseless sheep without the security and protection of a caring shepherd. The imagery is used often in the OT to describe the desperate condition of a nation without proper leadership (cf. Num 27:16-17; 1 Kgs 22:17; 1 Chron 18:16; Jer 50:6; Ezek 34:1-16; Zech 11:15). Probably the language of Ezek 34 is foremost in mind: "Woe to the shepherds of Israel who only take care of themselves! Should not shepherds take care of the flock? . . . You have not strengthened the weak or healed the sick or bound up the injured. You have not brought back the strays or searched for the lost. You have ruled them harshly and brutally. So they were scattered because there was no shepherd, and when they were scattered they became food for all the wild animals" (Ezek 34:2, 4-5).

However, Ezekiel also predicted that God one day will place over Israel "one shepherd, my servant David, and he will tend them; he will tend them and be their shepherd" (34:23).[17]

The reader knows that earlier Jesus was identified as the one who will "shepherd my people Israel" (2:7). Thus the reference of "shepherding" recalls the earlier prediction and provides a framework to understand Jesus' compassionate messianic involvement with the people.

9:37-38. In verses 37-38 the metaphor abruptly changes from "shepherding" to a great **harvest**, and the focus is to call the disciples to action. Although the imagery of a harvest is often employed to depict the coming judgment of God (Isa 27:12-13; Jer 51:33; Hosea 6:11; Joel 3:1,13; Amos 9:13-15; Matt 3:12; 13:8, 39-42), in this instance the saying is intended to stir the disciples to mission, not the execution of final judgment. While the imagery of a "great harvest" envisions abundant potentiality, concern is raised by the

---

[17]See Martin, "Image of Shepherd in Matthew," pp. 277-278; and J.P. Heil, "Ezekiel 34 and the Narrative Strategy of the Shepherd and Sheep Metaphor in Matthew," *CBQ* 55 (October 1993), 698-708.

few workers available to take advantage of the situation. The disciples ought to be equally concerned, and are called to specific action, i.e. prayer. No longer can the concern for the multitudes be Jesus' alone; the disciples must also identify personally with the plight of the crowds.

MATTHEW 10

F. A CALL TO MISSION (9:35–10:4) (Continued)

10:1. Remarkably, the disciple's prayer for additional workers is answered by Jesus taking action to enlist the disciples as laborers to be sent into the harvest fields (10:1-4). The number of disciples has grown from five (4:18-22; 9:9) to **twelve**, thus establishing them as the core of the new messianic community (cf. 19:28). As such, they are empowered with the same authority exhibited in Jesus to cast out demons and to heal illnesses. They are thus equipped to participate in Jesus' own ministry of relieving the oppressed from affliction and the tyranny of evil. It is Jesus' creative empowerment that enables them to fulfill their role as "fishers of men" (4:19).

10:2-4. The twelve are now identified as **apostles** (10:2), since they are to be "sent out" on a mission patterned after Jesus'. They are then introduced by name with only minimal information provided concerning their background. Four of the disciples are introduced by name only (**Philip**, **Bartholomew**, **Thomas**, and **Thaddaeus**). Four others are introduced with only a brief reference indicating family relationships (**his brother Andrew**, **James, son of Zebedee**, **his brother John**, **James, son of Alphaeus**). Two of the disciples are identified by their social or political affiliations (**Matthew, the tax collector**, and **Simon the Zealot**). The first and last names in the list are introduced with participial phrases that become descriptive of their respective roles in the ongoing story (**Simon, who is called Peter**, and **Judas Iscariot, who betrayed him**, cf. 16:18; 26:14-16). No longer will these disciples simply "follow Jesus," now they must emulate his ministry by a parallel mission. Jesus now gives them explicit instructions concerning their mission (10:5-42).

G. THE MISSIONARY DISCOURSE (10:5-42)

Although the structure of Jesus' second discourse has not found a consensus, it does appear that Weaver's proposal to divide the discourse into three parts (i.e., 10:5b-15; 16-23; 24-42) based on the threefold repetition of "I tell you the truth" (vv. 15, 23, and 42), followed by a warning or promise phrased in eschatological terms, is probably the best option.[1] Accordingly, an overview of 9:25–11:1 might be outlined as follows:

Narrative Introduction	9:35–10:5a
Instructions for Mission	10:5b-15
Persecution and Response	10:16-23
The Disciple's Relationship to Jesus	10:24-42
Narrative Conclusion	11:1

Two major themes dominate the discourse. First, the mission of the disciples is to be founded in the paradigmatic example of Jesus' own ministry. They receive his "authority" to do precisely what he has been doing (10:1). Like Jesus, their mission must be limited to the "lost sheep of Israel" (10:6). They are to proclaim the same message of the dawning kingdom (10:7; cf. 3:1; 4:17). Like Jesus, their proclamation will be accompanied with the same powers to "heal the sick, raise the dead, cleanse the lepers, drive out demons" (10:8). Their involvement in a ministry patterned after Jesus' also necessitates an itinerant lifestyle where one learns to trust in God for even the basics of life (10:9-14). Like Jesus they will be persecuted (10:23/23:34), flogged (10:17/20:19), brought before Gentile authorities (10:17-20/20:19; 27:11-26), and even put to death (10:28-30/16:21; 17:22; 20:17-19). In the face of all opposition the disciples must exhibit certain qualities and actions: "be as shrewd as snakes and as innocent as doves" (10:16); when you are persecuted in one city, "flee to another" (10:23); do not fear (10:26-31); never deny your allegiance to Jesus (10:32-33); constantly reexamine your priorities (10:37-39).

---

[1]For chapter 10 I am especially indebted to the helpful study of D.J. Weaver, *Matthew's Missionary Discourse: A Literary Critical Analysis* (JSNTSup 38; Sheffield: JSOT Press, 1990).

The second theme woven into the fabric of the discourse is the insistence that the disciples' shepherd-like mission has various eschatological consequences: For those who reject their message "it will be more bearable for Sodom and Gomorrah on the day of judgment" (10:15). Eventually, the coming of the Son of Man will validate Jesus' claims and confirm the testimony of the disciples by bringing judgment upon those who oppose them (10:23). The eternal destiny of the disciples depends on their willingness to acknowledge their faith no matter what the opposition (10:32-33). A favorable response given to the disciples means a positive response from the Father who will reward accordingly (10:40-42).

The overall function of the discourse is to establish the closest possible relationship between Jesus and his disciples in terms of their mission and the fate that awaits them. What it means to "follow" Jesus is about to take on significant new dimensions.

1. Instructions for Mission (10:5-15)

[5]These twelve Jesus sent out with the following instructions: "Do not go among the Gentiles or enter any town of the Samaritans. [6]Go rather to the lost sheep of Israel. [7]As you go, preach this message: 'The kingdom of heaven is near.' [8]Heal the sick, raise the dead, cleanse those who have leprosy,[a] drive out demons. Freely you have received, freely give. [9]Do not take along any gold or silver or copper in your belts; [10]take no bag for the journey, or extra tunic, or sandals or a staff; for the worker is worth his keep.

[11]"Whatever town or village you enter, search for some worthy person there and stay at his house until you leave. [12]As you enter the home, give it your greeting. [13]If the home is deserving, let your peace rest on it; if it is not, let your peace return to you. [14]If anyone will not welcome you or listen to your words, shake the dust off your feet when you leave that home or town. [15]I tell you the truth, it will be more bearable for Sodom and Gomorrah on the day of judgment than for that town.

[a]*8* The Greek word was used for various diseases affecting the skin—not necessarily leprosy.

The opening section of the discourse is dominated by imperatival statements (sixteen), as Jesus instructs his disciples, (1) where they are to go (10:5b-6), (2) what they are to do (10:7-10), and (3) how they are to deal with responses to their ministry (10:11-15).[2]

10:5-6. Concerning where they are to go, Jesus establishes the focus of their mission by two negative imperatives, followed by a positive command. The prohibitions not to go to the **Gentiles** or to the **Samaritans** are not racially motivated. As has been observed throughout Matthew, non-Jews are often viewed favorably and do benefit from Jesus' ministry (2:1-12; 3:9; 8:10-11; 15:21-28). Some see Jesus' prohibition as incongruent with a Gospel that ends with a commission to take the Good News to all the nations (28:19). Although not all are agreed how to resolve the seeming tension between Matthew's universalism and the limited particularism suggested by this text (cf. 10:5-6; 15:24), it would seem that the solution must be found in convenantal considerations of the OT, and the priority given Israel in prophetic promises.[3] In Pauline terms, God's covenantal faithfulness demands the salvific scheme of "to the Jew first and then to the Gentiles" (Rom 1:16).

10:7-8. The message they are to proclaim (**The kingdom of heaven is near**) is the same as that heralded by both John the Baptist and Jesus (3:1; 4:17, 23; 9:35). The message of God's impending reign is most appropriate for those deemed "subjects of the kingdom" (8:12). The authority granted to them (10:1) enables them to exhibit the reality of God's presence by healing sicknesses, raising the dead, cleansing lepers, and driving out demons. Like Jesus' own ministry the exhibition of these miraculous powers symbolically exemplified the Good News of the kingdom. Since they have freely received such authority, they must exercise their "gifts" free of charge. They must never turn the free gifts of God into a business venture (v. 8b).

10:9-10. The exhortation to engage in their ministry free of

[2]Ibid., pp. 83-84.

[3]See G.E. Ladd, *A Theology of the New Testament*, ed. D.A. Hagner (Grand Rapids: Eerdmans, 1993), pp. 104-105; *contra* G.B. Caird, *New Testament Theology*, ed. L.D. Hurst (Oxford: Clarendon Press, 1994), p. 56 who sees the primary focus to remind the church that the Gentile mission has not replaced a mission to Jews.

charge is followed by a series of imperatives highlighting the sacrificial nature of their ministry. The disciples are not only prohibited from profiting financially from their mission, they are forbidden to take with them any money (gold, silver, copper), or any other items that seemingly would be of necessity for the traveler: a bag for carrying extra food and provisions, a change of clothes, an extra pair of sandals, and a walking stick, that can also provide some protection from possible physical threats. Essentially, they are to travel unencumbered by anything that might restrict the haste of their mission. By embarking on their journey without basic provisions the disciples will learn to trust God's providential care, who will provide for them through those who favorably receive them.

10:11-13. Next, Jesus spells out the procedures to follow when they enter a **town or village**. The emphasis is upon how they are to respond to the reception given them and their message. They are to seek lodging only with those deemed **worthy**, meaning those who are positively disposed toward their mission and message. Thus daily needs are met through the hospitable good will of their host. Such a receptive home deserves the **greeting**: "peace be upon this house." Probably the offer of peace is intended to symbolize the blessings of the kingdom. On the other hand, those homes that are not receptive (=unworthy) do not benefit from God's *shalom* found in Jesus.

10:14-15. The section closes on a negative note by focusing on those who neither **welcome [them]** or **listen to [their] words**. The disciples are to respond to such rejection by publicly demonstrating their complete disassociation from those who reject them. The symbolic gesture of "shaking off the dust from the feet" upon departure would not have been missed by Jewish observers. It was typical of Jews to evoke this ritual when re-entering Jewish boundaries, having passed through Gentile territory. The gesture made a statement both with regards to the status of the home or community they were leaving and the intent to have nothing more to do with it. In fact, the city that rejects Jesus' disciples deserve a worse fate than Sodom and Gomorrah. The infamous cities of **Sodom and Gomorrah** (cf. Gen 18) were notorious for their wickedness, and very much deserving of God's consuming wrath. Yet, the fate of a town or home that rejects the Good News of the kingdom is far more serious than that experienced by Sodom and Gomorrah. Jesus could not stress to the disciples in more emphatic terms the decisive significance to be attached to their ministry.

2. Persecution and Response (10:16-23)

[16]I am sending you out like sheep among wolves. Therefore be as shrewd as snakes and as innocent as doves.

[17]"Be on your guard against men; they will hand you over to the local councils and flog you in their synagogues. [18]On my account you will be brought before governors and kings as witnesses to them and to the Gentiles. [19]But when they arrest you, do not worry about what to say or how to say it. At that time you will be given what to say, [20]for it will not be you speaking, but the Spirit of your Father speaking through you.

[21]"Brother will betray brother to death, and a father his child; children will rebel against their parents and have them put to death. [22]All men will hate you because of me, but he who stands firm to the end will be saved. [23]When you are persecuted in one place, flee to another. I tell you the truth, you will not finish going through the cities of Israel before the Son of Man comes.

At the end of the previous section (vv. 14-15) Jesus makes it clear that there will be those who reject the gospel of the kingdom. The rejection of the message resulted in the disciples leaving the area, and showing their disdain by the symbolic gesture of shaking the dust from their feet. Having introduced the negative side of their mission, Jesus now (vv. 16-23) details the extent of the opposition they will face as a result of their ministry, and instructs them how they are to respond. It should be observed that the details of Jesus' words go far beyond the immediate mission of the twelve. Jesus envisions the ongoing mission of the church that eventually resulted in being brought before Gentile "governors and kings" (v. 18). In this way the discourse speaks not only to the twelve, but to the later church.

10:16. Beginning with v. 16 Jesus moves beyond mere rejection to describe an escalation of violent hostility the disciples will ultimately face. The sheep/wolf imagery graphically depicts the disciples as defenseless sheep facing the ferocious attack of hungry wolves. The exact nature of the threat is spelled out in later texts. But Jesus does give instructions concerning how they are to respond to such danger: **be as shrewd as snakes and as innocent as doves**. In the heat of opposition two qualities are absolutely necessary. To be "shrewd" (φρόνιμος, *phronimos*) means to react to difficult situations with a prudent, clear-headedness that carefully thinks through one's actions. Comparison to the snake is drawn from Genesis 3:1 where the serpent is described as "more crafty than any of the wild animals the Lord has made." The disciples must also possess an innocence symbolized by the dove. The term literally means "unmixed" and describes an undivided loyalty and "purity of intention" to do what is right. These life threatening situations are countered by a practical sensibility along with a transparent innocence. Like Jesus, such a response reduces opponents to silence (cf. 22:46).

10:17-18. Jesus' general warning (v. 16) is followed by a series of examples detailing how hostility directed at the disciples will be manifested (vv. 17-18; 21-22). Once again, however, Jesus provides instructions concerning how the disciples should respond to adverse situations. They must exhibit caution to avoid those who would seek them harm. There are those who would seize them by force and turn them over (παραδώσουσιν, *paradōsousin*) to local authorities. The **councils** (συνέδρια, *synedria*) refer to the various forms of Jewish jurisprudence. In **their synagogues** they will be beaten, probably being careful to observe the dictates of Deuteronomy 25:1-3. The disciples will eventually find themselves in custody and interrogated by Gentile authorities. Jesus is emphatic that it is their association with him that is the dominant factor precipitating their persecution (**On my account**). Therefore, their interrogation before Gentile authorities should be viewed as an opportunity to give their witness. In Jesus' estimation, suffering and hardship not only must be endured; it should be embraced as an opportunity to further their mission. [4]

[4]Weaver, *Missionary Discourse*, p. 95.

10:19-20. The negative focus on persecution is supplemented with the promise of God's sustaining presence. They are not to be unduly "anxious" (μεριμνήσητε, *merimnēsēte*; cf. 6:25-34) about their witness in the midst of trying conditions. Jesus promises that both the "what" and the "how" of their verbal defense before their accusers will be provided by the **Spirit of your Father**. In the very moment of their need God will provide the disciples with their witness, both in terms of content and the manner of delivery. Although they may appear helpless and vulnerable before interrogating authorities, Jesus promises that the power of God will turn the threatening situation into an occasion for faithful witness. The reference to the Spirit as the "*Spirit of your Father*" serves to counter the shattered family relationships described in v. 21. The disciples are children of the heavenly Father and will not be left to their own devices in the critical hour of trial.

10:21-22. Jesus now returns to a rather grim scenario where persecution takes on an even more ominous tone. Jesus predicts a time will come when family members turn on one another, and are even responsible for handing over members of their own family to be put to death. Such persecution points to an experience beyond the immediate Galilean mission. Nevertheless, all disciples must be prepared for divisive hostile reactions that the message of the kingdom sometimes elicits. In v. 22 the hyperbolic **All men will hate you** indicates that persecution and rejection will come also from the general populace. There will be no "cities of refuge," nor should they expect that their message will find favor with the majority. Jesus indicates that the persecution they experience is directly related to their identification and allegiance to him. As such, their loyalty cannot be compromised if they hope to be saved in the end. It appears that the lot of the disciples is to face ongoing opposition, and even continual life-threatening situations, to which they must respond with a long-term commitment to steadfast faithfulness.

10:23. Although the disciples are called to uncompromising courage they are not to seek martyrdom by a reckless disregard for their own safety. When faced with persecution **in one place** it is not an act of cowardice to **flee to another**. Even Jesus prudently "withdraws" on occasion when faced with active resistance (cf. 12:15; 15:21). However, as Weaver argues, Jesus' call to flee may relate primarily to the urgency of their mission, rather than their escape from danger.[5] It follows that the reason (γάρ, *gar*) why they should move on to more receptive places is that their task of **going through the cities of Israel before the Son of Man comes** demands that they make progress, and not be delayed by those who reject their message.

The "termination point" of their mission to Israel is the "coming of the Son of Man." It is difficult to know precisely what Jesus meant by linking the disciples' missionary efforts among the "cities of Israel" to the termination of such efforts by the coming of the Son of Man. Did he mean that the coming of the Son of Man after his death and resurrection would empower the church to a worldwide mission, no longer limited to the "lost sheep of Israel"? Perhaps the text simply envisions an ongoing Jewish evangelism until the parousia of the Son of Man, i.e., end of time. Others have argued that Jesus had in mind that a mission to the Jews would continue until the Son of Man comes in judgment upon Israel in some catastrophic event like the destruction of Jerusalem (cf. ch. 24). While it is difficult to know with certainty what Jesus meant, the disciples can be assured that their mission will culminate in the vindication of their efforts.

3. The Disciples' Relationship to Jesus (10:24-42)

24"A student is not above his teacher, nor a servant above his master. 25It is enough for the student to be like his teacher, and the servant like his master. If the head of the house has been called Beelzebub,[a] how much more the members of his household!

26"So do not be afraid of them. There is nothing concealed that will not be disclosed, or hidden that will not be made known. 27What I tell you in the dark, speak in the daylight; what is whispered in your ear, proclaim from the roofs. 28Do not be afraid of those who kill the body but cannot kill the soul. Rather, be afraid of the One who can destroy both soul and body in hell. 29Are not two sparrows sold for a penny[b]? Yet not one of them will fall to

[5]Ibid., pp. 100-101.

**the ground apart from the will of your Father. [30]And even the very
hairs of your head are all numbered. [31]So don't be afraid; you are
worth more than many sparrows.**

**[32]"Whoever acknowledges me before men, I will also acknowl-
edge him before my Father in heaven. [33]But whoever disowns me
before men, I will disown him before my Father in heaven.**

**[34]"Do not suppose that I have come to bring peace to the
earth. I did not come to bring peace, but a sword. [35]For I have
come to turn**

"'a man against his father,
a daughter against her mother,
a daughter-in-law against her mother-in-law –
[36]a man's enemies will be the members of his own household.'[c]

**[37]"Anyone who loves his father or mother more than me is not
worthy of me; anyone who loves his son or daughter more than
me is not worthy of me; [38]and anyone who does not take his cross
and follow me is not worthy of me. [39]Whoever finds his life will
lose it, and whoever loses his life for my sake will find it.**

**[40]"He who receives you receives me, and he who receives me
receives the one who sent me. [41]Anyone who receives a prophet
because he is a prophet will receive a prophet's reward, and anyone
who receives a righteous man because he is a righteous man will
receive a righteous man's reward. [42]And if anyone gives even a cup
of cold water to one of these little ones because he is my disciple, I
tell you the truth, he will certainly not lose his reward."**

[a]*25* Greek *Beezeboul* or *Beelzeboul* [b]*29* Greek *an assarion* [c]*36* Micah 7:6

This section begins with a brief transitional saying linking the experience of the disciples to that of their "teacher" and "master" (vv. 24-25). The intent is to firmly ground their experience of persecution and hardship in their relationship with Jesus. Subsequent texts (vv. 26-42) build on that relationship by encouraging a fearless witness before men (vv. 26-33), and a loyalty that transcends even the closest of relationships (v. 34-39). The discourse closes (vv. 40-42) with the insistence that the reception given the disciples is equivalent to that extended to Jesus and the "one who sent" him. Thus Jesus concludes by establishing a bond that links the disciples, himself, and God in the closest of relationships.

10:24-25. Jesus first establishes the relationship of the disciples to himself by a twofold analogy based on student/teacher and slave/master relationships. The point of the analogy is obvious: By virtue of the disciples' relationship to Jesus they cannot expect to be treated any differently from that which their "teacher" and "Lord" experienced. In fact, the greatest aspiration of the disciple is to be "like" Jesus in both service and suffering. The "likeness" may entail the same negative assessment that was earlier given Jesus' person (cf. 9:34; 12:24): **the head of the house has been called Beelzebub.**[6] Certainly the ministry of the disciples performed in the name of Jesus will not escape such slanderous assessments. Thus, the disciples can expect to be participants in Jesus' rejection and suffering.

10:26-27. In spite of the adversity they will face, Jesus calls them to a "fearless witness" (vv. 26-33). Three times in this section Jesus encourages his disciples "not to fear" (vv. 26, 28, 31) and supports his exhortation by offering three reasons why they should not fear. First, they are not to fear those who oppose or malign their ministry because their opponents live in ignorance and darkness, while they are God's agents[7] to bring to light that which was formerly concealed. That which is to be revealed is none other than that which Jesus has made known to them. Although presently his words are uttered privately and in a somewhat cryptic form they will openly and with clarity proclaim his words in the most public of places (**from the roof**). Since God actively works within the ministry of the disciples to disclose his redemptive plan they should be bold in their proclamation.

10:28. The second reason why the disciples need not fear their opponents is that they have only limited power at their disposal: they can **kill the body but cannot kill the soul**. The intent of Jesus'

---

[6]The etymological background of the term is uncertain. Davies and Allison, *Matthew*, p. 195 conclude that the "best guess is that βεελζεβούλ is an ancient name for the Canaanite god Baal, the Lord of heavens." In the NT the meaning is "prince of demons," and is one of the many names for Satan.

[7]The passive verbs ἀποκαλυφθήσεται (*apokalyphthēsetai*) and γνωσθήσεται (*gnōsthēsetai*) are "divine passives" indicating that God is the ultimate source behind the ministry of the disciples.

words is not to argue for an extreme dualistic understanding of human nature, i.e., that humans can be separated into two unrelated parts, "body" and "soul." Rather, the point is that while those who persecute the disciples can harm the body, they have no power over the total person, composed of both "body and soul."[8] Although men may terminate physical bodily life, only God possesses the power to finally and ultimately destroy the total person (=body and soul) in *Gehenna* (see 5:22). Since it is God alone who has ultimate jurisdiction over one's eternal destiny, it would seem the wiser course to fear God rather than those who can only end one's physical existence.

10:29-31. The third **don't be afraid** comes as a conclusion to Jesus' illustration of God' providential care and concern for the disciples. Of all the birds used for food, **sparrows** (στρουθός, *strouthos*, lit. "little sparrow") were considered the least expensive.[9] Yet, the providential care of God is concerned with the fate of even the least of his creatures. The consolation is based on the fact that nothing, even something as trivial as the loss of a sparrow, goes unnoticed by God. The second illustration of numbering hairs is also intended to emphasize that nothing escapes God's notice, not even the trivial details of how many hairs are on one's head. The passive verb (**are numbered** ἠριθμημέναι, *ērithmēmenai*) emphasizes that God has counted and fully knows that which is beyond what any human can know. The intent of this proverbial saying is not to guarantee that the Lord will protect the disciples from all affliction (cf. 1 Sam 14:45; 2 Sam 14:17; 1 Kgs 1:52; Luke 21:18; Acts 27:34), but simply to assure them that even in their affliction, God is fully aware and is somehow working out his divine will. It follows "from the lesser to the greater," that since they are worth more than the sparrow they need not fear persecution, but simply trust that God in his unfathomable wisdom and knowledge will work the good in all things (Rom 8:28).

---

[8]Within Judaism the reference to "body and soul" constitutes a reference to the whole person, see I.H. Marshall, "Uncomfortable words: VI. 'Fear him who can destroy both soul and body in hell' [Mt 10:28, RSV]," *ExpTim* 81 (1970), 277, 279.

[9]Morris, *Matthew*, p. 263.

10:32-33. Jesus concludes his focus on "fearlessness" by spelling out the consequences of either **acknowledg[ing him] before men** or **disown[ing him] before men.**[10] To acknowledge Jesus "before men" is to openly and wholeheartedly express one's solidarity and allegiance with him. Notice that one's stance towards Jesus determines one's acceptance by the Father. If in the midst of persecution the disciple fearlessly acknowledges his or her allegiance to Jesus, then Jesus will come to his or her defense on the day of judgment. However, if in the heat of public scrutiny one rejects Jesus by denying a commitment to him, the result will be rejection by God. Obviously, Jesus stands in a special place of authority, as the final arbiter of one's eternal destiny.

10:34. Throughout the next section (vv. 34-39) the focus is upon the absolute priority of one's relationship to Jesus (note the personal pronouns "I," "me," and "my"). The tone of the section is set by Jesus' startling announcement that the purpose of his coming was not **to bring peace, but a sword**. The words are intended to counter the faulty notion (μὴ νομίσητε, *mē nomisēte*, cf. 5:17) that Jesus' messianic vocation means that an era of peace and tranquility has now come. Although some Jewish traditions anticipated an age of peace when the Messiah arrives (see Isa 9:5-7; 11:6; 66:25; Zech 9:9-10; 1 Chr 22:9; cf. Luke 2:14), the peace that Jesus offers does not insure the absence of conflict or social disruptions. In fact, Jesus has not come to bring a stability associated with the absence of fighting, but rather his presence provokes a hostility associated with open warfare. The symbol of the "sword," not the "dove," is more appropriate when describing the impact of Jesus' messianic vocation. The metaphor of "sword" is not intended to convey the use of violent force, but symbolizes divided loyalties, even within family units, because of the demands of the kingdom. As the next two verses make clear (vv. 35-36), the closest of human relationships are sometimes divided by the "sword" that Jesus brings.

10:35-36. Jesus' coming has the effect of turning members of the same household against one another. Using the language of Micah

---

[10]It should be observed that beginning in 10:32 the style of the discourse changes from an address directed to "you" (the twelve), to an emphasis on "whoever" and "anyone."

7:6 (see v. 21), Jesus envisions discord and animosity among family members because the message of the kingdom places people in a crisis of decision, either for or against. Basic conventional norms and loyalties are shattered by the priority of the kingdom of God as announced by Jesus. There is no neutrality or mutual toleration, one either responds favorably to the message or violently rejects it. The result is that **a man's enemies will be members of his own household**. Such disruptions are inevitable in households because light and darkness cannot mutually coexist.

10:37. In the midst of such conflict and the loss of familial security it is tempting to compromise one's loyalties. However, Jesus insists that absolute priority must be given one's relationship to him, even over family ties. In other words, when the "sword" of the kingdom results in family divisions the disciple must make his allegiance clear. The failure to be aligned with Jesus, even against family members, means the forfeiture of one's status as a disciple (=**not worthy of me**). Jesus' demand of total allegiance on such a personal level is certainly unprecedented within the rabbinic tradition.

10:38-39. The extravagant devotion called for by Jesus in verse 37 is graphically spelled out in verses 38-39. The vivid metaphorical reference to taking up one's **cross** captures the imagery of a condemned man forced to carry the means of his own execution. Jesus charges the one who would follow him to actively take up the cross and follow him in a voluntary act of self-denial and obedience. Their solidarity with Jesus demands that the disciples walk the same path of sacrificial obedience. As noted by Hagner: "Taking up one's cross refers not to the personal problems or difficulties of life that one must bear, as it is sometimes used in common parlance, but to a radical obedience that entails self-denial and, indeed, a dying to self. To take up one's cross is to follow in the footsteps of Jesus, who is the model of such radical obedience and self-denial (cf. 4:1-11)."[11] With these words Jesus has provided the most explicit reference to the violent fate that awaits him (cf. 16:21-24). The paradoxical saying of verse 39 reinforces the message of verse 38 and puts it into proper perspective.[12] If the disciples are to emulate Jesus' sacrificial

---

[11]Hagner, *Matthew*, p. 293.

[12]Weaver, *Missionary Discourse*, p. 116.

ministry they must embrace a perspective wherein "life" for Jesus' sake is perceived as of greater value than even one's physical life. While alignment with Jesus may result in the sacrifice of one's present life, in the end the faithful disciple reaps the reward of eternal life. It is thus in the interest of life in the fullest that the disciple fearlessly faces the prospects of death.

10:40. The concluding verses (vv. 40-42) open with a succinct pronouncement aptly underscoring the major theme of the discourse: **He who receives you receives me**. It follows that a positive reception of the disciples amounts to a positive reception of Jesus. However, Jesus extends the concept of solidarity to include himself and **the one who sent** him (i.e., God). Although Jesus now sends out his disciples into ministry, it was God who acted first by sending Jesus.[13] Since God is the original "sender," the mission of the disciples is ultimately grounded in God's authority. Therefore to reject their ministry is to scorn the favor of God.

10:41-42. The discourse closes by spelling out the positive results of a favorable reception of the disciples. The designations of **prophet** and **righteous man** are intended to be illustrative of the positive response that should be given the disciples, called "little ones" in v. 42. Since the "prophet" and "righteous man" represent God, those who warmly receive them are blessed accordingly. Although the disciples, called **little ones** (cf. 18:1-9), can claim no status or worldly clout, a simple act of kindness extended to them, such as the offer of **a cup of cold water**, will be richly rewarded by God. Thus these final words function as a powerful word of encouragement to impress upon the disciples the enormous significance of the task to which Jesus has called them.

[13]Ibid., p. 118.

MATTHEW 11

III. ISRAEL'S MISUNDERSTANDING AND REPUDIATION OF JESUS (11:1–14:12)

Following the discourse (10:5-42) Matthew marks the transition to the narrative by noting that Jesus "went on from there to teach and preach in the towns of Galilee" (11:1). Although Jesus continues also to heal and cast out demons (12:13, 15, 22), the tone of the language and series of events that comprise this section (i.e., 11:1–14:12) clearly indicate that such activity is now subsumed under the dominant motif of Israel's rejection of Jesus. While earlier portions of the story anticipate that Jesus' ministry in Israel would ultimately clash with established religious thinking (cf. 9:3-4, 14, 32-34; also 10:24-25), beginning in 11:2 through 14:12 the story turns on the negative reviews that Jesus' therapeutic activity received from various groups of Jews and certain individuals.

It is significant that the scenes comprising 11:2–14:12 are bracketed by episodes involving John (cf. 11:2ff.; 14:1ff.), and questions concerning how Jesus' miraculous powers are to be interpreted (11:3; 14:2). While John in Herod's prison finds Jesus' activities incongruent with his own messianic expectations, Herod speculates that Jesus' exhibition of miraculous powers may be evidence that John has risen from the dead. John's question in 11:2 heads a series of episodes showing Israel's largely negative response to Jesus and his ministry (11:16-19; 20-24; 12:1-14, 24; 13:13, 54-58). After the execution of John (14:3-12) the narrative scenes are marked by Jesus' strategic withdrawals (14:13; 15:21; 16:4) alongside a more exclusive concentration on the development of the disciples (14:13-16:20).

The fundamental reason for Israel's culpable rejection of Jesus is their failure to discern in Jesus' activity the "deeds of the

Messiah" (11:2, τὰ ἔργα τοῦ Χριστοῦ, *ta erga tou Christou*). Jesus' miracles are like the parables of the kingdom: they must be rightly interpreted and can only be understood by those who have "eyes to see and ears to hear." Furthermore, since it is the Father who truly knows the Son (11:27), understanding the person and mission of Jesus is ultimately dependent upon God's sovereign will to disclose the meaning of Jesus' activity (11:27; 13:11; 16:17). Accordingly, throughout 11:1–14:12 various groups misunderstand or interpret negatively Jesus' therapeutic action: John misunderstands (11:3); various Galilean cities see his miraculous powers but do not repent (11:20-24); Pharisees see his actions as a violation of Sabbath restrictions (12:1-14); other Pharisees attribute his powers to Beelzebub (12:24); his hometown looked upon his activities with suspicion (13:53-58); and Herod attributes Jesus' miraculous powers to the risen John (14:1-2). In spite of isolated positive glimpses of the disciples (11:25-27; 12:46-50; 13:10-17), for the most part 11:1–14:12 is dominated by a persistent negative tone that grimly anticipates the course of subsequent events (see 12:14).

A. JOHN'S QUESTION FROM PRISON (11:1-6)

[1]After Jesus had finished instructing his twelve disciples, he went on from there to teach and preach in the towns of Galilee.[a]

[2]When John heard in prison what Christ was doing, he sent his disciples [3]to ask him, "Are you the one who was to come, or should we expect someone else?"

[4]Jesus replied, "Go back and report to John what you hear and see: [5]The blind receive sight, the lame walk, those who have leprosy[b] are cured, the deaf hear, the dead are raised, and the good news is preached to the poor. [6]Blessed is the man who does not fall away on account of me."

[a]*1* Greek *in their towns* [b]*5* The Greek word was used for various diseases affecting the skin—not necessarily leprosy.

11:1. In typical fashion, Matthew closes the discourse (10:5-42) with the same basic saying used to mark the end of each of the five major discourses of Jesus (see on 7:28). However, the transition from discourse to narrative in 11:1 is somewhat surprising since after Jesus' instructions to his disciples (10:5-42) the focus shifts abruptly to Jesus' activity of "teaching" and "preaching," with nothing being said about the disciples' missionary efforts (cf. Mark 6:12-13, 30; Luke 9:6, 10; 10:17-20). As observed by Magness: ". . . whether or not the author intends for his reader to think that the journey took place immediately, took place later in Jesus' ministry, or could only occur after the resurrection and commission (Matthew 28:18-20), the expectation and visualization of a missionary tour has been created in the mind of the reader apart from any narration of it."[1] Be that as it may, the ominous threat of rejection and hostility foretold in chapter 10 becomes a reality in Jesus' ministry of teaching and preaching in the towns of Galilee.

11:2-3. The narrative section opens with a reference to John's imprisonment (cf. 4:12) and his genuine perplexity concerning the reports circulating about **what Christ was doing** (11:2, lit., "the deeds of the Messiah"). The phrase is comprehensive and is intended to summarize all of Jesus' activity in word and deed (4:23–9:35). While Matthew is quite definite about the messianic nature of Jesus' deeds (calling him the "Christ" = Messiah), John's inquiry indicates that Jesus' activity did not immediately settle in his mind the identity question: **Are you the one who was to come** [i.e., the Messiah, cf. 3:11-12]**, or should we expect someone else?** John's earlier predictions anticipated a messianic figure who would instigate God's vengeful wrath and eschatological judgment (3:10-12), and Jesus' deeds simply did not match his expectations. John, therefore, poses the question whether they should expect another (ἕτερον, *heteron*),[2] perhaps one possessing the qualities he had anticipated. John's ambivalence as suggested by his inquiry does set before the reader the central concern dominating both the previous narrative section (4:23–9:35), and subsequent episodes comprising 11:7–16:20: what is the proper conclusion to be drawn upon "seeing and hearing" the ministry of Jesus?[3]

---

[1]J.L Magness, *Sense and Absence: Structure and Suspension in the Ending of Mark's Gospel* (SBLSemSt; Atlanta: Scholars Press, 1986), p. 67.

[2]The use of ἕτερον may imply a Messiah of a different kind.

[3]As Held, "Miracles Stories," p. 251, observes, John's question serves a double function: "on the one hand it clearly expresses the decisive question

11:4-6. Jesus' response (11:4-5) calls for John to reevaluate his activity in terms of expectations associated with the messianic times (cf. Isa 35:4-6; 26:29; 29:18-19; 61:1-2). The particular deeds highlighted deliberately coincide with the events narrated in chapters 8 and 9. Although John had heard about the "deeds of Christ" (v. 2), Jesus' intent is to supply him with an interpretative suggestion by phrasing his response in terms reminiscent of Isaiah's vision of the messianic era. If John will consider these things carefully he will have the answer to his inquiry. Indeed, if John is to avoid being "put off" (σκανδαλίζω, *skandalizō*) by the character of Jesus' messiahship, he must move beyond his own narrow expectations to the realization that in Jesus God is manifesting a merciful response to the plight of his people. As Matthew's story consistently demonstrates, a one-sided messianic expectation always leads to a faulty appraisal of Jesus' mission and identity (cf. 16:21-23; 21:1-11).

B. THE PERSON AND MISSION OF JOHN (11:7-19)

1. Identification of John by Jesus (11:7-15)

[7]As John's disciples were leaving, Jesus began to speak to the crowd about John: "What did you go out into the desert to see? A reed swayed by the wind? [8]If not, what did you go out to see? A man dressed in fine clothes? No, those who wear fine clothes are in kings' palaces. [9]Then what did you go out to see? A prophet? Yes, I tell you, and more than a prophet. [10]This is the one about whom it is written:

"'I will send my messenger ahead of you,
who will prepare your way before you.'[a]

[11]I tell you the truth: Among those born of women there has not risen anyone greater than John the Baptist; yet he who is least in the kingdom of heaven is greater than he. [12]From the days of John

---

which comes out of what has gone before and so forms a conclusion which once again illuminates the Christological theme of the preceding chapters. On the other hand, the chapters which follow must be understood even more in the light of this question and the negative or positive answers to it."

the Baptist until now, the kingdom of heaven has been forcefully advancing, and forceful men lay hold of it. [13]For all the Prophets and the Law prophesied until John. [14]And if you are willing to accept it, he is the Elijah who was to come. [15]He who has ears, let him hear.

[a]*10* **Mal. 3:1**

Lest anyone think that Jesus' response to John is intended to detract from the significance of his ministry, Jesus next addresses the crowd concerning John's significance, his role in God's redemptive scheme, and his relationship to his own ministry. The section can be divided structurally according to a threefold thematic emphasis: (1) Through a series of questions, which Jesus answers, John is identified as "more than a prophet," being the messenger foretold by Malachi (vv. 7-10). (2) He functions as a transitional figure, signaling a major turning point from the old era of expectation and promise to the age of fulfillment and the realization of God's salvific purposes (vv. 11-15). (3) John's rejection parallels the way "this generation" has reacted to the ministry of Jesus (vv. 16-19). But as wisdom is proved right by her actions (*erga*, "works") (v. 19), so Jesus' works will ultimately be vindicated.

11:7-10. Jesus' series of question are intended to remind the **crowds** concerning their motivations for venturing into the desert to see and hear John (vv. 7-9). John's charismatic character was certainly not like **a reed swayed by the wind**. Both his courageous denunciation of Israel's leadership (3:7-10), and his focused call for repentance (3:2, 8) negate the conclusion that John was easily swayed by popular notions or public pressure. The rigors of his austere lifestyle and dress certainly do not correspond to the decorum and elegancy one might find in **kings' palaces** (cf. 3:4). John's attraction was never based on the supposition that he had the refinement and demeanor of a king, but rather because his ascetic lifestyle and powerful message conjured up images of Israel's prophetic tradition. However, in Jesus' estimation, John should be regarded as even **more than a prophet**. Even though he stands in the tradition of prophetic figures, his distinctive role ranks him as "something more" (περισσότερον, *perissoteran*) than a prophet. In fact, John's greatness arises because he is not only a prophet, but is himself the object of prophecy. Citing Malachi 3:1 (cf. also Exod 23:20), Jesus makes it clear that John had a pivotal role as a precursor ushering in the long expected "day of the Lord." By conforming the first line of the citation from Malachi to Exod 23:20 ("I am sending an angel ahead of you"), and altering a few pronouns (μου [*mou*], "me," to σου [*sou*], "you"), Malachi's prediction (3:1) of a **messenger** preparing the way for Yahweh is easily associated with John's preparing the way for God's Messiah. Of course, a high estimation of John's ministry necessarily leads to an even greater appreciation of Jesus' ministry.

11:11. The greatness of John is continued in verses 11-15, with the focus now on his relationship to the kingdom and the dawning of the new age in Jesus. First, from a human perspective, there has been no one **born of women** [=humans] **. . . greater than John**. The emphasis is upon his pivotal role in the transition from the *old* to the *new*, not his intrinsic personal worth. Yet, as valuable and important as John's ministry was, it does not compare to the participation of the **least in the kingdom**. While John's ministry established a critical link between the OT promises and their fulfillment, its function was nevertheless preliminary to the new order of the kingdom introduced by Jesus. As great as John was he must always be classed with those who preceded the kingdom and its blessings (cf. 8:11). As such, the privileges and blessings experienced by even the least in the kingdom far surpasses the limited experiences of John. Accordingly, the contrast between the least in the kingdom and John is not one of personal worth or achievements, but a contrast between the limitations of the old order represented in John, and the blessings and privileges experienced by those who fully participate in God's reign.

11:12. The interpretive difficulties associated with verse 12 are well known.[4] Essentially, the difficulty hinges on how one could interpret the two verbs βιάζεται (*biazetai*) and βιασταὶ (*biastai*). The first verb can be taken either as a passive ("kingdom suffers violence"), or as a middle ("kingdom comes forcefully"), largely depending on whether one views the statement as a positive (e.g.,

---

[4]For an overview of interpretive proposals see P.S. Cameron, *Violence and the Kingdom: The Interpretation of Matthew 11:12* (ANTJ 5; Frankfurt: Peter Lang, 1984).

the kingdom "forcefully advances") or as a negative (e.g., "forceful men") description of how the kingdom has been responded to. The NIV rendering translates the first verb as a positive middle (**has been forcefully advancing**), while rendering the second verb negatively as **forceful men lay hold of it**. Since the most natural meaning of βιαστής (*biastēs*) is negative (see *BAGD*, p. 141) meaning "violent person," it would seem that the first verb is also best understood negatively ("suffers violence") rather than positively ("forcefully advancing").[5] I therefore take the first verb to be passive and both verbs to be a negative description of the kingdom's experience, hence, "since the ministry of John the kingdom has been under attack, and violent men have laid hold on it." While it is difficult to be specific as to when and by whom such violence occurred, Jesus intends to highlight the fact that since the first heralder of the kingdom (i.e., John) to the present moment, the advance of God's reign has met with increasing opposition.

11:13-15. In verse 13 Jesus links John and his ministry to the prophetic intent of the entirety of OT Scriptures (=**the Prophets and the Law**). The usual word order of "the law and the prophets" (cf. 5:17; 7:12; 23:40) is reversed probably to stress the prophetic nature of the entire OT.[6] As a key transitional figure, John's ministry signaled that the era of promise and expectation has reached its culmination in Jesus and the presence of God's kingdom. As such, John is the last and greatest of the OT prophets, since in him the "law and prophets" find their climactic and definitive expression. He is indeed **the Elijah who was to come** (cf. 17:12; Mal 3:1-3; 4:5). Allison has demonstrated that at least in some Jewish circles, eschatological beliefs definitely associated the coming of Elijah as an event preceding the coming of the Messiah.[7] For some the mysterious disappearance of Elijah (2 Kgs 2:1-15) from this world was sufficient to generate speculations about his return and active role in the day of Yahweh (cf. 27:47-49). Jesus' words about John are not intended to imply some notion of reincarnation, where John is literally the returned Elijah (cf. John 1:21). Rather, John came in the "spirit and power of Elijah" (3:4; cf. 1 Kgs 1:8; Luke 1:17), and also

[5]*Contra* Carson, *Matthew*, pp. 265-268.

[6]Davies and Allison, *Matthew*, 1:257.

[7]D.C. Allison, "Elijah Must Come First," *JBL* 103 (June 1984), 256-258.

endured suffering at the hands of a ruthless king (cf. 1 Kgs 17-19). In view of John's imprisonment it might be difficult for some to see John as the expected Elijah, so Jesus exhorts his hearers, **He who has ears let him hear** (cf. 13:9, 43).[8] While the saying concerning John may present problems in the mind of some, those who truly "hear" (=understand) will see the validity of Jesus' assessment of John.

2. Rejection of John and Jesus (11:16-19)

16"To what can I compare this generation? They are like children sitting in the marketplaces and calling out to others:

17"'We played the flute for you, and you did not dance;
we sang a dirge, and you did not mourn.'

18For John came neither eating nor drinking, and they say, 'He has a demon.' 19The Son of Man came eating and drinking, and they say, 'Here is a glutton and a drunkard, a friend of tax collectors and "sinners."' But wisdom is proved right by her actions."

11:16. Having set forth the identity and significance of John, Jesus' concluding words castigate **this generation** for their obdurate resistance to the implications associated with John's ministry. Furthermore, the same superficial judgment and obstinate behavior that resulted in John's rejection, necessarily resulted in a faulty appraisal of Jesus' character and mission. Although both Jesus and John, in their respective ministries, made their appeal to Israel, they are both rejected because neither squared with conventional expectations or preconceived notions of acceptable behavior.

11:17. The contemporaries of Jesus and John (="this generation") are compared to children who are playing games in the marketplace. One group of children complain that no matter what game they attempted to play, either a pretend wedding or some other joyous occasion (**played the flute**), or a make believe funeral (**sang a dirge**), the other group refused to participate, neither

[8]As noted by Hill, *Matthew*, p. 201, "to regard John, who was now lying in Herod's prison, as having come in the spirit and power of Elijah was difficult for those who clung to preconceived and apocalyptic notions."

dancing or **mourning**. The simile is intended to illustrate the obstinate behavior of Israel no matter what the appeal or evidence offered by either John or Jesus.[9]

11:18-19. With respect to John's ministry, his extreme asceticism and the demands of his message resulted in the assessment that he was possessed. Thus John and his message are treated with disdain and cavalierly dismissed as the rantings of a mad man. On the other hand, Jesus is vilified because his social involvement lacked conventional sensitivities regarding table fellowship (see 9:10-13). His free indulgence in food and drink brought the charge of being a **glutton and a drunkard**; and furthermore, his table companions consisted of those that should have been avoided (i.e., **tax collectors and "sinners"**). Their criticism and repudiation is brought into sharper focus by the use of the designation **Son of Man**. Just who do they think they are insulting and treating with such contempt? Fundamentally, "this generation's" rejection of both John and Jesus is ultimately related to their stubborn refusal to be persuaded no matter what the evidence. But in spite of their evaluation, Jesus affirms that like wisdom's "mighty deeds" are proven right, so his "mighty deeds" will ultimately be vindicated.[10]

C. UNREPENTANT CITIES (11:20-24)

[20]Then Jesus began to denounce the cities in which most of his miracles had been performed, because they did not repent. [21]"Woe to you, Korazin! Woe to you, Bethsaida! If the miracles that were performed in you had been performed in Tyre and Sidon, they would have repented long ago in sackcloth and ashes. [22]But I tell

[9]*Contra* Davies and Allison, *Matthew,* 1:262 who interpret the illustration as indicating that Jesus' and John's contemporaries are "like disagreeable children who complain that others will not act according to their desires and expectations."

[10]Based on this and subsequent text (11:20-30) many have argued for a wisdom christology as fundamental to Matthew's understanding of Jesus. For a defense of Wisdom Christology see Ben Witherington, *The Christology of Jesus* (Minneapolis: Fortress, 1990), pp. 51-55; see also the discussion by F.W. Burnett, "Wisdom," *DJG*, pp. 873-877.

you, it will be more bearable for Tyre and Sidon on the day of judgment than for you. [23]And you, Capernaum, will you be lifted up to the skies? No, you will go down to the depths.[a] If the miracles that were performed in you had been performed in Sodom, it would have remained to this day. [24]But I tell you that it will be more bearable for Sodom on the day of judgment than for you."

[a]***23* Greek *Hades***

11:20. The portrayal of Jewish obstinacy (11:16-19) leads naturally into the invectives directed against **cities in which most of his miracles** [δυνάμεις, *dynameis*] **had been performed**. The term *dynameis* (="deeds of power") is linked to the previous section (11:2-19) by keeping the focus on how Jesus' miraculous powers were responded to. In the case of several Galilean cities the miracles did not produce the desired results, i.e., repentance.

After the introductory sentence Comber observes that the overall structure of this section "consists of a double series of (1) pronouncement of judgment; (2) explanation for judgment; and (3) comparison of eschatological fates."[11] Thus this brief section marks a new stage in the relationship between Jesus and Israel, as Jewish cities reject their Messiah and thus incur God's eschatological condemnation. Their failure to repent leaves them susceptible to a negative evaluation of Jesus' supernatural powers (cf. 9:34; 12:24). This tragic turn of events will soon degenerate into heated disputes and deadly plots perpetuated by Israel's leadership (ch. 12).

When one recalls that Jesus' message about the kingdom necessarily entailed the exhortation to repent (4:17; cf. 3:2), it is clear that the refusal to repent in the face of Jesus' "mighty deeds" is the result of a failure to interpret Jesus' deeds in terms of their disclosure of God's presence. While his miraculous deeds were a source of interest and wonder, they cannot be separated from the demands of his message.

11:21-22. Three coastal cities along the Sea of Galilee (Korazin, Bethsaida, and Capernaum)[12] are singled out for their stubborn

---

[11]See J.S. Comber, "The Composition and Literary Characteristics of Matt 11:20-24," *CBQ* 39 (1977), 498.

[12]For background information see R. Riesner, "Archeology and Geography," *DJG*, p. 39.

refusal to be moved to repentance by Jesus' mighty works. Jesus' expression of **woe** upon **Korazin** and **Bethsaida** is both an expression of sorrow and warning. Their culpability is forcefully brought into focus by comparing them to the infamous cities of **Tyre and Sidon** (see Isa 23 and Ezek 28). These cities, which all Jews would have judged to be evil, are made to look good by comparison to contemporary cities of Jesus' day.[13] As noted by Davies and Allison, Korazin and Bethsaida were Jewish cities while Tyre and Sidon were not. "Thus Jesus, with the hyperbole of a prophet, is exclaiming that Jews failed to respond to phenomena which would have persuaded even pagans – and what is more, notorious pagans."[14] Jesus concludes with a dramatic reversal of expectations whereby Israelites suffer a worse fate than the pagans inhabiting Tyre and Sidon. It appears that God's judgment expects more from those with greater opportunities, and they will be judged more severely than those who had less.[15]

11:23-24. Next Jesus singles out **Capernaum**, a city especially blessed by Jesus' presence, being earlier described as his "own town" (9:1; cf. 4:13; 8:14). As such, Jesus uses even stronger language in his denunciation of Capernaum. The question **will you be lifted up to the skies** is a typical prophetic taunt addressed to proud individuals or cities (cf. Isa 14:13; Ezek 26:20), it thus expects a negative response. Indeed, rather than being exalted, Capernaum is poised for a fall, all the way to Hades (ᾄδου, *hadou*; gen. of *hadēs*), the realm of the dead. Like the two previous cities, Capernaum is also compared to an infamous OT city, **Sodom** (see 10:15). In spite of the legendary wickedness of Sodom, if the mighty deeds performed by Jesus would have been performed in Sodom, they would have repented, and the city would never have been destroyed. Judgment will therefore be more severe for Capernaum than for Sodom. Although Jesus is the humiliated and rejected Son of Man (11:19), his activity in Galilee obviously has serious eschatological consequences.

---

[13]See discussion of Tannehill, *Sword of His Mouth*, pp. 122-128.

[14]Davies and Allison, *Matthew*, 2:267.

[15]Morris, *Matthew*, p. 290.

D. JESUS' RESPONSE AND INVITATION (11:25-30)

[25]At that time Jesus said, "I praise you, Father, Lord of heaven and earth, because you have hidden these things from the wise and learned, and revealed them to little children. [26]Yes, Father, for this was your good pleasure.

[27]"All things have been committed to me by my Father. No one knows the Son except the Father, and no one knows the Father except the Son and those to whom the Son chooses to reveal him.

[28]"Come to me, all you who are weary and burdened, and I will give you rest. [29]Take my yoke upon you and learn from me, for I am gentle and humble in heart, and you will find rest for your souls. [30]For my yoke is easy and my burden is light."

The abrupt and remarkable change of tone from invective to praise beginning in 11:25 is intended to represent Jesus' ensuing words as a response (note ἀποκριθεὶς, *apokritheis*) to Israel's hardened opposition. As such, 11:25-30 brings to a climactic closure Jesus' exposure of Israel's guilt and the stubbornness of unbelief. First, Jesus explains his rejection as due to God's sovereign will, which withholds insight to the "wise and learned," but discloses his will to "little children" (vv. 25-26). Next, Jesus boldly affirms that only God truly knows the identity and character of the Son (cf. 16:17), and only the Son truly knows and reveals the Father (v. 27). This extraordinary claim is followed by an invitation for the "weary and burdened" to accept his yoke and rest by coming to learn of him (vv. 28-30). The following controversies provide a concrete illustration of Jesus' "easy yoke" in contrast to the burdens placed on the people by the Jewish leaders (12:1-14). It is interesting that the controversies are bracketed by explicit characterizations of Jesus' person and ministry (cf. 11:28-30 and 12:15-21).

11:25-26. Jesus praises his Father because he has **hidden these things from the wise and learned, and revealed them to little children.** The most natural antecedent of "these things" is the reality which Israel failed to see in Jesus' mighty deeds, as noted in 11:2-24. The opposition and rejection of Jesus is no accident, because those who deem themselves to be "wise" and claim prior knowledge of God's will (cf. 11:23; 1 Cor 1:19ff.) will always be offended by Jesus' activity and teaching. The very nature of God's revelation in Jesus is offensive to those filled with worldly pride, and whose intellectual sophistication has convinced them that they have nothing to learn from a humble Galilean peasant. On the other hand, the Father's revelatory disclosure of the significance of Jesus' deeds finds a receptive spirit among those who have no illusions of grandeur or sense of their own self-sufficiency (νήπιος, *nēpios*). Contextually, it would seem that Jesus' words are intended to contrast the arrogance and haughty spirit of Israel's leadership with those who humbly acknowledge their dependency upon God, and thus are willing to be taught. While, as noted by Hagner, God's mysterious sovereignty lies behind both belief and unbelief, it never precludes the accountability of those who fail to believe.[16]

11:27. Jesus then grounds his claim to be the recipient and ultimate mediator of God's will in his unique filial relationship with God. He is qualified to be the discloser of God because **all things** (πάντα [*panta*]; cf. ταῦτα [*tauta*, "these things"], v. 25) **have been committed** (παρεδόθη [*paredothē*], a term typically used in the handing down of rabbinic tradition) to him by his Father. Not only does Jesus have exclusive knowledge of God, but the Son's true identity is known only by the Father. The implication is that truly perceiving the significance of Jesus comes only by God's gracious gift (cf. 12:11; 16:17). This claim of a reciprocal knowledge shared by Jesus and his Father is certainly reflective of a profound christology. The saying implies a filial consciousness and a degree of intimacy with God unlike anything found in Judaism prior to Jesus' day.[17] While some would want to dismiss the text as the mere creation of the early church, there is no persuasive evidence that this saying lacks authenticity. The language of the text has been traced to either a Mosaic typology based on Exodus 33:12-14,[18] or to traditions concerning wisdom's relationship to God (cf. Job 28:1-27; Sir 1:6, 8; Bar 3:15-32; Prov 8:12; Wis 7:25; 8:3-8; 9:4, 9, 11).[19] Whatever

---

[16]Hagner, *Matthew*, 1:318; see also Blomberg, *Matthew*, p. 193.

[17]For a helpful discussion see Witherington, *Christology of Jesus*, pp. 221-228. The amazing similarities with the language of John has led to the characterization of this text as a "Johannine thunderbolt," seemingly coming out of nowhere.

[18]Argued by Davies and Allison, *Matthew*, 2:282-287.

[19]Accepted by Hagner, *Matthew*,1:320.

the background, Jesus' words testify to an exclusive awareness of God that can only be explained on the basis of his unique transcendent relationship to God.

11:28. Based on the extraordinary claim of verse 27 Jesus calls the **weary and burdened** to himself as one who gives "rest." Earlier Jesus identified his mission as a shepherd-like ministry designed to give guidance and direction to those termed "oppressed" and "helpless" (9:36). The reference led naturally into the discourse to the twelve (10:5-42), who are called as "workers" sent into the "harvest field" (9:37–10:4). Now the metaphors change in anticipation of subsequent scenes wherein Jesus' "yoke" and "light burden" are contrasted with the heavy burdens placed upon the people by Pharisaic legalism (12:1-14).

11:29. Jesus appeals to the "weary and burdened" to accept his **yoke** by becoming a "learner" (μάθετε [*mathete*]; cf. μαθητής [*mathētēs*] = disciple). Since Jesus has an exclusive claim on resources from the Father, the invitation is to come to *him.* The invitation is extended to all those weighed down to the point of exhaustion, whether by the awareness of personal sin, or more likely in this context, by the sheer weight of law keeping as advocated by Pharisaic casuistry: "They tie up heavy loads and put them on men's shoulders, but they themselves are not willing to lift a finger to move them" (23:4).

11:30. In contrast, the **yoke** Jesus offers is **easy** and his **burden is light**. Jesus' words should not be construed to imply that discipleship is easy or that the rigors of his demand are not challenging (cf. chs. 5-7). Jesus grounds the nature of his "yoke" and "burden" in the unique quality of his own character: **I am gentle and humble in heart** (v. 29). This explicit self-characterization serves to indicate that his "yoke" and "burden" are not to be found in the precision of law keeping, but in a relationship with one who is filled with compassion and devoted to humble service on behalf of his people. It is not at all tiresome to follow such a one in devoted service.[20]

[20]As G. Barth, "Matthew's Understanding of the Law," *TIM*, p. 148 observes, Jesus' yoke "does not throw a man upon his own efforts but brings him into fellowship with the πραΰς" [*praüs* = "gentle, humble, considerate, meek," *BAGD*, p. 600].

While the scribes "learn Torah," Jesus' followers are called to enroll "in his school of wisdom where he is both the teacher and core curriculum."[21] By doing so they will experience rest for their souls, meaning an inner well-being and tranquility grounded in the assurance of God's faithfulness and sustaining power; not the fickleness of human performance in keeping the rules. Jesus is therefore the definitive interpreter of God's will who cuts "through the thicket of elaborate human rules and regulations," and charts a course directly to the heart of the Father. This will become apparent in the scenes to follow.

---

[21]Garland, *Reading Matthew*, p. 133.

MATTHEW 12

E. SABBATH CONTROVERSY: INCIDENT IN THE GRAINFIELD (12:1-8)

As noted earlier, the following two conflict scenes provide concrete illustrations of Jesus' "easy yoke" in contrast to the heavy burdens placed on the people by the religious authorities. The phrase "at that time," connects with 11:25, and "is not intended to supply chronological information but to serve as a thematic bridge."[1] The one who supplies the "weary and burdened" with "rest," now challenges the way the Pharisaic legal concerns have reduced the "day of rest" (=Sabbath) to a burden, thus nullifying its original intention.

Essentially, public conflict between Jesus and his critics centered largely on fundamental differences concerning how one determines and observes God's will as expressed in Scripture. Sabbath observance was considered a fundamental expression of covenantal faithfulness. The sacredness of the seventh day was linked both to creation motifs (Gen 2:1-2; Exod 20:11), and Israel's liberation from Egypt (Deut 5:15). Its observance was basic to Israel's ethnic identity, and was considered a clear "boundary marker" distinguishing the Jew from the Gentile.[2] Because its strict observance was integrally bound up with Jewish self-understanding and identity, legal experts sought to stipulate in precise terms what constituted violations of Sabbath observance. Since Scripture was emphatic that no "work" was to be done on the Sabbath (Exod 20:10; 31:14; Deut 5:14) legal discussion centered on the question, "what actions constitute work

---

[1]Davies and Allison, *Matthew*, 2:305.

[2]See James D.G. Dunn, *The Partings of the Ways* (Philadelphia: Trinity Press, 1991), p. 30.

and hence a violation of Sabbath regulations?" The OT Scriptures offered only minimal restrictions: no fire in your dwellings on the Sabbath (Exod 35:3); no plowing or harvesting (Exod 34:21); do not carry a load on the Sabbath (Jer 17:21-22); and excessive travel was prohibited (Isa 58:13; cf. Acts 1:12). However, scribal concerns for exact compliance to God's Law, felt compelled to greatly expand explicit legislation by further defining and categorizing precisely what kind of activities constituted "work." Eventually, their discussions were collected in the Mishna, resulting in thirty-nine distinct categories, with sub-groupings, of activities prohibited on the Sabbath (see the three tractates, *Shabbath* [Sabbath], *Erubin* [Sabbath limits], and *Betzah* [festival days]. It is precisely this tradition (=*halakah*) that Jesus opposes as burdensome and a distortion of God's true intent with respect to the Sabbath.

[1]At that time Jesus went through the grainfields on the Sabbath. His disciples were hungry and began to pick some heads of grain and eat them. [2]When the Pharisees saw this, they said to him, "Look! Your disciples are doing what is unlawful on the Sabbath."

[3]He answered, "Haven't you read what David did when he and his companions were hungry? [4]He entered the house of God, and he and his companions ate the consecrated bread – which was not lawful for them to do, but only for the priests. [5]Or haven't you read in the Law that on the Sabbath the priests in the temple desecrate the day and yet are innocent? [6]I tell you that one[a] greater than the temple is here. [7]If you had known what these words mean, 'I desire mercy, not sacrifice,'[b] you would not have condemned the innocent. [8]For the Son of Man is Lord of the Sabbath."

[a]*6* Or *something*; also in verses 41 and 42 [b]7 Hosea 6:6

12:1-2. The setting for the first Sabbath controversy is described in verses 1-2. While going **through the grainfields on the Sabbath** (σάββασιν, *sabbasin*, names of Jewish festivals are typically rendered by the plural), Jesus' **disciples were hungry** (only in Matthew; cf. Mark 2:23; Luke 6:1) **and began to pick some heads of grain and eat them**. The Pharisees interpret their actions as a violation of the prohibition of work on the Sabbath. Evidently, their charge was based on Exodus 34:21. Thus, they interpreted the disciples' "picking some heads of grain" as a form of harvesting (cf. m. Sabb. 7:2). Such a charge could not be passed off lightly.

12:3-4. Jesus responds first by chiding his opponents for their failure to perceive the implications of David's actions recorded in 1 Samuel 21. The rhetorical question, **Haven't you read . . .** , certainly has a element of sarcasm, as Jesus addresses those who prided themselves in their understanding and compliance to the literal words of Scripture. With respect to David, the actions of he and his men must technically be viewed as a violation of the strict provisions of the Law. The Law is clear (see Lev 24:9) that only Aaron and his sons were allowed to eat the bread "set out before the Lord." Jesus is asking why there is no condemnation of David and his men for their violation of the letter of the Law? The same grounds that legitimize David's actions also justify the conduct of Jesus' disciples. Given the special circumstances of David's predicament (his flight from Saul), along with the dignity of the special role he was to occupy on behalf of the nation (anointed king) his technical breach of the Law must be seen in the light of broader circumstances. For the sake of the greater good (i.e., the preservation of David) the letter of the Law cannot always be rigidly enforced. Not only must discernment of God's will take into consideration higher priorities, the Law of God cannot be interpreted in isolation, but must be understood in light of God's total will. With respect to David's actions, Jesus reasons in typical rabbinic fashion, i.e., from the "light to the weighty" (*qal wahomer*).[3] If one can justify David's actions in the light of his special circumstances and the dignity of his person, how much more are the actions of Jesus' disciples justified in light of the eschatological circumstances surrounding Jesus' kingly presence? If David and his men were justified in transgressing the letter of the Law, how much more are Jesus and his disciples justified in ignoring mere scribal tradition?

12:5-6. Next, Jesus appeals directly to the priestly prerogative of offering sacrifices on the Sabbath. Such practice could technically be viewed as a violation of the prohibition of work on the Sabbath.

---

[3]Longenecker, *Biblical Exegesis*, pp. 68-69.

Yet the fulfillment of priestly duties demands that the offering of sacrifices by given precedence over Sabbath regulations (Num 28:9-10).[4] Hence, since the priests are performing their God-assigned tasks they are regarded as **innocent**, though the rigor of their priestly duties could easily be categorized as work. The priests are justified in their performance of their sacrificial duties because the temple cult takes precedence over the strict observance of the Sabbath. However, Jesus makes the startling claim that his disciples are justified in their actions because they are associated with "something" (*contra* NIV **one**) **greater than the temple**. While the use of the neuter μεῖζον (*meizon*) can refer to a "person," its usage here is probably intended as a general reference to Jesus' ministry and the greater blessings associated with the new era being inaugurated in him. What God was doing in Jesus far surpasses what the temple cult could offer. In fact, the new *locus* of God's holy presence is to be found in Jesus (cf. 1:23; 21:12-14), and his merciful acts. It follows that Pharisaic criticism of the disciples is unjustified because by their association with Jesus they are involved in a sacrificial service that transcends anything connected to the temple cult.

12:7. By the second use of Hosea 6:6 (cf. 9:13), Jesus stresses that the Pharisees have failed to learn the lesson that God's will places a priority on mercy over sacrifice. Although they pride themselves in their mastery of Scripture, Jesus chides them for the failure to understand. They use the Law as "a blunt weapon . . . to condemn the untutored in the Law, people who are nevertheless the truly innocent ones, the poor and the meek."[5] That is why their teaching constituted a heavy yoke burdening the people (11:28). In contrast, Jesus' view of God's will did not revolve around legal niceties designed to ensnare the innocent. Had the Pharisees truly understood Hosea's words they would not have been so hasty in their denunciation of the disciples. While they knew the letter of the Law, they failed miserably in the apprehension of the heart of the Lawgiver.

12:8. Jesus' climactic christological affirmation (**the Son of Man is Lord of the Sabbath**) builds on his previous claims (note γάρ,

---

[4]Circumcision on the eighth day was also given precedence over Sabbath regulations.

[5]Meier, *Vision of Matthew*, p. 84.

gar) and affirms the priority of his person and mission for determining behavior that is acceptable on the Sabbath. Such a view is anchored in his prior, more fundamental awareness of God's will and character, and his determination to manifest the presence of God in terms of a ministry of mercy. Ironically, the "Son of Man" who has no place to rest (8:20), and is rejected as a "friend of tax collectors and sinners" (11:19), possesses authority and glory greater than one of Israel's most sacred cultic expressions. He will demonstrate the true meaning of the Sabbath, and thereby bring "rest" to his people. As the next scene illustrates, Jesus is the revealer of God's merciful character, and will not be intimidated by Pharisaic threats or maneuvers.

F. SABBATH CONTROVERSY: HEALING IN THE SYNAGOGUE (12:9-14)

9Going on from that place, he went into their synagogue, 10and a man with a shriveled hand was there. Looking for a reason to accuse Jesus, they asked him, "Is it lawful to heal on the Sabbath?"

11He said to them, "If any of you has a sheep and it falls into a pit on the Sabbath, will you not take hold of it and lift it out? 12How much more valuable is a man than a sheep! Therefore it is lawful to do good on the Sabbath."

13Then he said to the man, "Stretch out your hand." So he stretched it out and it was completely restored, just as sound as the other. 14But the Pharisees went out and plotted how they might kill Jesus.

12:9-10. The transitional phrase "going on from that place" marks Jesus' movement from the grainfields to inside one of "their synagogues."[6] The impression from Matthew's account is that this scene happens on the same day (i.e., the Sabbath) as the grainfield incident (cf. Luke 6:6, "on another Sabbath"). As Kingsbury has

[6]It should be noted that the designation "their synagogue" is a clear indication of the distance between Matthew's own community and the contemporary Jewish community.

observed, this scene represents a progression in the confrontational stance of the Pharisees: "In the first debate [12:1-8], the Pharisees confront Jesus, but the charge they raise is against the disciples . . . In the second debate, the Pharisees again confront Jesus, but this time, and indeed for the first time in Matthew's story, the accusation they make in the question they raise concerns an act Jesus himself intends to perform."[7]

The scene opens with Jesus in **their synagogue** along with a man suffering with a paralyzed hand. It is not at all improbable to imagine Jesus' opponents staging the encounter by using the man's infirmity for their own evil intentions. Matthew provides an insight into their motivations by noting that they were **Looking for a reason to accuse Jesus**. Their question, **Is it lawful to heal on the Sabbath**, was not a genuine inquiry for information, but was calculated to put Jesus at odds with their tradition. It was the general consensus among most Jewish groups that unless one's life was in immediate danger, it was not lawful to heal on the Sabbath (cf. m.Yoma 8:6: "Every case where life is in danger supersedes the Sabbath").[8] In this case, the man was not in immediate danger, thus respect for the Sabbath mandates that his healing be delayed, at least for another day.

12:11-12. Jesus' response indicates his refusal to have his mission stifled by legalistic discriminations that militate against the immediate expression of God's mercy. Once again, Jesus reasons *a fortiori* and thereby cuts through legalistic entrapments by going directly to the heart of God's intentions for the Sabbath. Most Jews would think nothing of rescuing a sheep that had fallen into a pit on the Sabbath.[9] Jesus reasons, if it is right and proper to assist a sheep in trouble on the Sabbath, how much more should the plight of human beings be mercifully responded to. Their own practice with respect to animals justifies the affirmation, **Therefore it is lawful to do good on the Sabbath**. In Jesus' view the Sabbath presents an

---

[7]Kingsbury, *Matthew as Story*, p. 120.

[8]For Qumran text pertaining to the Sabbath see S.T. Kimbrough, "The Concept of Sabbath at Qumran," *RevQ* 5 (1966), 482-502. See also the treatment in *Jubilees* 2 and 50.

[9]However, the Qumran community did disallow even this activity on the Sabbath (*CD* 11:13- 14).

opportunity to do good (=God's will), while the religious authorities use the occasion to find fault (12:10) and to condemn the innocent (12:14).

12:13-14. Having established the appropriateness for doing good on the Sabbath, Jesus proceeds to do good by restoring the man's hand to a healthy wholeness (ὑγιής, *hygiēs*). Once again, when Jesus' authoritative command is accepted in faith the seemingly impossible becomes a reality. The exhibition of Jesus' miraculous powers have provided sufficient evidence validating his words concerning what was permissible on the Sabbath. However, the Pharisees are only provoked to hostility and begin to plot their murderous intentions. The obsession with legalistic law keeping and the security it affords is not often open to alternative proposals and frequently responds by attempting to eliminate those who challenge their dependence on a rules-oriented form of religion. With this negative turn of events, "the conflict between Jesus and the Jewish leaders has intensified to the point of becoming irreconcilably hostile and will remain as such throughout the rest of the story."[10]

G. THE CHARACTER AND MISSION OF GOD'S SERVANT (12:15-21)

15Aware of this, Jesus withdrew from that place. Many followed him, and he healed all their sick, 16warning them not to tell who he was. 17This was to fulfill what was spoken through the prophet Isaiah:

18"Here is my servant whom I have chosen,
the one I love, in whom I delight;
I will put my Spirit on him,
and he will proclaim justice to the nations.
19He will not quarrel or cry out;
no one will hear his voice in the streets.
20A bruised reed he will not break,

[10]J.D. Kingsbury, "The Developing Conflict between Jesus and the Jewish Leaders in Matthew's Gospel: A Literary Critical Study," *CBQ* 49 (January 1987), 69-70.

and a smoldering wick he will not snuff out,
till he leads justice to victory.
[21]In his name the nations will put their hope."[a]

[a]*21* **Isaiah 42:1-4**

Matthew now interrupts the flow of the narrative by comments designed to underscore Jesus' ongoing ministry as his response to Pharisaic intentions (v. 14; 12:15-16). Jesus' withdrawal in the face of his rejection, his continual therapeutic involvement with the people, and his order "not to tell who he was," all find their explanation in what was foretold by Isaiah (vv. 17-21). The immediate effect of Matthew's intrusive comment is to validate Jesus' claim that his actions are in fulfillment of God's will as expressed in Scripture. As such, the fulfillment citation functions thematically to reiterate certain points expressed earlier and to lead the reader to expect that they will be further developed in scenes that follow.

12:15-16. Matthew makes it clear that Jesus' knowledge of their deadly plot (**Aware of this**) prompted his withdrawal so as to avoid further provocation. Nevertheless, his tactical withdrawal was not an attempt to hide from his opponents, since large crowds had no trouble finding him. While he continues to heal the sick, it is clear that he does not seek undue publicity. The warning **not to tell who he was** is not motivated by fear of his opponents, but is reflective of the unassuming nature of his ministry, and the inability of the crowds to correctly interpret his therapeutic activity. The description also prepares the reader for the fulfillment citation where the character of God's Servant and the contours of his mission are described.

12:17-18. Matthew's independent translation of Isaiah 42:1-4[11] serves to align Jesus' character and ministry with Israel's depiction of Yahweh's Spirit-endowed Servant (cf. 3:16; 17:5). Contextually, Matthew uses the Isaianic quotation to emphasize that while the essential features of Jesus' ministry evoke God's good pleasure, these same elements have become a source of offense and rejection

[11]Although Matthew may have drawn upon an unknown source or Targum it is probably best to see the citation as Matthew's original translation adapted to suit his purposes; so Davies and Allison, *Matthew*, 2:323-324.

in Israel.[12] While God delights in his servant, having chosen him and empowered him with his Spirit to carry out his redemptive mission, Israel's leaders have repudiated his authority by attributing his "powers" to the "prince of demons" (cf. 9:34; 10:25; 12:24). The ultimate goal of his ministry is described as to **proclaim justice to the nations**, to lead **justice to victory** with the result that **In his name the nations will put their hope**. However, it was precisely the character and extent of Jesus' outreach that stirred hostility and indignation within Israel (cf. 9:9-13, 16:19). The reference serves to anticipate the Gentile mission and to underscore that a fundamental feature of Jesus' compliance to the divine will becomes a major source of offense and conflict among the Jewish leaders.

12:19-21. The negatives that characterize the Servant's vocation remind the reader that the Son who is gentle and humble in heart (11:28-30) is compassionately responsive to the downtrodden in Israel; those elsewhere characterized as "oppressed and helpless" (9:36), and "weary and burdened" (11:28). The unobtrusive and judicious character of Jesus' ministry exhibited by his withdrawals (v. 15) and warnings "not to tell who he was" (v. 16), is in compliance to God's will which affirmed that **he will not quarrel or cry out** (v. 19). Matthew shows, by his longest OT citation, that both Jesus' incomparable authoritative power and the humble unassuming contours of his ministry are best understood in terms of his role as God's Servant, who sets his heart on fulfilling his Father's will. As such, it is he, not Israel's leadership, who truly understands and obeys God's will.

H. THE BEELZEBUB CONTROVERSY (12:22-37)

After demonstrating the correct evaluation of Jesus and his ministry as God's endowed Servant (12:17-21), the next narrative scene stands in stark contrast, as the Pharisees attribute the origin of his powers to Beelzebub (see 10:25). The setting for the controversy is reminiscent of 9:32-34 where an exorcism of a deaf-mute stirred

---

[12]See J.H. Neyrey, "The Thematic Use of Isaiah 42, 1-4 in Matthew 12," *Bib* 63 (1982), 457-473 for an excellent overview of the citation's connections to chapter 12.

differing assessments of Jesus' miraculous powers. In this instance, the crowds and Pharisees once again offer conflicting interpretations of Jesus' exorcism (12:22-24). But unlike the previous episode where Jesus does not respond to their charge, in this case Pharisaic accusations elicit a stinging rebuttal (vv. 25-37). Jesus first demonstrates why their evaluation is incorrect (vv. 25-29); he goes on to show the seriousness of their charge (vv. 30-32), and the external consequences of their evil intentions and hasty conclusions (vv. 33-37).

22Then they brought him a demon-possessed man who was blind and mute, and Jesus healed him, so that he could both talk and see. 23All the people were astonished and said, "Could this be the Son of David?"

24But when the Pharisees heard this, they said, "It is only by Beelzebub,[a] the prince of demons, that this fellow drives out demons."

25Jesus knew their thoughts and said to them, "Every kingdom divided against itself will be ruined, and every city or household divided against itself will not stand. 26If Satan drives out Satan, he is divided against himself. How then can his kingdom stand? 27And if I drive out demons by Beelzebub, by whom do your people drive them out? So then, they will be your judges. 28But if I drive out demons by the Spirit of God, then the kingdom of God has come upon you.

29"Or again, how can anyone enter a strong man's house and carry off his possessions unless he first ties up the strong man? Then he can rob his house.

30"He who is not with me is against me, and he who does not gather with me scatters. 31And so I tell you, every sin and blasphemy will be forgiven men, but the blasphemy against the Spirit will not be forgiven. 32Anyone who speaks a word against the Son of Man will be forgiven, but anyone who speaks against the Holy Spirit will not be forgiven, either in this age or in the age to come.

33"Make a tree good and its fruit will be good, or make a tree bad and its fruit will be bad, for a tree is recognized by its fruit. 34You brood of vipers, how can you who are evil say anything good? For out of the overflow of the heart the mouth speaks.

[35]The good man brings good things out of the good stored up in him, and the evil man brings evil things out of the evil stored up in him. [36]But I tell you that men will have to give account on the day of judgment for every careless word they have spoken. [37]For by your words you will be acquitted, and by your words you will be condemned."

[a]*24* Greek *Beezeboul* or *Beelzeboul*; also in verse 27

12:22-24. The conflict scene comprising 12:22-37 opens with a brief narration of Jesus healing a blind and mute demoniac. Although there are similarities with the episode described in 9:32-34, the differences should not be downplayed.[13]

In this instance the demoniac is **blind and mute,** whereas the previous scene involved a deaf mute (9:32-34). The crowd's earlier response was the affirmation that "nothing like this has ever been seen in Israel" (9:33), while in 12:23, they entertain the possibility that Jesus may be the Davidic Messiah, though they do expect a negative response to their question (μήτι, *mēti*). But like the previous episode (9:34), the mere suggestion of a positive response to Jesus' ministry evokes a swift response from the religious establishment (note ἀκούσαντες, *akousantes*, v. 23). Any suggestion of a royal Davidic claim is countered once again by attributing Jesus' power to **Beelzebub, the prince of demons** (cf. 9:34; 10:25). The desperate attempt to counter any positive assessment of Jesus results in the bizarre notion that the source of Jesus' powers is Satanic. It is probably no accident that healings of blindness juxtapose scenes highlighting the blindness of Israel's leaders. It should also be observed that they never question the reality of Jesus' supernatural power, but find their only recourse (other than faith) to attribute them to evil forces.

12:25-26. This time instead of remaining silent (9:34-35) or withdrawing (12:15), Jesus, who knows their hearts, counters their charge by demonstrating the logical absurdity of their assessment (vv. 25-27). No **kingdom**, **city**, or **household** can survive if there are

[13]See for example the conclusions of J.C. Anderson, "Double and Triple Stories, the Implied Reader, and Redundancy in Matthew," *Semeia* 31 (1985), 73ff.

internal divisions or dissensions that undermine their solidarity. The same applies to the "kingdom of Satan," which assumes some sort of structure or organization under the ruling authority of Satan. If the agents of Satan's rule are opposing one another by a relentless war against demonic influence, it would seem that Satanic influence is being undermined and his influence diminished. Thus, assuming their charge against Jesus to be accurate, it logically follows that Satan's kingdom is being seriously weakened by Jesus' activity. The question remains, does Jesus function as an agent of Satan in his assault against evil, or should his efforts be understood radically differently?

12:27. Jesus reasons that both he and other Jewish exorcists[14] (**your people**, lit., "your sons") have been active in expelling demons, yet they attribute the same activity of exorcism to radically different sources: God is at work in their people, but Beelzebub in Jesus' activity. If they would vehemently deny that the exorcisms performed by their own colleagues prove they are in league with Satan, by what logic do they attribute evil forces to Jesus' exorcisms? Jesus concludes that their own people will stand in judgment of them for hastily ascribing to Satanic forces that which obviously comes from God.

12:28-29. The proper assessment of Jesus' exorcisms is to see in them the presence of God's powerful reign. While others may exercise the power to cast out demons (v. 27), in Jesus, exorcisms are only one in a plethora of manifestations confirming the reality of God's mighty presence. Jesus is emphatic that the source of his power is the **Spirit of God** (cf. v. 18), not Beelzebub (v. 27; cf. Luke 11:20). The liberation of people from Satan's tyrannical hold is fundamental to the manifestation of God's kingdom. The presence of God's reign means a full frontal assault against the kingdom of Satan, resulting in many captives being liberated. The language of verse 29 graphically captures the notion of a direct assault against Satan and the plundering of his possessions. Far from being in league with Satan, Jesus describes his intentions as the complete overthrow of Satan and the liberation of all those under his authority. Jesus is

---

[14]For sources detailing stories about Jewish exorcists see Davies and Allison, *Matthew* 2:338-339.

stronger than the **strong man** and will render him powerless (**ties up**), thus effectively neutralizing his oppressive control over people. However, while the exorcisms signal Satan's ultimate defeat, he continues to wield considerable power and influence until the time of his total destruction (see Rev 20:2-15).

12:30. In the conflict against evil forces, neutrality is not an option. Those who do not see the presence of God and the mighty work of God's Spirit in Jesus' ministry stand diametrically opposed to him and do not contribute to the gathering of God's people, but to their scattering (cf. the harvest theme in 9:36-38). Simply put, there is no middle ground; one is either aligned with Jesus and his mission or one stands with Satan in opposition to the kingdom of God.

12:31-32. But opposition and repudiation of the power at work in Jesus carries with it serious eschatological consequences. While one can be forgiven for having difficulty with the humbled unpretentious role assumed by the Son of Man (cf. 11:2-3), attributing his divine power to a diabolical source constitutes a direct repudiation of God's Spirit at work in him, and as such, cannot be forgiven. It is unfortunate that Jesus' words have become a source of anxiety and concern for many Christians who have wondered if they may have committed the unpardonable sin. Notice that Jesus prefaces his remarks with the assurance that **every sin and blasphemy will be forgiven men**. Jesus makes it clear that the **blasphemy** that **will not be forgiven** is not the mere formation of words or thoughts, or deeds done in ignorance, but rather a hardened form of opposition that attributes the works of God's Spirit to Satan, and thereby rejects God's salvific offer in Jesus. With such a response one is cut off from any hope of forgiveness **either in this age or in the age to come**. The actions of the Pharisees and their slanderous rejection of God's Spirit at work in Jesus is the result of a willful, obstinate hardness that has therefore determined their eternal fate.

12:33-35. Jesus then offers an explanation for their blasphemous assessment of his ministry. Their words are simply the reflection of an evil heart which cannot **say anything good**. In words reminiscent of 7:16-20, Jesus illustrates the corruption of the Pharisees by noting that the fruit of a tree is ultimately determined by the health of the tree itself. The deeds and accusations (=fruits) of the Pharisees are simply indicative of an internal rottenness that has no chance of producing anything good. Since their hearts are fundamentally evil their words will necessarily reflect their basic character. Jesus makes it clear that one's deeds are always reflective of the core of one's inner being. As surely as a good man will produce that which is good, so the evil man can only produce evil. Jesus is not suggesting that change is impossible, only that as long as the heart remains corrupt, one's words and behavior will correspond accordingly.

12:36-37. Jesus concludes this section (vv. 22-37) with an indirect response to the verbal abuse he received from the Pharisees. Since words are reflective of one's basic character, even **careless words**[15] are not to be taken lightly because of what they can reveal about a person. A critical factor in God's ultimate evaluation of one's life involves the very words that one utters. Since words are both an insightful indicator of character, and a powerful instrument to incite behavior patterns, it is critical that the Lord's disciples carefully weigh the worth and implications of every word spoken.

I. THE REQUEST FOR A SIGN (12:38-42)

[38]Then some of the Pharisees and teachers of the law said to him, "Teacher, we want to see a miraculous sign from you."

[39]He answered, "A wicked and adulterous generation asks for a miraculous sign! But none will be given it except the sign of the prophet Jonah. [40]For as Jonah was three days and three nights in the belly of a huge fish, so the Son of Man will be three days and three nights in the heart of the earth. [41]The men of Nineveh will stand up at the judgment with this generation and condemn it; for they repented at the preaching of Jonah, and now one[a] greater than Jonah is here. [42]The Queen of the South will rise at the judgment with this generation and condemn it; for she came from the ends of the earth to listen to Solomon's wisdom, and now one greater than Solomon is here.

[a]*41* Or *something*; also in verse 42

---

[15]ῥῆμα ἀργόν, *rhēma argon*, can mean "without thought" or "useless in the sense of accomplishing nothing" (see J.P. Louw and E.A. Nida, eds. *Greek-English Lexicon of the New Testament*, [New York: UBS, 1988] 1:355, 625).

12:38. The paragraph opens with words that indicate that the Pharisee's request for a sign comes as a response to Jesus' words in the preceding section (i.e., 12:25-38; τότε ἀπεκρίθησαν αὐτῷ, *tote apekrithēsan autō*). Their words constitute a further indictment of their hardened hearts since they have already witnessed numerous convincing signs validating Jesus' message, but they refused to believe, and even attributed his works to Beelzebub. Perhaps they desire something more spectacular (cf. 11:4-6), geared especially to meet their expectations and approval. They were obviously not impressed with Jesus' healings and exorcisms, evidently being persuaded that such activity either could be duplicated by others or could be accounted for by factors other than that God was at work within him. They wanted an irrefutable sign that God was behind Jesus' miraculous deeds (cf. 16:1, where their request is identified as a "test"). It is precisely this "signs on demand" performance for the sake of impressing others that Jesus has always resisted. His ministry will not be reduced to a mere circus performance calculated to win the applause of men (cf. 4:1-11).

12:39-40. Accordingly, Jesus responds that the only "sign" given this **wicked and adulterous generation** (cf. 11:16) is the **sign of the prophet Jonah**. Because of the evil character of "this generation" they will not be convinced by further miraculous exhibitions. There is only one irrefutable sign that will be offered this generation, i.e,. the sign of Jonah. Jesus immediately explains the meaning of his words (v. 40, *gar*) by drawing a parallel between the experience of Jonah and the future experience of the Son of Man. Although Jonah was humbled and rendered powerless by his experience with a great fish, God's deliverance validated his commission and led to a successful campaign in Nineveh (v. 41). In like manner, the Son of Man will suffer humiliation and even death, and yet, God will validate the mission of his Son by raising him from the dead. Thus, this one remaining sign will be even more stunning than the return of Jonah from the belly of a fish. Jesus' death and subsequent return to life was heralded by the early church as the ultimate sign authenticating his person and mission (Acts 2:24, 32, 26; 3:15 etc.).

12:41-42. Once again, Jesus cites pagan examples to sharpen his criticism of his Jewish contemporaries (cf. 11:20-24). When the

Ninevites were confronted with Jonah's preaching they responded by repenting (Jonah 3:3-5). The **Queen of the South** was so impressed by Solomon's wisdom that she traveled a great distance for the opportunity to listen to him (1 Kgs 10:1-10). If both Jonah and Solomon merit such a positive response how much more Jesus, since with him this generation has been introduced to something greater (see 12:6) than both Jonah and Solomon. The ministry of Jesus is greater than Jonah's because Jesus embodies God's divine will and therefore both his teachings and actions constitute a revelation of God in the midst of his people. The **wisdom** of Jesus is **greater than Solomon** because he speaks as one divinely endowed and empowered by God's Spirit (3:17; 12:28; cf. 10:19-20). Jesus' affirmation is remarkable in its content, and is calculated to enhance the guilt of this generation which has so adamantly opposed his ministry.

J. A CONCLUDING ANALOGY (12:43-45)

43"When an evil[a] spirit comes out of a man, it goes through arid places seeking rest and does not find it. 44Then it says, 'I will return to the house I left.' When it arrives, it finds the house unoccupied, swept clean and put in order. 45Then it goes and takes with it seven other spirits more wicked than itself, and they go in and live there. And the final condition of that man is worse than the first. That is how it will be with this wicked generation."

[a]*43* Greek *unclean*

12:43. Jesus' confrontation with the Pharisees began with their faulty assessment of Jesus' exorcism (12:23), and now the discussion ends with an illustration implying that they, not he, have been completely taken over by evil forces. Since the analogy is not intended to provide detailed information about the demonic world, one should be cautious about extrapolating from this text to general speculative theories about demonic activity. The illustration has the primary function of dispelling any notion that one can benefit from Jesus' divine powers and yet continue to live non-committal empty lives.

12:44-45. Once a demon is driven out of a man it searches for another suitable host. If it is unable to find one it returns to its previous host, where conditions have been made even more favorable (**unoccupied, swept clean, and put in order**). As a result, the host is susceptible to a new invasion, this time, however, the demon is accompanied by additional evil spirits (seven) even more wicked than itself. The parable concludes with a line highlighting its central thought: **And the final condition of that man is worse than the first**.

Jesus' words certainly indicate that once one has been liberated from an evil spirit, it is essential that the Spirit of God take up residence within. A mere vacuum will not stay vacant for long. Nevertheless, by the concluding words, **That is how it will be with this wicked generation**, Jesus applies the parable to his contemporaries, especially unrepentant Jews who have seen his powerful deeds. Although they have greatly benefitted from his cleansing powers they have not repented, thus leaving themselves open to an even greater deception and control by evil forces. If Jesus' ministry does not generate both moral reform and a new allegiance there is created a void which Satan will surely exploit. Thus the final condition of this generation will be worse than their former state.

K. JESUS' TRUE FAMILY (12:46-50)

46 While Jesus was still talking to the crowd, his mother and brothers stood outside, wanting to speak to him. 47 Someone told him, "Your mother and brothers are standing outside, wanting to speak to you."[a]

48 He replied to him, "Who is my mother, and who are my brothers?" 49 Pointing to his disciples, he said, "Here are my mother and my brothers. 50 For whoever does the will of my Father in heaven is my brother and sister and mother."

[a]*47* Some manuscripts do not have verse 47.

12:46. With the lengthy exchange between Jesus and the Pharisees concluded (vv. 22-45), Jesus now addresses a new audience (**the crowd**), and shifts the focus of his attention from his opponents to those who constitute his true family (vv. 49-50). The "crowd" is therefore confronted with an implicit invitation (cf. 11:29-30) to become part of the messianic family by embracing a common commitment with Jesus to do the will of the Father. Obviously, such a proposal constitutes a serious indictment of the Pharisaic claim to be doers of the divine will.

No explanation is provided by Matthew concerning why Jesus' **mother and brothers** wish to speak to him. The fact that they remain **outside** may indicate their reluctance to be directly associated with Jesus' activities. It does appear from Mark 3:21 that they were at least concerned about the implications of his activity. Nevertheless, they seem to be under the impression that because of family ties they can immediately summon a private meeting with Jesus.[16] Mary has not been mentioned since chapter two, and this is the first reference to Jesus' extended family (cf. 13:55). However, their introduction here is not necessarily to cast Jesus' relatives in a negative light, they serve only as "a foil to highlight the true family of Jesus . . ." (cf. Mark 3:20-21).[17]

12:47-49. When Jesus is made aware of their desire to speak with him he immediately poses a question designed to challenge the priority extended to earthly family ties: **"Who is my mother, and who are my brothers?"** Jesus answers his own question by **Pointing to his disciples** and identifying them as his true family. Old earthly ties have either been replaced or renewed by the presence of God's kingdom. The service of God and the work of the kingdom must be given priority over even the most intimate of human relationships (4:22; 8:21; 10:35-37). In fact, there are no structures of authority or basic relationships that are not radically effected by the dawn of God's reign in Jesus.

---

[16]See Bruce J. Malina and Richard L. Rohrbaugh, *Social-Science Commentary on the Synoptic Gospels* (Minneapolis: Fortress, 1992), pp. 100-101, who point out the importance of the family unit over all individualism. The public role of a male definitely, in the ancient world, has serious implications for the family unit from which he came.

[17]Meier, *Vision of Matthew*, p. 89. It should also be observed that there is no reason, other than the promotion of Mary's perpetual virginity, to regard the "brothers" of Jesus as anything other than the offspring of Mary and Joseph, who were born subsequent to the birth of Jesus. See Carson, *Matthew*, p. 299 for a response to counter proposals.

12:50. The essence of discipleship is defined as a wholehearted commitment to do the will of the Father. Those who follow Jesus and allow the Father's will to be the guiding principle controlling both actions and the way persons and events are evaluated are part of an extended family whose bonds transcend all earthly ties. This invitation is extended to **whoever**, thus shattering ethnic and gender restrictions characteristic of contemporary Judaism. The intimacy that Jesus experiences with God as his Father is offered to all who take seriously conformity to God's will. Jesus is therefore not repudiating family relationships or necessarily rejecting all of Israel. He is, however, equating following him with doing the will of God, and therefore intends his new family to emulate his sacrificial obedience to the will of the Father. Of course, Jesus' language seriously undermines and directly challenges the Pharisaic claim that they are representative of compliance to God's will. To the contrary, it is the Son's intimate knowledge of his Father's will and his conformity to it that constitute the basis of the new family of God.

MATTHEW 13

L. THE PARABLES OF THE KINGDOM (13:1-52)

In the discourse to follow (i.e., 13:1-53), Jesus assumes the role of a storyteller, and relates a series of parables wherein the kingdom is like what happens in the story. Oftentimes, the parables of Jesus have been interpreted in isolation from the ongoing story in which they are embedded, resulting in rather elaborate and arbitrary allegorizing of virtually every element within a given parable. While there are certainly allegorical elements in the parables, the modern reader must be careful not to impose ideas that would be completely foreign to a first-century Galilean Jewish audience.[1] Typically, Jesus' illustrative language draws from imagery well known in ancient Judaism. Thus, given the metaphoric nature of parables, if a metaphor is to have its desired impact, the modern reader must learn to hear the parable in terms of its first century setting.[2] Parables are not intended to merely communicate factual data, but to draw the reader into a new reality and thereby to dramatically subvert, alter, confirm, and radically transform the world of the reader.

Although Jesus has used parabolic language on other occasions (e.g., 5:25-26; 11:16-19; 12:43-45), for the first time his entire discourse consists of seven parables. The parables are united around the central theme of God's kingdom, as six out of seven parables

---

[1]The works of K.E. Bailey, *Poet and Peasant: A Literary Cultural Approach to the Parables in Luke* (Grand Rapids: Eerdmans, 1976); idem, *Through Peasant Eyes: More Lucan Parables, Their Culture and Style* (Grand Rapids: Eerdmans, 1980), are a helpful corrective to this tendency.

[2]The works of C.L. Blomberg, *Interpreting the Parables* (Downers Grove, IL: InterVarsity, 1990), and R.H. Stein, *An Introduction to the Parables of Jesus* (Philadelphia: Westminster, 1981), are helpful introductions to the study of the parables.

are introduced with the words, "the kingdom of heaven is like" (13:24, 31, 33, 44, 45, 47). The focus on "the kingdom and its fate in the world"[3] in chapter 13 serves to explain the diverse reactions to Jesus' ministry encountered in chapters 11 and 12. In addition, Jesus' parabolic discourse dramatizes a decided shift as Jesus moves from a lakeside setting where he addresses large crowds (vv. 1-2), to a private setting in a house where his disciples are instructed privately concerning the "secrets of the kingdom" (vv. 34-36).[4] Thus, Jesus turns from those who are "ever hearing and never understanding" and "ever seeing but never perceiving" to those who have been blessed to "see and hear" (cf. vv. 11-17). The disciples must be "instructed about the kingdom of heaven" (v. 52) so they will remain faithful in spite of adverse reactions given God's reign, and fulfill their mission to be "fishers of men" (4:19).

It is important to read the parables of chapter 13 against the background of the previous "twelve chapters of narrative about the reign."[5] As Carter observes, "the parables of chapter 13 seem more to confirm what is already known about the 'reign of the heavens' than to reveal new insights." The illustrative language of Jesus is therefore calculated to reaffirm, clarify, and make vivid important aspects of God's reign.[6] Thus, the parables, at this point in the story challenge the reader to rethink and to experience afresh the significance of God's kingdom. The intent is to cultivate a deeper understanding of God's active and transforming presence, and thereby to equip disciples with a vision and power for living that will enable them to endure an ongoing ministry of repudiation and suffering. Being "discipled in the kingdom of heaven" (v. 52) means having one's expectations and ongoing lifestyle continually challenged and radically altered by God's abiding presence (cf. 1:23; 28:20). Accordingly, all the parables of chapter 13 are illustrative of what happens when God's kingship impacts human lives.

---

[3]Davies and Allison, *Matthew*, 2:449.

[4]For various proposals concerning the structure of chapter 13 see Hagner, *Matthew*, 1:362-364.

[5]See the helpful treatment by Warren Carter, "Challenging by Confirming, Renewing by Repeating: The Parables of 'the Reign of the Heavens' in Matthew 13 as Embedded Narratives," *SBLASP* (Atlanta: Scholars Press, 1995), 399-424.

[6]Ibid., p. 422.

1. The Parable of the Four Soils (13:1-9)

[1]That same day Jesus went out of the house and sat by the lake. [2]Such large crowds gathered around him that he got into a boat and sat in it, while all the people stood on the shore. [3]Then he told them many things in parables, saying: "A farmer went out to sow his seed. [4]As he was scattering the seed, some fell along the path, and the birds came and ate it up. [5]Some fell on rocky places, where it did not have much soil. It sprang up quickly, because the soil was shallow. [6]But when the sun came up, the plants were scorched, and they withered because they had no root. [7]Other seed fell among thorns, which grew up and choked the plants. [8]Still other seed fell on good soil, where it produced a crop – a hundred, sixty or thirty times what was sown. [9]He who has ears, let him hear."

13:1-2. The setting for the discourse is described both temporally and with respect to location. Jesus delivers his parabolic discourse on the **same day** of his heated exchange with the Pharisees (12:22-45). He has left the **house** where evidently his mother and brothers sought to speak to him (12:46, ἔξω, *exō*). He now takes a position in a boat, just off shore, and begins to address a large crowd now standing on the shore. Later Jesus will leave the crowds, return to the house, and from inside the house privately instruct the disciples (vv. 34-36). The different locations and change of audiences form clear transitional brackets marking a decided shift away from speaking to the "crowds" to teaching directed exclusively to the disciples.

13:3. Jesus now assumes a form of speech where his teachings are communicated by short stories called **parables** (παραβολή, *parabolē*, lit., "cast alongside"). The Greek term *parabolē* is derived from the Hebrew משׁל (*māšāl*, lit., "to liken to," see LXX), which can refer to a wide variety of figurative expressions (e.g., proverbs, similes, riddles, and simple stories).[7] However, the common element is some form of comparison, where everyday events and terms familiar to the audience serve to illustrate a spiritual or transcendent

[7]See K.R. Snodgrass, "Parable," *DJG*, p. 593.

reality. His purpose for teaching in parables will be explained in verses 10-17.

The first parable begins with a familiar scene: **A farmer went out to sow his seed**. While one may explain the seemingly careless casting of seed by claiming that in the ancient world sowing preceded plowing,[8] it is not necessary to find realistic explanations for such details.[9] Furthermore, recent evidence has demonstrated that there was no uniform practice of sowing always preceding plowing.[10] Therefore, the imagery is intended to depict a farmer who sows with abandon hoping for a fruitful yield. As it turns out, the parable is not about the sower, but about the different types of soil upon which the seed falls. While the meaning and significance of the parable may be lost on the crowd, Jesus will ultimately provide his disciples with an explanation (vv. 18-23).

13:4-7. Jesus devotes considerable attention to the various types of ground upon which the seed falls and the inevitable results for the crop. Some seed fell upon the beaten path with little chance of penetrating the soil. As a result, such seed remained exposed and therefore susceptible to being eaten by birds. Other seed fell upon ground where a solid bedrock lies very close to the surface, and hence there was very little depth to the soil. The situation meant that the topsoil was too shallow to enable a sufficient root system to develop to sustain the plant. Thus, while the soil was conducive to rapid growth, it lacked sufficient depth to enable the roots to absorb sufficient moisture to withstand hot weather. The result was inevitable: **the plants were scorched and they withered because they had no root**. The third unfavorable environment for the seed's survival is described as **among thorns**. Within this environment the seed germinates and survives for awhile,[11] only to lose its struggle for life to more sturdy and robust plants which deprive it of needed nourishment.

---

[8]See, e.g., J. Jeremias, *The Parables of Jesus*, 2nd ed. (New York: Charles Scribner's Sons, 1972), pp. 11-12.

[9]Garland, *Reading Matthew*, p. 145.

[10]See P.B. Payne, "The Order of Sowing and Ploughing," *NTS* 25 (1978), 123-129.

[11]Davies and Allison, *Matthew* 2:384, observe that "the lifetime of the various seeds becomes greater as one moves toward the parable's climax."

13:8. Finally, we come to seed that happens to fall upon **good soil**, with the results dramatically different from the previous examples. The focus is upon the sheer productivity and varying yields of crops when the seed is planted in good soil (**a hundred, sixty, or thirty times what is sown**). While some see the numbers associated with the yield as fantastically high, others do not see the varying yields as particularly high by ancient standards.[12] The cautionary observation by France seems appropriate: ". . . the experts differ as to what was a typical yield depending on the method of reckoning, but the point of the parable does not lie in the size of the yield, but in the variety of the fate of the seed. This is not a general description of Palestinian agriculture, but a story designed to teach a specific lesson."[13]

13:9. With the final words, **He who has ears, let him hear**, Jesus indicates the importance of truly understanding the underlying reality to which this parable points. To have "ears" is to listen with a receptive spirit, open to the hidden truths contained in the parable. The reader will learn that the disciples have "ears to hear" (v. 16), and thus they will be recipients of the parable's interpretation (vv. 18-23).

2. The Purpose of the Parables (13:10-17)

[10]The disciples came to him and asked, "Why do you speak to the people in parables?"

[11]He replied, "The knowledge of the secrets of the kingdom of heaven has been given to you, but not to them. [12]Whoever has will be given more, and he will have an abundance. Whoever does not have, even what he has will be taken from him. [13]This is why I speak to them in parables:

"Though seeing, they do not see;
though hearing, they do not hear or understand.

[14]In them is fulfilled the prophecy of Isaiah:

"'You will be ever hearing but never understanding;
you will be ever seeing but never perceiving.

---

[12]Cf. Malina and Rohrbaugh, *Social-Science Commentary*, p. 102; and Carson, *Matthew*, p. 305.

[13]France, *Matthew*, p. 218.

[15]For this people's heart has become calloused;
they hardly hear with their ears,
and they have closed their eyes.
Otherwise they might see with their eyes,
hear with their ears,
understand with their hearts
and turn, and I would heal them.'[a]

[16]But blessed are your eyes because they see, and your ears because they hear. [17]For I tell you the truth, many prophets and righteous men longed to see what you see but did not see it, and to hear what you hear but did not hear it.

[a]*15* Isaiah 6:9,10

13:10-12. The parabolic discourse is temporarily suspended in order to explain why parables are the most appropriate form of speech with which to address the crowds. In verse 10 the disciples ask Jesus not the meaning of the preceding parable, but why he has resorted to the use of parables, and seemingly abandoned the use of plain speech (cf. Mark 4:10). Their concern with Jesus' manner of speaking is probably indicative of their own feelings of ineptness in understanding Jesus' words (cf. v. 36). Yet, Jesus responds by assuring them that they are indeed blessed by God to have **the secrets** [μυστήριον, *mystērion*] **of the kingdom** disclosed (note passive δέδο–ται, *dedotai*) to them. They will be provided with insight not only into the kingdom's presence in Jesus, but also into "both faith (eschatology) and life (ethics) that together constitute the Christian existence between the Resurrection and the Parousia as it is governed by the rule of God."[14] In contrast to the crowds who either reject the message or assume a posture of neutrality, the disciples who have basic knowledge will be given even more understanding, while the crowds only increase in their confused and darkened state of mind.[15] Thus, the parables both *conceal* and *reveal* at the same time, depending on the heart condition of the hearer.

---

[14]J.D. Kingsbury, *The Parables of Jesus in Matthew 13* (London: SPCK, 1978), p. 145.

[15]France, *Matthew*, p. 221, refers to the "laws of capitalist economics" as illustrative of this verse: "capital breeds income; lack of capital spells ruin."

13:13. Jesus explains why his parabolic form of speech is appropriate when addressing the crowds: **This is why I speak to them in parables . . . .** Unlike Mark 4:12, Jesus does not speak to the crowds "in order to" (ἵνα, *hina*) make them blind or deaf, but because (ὅτι, *hoti*) they already shut their eyes and refuse to hear, they lack the capacity to understand the message of the kingdom. The parables merely confirm the fact that they are not ready to hear the mysteries of the kingdom. As noted by Davies and Allison, "until hostility raised its ugly head,"[16] Jesus did not resort to the use of parables. The parables are therefore an appropriate means of discourse, revealing deeper mysteries of the kingdom to those who honestly seek their meaning, while to those with hardened hearts they appear as mere riddles with little communicative value.

13:14-15. To further condemn Israel's rebellion and unbelief, Jesus cites Isaiah 6:9-10 (almost verbatim from the LXX), a favorite text in the NT to explain Israel's unbelief (see John 12:40; Acts 28:26-27; Rom 11:8). There are clear topological parallels between Isaiah's prophetic commission and task and Israel's response to Jesus' divinely appointed mission. The citation continues the thought of verse 13 and makes it clear that Israel's spiritual blindness is the result of a calloused heart, not some predetermined plan of God. While their unbelief and hardened hearts certainly fall within the preview of God's sovereign will, they are nevertheless accountable for their action: they refuse to hear and have closed their eyes. The result is that in their refusal to repent they do not benefit from Jesus' saving powers. Like the generation in Isaiah's day, Israel remains a hardened people and thus stands under God's judgment.

13:16-17. In contrast to the people who fall under prophetic condemnation (vv. 13-15), the disciples are blessed to "see and hear" that which **many prophets and righteous men longed to see** and **hear** (cf. 11:4-6). They are blessed in that they experience the era of fulfillment and the presence of God's powerful reign. The privileged status of the disciples is both a gift from God and a result of their initial positive response to Jesus' message. As a result, Jesus will interpret for them the meaning of the parables, thus revealing to them the secrets of the kingdom (vv. 18-23; 36-43).

[16]Davies and Allison, *Matthew*, 2:392.

3. The Interpretation of the Parable of the Soils (13:18-23)

[18]"Listen then to what the parable of the sower means: [19]When anyone hears the message about the kingdom and does not understand it, the evil one comes and snatches away what was sown in his heart. This is the seed sown along the path. [20]The one who received the seed that fell on rocky places is the man who hears the word and at once receives it with joy. [21]But since he has no root, he lasts only a short time. When trouble or persecution comes because of the word, he quickly falls away. [22]The one who received the seed that fell among the thorns is the man who hears the word, but the worries of this life and the deceitfulness of wealth choke it, making it unfruitful. [23]But the one who received the seed that fell on good soil is the man who hears the word and understands it. He produces a crop, yielding a hundred, sixty or thirty times what was sown."

13:18. Jesus now illustrates the blessed status of the disciples by providing them with the interpretation of his earlier parable (vv. 3-9). The explanation naturally assumes that the disciples have the capacity to understand the intent of Jesus' words (vv. 11-12). It has been customary for some scholars to analyze the parable of the soils (vv. 3-9) and its interpretation (vv. 19-23) in isolation, assuming that the somewhat allegorical interpretation is the product of the early church, not the historical Jesus. However, only prior conclusions about the complete absence of allegorization in parables, or assumptions about the early church's inappropriate use of the parable seem to undergird its alleged lack of authenticity.[17] The fact is, the interpretation so clearly fits the parable that there is no compelling reason to dispute that the interpretation was provided by Jesus.[18] As such, we have a somewhat rare phenomena where the storyteller informs his hearers/readers explicitly how they are to understand his words.

---

[17]See P.B. Payne, "The Authenticity of the Parables of Jesus," in *Gospel Perspectives,* ed. R.T. France and D. Wenham (Sheffield: JSOT, 1981), 2:329-344.

[18]B. Gerhardsson, "The Parable of the Sower and Its Interpretation," *NTS* 14 (1967-68), 192, observes that the interpretation fits the parable like a hand fits a glove.

Jesus' interpretation of the parable makes it clear that its intent was to identify factors which influence negative and positive responses to Jesus' proclamation of the kingdom. Jesus is in fact the **sower** who scatters the seed (=**message about the kingdom**). The central focus of the parable concerns the diverse reactions given Jesus and his message. Each of the scenes in the original parable depicting how the seed fares within various types of soil upon which it falls, is now interpreted in terms of how, given varying circumstances, people have responded to the message about the kingdom (cf. 4:23; 9:35).

13:19. Jesus first explains the meaning of the **seed sown along the path**. In this instance, the proclaimed word is not understood (συνίημι, *syniēmi*, cf. v. 23), meaning the hearer lacks comprehension and thus fails to take appropriate action. Since the word makes no penetrating impression it is easily snatched (ἁρπάζω, *harpazō*) away by the **evil one** (=birds). The failure to understand is not attributable to the proclaimer or the obscurity of the word, but to the hardhearted condition of the receptor's heart (see. vv. 13-15). No doubt the hardened Pharisaic response to Jesus comes readily to mind (cf. 9:3-4; 11:34; 12:22-45).

13:20-21. Next, Jesus discusses the fate of the seed that fell **on rocky places**. As was the case in the original parable (vv. 5-6), where the sown seed lodged in an environment conducive to rapid growth, so the words of Jesus are met initially by some with a favorable response. However, their joy and commitment are short-lived because like seed in shallow soil, they lack sufficient depth to sustain their spiritual lives. They have misconstrued the message about the kingdom as meaning a life without hardship and demands. Hence, at the first sign of opposition and trouble the shallow enthusiast quickly abandons faith and prior loyalties (σκανδαλίζεται, *skandalizetai*). Jesus has made it clear that persecution and physical affliction is the lot of the disciple (5:11-12; 10:21-34). Therefore, a positive response to the message of the kingdom means an unconditional commitment to follow Jesus even in the hard times, not just when conditions appear favorable.

13:22. The seed that fell among the thorns becomes representative of a disciple's constant struggle against worldly influences. Thorns are analogous to the worries of this world (cf. 6:25-33) and the seduction of riches (cf. 6:19-24). When life is crowded by worldly concerns and the pursuit of wealth, these commitments tend to stifle and eventually snuff out spiritual life. Because worry can become so commonplace, and devotion to wealth so deceptively subtle, it is essential that disciples constantly monitor the productivity of their spiritual lives.

13:23. The **good soil** with yields of varying amounts (**a hundred, sixty, and thirty times what was sown**) is identified as **the man who hears the word and understands it** (cf. v. 19). Truly understanding Jesus' words means not only intellectually grasping its content, but responding with a wholehearted allegiance and devotion. The theme of "understanding" is important in Matthew's Gospel, since it goes to the heart of what it means to be a disciple. Jesus calls the whole person (cf. 22:37) to an undivided loyalty where hearing results in doing.

4. Parable of the Weeds (13:24-30)

24Jesus told them another parable: "The kingdom of heaven is like a man who sowed good seed in his field. 25But while everyone was sleeping, his enemy came and sowed weeds among the wheat, and went away. 26When the wheat sprouted and formed heads, then the weeds also appeared.

27"The owner's servants came to him and said, 'Sir, didn't you sow good seed in your field? Where then did the weeds come from?'

28"'An enemy did this,' he replied.

"The servants asked him, 'Do you want us to go and pull them up?'

29"'No,' he answered, 'because while you are pulling the weeds, you may root up the wheat with them. 30Let both grow together until the harvest. At that time I will tell the harvesters: First collect the weeds and tie them in bundles to be burned; then gather the wheat and bring it into my barn.'"

Jesus' second parable continues the use of agricultural metaphors in order to illustrate aspects of God's kingdom (e.g., "field," "seed," "sowing"). Also, like the first parable (vv. 3-9), this parable is accompanied by an interpretation, reserved for the disciples in a later private setting (vv. 36-43). Both parables make it clear that although God's active reign will continue to have a powerful impact in the world, the presence of evil and hostile opposition will also continue until the consummation of God's victory in Jesus.[19] Between the resurrection and the *parousia* there will always be those who respond to the message about the kingdom with hostility and seek to undermine its influence. Later Jesus will identify the "evil one" (=Satan) as behind all efforts to diminish the effectiveness of God's reign (vv. 38-39).

13:24. Jesus now returns to his discourse directed to the "crowds" (αὐτοῖς, *autois*, **them**; cf. vv. 34-36), once again speaking of seed and a sower, but this time the focus is not upon the ground upon which the seed falls, but on two different kinds of seed, and on the distinction between two different sowers. The **kingdom of heaven** is compared to a man who sows **good seed**. The aorist passive ὡμοιώθη (*hōmoiōthē*, **like**) serves to indicate that "the kingdom of heaven . . . is a present reality and already has a certain history behind it."[20] The significance is best communicated not by the translation "like" (NIV), but by the phrase "it has been the case with the kingdom of heaven as with a man . . . ." In reality it is not the man who sowed who is being compared to the kingdom of heaven, "but the situation resulting from the sowing."[21]

13:25-26. After the man had prepared his field by sowing good seed (cf. "good soil," v. 19), he then rested from his labor. Reference to the **sleeping** servants intends no negative indictment of the servants, but does underscore the malicious character of the enemy who hopes to escape detection by performing his sinister act under the cover of darkness. The enemy sows seed that results in **weeds**, which probably refers to a troublesome weed called darnel which can only be distinguished from wheat when it fully ripens.[22] Thus with time it becomes apparent that the once carefully prepared field has now become contaminated with weeds.

---

[19]See Davies and Allison, *Matthew*, 2:408.

[20]Kingsbury, *Parables*, p. 67.

[21]France, *Matthew*, p. 225.

[22]See I. Jacob and W. Jacob, "Flora," *ABD* 2:816.

13:27. The servants address the sower, now identified as the **owner** (lit., "master of the house"), and pose a question anticipating a positive response: **"Sir** [κύριε, *kyrie*] **didn't you sow good seed in your field?"** Given that only "good seed" was used by the sower, the next question logically follows: **"Where then did the weeds come from?"** The servants are surprised to discover the presence of weeds in a field that they know to be sowed only with "good seed."

13:28-30. But the householder promptly and accurately recognizes the hand of an enemy as responsible for the field's condition. The servants then respond with a question, which amounts to a proposal to immediately rectify the situation by uprooting the weeds from the field. The householder denies their request, citing the difficulty of separating the weeds from the wheat. The problem is not in distinguishing between the two plants, but because their root systems have become so intertwined one cannot pull up the one without damaging the other. The householder therefore proposes an alternative plan whereby the wheat and weeds are allowed to coexist until harvest time. At that time, once the plants have reached maturity, the weeds will then be gathered up and burned, while the wheat will be gathered for storage in the barns.

Although both the crowds and the disciples hear the parable, its meaning was not immediately obvious to its original hearers. Later the disciples will inquire about its meaning and Jesus will provide them with an explanation (vv. 36-42).

5. Parable of the Mustard Seed (13:31-32)

31He told them another parable: "The kingdom of heaven is like a mustard seed, which a man took and planted in his field. 32Though it is the smallest of all your seeds, yet when it grows, it is the largest of garden plants and becomes a tree, so that the birds of the air come and perch in its branches."

13:31-32. A third parable becomes illustrative of the kingdom by means of the imagery of sowing seed. In this instance, the point of the analogy consists in the particular type of seed that was planted, i.e,. a **mustard seed**. The use of a mustard seed to illustrate certain aspects of the kingdom was especially well-suited, as noted by Kingsbury: "First, although technically speaking, the mustard seed is not in reality 'the smallest of all seeds' (v. 32a), it was nevertheless proverbial among the Jews as the most minute of qualities (cf. Mt. 17:20; Luke 17:6). Second, of no other small seed did the fully grown plant attain the size of the mustard herb."[23] Once again Jesus captures the imagination by reminding his hearers that external appearances can be deceptive. One would not naturally expect that from a tiny mustard seed would come a tree-like shrub attaining a height of ten to twelve feet, suitable for even birds to find a resting place. Yet, this remarkable natural phenomenon has its spiritual counterpart in the kingdom of God.

The parable is intended to accent both the qualities of growth and contrast. Like the mustard seed, the kingdom's humble beginnings and unpretentious character offer no visible indication of its future growth and glory, but just as there is continuity between the tiny mustard seed and the resulting "tree," so there is continuity from the seemingly inconsequential beginnings in Jesus' ministry and the future glory of God's consummating reign. Thus even though the beginnings of God's kingdom as manifested in Jesus may appear unimpressive, it is casually dismissed at one's own peril.

6. Parable of the Leaven (13:33)

[33]He told them still another parable: "The kingdom of heaven is like yeast that a woman took and mixed into a large amount[a] of flour until it worked all through the dough."

[a]*33* Greek *three satas* (probably about ½ bushel or 22 liters)

13:33. The fourth parable brings to a closure the public aspect of Jesus' parabolic discourse. Although the imagery is different, this parable is closely related to the parable of the mustard seed. The effect of a small amount of leaven[24] on a large amount of dough

[23]Kingsbury, *Parables*, p. 79.

[24]Morris, *Matthew*, p. 353, observes that the rendering "yeast" is not strictly accurate. "Leaven was a piece of last week's dough, which certainly made this week's dough rise, but was not strictly 'yeast.'"

makes essentially the same point as the contrast between a tiny mustard seed and the resulting shrub. Usually, leaven symbolized the influence of corrupting forces (cf. 16:6, 11-12; 1 Cor 5:6; Gal 5:9), but here its usage serves to highlight the effect even a small amount of leaven can have on a large batch of dough. As such, leaven, like a small mustard seed serves as a fitting illustration of the dynamic, permeating impact of the kingdom in the world.

The woman in the parable mixes (lit., "hides or conceals") a small amount of leaven in a large amount of flour (σάτα τρία [*sata tria*] = "three measures," or roughly equivalent to forty pounds of dough; enough to feed over one hundred people).[25] The exaggerated numbers are designed to create a powerful image of the eventual pervading influence of God's kingdom. Do not be put off by its unimpressive beginnings, for its unobtrusive transforming effect will far surpass all expectations.

7. The Purpose of Parables (13:34-35)

[34]Jesus spoke all these things to the crowd in parables; he did not say anything to them without using a parable. [35]So was fulfilled what was spoken through the prophet:

"I will open my mouth in parables,
I will utter things hidden since the creation of the world."[a]

[a]*35* Psalm 78:2

13:34. With these words Matthew now formally brings to an end the first half of Jesus' discourse, which was primarily directed to the Jewish crowd (vv. 1-3). From now on Jesus' typical mode of speech before the crowds will be parabolic (see ἐλάλει, *elalei*, imperfect tense, implying a habitual mode of instruction). While earlier his parabolic speech fulfilled the words of Isaiah 6:9-10, now his use of parables when speaking to the crowds fulfills Psalm 78:2.

13:35. In what way might Jesus' use of parables be said to fulfill the words of Asaph as recorded in Psalm 78:2? As with several of

[25]Although the numbers are subject to varying interpretations, see Patte, *Matthew*, p. 195; and Hagner, *Matthew*, 1:390.

Matthew's citations from the OT, "fulfillment" is to be understood typologically, where certain features from an OT text are highlighted because they have certain parallels in Jesus' ministry. In Psalm 78, Asaph, who was regarded as a prophetic figure (1 Chr 25:2; 2 Chr 29:30), rehearses Israel's sacred history in terms that highlight a pattern of God's salvific involvement with his people.[26] Asaph's language is parabolic in the sense that it intends to reveal and make clear that which may not be immediately apparent. Thus, on the one hand, while Jesus' parabolic speech functioned to conceal divine truths from the hardhearted, it also revealed God's presence in Jesus for those who have "eyes to see." It should also be observed that Jesus understands his parables as a disclosure of that which God has **hidden since the creation of the world**, therefore testifying to Jesus' unique role of mediating divine revelation.[27]

8. The Interpretation of the Parable of the Weeds (13:36-43)

36Then he left the crowd and went into the house. His disciples came to him and said, "Explain to us the parable of the weeds in the field."

37He answered, "The one who sowed the good seed is the Son of Man. 38The field is the world, and the good seed stands for the sons of the kingdom. The weeds are the sons of the evil one, 39and the enemy who sows them is the devil. The harvest is the end of the age, and the harvesters are angels.

40"As the weeds are pulled up and burned in the fire, so it will be at the end of the age. 41The Son of Man will send out his angels, and they will weed out of his kingdom everything that causes sin and all who do evil. 42They will throw them into the fiery furnace, where there will be weeping and gnashing of teeth. 43Then the righteous will shine like the sun in the kingdom of their Father. He who has ears, let him hear.

13:36. Matthew marks a major transition as Jesus leaves the crowd and enters into the privacy of a **house** (see 13:1). The transition

---

[26]See Carson, *Matthew*, pp. 320-323.

[27]Suggested by Kingsbury, *Parables*, p. 91.

provides the setting for the rest of his parabolic discourse directed exclusively to the disciples. Although they are earlier contrasted with the crowds as having "eyes that see" and "ears that hear" (v. 16), they nevertheless need further explanation in order to understand Jesus' parable of the weeds. They are therefore not distinguished from the crowd by "their instant and intuitive understanding but by their persistence in seeking explanations."[28] Jesus is sensitive to their deficiency and as with the parable of the soils (vv. 3-9; 18-23), Jesus provides the disciples with a private explanation of his earlier parable (vv. 24-30).

13:37-39. Jesus begins by allegorizing seven critical elements found in the previous parable. First, the **Son of Man** is identified as the sower of the **good seed**. It has been typical to highlight aspects of Jesus' earthly ministry with the designation "Son of Man" (cf. 8:20; 9:6; 11:19). The **field** is explicitly identified as the **world** not the church. As rightfully noted by Carson, "The parable does not address the church situation at all but explains how the kingdom can be present in the world while not yet wiping out all opposition."[29] The product produced from the "good seed" are those who belong to and participate in the kingdom (=**sons of the kingdom**). The **weeds** are identified as those who belong to and support the reign of the **evil one**. The **devil** is identified as the **enemy**, responsible for contaminating the field with poisonous plants. He is a rival sower whose intentions are to undermine the efforts of the Son of Man. The **harvest** is intended to symbolize the **end of the age**, meaning "the termination of the existing world order, when present history has run its course (cf. 24:3; 28:20)."[30] Finally, the **angels** are represented by the **harvesters** and are responsible for burning the weeds and gathering the wheat into the barns (see also 16:7; 24:31; 25:41).

13:40-42. With the critical details of the parable explained, Jesus proceeds to highlight the fate of the weeds sown by the "evil one," and the ultimate reward of the righteous. The burning of the weeds **at the end of the age** refers to God's final judgment which effects a

---

[28]Carson, *Matthew*, p. 325.
[29]Ibid., p. 317.
[30]Kingsbury, *Parables*, p. 107.

great separation between the ungodly and the righteous. **The Son of Man** (=Jesus) is accompanied by **his angels** in the accomplishment of the removal of **everything that causes sin and all who do evil**. It may appear problematic that evil people are said to be gathered **out of his kingdom**. Since the field is identified as the world (v. 38) not the kingdom, how can it be said that the angels will **weed out of his kingdom everything that causes sin and all who do evil**? It appears that the kingdom is now idealized as encompassing the entire world. Therefore, as articulated by Hagner, "The wicked are gathered from the kingdom, not in the sense that they actually were a part of the Church (nor does the kingdom exactly equal the field/world) but in the sense that they were in the world, had existed alongside the righteous (cf. v. 30), hence were even in the visible church and are now finally distinguished and separated from them."[31] Their fate will be a total destruction (see 7:19; 8:12; 13:41; 25:32, 41), accompanied by extreme anguish and remorse.

13:43. On the other hand, the **righteous** [cf. 10:41; 25:37, 46] **will shine like the sun in the kingdom of their Father**. The language has parallels with Jesus' transfiguration (cf. 17:2), and is descriptive of an existence that partakes of God's glory (cf. Dan 12:3). The fiery furnace for the wicked stands in dramatic contrast to the bliss of God's eternal kingdom. At last the wicked will be revealed for who and what they are, and the righteous will also be manifested as the true partakers of God's kingdom.

9. Parable of the Hidden Treasure and the Pearl (13:44-46)

44"The kingdom of heaven is like treasure hidden in a field. When a man found it, he hid it again, and then in his joy went and sold all he had and bought that field.

45"Again, the kingdom of heaven is like a merchant looking for fine pearls. 46When he found one of great value, he went away and sold everything he had and bought it.

[31]Hagner, *Matthew* 1:394; so also Davies and Allison, *Matthew*, 2:430; see also Gundry, *Matthew*, p. 275; and Schweizer, *Good News According To Matthew*, p. 311.

These brief parables build on the preceding verse by highlighting the tremendous worth and glory of the kingdom. They are also linked to earlier parables "by the continuing motif of hiddenness and smallness."[32] The two parables can be treated together since they both, by means of different imagery, stress similar themes: (1) the value of discovered objects; (2) a sacrificial investment to possess the object discovered.

13:44. It was not unusual in the ancient world to hide valuables by burying them in the ground. Once the treasure is hidden, its presence is no longer obvious to those who may pass by. But the one who happens to discover the hidden treasure takes great pain to assure that he will be able to obtain the treasure. He not only reburies the treasure, but also with great personal sacrifice he purchases the entire field in order to secure what he has found. There is no need to build an elaborate defense of the man's ethical choices, since the details of the story are not sufficient to argue one way or the other.[33] Nonetheless, the point of the story is not the man's morality, but the joy of his discovery and the extreme measures he took to obtain what he had found. In the same way, those who discover the value and worth of the kingdom will go to great personal sacrifice for their participation.

11:45-46. Jesus reinforces the point with a second parable depicting **a merchant** who discovers and purchases a costly pearl. In the ancient world pearls were highly prized, being even more valuable than gold.[34] Unlike the man in the previous parable who happens across his treasure, the merchant was in search of **fine pearls**, and happens to discover one especially exquisite. His actions are as decisive as the previous man in that he sells everything he owns in order to purchase this one pearl. Once one recognizes the incalculable value of the kingdom, no sacrifice is too great. Both the action of the man in the previous parable and the merchant exhibit a fundamental element of genuine discipleship, i.e., a total commitment to live under the reign of God without reservations.

---

[32]Hagner, *Matthew*, 1:396.

[33]See, e.g., J.D.M. Derrett, "Law in the New Testament: The Treasure in the Field (Mt 13:44)," *ZNW* 54 (1963), 35-41.

[34]See Jeremias, *Parables*, p. 199.

10. Parable of the Dragnet (13:47-50)

[47]"Once again, the kingdom of heaven is like a net that was let down into the lake and caught all kinds of fish. [48]When it was full, the fishermen pulled it up on the shore. Then they sat down and collected the good fish in baskets, but threw the bad away. [49]This is how it will be at the end of the age. The angels will come and separate the wicked from the righteous [50]and throw them into the fiery furnace, where there will be weeping and gnashing of teeth.

13:47-48. The seventh and final parable draws on a familiar sight along the Galilean coastline. Dragnets (σαγήνη, *sagēnē*) were large nets with floats along the top and weights fitted to the bottom. With one side fastened to the shore, a boat would drag the net through the water in a semicircle, thus trapping fish between the shore and the net. Once the maneuver had been completed the net would be drawn to shore, then fishermen would sit on the shore, sorting the day's catch, keeping the good fish and disposing of the bad ones (cf. John 21:6-8).[35]

11:49-50. This familiar scene becomes illustrative of the eschatological judgment of God where the righteous (=**good fish**) are finally separated from the wicked (=**bad fish**). Although the parable has similarities with the parable of the weeds (cf. vv. 24-30; 36-43), it does not focus on the earthly co-existence of the righteous and the wicked, but on the final act of God's end-time separation. The language of a fiery destruction mentioned in verse 42 is repeated verbatim in verse 50. However, there is no corresponding repetition of the bliss of the righteous (cf. v. 43), only the fate of the wicked is depicted. Since the parable is directed to the disciples, its message calls for vigilance and untiring commitment to the will of the Father. Not all that are attracted by the message of the kingdom exhibit genuine discipleship and are thus suitable for participation in God's eternal kingdom.

---

[35]See C.G. Rasmussen, "Net Scene," *ISBE* 3:523-524.

11. Trained in the Kingdom (13:51-52)

[51]"Have you understood all these things?" Jesus asked.

"Yes," they replied.

[52]He said to them, "Therefore every teacher of the law who has been instructed about the kingdom of heaven is like the owner of a house who brings out of his storeroom new treasures as well as old."

13:51. The parabolic discourse concludes with Jesus' question to the disciples, **"Have you understood all these things?"** "All these things" (ταῦτα πάντα, *tauta panta*) most likely refers to the entire discourse (cf. v. 34), and not just the material comprising verses 36-50.[36] As noted earlier, "understanding" is a fundamental component of discipleship in Matthew (cf. 13:23; 15:10; 16:12; 17:13). It is not merely intellectually comprehending, but involves the entire person putting into practice what one has understood. Although the disciples answer in the affirmative that they have understood, in subsequent scenes the depth of their perception will be called into question (cf. 15:15-16; 16:9). Nonetheless, they are distinguished from the crowds as enlightened recipients of Jesus' teachings.

13:52. Jesus responds to their affirmation by underscoring what true understanding necessarily implies. A **teacher** (γραμματεύς [*grammateus*] = "scribe") thoroughly trained or **instructed** (μαθη–τευθεὶς, *mathēteutheis*, lit., "discipled") in the truths concerning the nature of the kingdom is compared to an **owner of a house** who provides for his family from a well-stocked storeroom, materials both old and new (cf. the portrait of a scribe in Sirach 39:1-11).[37] The well trained "Christian scribe" who truly understands is equipped to interpret that which is old (=Old Testament) in light of (*contra* NIV "the new is not added to the old"[38]) the new order and revelation coming to pass in Jesus. Therefore, the Old Testament continues to have relevance for the disciple, but only as it is

---

[36]So O.L. Cope, *Matthew: A Scribe Trained for the Kingdom of Heaven* (Washington, DC: Catholic Biblical Association of America, 1976), p. 25.

[37]For a discussion on "scribes" see D.E. Orton, *The Understanding Scribe: Matthew and the Apocalyptic Ideal* (JSNTSup 25; Sheffield: JSOT, 1989).

[38]Carson, *Matthew*, p. 332.

understood in the light of Jesus' new teachings (cf. 5:17-19). Being trained in the priorities and values of the kingdom provides disciples with a hermeneutical lens through which to read and interpret Scripture. Such training is critical if the disciples are to realize their calling to become "fishers of men."

M. REJECTION AT NAZARETH (13:53-58)

The progressive drama of the story carries the motifs of opposition and misunderstanding to a high point in Jesus' rejection at Nazareth (13:53-58), followed by the execution of John the Baptist (14:1-12). As such, these two incidents bring the narrative section of 11:2–14:12 to a close and constitute the background for the evasive actions characterizing Jesus in the scenes to follow, and the decided shift of focus to his disciples (14:13–16:20).

The episodes involving Jesus' rejection at Nazareth, followed by Herod's response to Jesus' miraculous deeds in terms of his Messianic mission and transcendent status inevitably lead to misunderstanding and rejection. The reader has already encountered several scenes throughout 11:2–14:12 wherein Jesus' miraculous powers and authoritative teachings do not evoke the proper response or a correct identity assessment (cf. 11:2, 20-24; 12:24, 41-42). It is significant that two additional scenes illustrating the blindness of unbelief (13:53–14:12), are followed in the next section (14:13–16:20) by scenes illustrating the insights granted to those who have "eyes to see."

53When Jesus had finished these parables, he moved on from there. 54Coming to his hometown, he began teaching the people in their synagogue, and they were amazed. "Where did this man get this wisdom and these miraculous powers?" they asked. 55"Isn't this the carpenter's son? Isn't his mother's name Mary, and aren't his brothers James, Joseph, Simon and Judas? 56Aren't all his sisters with us? Where then did this man get all these things?" 57And they took offense at him.

But Jesus said to them, "Only in his hometown and in his own house is a prophet without honor."

[58]And he did not do many miracles there because of their lack of faith.

Jesus' rejection in a Nazareth synagogue provides a fitting illustration of people who "hear but do not hear, who have eyes but do not see" (13:13-15). It should be observed that the "failure to understand leads not to indifference but to hostility."[39] Jesus had earlier warned John that the failure to understand his messianic activity in terms of his mission and identity put him in danger of "falling away" (see 11:2-6). Now the failure of his hometown to correctly assess his "wisdom and mighty powers" results in their being "offended by him" (ἐσκανδαλίζοντο, *eskandalizonto*, v. 57). The reference to a prophet's being rejected by his own "household" also connects this scene with 12:46-50. It is significant that the parabolic discourse is bracketed by scenes that relativize both natural and social connections in light of a higher calling.

13:53-56. For the third time the reader is confronted with Matthew's typical phrase marking the end of a major discourse (cf. 7:28; 11:1). As is usual, when Jesus finishes a major speech there is a radical change of locations. On this occasion, Jesus returns to his **hometown** (=Nazareth), and begins teaching in **their synagogue**. Although the people in the synagogue are **amazed** and readily acknowledge his wisdom and miraculous powers, they are "scandalized" by him because the origin of his powers seemed incongruent with his paternity. Twice they raise the question concerning the origin of Jesus' **wisdom** and **miraculous powers**. Their question necessarily allows for only two possibilities: God or Satan (cf. 12:22-30; 21:23-27). The questions regarding Jesus' family relationships are all assumed to be true, therefore their claim to familiarity breeds only suspicion and contempt. Jesus is a mere "hometown boy" with no claim of inherited honor, social status, or familial accomplishments, therefore how can one born to a mere "woodworker" (τέκτονος, *tektonos*[40]) make such claims and exhibit such

[39]Davies and Allison, *Matthew*, 2:453.

[40]Louw and Nida, *Greek-English Lexicon of the New Testament* 1:520; "There is every reason to believe that in biblical times one who was regarded as a τέκτων would be skilled in the use of wood and stone and possibly even metal."

power? Their repudiation is based on a faulty assessment of Jesus' true paternity (cf. 3:17), therefore they found his claims intolerable.

13:57-58. Jesus responds with a proverbial saying acknowledging that the prophetic status of many true prophets have often experienced rejection in their own hometown. The validity of the saying has been verified on many occasions in the experience of Jesus' followers. It is often the case that those who claim to know someone from an early age find it difficult to accept that that same person is spiritually gifted or an insightful teacher. In Nazareth, their rejection and unbelief, with respect to Jesus' person, resulted in few miracles being performed (cf. Mark 6:5). It was not a question of power but a refusal to respond to unbelief with the exercise of the miraculous (cf. 12:38-42; 16:1-4).

MATTHEW 14

N. THE DEATH OF JOHN THE BAPTIST (14:1-12)

The themes of misunderstanding and rejection dominating 11:2–14:12 now reach their climactic closure with Herod's execution of John the Baptist (14:1-12).[1] The reader knows from 11:2 that John is in prison (cf. 4:12), but now learns that John is dead (v. 2), having been put to death by Herod (vv. 3-12). Just as John's initial imprisonment prompted Jesus to make a decisive move (4:12), so upon hearing of Herod's assessment of John (v. 2), Jesus "withdraws" (v. 13), and his ministry takes on a different emphasis (14:13–16:20). Matthew's flashback narration of John's death is ironically juxtaposed with 11:2-6 where John in Herod's prison finds Jesus' activities difficult to square with his own messianic expectations. Now, after John's brutal execution, Herod speculates that Jesus' exhibition of miraculous powers may in fact be proof of John's resurrection (cf. 16:14). While on the one hand, the faulty assessment of Jesus' mighty words by Herod links this episode with previous misconceptions found throughout 11:2–14:12 (cf. 11:3-6, 20-24; 12:12-24; 13:53-58), the flashback detailing John's death provides an ominous foreshadowing of what is in store for Jesus. In this way Matthew concludes 11:2–14:12 by underscoring the menacing threat of unbelief already pictured in preceding scenes, and thereby prepares the reader for subsequent scenes leading to Jesus' passion.

---

[1]For structural proposals of chs. 14-17 see J. Murphy O'Connor, "The Structure of Matthew XIV-XVII," *Revue Biblique* 75 (July 1975), 360-384. I do not find his proposal that 13:53-58 and 14:1-12 constitute an introduction to the section comprising chapters 14-17 convincing. See also D.J. Verseput, "The Faith of the Reader and the Narrative of Matthew 13:53-16:20," *JSNT* 46 (1992), 3-24.

[1]At that time Herod the tetrarch heard the reports about Jesus, [2]and he said to his attendants, "This is John the Baptist; he has risen from the dead! That is why miraculous powers are at work in him."

[3]Now Herod had arrested John and bound him and put him in prison because of Herodias, his brother Philip's wife, [4]for John had been saying to him: "It is not lawful for you to have her." [5]Herod wanted to kill John, but he was afraid of the people, because they considered him a prophet.

[6]On Herod's birthday the daughter of Herodias danced for them and pleased Herod so much [7]that he promised with an oath to give her whatever she asked. [8]Prompted by her mother, she said, "Give me here on a platter the head of John the Baptist." [9]The king was distressed, but because of his oaths and his dinner guests, he ordered that her request be granted [10]and had John beheaded in the prison. [11]His head was brought in on a platter and given to the girl, who carried it to her mother. [12]John's disciples came and took his body and buried it. Then they went and told Jesus.

14:1-2. Although the transitional phrase **At that time** (cf. 11:25; 12:1) lacks chronological precision, it does link this scene with the previous episode in Nazareth (13:53-58). Like the people in Nazareth, Herod[2] seeks an explanation for the **reports** of mighty powers being exhibited in Jesus (cf. 13:54). However, unlike the people in the synagogue who are offended by Jesus' seeming lack

---

[2]Herod Antipas was the son of Herod the Great and his second wife Malthace, the Samaritan mother of Archelaus also. With the death of Herod the Great (4 B.C.) his domain was divided among his three sons, Archelaus, Philip, and Antipas. Both Antipas and Archelaus attempted to eliminate the other as an heir to Herod's will. After lengthy efforts to establish his right to be designated king, Antipas lost his claim and was given the title "tetrarch," while his brother Archelaus was made an ethnarch with the promise that he would be made king if he served his position well. Herod Antipas was only called "king" out of "courtesy or local custom," not because he had any claim to the royal title. Nevertheless he was an able ruler who reigned over Galilee and Perea from 4 B.C. to A.D. 39 (For additional details see Harold W. Hoehner, *Herod Antipas: A Contemporary of Jesus Christ* [Grand Rapids: Zondervan, 1972]).

of paternal credentials, Herod mistakenly identifies Jesus as John the Baptist risen from the dead (cf. 16:14). The basis of this superstitious conclusion seems to stem from his recognition of John's prophetic status and the guilt he felt for ordering his execution.

14:3-5. Although early in his story Matthew notes in passing that "John had been put into prison" (4:12), he now provides explanatory background detailing the arrest and subsequent events leading to John's execution (cf. the account of Josephus, *Ant.* 18:116-119). Herod arrested John and had him bound in prison because John publicly denounced Herod's marriage to his brother Philip's wife. The identification of Philip has posed some problems since Josephus indicates that Philip the tetrarch (cf. Luke 3:1) was married not to Herodias but to her daughter Salome (*Ant.* 180.5.4.136). The problem has been resolved by claiming that the brother mentioned in Matthew is not Philip the tetrarch, but rather Herod Philip, the son of Herod the Great and Mariamne II (not Malthace, the mother of Herod Antipas), and therefore the half brother of Antipas.[3] Whatever the solution, John was critical of the marriage between Herod and Herodias because it violated restrictions reflected in Leviticus 18:16: "Do not have sexual relations with your brother's wife; that would dishonor your brother." Given John's persistent denunciation (ἔλεγεν, *elegen*, "he kept saying") of this arrangement, and the political overtones accompanying his public condemnation, Herod could not tolerate his inflammatory opposition so he had him arrested. Matthew reports (cf. Mark 6:19-20) that Herod wanted to permanently silence John by having him killed, but he knew that since the people regarded John to be a prophet such actions would have serious political consequences.

14:6-8. The scene now changes to a great banquet in honor of Herod's birthday. Part of the celebration included a dance performed by the **daughter of Herodias** (identified by Josephus as Salome, *Ant* 18.5.4, 136), that so pleased Herod that he recklessly made a vow to **give her whatever she asked**. Since Salome was a young adolescent (estimates run from 12 to 14 years old), she consulted her mother, who immediately seized on the opportunity to be rid of John. Hence the girl followed her mother's "prompting,"

---

[3]See discussion in Hoehner, *Herod*, pp. 131-136.

and requested that John's head be given her on a platter. Such a gruesome request indicates the extent that John had aroused the indignation of the royal court.

14:9-12. Although Herod was greatly **distressed** with such a request, he felt compelled both by his **oaths** and his unwillingness to lose face before his **dinner guests** to grant her request. He would rather see John put to death than to admit before his guests that he had been unduly rash, and must rescind his promise. Later we will see another reluctant political leader bow before pressure brought upon him to have an innocent man put to death (cf. 27:11-26). Although Herodias was the instigator of the horrendous crime, Herod gives the orders that the execution be carried out. While the head of John is carried to Herodias as proof of John's death, John's disciples retrieve his body for burial. The Baptist's close ties with Jesus is noted as John's disciples immediately after the burial rush to inform Jesus of his death. Thus this brief episode involving John is not only bracketed by language highlighting the closeness of Jesus to John (cf. vv. 1-2; 12), the details of John's arrest and execution also foreshadow the fate of Jesus.[4]

IV. EDUCATING THE DISCIPLES: IDENTITY AND MISSION (14:13–16:20)

Subsequent episodes comprising 14:13–16:20 exhibit a clear shift in the major focus of Jesus' active ministry. Although Jesus continues his therapeutic activity among the masses (14:14, 34-36; 15:29-31), this section is also marked by three nontherapeutic miracles worked primarily for the disciples to reveal and clarify aspects of his identity (14:22-33), as well as the contours of his mission (14:14-21; 15:32-39).[5] While Jesus' opponents appear in two brief episodes (15:1-9; 16:1-4), the incidents are followed immediately by teaching directed to the disciples, warning them not to be deluded by "blind guides" (15:14), and to be on their guard "against the

[4]For a detailed list of parallels see Davies and Allison, *Matthew* 2:476.

[5]As noted by Gerhardsson, *Mighty Acts*, p. 54, the nontherapeutic miracles are always worked for the disciples ". . . as revelations, clarifying the mysteries of the Reign for the disciples."

teaching of the Pharisees and Sadducees" (16:5-12). Matthew underscores Jesus' effort to distance himself from his opponents by the words "Jesus withdrew" (ἀνεχώρησεν, *anechōrēsen*, 14:13; 15:21), and the culminating "he left them (καταλιπών, *katalipōn*) and went away" (16:4).[6] Within this oscillation of events significant evaluative assessments of Jesus' person are enunciated; first by the disciples (14:33, "truly you are the Son of God"), then by a Gentile woman (15:22ff., "Lord, Son of David"). The section closes with Peter's confessional appraisal, wherein both Jesus' messiahship and divine Sonship are brought together by divine disclosure: "You are the Christ; the Son of the living God" (16:16).

It is clear from an overview of episodes comprising 14:13–16:20 that the welfare of the people was a major concern of Jesus. Of the five miracle accounts narrated, four are concerned with large numbers: two feeding stories (14:13-21; 15:32-39), and two healing summaries (14:34-36; 15:29-31). These episodes are punctuated by explicit references to Jesus' compassionate spirit (14:14; 15:32), reminding the reader of Matthew's earlier disclosure of Jesus' inward reaction to the condition of the crowds (9:36). Jesus' actions give concrete expression to his compassionate regard for the people. His relationship with the crowds also functions to impress the disciples with their responsibility to be an extension of his care for the people. Furthermore, the movement from Jewish to predominantly Gentile territory illustrates that ultimately (cf. 28:18-20) such compassion is to have no ethnic limitations.

A. FEEDING OF THE FIVE THOUSAND (14:13-21)

13When Jesus heard what had happened, he withdrew by boat privately to a solitary place. Hearing of this, the crowds followed him on foot from the towns. 14When Jesus landed and saw a large crowd, he had compassion on them and healed their sick.

15As evening approached, the disciples came to him and said, "This is a remote place, and it's already getting late. Send the

---

[6]J. Murphy-O'Conner, "Structure of Matthew," p. 372, observes that the departure of 16:4 has a more absolute quality to it, being a turning away in judgment.

crowds away, so they can go to the villages and buy themselves some food."

[16]Jesus replied, "They do not need to go away. You give them something to eat."

[17]"We have here only five loaves of bread and two fish," they answered.

[18]"Bring them here to me," he said. [19]And he directed the people to sit down on the grass. Taking the five loaves and the two fish and looking up to heaven, he gave thanks and broke the loaves. Then he gave them to the disciples, and the disciples gave them to the people. [20]They all ate and were satisfied, and the disciples picked up twelve basketfuls of broken pieces that were left over. [21]The number of those who ate was about five thousand men, besides women and children.

Given the parenthetical nature of verses 3-12 it appears that verse 13 connects most naturally with verse 2, and thus Jesus' withdrawal is primarily precipitated by Herod's assessment of his ministry.[7] Earlier when Jesus heard of the imprisonment of John he *withdrew* into Galilee to begin his public ministry (4:12), now Herod's identification of Jesus as the embodiment of the murdered prophet (vv. 1-2) prompts his withdrawal again, this time out of public view (v. 13). Certainly both the events surrounding John's death and Herod's paranoid assessment contributed to Jesus' hasty retreat so as to avoid a premature confrontation with political authorities. Jesus must also seek privacy in order to focus his attention upon his disciples to prepare them for a mission patterned after his own.

14:13-14. The withdrawal **by boat** to a **solitary place** takes Jesus outside the boundaries of Antipas' control. He nevertheless could not escape the crowds, who observed his movement from the shoreline, and "on foot" rushed to the place where he would come ashore. The result was that instead of the solitude he sought he was met by a large crowd who had anticipated his arrival. However, Jesus does not view them as an annoying inconvenience, but

---

[7]See Carson, *Matthew*, p. 337; Blomberg, *Matthew*, p. 231; Morris, *Matthew*, p. 376; *Contra* Hagner, *Matthew*, 2:417.

instead is moved by **compassion** (ἐσπλαγχνίσθη, *esplangchnisthē*, cf. 9:36; 15:32). Seldom is the reader provided an inside glimpse of Jesus' emotional state, detailing the motivating factor for his actions. In this instance, Jesus heals their sick because he is touched by the plight of the people, as well as their persistent efforts to seek out his presence. If the disciples are going to understand Jesus' person and mission, and embark on their own ministry of compassion they must learn to see the "crowds" through the eyes of Jesus, and take personal responsibility for their needs.

14:15. As the day draws to a close, Matthew records a significant exchange between Jesus and his disciples which will set the stage for a truly remarkable event (vv. 15-18). On one level, the disciples are responsive to the plight of the crowd, suggesting that due to the late hour and the remoteness of their location, the welfare of the crowd would be best served by dismissing them so as to allow them to secure provisions in the neighboring towns. That certainly sounds like a reasonable request and is reflective of a certain level of concern for the well-being of the people.

14:16-17. Nevertheless, Jesus' response to their suggestion insists that there is no need to dismiss the crowd, but rather they should personally take action to relieve the situation. Jesus' reply puts the burden of responsibility squarely on the shoulders of the disciples.[8] By highlighting their meager resources (**five loaves of bread and two fish**), the disciples hope to demonstrate the absurdity of their being able to provide sufficient provisions for such a large crowd. While their response reflects an accurate assessment of their limitations, they had failed to perceive that Jesus' commands are always accompanied by sufficient resources and empowerment to accomplish that which he commands. The disciples must learn that he who calls them for service will also equip them for the task at hand.

14:18-19. Jesus then takes charge and demonstrates what God can accomplish with even limited human resources (vv. 17-21).

---

[8]Robert Fowler, *Loaves and Fishes: The Function of the Feeding Stories in the Gospel of Mark* (SBLDS 54; Chico, CA: Scholars, 1981), p. 82, suggests that "Jesus tries to get the disciples to assume responsibility for the care of the 'sheep,' but they are offended at what they understand to be a demand calculated to empty their wallets."

Jesus simply takes the provisions available and, in an astonishing move, prepares the crowd for a great banquet (ἀνακλιθῆναι, *anaklithēnai*, lit., "to recline," the normal posture at a banquet). Although the giving of thanks followed by the breaking of the loaves and the distribution of the food is quite typical of a Jewish meal, it is hard not to see some allusion or foreshadowing of the Last Supper (26:26-28). However, the distribution of the bread by means of the disciples is intended to remind them of their vital intermediary role in bringing heaven's blessings to bear on the human predicament. They must learn from this event to be true shepherds, who minister to the flock by relying on divine resources to supply whatever is needed to "feed" the people of God.

14:20. While the actual miracle of multiplying the loaves and fish is not described, the effect on satisfied consumers is duly noted: **they all ate and were satisfied**. The abundant provisions are reminiscent of God's care of his people in the wilderness when he provided manna in response to their physical needs (cf. Exod 16; Ps 78:18-30; 81:17; 105:40).[9] While some dispute that the "twelve baskets" of leftovers has any symbolic value,[10] it does appear from 16:9-11 that Jesus intended the disciples to see some significance in the gathered baskets (cf. 19:28). It does not seem far-fetched to understand the "twelve baskets" to symbolize the twelve tribes of Israel, and thus this feeding account is performed on behalf of a Jewish audience, perhaps to foreshadow the end time messianic banquet. Of course, it is the disciples who are blessed with eyes to see its significance (cf. 16:19).

14:21. The scene concludes not with a reference to the response of the "crowd," since they are probably unaware that anything miraculous had taken place. Matthew is concerned to provide an approximation of the number that were miraculously fed. Since the figure 5000 only included the males, the inclusion of women and children could have easily made the crowd three times the number mentioned. Whatever the enormity of the crowd it posed no obstacle to Jesus' awesome power.

---

[9]For various proposals concerning possible thematic interests see Davies and Allison, *Matthew*, 2:180-485.

[10]E.g., France, *Matthew*, p. 238.

B. WALKING ON THE WATER (14:22-33)

In an earlier episode involving the disciples in a boat, the scene closes with the disciples posing the decisive question concerning the identity of the one who exhibited such authoritative powers: "What kind of man is this? Even the winds and waves obey him!" (8:27). A second scene involving the disciples in a boat (14:22-33) is linked to the first episode by various verbal and thematic similarities. In both scenes the disciples are characterized as "fearful" (8:26/14:26), and the typical Matthean label of "little faith" (8:26/14:31) also appears in both episodes. Just as the group cried out, "Lord save us" (8:25), so Peter in the second scene petitions Jesus with the identical terminology (14:30). While in the first episode the disciples raise the identity question, wondering "what kind of man is this?" in the second boat scene they answer their own question by confessing him to be the "Son of God" (14:33). These verbal and thematic similarities engage the reader's memory and encourage comparisons between the two episodes. The reader will perceive definite progress in the disciples' perception concerning Jesus' person. Their confession marks the first time in the story that any of the human characters in the story penetrate the mystery of Jesus' identity (cf. 8:29).

This episode is closely linked to the preceding story of the miraculous feeding (cf. Mark 6:45ff.; John 6:16ff.) by an unbroken narrative sequence where one event naturally follows the other. As in the miraculous feedings where the disciples are given insight and are privileged to experience dimensions of Jesus' authority and power unknown to the crowds, so in Jesus' appearance on the water it is the disciples who are led into a deeper understanding of Jesus' person. In view of their eventual mission Jesus grants them revelatory insight into his identity and mission. Their confession in 14:33 is anticipatory of another scene where Peter, representing the disciples, confesses Jesus to be Israel's long-awaited Messiah who possesses a unique relationship to God (16:16).

22Immediately Jesus made the disciples get into the boat and go on ahead of him to the other side, while he dismissed the crowd. 23After he had dismissed them, he went up on a mountainside by himself to pray. When evening came, he was there alone, 24but the boat was already a considerable distance[a] from land,

buffeted by the waves because the wind was against it.

[25]During the fourth watch of the night Jesus went out to them, walking on the lake. [26]When the disciples saw him walking on the lake, they were terrified. "It's a ghost," they said, and cried out in fear.

[27]But Jesus immediately said to them: "Take courage! It is I. Don't be afraid."

[28]"Lord, if it's you," Peter replied, "tell me to come to you on the water."

[29]"Come," he said.

Then Peter got down out of the boat, walked on the water and came toward Jesus. [30]But when he saw the wind, he was afraid and, beginning to sink, cried out, "Lord, save me!"

[31]Immediately Jesus reached out his hand and caught him. "You of little faith," he said, "why did you doubt?"

[32]And when they climbed into the boat, the wind died down. [33]Then those who were in the boat worshiped him, saying, "Truly you are the Son of God."

[a]*24* **Greek** ***many stadia***

14:22. After the miracles of the feeding, Jesus compels (ἀναγκάζω, *anankazō*, the term signifies strong action, either by force or persuasion) his disciples to depart to the other side of the lake. Although Matthew does not inform the reader why Jesus is insistent that his disciples leave the area, it has been suggested, based on John 6:15, that the feeding scene had turned into a political rally, with revolutionary overtones, and Jesus knew that his disciples were susceptible to such suggestions. With the disciples out of the way, Jesus could then focus his attention on disbursing the crowd, thus defusing a potentially dangerous situation.

14:23. Jesus also sought the dismissal of the crowd so he could seek a place of solitude for prayer. The day's events, as well as the ominous foreshadowing suggested by John's death, sent Jesus to find solace in communion with his Father. Heil also observes that "the uniquely divine action of walking on the sea proceeds from Jesus' intimate union with his Father."[11] Thus God empowers his

---

[11]See J.P. Heil, *Jesus Walking on the Sea* (Rome: Biblical Institute Press, 1981), pp. 55-57.

Son to overcome the chaotic forces that threaten his disciples, and thereby to manifest Yahweh's sovereignty over the sea.

14:24. While Jesus prayed, the disciples struggled on the lake **a considerable distance from land** (σταδίους πολλοὺς [*stadious pollous*]; one stadium equaled approximately 600 feet; cf. John 6:19, the disciples were "three to three and a half miles" offshore). Weather conditions were such that the waves "harassed" (βασανιζόμένον, *basanizomenon*) the boat, and strong head winds prohibited much progress. They had evidently battled the conditions most of the night, and even these seasoned fishermen would have cause for some concern.

14:25-27. During the predawn hours between 3:00 and 6:00 A.M. (=**fourth watch**), Jesus comes walking on the stormy seas, and terrifies the disciples by his presence. They were not at all prepared for such a bewildering sight, and thus respond with fear and the conclusion that they are seeing an apparition. Given the conditions of the sea, and the "popular belief that the sea was the home of evil spirits,"[12] it is possible that the disciples thought their lives were in mortal danger. Jesus must **immediately** identify himself in order to calm their fear. The verb translated **take courage** (θαρσεῖτε, *tharseite*; cf. 9:2, 22) calls for their fear to be replaced with confidence and joyous relief. Jesus identifies himself with the words "it is I" (ἐγω εἰμὶ, *egō eimi*), thus assuring them of imminent divine assistance to meet their crisis. While the full force of the words *egō eimi* ("I am") may have been lost on the disciples, the reader finds Jesus' reassuring words as an allusion to Yahweh's identification of himself in Exodus 3:14: "I am who I am." Such an allusion is not surprising since only God possesses dominion over the sea and rescues his people from its chaotic destructive powers (see Job 9:8; 38:16; Ps 77:19; Isa 43:16; Hab 3:15). Since God has drawn near in the person of Jesus, fear must give way to faith and worship.

14:28-31. Only in Matthew does Peter take center stage[13] by exhibiting a willingness to emulate his Lord by walking on the sea. The words **Lord, if it is you** do not express doubt but a reality assumed to be true (first class condition), hence his willingness, if

[12]Hagner, *Matthew*, 2:423.

[13]This is the first of several key scenes where Peter occupies a central role (cf. 15:5; 16:17-19; 17:1-9, 24-27; 18:21).

the Lord so commands, to join Jesus on the sea. Jesus responds with a one word command **come**, thus challenging him to make good on his word. Once again Jesus' command makes possible the impossible. Peter initially becomes a model of great faith with his willingness to get out of the boat and emulate his Lord by also walking on the water. Peter's problems arose when his focus upon Jesus was replaced with a fear of the driving wind. The result was a failure to participate in Jesus' power, thus he begins to sink in the waves. To Peter's credit he responds to his crisis with the petition **Lord, save me** (cf. 8:25). The most dire of circumstances can only be met with the Lord's saving hand. Peter's desperate cry is immediately (εὐθὺς, *euthus*) responded to by Jesus who delivers him from his peril. However, Jesus challenges his faltering faith (ὀλιγόπιστε, *oligopiste*, cf. 6:30; 8:26; 16:8; 17:20) with the question, **why did you doubt?** The term translated "doubt" (ἐδίστασας, *edistasas*) pinpoints Peter's problem: he lost his single-minded focus on Jesus. Nevertheless, the experience of Peter is prototypical of discipleship, and Peter's wavering faith is met by Jesus' willingness to rescue him, even in the darkest of crisis (cf. Ps 18:16-17).

14:32-33. When Jesus and Peter climb into the boat, two significant events occur. First, the storm suddenly and miraculously ceases; not as earlier with a command of Jesus (8:26), but evidently his mere presence in the boat brought calm to the raging storms (cf. Job 26:11-12; Ps 65:7; 89:9-10; 107:29). Second, the disciples' fear is replaced by "worship" (προσεκύνησαν, *prosekynēsan*, cf. 2:2, 8, 11; 8:2; 9:18; 15:25; 28:9, 17), and the confession, **Truly you are the Son of God**. As noted earlier, their confession shows definite progress in the disciples' understanding of Jesus' person (cf. 8:27). However, the level of perception associated with the confession must be tempered by the fact that it is annunciated as a spontaneous response to the exhibition of Jesus' miraculous powers. Although the post-resurrection church would understand much more by the titular designation *Son of God*, the confession of the disciples remains inadequate until Sonship is understood in terms of Jesus' redemptive mission. His identity as God's Son is best understood not by his mighty acts of power, but in his singular devotion to a mission of suffering and sacrifice in compliance to his Father's will. Later Jesus will begin to shape their understanding of

Sonship by explicitly setting before his disciples the fate awaiting him in Jerusalem (cf. 16:21; 17:22-23; 20:17-19). At least at this point in the story the disciples do understand that Jesus is no ordinary man, and is deserving of their adoration.

C. SUMMARY: HEALINGS AT GENNESARET (14:34-36)

[34]When they had crossed over, they landed at Gennesaret. [35]And when the men of that place recognized Jesus, they sent word to all the surrounding country. People brought all their sick to him [36]and begged him to let the sick just touch the edge of his cloak, and all who touched him were healed.

Matthew's repetitive use of summaries (cf. 4:23-25; 8:16; 9:35; 11:1; 12:15; 14:13-14; 14:34-35; 15:29-31) function to create the general atmosphere and the background against which specific incidents are to be viewed. In the central portion of Matthew's story the summaries repeatedly emphasize the itinerant nature of Jesus' ministry, his therapeutic involvement with the people, and presence of large crowds attracted by his activity (cf. 15:29-31). By repeatedly telescoping Jesus' movement, activity, and influence by means of summary statements, Matthew helps the reader to see the extent and magnitude of Jesus' very active ministry.

14:34-35. Jesus and his disciples cross the sea, landing on the northwest shore in the area of the fertile plains of **Gennesaret.**[14] The region is just a few miles south of Capernaum, and therefore heavily populated with those who knew of Jesus' extraordinary deeds. It is therefore not surprising that his arrival was met with recognition and immediate efforts to take advantage of his presence. The word goes out to the surrounding region, and before long the place turns into a clinic full of sick people, with Jesus as the attending physician.

---

[14]It is not entirely clear whether the reference is to the city overlooking the plain, or to the plain which drew its name from the city. For background see D.R. Edwards, "Gennesaret," *ABD*, 2:963.

14:36. In desperation the people sought merely to **touch the edge of his cloak** (cf. 9:21), firmly believing in Jesus' healing powers. Matthew is emphatic that everyone who touched him were healed (διεσώθησαν, *diesōthēsan*; the term is stronger than σῴζω [*sōzō*] having "the added implication of having rescued such persons from a state of illness" [Louw and Nida, *Greek-English Lexicon of the New Testament*, p. 269]). Such healings demonstrate Jesus' concern to bring restoration and wholeness to his people by overcoming all afflictions and ritually contaminating defects (cf. Lev 21:18-23) by his cleansing power. It is no accident that the next scene (15:1-20) is concerned with the issue of "clean and uncleanness."

MATTHEW 15

D. JESUS AND THE TEACHINGS OF THE PHARISEES (15:1-20)

As noted earlier, the section comprising 14:13–16:20 has two conflict scenes which portray Jesus' interaction with the Jewish leaders (15:1-9; 16:1-4), which lead to specific instructions and warnings to the disciples not to be swayed by their teachings (15:10-20; 16:5-12). It is critical that the disciples distance themselves from the destructive influence of Pharisaic teaching. Their "traditions" have resulted in a serious distortion of God's will, especially as it relates to holiness and true defilement. In spite of Jesus' efforts to explain the dangers of following the teachings of the Pharisees the disciples continue to exhibit a lack of understanding (v. 16, ἀσύνε-τοι, *asynetoi*). Jesus then proceeds into Gentile territory (v. 21), and two significant events (the Canaanite woman 15:21-28, and the feeding of the four thousand 15:29-39), provide concrete illustrations that endorsement of Pharisaic notions of defilement would stand in opposition to the advancing reign of God. When an "unclean" Canaanite woman petitions Jesus on behalf of her daughter who is possessed by an "unclean" spirit, he does not let legalistic niceties dictate what he should or should not do. It is her "great faith" that determines his course of action (v. 28). When he is surrounded by "unclean" Gentiles who bring their sick to him, and are in desperate need, rather than attempt to escape their contaminating touch, Jesus is moved by compassion to heal and feed the hungry (15:29-39). Obviously, if the disciples are persuaded by Pharisaic teaching, they too would find Jesus' activity offensive, and would be unwilling to emulate his unrestrictive ministry of compassion.

After a second brief controversy scene (16:1-4), Jesus explicitly warns his disciples to "be on guard against the yeast of the

Pharisees and Sadducees" (16:6-12). Only after some discussion do the disciples finally "understand" (v. 12) what their attitude should be toward the teachings of Israel's religious leadership (16:12). Thus, the scenes comprising 15:1–16:12 are dominated by the central theme of "Jesus' and the disciples' relationship with the Pharisees and their teaching."[1] There is a radical difference between how Jesus discerns and does the will of God and how Pharisaic tradition interprets and performs God's will. If the disciples are to be "trained in the kingdom" (13:52) they must discern the difference.

1Then some Pharisees and teachers of the law came to Jesus from Jerusalem and asked, 2"Why do your disciples break the tradition of the elders? They don't wash their hands before they eat!"

3Jesus replied, "And why do you break the command of God for the sake of your tradition? 4For God said, 'Honor your father and mother'[a] and 'Anyone who curses his father or mother must be put to death.'[b] 5But you say that if a man says to his father or mother, 'Whatever help you might otherwise have received from me is a gift devoted to God,' 6he is not to 'honor his father[c]' with it. Thus you nullify the word of God for the sake of your tradition. 7You hypocrites! Isaiah was right when he prophesied about you:

8"'These people honor me with their lips,
but their hearts are far from me.
9They worship me in vain;
their teachings are but rules taught by men.'[d]"

10Jesus called the crowd to him and said, "Listen and understand. 11What goes into a man's mouth does not make him 'unclean,' but what comes out of his mouth, that is what makes him 'unclean.'"

12Then the disciples came to him and asked, "Do you know that the Pharisees were offended when they heard this?"

13He replied, "Every plant that my heavenly Father has not planted will be pulled up by the roots. 14Leave them; they are

[1]Patte, *Matthew*, p. 215.

blind guides.[e] If a blind man leads a blind man, both will fall into a pit."

[15]Peter said, "Explain the parable to us."

[16]"Are you still so dull?" Jesus asked them. [17]"Don't you see that whatever enters the mouth goes into the stomach and then out of the body? [18]But the things that come out of the mouth come from the heart, and these make a man 'unclean.' [19]For out of the heart come evil thoughts, murder, adultery, sexual immorality, theft, false testimony, slander. [20]These are what make a man 'unclean'; but eating with unwashed hands does not make him 'unclean.'"

[a]*4* Exodus 20:12; Deut. 5:16 [b]*4* Exodus 21:17; Lev. 20:9 [c]*6* Some manuscripts *father or his mother* [d]*9* Isaiah 29:13 [e]*14* Some manuscripts *guides of the blind*

Our text evinces a clear threefold structural outline based on three distinct scenes: Jesus with the Pharisees and teachers of the law (vv. 1-9); Jesus and the crowd (vv. 10-11); Jesus and his disciples (vv. 12-20). The issue of how one interprets God's will with respect to ritual purity/uncleanness dominates the entire section (cf. vv. 2, 20).[2]

15:1-2. It appears that the **Pharisees and teachers of the law** who come to Jesus are on an official fact-finding mission to determine Jesus' stance on critical matters central to Israel's identity. Of fundamental concern was the failure of Jesus' disciples to be observant of the **tradition** (παράδοσις, *paradosis*)[3] **of the elders** with regard to the ceremonial washing they felt mandatory before every meal (cf. Mark 7:3-4). Although there is no OT commandment demanding ceremonial handwashing before everyday meals, scribal tradition reasoned that since all Israel was to be a "kingdom of priests" (Exod 19:6), every Jew should scrupulously observe priestly regulations regarding ceremonial defilement and ritual impurity.

---

[2]See the observations by Davies and Allison, *Matthew*, 2:516.

[3]The term is a technical expression referring to the handing down of oral tradition. Pharisaic tradition held to the belief that "Moses received the Law from Sinai and committed it to Joshua, and Joshua to the elders, and the elders to the Prophets; and the Prophets committed it to the men of the Great Synagogue. They said three things: Be deliberate in judgment, raise up many disciples, and make a fence around the Law" (m. Aboth 1:1).

The cleansing of Aaron and his sons before entering the "Tent of Meeting" (Exod 30:17-21) establishes a precedent for all Israel observing every meal as if it were a sacred priestly act, thus demanding a state of ritual purity. Since according to Leviticus 15:11 rinsing hands with water prevents ritual contamination from a bodily discharge, so ceremonial handwashings are thought to remove all ritual uncleanness and enable one to eat ordinary meals in a state of ritual purity. While it is difficult to determine how successful the Pharisees were in convincing the general populace to adopt their practice, Pharisaic leaders were extremely zealous "to spread their influence and ideas over all Israel"[4] (cf. 23:15).

15:3. Rather than directly defend the actions of the disciples, Jesus' response intends to undercut the fundamental assumption upon which their charge is founded, i.e., violation of their oral tradition is tantamount to breaking God's written law. Jesus contends that their elevation of human tradition over Scriptural authority has resulted in views that undermine the written law of God and lead to practices in direct violation of God's commandments. Ironically, a casuistic tradition intended to assist people in the rigorous observance of the law (see m. Abot 3:14) had become the prime means (δία, *dia*) whereby the force of God's laws were blunted and blatant transgressions were justified through legal loopholes.

15:4. Jesus then offers a concrete example of how scribal tradition has led to the violation of God's commandments (vv. 4-6). First, Jesus distinguishes the divine origin of the written commandment (**God said**) from scribal tradition (cf. "you say," v. 5). The specific commandments cited come from Exod 20:12/Deut 5:16 (LXX). Both passages stress the importance of caring for one's parents and showing them proper respect. Certainly, financial support and providing physical necessities are inherent in the command to **honor** (τίμα, *tima*, cf. 1 Tim 5:3) one's parents. To emphasize the seriousness of the commandment, Jesus also cites Exodus 21:17 (cf. Lev 20:9; Deut 27:6) which emphasizes that "cursing" (καταλογῶν, *katalogōn*, lit., "to speak evil of ") one's parents

[4]S. Westerhold, *Jesus and Scribal Authority* (ConNT 10; Lund, Sweden: C.W.K. Gleerup, 1978), p. 72.

was a capital offense. Withholding of financial support due one's parents amounted to a dishonoring of them, and thus was deserving of severe punishment.

15:5-6. Pharisaic tradition had in effect developed a practice that not only violated the spirit of the fifth commandment but actually contravened the letter of the written code. Assistance rightfully due one's parents could be avoided if all one's financial resources and possessions were declared sacred and pledged to the support of the temple upon one's death.[5] Once such a "vow" had been made, these resources could not be used by anyone else, although they could be used for one's personal benefit while still living. Based on the binding force of vows (cf. Num 30:2-3; Deut 23:21-23), Pharisaic tradition argued that regardless of the plight of one's parents, or the circumstances in which a vow was made, a Corban vow could not be revoked.[6] Thus, while the tradition about vows was scrupulously observed, the explicit commandment of God was treated as having no binding authority (ἀκυρόω, *akyroō*). Of course such a flagrant disregard for God's law stands in dramatic contrast with Jesus' resolve to fulfill God's will as expressed in Scripture.

15:7-9. Jesus culminates his counter accusation against the Pharisees by citing Scripture to illustrate their hypocritical conduct. The inconsistency between their claims to please God and their maneuvering to avoid the force of God's will is reminiscent of the generation that Isaiah opposed (see Isa 20:13ff., LXX). They are **hypocrites** because their external claims are a mere pretense concealing a heart bent on doing its own will. Isaiah's description of his contemporaries parallels the superficial externalism of those who oppose Jesus and his disciples. Although they say the right things and profess their devotion, their hearts remain far from God. Even though they continue to worship, it has become nothing more than a sham, because they have replaced God's will with human rules and regulations. How can one purport to genuinely worship God when mere human teachings are given precedence over the

[5]The technical term for the practice is Corban (κόρβαν, cf. Mark 7:11), meaning "gift or offering," (see m. Ned. 1:2-4; 9:7).

[6]Later rabbinic discussions do indicate a willingness not to enforce a rash vow (see m. Ned. 9:1; 4:7-8).

expressed will of God? Jesus' pronouncement makes it clear that mere sentiment and sincerity counts for nothing; if worship is not grounded in sound teaching it will ultimately be in vain.[7] Jesus' opposition to a religion based on barren legalism and human tradition is brought to a climax in chapter 23.

15:10-11. Jesus now turns from his opponents to address the crowd in terms that completely undermine Pharisaic notions of defilement. The absolute importance of what he is about to say is prefaced by the exhortation to **listen and understand** (cf. 13:13-15, 23). Too often Jesus' words are met with superficial conclusions, lacking little reflective thought or insight. However, Jesus' words in verse 11 must be given careful thought since the implications seem to challenge basic Jewish sensitivities about ceremonial purification and the rules of defilement. Does Jesus' affirmation in verse 11 intend to dispense with all ritual washings and dietary restrictions so fundamental to the Jewish way of life? Although Mark highlights the radical implications of Jesus' words by emphatically telling his readers that "in saying this, Jesus declared all foods clean" (Mark 7:19), Matthew's account lacks this emphatic assertion and is content to emphasize the nature of true defilement without emphatically setting aside all laws concerning purity and defilement. Certainly the implications of Jesus' words do undermine the importance that Pharisaic Judaism placed upon defilement by physical contact or food intake. However, it does not appear that these implications were fully understood and practically embraced until after the events recorded in Acts 10[8] (cf. Rom 14:14, 20). Jesus' words are therefore intended to highlight that genuine defilement, the kind that causes true alienation from God, stems from a corruptible heart, not the mere neglect of external washings. Thus, Jesus is not extolling inward piety at the expense of all external forms (cf. 9:13; 12:7; 23:23-24).

15:12. In contrast to the crowd who are exhorted to listen and understand, the disciples report that the Pharisees were **offended**

---

[7]See the helpful discussion on "worship" in Matthew by M.A. Powell, *God With Us: A Pastoral Theology of Matthew's Gospel* (Minneapolis: Fortress Press, 1995), esp. pp. 59-61.

[8]As noted by Blomberg, *Matthew*, p. 229.

(ἐσκανδαλίσθησαν, *eskandalisthēsan*) by the teaching (τόν λογόν, *ton logon*, lit., by hearing "the word") of Jesus.[9] The disciples' statement reflects their personal concern that Jesus not antagonize Israel's religious leaders. Evidently, they still entertain the notion (and perhaps hope) that Jesus' teachings will meet with Pharisaic approval. Hence their report casts the disciples in a negative light, as unduly concerned with incurring the irritation and offense of Israel's most revered teachers.

15:13-14. Jesus' response exhibits no remorse or cautious restraint in his denunciation of the Pharisees. The disciples must understand that the religious form of Pharisaic Judaism does not have its origin with God. By use of a horticultural metaphor, the Pharisees and their legalistic system are compared to plants not planted by God, therefore deserving only to be rooted up. Since God is neither responsible for or endorsing of Pharisaic teaching it has no future. It follows that the Pharisees are mere **blind guides**, and one follows their teachings at one's own peril. The disciples, therefore, must not be caught up with the popular regard and esteem extended the Pharisees; but must forsake any involvement with them, lest they be swayed by Pharisaic concerns. Since they are blind guides, they cannot possibly offer reliable religious guidance that results in the favor of God. Thus, to heed their teachings is to court inevitable spiritual disaster.

15:15-17. Then Peter, as a spokesperson for the rest of the disciples, asks Jesus for an explanation of the **parable** (cf. 13:36). Evidently, Peter refers to the proverbial statement of verse 11. One may wonder why, if the Pharisees understood enough to be offended (v. 12), the disciples have difficulty comprehending Jesus' meaning (cf. 13:11). Even Jesus seems somewhat outraged by their failure to comprehend the significance of his words. His questions constitute a rebuke for their seeming obtuse inability to pick up on his meaning. Jesus then proceeds to explain, in literal terms, the nature of true defilement. First, he tells them what cannot possibly contribute to one's spiritual defilement. Food that is taken into the **mouth**, passes through the digestive system (τήν κοιλίαν, *tēn koilian*), and eventually winds up in the toilet (ἀφεδρῶνα, *aphedrōna*) has virtually no impact

---

[9]Patte, *Matthew*, p. 218, notes the parallels with the parable of the sower.

on one's spiritual state. Since the body discards that which may be deemed **"unclean,"** the mere intake of certain foods has no bearing on the question of one's defilement. With one sweeping authoritative pronouncement Jesus dismisses all external causes as being without ultimate value for determining spiritual purity.

15:18-19. Having explained what does not produce spiritual defilement, Jesus now explains the true source of defilement. Instead of what one *puts into the mouth* defiling a person Jesus identifies the ultimate cause of defilement as that which *comes out of the mouth*. The reason for this is that one's words come from the **heart**, and are therefore a reliable indicator of one's true spiritual state. Jesus then proceeds to identify various vices (seven, cf. Mark 7:21-23, thirteen) that owe their origin to a corruptible inner nature. The list is headed by **evil thoughts** followed by six actions that stem from evil thoughts: **murder** (φόνοι, *phonoi*), **adultery** (μοιχεῖαι, *moicheiai*), **sexual immorality** (πορνεῖαι, *porneiai*), **theft** (κλοπαί, *klopai*), **false testimony** (ψευδομαρτυρίαι, *pseudomartyriai*), and **slander** (βλασφημίαι, *blasphēmiai*). Jesus' stress on the heart, on the importance of the internal dimension of one's religion, is central to his teaching and fundamental in the discernment of God's will (cf. 5:20-48). Hence these vices are indicative of an inward defilement, deemed much more serious than unwashed hands. It should be observed, as noted by Garland, that "the opponents of Jesus are guilty of nearly all these things in Matthew's story."[10]

15:20. Jesus' concluding words round off the section by repeating the central issue raised in verse 2. It is apparent that the Pharisaic insistence on ritual hand washing is only symptomatic of a completely flawed system where legal niceties and a hyperexternalism have come to dominate religious expression. Jesus will have nothing to do with a "tradition" that continually stresses the external forms to the almost total neglect of the cultivation of one's interior character. The observation by Westerholm is particularly poignant:

> . . . the punctilious observance of such concrete commands as . . . ritual purity may easily become a preoccupation overshadowing the demands placed on the heart, which are less susceptible to halakhic definition . . . Jesus, who found the will of

---

[10]Garland, *Reading Matthew*, p. 162.

God not in statute but in a heart in tune with the divine purposes, avoided these dangers, but inevitably offended the proponents of halakhah in the process.[11]

E. THE CANAANITE WOMAN (15:21-28)

[21]Leaving that place, Jesus withdrew to the region of Tyre and Sidon. [22]A Canaanite woman from that vicinity came to him, crying out, "Lord, Son of David, have mercy on me! My daughter is suffering terribly from demon-possession."

[23]Jesus did not answer a word. So his disciples came to him and urged him, "Send her away, for she keeps crying out after us."

[24]He answered, "I was sent only to the lost sheep of Israel."

[25]The woman came and knelt before him. "Lord, help me!" she said.

[26]He replied, "It is not right to take the children's bread and toss it to their dogs."

[27]"Yes, Lord," she said, "but even the dogs eat the crumbs that fall from their masters' table."

[28]Then Jesus answered, "Woman, you have great faith! Your request is granted." And her daughter was healed from that very hour.

The episode involving the Canaanite woman is pivotal in the sequence of scenes comprising 14:13–16:20. Jesus now leaves a predominantly Jewish location to venture into a region inhabited largely by Gentiles (v. 21). However, in contrast to the "Pharisees and teachers of the law" who come from Jerusalem to find fault with Jesus (15:1-2), in Gentile territory Jesus is met by a Canaanite woman who acknowledges his messianic authority with the words, "Lord, Son of David, have mercy on me" (v. 22). Such an insight from this Gentile woman is clearly intended as a foil against which is heightened the blindness of Israel's leaders (15:14, 24; cf. 2:1-4). This Gentile woman not only exhibits a reverent regard for Jesus (she calls him "Lord" three times and worships him), her persistent

[11]Westerholm, *Scribal Authority*, p. 91.

expression of faith overcomes all obstacles and culminates in a willingness to receive mere "bread crumbs" (v. 27). It is her "great faith" that provides Jesus the occasion to stretch the disciples' perspective concerning the contours of his compassionate ministry. In the face of such faith, exhibited by a foreigner, contemporary standards of "uncleanness," and the ideology of separation so prevalent in Pharisaic teaching must be set aside. As such, this scene provides an object lesson reinforcing the principles enunciated in 15:1-20.

15:21. A transitional phrase sets the stage for Jesus' encounter with the Canaanite woman. Once again **Jesus withdrew** in the face of opposition (cf. 14:13), this time going outside Jewish territory, **to the region of Tyre and Sidon**. The mention of Tyre and Sidon is not merely to document Jesus' geographical location, but to conjure up images of some of Israel's most hated enemies (see, e.g., Isa 23; Ezek 26-28; Joel 3:4).[12] Given Jesus' decidedly Jewish mission (cf. 10:6) it is probable that his venture into Gentile lands was an effort to escape Jewish opposition, as well as to find some solace away from the crowds. Nevertheless, even in Gentile territory huge crowds were attracted to him (15:29-39).

15:22. Matthew accentuates the religious and national distance between Jesus and the woman who approaches him by calling her a **Canaanite** (cf. Mark 7:26), thus conjuring up a long standing animosity, with deep roots in Israel's history. Nevertheless, the woman's petition, **"Lord, Son of David, have mercy on me"** (cf. 9:27; 20:31-32) indicates a remarkable insight into Jesus' messianic authority. Just how she came to have this conviction is not said. The reader is reminded of another Gentile in Matthew's story who also exhibits an exceptional understanding of Jesus' authority (cf. 8:5-13).[13] In both episodes the faith of a Gentile stands in stark contrast to the unbelief and blindness of Israel. Therefore, the woman's confessionary petition becomes illustrative of the response that should have characterized all Israel.[14] Her petition concerns her **daughter**

---

[12]On the symbolic value of Tyre in the OT, see Carol Newsom, "A Maker of Metaphors–Ezekiel's Oracle Against Tyre," *Int* 38 (1984) 151-164.

[13]For a detailed comparison of the two scenes see Davies and Allison, *Matthew*, 2:558-559.

[14]See W.R.G. Loader, "Son of David, Blindness, Possession, and Duality in Matthew," *CBQ* 44 (1982), 578; and Donald J. Verseput, "The Role and

who **is suffering terribly from demon-possession**. Her words are intended to amplify the serious condition of her daughter.

15:23. Given the urgency of the situation one might expect Jesus to respond immediately to resolve the situation (cf. 8:7). But, instead her continual cries for help (ἔκραζεν, *ekrazen*, v. 22, the imperfect tense suggests repeated efforts to get the attention of Jesus), were met with silence. To make matters worse, the disciples are quick to judge the woman as a nuisance, and respond in the same way they did to the hunger of the crowds, i.e., **Send her away** (ἀπόλυσον αὐτήν, *apolyson autēn*, cf. 14:15; see also 15:32). It is difficult to be sure if they simply wanted to be rid of her, being an unclean Canaanite, or if they are requesting that Jesus shut her up by giving her what she wants. In either case, the disciples' response is less than compassionate, revealing a calloused lack of sensitivity to the woman's desperate appeal.

15:24-25. Jesus seems temporarily to align himself with the disciples as he reiterates the limitations of his mission: **"I was sent only to the lost sheep of Israel"** (cf. 10:6). Convenantal faithfulness demanded that Israel be given priority in God's dealings with humanity (see 10:6). Yet, the reader knows that earlier Jesus was responsive to a Gentile supplicant, and even affirmed that "he had not found anyone in Israel with such great faith" (8:10). Jesus' words are therefore calculated to elicit from the woman a basis for the inclusion of Gentiles in blessings reserved for Israel. Her only response is to assume the posture of worship (προσεκύνει, *prosekynei* ["worshiped" in older versions, NIV **knelt before**], carries the root sense of bowing or bending the knee before the object of one's adoration), and with deep reverence plead for his **help** (βοηθέω, *boētheō*). It is her expression of total dependency and confidence in Jesus that begins to undermine the exclusivism of the preceding statement. Certainly, few Israelites have demonstrated such a remarkable persistence and dauntless faith in Jesus' authoritative power.

15:26-27. But Jesus places another hurdle before her faith, by reminding her of the privileged status of Israel in terms that appear unduly harsh and completely lacking in any conciliatory

---

Meaning of the 'Son of God' Title in Matthew's Gospel," *NTS* 33 (1987), 544.

overtones.[15] With a brief parabolic saying Jesus resorts to conventional Jewish language highlighting Israel's privileged status in contrast to pagan Gentiles. The Israelites are the **children** who are blessed to receive the messianic blessings (=**bread**), while Gentiles were typically referred to as "unclean dogs," mere scavengers that roamed the streets. Although Jesus uses the diminutive form of κύων (*kyōn*) (κυνάριον [*kynarion*]="house dog, or lapdog in contrast to a dog of the street," *BAGD,* p. 457), it is still difficult to see how the woman would interpret his words as anything other than an insult. Of course, as has been pointed out,[16] we do not know the body language or the tone of voice that accompanied such a saying, hence Jesus' spoken words may have come across as less offensive. At any rate, the woman is not deterred by Jesus' words. In fact, she is in agreement that the needs of the children (=Israel) should take priority over care for the family dogs (=Gentiles). She is thus willing to recognize her secondary status, but adopts Jesus' metaphoric language to draw out implications in support of her cause. She points out that the children of a household are not deprived by the **dogs** eating mere **crumbs that fall from the master's table**. So even though she could make no claim to belonging to the chosen people, granting her request in no way would diminish Israel's privileged status.

15:28. Her insightful response and humble persistency are recognized by Jesus with the words, **"Woman, you have great faith"** (cf. 8:10). "Great faith" necessarily involves a humble recognition of Jesus' authoritative power, along with a level of understanding concerning his messianic vocation. Although this unnamed woman never reappears in the story or becomes part of the inner circle of disciples, her great faith stands in stark contrast to Israel's unbelief (cf. 13:58), and even the "little faith" of the disciples (14:31). Jesus grants her request and her daughter experienced immediate healing. Jesus' positive appraisal of this Gentile woman, and the granting of her request should cause the disciples to rethink contemporary Jewish standards of uncleanness and ethnic boundaries. Should such great faith be ignored simply because it is expressed

---

[15]Davies and Allison, *Matthew,* 2:552.

[16]See discussion in France, *Matthew,* p. 247; and Morris, *Matthew,* pp. 404-405.

by a foreigner, one outside national Israel? The two scenes involving Gentiles (8:5-13; 15:21-28) clearly foreshadow a mission to all the nations (28:18-20), when the true people of God will transcend all boundaries of race and cultural peculiarities.

F. FEEDING OF THE FOUR THOUSAND (15:29-39)

[29]Jesus left there and went along the Sea of Galilee. Then he went up on a mountainside and sat down. [30]Great crowds came to him, bringing the lame, the blind, the crippled, the mute and many others, and laid them at his feet; and he healed them. [31]The people were amazed when they saw the mute speaking, the crippled made well, the lame walking and the blind seeing. And they praised the God of Israel.

[32]Jesus called his disciples to him and said, "I have compassion for these people; they have already been with me three days and have nothing to eat. I do not want to send them away hungry, or they may collapse on the way."

[33]His disciples answered, "Where could we get enough bread in this remote place to feed such a crowd?"

[34]"How many loaves do you have?" Jesus asked.

"Seven," they replied, "and a few small fish."

[35]He told the crowd to sit down on the ground. [36]Then he took the seven loaves and the fish, and when he had given thanks, he broke them and gave them to the disciples, and they in turn to the people. [37]They all ate and were satisfied. Afterward the disciples picked up seven basketfuls of broken pieces that were left over. [38]The number of those who ate was four thousand, besides women and children. [39]After Jesus had sent the crowd away, he got into the boat and went to the vicinity of Magadan.

This episode exhibits such a remarkable similarity with the feeding of the five thousand (14:13-21) that many have concluded that one or the other of the accounts is a mere literary fabrication based on a single event.[17] While it is true that numerous verbal and

[17]For discussion see Hagner, *Matthew*, 2:449-450; Davies and Allison, *Matthew*, 2:562-565; Carson, *Matthew*, pp. 357-358.

conceptual parallels can be found in both accounts, the differences should not be downplayed.[18] Furthermore, if two separate feeding events actually did take place, is it unreasonable to expect the accounts to be narrated in similar terminology? In fact, there are good reasons why a second feeding story makes good sense. Although the proposal has been disputed,[19] seeing the crowd in the first feeding as predominantly Jewish and the crowd in the second feeding as predominantly Gentile does have some contextual support. Even though not as emphatic as Mark 7:21, it would seem that Matthew does expect his readers to understand that Jesus is still in Gentile territory when the events comprising 15:29-39 take place (cf. v. 21 and v. 39). In addition, when the crowds praise "the God of Israel" (v. 31) this makes the best sense if the crowds are Gentile praising Israel's God, Yahweh. Although not as conclusive, it may be significant that the term translated "basketful" in v. 37 is distinctly Hellenistic in contrast to the typically Jewish term for "basket" in 14:20. It is therefore reasonable to see Jesus providing for Gentiles in the same manner that he earlier provided for Jews. Furthermore, coming after the Canaanite woman episode (15:21-28), this scene reinforces the universal implications of Jesus' ministry, in contrast to the exclusiveness inherent in the teaching of the Jewish leaders.

15:29-31. Like the earlier feeding, the feeding of the four thousand is prefaced by a summary highlighting Jesus' therapeutic involvement with the crowds (cf. 14:13-14). Jesus takes a position **on a mountainside**, while large **crowds** come before him bringing their sick (**lame**, **blind**, **crippled**, **mute**, **and many others**, cf. 11:3-5). They are **amazed** with Jesus' healing powers and **praised the God of Israel**. These same crowds are then blessed to participate in a great messianic banquet (vv. 32-39), with the provisions miraculously provided by Jesus. Donaldson has argued that the "mountain" as a "place of gathering, healing, and feeding," is intended to conjure up images of the eschatological promises associated with

---

[18]See the discussion by Gundry, *Matthew*, pp. 318-322.

[19]*Contra* Hagner, *Matthew*, 2:445; and T. Donaldson, *Jesus on the Mountain: A Study in Matthean Theology* (JSNTSup 8; Sheffield: JSOT, 1985), see pp. 122-135.

Mt. Zion (cf. Isa 35:5f; 25:6-10; Jer 31:10-14; Ezek 34:14, 26ff).[20] Although these overtones may be present in 15:29-31, like 8:11-12, it is not Jews who are depicted as enjoying these blessings, but Gentiles. They are the ones who came to Jesus in faith, and are participants in the Isaianic promises: "Then will the eyes of the blind be opened and the ears of the deaf unstopped. Then will the lame leap like a deer, and the mute tongue shout for joy" (Isa 35:5-6). While the Jewish leaders worship "in vain," these Gentile crowds praise "the God of Israel." Although a formal charge to minister to the Gentiles would not come until after the resurrection (28:18-20), certainly scenes such as this anticipate such an endeavor.

15:32. Without any interruption, the narrative moves from the summary to the feeding of the four thousand (vv. 32-39). Unlike the earlier feeding, it is Jesus who takes the initiative to identify the plight of the crowd (vv. 32-33; cf. 14:15). Whereas earlier Matthew the narrator emphasized Jesus' "compassion" (14:14), in this instance Jesus speaks personally of being moved by compassion. The crowds have been with Jesus for the better part of **three days**, and provisions have been depleted. To send them away without food would run the risk that some, in a weakened state, would have undue hardship in their travels home.

15:33. By setting before the disciples his concerns Jesus hoped to stimulate them into action. Instead, the disciples focus on the impossibility of the task to secure enough food to meet the demands of so many people. It is difficult to understand the reaction of the disciples since they had but a short time earlier witnessed how an identical problem had been solved (14:13-21). It has been suggested that their response in verse 33 is intended to put stress on the emphatic "we," thus "to indicate their own helplessness, and to leave the way open for Jesus to make provisions again."[21] If Jesus' previous remarks about the condition of the crowds (v. 32) were intended to suggest that the disciples should miraculously provide food, then their statement in verse 33 could be construed as an expression of their own inability. Be that as it may, the disciples

---

[20]Donaldson, *Jesus on the Mountain*, pp. 128ff.; Davies and Allison, *Matthew*, 2:566-567 are in agreement.

[21]So France, *Matthew*, p. 249; cf. also Blomberg, *Matthew*, p. 246.

exhibit no awareness of the awesome power available through Jesus, but instead focus on the seeming impossibility of the task.

15:34-37. Using words reminiscent of the first feeding story, Jesus once again takes charge of the situation (vv. 34-36). He first inquires about the provision available. This time they specify **seven** loaves, and a **few fish** (cf. 14:17). As in the previous miracle of feeding, Jesus commands the people to prepare for a banquet by "reclining" **on the ground** (cf. "grass," 14:19). He then *took* the provisions available, *gave thanks* (cf. 14:19), and *broke* the loaves, and *gave* them to the disciples, who in turn distributed the food to the multitudes. As in the first feeding (14:20), **They all ate and were satisfied.** Once again the surplus of provisions is stressed by noting the number of baskets (σπυρίς, *spyris*)[22] needed for the leftovers (seven, cf. twelve in 14:20). If the "twelve baskets" had symbolic value, it is not unreasonable that Matthew intended his readers to see some symbolism by the reference to **seven basketfuls** (cf. 16:9-10). However, exactly what the significance may be is certainly not obvious to the modern reader.[23]

15:38-39. The number fed is identified as **four thousand, besides women and children**. The numbers are obviously only an estimate, and there appears no reason to read symbolic value into the number fed.[24] Like the feeding of the five thousand, this episode closes with Jesus dismissing the crowd (v. 30; 14:22), followed by a boat trip. This time their voyage takes them into the **vicinity of Magadan** (cf. Mark 8:10), the exact location of which is uncertain. However, in view of their subsequent encounter with the "Pharisees and Sadducees" (16:1ff.) it is likely that they are back in Jewish territory, on the western side of the Sea. The stage is thus set in verse 39 for a return to Jewish territory followed immediately by a less than friendly welcoming committee (16:1-4).

---

[22]The distinction between the two words for basket (v. 37, σπυρίς, *spyris*, while in 14:20 it was κόφινος, *kophinos*), may be an emphasis either on the difference in size, or the materials they were made of.

[23]The number "seven" has been linked to "completion or perfection," the "seventy Gentile nations," and even the "seven deacons of Acts 6:1-6."

[24]Hagner, *Matthew* 2:452, suggests that if the four thousand were Gentiles (which he disputes), then the smaller number fed "may subtly point to Israel's priority in the reception of the abundance of eschatological blessing."

MATTHEW 16

G. REQUEST FOR A SIGN (16:1-4)

[1]The Pharisees and Sadducees came to Jesus and tested him by asking him to show them a sign from heaven.

[2]He replied,[a] "When evening comes, you say, 'It will be fair weather, for the sky is red,' [3]and in the morning, 'Today it will be stormy, for the sky is red and overcast.' You know how to interpret the appearance of the sky, but you cannot interpret the signs of the times. [4]A wicked and adulterous generation looks for a miraculous sign, but none will be given it except the sign of Jonah." Jesus then left them and went away.

[a]2 Some early manuscripts do not have the rest of verse 2 and all of verse 3.

16:1. No sooner had Jesus arrived back on Jewish soil (note "withdrew" in 15:21) than he again finds himself the target of opposition. This time the Pharisees have joined forces with their bitter rivals, the Sadducees (cf. 3:7), in order to deal with one, who in different ways posed a threat to both sects. By linking the Pharisees and Sadducees together it need not be inferred that Matthew exhibits no awareness of their distinctive theological and political differences.[1] His intent is to show the hardened obduracy characterizing "official Judaism." Although they are doctrinally miles apart, differences could be temporarily set aside in order to address such a formidable threat to their status and welfare.

For the second time the religious leaders request a **sign** to validate the divine origin of Jesus' ministry (cf. 12:38-39). They are not really interested in Jesus' providing compelling evidence to

---

[1]See discussion of D.A. Carson, "The Jewish Leaders in Matthew's Gospel: A Reappraisal," *JETS* 25 (June 1982), 161-174.

substantiate his claims. Matthew makes it clear that their request was simply a means to "test" (πειράζω, *peirazō*, cf. 4:1) him. Like Satan who demanded that Jesus orchestrate a situation whereby God is forced to miraculously confirm his Sonship (4:1-11), so the religious authorities expect Jesus to compel God to show a miraculous sign on his behalf. Obviously, they do find Jesus' healings and exorcisms as sufficient evidence that God is at work in him. The fact is, no matter what the evidence, unbelief can readily distort its significance so as to justify even the most outlandish conclusions (cf. 12:24-27). Jesus therefore refuses to countenance the demands of unbelief by performing some extraordinary feat.

16:2-3. There are some questions about the exact wording of Jesus' response in verses 2b-3. As noted in the NIV footnote, "some early manuscripts do not have the rest of verse two and all of verse three." Metzger, in his *Textual Commentary on the Greek New Testament*, observes that "the external evidence for the absence of these words is impressive . . ." (cf. Luke 12:54-56). The passage is, however, retained in the UBSGNT, but is found in brackets to indicate the uncertainty of the text. It has been argued that the absence of these words in a small but important group of textual witnesses may be explained by their being deleted by scribes who did not live in climatic conditions where a red sky in the morning was a reliable precursor of approaching stormy weather.[2] Since the evidence against the words being original is not conclusive, and given the many texts that have the saying, it is probably best to include them, but with some indication of their uncertainty.

Jesus chides his opponents for their ability to discern and anticipate certain climatic changes, while being totally void of discernment when it comes to interpreting the **signs of the times**. Jesus is referring to the many "signs" accompanying his ministry, powerfully testifying to the dawn of the messianic age. Their failure to **interpret** (διακρίνειν, *diakrinein*) the signs of the times is sufficient evidence that they are "blind guides," totally lacking in spiritual discernment.

16:4. Jesus concludes his denunciation of the Jewish leaders with language virtually identical to his earlier response to their

[2]See Metzger, *Textual Commentary*, p. 41.

request for signs (12:39-40). They are representative of a **generation** perverse and hardened in unbelief. Hence, as he said earlier, there remains only one sign to be given this generation, i.e., **the sign of Jonah** (see comments 12:40). Following these words Matthew informs the reader that **Jesus then left them and went away**. Discussion is brought to an abrupt halt, and Jesus seeks to distance himself from Israel's leadership by retreating once again into Gentile territory (v. 5).

H. THE LEAVEN OF THE PHARISEES AND SADDUCEES (16:5-12)

5When they went across the lake, the disciples forgot to take bread. 6"Be careful," Jesus said to them. "Be on your guard against the yeast of the Pharisees and Sadducees."

7They discussed this among themselves and said, "It is because we didn't bring any bread."

8Aware of their discussion, Jesus asked, "You of little faith, why are you talking among yourselves about having no bread? 9Do you still not understand? Don't you remember the five loaves for the five thousand, and how many basketfuls you gathered? 10Or the seven loaves for the four thousand, and how many basketfuls you gathered? 11How is it you don't understand that I was not talking to you about bread? But be on your guard against the yeast of the Pharisees and Sadducees." 12Then they understood that he was not telling them to guard against the yeast used in bread, but against the teaching of the Pharisees and Sadducees.

Like the earlier conflict scene (15:1-9), which led to specific instructions and warnings given to the disciples (15:10-20), so the request of the Pharisees and the Sadducees for a sign (16:1-4) is followed by Jesus warning the disciples not to be swayed by the teachings of Israel's leaders (16:5-12). The repeated reference to the "Pharisees and Sadducees" (vv. 1, 6, 11, 12) serves to link the two scenes into an interwoven unit. Furthermore, the twice repeated warning to be on "guard against the yeast of the Pharisees and Sadducees" (vv. 6, 11), followed by its literal interpretation ("yeast" = "the teaching of the Pharisees and Sadducees," v. 12) indicates that the dominant focus of verses 5-12 is to warn the disciples of the corrupting influence of the Jewish leaders. However, a secondary theme is suggested by the disciples' concern for having forgotten to bring bread on their journey (v. 1). Jesus rebukes their petty concerns with the words "you of little faith" (v. 8), and by reminding them of the provisions that God provided in the earlier feeding episodes (vv. 9-10). Their preoccupation with "bread" is indicative of their mundane concerns that Jesus expects them to rise above (cf. 6:25-33). These two themes are interwoven and explain the alterations between "bread," "leaven" (="yeast"), and "teachings."

16:5-7. As noted in verse 4 Jesus withdraws from hostility, coming once again to the eastern shores of the Sea of Galilee. Having arrived on the other side of the lake (cf. Mark 8:14) the disciples realize they have forgotten to bring sufficient provisions (=**bread**). It appears that it is their concern for literal bread that prompts Jesus to issue his warning about the dangers of **the yeast of the Pharisees and Sadducees**. Although the disciples are consumed with their lack of physical provisions, Jesus points to an even greater threat to their welfare. The insidiously dangerous influence of the Pharisees and Sadducees undermines all that Jesus would have his disciples to be and do. However, Jesus' point seems to go right over their heads. They remain fixated on their lack of bread, and therefore conclude that Jesus' remarks about "leaven" must have something to do with their lack of provisions.

16:8-11. Jesus, being fully **aware** (γνούς, *gnous*)[3] of their discussion rebukes them for their trivial concerns, addressing them with the words **you of little faith** (ὀλιγόπιστοι, *oligopistoi*, cf. 6:30; 8:26; 14:31). Jesus then asks a series of questions (vv. 8b-11a) designed to remind them of the important lessons they should have learned with the two feeding episodes.[4] First, the disciples should have learned to trust God to meet their physical needs and not have

[3]Hagner, *Matthew* 2:459; notes that the "participle γνούς, "knowing" suggests an unusual or miraculous ability of Jesus to know what has not been told to him" (cf. 12:15; 22:18; 26:10; 9:4).

[4]Davies and Allison, *Matthew* 2:591, observe that the verb μνημονεύω (*mnēmoneuō*) in verse 9 connotes more than an intellectual activity. "The disciples should not just recall a miraculous fact but should responsibly engage its implications for the present."

allowed their preoccupation with securing physical provisions to have caused them to fail to comprehend Jesus' spiritual warnings. Second, the specific emphasis on the numbers fed and the number of baskets needed to contain the surplus of leftovers, should have reminded the disciples that God's provisions were both abundant and not ethnically motivated. In both feedings Jesus is moved by "compassion" (cf. 14:13; 15:32), and ministers to the needs of the people. If the disciples are swayed by the teachings of "official Judaism," their involvement with people will be greatly curtailed. Although the sects of the Pharisees and Sadducees differed in their "teaching" about a lot of matters, they were pedagogically united in their opposition to the ministry of Jesus. For the disciples to give their teachings any credence whatsoever is to seriously undermine their relationship to Jesus, and thereby to jeopardize their involvement with his mission.

16:12. The section closes with Matthew informing the reader that the disciples have come to understand (συνῆκαν, *synēkan*) Jesus' metaphoric use of "leaven." Once again Jesus has assisted his disciples to understand his parabolic sayings (cf. 13:10, 36; 15:15). Even though they are at times obtuse and unperceptive (cf. 17:14-20; 29:17), the disciples are portrayed in the end as making some progress.

I. CONFESSION AT CAESAREA PHILIPPI (16:13-20)

13When Jesus came to the region of Caesarea Philippi, he asked his disciples, "Who do people say the Son of Man is?"

14They replied, "Some say John the Baptist; others say Elijah; and still others, Jeremiah or one of the prophets."

15"But what about you?" he asked. "Who do you say I am?"

16Simon Peter answered, "You are the Christ,[a] the Son of the living God."

17Jesus replied, "Blessed are you, Simon son of Jonah, for this was not revealed to you by man, but by my Father in heaven. 18And I tell you that you are Peter,[b] and on this rock I will build my church, and the gates of Hades[c] will not overcome it.[d] 19I will give you the keys of the kingdom of heaven; whatever you bind on earth will be bound in heaven, and whatever you loose on earth

will be[e] loosed in heaven." [20]Then he warned his disciples not to tell anyone that he was the Christ.

[a]*16* Or *Messiah*; also in verse 20 [b]*18 Peter* means *rock.* [c]*18* Or *hell*
[d]*18* Or *not prove stronger than it* [e]*19* Or *have been*

The scene at Caesarea Philippi brings to a dramatic closure the long central portion of Matthew's story detailing Jesus' active mission to call Israel to repentance in view of God's impending reign (4:17-16:20). Jesus' activity produced amazement and wonder among the crowds (7:28-29; 9:8, 26, 31, 33; 13:54; 15:31), leading to speculations about his identity and the significance of his deeds (12:23; 16:1-4). Israel's leadership responded with suspicious skepticism (cf. 9:3, 11), leading to vitriolic confrontations and hostile repudiation (9:34; 12:1-14, 22-45; 15:1-9; 16:1-4). In contrast to both the crowds and Israel's leaders, Jesus calls disciples to be "trained in the kingdom of God" (4:18-22; 9:9; 10:1-4; 13:52; cf. 8:18-22), in order that they might embark upon a mission similar to his own (cf. 4:17; 9:36-38; 10:5-42; 14:14ff.; 15:32ff.). They constitute the true messianic community (12:46-50), and thus several scenes comprising 11:2-16:20 are exclusively devoted to depicting Jesus stretching and shaping their faith and understanding (cf. 13:13-17, 36-52; 14:13-21, 22-33; 15:10-20, 24-33; 16:5-12). Although the disciples often exhibit a lack of understanding (13:10, 36; 14:15; 15:16, 23, 33; 16:8-13), and are chided for their "little faith" (14:31; 16:8), they do on occasion exhibit a flash of insight (13:51; 14:33; 16:12).

But now, in a setting far removed from the crowds and the pressure of popular opinion, Jesus elicits from the disciples a thoughtful and carefully reasoned personal assessment of their understanding concerning his identity (16:13-15). Peter, on behalf of all the disciples, articulates a confessionary stance which constitutes the most insightful appraisal of Jesus' person by any character so far in the narrative: "You are the Christ, the Son of the living God" (16:16). Although Peter's confession is correct, the disciples are prohibited from telling anyone (v. 20) until they learn to properly integrate Jesus' transcendent glory and status with his humble sacrificial mission on behalf of his people. Since identity and mission are integrally related, one cannot truly understand Jesus' Sonship and messianic status until they are defined in terms of his mission.

In the next section (16:21–20:34) the disciples will be challenged to understand Jesus' person in terms of his suffering and death.

16:13. Jesus travels once again into Gentile territory, this time heading north of the Sea of Galilee approximately twenty-five miles, to the largely Gentile-populated city of **Caesarea Philippi**. It is here that Jesus poses the decisive question to his disciples: **"Who do people say the Son of Man is?"** The question is not intended to gather information about popular assessments about his person, but to stimulate reflection among the disciples about his identity. The disciples evidently had no problem in understanding the designation "Son of Man" as Jesus' personal reference to himself (cf. Mark 8:27). The usage here reminds the reader of Jesus' humble earthly service (8:20; 10:23; 12:8, 32; 13:37, 41). Jesus, therefore, questions the disciples concerning how the general populace has assessed his active ministry in Israel.

16:14. The disciples respond by cataloging four evaluative viewpoints of popular opinion. Notably the disciples only mention those views which they deem to be complimentary. The equation of Jesus with **John the Baptist** probably owes its origin to Herod (cf. 14:2), whose guilt over the execution of John stimulated the notion that Jesus was the risen John. Perhaps Jesus' preaching and miracles encouraged some to speculate that Jesus may be the returned **Elijah**, come to herald the arrival of the messianic age (cf. Mal 3:1; 4:5-6; see 11:9-10, 14; 17:12-13). Still others found certain similarities that seemed to link Jesus to **Jeremiah**. It may be Jesus' many allusions to sayings from Jeremiah or possibly the parallels in their respective ministries[5] stimulated such an assessment. Finally, Jesus' prophetic character and activity produced the general assessment that one of the revered prophetic figures of Israel's past has returned to herald the end times (cf. 21:11). As flattering as all of these assessments may be, they are woefully inadequate in their appraisal of Jesus' person.

16:15-16. Jesus then asks the disciples for their perception concerning his identity. Although the question is directed to the group,

---

[5]For possible connections to Jeremiah see B.T. Dahlberg, "The Typological Use of Jeremiah 1:4-19 in Matthew 16:13-23," *JBL* 94 (1975) 73-80; M.J.J. Menken, "The References to Jeremiah in the Gospel According to Matthew (Mt 2:17; 16:14; 27:9)," *ETL* 60 (1984) 5-24.

Peter answers as their spokesperson, identifying Jesus as **the Christ, the son of the living God**. Essentially, Peter has verbalized two conceptual expressions which capture the essence of Jesus' identity and mission. As the designation "Christ" implies, Jesus is the fulfillment of Israel's messianic hopes, who has come to gather his people under the reign of God (cf. 1:1, 16-17; 11:2). The designation reminds the reader of Jesus' redemptive involvement with the people (1:21; 2:6; 3:11-12; 4:15-16, 21-25; 9:36-38; 11:2-6), and necessarily assumes the validity of other designations which cast Jesus as Israel's long awaited Messiah: e.g., "Son of David," "Son of Abraham," "King of the Jews," "Ruler," "Coming One," and "Shepherd."

While the confessional appraisal "Son of God" does carry with it elements of Jesus' royal messianic rule,[6] it adds dimensions to Jesus' messiahship not immediately apparent within Davidic categories. Rather than the conquering victor, the title "Son of God" emphasizes that his extraordinary power and authority are ultimately tied to his humble obedience and dependency upon his Father. In fact, it is Jesus' unique Sonship, with its accent upon conformity to his Father's will, that validates the manner that his messiahship comes to expression. As God's Son, Jesus fulfills his messianic task as one chosen by God to fulfill a mission expressive of God's merciful presence in the midst of his people. It is his filial obedience to the plan of God which explains the unexpected "unmessianic gentleness"[7] (cf. 11:2-6) of his role in Israel.

16:17. While it will become obvious that the disciples lack sufficient depth to appreciate the full force of these Christological titles, Jesus, nevertheless, accepts Peter's confession without qualification. In fact, Peter[8] is to be congratulated (μακάριος, *makarios*), because

---

[6]As argued by Kingsbury, "The Title Son of God in Matthew's Gospel," *JBL* 95 (1976), 591-602.

[7]Verseput, "Son of God," 548.

[8]In John 1:42 Peter is referred to as the "son of John." Morris, *Matthew*, p. 421, n. 24, suggests several options for harmonizing the references: "His father may have borne two names, or perhaps Ἰωνᾶ is a contraction of Ἰωάνης. Jona is a very infrequent name, and it is possible that "son of Jona" means "someone very like Jona." For other options see Jeremias, "Ἰωνᾶς," *TDNT*, 3:410.

such insight did not come through mere human agency (**man**; lit., flesh and blood), but by means of God's revelatory disclosure. Jesus' appraisal of the source of Peter's perception accords well with his earlier announcement that it is only by the Father's disclosure that "one knows the Son" (11:27). However, Peter's Christological insight should not be construed as a sudden flash of insight, but was fundamentally grounded in his observation of Jesus' performance in word and deed. As a matter of fact, Jesus' entire ministry was performatively God's revelation concerning the mystery associated with his person.

16:18. The next two verses have constituted some of the most difficult and certainly some of the "most controversial of all of Scripture."[9] Two extremes need to be avoided. On the one hand, Roman Catholicism has read into these verses an elaborate doctrine of Papal succession and infallibility based on a supposed investiture of Peter with exclusive authority and status. Protestants have responded by downplaying Peter's importance and pivotal role by these texts. Peter is either viewed as the "typical disciple" or merely a representative of all the other disciples.[10] However, it is difficult to ignore the intensely personal focus of verses 18-19. After Peter makes his evaluative affirmation concerning Jesus, Jesus in turn addresses Peter personally (note singular pronouns, σοι [*soi*] and σὺ εἶ [*su ei*], cf. v. 16), making a play upon his name ("you are Peter" = πέτρος, *petros*). Peter's name in Greek is probably derived from the Aramaic כֵּיפָא (*kēypha*), meaning a "rock" or "crag."[11] Since Jesus probably originally responded to Peter in Aramaic,[12] the wordplay suggested in verse 17 becomes readily apparent: "you are *kēypha* and upon this *kēypha* I will build my

[9]See J.A. Burgess, "A History of the Exegesis of Matthew 16:17-19 from 1781 to 1965," (Ann Arbor, MI: Edwards Brothers Inc., 1976), for an overview of some of the difficulties.

[10]See the balanced treatment of J.D. Kingsbury, "The Figure of Peter in Matthew's Gospel as a Theological Problem," *JBL* 98 (1979), 67-83.

[11]See the study of J.A. Fitzmyer, "Aramaic Kepha and Peter's Name in the New Testament," in *To Advance to Gospel: New Testament Studies* (New York: Crossroad, 1981), p. 115.

[12]It should not be construed that Jesus did not know Greek or use it on occasion; see S.E. Porter, "Did Jesus Ever Teach in Greek?" *TynBul* 44 (1993), 195-235.

church." In Greek the wordplay is not as apparent since the feminine noun πέτρα (*petra*) must become masculine (*petros*) when referring to a man's name. Hence the argument that the **rock** upon which Jesus builds his church could not be Peter because the genders fail to match cannot be grammatically sustained. There does not appear to be good reason to see the "rock" (*petra*) upon which Jesus builds his church as anything other than Peter (*petros*).[13] But as Kingsbury has pointed out, Peter should be seen as "first among equals, and his 'primacy' . . . is 'salvation-historical' in character."[14] This means that Jesus' words are intended to assign to Peter a pivotal role in the new phase of redemptive history involving the church (cf. Acts 1-12), not to give him special status with respect to some ecclesiastical office. In this respect France's words are particularly cogent:

> It is only Protestant overreaction to the Roman Catholic claim (which of course has no foundation in the text), that what is said of Peter applies also to the later bishops of Rome, that has led some to claim that 'rock' here is not Peter at all but the faith which he has just confessed. The wordplay and the whole structure of the passage, demands that this verse is every bit as much Jesus' declaration about Peter as v. 16 was Peter's declaration about Jesus.[15]

So Jesus promises Peter that he will have a foundational role when he (i.e., Jesus) builds (οἰκοδομήσω, *oikodomēsō*) his "church" (ἐκκλησία, *ekklēsia*). The imagery of "building" the "church" upon a foundational "rock" comes from the background of perceiving God's people as a "temple" or "house of God."[16] This is the first use of the term **church** (cf. 18:17), and many would dispute that Jesus actually used the term, claiming that its usage in Matthew was a later insertion. However, there is no need to read into the term *ekklēsia* elaborate church structures and organizational patterns

---

[13]For an able defense that the "rock" was Peter's confession see C.C. Caragounis, *Peter and the Rock* (BZNW 58; Berlin: de Gruyter, 1989).

[14]Kingsbury, "The Figure of Peter," p. 71.

[15]France, *Matthew* p. 254; see also Carson, *Matthew*, p. 368; Blomberg, *Matthew*, p. 252.

[16]Davies and Allison, *Matthew* 2:628-629.

typical of a later period. The term *ekklēsia* is found throughout the LXX (translating the Hebrew קָהָל, *qāhāl*), and means nothing more than an "assembly or community" of people, gathering for a particular purpose. It is not at all surprising that Jesus intends to establish a fellowship of believers who assemble in his name; after all, "a messiah without a messianic Community would be unthinkable to any Jew . . ."[17]

After announcing Peter's important role in the "building of the church," Jesus then assures Peter that **the gates of Hades will not overcome it**. Although the antecedent of αὐτῆς (*autēs*, "it") has been much debated, it seems that the most natural referent is the church, not Peter. However, the imagery of "gates" actively seeking to "overpower" (κατισχύσουσιν, *katischysousin*, active, not passive) the church is conceptually difficult to understand.[18] Probably the metaphor "gates of Hades" is intended to stand for the abode of the dead, not to a place of punishment, as suggested by the KJV translation *hell.*[19] Many have extended the metaphor by understanding ῞Αιδης (*Haidēs*) as the realm of evil powers of the underworld. The church will emerge victorious in the end.[20] While it is true that the church will have to endure evil assaults, and in the end will be victorious, it is difficult to find such suggestions in the imagery of "gates." The metaphor does not conjure up imagery of aggressive assaults, but rather gates are most naturally seen as defensive, keeping people either in or out. As noted by C. Brown, "the gates themselves do not attack, they serve as vivid reminders that those who go to the realm of the dead do not return to the land of the living."[21] Therefore the gates of Hades, meaning "death," will

---

[17]W.F. Albright and C.S. Mann, *Matthew*, Anchor Bible, vol. 26 (New York: Doubleday, 1971), p. 196.

[18]See the helpful historical survey by J.P. Lewis, "The Gates of Hell Shall Not Prevail Against It (Matt 16:18): A Study of the History of Interpretation," *JETS* 38/3 (September 1995), 349-367; Davies and Allison, *Matthew* 2:630-632, also survey twelve possible interpretations.

[19]Lewis, "Gates of Hell," 353, discusses the translation problems associated with this verse.

[20]See, e.g., Joel Marcus, "The Gates of Hades and the Keys of the Kingdom (Matt 16:18-19)," *CBQ* 50 (July 1988), 443-445; see also Davies and Allison, *Matthew* 2:633.

[21]Colin Brown, "The Gates of Hell: An Alternative Approach," *SBLASP*

neither be successful in prohibiting Christ from "building his church," nor will the death of its members signal its ultimate defeat. In view of Jesus' efforts in 16:21–20:34 to prepare his disciples for his fate in Jerusalem, Jesus' words may be a subtle allusion to his eventual overcoming of Hades by his resurrection.[22]

16:19. Jesus now defines in what way Peter plays an active role in the "building" of the new community of God. Peter receives the **keys of the kingdom of heaven**, a symbol of power and authority (cf. Isa 22:22; Rev 3:7; 9:1; 10:1). However, the imagery is not intended to portray Peter as a kind of gatekeeper who controls admission into heaven. Rather, his authority is exercised by bringing God's heavenly reign to bear on matters pertaining to the church. The "kingdom" is therefore not to be equated with the "church." Reference to the "kingdom" is always a focus on God who actively reigns over his people, while the "church" refers to the people over which God reigns. Hence, although the terms overlap, the arbitrary equation of the two concepts is not justified.

Peter's authority is forcefully brought out by the use of the terms "binding" and "loosing." These terms have a technical background in rabbinic Judaism, and refer to pronouncements made concerning conduct allowed and that which is forbidden, based upon rabbinic interpretations of the Law.[23] There is no reason to understand the terms "binding" and "loosing" in the sense of "excluding" or "admitting" certain people from participation in the Christian community (note "whatever" is neuter). The saying clearly means that Peter is authoritatively endowed (as are the other disciples, 18:17-18) to declare what things are forbidden and what things are acceptable in view of God's sovereign reign (cf. 6:10).

Although the syntactical force of the periphrastic perfect participles (ἔσται δεδεμένον [*estai dedemenon*] / ἔσται λελυμένον [*estai*

(Atlanta: Scholars Press, 1987), 361; see also his fuller treatment, "The Gates of Hell and the Church," in *Church, Word and Spirit: Festschrift in Honor of G.W. Bromily*, eds. J. Bradley and R. Muller (Grand Rapids: Eerdmans, 1987), pp. 15-43.

[22]Suggested by Brown, "Gates of Hell," 365-367.

[23]See the survey of texts in Herbert W. Basser, "Derrett's 'Binding' Reopened," *JBL* 104 (June 1985), 297-300.

lelymenon]) has been much debated,[24] there seems to be no contextual reason why they should not be given their full perfect force. Hence the translation, "will have been bound"/ "will have been loosed" is a viable rendition of the terms. Thus the texts envision authoritative teachings that are not grounded in some sort of inherent authority or the arbitrary initiation of Peter (or the rest of the disciples). Rather, their authoritative instructions and decisive decrees are in accord with what is already settled in heaven, and are therefore reflective of God's sovereign will. In contrast to the Pharisees who "shut the kingdom of heaven in men's faces" (23:13-24), the disciples are "trained in the kingdom" and will eventually go forth to summon both Jew and Gentile under the reign of God (28:18-20). The early believers recognized their authority and "devoted themselves to the apostles' teaching" (Acts 2:42). In this way it can legitimately be said that "God's household [was] built on the foundation of the apostles . . ." (Eph 2:19-20). With respect to Peter, an examination of Acts 1-12 will confirm his important leadership role in the early history of the church.

16:20. It may come as a surprise, in view of Jesus' positive remarks and promises to Peter, that he and the rest of the disciples are forbidden to tell anyone that Jesus is the Messiah. The best explanation for Jesus' prohibition is the likelihood that while the disciples have come to understand Jesus in terms of his transcendent authoritative status, his identity as Messiah must be integrated into a mission that involved suffering and death. Beginning with 16:21 Jesus will attempt to lead the disciples into an understanding of his messianic fate.

V. THE WAY OF THE CROSS (16:21–20:34)

As was observed in 4:17 the phrase, "From that time on Jesus began" (ἀπὸ τότε . . ., *apo tote* . . .) clearly introduces major story developments, as a new phase of Jesus' ministry is introduced. The first time the phrase occured (4:17), it signaled the beginning of Jesus' Galilean ministry, and succinctly summed up the content of

[24]Carson, *Matthew*, pp. 370-374, provides a good overview of the discussion.

his proclamation in Israel (i.e., "Repent for the kingdom of heaven is near"). The second occurrence signals the closure of Jesus' Galilean ministry (4:17-16:20),[25] and subsumes subsequent material under the dominant motif of Jesus' journey to Jerusalem, culminating in his suffering, death, and resurrection (16:21-28:20). As Kingsbury notes, the travels prior to 16:21, "have the character of withdrawal in the face of danger (cf. 12:15; 14:13; 15:21; 16:4)," while "from 16:21 on, Jesus' travels assume the character of a 'divinely ordained' journey to Jerusalem (cf. δεί, *dei* "it is necessary")."[26] If one simply notes major thematic developments, the following pattern emerges:

A Conflict 11:1–14:12 (In Galilee)
  B Education of the Disciples 14:13–16:20 (Identity)
  B Education of the Disciples 16:21–20:34 (Mission)
A Conflict 21:1–25:46 (In Jerusalem)

Like the scenes comprising 14:13–16:20, in 16:21–20:34 the disciples are present in every scene and are the major focus of Jesus' instruction. Jesus begins to "show" them (16:21) that humble compliance to the will of God demands his journey to Jerusalem to suffer and die. On three occasions (16:21; 17:22-23; 20:17-19) Jesus explicitly foretells his fate in Jerusalem. This disclosure becomes the major backdrop against which Jesus challenges his disciples to adopt values and priorities that will enable them to emulate his sacrificial mission.

The disciples must come to see the way of the cross as the fulfillment of Jesus' messianic mission, and as the ultimate expression of his divine Sonship. They must deny themselves and resolve to follow Jesus in selfless devotion to God's will (16:24). Such a commitment demands a radical shift of values where one's spiritual life takes priority over the loss of one's physical existence (16:25-26). If they are to "have in mind the things of God" and "not the things of man" (16:23) they need to "listen" to Jesus (17:5), as he confronts them with a radical vision of his messiahship. Their dependency must be upon God, who through faith will empower his servants so

---

[25]Although Jesus does not actually leave Galilee until 19:1, in 16:21 Jerusalem is first mentioned as the place of the passion.

[26]Kingsbury, *Matthew As Story*, pp. 77-78.

that "nothing will be impossible" (17:21). They must not insist on their own rights, but make every effort not to carelessly alienate others (17:24-27; 18:5-9). Like "good shepherds" they must come to value even one "sheep" that has wandered from the fold (18:15-20). Regardless of how they are treated, they cannot harbor ill-feelings, but must respond to personal hurt with a forgiving spirit (18:21-35). Such an attitude demands a childlike dependency upon God (18:1-4; 19:13-15), and not in earthly securities of wealth and status (19:16-26). The disciples are therefore not to insist on their own authority over others, but are rather to emulate Jesus' sacrificial service on behalf of others (20:20-28). Although the disciples exhibit some understanding (17:13), and remain devoted to following Jesus, their reactions and questions indicate that they do not fully perceive the nature of Jesus' mission and the demands it entails (cf. 16:23; 17:10, 17, 23; 18:21; 19:10, 25; 20:24-25, 27).

Even though the disciples struggle to accept the way of the cross, Jesus is resolved to exhibit before them its necessity (16:21). If they are to "think the things of God," they must "listen" to Jesus as he confronts them with the ultimate values, priorities, and intentions that govern his messianic mission.

A. THE THINGS OF GOD VERSUS THE THINGS OF MEN (16:21-28)

21From that time on Jesus began to explain to his disciples that he must go to Jerusalem and suffer many things at the hands of the elders, chief priests and teachers of the law, and that he must be killed and on the third day be raised to life.

22Peter took him aside and began to rebuke him. "Never, Lord!" he said. "This shall never happen to you!"

23Jesus turned and said to Peter, "Get behind me, Satan! You are a stumbling block to me; you do not have in mind the things of God, but the things of men."

24Then Jesus said to his disciples, "If anyone would come after me, he must deny himself and take up his cross and follow me.
25For whoever wants to save his life[a] will lose it, but whoever loses
his life for me will find it. 26What good will it be for a man if he

gains the whole world, yet forfeits his soul? Or what can a man give in exchange for his soul? [27]For the Son of Man is going to come in his Father's glory with his angels, and then he will reward each person according to what he has done. [28]I tell you the truth, some who are standing here will not taste death before they see the Son of Man coming in his kingdom."

[a]*25* The Greek word means either *life* or *soul*; also in verse 26.

16:21. Following Peter's confession that Jesus is "the Christ, the Son of the living God," Matthew now highlights a new stage in the life of Jesus. The term **began** (ἤρξατο, *ērxato*) definitely signals the beginning or start of a new emphasis in Jesus' ministry. Not only does Jesus speak emphatically concerning his fate in Jerusalem, he also impresses upon his disciples the absolute necessity (*dei*) for his course of action. The events in Jerusalem should not be construed as a tragic twist of impersonal fate or the mere haphazard working of blind chance. Jesus intends to **explain** (δείκνυμι, *deiknymi*, lit., "show" or "exhibit"; cf. 4:8; 8:4), or vividly demonstrate not only by what he says, but also by what he does, that it is in accordance with God's will that he suffer and die.[27] It is precisely this dimension of Jesus' messianic mission and divine Sonship that Peter's confession (16:16) lacked.

Jesus' passion predictions (16:21; 17:22; 20:17-19) exhibit a progression of specificity and detail. In verse 21 the reader learns that it is of divine necessity (*dei*)[28] that Jesus "suffer many things." Three groups are identified as responsible for what Jesus will suffer: "elders, chief priests, and teachers of the law." It is probable that the three groups are representative of the Sanhedrin, Israel's highest judicial and legislative body. Hence, although Jesus' suffering and death were according to God's divine plan, his suffering and execution were inflicted upon him by the highest Jewish court in the land. Nevertheless, God's divine sovereignty never diminishes either

---

[27]Bauer, *Structure of Matthew's Gospel*, pp. 104-105.

[28]Hagner, *Matthew*, 2:479. The verb δεῖ points to the fulfillment of God's will (cf. 26:54). "It is thus the compulsion of God's will that lies behind the following four infinitives [ἀπελθεῖν, παθεῖν, ἀποκτανθῆναι, ἐγερθῆναι; *apelthein, pathein, apoktanthēnai, egerthēnai*], which are syntactically governed by dei."

moral responsibility or human culpability. But God does vindicate his Son by raising him from the dead (note passive ἐγερθῆναι, *egerthēnai*). It is significant that in all three passion predictions Jesus' view of what lies ahead concludes with confidence that God's vindication will take the form of his restoration to life. Hence, the performance of God's will should never be compromised by the fear of death.

16:22. Peter found Jesus' words totally incongruent with his understanding of Jesus' messianic mission and divine Sonship. His consternation with Jesus' prediction compelled him privately, but sternly, to reprove Jesus for such a thought. Remarkably, Peter is so fixed on his own understanding of Jesus' mission, that even though he confessed him to be the Messiah, Son of God (v. 16), and addresses him as **Lord**, he thinks Jesus must be mistaken concerning the fate awaiting him in Jerusalem. The words, **Never, Lord** translate a Septuagintal idiom meaning something like "far be it from you, Lord."[29] This is followed by the strongly emphatic, **This shall never happen to you** (note the double negative οὐ μή, *ou mei*). Even though well intentioned, Peter has taken a stance that both put him at odds with God's will and placed him as a major obstacle in the path that Jesus is resolved to walk.

16:23. The seriousness of Peter's assertion (v. 22) becomes evident with Jesus' response. Peter had unwittingly assumed the role of Satan who earlier sought to deter Jesus from walking the path of true Sonship (4:1-11; esp. v. 10). Jesus' rebuke stands in stark contrast to his earlier "blessing" pronounced upon Peter (v. 17). While his earlier confession was inspired by God (v. 17), his present effort to thwart the plan of God emanates from Satan. Peter was susceptible to being used by Satan because he did **not have in mind the things of God, but the things of men**. Like many of his contemporaries, Peter's agenda and aspirations for the Messiah involved triumphant glory, not a seeming defeat at the hands of his enemies. If Peter is to understand the "wisdom of the cross" he must set aside personal ambitions driven by natural inclinations, and set his mind on "the things of God." In order for Peter and the other disciples to emulate Jesus' sacrificial ministry they must come to see his

[29]See Davies and Allison, *Matthew* 2:662.

mission of suffering and death as a positive expression of God's will.

16:24. Jesus then addresses all the disciples and insists that just as he "orients his life around the cross, so the disciples are to orient their lives around the cross."[30] In fact, it is incumbent upon all who would be a committed follower of Jesus (=disciple) to renounce self-oriented ambitions and personal interests, and give absolute priority to the doing of God's will. The ultimate expression of self-denial involves a willingness to emulate Jesus in the way of the cross; i.e., to embark upon a ministry of selfless devotion and service on behalf of others. Jesus' words are obviously descriptive of a lifestyle driven by a radically different worldview. He was not talking about minor inconveniences or enduring the common maladies of life.[31] The metaphorical expression "to take up one's cross" graphically recalls the actions of a condemned man who must bear his cross to the place of execution. Jesus thus calls upon his followers to assume the mentality of a man who is already condemned to die.[32] Rather than preserve one's life at any cost, Jesus' disciples must assume an attitude of self-denial, voluntarily surrendering his/her life for the sake of the kingdom (=God's will). This sort of discipleship is not a matter of convenience, but a way of life, that faithfully and humbly walks the same path of sacrificial devotion and service first walked by Jesus.

16:25. As indicated by the conjunction γάρ (*gar*), verse 25 is intended to further clarify and elucidate verse 24. The reason that Jesus' followers must live sacrificially, even renouncing their own lives for the sake of others, is that true spiritual life can only be realized by such devotion. Paradoxically, those who seek to preserve their physical lives at any cost, forfeit an existence that transcends the physical. As Meier aptly observes, "The paradox of temporal loss for eternal gain is *the law* of Christian existence."[33]

---

[30]Bauer, *Structure of Matthew's Gospel*, p. 104.

[31]As is sometimes suggested by the common saying, "We all have our cross to bear."

[32]See I.H. Marshall, *Commentary on Luke*, NIGTC (Grand Rapids: Eerdmans, 1978), p. 373.

[33]J.P. Meier, *Matthew* (NTM 3; Wilmington, DE: Michael Glazier, 1989), p. 187.

Jesus makes it clear that it is not sacrificial devotion to any cause that results in true spiritual life. It is service based on and motivated by one's allegiance to Jesus (**for me**, ἕνεκεν ἐμοῦ, *heneken emou*, lit., "on my account," cf. 5:11; 10:18, 39; 19:29) that results in **life** that transcends death. The disciple belongs to Jesus and obediently submits to his will. Jesus certainly exhibits a remarkable self-appraisal when he locates the fullness of spiritual life in service on his behalf. In contrast to those who would preserve their lives at any cost, it is the person who dies to self, and loses selfish concerns in service to Christ that discovers the true essence of life.

16:26. The supreme importance of spiritual life is next driven home (note *gar*) by two rhetorical questions. The first question assumes the primacy and ultimate value of one's **soul** (ψυχή, *psychē*) over even the possibility of taking possession of the entire world. When weighed in the balance, possession of all the world has to offer cannot possibly transcend the value of one's "life." The supreme value of one's life over all the world is forcefully brought out by the second question. There is virtually nothing in the world that could be given **in exchange for** one's life. Given the value of the soul (i.e., the essence of one's being), there is no earthly possession that could possibly warrant a tradeoff. These truisms are intended to cultivate a sense of values and priorities so that the disciples will come to perceive that self-denial and the way of the cross is an ultimate good to be pursued.

16:27. The third reason (*gar*) why the disciples should deny themselves and take up their crosses is that life in the human realm should take into account the return of the Son of Man as eschatological judge. The Son of Man who experienced humiliation in this world (8:20), and who will suffer and die at the hand of his enemies (v. 21) will also return and hold **each person** accountable for **what he has done**. This time he will come in transcendent glory and authority, accompanied by his angels (cf. 13:41; 24:31; 25:31), and all those who despised and rejected him must then have their eternal destiny decided by him. Indeed, Jesus will participate in the eschatological judgment of all humanity, deciding the value and worth of every deed. It therefore behooves the disciples to devote the entirety of their lives to a ministry patterned after Jesus' selfless devotion.

16:28. Jesus closes his remarks to the disciples with an especially important promise, introduced with the words, **I tell you the truth** (ἀμήν, *amēn*, "truly"). Jesus announces that some among his present audience (i.e., the disciples) will not die before they witness **the Son of Man coming in his kingdom**. In verse 27 Jesus foretells his coming as the Son of Man in judgment; now he promises that some of his disciples will see his coming in kingly power. Like 10:23 this text has been interpreted to mean that Jesus anticipated the end-time and the final triumph of the kingdom in the lifetime of at least some of his disciples. But elsewhere Jesus refuses to set time parameters for his return (24:42f.), and even affirmed that he did not know when the end would come (24:36). It is doubtful, therefore, that the text should be understood as predicting the parousia sometime in the first century.

But what event took place within the lifetime of some of his disciples that could be construed as a manifestation of Jesus' kingly presence? Some point to the very next scene, a mere six days later (17:1-8), when Jesus is transfigured before "some" of the disciples, and his awesome glory was manifested, as the fulfillment of Jesus' words. But the language of v. 28 does not fit well with an event that occurs just six days later. Other options proposed include, (1) the resurrection and ascension; (2) the day of Pentecost; (3) the empowering of the church for a worldwide mission; (4) the destruction of Jerusalem; (5) the second coming of Jesus; (6) or possibly some combination of the various proposals.[34] It is difficult to decide on any one event since the manifestation of the Son of Man in kingly glory and power can come in a variety of ways and events. In my judgment options 1, 2, and 4 have the greatest likelihood of being what Jesus meant by the "coming of the Son of Man in his kingdom." But be that as it may, Jesus' words were ultimately intended to cultivate among the disciples a lifestyle that takes seriously Jesus' sovereign authority and his path of selfless service.

---

[34]For surveys of the various options see Davies and Allison, *Matthew* 2:676-681; and Hagner, *Matthew* 2:485-487.

MATTHEW 17

B. TRANSFIGURATION (17:1-8)

[1]After six days Jesus took with him Peter, James and John the brother of James, and led them up a high mountain by themselves. [2]There he was transfigured before them. His face shone like the sun, and his clothes became as white as the light. [3]Just then there appeared before them Moses and Elijah, talking with Jesus.

[4]Peter said to Jesus, "Lord, it is good for us to be here. If you wish, I will put up three shelters – one for you, one for Moses and one for Elijah."

[5]While he was still speaking, a bright cloud enveloped them, and a voice from the cloud said, "This is my Son, whom I love; with him I am well pleased. Listen to him!"

[6]When the disciples heard this, they fell facedown to the ground, terrified. [7]But Jesus came and touched them. "Get up," he said. "Don't be afraid." [8]When they looked up, they saw no one except Jesus.

It is unusual for Matthew to link events together by documenting how much time elapsed between episodes (v. 1 "after six days"). It is doubtful that the notation of time was simply to indicate how long it took them to travel from Caesarea Philippi (16:13) to the mountain where the transfiguration takes place (17:1f.). The temporal reference is intended to closely tie the transfiguration scene with the events that occurred in Caesarea Philippi (16:13-28). It is significant that the transfiguration happens only a few days after Peter's confession (16:16), and Jesus' prediction of his suffering and death (16:21). Once again the revelatory action of God (cf. 16:17) reveals to a select few Jesus' transcendent glory and status

(17:1-8). However, as emphasized in 16:21-23, Jesus' exalted status is qualified by his role as God's Suffering Servant (17:5).

It has also been observed that the account of Jesus' transfiguration has many parallels with the experience of Moses on Mt. Sinai (cf. Exod 24 and 34). Both Jesus and Moses ascend a mountain, and after a "six day" interval the glory of the Lord is revealed (cf. Exod 24:15-16).[1] In both incidents three men are specifically named as being present (Exod 24:1, "Aaron, Nadab, and Abihu"; 17:1 "Peter, James, and John"). Both scenes mention the presence of a cloud (Exod 24:15f.), and the glory of God being revealed. Both Jesus and Moses experience an alteration of their appearances. However, while Moses' shining face reflected God's glory, Jesus' transformed appearance radiated from within, reflecting the glory of God's presence in him. In both instances the voice of God was heard (cf. Exod 24:16; Matt 17:5), and in the Matthean context, God's exhortation to "listen" to Jesus (17:5), may be an allusion to Deuteronomy 18:15 where Moses predicts that God will raise up a prophet like him, and all the people "must listen to him" (Deut 18:15-18). It certainly appears that Matthew does intend his readers to see Sinai motifs behind his narration of Jesus' transfiguration.[2]

17:1-2. Jesus leads three of his disciples (**Peter, James, and John**) onto a very **high mountain**. The precise location is not named, possibly "so that the reader is free to make symbolic associations with mountains of biblical importance, such a Sinai, Carmel, or Moriah."[3] In the privacy of this setting, Jesus' physical appearance was dramatically altered (μετεμορφώθη, *metemorphōthē*), so that **his face shone like the sun, and his clothes became as white as light** (cf. Exod 34:29; 2 Cor 3:7, 11). The brilliance of Jesus' true

---

[1]Although Moses and his companions were already on the mountain for a six day period, both accounts indicate that God spoke and his glory was revealed after a six day period (cf. Exod 24).

[2]See W.L. Liefeld, "Theological Motifs in the Transfiguration Narrative," in *New Dimensions in New Testament Study*, eds. R.N. Longenecker and M.L. Tenney (Grand Rapids: Zondervan, 1974), pp. 162-179; also Davies and Allison, *Matthew* 2:705-706, who also notes how the transfiguration narrative has many parallels to the account of Jesus' execution (27:32-54).

[3]Liefeld, "Transfiguration," p. 167. Although Mt. Tabor is the traditional site, Liefeld makes a case for Mt. Meron, the highest mountain within Israel (3,926 ft.).

glory is God's revelatory disclosure to the disciples (note the passive). They are privileged to experience firsthand a remarkable disclosure of Jesus' transcendent glory and status. Certainly they would never look at Jesus in the same way after such a remarkable event.

17:3. The astonishing character of the scene is even further enhanced by the appearance of two of Israel's most illustrious figures, **Moses and Elijah**. The presence of Israel's great lawgiver, Moses, accompanied with Elijah, the famed prophet, may be intended to represent the "law and the prophets." Thus, while their conversing with Jesus indicates a degree of continuity between their work and the mission of Jesus, their ultimate departure (v. 8) indicates the surpassing greatness of Jesus' person and role, in terms of fulfillment. It may also be that general expectations concerning the return of Moses and Elijah in the Messianic Age (cf. Deut 18:15-18; Mal 3:1; 4:6) prompted Matthew to mention their presence. Whatever the precise significance of their presence, the ensuing narrative makes it clear that in Jesus the line of God's faithful servants has reached its ultimate fulfillment.[4]

17:4. The majestic and imposing aura surrounding the scene prompted Peter's proposal to erect **three shelters**, one for each of the notable figures before him. The flaw in Peter's honorary proposal is that it seemed to relativize Jesus by equating him in importance with Moses and Elijah. Although Peter does acknowledge Jesus' authority (**if you wish**), by equating Jesus with Moses and Elijah he has adopted a human point of view (cf. 16:23), similar to the popular proposals noted in 16:14. Once again, while good intentioned, Peter reveals his failure to see the real significance of Jesus transfigured state and the appearance of Moses and Elijah.

17:5. While still speaking, Peter is interrupted by an awesome sight signaling the very presence of God. Suddenly **a bright cloud enveloped them** (ἐπισκιάζειν, *episkiazein*, cf. Exod 19:19), not casting a shadow, but flooding the place with dazzling light. The imagery is reminiscent of the Shekinah glory of God (Isa 4:5), and the glory of the Son of Man described in Daniel 7:13.[5] From the

---

[4]France, *Matthew*, p. 263.
[5]Liefeld, "Transfiguration," pp. 169-170.

midst of the cloud God once again offers his evaluative point of view concerning Jesus' identity and role. In language virtually verbatim to the announcement made at his baptism (3:17), Jesus is identified as God's Son, in whom he delights. The allusion to Psalm 2 (**this is my Son**) recalls Jesus Messianic status, especially his Kingly role as the Son of David. The allusion to Isaiah 42 (**with him I am well pleased**) is suggestive of Jesus' role as God's Suffering Servant who conforms to his Father's will. This emphasis is especially poignant in light of Jesus' prediction concerning his fate in Jerusalem (e.g., 16:21). The command to **Listen to him** is not found in the baptism announcement. As noted earlier the exhortation may be an allusion to Deuteronomy 18:18-19, and thus show Jesus to be God's authoritative spokesman. If the disciples are to grasp the significance of Calvary they must put aside their own agendas and personal ambitions and learn from the authoritative words of Jesus.

17:6-8. The disciples were overcome with fear upon hearing the voice of God, and hid their faces in terror. Nevertheless, Jesus by his "touch" (cf. 8:3, 15; 9:29; 20:34) seeks to still their fears as he orders them to get up and stop being afraid. It is critical that they not allow their terrifying experience to stifle the work at hand. The transcendent glory of Jesus is always balanced by his compassionate response to human frailty. When the disciples who had **fallen face-down to the ground** looked up, only Jesus was before them. The absence of Moses and Elijah reinforces the centrality of Jesus as the pivotal figure in God's salvific plan.

Although the disciples must come to understand Jesus' mission in terms of suffering and death (16:21), the transfiguration, along with God's assessment of his Son (v. 5), foreshadow Jesus' ultimate vindication and subsequent glorification. The themes of Jesus' glory and divine status alongside his humble obedience continue to dominate Matthew's portrayal of Jesus.

C. THE COMING ELIJAH (17:9-13)

9As they were coming down the mountain, Jesus instructed them, "Don't tell anyone what you have seen, until the Son of Man has been raised from the dead."

[10]The disciples asked him, "Why then do the teachers of the law say that Elijah must come first?"

[11]Jesus replied, "To be sure, Elijah comes and will restore all things. [12]But I tell you, Elijah has already come, and they did not recognize him, but have done to him everything they wished. In the same way the Son of Man is going to suffer at their hands." [13]Then the disciples understood that he was talking to them about John the Baptist.

17:9. While coming down from the mountain Jesus prohibits his disciples from telling anyone what they had just witnessed (ὅραμα, *horama*). The command to silence is motivated by the inappropriateness of proclaiming Jesus' glorious status apart from the reality of the cross. It is only after the cross, and his vindication by God in the resurrection, that the significance of the transfiguration can rightly be understood. Hence, these verses, (i.e., 9-13) link the transfiguration to the resurrection and therefore tie the transfiguration vision to the passion predictions (cf. 16:21; 17:23; 20:19). The Son of Man, who is the "Christ, the Son of the living God" (16:16, 17:5), who radiates God's divine presence (17:2-3), is also the one who will suffer and die (16:21, 17:12), but will be raised in glory (17:9), and one day return as eschatological judge (16:27). The reader is therefore encouraged to read the exalted titles in terms of a mission involving suffering and death.

17:10. Although one might expect the disciples to question Jesus about their experience on the mountain, or perhaps the reason for his prohibition (v. 9), they instead seek his response to the scribal contention that **Elijah must come** before the inauguration of the messianic era (cf. 11:14). Presumably, Jewish belief about Elijah's reappearance was based on Malachi 4:5, where Elijah is depicted as a messianic precursor.[6] It may be that the religious authorities had earlier used this text in opposition to the messianic claims surrounding Jesus. Hence, they would argue that Jesus could

---

[6]For a discussion addressing the question whether Elijah was viewed in Judaism as a forerunner of the Messiah, see M.M. Faierstein, "Why Do the Scribes Say that Elijah Must Come First?", *JBL* 100 (1981), 75-86; D.C. Allison, "Elijah Must Come First," *JBL* 103 (1984) 256-258; and J.A. Fitzmyer, "More About Elijah Coming First," *JBL* 104 (1985), 295-296.

not be the Messiah since no figure comparable to Elijah had arisen. The disciples are therefore soliciting Jesus' response to the scribal contention that Elijah would have an active part in the messianic era (= "day of the Lord," Mal 4:5-6).

17:11-12. Jesus is in agreement with the scribal interpretation that Elijah must come first, but insists that **Elijah as already come**. His task is described as to **restore all things** (ἀποκαταστήσει, *apokatastēsei*). It is difficult to define precisely what is meant by the task of "restoration."[7] Most likely the idea behind "restoration" points to the preparatory renewal and reform suggested by Malachi 3:1.[8] Although it may be difficult for some to accept, in view of his brutal treatment in the hands of Herod, the preparatory work of John the Baptist is to be identified with the Elijah who was to come (cf. 11:14). The failure of the religious and political leaders to recognize and accept the pivotal role of John led them to act "toward him as though there was nothing to be considered but their own will"[9] (= **done to him everything they wished**).

But their treatment of John was only a foreshadow of Jesus' fate. Their failure to see the significance of John virtually guaranteed that Jesus' role as the promised Messiah would also be rejected. Nevertheless, although his inevitable suffering comes about by the hands of evil men, Jesus has accepted his fate as the ultimate expression of his Father's will (16:21). Hence, the glorious transfigured Son of Man is destined for a similar fate as that suffered by John.

17:13. Matthew closes the section by observing that the disciples finally make the connection between Elijah and John the Baptist. Perhaps their memories were jogged to remember the earlier explicit identification of John with Elijah (11:14). The theme of "understanding" is an important concept in Matthew since discipleship demands a level of apprehension (cf. 13:13-17, 51; 15:16; 16:12). The major question confronting the disciples is their ability to integrate the reality of the passion with their exalted estimation of Jesus.

---

[7]On the significance of the verb and the options proposed see Davies and Allison, *Matthew* 2:714-715.

[8]So Hagner, *Matthew* 2:499.

[9]Morris, *Matthew*, p. 444.

D. THE POWER OF FAITH (17:14-21)

[14]When they came to the crowd, a man approached Jesus and knelt before him. [15]"Lord, have mercy on my son," he said. "He has seizures and is suffering greatly. He often falls into the fire or into the water. [16]I brought him to your disciples, but they could not heal him."

[17]"O unbelieving and perverse generation," Jesus replied, "how long shall I stay with you? How long shall I put up with you? Bring the boy here to me." [18]Jesus rebuked the demon, and it came out of the boy, and he was healed from that moment.

[19]Then the disciples came to Jesus in private and asked, "Why couldn't we drive it out?"

[20]He replied, "Because you have so little faith. I tell you the truth, if you have faith as small as a mustard seed, you can say to this mountain, 'Move from here to there' and it will move. Nothing will be impossible for you.[a]"

[a]*20* **Some manuscripts** *you. [21]But this kind does not go out except by prayer and fasting.*

It may be that Matthew intended this episode to be reminiscent of Moses' descent from the mountain when he was confronted with Israel's rebellion and apostasy (Exod 32).[10] In this instance, Jesus is confronted with an "unbelieving and perverse generation" (v. 17) that exhibits "little faith" (v. 10) in God's power to resolve a spiritual crisis. Jesus therefore becomes a model of great faith, thus indicating that his fate in Jerusalem should not be construed as an indication of his powerlessness, but of his resolve to do the Father's will. If the disciples are to accept the cross, they must see it as an expression of faith not weakness.

17:14-16. When Jesus and the three disciples come down from the mountain, they encounter a crowd from which a man emerges to make a request of Jesus. The man exhibits an attitude of deep respect, assuming the posture of worship. The supplicant is described as kneeling (γονυπετῶν, *gonypetōn*), and addressing Jesus with reverential words (**Lord, have mercy on my son**). The condition of his son is described as having **seizures** (σεληνιάζεται, *selēniazetai*, lit.,

---

[10]Suggested by France, *Matthew*, p. 266.

"moonstruck," i.e., epileptic seizures were "associated in ancient times with the supernatural power of the moon" [Louw and Nida, *Greek English Lexicon*, 1:272]). The result of his severe condition was the loss of motor skills, often resulting in self-destructive behavior (**falls into the fire or into the water**). The reader subsequently will learn that the boy's condition was ultimately caused by demon possession (v. 18). The man also informs Jesus that he had brought his son to his disciples (i.e., the nine who did not accompany Jesus onto the mountain), and they were unable to relieve the boy's condition. In spite of their earlier empowerment to cast out demons (10:1, 8), they had miserably failed in their efforts to expel the demon from this stricken boy.

17:17-18. Seemingly frustrated with his powerless followers, Jesus indicts the entire **generation** as **unbelieving and perverse** (cf. Deut 32:5). Their powerless condition undermined the reality of God's powerful presence and his sovereign reign. In a kind of "prophetic lament"[11] Jesus poses the rhetorical question, **"How long shall I put up with you?"** The words spell out in graphic terms Jesus' exasperation with the faithless impotency of his disciples. Rather than exercise the divine authority given them, in Jesus' absence they had become part of a "faithless" generation. With a note of flustered impatience, Jesus orders the boy to be brought to him. With nothing more than a "rebuke" the demon is compelled to leave the boy and he is instantly **healed** (cf. Mark 9:20-17).

17:19-20. The disciples then inquire privately concerning the reason they were unable to drive the demon from the boy. Jesus is emphatic that their inability to cast out the demon was to be attributed to their **little faith**. It may be that they had become infatuated with previous successes and had forgotten the true source of their power. Or, possibly the absence of Jesus, coupled with the seriousness of the boy's condition, caused them to doubt their ability to remedy the situation. Whatever the exact reason for their "little faith," their focus was more on themselves than on the God who could empower them.

Although the disciples have "little faith," Jesus insists that if they possessed even a small amount of genuine faith that truly trusted in

[11]Hagner, *Matthew* 2:504.

God, they would have access to unlimited resources through the power of God. Jesus' proverbial and hyperbolic illustration of faith the size of **a mustard seed** commanding mountains to be removed, drives home the enormous potentiality of faith. In fact, Jesus promises that with such faith **Nothing will be impossible for you**. Contextually Jesus' words have reference to those things that promote and announce God's dynamic kingdom. Jesus assures his disciples that within the parameters of God's will nothing shall be impossible for the one who truly believes. However, lest we reduce faith to a kind of mind-over-matter technique, the observation by France is particularly noteworthy: "It is important to observe here that it is not the 'amount' of faith which brings the impossible within reach, but the power of God, which is available to even the 'smallest' faith.[12]

E. THE SECOND PASSION PREDICTION (17:22-23)[13]

22When they came together in Galilee, he said to them, "The Son of Man is going to be betrayed into the hands of men. 23They will kill him, and on the third day he will be raised to life." And the disciples were filled with grief.

With another passion prediction Matthew reminds the reader that everything comprising 16:21–20:34 must be seen under the shadow of the cross. The glorious transfigured Son of God (17:1-9), who has faith so as to remove mountains (17:20) will face suffering and death in Jerusalem.

17:22-23. Although the disciples "gather around" Jesus in **Galilee**, Jesus' focus is upon his fate awaiting him in Jerusalem. For the first time the reader learns that Jesus will be **betrayed** (παραδί-δοσθαι, *paradidosthai*) **into the hands to men**. It may be that the term does not refer specifically to his betrayal by Judas, but rather

[12]France, *Matthew*, p. 266.

[13]Verse 21 with the words "but this kind does not go out except by prayer and fasting" (see NIV footnote), lacks sufficient manuscript evidence and its presence in some MSS can be explained as an assimilation to Mark 9:29. See Metzger, *Textual Commentary*, p. 43.

to God's handing over of his Son to suffer and die (cf. 26:45). It is not at all improbable that Jesus' words are intended to allude to the fate of God's suffering servant as portrayed in Isaiah 53:6, 12. Once Jesus is "delivered" into the hands of men **They will kill him**, but God will raise him from the dead (cf. 16:21; 20:19). Unlike Peter's earlier response to the first passion prediction ("This shall never happen to you," 16:22), this time the disciples are deeply saddened by Jesus' prediction. At least they are listening to him (cf. 17:5) and are beginning to fathom the seriousness of the course of events.

F. JESUS AND THE TEMPLE TAX (17:24-27)

[24]After Jesus and his disciples arrived in Capernaum, the collectors of the two-drachma tax came to Peter and asked, "Doesn't your teacher pay the temple tax[a]?"

[25]"Yes, he does," he replied.

When Peter came into the house, Jesus was the first to speak. "What do you think, Simon?" he asked. "From whom do the kings of the earth collect duty and taxes – from their own sons or from others?"

[26]"From others," Peter answered.

"Then the sons are exempt," Jesus said to him. [27]"But so that we may not offend them, go to the lake and throw out your line. Take the first fish you catch; open its mouth and you will find a four-drachma coin. Take it and give it to them for my tax and yours."

[a]*24* Greek *the two drachmas*

Why Matthew included this scene at precisely this point in the narrative is not easy to discern. However, if one observes that the issue of paying the temple tax is resolved by the principle of not needlessly offending (σκανδαλίσωμεν, *skandalisōmen*, v. 27) others, then the episode does prepare the reader for a major theme developed in ch.18.[14] But also the principle reminds the readers of the

[14]See the treatment by W.G. Thompson, *Matthew's Advice to a Divided Community: Matthew 17:22-18:35* (Rome: Pontifical Biblical Institute, 1970); and Patte, *Matthew*, pp. 244-260.

way of the cross earlier articulated by Jesus (16:24-25). Jesus' followers must forgo their own prerogatives (="deny yourself") for the sake of a higher value. As Patte has shown, the various topics and issues enumerated in 17:24–18:35 are calculated to teach the disciples that self-denial and submission constitute the greater good, while self-preservation at the expense of others should be viewed negatively.[15]

17:24. Having returned to Capernaum, Peter is questioned about Jesus' policy regarding payment of the temple tax. The question is phrased in such a manner that a positive answer to their question is expected. Although there were some exemptions to the tax,[16] for the most part, all male Jews, twenty years and older, submitted to the tax as a matter of patriotic duty. The payment of **two drachmas** (=half shekel, or about one day's wages) was based on Exod 30:11-16 (cf. Neh 10:32-33), and was used to fund the daily activities associated with the temple cult. Although Jesus may have some grounds for exemption, a refusal to pay certainly could generate some hard feelings. Apparently for Peter there was no question that the Lord would fulfill his patriotic responsibility and pay the tax. Although he gives the right answer, he needs instruction concerning the principle involved.

17:25-26. Later, while in the **house** (probably Peter's) Jesus takes the initiative to revisit the issue of the temple tax. As a means to get Peter to look at the issue from a different perspective, Jesus asks Peter for his opinion regarding the collection of taxes: Do kings collect taxes from their immediate family or from the citizens over which they have authority? Peter correctly answers **from others**. Jesus then draws the necessary conclusion: **"Then the sons are exempt."** By analogy, the exemption extended to the "sons" of earthly kings would also apply to Jesus and his followers by virtue of their relationship to God as Father. It follows that not only does Jesus affirm that he and his disciples constitute God's immediate

[15]Patte, *Matthew*, p. 244f.

[16]See T.E. Schmidt, "Taxes" *DJG*, pp. 804-807. Schmidt contends that the "tax was voluntary and was paid almost exclusively by Pharisees." However, Josephus (*Ant.* 18.9.1) says it was collected every year from every Jew twenty years of age, both in the land of Israel and abroad. See also D.C. Snell, "Taxes and Taxation," *ABD* 6:338-340.

household, he also views "the temple cult as being irrelevant to Christians" (cf. 12:6; 24:1f.).[17]

17:27. However, the primary focus of the episode comes in v. 27. In order not to **offend** (*skandalisōmen*) Jesus is willing to forgo his rights and pay the tax. Payment is not a matter of necessity or obligation but a willingness to surrender one's own rights out of concern for the interest of others. Thus, although Peter was correct that Jesus will pay the tax, the reason for doing so is based on principle, not a mere customary obligation.

The usual manner of securing payment reinforces Jesus' unique relationship to God, who provides sufficient funds for his Son to pay the tax. In fact, the coin to be found in the mouth of a fish (στατῆρα [*statēra*] = shekel) was sufficient to provide payment for both Jesus and Peter. There is no contextual reason not to take the incident at face value, and recognize Jesus' supernatural foreknowledge in predicting the discovery of the coin in the mouth of a fish. Hence, the episode underscores the importance of not being sidetracked by trivial concerns that can only generate hostility and alienation. The reader is therefore prepared for a major thematic emphasis in ch.18.

[17]Hagner, *Matthew* 2:512.

MATTHEW 18

G. FOURTH DISCOURSE: LIFE IN THE CHRISTIAN COMMUNITY (18:1-35)

Jesus' fourth discourse (cf. 5-7; 10; 13) builds on the general themes of self-denial and sacrifice pervading 16:21–20:34, by describing "concrete expression of humility and self-denial within the life of the community."[1] Greatness in the kingdom is not determined by one's preeminence or social clout, but by a childlike humility (18:1-4) that sacrificially seeks the welfare of those who lack worldly significance and are weak and vulnerable (18:6-9). The disciples must learn to see the value of these "little ones" and their special relationship to the Father (18:10). Like an ever vigilant shepherd who is concerned for the welfare of every sheep, so the Father "is not willing that any of these little ones should be lost" (18:12-14).

Even an offending brother must be extended every opportunity for reconciliation (18:15-17). Only if he is adamant in his refusal, should he be regarded as an outsider (18:17). The activity of "binding and loosing" is predicated upon the efforts that are put forth on behalf of another, to restore brotherly relations with the offending one (18:18). Such efforts have the endorsement of the Father in heaven (18:19), and the assurance of the Lord's presence (18:20). But even if one is mistreated by others a forgiving spirit must prevail in order to hold out the possibility of reconciliation and the restoration of a relationship (18:21-27). To reinforce the point, Jesus tells a story contrasting a merciful king who pardons an offender (18:26-27, 33), with an unmerciful servant who does not possess a forgiving spirit (18:20-22a). The ultimate expression of humility and sacrificial service is the willingness to "forgive your

---

[1]Bauer, *Structure of Matthew's Gospel*, p. 131.

brother from your heart" (18:35). The character of the new community must be defined and shaped by the character of Jesus, who humbly and sacrificially gives himself up for the welfare of others.

The structure of the chapter naturally divides into five basic sections, corresponding to the paragraphs founds in the UBSGNT:[2]

vv. 1-5	Becoming like a child
vv. 6-9	Avoiding offense
vv. 10-14	Value of the "little ones" (Parable)
vv. 15-20	Reconciling an offending brother
vv. 21-35	Importance of forgiveness (Parable)

1. Becoming Like a Child (18:1-5)

[1]At that time the disciples came to Jesus and asked, "Who is the greatest in the kingdom of heaven?"

[2]He called a little child and had him stand among them. [3]And he said: "I tell you the truth, unless you change and become like little children, you will never enter the kingdom of heaven. [4]Therefore, whoever humbles himself like this child is the greatest in the kingdom of heaven.

[5]"And whoever welcomes a little child like this in my name welcomes me.

18:1. Not long after the episode closing the previous chapter (**at that time**), the disciples raise the question concerning **Who is the greatest in the kingdom of heaven**. Their question assumes a hierarchal pecking order in which status and clout are determined by one's rank. Once again they are "thinking the things of men," and view their life in the kingdom in terms of status and privilege, not self-denial and sacrifice. Their interest in prestige and power demonstrates that they did not fully grasp Jesus' recent prediction of his passion and sacrificial death (16:21; 17:22-23). Sadly, their preoccupation with such mundane concerns becomes evident when the issue of greatness surfaces again later, just prior to Jesus' entry into Jerusalem (20:20-28).

[2]See also Davies and Allison, *Matthew* 2:752, 781.

18:2. Jesus responds to the disciples by radically challenging and undermining their worldly values. By means of a **little child** (παιδίον, *paidion*) Jesus illustrates a core value fundamental to the kingdom. Jesus' actions were not calculated to call attention to some innate quality within children, such as innocence, humility, or being teachable. Rather, it is the status of children as the "weakest, most vulnerable members of society"[3] that is the focal point of Jesus' illustration. Children had no social clout or independent rights in the ancient world. They were utterly dependent on others for their livelihood and protection. They had no illusion of greatness or power according to worldly standards. Jesus' use of a child was to remind the disciples that in the kingdom greatness is measured by one's own sense of vulnerability and helplessness, and ultimate dependency upon God.

18:3-4. Rather than embrace the world's standards of greatness, Jesus challenges his disciples to **change and become like little children**. It is incumbent upon all disciples, if we are to experience fully God's reign, to exhibit a childlike indifference to worldly power and prestige. To become "humble" like a child is to understand that in the kingdom one's security and sense of identity (="greatness") are grounded not in human accomplishments or accolades, but in a relationship to God as Father.

18:5. The focus of vv. 2-4 is not about children *per se*, but about disciples who are viewed by the world as without worth and significance. In v. 5 the emphasis is not upon receiving literal children (cf. 19:13), but upon the reception of those disciples whom the world may view as weak and dispensable. To exhibit a hospitable reception of a disciple is tantamount to welcoming Jesus (cf. 10:40-42; 25:40, 45). Unlike the world which extends honor only to those possessing fame and power, in the kingdom the disciple emulates his/her Lord by welcoming the "least."

2. Avoiding Offense (18:6-9)

6But if anyone causes one of these little ones who believe in me to sin, it would be better for him to have a large millstone hung

[3]Malina and Rohrbaugh, *Social-Science Commentary*, p. 117.

around his neck and to be drowned in the depths of the sea.

[7]"Woe to the world because of the things that cause people to sin! Such things must come, but woe to the man through whom they come! [8]If your hand or your foot causes you to sin cut it off and throw it away. It is better for you to enter life maimed or crippled than to have two hands or two feet and be thrown into eternal fire. [9]And if your eye causes you to sin, gouge it out and throw it away. It is better for you to enter life with one eye than to have two eyes and be thrown into the fire of hell.

18:6. From the emphasis on the emulation of a childlike attitude (vv. 2-4), and the reception of those the world may deem as less than worthy (v. 5), Jesus now emphasizes the extreme measures to which one should go so as to avoid being instrumental in the downfall of a "little one." The repeated use of the term (*skandalizō* = to stumble or fall into sin, vv. 6-9), indicates that Jesus is concerned that among his followers there be a sensitive regard for the vulnerability of others. It is a serious matter to contribute to the downfall of a fellow believer. To illustrate the severity of God's judgment upon one who causes another to fall, Jesus affirms that **it would be better for him to have a large millstone** (= large, heavy stone usually turned by donkey power) **hung around his neck and to be drowned in the depths of the sea**, than to be instrumental in causing a "little one" to fall. Drowning at sea is to be preferred to the eschatological judgment that awaits the one who undermines the faith of those who believe in Jesus.

18:7. Jesus recognizes that in a fallen world numerous factors may contribute to the downfall of one of his disciples (cf. 13:37-43). Nevertheless, those who cause others to stumble will be held accountable. Thus, while there is a certain inevitability in the course of things, there is never a lessening of human responsibility (cf. 26:24, as in the case of Judas).

18:8-9. The language of these two verses is virtually the same as that recorded in 5:19-20. Previously, Jesus used this hyperbolic emphasis to underscore the drastic measures to which one should go in order to avoid lustful desires. In this instance, the language calls for drastic action so as to avoid sin of any kind. It is far better to suffer a self-imposed limitation in this life than to suffer the eternal loss of one's very being. Once again the priorities of the kingdom demand decisive action that may not square with worldly ambitions or the maintaining of our rights and privileges. Priority must be given the eternal state, even if it means an earthly existence of deprivation and repression.

3. Value of the "Little Ones" (18:10-14)

[10]"See that you do not look down on one of these little ones. For I tell you that their angels in heaven always see the face of my Father in heaven.[a]

[12]"What do you think? If a man owns a hundred sheep, and one of them wanders away, will he not leave the ninety-nine on the hills and go to look for the one that wandered off? [13]And if he finds it, I tell you the truth, he is happier about that one sheep than about the ninety-nine that did not wander off. [14]In the same way your Father in heaven is not willing that any of these little ones should be lost.

[a]*10* Some manuscripts *heaven. [11]The Son of Man came to save what was lost.*

18:10-11. These verses reinforce the value and worth of every disciple by highlighting the special relationship and care extended to them by the Father. Not only must Jesus' followers avoid any action that might cause a "little one" to be tripped up (*skandalizō*), they must not exhibit a disdainful attitude that results in devaluing or belittling a little one. The reason is (*gar*) that each of these **little ones** have a heavenly representative with direct access to the very presence of God. Elaborate Jewish angelogy proliferated a number of ideas about angelic involvement with God's people.[4] In Scripture angels are linked to God's people as a nation (Dan 10:13; 12:1), and with individual churches (Rev. 1:20). While Jesus does not develop in detail the role that angels may play in the life of the individual believer (cf. Heb 1:14), his words do imply that every disciple benefits from an angelic representative who brings their situation before the Father. The text, however, stops short of calling these angelic

[4]See D.F. Watson, "Angels," *ABD* 1:248-255.

representatives "guardian angels." It should be observed that these angels are in heaven, not upon the earth providing human protection. Nonetheless, Jesus' point is that if angels are concerned with the little ones then any maltreatment of them will surely not go unnoticed.

18:12. To illustrate the Father's concern for every disciple Jesus tells a parable in which the value of even one that has gone astray becomes the object of intense concern (vv. 12-14; cf. Luke 15:4-7). The imagery of a good shepherd who pastorally cares for all the sheep recalls the language of Ezekiel 34 where "the Sovereign LORD says: 'I myself will search for my sheep and look after them . . .'" (see 34:11-16). As noted earlier, the shepherd theme is important in Matthew's portrayal of Jesus (cf. 2:6; 9:36; 14:15; 15:29-39).

18:13-14. The shepherd in Jesus' parable who seeks out even one sheep gone astray is representative of the great value that God places upon the restoration and preservation of even one little one who has wandered away. It is the finding and rescuing of one sheep gone astray that produces a greater joy than remaining with the ninety-nine who stayed in the security of the fold. For that reason the shepherd does not hesitate to focus his concern upon the lost sheep, in order to experience the joy of restoration. Since it is God's will that none **of these little ones should be lost**, the disciples should exhibit the same regard, and go out of their way to assure the eternal welfare of all that are a part of God's flock. A disciple therefore will not despise that which God so highly values.

4. Reconciling an Offending Brother (18:15-20)

15"If your brother sins against you,[a] go and show him his fault, just between the two of you. If he listens to you, you have won your brother over. 16But if he will not listen, take one or two others along, so that 'every matter may be established by the testimony of two or three witnesses.'[b] 17If he refuses to listen to them, tell it to the church; and if he refuses to listen even to the church, treat him as you would a pagan or a tax collector.

18"I tell you the truth, whatever you bind on earth will be[c] bound in heaven, and whatever you loose on earth will be[c] loosed in heaven.

[19]"Again, I tell you that if two of you on earth agree about anything you ask for, it will be done for you by my Father in heaven. [20]For where two or three come together in my name, there am I with them."

[a]*15* Some manuscripts do not have *against you* [b]*16* Deut. 19:15 [c]*18* Or *have been*

If the disciple is to go to extreme measures to rescue a fallen brother or sister (vv. 10-14), how should the disciple respond to a personal offense committed by a fellow believer?[5] Essentially, Jesus calls for the same shepherd-like response, which pursues every avenue for possible reconciliation and the mending of relationships. It is not acceptable to cavalierly dismiss an offending brother without a concerted effort to effect reconciliation. It is not only the welfare of the offending brother or sister that is at stake. The solidarity of the Christian community has been seriously undermined and thus every effort must be exerted so as to restore the offending one to fellowship. Jesus' disciples must learn to value relationships and therefore accept the responsibility to hold others accountable for behavior that undermines Christian unity.

18:15. Jesus carefully outlines a judicious procedure for enabling an offending brother to acknowledge his sin and repent. First, since the offense is personal and of a private nature, the offended should confront the offender privately in order to make him aware (ἔλεγχον, *elengchon,* "to state that someone has done wrong with the implication that there is adequate proof of such wrongdoing" [Louw and Nida, *Greek-English Lexicon,* 2:436]) of his wrongdoing. If the individual **listens** (ἀκούσῃ, i.e., is persuaded of his guilt and seeks forgiveness) then the severed relationship has been restored (**you have won your brother over**). Thus, the sinner benefits and the disciple is no longer at risk of losing a brother or sister.[6]

---

[5]If εἰς σέ is original, then the offense appears to be something committed against a fellow believer, and not sin in general; see Gundry, *Matthew,* p. 367, as opposed to France, *Matthew,* p. 274. It seems from v. 21 that Peter's question understood the offense as personal.

[6]See discussion in Patte, *Matthew,* p. 253.

18:16. If the one-on-one effort proves fruitless, the disciple is to broaden the participants in the process to **two or three witnesses** (cf. Deut 19:15). Efforts are then made by a small number of disciples to persuade the offending brother to acknowledge his sin and repent. Care is taken not to escalate the problem beyond what is needed to effect a penitent response.

18:17. With the failure of a small group of disciples to bring about a change in the situation, Jesus advises to take the matter before the **church** (*ekklēsia*, cf. 16:18). Now the entire Christian community is brought into the process, not to punish the offender, but to add further weight to the effort of reconciliation. If the brother obstinately refuses to be moved by the persuasion of the Christian community, he is then to be regarded as an outsider, severed from the fellowship of the church. The Jewish proverbial designation of **pagan or a tax-collector** indicates that this brother has aligned himself with those outside the covenant and thus is to be socially avoided. However, the categorization of the fallen brother does not mean that the church should have no further contact with him. Since the church now relates to him as an outsider, classed among the worst of sinners, further contact must take the form of remedial association. It should be observed that in the expression **treat him as you would . . .** , the "you" is singular indicating that each member of the church is to abide by the corporate judgment,[7] and thus each member should accept the responsibility for holding the brother accountable for his actions. It is often the failure of the church to speak and act with a united front that results in seriously weakening the discipline process.

18:18. To reinforce the importance of the church responding to conduct unbecoming a disciple, Jesus assures his followers that their disciplinary actions have the endorsement of heaven's authority. Jesus' words are virtually identical to those addressed earlier to Peter (cf. 16:17). However, in this instance the authority to **bind . . . and . . . loose** extends to all the disciples, and is directly concerned with church discipline. Nevertheless, like 16:17 (see comments), the future perfect participles should be given their full perfect force, hence the translation, "will have been bound in heaven" . . . "will

[7]Carson, *Matthew*, p. 403.

have been loosed in heaven," best conveys the sense of the passage.[8] Therefore, the church's identification of sin and the appropriate discipline needed to effect repentance simply manifest that already decreed in heaven.

18:19-20. The section closes with the promise that when the Christian community is decisively one in its commitment, God will provide his guidance and resources to back such efforts. Contextually, the **anything** (πράγματος, *pragmatos*) to which God will be responsive has to do with the discipline of an erring brother. The text should not be read as a *carte blanche* assurance that God will provide "anything" that two or three agree upon. Jesus is simply assuring the Christian community that God's presence and his resources are available to a church that exhibits a united prayerful concern for the welfare of one of its members. The reason that the Father will do what is asked if two agree is because Jesus is present when **two or three come together in** his **name**. The sense may be that "if you gather in my name, I am there, and my presence will lead to the Father's support of your requests."[9] The theme of God's presence in Jesus is an important one in Matthew's Gospel (cf. 1:23; 28:20).

5. Importance of Forgiveness (18:21-35)

21Then Peter came to Jesus and asked, "Lord, how many times shall I forgive my brother when he sins against me? Up to seven times?"

22Jesus answered, "I tell you, not seven times, but seventy-seven times.[a]

23"Therefore, the kingdom of heaven is like a king who wanted to settle accounts with his servants. 24As he began the settlement, a man who owed him ten thousand talents[b] was brought to him. 25Since he was not able to pay, the master ordered that he and his wife and his children and all that he had be sold to repay the debt.

---

[8]See the discussion in D.A. Carson, *Exegetical Fallacies* (Grand Rapids: Baker, 1984), pp. 79-80.

[9]See R.A. Edwards, "Narrative Implications of *Gar* in Matthew," *CBQ* 52 (October 1990), 648.

26"The servant fell on his knees before him. 'Be patient with me,' he begged, 'and I will pay back everything.' 27The servant's master took pity on him, canceled the debt and let him go.

28"But when that servant went out, he found one of his fellow servants who owed him a hundred denarii.[c] He grabbed him and began to choke him. 'Pay back what you owe me!' he demanded.

29"His fellow servant fell to his knees and begged him, 'Be patient with me, and I will pay you back.'

30"But he refused. Instead, he went off and had the man thrown into prison until he could pay the debt. 31When the other servants saw what had happened, they were greatly distressed and went and told their master everything that had happened.

32"Then the master called the servant in. 'You wicked servant,' he said, 'I canceled all that debt of yours because you begged me to. 33Shouldn't you have had mercy on your fellow servant just as I had on you?' 34In anger his master turned him over to the jailers to be tortured, until he should pay back all he owed.

35"This is how my heavenly Father will treat each of you unless you forgive your brother from your heart."

[a]*22* Or *seventy times seven* [b]*24* That is, millions of dollars [c]*28* That is, a few dollars

The discourse closes with a parable stressing the importance of forgiveness. Like the earlier parable (vv. 12-13), which is bracketed by sayings interpreting the parable (vv. 10, 14), so this parable is bracketed by Jesus' exchange with Peter about forgiveness (vv. 21-22), and concludes with Jesus' application of the parable (v. 35).[10] The focus on forgiveness continues the dominant theme of the discourse by stressing the importance of seeking reconciliation and a restored relationship by learning to forgive one another from the heart. The previous effort to restore an offending brother (vv. 15-20) assumes a forgiving spirit that seeks a restored relationship. The subversion of conventional values dominates the discourse and is climaxed by Jesus' startling teaching on forgiveness found in the parable.

18:21-22. Peter, perhaps sensing Jesus' radical emphasis upon reconciliation and his call for forbearance, asks Jesus concerning

---

[10]Suggested by Garland, *Reading Matthew*, p. 194.

the limits of forgiveness. Peter's tentative suggestion of **seven** offenses before forgiveness is exhausted does surpass conventional thinking.[11] However, to even pose the question concerning the limitations of forgiveness demonstrates that Peter still thinks in worldly categories (cf. 16:23). Instead of a legalistic mindset that calculates how many offenses can be forgiven before retaliation is justified, Jesus insists that there are no limits to forgiveness (**seventy-seven times** [or "seventy times seven" as in NIV fn.] means always).[12] Rather than keeping track of the number of times we grant forgiveness, Jesus calls his followers to a basic mindset that is ever open to forgiveness and reconciliation. The point is graphically illustrated by the parable to follow.

As indicated by the introductory line, **the kingdom of heaven is like . . .** (v. 23), Jesus' parable is intended to delineate certain values characteristic of life under the reign of God (cf. 13:24, 31, 33, 44, 45, 47; 20:1; 22:2; 25:1). Those who embrace God as King must exhibit the same forgiving spirit toward others that God in his mercy has manifested toward us. The parable exhibits a threefold structure based on three distinct scenes: the king's accounting, vv. 23-27; the servant's accounting, vv. 28-31; the king's response, vv. 32-34.[13] The chapter concludes with Jesus' drawing out the principle concern of the parable (v. 35).

18:23-25. The first scene opens with a king who decides to **settle accounts** (συνᾶραι, *synarai*; cf. 24:45-51; 25:14-30) **with his servants**, probably meaning high ranking officials within the royal court. One particular "servant" is brought in who owed the king **ten thousand talents**. The figure is deliberately astronomical, juxtaposing the highest numeral (10,000), with the highest unit of currency (talent). Perhaps the figure of a "billion dollars" would be comparable to the debt owed the king. The fantastic sum is

---

[11]Rabbinic texts cited in Str-B 1:795-796, indicate that rabbinic tradition generally placed some limitation on the number of times forgiveness should be extended (e.g., three times, b. Yoma 86b-87a). Thus Peter's suggestion of seven times may appear extremely generous.

[12]It is possible that Jesus' reference to "seventy-seven times" is an allusion to Gen 4:23-24 to counter Lamech's unlimited desire for revenge.

[13]Suggested by B.B. Scott, "The King's Accounting: Matthew 18:23-24," *JBL* 104 (September 1985), 433-434.

intended to emphasize the human impossibility of ever repaying such a debt. However, the punishment for nonpayment was the confiscation of all his property, and the selling of his wife and children into slavery. Such actions were punitive, and could never begin to compensate for the debt owed. The exaggerated sum owed and the actions of the king are not intended to be read as a realistic account, with every detail corresponding to historical reality. The language is hyperbolic in order to illustrate the enormity of our debt to God.[14]

18:26-27. The servant pleads his case, knowing that his fortune rests solely with the graciousness of the king. In desperation he begs for patience and promises (unrealistically!) to pay back all that he owes. Hearing his servant's anguished petition the king **took pity upon him** (σπλαγχνισθείς, *splangchnistheis*, cf. 9:36; 14:14; 15:32; 20:34) and unexpectedly cancels the man's debt (δαίνειαν, *daineian*, lit., "cancel the loan," *BAGD*, p. 171). The king's unconditional gracious response ignores the request for more time and mercifully forgives the entire loan. Such an expression of compassion goes far beyond anything the servant could ever dare to ask or even imagine. Of course, the king's actions are illustrative of the enormity of God's incalculable graciousness toward the human condition.

18:28-31. In the second scene the story takes an unexpected turn. Instead of immediately sharing his good fortune with others, he seeks out a **fellow servant** who owes him a relatively small debt of **a hundred denarii**. Even though a hundred denarii would be equivalent to one hundred days' wages, it was a paltry sum in comparison to what the man had just been released from (i.e., ten thousand talents). Estimates are that it took anywhere from six to ten thousand denarii to equal the value of one talent. It follows that the second servant owed the first only a small fraction of what the king had forgiven (from six hundred thousand to one million times greater). But instead of being gracious to his fellow servant, the first servant responds with brutality, demanding full payment for the debt owed. Even when his fellow debtor responds with a plea for mercy, patterned after his own petition before the king, still the first

[14]As noted by Hagner, *Matthew* 2:538.

servant refuses to listen and has **the man thrown into prison until he could pay the debt**. Such a cold and heartless response to a fellow servant's plea is as unexpected and surprising as the king's gracious response to the unforgiving servant's pitiful condition. However, the outrageous injustice and ingratitude exhibited by the first servant does not go unnoticed. **Other servants** of the king had witnessed the injustice and are **greatly distressed** by the servant's actions. They recognize the inequity of the situation and promptly inform their master concerning the servant's behavior.

18:32-34. In the final scene the servant is once again summoned before the king. This time the king addresses him as a **wicked servant**, and calls him to account for the treatment of his fellow servant. It is clear that this time the king will have no mercy on the unforgiving servant. His failure to emulate the king's response to his own pleas for mercy has resulted in the withdrawal of the cancellation of his debt. He must now face his imprisonment and the "torturers" who will vent the king's wrath. Since the enormity of the debt can never hope to be repaid, the punishment is unending, thus typifying the eschatological destruction of the wicked.

18:35. The discourse concludes with Jesus drawing out the central point illustrated by the parable, if not the entire discourse. A forgiving spirit is fundamental to life in the kingdom. If you refuse to **forgive your brother from your heart**, you cannot expect God's forgiveness. We are called to emulate the Father's forgiving spirit by being ever accessible to reconciliation and forgiveness. As noted by Patte, "this is not a law that *stands above* the disciple and that they *simply must obey*. It is perceiving things from the perspective of the kingdom and, as a consequence, having *internalized* God's will" (emphasis added).[15]

---

[15]Patte, *Matthew*, p. 258.

MATTHEW 19

H. TRANSITION FROM GALILEE TO JUDEA (19:1-2)

An overview of the various episodes comprising chapters 19 and 20 reveals a series of events wherein Jesus radically challenges conventional values and personal rights.[1] Jesus calls for the stabilization and permanency of marriage, thus challenging a legal system that perpetuated divorce (19:3-9). Jesus' call to renounce the option of divorce seemed extraordinarily difficult for the disciples (19:10). But Jesus insists, that for the sake of the kingdom, some may even be called upon to renounce their right to marry (19:11-13).

Those deemed by society as weak and vulnerable (like children, 19:13-15), must not be marginalized, but accepted and even esteemed as a model of life in the kingdom. In a society where one's status and security were grounded in wealth and riches, Jesus calls for the renunciation of all possessions in view of the higher priority of following him (19:16-30). The parable of the landowner graphically illustrates a reversal of values based upon sheer generosity (20:1-16). In contrast, to the Gentile way of lording it over others, Jesus calls for his disciples to be servants, modeled after his own sacrificial mission (20:20-28). The section concludes with Jesus modeling a compassionate response toward those who cry out for mercy (20:29-34).

1When Jesus had finished saying these things, he left Galilee and went into the region of Judea to the other side of the Jordan. 2Large crowds followed him, and he healed them there.

---

[1]For an overview see W. Carter, *Households and Discipleship: A Study of Matthew 19-20* (JSNTSup 103; Sheffield: JSOT, 1994).

19:1. Once again the formulaic phrase, **when Jesus had finished saying these things** closes the discourse and sets the stage for the narrative to follow (cf. 7:28; 11:1; 13:53). The geographical note (**he left Galilee and went into the region of Judea . . .**) suggests to the reader that Jesus is on his way to Jerusalem to fulfill the divine will (cf. 16:21). The text thus signals an end to Jesus' Galilean ministry, not to return until after the resurrection (28:16).

Jesus enters Judea from east of the Jordan river, probably indicating that his travels from Galilee to Judea were done on the eastern side of the Jordan. It was customary for Jesus to take such a route in order to avoid Samaritan territory.

19:2. Reference to the **crowds** and Jesus' ongoing ministry of healing functions to stress the continuity between the Galilean and Judean ministry. In light of his ultimate rejection and death in Jerusalem, Matthew wants the reader to see that Jesus continued his compassionate ministry of healing (cf. 20:29-34).

I. MARRIAGE AND DIVORCE (19:3-9)

[3]Some Pharisees came to him to test him. They asked, "Is it lawful for a man to divorce his wife for any and every reason?"

[4]"Haven't you read," he replied, "that at the beginning the Creator 'made them male and female,'[a] [5]and said, 'For this reason a man will leave his father and mother and be united to his wife, and the two will become one flesh'[b]? [6]So they are no longer two, but one. Therefore what God has joined together, let man not separate."

[7]"Why then," they asked, "did Moses command that a man give his wife a certificate of divorce and send her away?"

[8]Jesus replied, "Moses permitted you to divorce your wives because your hearts were hard. But it was not this way from the beginning. [9]I tell you that anyone who divorces his wife, except for marital unfaithfulness, and marries another woman commits adultery."

[a]*4* Gen. 1:27 [b]*5* Gen. 2:24

19:3. Jesus' arrival back in the **region of Judea** (vv. 1-2; cf. 2:1, 5, 22; 4:25) is immediately met with Pharisaic opposition. Matthew informs the reader that the Pharisees came to "test" (πειράζοντες, *peirazontes*, cf. 4:1; 16:1; 22:35) Jesus. They evidently hope to legally discredit him by drawing him into the rabbinic debate concerning the legitimate grounds for divorce (for the various schools of thought see comments on 5:32). Hence, they pose the question: **"Is it lawful for a man to divorce his wife for any and every reason?"** (cf. Mark 10:32). The question calls for Jesus to take sides in the contemporary debate. Perhaps they had heard about Jesus' absolute prohibition of divorce (cf. Mark 10:11-12; Luke 16:18), and therefore hoped to expose his failure to take seriously the Mosaic legislation in Deuteronomy 24. Whatever their exact motives, they certainly hoped that their exchange would provide sufficient leverage to call for Jesus' absolute repudiation.

19:4-6. Jesus responds by first underscoring their ignorance of Scripture by sarcastically asking, **"Haven't you read . . . ?"** (cf. 12:3, 21: 21:16, 42; 22:31) your own creation story (i.e., LXX Gen 1:27 and 2:24). Jesus thus speaks authoritatively about God's original intention with respect to marriage. Originally God created **male and female** (Gen 1:27), and decreed that in marriage the husband is **united to his wife and the two will become one flesh** (Gen 2:24). Since the woman was originally taken out of man, the joining of a man and woman in marriage was a reuniting, where two distinct beings become one again. The "one flesh" symbolism spells out in the strongest possible terms the relational and personal intimacy that should characterize the marital union.[2] Since God originally ordained that marriage be an inseparable bond, grounded in covenantal commitment, "man is to stop separating what God has united" (μὴ χωρίζετο, *mē chōrizeto*). Thus, Jesus' initial response goes beyond major rabbinic interpretations to label all divorce as a violation of God's original intention for the one-flesh union in marriage.

19:7-8. The Pharisees respond to Jesus' words by appealing to Deuteronomy 24:1, which they interpret as a Mosaic command (ἐνετείλατο, *eneteilato*, cf. Mark 10:3), giving authorization to divorce. In effect, Deuteronomy 24:1-4 was read as setting forth the

---

[2]See W.A. Heth, "Divorce and Remarriage: The Search for an Evangelical Hermeneutic," *TrinJ* 16 (1995), 82-84; also Gary Collier, "Rethinking Jesus on Divorce," *RQ* 37 (1995), 85.

conditions legitimizing divorce. Thus rabbinic debate shifted to defining precisely what the "indecency" (Deut 24:1; cf. m. Gitt. 9.10) was that virtually mandated divorce. However, Jesus reads the text not as a "command" but as a *concession* to their hardness of hearts. The Torah should not be read as either endorsing or mandating the practice of divorce. In fact, Deuteronomy 24:1-4 presupposes the practice of divorce and attempts to bring an element of restraint and legal protection for an already abusive situation. Jesus thus undermines any reading of Deuteronomy 24 that attempts to use this text as a basis for legitimizing the practice of divorce. The text must be read in light of God's original intention **from the beginning**. Jesus' reading of the Torah counters any manipulation of texts or faulty hermeneutic that attempts to circumvent the ultimate intention of God. Those who take seriously God's reign will understand the marital union in terms of God's original creative will.[3]

19:9. Having escaped the Pharisaic effort to discredit him as opposing Moses (v. 7), Jesus closes the discussion with his own pronouncement concerning marriage: **anyone who divorces his wife, except for marital unfaithfulness** [πορνεία, *porneia*], **and marries another commits adultery**. As noted in 5:32, the Matthean exemption clause (except for marital unfaithfulness) has been the primary focus of scholarly attention. It should be observed that the text simply reinforces the sanctity of marriage and thereby effectively counters popular *halakah* regarding divorce. In one sense, Jesus is in agreement with the school of Shammai in that some form of sexual impropriety makes divorce permissible (see m. Gitt. 9.10). However, it should also be noted, that for Jesus Genesis 1 and 2 (not Deuteronomy 24) provides the primary framework for understanding the covenant of marriage. One of the problems with the Pharisaic fixation on Deuteronomy 24 is that they neglected the normative vision for marriage as revealed in the creation story. Ironically, Matthew's exception clause has been treated in much the same way today. Preoccupation with the grounds for severing a

---

[3]Richard Hays, *The Moral Vision of the New Testament: A Contemporary Introduction to New Testament Ethics* (San Francisco: Harper, 1996), pp. 347-378, observes Jesus' "bold hermeneutical moves" in opposition to the Pharisaic interpretation of Deut 24.

marital union has often been done at the expense of affirming the permanently binding commitment of marriage.

It would seem that Matthew's Jewish male readers would have taken for granted that a marriage would be irreparably damaged by any form of sexual impropriety on the part of one's wife. Some rabbis went as far as to recommend divorce of one's wife who even "gives the impression of having betrayed her husband."[4] Given Jewish sensitivities to the state of impurity that incurs if one remains in a relationship with an immoral woman,[5] the exception clause probably speaks to that issue. It would appear that Jesus' general unconditional prohibition of divorce found elsewhere (cf. Mark 10:11-12; Luke 16:18) is adapted and applied in the interest of Matthew's Jewish-Christian readers. The exception clause is therefore another concession to the fallen state of humanity. Divorce, for whatever reason, must always be viewed as a tragic failure and a serious perversion of God's original intention regarding marriage.

Those who purport to live under the reign of God will treat marriage as a sacred covenant, demanding loyalty and faithfulness. Our intent ought to be the enhancement and improvement of marriage rather than the contemplation of how one can avoid marital commitments. While being sensitive to human frailty and failure we must not dilute Jesus' vision of marriage as a permanent one-flesh union that cannot be dissolved except by the most grievous of circumstances.[6] However, when divorce happens the church must exhibit a redemptive response that seeks to love, encourage, and rebuild shattered lives.[7]

---

[4]See discussion in Tal Ilan, *Jewish-Women in Greco-Roman Palestine* (Peabody, MA: Hendrickson, 1995), p. 142.

[5]M. Bockmuehl, "Matthew 5:32; 19:9 in Light of Pre-Rabbinic Halakhah," *NTS* 35 (1989), 291-295; has demonstrated that divorce for adultery was not optional but mandatory among many groups in ancient Judaism; see also the discussion of D.C. Allison, "Divorce, Celibacy and Joseph (Matthew 1.18-25 and 19.1-12)," *JSNT* 49 (1993), 3-10.

[6]On the question of other possible grounds for divorce, other than sexual infidelity or possibly desertion (e.g., spousal abuse), see the remarks by Hays, *Moral Vision*, p. 372f.

[7]In defense of a person's right who has been legally divorced to remarry see C.S. Keener, . . . *And Marries Another*.

J. THE BEWILDERED RESPONSE OF THE DISCIPLES (19:10-12)

[10]The disciples said to him, "If this is the situation between a husband and wife, it is better not to marry."

[11]Jesus replied, "Not everyone can accept this word, but only those to whom it has been given. [12]For some are eunuchs because they were born that way; others were made that way by men; and others have renounced marriage[a] because of the kingdom of heaven. The one who can accept this should accept it."

[a]*12* Or *have made themselves eunuchs*

19:10. The disciples respond to the rigors of Jesus' words regarding divorce by suggesting (perhaps facetiously) that marriage might as well be avoided. As Hill observes, "They are virtually making the attractiveness of marriage contingent upon the possibility of easy divorce."[8] At least they recognize the extraordinary demands associated with discipleship.[9]

19:11-12. Jesus' reply indicates that "this word" (τὸν λόγον, *ton logon*), is not necessarily applicable to everyone. The referent of **this word** could apply either to Jesus' teaching comprising vv. 3-9, or, as is more likely, is intended to respond directly to the disciples' complaint and proposed renunciation of marriage in the preceding verse. Hence, Jesus in essence concurs with the disciples' conclusion (v. 10), that for some marriage may not be an option. He then provides some examples of those who either by physical necessity (**eunuchs . . . born that way**, or **made that way by men**), or those who for higher purposes have figuratively become eunuchs (cf. the language of 18:8-9) for the sake of the kingdom, and have therefore renounced their right to marry (e.g., as both Jesus and Paul, cf. 1 Cor 7). Jesus' words are intended to impress the disciples with the absolute claim that the kingdom must have over one's life, even for

[8]Hill, *Matthew,* p. 281.

[9]As Keener, " . . . *And Marries Another,*" p. 46, points out, the disciples are astonished that Jesus would absolve their right to get out of a bad marriage, which normally in the ancient world would have been pre-arranged by well-meaning parents.

some resulting in the renunciation of marriage. It should be observed that Jesus is not suggesting that celibacy be enforced upon a select few, or that celibacy be regarded as a holier state than being married. But for those whose ministry may demand it, and who are "gifted by God" (cf. 1 Cor 7:1-7), the celibate life may be of necessity. In all things, including marriage, life and service in the kingdom must be given priority.

K. THE LITTLE CHILDREN (19:13-15)

13Then little children were brought to Jesus for him to place his hands on them and pray for them. But the disciples rebuked those who brought them.

14Jesus said, "Let the little children come to me, and do not hinder them, for the kingdom of heaven belongs to such as these." 15When he had placed his hands on them, he went on from there.

19:13. The brief episode involving the children and the disciples' response to those who brought them to Jesus highlights the disciples' failure to perceive the inner qualities essential for the realization of the divine will. Once again the disciples embrace an ideological stance which reflects more the "things of men" than the"things of God" (cf. 16:23). They had evidently failed to learn the earlier lesson that "whoever welcomes a little child . . . in my name welcomes me" (18:5).

As noted earlier (cf. 18:1-4), children in the ancient world, while cherished within the family unit, were extremely vulnerable to the harshness of life within Palestinian peasantry. Various types of sickness stemming from malnutrition and poverty made childhood in the ancient world extremely precarious. Infant mortality rates were extremely high within peasant communities.[10] Concerned parents bringing their children to Jesus in hope of healing and protection is reflective of their deep concerns.

---

[10]See R.L. Rohrbaugh, "Introduction," *The Social Sciences and New Testament Interpretation* ed. R.L. Rohrbaugh (Peabody, MA: Hendrickson, 1996), pp. 4-5.

19:14-15. Remarkably, the conditions of childhood become a model of dependency and humility that is essential for God's will to be accomplished. By rejecting the children the disciples were essentially rejecting a mindset and quality of life fundamental to the kingdom of heaven. As such, Jesus' words radically challenge and reverse conventional values by extolling the qualities and virtues of those deemed by society as without social status and importance. Therefore, Jesus does not hesitate to lay his hands upon the little children and to bless them. Their childlike dependency stands in vivid contrast to the next scene involving a self-sufficient rich young man (19:16-22).

L. THE RICH YOUNG MAN (19:16-22)

Although the children of the previous scene represented the have-nots, the dependent and vulnerable, as it turns out they exemplify qualities associated with the kingdom, while the rich man, with all his possessions, exhibits a commitment and values antithetical to life in the kingdom. Social conventions that tie one's identity and sense of security to material possessions are not applicable to one's standing in the kingdom. Neither should divine favor be gauged by the accumulation of wealth or social prestige. In fact, a serious commitment to follow Jesus demands a willingness to share our resources with those in need, and, if the necessity arises, to even divest ourselves of all our possessions for the sake of bearing witness to God's presence in his kingdom. Hence, the relationship of wealth to discipleship is a critical lesson for the disciples to learn. The economics of the kingdom of God necessarily entails a radical worldview where true profit is realized in sacrificial sharing, and the renunciation of worldly goods for the sake of others becomes an investment in treasures not subject to earthly loss or corruption (cf. 6:20). In the scene that follows, a rich man is confronted with the radical demands of participation in the kingdom.

16Now a man came up to Jesus and asked, "Teacher, what good thing must I do to get eternal life?"

17"Why do you ask me about what is good?" Jesus replied. "There is only One who is good. If you want to enter life, obey the commandments."

[18]"Which ones?" the man inquired.

Jesus replied, "'Do not murder, do not commit adultery, do not steal, do not give false testimony, [19]honor your father and mother,'[a] and 'love your neighbor as yourself.'[b]"

[20]"All these I have kept," the young man said. "What do I still lack?"

[21]Jesus answered, "If you want to be perfect, go, sell your possessions and give to the poor, and you will have treasure in heaven. Then come, follow me."

[22]When the young man heard this, he went away sad, because he had great wealth.

[a]*19* Exodus 20:12-16; Deut. 5:16-20 [b]*19* Lev. 19:18

19:16. Jesus meets a man (later described as a "young man" who had great wealth, v. 22; cf. Luke 18:18, 23 "a certain ruler") who addresses him as **Teacher** (=rabbi, a noncommittal title of respect), and poses a most fundamental question: **what good thing must I do to get eternal life?**[11] It appears that the man was entirely sincere in his effort to have Jesus identify some notable deed that would ensure divine favor. He is, however, conscious of his own deficiency, and therefore seeks from Jesus some definitive act he has yet to perform. Unlike the helpless children in the preceding episode, the rich man appears totally confident in his ability to perform the necessary "deed," once the requirement for "life" is made known.

19:17. Jesus responds to the man with a question concerning **what is good?**, followed by an explicit statement identifying the true standard of goodness and how it is to be realized. Only God is to be regarded as **good**, and conformity to his **commandments** is an acknowledgment of his authority to define the good that should be done. Keeping the commandments is therefore not to be viewed as "an automatic passport to life, but as a pointer to the absolute goodness of the one who gave them."[12] As such, God's will as expressed

[11]Cf. Mark 10:17 "Good teacher, what must I do to inherit eternal life" (also Luke 18:18). For a plausible harmonization of the accounts see Carson, *Matthew*, pp. 422-423.

[12]France, *Matthew*, p. 285.

in Scripture undermines any notion that what is "good" can either be known or accomplished solely through human resources.

19:18-20. When the young man inquires **which ones** (ποίας, *poias*, lit., "what kind, or sort of commandments"), he evidently sought a commandment of a different sort, perhaps more weighty and fundamental in the eyes of God (cf. 22:36). Instead, Jesus directs his attention to five of the ten commandments (i.e., the fifth through the ninth; cf. order in Exod 20:12-16; Deut 5:16-20), with the addendum of Leviticus 19:18 concerning loving one's neighbor as oneself. These commandments are representative of the whole of the Torah and are fundamental for understanding God's standard of goodness. Of course, the reader knows that Jesus' understanding of observing God's commandments goes far beyond any external system or rabbinic *halakah* (cf. 5:17-48). But, like Saul of Tarsus who can claim that "as for legalistic righteousness faultless" (Phil 3:6), so this young man can confidently affirm, **"All these I have kept."** And certainly, given contemporary standards of legalistic righteousness, there is no reason to dispute the boast of the young man. But there appears to be a nagging suspicion within the young man that his conformity to mere external requirements may not be sufficient to assure divine favor, hence the question, **What do I still lack?**

19:21. Jesus now elevates the discussion beyond mere legalism to a life wholly devoted to the will and character of God (cf. 5:48). Such undivided, wholehearted devotion constitutes a call to "perfection" (τελείος, *teleios*, cf. Deut 18:13), and a righteousness far surpassing that of Pharisaic and scribal adherence (cf. 5:20). The young man is now confronted with the essential elements necessary for true "life" to be realized. First, he must be willing to part with everything he so highly valued and which gave him personal identity and social clout (cf. Luke 18:22). He is to totally identify with the **poor** (πτωχοῖς, *ptōchois*) by redistributing his wealth to those in need. Such conduct would constitute a practical exhibition of what it means to "love your neighbor as yourself" (Lev 19:18).[13] But Jesus

---

[13]Tom Wright, *Jesus and the Victory of God* (Minneapolis: Fortress Press, 1996), pp. 301-303, suggests that Jesus' command to sell his possessions and follow him replaces the commandments to get rid of all idols and to give total allegiance to a way of life like that suggested in the first com-

was not merely legislating charitable acts for the sake of the poor. His demand goes to the heart of the young man's personal weakness, hindering his full allegiance to the will of God. While total divesture of all he possessed may seem unduly demanding,[14] it was precisely his attitude toward his possessions that would keep him from the "life" he sought (cf. v. 16). Jesus' focus is upon discipleship as indicated by the closing words, **"Then come, follow me"** (cf. 4:18, 22; 9:9). If the rich man is **to be perfect** in his devotion to God, he must demonstrate a radical trust in God by divesting himself of all he has, and find a new sense of identity and purpose by following Jesus on a mission of self-denial and sacrifice.

19:22. The man's response indicates that Jesus has indeed spoken to his most fundamental need. Jesus' radical demands (*ton logon*; cf. 19:11) produces only "sadness" (λυπούμενος, *lypoumenos*, cf. the man in the parable who with great joy sold everything, 13:44). The reason the man was filled with sorrow is that **he had great wealth** (lit., "many possessions").[15] His preoccupation with his wealth made the demand of Jesus' words simply out of the question. It may be, as proposed by Garland, "His thumbs down on Jesus' proposal reveals that he wanted from him only some reassurance that would allow him to live out his days comfortable in the knowledge that eternal life had been added to the many other goods he had."[16]

M. WEALTH, REWARD, AND DISCIPLESHIP (19:23-30)

[23]Then Jesus said to his disciples, "I tell you the truth, it is hard for a rich man to enter the kingdom of heaven. [24]Again I tell

---

mandment. Now, however, instead of Torah, the young man is summoned to live under Jesus.

[14]Jesus' disciples are still called to share our goods generously with those in need. For a challenging discussion on sharing possessions see S.E. Wheeler, *Wealth as Peril and Obligation: The New Testament on Possessions* (Grand Rapids: Eerdmans, 1995).

[15]As Hagner, *Matthew* 2:558, observes, "the periphrastic construction ἦν ἔχων, with its emphasis on continuing action, suggests a preoccupation with his wealth."

[16]Garland, *Reading Matthew*, p. 203.

you, it is easier for a camel to go through the eye of a needle than for a rich man to enter the kingdom of God."

25When the disciples heard this, they were greatly astonished and asked, "Who then can be saved?"

26Jesus looked at them and said, "With man this is impossible, but with God all things are possible."

27Peter answered him, "We have left everything to follow you! What then will there be for us?"

28Jesus said to them, "I tell you the truth, at the renewal of all things, when the Son of Man sits on his glorious throne, you who have followed me will also sit on twelve thrones, judging the twelve tribes of Israel. 29And everyone who has left houses or brothers or sisters or father or mother[a] or children or fields for my sake will receive a hundred times as much and will inherit eternal life. 30But many who are first will be last, and many who are last will be first.

[a]*29* **Some manuscripts** ***mother or wife***

The arduous demand of Jesus, coupled with the young man's unwillingness to accept the call to discipleship, necessitates further explanation. Jesus must help the disciples to understand the dangers of earthly wealth, as well as the eschatological blessings that await those who forsake worldly securities and even human relationships for the sake of allegiance to him ("for my sake," 19:29). Until they embrace the higher values and principles associated with devotion to God's reign, Jesus' sacrificial ministry will not be seen in its proper light.

19:23-24. Jesus makes it clear that it is extremely difficult (δυσκόλως, *dyskolōs*) for the rich to embrace wholeheartedly the priorities and values of the kingdom. Obviously, the more one has the more difficult to sacrificially share one's goods, and to renounce the seductive tendency to rely upon one's wealth for security and sense of well-being. Jesus then illustrates the point by comparing **a rich man** entering the kingdom to a **camel** (the largest animal in Palestine) attempting to go through **the eye of a needle** (the smallest opening). Jesus' proverbial analogy should not be weakened by reading κάμηλον (*kamēlon*, camel) as κάμιλον (*kamilon*, meaning "rope"), as several later textual witnesses attempt to do.[17] Neither should we imagine some fictitious gate called "the Needle's Gate," where camels found it difficult to squeeze through.[18] In fact, "the parable deliberately presents a picture of something *quite impossible.*"[19] Contrary to a culture that tended to see wealth as a sign of divine favor, Jesus is emphatic that riches constitute a major deterrent to life in the kingdom.

19:25-26. The disciples, perhaps reflecting contemporary values, respond with utter amazement (ἐκπλήσσω, *ekplēssō,* the term is a particularly strong expression: "to be so amazed as to be practically overwhelmed" [Louw and Nida, *Greek-English Lexicon,* 1:312]), **"Who then can be saved?"** Jesus' words seem to undermine their basic assumptions about wealth as an indicator of divine approval. If such illustrious wealthy figures as Abraham, Solomon, David, and even this well-respected young man experience difficulty in entering the kingdom, how could lesser mortals ever hope to enjoy salvation? Jesus replies that if salvation were dependent upon human resources then no one, including the rich, could have any hope of salvation. It is therefore only by means of God's unlimited power that human salvation is possible (cf. Gen. 18:14; see also Joseph of Arimathea, 27:57). Once again the disciples are challenged to assess things not according to the "things of men" but according to the "things of God" (cf. 16:23). The fact is, it is God who works mightily in people's lives so as to bring about salvation. Thus, while wealth may greatly hinder one's spiritual progress, God can effectively work so as to overcome all earthly circumstances.

19:27. Peter, perhaps finding renewed confidence raises the question concerning their own reward, since they had indeed, contrary to the rich young man, **left everything to follow** Jesus. While Peter's question may appear somewhat crass and self-promoting, Jesus gives no indication that the question was totally out of line. They had indeed made significant sacrifices and such will be richly rewarded (vv. 28-29). However, they must realize that their reward greatly overshadows any sacrifice they might have made.

---

[17]See discussion in Metzger, *Textual Commentary*, p. 169.

[18]Carson, *Matthew*, p. 425 suggests that "this conjecture may come from some of Jerome's allegorizing."

[19]See K.E. Bailey, *Through Peasant Eyes* (Grand Rapids: Eerdmans, 1980), p. 166.

19:28. Those who have initially followed Jesus shall have meaningful roles in the world that is to come (παλιγγενεσία, *palingenesia*).[20] They will be enthroned with **the Son of Man** in his glory, sharing judgment over **the twelve tribes of Israel**. France rightly calls attention to the background of Daniel 7 to explain "the themes of thrones, glory, judgment, and Kingship associated with one like the son of man." As in Daniel 7:22, 27 where the "saints of the most High" participate in the "authority" and "sovereign power" of the "son of man," so now Jesus' followers, who take the place of national Israel, participate in his kingship and sovereign authority. "This remarkable transfer of imagery graphically illustrates the theme of 'true Israel' of the followers of Jesus who take the place of the unbelieving nation, a theme that runs through much of the teaching of Jesus in this Gospel (cf. 8:11-12, 21:43)."[21]

19:29. Jesus then broadens his remarks to include **everyone who** has suffered loss of family and possessions for the sake of Jesus (ἕνεκεν τοῦ ὀνόματος μου, *heneken tou onomatos mou*). The language is typically hyperbolic describing the bountiful blessings and reversal of fortunes that will characterize life in the age to come (cf. Mark 10:30). The hundredfold compensation is not to be taken literally, but rather graphically illustrates that whatever possessions or relationships one has lost for Jesus' sake cannot possibly compare with the "new heavens and new earth," and life with the eternal family of God. Earlier the rich man sought "eternal life" (v. 16) and went away sad because he valued his earthly possessions more than "treasures in heaven." Jesus now promises his followers true wealth, along with life of the highest quality (i.e., "eternal life").

19:30. The inevitable reversal of fortunes to come is illustrated by the proverbial slogan: **many who are first will be last, and many who are last will be first**. The saying may have a twofold purpose: On the one hand, while the world gives preferential treatment to the wealthy and powerful, in the eschaton those who are deemed of little worth (i.e., disciples) will be exalted to a place of priority. However, the saying may also be intended as a warning to the disciples

---

[20]On the significance of the term see D.C. Sim, "The Meaning of παλιγγενεσία in Matthew 19:28," *JSNT* 50 (1993) 3-12.

[21]France, *Matthew*, p. 288.

not to think of themselves too highly, because as the following parable illustrates, God's rewards are not based on length of service (cf. 20:1-16).

MATTHEW 20

N. THE GENEROUS LANDOWNER (20:1-16)

Jesus now illustrates by means of a parable the proper perspective the disciples should have concerning rewards. The parable amplifies on the principle the "first will be last and . . . the last will be first" (19:30), as indicated by the repetition of the language in 20:16 (albeit in reverse order). The parable demonstrates that the concept of "reward" in terms of God's kingdom cannot be determined by what might be considered fair and equitable labor practices. Human standards of fairness and justice are not the norm in the dispensing of eschatological rewards. Once again Jesus challenges his disciples with a radical reversal of values commensurate with the dawn of God's kingdom. The incomprehensible goodness of God can only become a stumbling-block to those who assess things based upon human ideas of worth and merit.[1] The disciples must therefore learn to "think the things of God" and not construe eschatological rewards in terms of human accomplishment.

**1"For the kingdom of heaven is like a landowner who went out
early in the morning to hire men to work in his vineyard. 2He
agreed to pay them a denarius for the day and sent them into his
vineyard.**

**3"About the third hour he went out and saw others standing in
the marketplace doing nothing. 4He told them, 'You also go and
work in my vineyard, and I will pay you whatever is right.' 5So
they went.**

**"He went out again about the sixth hour and the ninth hour
and did the same thing. 6About the eleventh hour he went out and**

[1]Schweizer, *Good News According to Matthew*, p. 394.

found still others standing around. He asked them, 'Why have you been standing here all day long doing nothing?'

7"'Because no one has hired us,' they answered.

"He said to them, 'You also go and work in my vineyard.'

8"When evening came, the owner of the vineyard said to his foreman, 'Call the workers and pay them their wages, beginning with the last ones hired and going on to the first.'

9"The workers who were hired about the eleventh hour came
and each received a denarius. 10So when those came who were
hired first, they expected to receive more. But each one of them
also received a denarius. 11When they received it, they began to
grumble against the landowner. 12'These men who were hired last
worked only one hour,' they said, 'and you have made them equal to us who have borne the burden of the work and the heat of the day.'

13"But he answered one of them, 'Friend, I am not being
unfair to you. Didn't you agree to work for a denarius? 14Take
your pay and go. I want to give the man who was hired last the
same as I gave you. 15Don't I have the right to do what I want with my own money? Or are you envious because I am generous?'

16"So the last will be first, and the first will be last."

20:1. Matthew's Gospel contains no fewer than ten parables prefaced with the opening line, **the kingdom of heaven is like . . .**[2] A survey of Matthew's kingdom parables reveals that the kingdom of heaven has both a present and a future reality. In this parable (i.e., 20:1-16) the focus is upon the consummation of the kingdom, and God's unexpected standards of reward.

20:2-7. To illustrate the point, Jesus compares the way of the kingdom to a landowner who seeks day laborers to work in his vineyard (vv. 1-2).[3] He goes out **early in the morning** (6:00 A.M.) and forms a contractual agreement with certain men to work, promising

---

[2]Cf. 13:24-30; 13:31f.; 13:33; 13:44; 13:45f.; 13:47-50; 18:23-35; 20:1-16; 22:1-14; 25:1-13.

[3]As noted by Malina and Rohrbaugh, *Social Science Commentary*, p. 124, "Day laborers were economically among the poorest persons in society. They were usually landless peasants who had lost their ancestral lands through debt and drifted into cities and villages looking for work."

for the day's labor **a denarius** (usual payment for a day's work, cf. 18:28). A few hours later (9:00 A.M.) the man returns to the marketplace and hires additional workers promising to pay them **whatever is right**. He repeats his hiring practices throughout the day, hiring additional workers at noon and at 3:00 P.M.[4] Finally, with only one hour left in the working day (5:00 P.M.), he returns to the marketplace still in pursuit of more workers. This time, finding some still seeking employment, he asks them why they have been standing around idle all day. The question expresses an element of surprise that the men have not found employment. Their response indicates that their situation was not because of an unwillingness to work, but because no one had hired them.[5] Perhaps these were the workers nobody wanted, the "ones rejected by other employers as unworthy."[6] Nevertheless, and in spite of the late hour, they are invited to work in the vineyard.

20:8-12. At the close of the day the workers are gathered for payment, in accord with the Jewish law (cf. Lev 19:13; Deut 24:15). The **foreman** (ἐπίτροπος, *epitropos*) is specifically told to pay the laborers beginning with the last hired, and going on to the first. The language describing a reversal of order recalls 19:30. However, a truly unexpected turn of events occurs when the last hired are paid the exact wages as those hired early that morning (i.e., **a denarius**). Understandably, those who worked since early morning expected to receive more than those who only worked one hour. When they received the same wages **they began to grumble** (the verb is imperfect, ἐγόγγυζον, *egongyzon*; cf. Exod 16:7-12; Num 14:27; Deut 1:27). Essentially, as articulated by Morris, their complaint was twofold: " . . . the latecomers did very little work, and what they did they did under the best of conditions in the cool of

---

[4]Although Jeremias, *The Parables*, p. 136, suggests that the efforts to hire workers throughout the day "shows that the work was unusually urgent," Stein, *Parables of Jesus*, p. 125 disputes such a claim by observing that "the treatment by the owner of those who worked only one hour is seen as an act of generosity and goodness and not recompense for helping the owner out in his time of need."

[5]*Contra* Jeremias, *The Parables*, p. 137, who contends: "The poor excuse conceals their characteristic oriental indifference."

[6]So Hagner, *Matthew*, 2:571.

the day."[7] No doubt those who had labored all day long fully expected payment that exceeded a denarius.

20:13-15. The landowner responds to the complaint by addressing the chief objector with a word that is "both friendly and reproachful," **friend** (ἑταῖρε, *hetaire,* cf. 22:12; 26:50).[8] The owner of the vineyard then makes a threefold defense of his actions. First, there has been no injustice done them since he has kept his contractual agreement to pay them a denarius for their day's work. Second, one has a right to use his own possessions to exhibit a gracious spirit to those to whom he will. And thirdly, their complaint is indicative of a spirit of jealousy (lit., "an evil eye," cf. 6:20) that begrudges goodness and mercy extended toward others.

20:16. The parable closes by repeating the saying of 19:30, but reverses the order so that **the last will be first** now comes before **the first will be last** (cf. 19:30). The point being that those deemed unworthy by others, and who come later into the kingdom will be blessed with the same reward as those who labored from the first. The parable thus effectively counters any notion that eschatological rewards are conditioned upon rank or length of service. Salvation is ultimately grounded in the sheer goodness of God and cannot be calculated in legal terms. Since all kingdom rewards depend on God's grace there should be no place for self-promotion or jealousy over how God treats the undeserving. As Stein observes:

> . . . if we were truly good and loving, even if we were the first workers, would we not as good people rather than grumbling reply something like, 'Is it not wonderful that those who worked only one hour also received a denarius as we did?' . . . It is frightening to realize that our identification with the first workers, and hence with the opponents of Jesus reveals how loveless and unmerciful we basically are. We may be more 'under law' in our thinking and less 'under grace' than we realize.[9]

---

[7]Morris, *Matthew,* p. 503.
[8]Jeremias, *The Parables,* p. 137.
[9]Stein, *Parables of Jesus,* p. 128.

O. THIRD PASSION PREDICTION (20:17-19)

[17]Now as Jesus was going up to Jerusalem, he took the twelve disciples aside and said to them, [18]"We are going up to Jerusalem, and the Son of Man will be betrayed to the chief priests and the teachers of the law. They will condemn him to death [19]and will turn him over to the Gentiles to be mocked and flogged and crucified. On the third day he will be raised to life!"

Although Jesus probably alluded to his death on several occasions (cf. 10:38; 16:21; 17:12, 22-23) this prediction constitutes the third major prediction concerning the events that await him in Jerusalem. In this instance Jesus no longer sought to convince the disciples concerning the necessity of the passion, but emphasizes from the shift from the third person references in 16:21 and 17:22-23 to the first person plural, their association with him ("we are going up . . . ," v. 18).[10] Jesus' words stand in sharp contrast to the disciples' preoccupation with rewards (19:27-30), and the following scene depicting the worldly ambitions of the sons of Zebedee (20:20-28).

20:17-19. The third passion prediction takes on an even more ominous tone since Jesus and his disciples are about to start their climactic ascent to Jerusalem. In spite of the joyous festive occasion, as many pilgrims made their way to Jerusalem to observe the Passover, Jesus privately reveals to the twelve the solemn purpose of their journey to the Holy City. The main elements of Jesus' previous passion predictions are now repeated. **The Son of Man will be betrayed** (παραδοθήσεται, *paradothēsetai,* "handed over," probably a "divine passive" indicating the fulfillment of God's will; cf. δει (*dei*) "it is necessary," 16:21). Through a formal legal proceeding Jesus will be condemned by official Judaism as deserving of death. However, since Jews were forbidden to exercise the death penalty (John 18:31), for the first time Jesus mentions the role of Gentile authorities, and the manner of his suffering and execution. At the hand of the Romans Jesus will suffer both verbal and physical assaults (**mocked and flogged**, cf. 27:27-31). In the end they will

[10]Observed by Patte, *Matthew*, p. 289, n. 3.

inflict the death penalty by means of crucifixion,[11] thus leaving no doubt as to his ultimate repudiation by his own people. Remarkably, the prediction ends on a hopeful note by repeating his earlier assurances that God will have the last word by raising him to life (cf. 16:21; 17:23). Thus, no matter the horror awaiting him in Jerusalem, Jesus expresses his confidence in God's sovereign guidance and direction in the course of events.

P. REQUESTS ON BEHALF OF THE SONS OF ZEBEDEE (20:20-28)

In spite of the fact that Jesus has insisted that a cross awaits him in Jerusalem (20:17-19), the disciples seem to envision a glorious throne, surrounded by places of honor and prestige (20:20-23). The request of the mother on behalf of her two sons, James and John, is indicative of a viewpoint that has failed to understand that the Son of Man will sit upon his glorious throne (19:28) only after his humiliation and suffering. If the disciples are to be aligned with him in glory and authority (19:28), they must also become sharers of his passion (cf. 16:24). True greatness can only be realized in sacrificial service, of which Jesus himself becomes the ideal model.

20 Then the mother of Zebedee's sons came to Jesus with her sons and, kneeling down, asked a favor of him.

21 "What is it you want?" he asked.

She said, "Grant that one of these two sons of mine may sit at your right and the other at your left in your kingdom."

22 "You don't know what you are asking," Jesus said to them. "Can you drink the cup I am going to drink?"

"We can," they answered.

23 Jesus said to them, "You will indeed drink from my cup, but to sit at my right or left is not for me to grant. These places belong to those for whom they have been prepared by my Father."

---

[11]On crucifixion as a Roman means of capital punishment see J.B. Green, "Death of Jesus," *DJG*, esp. 147-148.

[24]When the ten heard about this, they were indignant with the two brothers. [25]Jesus called them together and said, "You know that the rulers of the Gentiles lord it over them, and their high officials exercise authority over them. [26]Not so with you. Instead, whoever wants to become great among you must be your servant, [27]and whoever wants to be first must be your slave — [28]just as the Son of Man did not come to be served, but to serve, and to give his life as a ransom for many."

20:20-21. The **mother of Zebedee's sons** was probably Salome, the sister of Mary (cf. 27:56). In which case her request was given added leverage because of her family connection.[12] She approaches Jesus in a posture of adoration (προσκυνοῦσα, *prokynousa*) and makes her request known. It was not unusual for Mediterranean mothers to seek status and prestige through their sons.[13] Perhaps she, along with all the disciples, imagined that with their arrival in Jerusalem Jesus would be swept up in regal glory (cf. Luke 19:11), and thus she wanted to stake her claim on behalf of her two boys. Hence she sought the two highest places of honor, seats next to the royal throne.

20:22-23. Jesus responds to her request by addressing the brothers directly. His words, **you don't know what you are asking**, indicates that they have a faulty understanding of the nature of the kingdom and how true greatness is to be realized. Jesus attempts to jar their self-promoting agenda by asking if they are willing to **drink the cup** he is about to drink. The metaphorical use of the term "cup" is rooted in the OT symbolizing suffering and even the outpouring of God's wrath (e.g., Ps 75:8; Isa 51:17, 22; Jer 25:15-16). Hence, Jesus is asking them if they are prepared to experience suffering and rejection as a prerequisite to glory and exaltation. Their immediate response (**we can**), is indicative of their little understanding and shallow reflection on the significance of Jesus' words. However, Jesus does grant that one day they shall **drink from my cup**, meaning there will come a time when they shall experience

[12]Note that in Mark 10:35 it is James and John who take the initiative to request honorific positions.

[13]Malina and Rohrbaugh, *Social Science Commentary*, p. 126.

suffering and even death because of their allegiance to him. But even under those circumstances it is God's sovereign authority who prepares and assigns places of honor and reward. Rather than spending time calculating rank and jockeying for positions, the disciples need to learn the lesson of selfless service. Jesus shows himself to be the subordinate Son who seeks his Father's will, not his own.

20:24. When the manipulative tactics of John and James became known among the other disciples they were **indignant** [ἀγανάκτεω, *aganakteō*] **with the two brothers**. Their source of irritation was not that they thought the request inappropriate, but that the two had selfishly advanced their own interest at the expense of the others. Lest the dispute decline into a petty squabble over personal rights and privileges, Jesus calls the disciples together for a lesson about kingdom values.

20:25-27. Their petty disputes over positions of status and authority are reflective of secular values, not those of the kingdom. As the Jews were painfully aware, Gentile rulers and prominent pagan figures were driven by the quest for power, and exercised their authority and domination in the interest of self-promotion and personal preservation. In fact, all political systems are tainted to some degree by selfish concerns and personal ambitions. In the world of politics, humility and a refusal to advance oneself at the expense of others, are not considered virtues and a formula for political success. However, in the kingdom those who would be **great** must take the path of lowly service on behalf of others. Assuming the position of a **slave** meant to renounce all individual rights, and to live one's life in service of others. Therefore, to be governed by visions of grandeur, self-importance, and the ambition to impose one's will over others, are more reflective of secular values than the priorities of the kingdom.

20:28. The very essence of Jesus' messianic task is illustrative of the higher priority of seeking not one's own but the welfare of others: **the Son of Man did not come to be served, but to serve, and to give his life as a ransom for many**. Repeatedly, Jesus impresses his disciples with values and priorities that either reverse or transcend the human perspective. Contrary to their ambition, Jesus is not motivated by the pursuit of honor, glory, or social prestige. He came to fulfill the role of God's faithful servant (cf. Isa 52:13–53:12), who humbles himself before the Father and carries out his will on behalf of others.[14]

Jesus' self-giving service, culminating in his death as a ransom (λύτρον, *lytron*) for others, establishes a definitive interpretation of the events awaiting him in Jerusalem. The term "ransom" indicates that Jesus' death is to be understood, not as a penalty for his own sin, but as a means to procure the liberation and freedom of others from the tyrannical hold of sin.[15] The substitutionary nature of Jesus' messianic task is clearly articulated by the words ἀντὶ πολλῶν (*anti pollōn,* meaning "in the place of many" rather than the vague "for . . .").[16] Hence, the contours of Jesus' messianic mission on behalf of his people are most clearly seen at Golgotha. Those who seek "greatness" in the kingdom must follow Jesus in humble service and self-renunciation on behalf of others.

Q. TWO BLIND MEN RECEIVE SIGHT (20:29-34)

Immediately prior to Jesus' entry into Jerusalem Matthew records a second incident wherein Jesus is confronted by a pair of blind men who petition him with the words, "Lord, Son of David, have mercy on us" (20:29-34; cf. 9:27-31). The scene brings together themes and motifs reminiscent of previous episodes, as well as foreshadowing subsequent events to come. Once again the outcasts recognize the messianic significance of Jesus' healing activity. They function as a foil against which the unbelief and hardness of Israel's leaders are brought into sharp relief. The episode with the blind men, coming immediately after Jesus' emphasis on sacrificial service (20:20-28), is illustrative of a ministry of compassion that seeks to be responsive to the needs of others.

---

[14]See B. Gerhardsson, "Gottes Sohn als Diener Gottes," *Studia theologica* 27 (1973), 85.

[15]See A. McGrath, *Understanding Jesus* (Grand Rapids: Zondervan, 1987), pp. 126-127.

[16]See discussion by M. Harris, "Prepositions and Theology in the Greek New Testament," *NIDNTT* 3:1179-80; and D.W. Wallace, *Greek Grammar Beyond the Basics* (Grand Rapids: Zondervan, 1996), pp. 365-367.

The "crowd" is cast in an unfavorable light as the people exhibit a lack of compassion by their efforts to silence the handicapped men (v. 31). As was the case with the disciples who rebuked those who brought children to Jesus (19:13), so the crowd exhibits a misunderstanding concerning the basic thrust of Jesus' messianic mission. In fact, the issue of how one understands Jesus' identity and mission as the Son of David becomes a critical point of controversy when Jesus arrives in Jerusalem (cf. 21:9, 14-15; 22:41-45).

29As Jesus and his disciples were leaving Jericho, a large crowd followed him. 30Two blind men were sitting by the roadside, and when they heard that Jesus was going by, they shouted, "Lord, Son of David, have mercy on us!"

31The crowd rebuked them and told them to be quiet, but they shouted all the louder, "Lord, Son of David, have mercy on us!"

32Jesus stopped and called them. "What do you want me to do for you?" he asked.

33"Lord," they answered, "we want our sight."

34Jesus had compassion on them and touched their eyes. Immediately they received their sight and followed him.

20:29. Jesus and his disciples are now approximately fifteen miles from Jerusalem, having just left Jericho.[17] The closer they get to Jerusalem the more the crowds increase in anticipation of arrival in the Holy City. Both the festive occasion of Passover, along with a mounting "messianic interest and enthusiasm"[18] combined to fill the air with excitement and expectancy.

20:30-33. Two blind men who had positioned themselves beside the road, probably to beg for alms, heard that among the crowd passing by was Jesus. They evidently knew of his reputation as a healer, so they cry out, **"Lord, son of David, have mercy on us!"** Their petition thus construes the messianic significance of the title, Son of David, in terms of a mission of mercy and compassion. Jesus' kingly power and authority are not exercised as the Gentiles,

[17]For a possible harmonization with Luke's "as Jesus was approaching Jericho" (18:35), see C.L. Blomberg, *The Historical Reliablilty of the Gospels* (Downers Grove, IL: InterVarsity, 1987), pp. 128-130.

[18]Hill, *Matthew*, p. 290.

who love to lord it over (20:25-26), but rather in compassionate service on behalf of others. However, the crowd, who will also acknowledge Jesus as "Son of David" (21:9), considers such service as beneath his messianic dignity, and thus they consider the blind men as a mere annoyance hindering progress to the capital city. Their efforts to silence the blind men only result in their more persistent effort to attract the attention of Jesus.

20:34. For the fourth time Matthew informs the reader that Jesus' response to human need was motivated by **compassion** (cf. 9:36; 14:14; 15:32). In spite of the traumatic events awaiting him in Jerusalem, Jesus is easily moved by the plight of others and responds to alleviate their suffering. Jesus' powerful touch results in their ability to see, and they immediately become followers of Jesus.[19] Certainly, their response forms an interesting contrast to the rather dim-sighted vision of the disciples in the previous episode.

[19]On the issue of whether the verb ᾿ ΄ (*akoloutheō*) indicates they became "disciples," see France, *Evangelist and Teacher*, pp. 262-263.

MATTHEW 21

VI. CONFLICT IN JERUSALEM (21:1–25:46)

In the narrative block comprising 21:1–25:46 the earlier predictions about his fate in Jerusalem build to a climax, as Jesus' interaction with the Jewish leaders leads to an intensifying of conflict. Upon entering Jerusalem Jesus' provocative activities take place in the temple area (cf. 21:12, 14, 15, 23; 24:1). His healings of "the blind and the lame," coupled with the confessionary cries of the children ("hosanna to the Son of David"), incite the "chief priests and teachers of the law" to become "indignant" at him (21:15). Although Jesus has been in conflict with the religious leaders earlier in the story, the ensuing conflict over his "authority" (21:24-27), followed by three stinging parables underscoring Israel's rebellion and hardness of heart, results in decided efforts to have him arrested and killed (21:45).

It appears that the religious leaders' initial strategy was to alienate Jesus from the favor of the "crowds" (cf. 21:46) by forcing him to take a side on contemporary controversial issues (22:15-48). Although 22:15-45 portrays several groups confronting Jesus with controversial questions, the exchanges are introduced with Matthew's observation that the Pharisaic agenda was "to trap him in his words" (22:15). Thus, as Kingsbury observes, the various groups together comprise "the whole gamut of Jewish officialdom."[1] In the end, all of his opponents are reduced to silence (22:46), and are thus forced to withdraw from the scene. However, the reader will soon learn that their momentary retreat

[1]J.D. Kingsbury, "The Developing Conflict between Jesus and the Jewish Leaders in Matthew's Gospel: A Study in Literary-Criticism," *CBQ* 49 (January 1987), 73.

only culminates in a behind-the-scenes plot to arrest Jesus and have him put to death (26:3-5).

Once Jesus enters Jerusalem the narrative turns on how the Jerusalem authorities respond to the exhibition of Jesus' messianic credentials (21:1-17), and his subsequent authoritative teachings and affirmations concerning his identity (21:23–22:46). The refusal of Israel's religious leaders to accept Jesus' messianic status results in Jesus seizing the offensive by exposing and denouncing Pharisaic hypocrisy (23:1-39), and pronouncing apocalyptic doom over Jerusalem (24:1-34), followed by exhortations directed to the new people of God (24:36–25:46). The eschatological discourse becomes a warning to the community to "keep watch" (24:42; cf. 25:1-13), be "faithful and wise" (24:45; 25:14-30), and to continue in a ministry motivated by allegiance to Jesus (25:31-46). The entire section comprising 21:1–25:46 is united by Jesus' actions, debates, and teachings performed in the shadow of the temple as a challenge to Jerusalem concerning his identity.

A. JESUS' ENTRY INTO JERUSALEM (21:1-11)

Jesus' entry into Jerusalem and the subsequent "cleansing of the temple" (21:1-17) confront Jerusalem with a clear and public challenge concerning his messianic status. These two public acts are supplemented by another symbolic act, witnessed only by the disciples (cursing of the fig tree, 21:18-22), that prophetically underscores Israel's barrenness and the ultimate destruction of the temple. These events constitute the antecedent to the Jewish leader's question, "By what authority are you doing these things" (21:23). Together these symbolic prophetic acts constitute a deliberate and sustained question to Israel: "Who do you say I am?"[2]

From 16:21 on Matthew has created a "suspense of anticipation," as Jesus' earlier predictions of his fate in Jerusalem (cf. 16:21; 17:22-23; 20:17-19) have prepared the reader to expect an escalation of conflict between Jesus and the religious leaders. Matthew is careful to delineate Jerusalem's rejection of Jesus as a refusal to

---

[2]Ben F. Meyer, *The Arms of Jesus* (London: SCM Press, 1979), p. 199f.

accept their long-awaited Davidic Messiah. Jesus' entry into Jerusalem begins with 20:29-34 where two blind men acknowledge Jesus' Davidic messiahship and join Jesus' entourage in the final approach to Jerusalem.[3] The entry into Jerusalem is dominated by Davidic overtones (21:1-11). The crowds from Galilee take up the petition of Psalm 118:25-26, and cry out with the acclamation, "Hosanna to the Son of David; Blessed is he who comes in the name of the Lord" (21:9). Later in the temple area the children repeat the shouts of the crowd, "Hosanna to the Son of David" (21:15). It is his messianic activity, coupled with the Davidic designation that serves as the background for the controversy that follows (21:23–22:34). In the end, Jesus reduces his opponents to silence by posing a question concerning the relationship of the Messiah to King David (22:41-46). Their failure to understand that Jesus is *both* David's Son and Lord assures that they will never perceive the basis or source of Jesus' authority. Jesus' transcendent messianic role completely shatters all earthly political ambitions popularly associated with the Davidic Messiah.

[1]As they approached Jerusalem and came to Bethphage on the Mount of Olives, Jesus sent two disciples, [2]saying to them, "Go to the village ahead of you, and at once you will find a donkey tied there, with her colt by her. Untie them and bring them to me. [3]If anyone says anything to you, tell him that the Lord needs them, and he will send them right away."

[4]This took place to fulfill what was spoken through the prophet:

[5]"Say to the Daughter of Zion,
'See, your king comes to you,
gentle and riding on a donkey,
on a colt, the foal of a donkey.'"[a]

[6]The disciples went and did as Jesus had instructed them. [7]They brought the donkey and the colt, placed their cloaks on them, and Jesus sat on them. [8]A very large crowd spread their cloaks on the road, while others cut branches from the trees and

---

[3]D.J. Verseput, "Jesus' Pilgrimage to Jerusalem and Encounter in the Temple: A Geographical Motif in Matthew's Gospel," *NovT* 36 (1994), 115.

spread them on the road. [9]The crowds that went ahead of him and those that followed shouted,

"Hosanna[b] to the Son of David!"
"Blessed is he who comes in the name of the Lord!"[c]
"Hosanna[b] in the highest!"

[10]When Jesus entered Jerusalem, the whole city was stirred and asked, "Who is this?"

[11]The crowds answered, "This is Jesus, the prophet from Nazareth in Galilee."

[a]*5* Zech. 9:9 [b]*9* A Hebrew expression meaning "Save!" which became an exclamation of praise; also in verse 15 [c]*9* Psalm 118:26

21:1-3. Jesus' entrance into Jerusalem marks an important transition from Jesus' Galilean ministry and the completion of his journey to Jerusalem (cf. 16:21; 19:1; 20:28, 29-34). On his approach to Jerusalem from Jericho, Jesus comes **to Bethphage**, evidently just outside of Jerusalem in the vicinity of **the Mount of Olives**. Since both Mark (11:1) and Luke (19:28) connect Bethphage to Bethany, the village just ahead to which Jesus sends two disciples was probably Bethany.

It is doubtful, as noted by France, that Jesus' instructions for obtaining a donkey were simply to secure transportation for the final two miles of his journey.[4] Rather, it appears that Jesus intends to deliberately stage the manner of his entrance into Jerusalem in terms of the prophetic expectations of Zechariah 9:9. Thereby, his entrance becomes a prophetic act which implicitly makes a Christological statement. The focus of the account is upon the Lord's foreknowledge and sovereign awareness of his conformity to God's will as expressed in OT prophecies. Jesus not only knows that a donkey and a colt will be available for his service in the next village, he is also confident that any questions concerning the requisition of these animals will be fully satisfied merely by the explanation, **the Lord needs them**. Thus, with Jesus' authoritative command everything is put at his disposal for the orchestration of his entry into Jerusalem.

---

[4]France, *Matthew*, p. 296.

21:4-5. Matthew makes it clear by a fulfillment citation that Jesus' staging of events is calculated as a challenge to Jerusalem to receive her kingly Messiah. The citation comes from Zechariah 9:9, with possibly the opening line (**Say to the daughter of Zion**), drawn from Isaiah 62:11. The Zechariah citation is somewhat abridged by leaving out the line, "righteous and having salvation" (Zech 9:9), in order to keep the focus on Jesus' humble and peaceful entry into the city. Rather than an entry with all the trappings of power and militaristic overtones, Jesus enters Jerusalem on the **foal of a donkey**, thereby making a powerful statement concerning his non-political purpose and character.

21:6-7. The disciples do as they have been instructed. They secure a donkey with her colt in perfect accord with the language of Zechariah (v. 5). It may be, as suggested by Morris that "the mother's presence would help to calm the colt being ridden for the first time, and in the middle of a noisy demonstration."[5] There is no reason to think that Matthew intended his readers to imagine that Jesus rode both the mother and the colt into Jerusalem. The most natural antecedent for **Jesus sat on *them*** is the *cloaks* placed upon the animals. Although the mere fact that Jesus rode into town had definite royal and messianic implications, the use of a donkey is calculated to define his messianic intent in terms of humble service.

21:8. The crowds react by extending him honor and prestige due the extraordinary nature of his person. The garments and branches cover the ground "so that the feet of the ass do not even touch the soil or stones that ordinary people tread." This sort of "red carpet" treatment is reserved for only one who is "marked off as apart from and superior to ordinary human affairs and conditions."[6] Jesus, in effect is escorted into the capital city in a manner befitting royalty. The actions of these Galilean pilgrims clearly constitute a challenge to the residents of Jerusalem to welcome Jesus as their Davidic Messiah.

21:9. The political implications of the event may be suggested by the waving of palm branches, recalling the action of the first

---

[5]Morris, *Matthew*, p. 522.

[6]Observations by Malina and Rohrbaugh, *Social-Science Commentary*, p. 128.

Hanukkah, celebrating the cleansing of the temple from Seleucid control (see 2 Macc. 10:5-8). The crowds take up a petition based upon the Hallel-Psalm 118:25-26: **"Hosanna to the son of David; Blessed is he who comes in the name of the Lord; Hosanna in the highest!"** The term *hosanna* is a transliteration of the Hebrew הוֹשִׁיעָה נָּא (*hôšî'āh nā'*, or Aramaic equivalent) originally meaning "please help or save." Although the term "became an exclamation of praise" (see NIV footnote) it nevertheless retained an element of urgency for help and divine assistance.[7] Hence their shouts of adoration are mixed with nationalistic hopes of Jerusalem's liberation.

21:10-11. The commotion caused by the escorting of Jesus into Jerusalem resulted in **the whole city** being "shaken" (ἐσείσθη, *eseisthē*, cf. 27:51). The reader will recall that when the Magi came looking for the King of the Jews all Jerusalem was "troubled" (2:3). When the residents of Jerusalem confront the crowds with the identity question, **Who is this?**, the crowds are consistent with their earlier appraisal that Jesus' identity is best understood in terms of "one of the prophets" (cf.16:14). While Jesus' ministry has prophetic significance, the reader knows that the crowds' assessment, though not false, fails to adequately communicate to the city Jesus' messianic significance. However, the conclusion of the crowds was sufficient to raise the concerns of Israel's leaders (cf. 21:26, 46) and is anticipatory of the prophetic manner in which Jesus confronts Jerusalem (21:12-16; 23:34). The reference to **Nazareth** reminds the reader of the humble, unlikely beginnings of one so highly esteemed (cf. 2:23). It is noteworthy that Jerusalem's residents do not join the crowds' confessionary welcome of Jesus to the Holy City.

---

[7]See the discussion by M.H. Pope, "Hosanna–What It Really Means," *BibRev* 4 (1988), 16-25; also the different proposal by J.A. Fitzmyer, "Aramaic Evidence Affecting the Interpretation of Hosanna in the New Testament," in *Tradition and Interpretation in the New Testament*, festschrift for E.E. Ellis, ed. G.F. Hawthorne and O. Betz (Grand Rapids: Eerdmans, 1987), pp. 110-118.

B. DEMONSTRATION IN THE TEMPLE (21:12-17)

By directly combining the entry scene (21:1-11) with the temple incident (21:12-13; cf. Mark 11:1-19), Matthew further dramatizes the messianic implications of Jesus' activities in Jerusalem. Israel's Davidic Messiah, who is "greater than the temple" (12:6), upon entry into Jerusalem goes immediately to the temple and prophetically dramatizes the temple's inevitable destruction. His actions constitute an "acted parable of judgment,"[8] which will later be verbally reinforced (ch. 24). Moreover, the actions and teachings of Jesus associated with the temple constitute a stinging indictment of the entire ideology connected to the temple cult. Borg succinctly summarizes the importance of the temple for first century Judaism:

> As the place of God's presence, a sign of Israel's election, and the sole locus of the cult where atonement was made for sins and impurity, it was an institution substantive to the definition and existence of Israel. Representing for most Jews "the *nexus* between heaven and earth," the *axis mundi* by which the holy was connected to the earth, its proper operation was essential for the holiness of the land. As the center of holiness, it needed to be protected from defilement.[9]

Is it any wonder that Jesus' entry into Jerusalem and his prophetic denunciation of the temple gave rise to questions regarding his identity (21:10) and authority (21:23)? The religious leaders respond with "indignation" (21:15), and later Jesus' prediction concerning the temple's destruction becomes a charge at his trial (26:61), and a taunt during his crucifixion (27:40). His disrupting of temple operations was reflective of a prophetic indignation that repudiated the nationalistic pride and false sense of security entrusted in the temple as a place of salvation and hope.

[12]Jesus entered the temple area and drove out all who were buying and selling there. He overturned the tables of the money

---

[8]N.T. Wright, *Jesus and the Victory of God* (Minneapolis: Fortress Press, 1996), p. 416.

[9]Marcus Borg, *Conflict, Holiness, and Politics in the Teachings of Jesus* (New York: Edwin Mellen Press, 1984), p. 164.

changers and the benches of those selling doves. [13]"It is written," he said to them, "'My house will be called a house of prayer,'[a] but you are making it a 'den of robbers.'[b]"

[14]The blind and the lame came to him at the temple, and he healed them. [15]But when the chief priests and the teachers of the law saw the wonderful things he did and the children shouting in the temple area, "Hosanna to the Son of David," they were indignant.

[16]"Do you hear what these children are saying?" they asked him.

"Yes," replied Jesus, "have you never read,
"'From the lips of children and infants
you have ordained praise'[c]?"

[17]And he left them and went out of the city to Bethany, where he spent the night.

[a]*13* Isaiah 56:7 [b]*13* Jer. 7:11 [c]*16* Psalm 8:2

21:12. Jesus' activities associated with the temple probably took place in one of the outer courts, most likely the court of the Gentiles. It was not the mere presence of **the money changers** and the **buying and selling** of sacrificial animals that provoked Jesus' outrage. As noted by France, "The market performed a useful and indeed necessary role in providing the animals needed for sacrifice by those who traveled from a distance [cf. John 2:14; m. Seqalim 1:3; 2:4], the Syrian currency [cf. Exod 30:11-14] which was required for temple dues (see on 17:24), and the market's location in the Court of the Gentiles was sanctioned by priestly authorities."[10] In this author's view, there is also nothing in the text to suggest that Jesus was provoked by dishonest business practices or profiteering. After all, both the "buyers and sellers" were driven out of the courtyard. Jesus' actions were not primarily an attempt to reform temple proceedings, since he knew that the future destruction of the temple was not far off. Instead, it can be viewed as a symbolic act foreshadowing its destruction. With the removal of those buying and selling, and the scattering of the money changers, Jesus had in effect symbolized the end of the temple as a place of sacrifice. As

[10]France, *Matthew*, p. 301.

Wright observes, "Without the Temple-tax the regular daily sacrifice could not be supplied. Without the right money, individual worshipers could not purchase their animal sacrifices. Without animals, sacrifice could not be offered. Without sacrifice the Temple had lost its whole *raison d'être*."[11]

21:13. Jesus justifies his action by a composite citation from Scripture. The reference to the temple as a **house of prayer** comes from Isaiah 56 (v. 7), which affirms God's ultimate intention that the temple be open to all, including foreigners and eunuchs, if they are willing to keep his covenant. The characterization of the temple precincts as a **den of robbers** comes from Jeremiah's sermon denouncing Israel's desecration of the temple's holy function (7:1-11). In spite of Israel's corruption and unrighteous behavior, the people nevertheless entertained an unrealistic trust in the temple as a safe haven guaranteeing their protection and security. However, Jeremiah warns, "Do not trust in deceptive words and say, 'This is the temple of the LORD, the temple of the LORD, the temple of the LORD'" (7:4). As a result of their corruption the temple is to be destroyed (7:14).

Jesus' indictment of the temple as a **den of robbers** is intended to draw attention to the same abuses that Jeremiah condemned. The reference to "buying and selling' possibly has nothing to do with the business practices of those buying and selling in the outer courts of the temple. The term translated "robber" (λῃστῶν, *lēstōn*) is consistently used "throughout the Septuagint, apocrypha, New Testament and Josephus" as "one who killed and destroyed while plundering, not simply one who covertly thieved without violence . . . "[12] The "den" of these bandits refers to the place where they retreat for refuge after having committed their criminal acts. By calling the temple a den of robbers Jesus is indirectly condemning an attitude that views the temple as a place of nationalistic security and safe haven, no matter the violence associated with its cultic propagation. The ideology associated with the temple has resulted in the temple becoming a fortress, promoting nationalistic pride and exclusivism. Jesus' actions undermine any confidence that one

[11]Wright, *Jesus*, p. 423.

[12]Borg, *Conflict*, p. 124; see Josephus *Ant.* 14.415f.; 15.345-348; *War* 1.304-311.

might place in the temple's sacrificial system by boldly foreshadowing God's judgment upon it.

21:14. After Jesus' prophetic acts with respect to the temple, Jesus heals **the blind and the lame** who come to him in the temple area. As noted earlier (see chs. 8-9) the blind and the lame were not allowed access to the sanctuary of God's presence (cf. Lev 21:17-23; 2 Sam 5:8; m. Hagiga 1:1). But they came to one "greater than the temple," who mediates the very presence of God (cf. 1:23), and are healed from those defects that prohibited full participation with the people of God. The temple and its sacrificial system could only stigmatize and exclude those not meeting the various purity stipulations.

21:15-16. Jesus' acceptance of those considered "outcasts," along with the presence of **children** who persistently call attention to Jesus' Davidic Sonship by picking up on the shout of the crowd (**"Hosanna to the Son of David"**), results in the Jewish leaders becoming "indignant" (ἠγανάκτησαν, *ēganaktēsan*). Children, therefore, perceive the reality of Jesus' messianic status, while Israel's leaders are only aroused to anger by such a proposal. They seem to expect Jesus to silence the children in view of the implications of their shouts. Instead, Jesus chides them for their failure to seriously consider the language of Psalm 8:3 (LXX). As children respond spontaneously in praise of God's creation, so these children appropriately offer their praise of Jesus as the Son of David.

21:17. As was customary during the Passover, pilgrims sought accommodations in nearby villages. Jesus spends the night in Bethany, probably at the house of his friends Mary, Martha, and their brother Lazarus. Although the words **he left them** mark the transition to Bethany, it may also signal the fundamental break between Jesus and Israel's religious leaders.

C. THE FIG TREE (21:18-22)

18Early in the morning, as he was on his way back to the city, he was hungry. 19Seeing a fig tree by the road, he went up to it but found nothing on it except leaves. Then he said to it, "May you never bear fruit again!" Immediately the tree withered.

20When the disciples saw this, they were amazed. "How did the fig tree wither so quickly?" they asked.

21Jesus replied, "I tell you the truth, if you have faith and do not doubt, not only can you do what was done to the fig tree, but also you can say to this mountain, 'Go, throw yourself into the sea,' and it will be done. 22If you believe, you will receive whatever you ask for in prayer."

The fig tree episode follows the temple cleansing and forcefully dramatizes God's judgment upon barren Israel.[13] Jesus' actions should not be seen as a mere temper tantrum or a petty vindictive outburst. The prophetic symbolism of the barren fig tree is intended to reinforce the impending judgment of God upon unfruitful Israel.

21:18-19. After spending the night in Bethany, **on his way back** to Jerusalem, Jesus encounters **a fig tree** that had all the appearances of yielding fruit (i.e., the presence of leaves). In spite of appearances, the fig tree was fruitless, and Jesus uses the occasion to dramatize a parable of judgment. Jesus has come to Jerusalem seeking fruit, and finding none, the temple is therefore doomed to destruction. The withering of the fig tree is therefore a prophetic sign of the future destruction of Israel's most important sacred shrine.

21:20-22. The disciples appear to be more amazed with the immediate impact of Jesus' words on the fig tree than they were about the meaning of the event. Although Jesus' subsequent teachings about the power of faith may seem unrelated to the point of the fig tree cursing, Jesus' explanation for the withering of the fig tree highlights the importance of a complete loyalty and commitment to God. Jesus' fidelity to God is proven true by his symbolic actions regarding the fig tree, while the destruction of the temple clearly demonstrates Israel's lack of faithfulness. It follows that Jesus is not suggesting that faith guarantees the reception of anything one may desire. The promise necessarily assumes a commitment to the will of God, and a willingness to forgo individual rights

[13]See W.R. Telford, *The Barren Temple and the Withered Fig Tree* (JSNTSup 1; Sheffield: JSOT, 1980), for the symbolic value of the fig tree cursing.

for the sake of the purposes of God. Jesus is the paradigm *par excellence* of what it means to "have faith and not doubt."

D. THE AUTHORITY QUESTION (21:23-27)

[23]Jesus entered the temple courts, and, while he was teaching, the chief priests and the elders of the people came to him. "By what authority are you doing these things?" they asked. "And who gave you this authority?"

[24]Jesus replied, "I will also ask you one question. If you answer me, I will tell you by what authority I am doing these things. [25]John's baptism – where did it come from? Was it from heaven, or from men?"

They discussed it among themselves and said, "If we say, 'From heaven,' he will ask, 'Then why didn't you believe him?' [26]But if we say, 'From men' – we are afraid of the people, for they all hold that John was a prophet."

[27]So they answered Jesus, "We don't know."

Then he said, "Neither will I tell you by what authority I am doing these things.

In the controversial exchanges comprising 21:23–22:46 the Jewish leaders are confronted with decisive indications concerning Jesus' identity and the contours of his mission. Fundamental in the discussion is the question regarding the source and the basis of Jesus' authority (21:23). While Jesus does refuse a direct response to their question regarding his authority, the three parables that follow (21:28–22:14) do address their question indirectly, in terms of God's saving presence being realized in his own person and ministry.

21:23. When Jesus returns to the temple courts he is confronted by representatives of the Sanhedrin (i.e., **chief priests and elders**), who interrogate him regarding the *basis* of his authority for **doing these things** (ταῦτα, *tauta*, i.e., his activities in connection with the temple), and the *source* of such authority. They understand that such actions necessitate authorization from a superior source. Yet, Jesus has no formal training or priestly credentials that might lend support to his teachings and actions in the temple courts. Of course, any claim of divine authorization would only fuel their hostility and be interpreted as blasphemous.

21:24-26. Instead of responding directly to their question, Jesus counters with a question of his own, designed to expose their insincere motives behind their original question. Since the ministry of John is in continuity with his own, their assessment of John's authority would have a direct bearing on how his own authority should be construed. There are only two alternatives concerning authorization for John's baptism: ***from heaven*** **or** ***from men***. Jesus' counter question is intended to show that these religious leaders are not really concerned with establishing whether heaven has authorized certain actions or not. As their subsequent deliberations indicate, they are more concerned with their own agenda, and with the possibility of losing credibility with the crowd, than in acknowledging heaven's authority.

21:27. The fact that their fear of the people takes precedence over their fear of heaven (i.e., God) shows conclusively that their own authority is of a mere human origin. Furthermore, their response (**We don't know**), is indicative of their refusal to honestly face the fallacy of their own position. At the least, their claim of ignorance undermines their own claim of competency for determining what is from God and what is of mere human origin. Jesus therefore refuses to indulge their deceitful and manipulative tactics. By their refusal to take a position regarding the authority of John, they have completely undermined their own ability to properly assess the authority by which Jesus acts.

E. PARABLE OF THE TWO SONS (21:28-32)

28"What do you think? There was a man who had two sons. He went to the first and said, 'Son, go and work today in the vineyard.'

29"'I will not,' he answered, but later he changed his mind and went.

30"Then the father went to the other son and said the same thing. He answered, 'I will, sir,' but he did not go.

31"Which of the two did what his father wanted?"

"The first," they answered.

Jesus said to them, "I tell you the truth, the tax collectors and the prostitutes are entering the kingdom of God ahead of you. 32For John came to you to show you the way of righteousness, and you did not believe him, but the tax collectors and the prostitutes did. And even after you saw this, you did not repent and believe him.

The religious leaders, being "outsiders" (cf. 13:11-17), are now addressed in parabolic speech (21:28–22:14). A series of three parables clearly indicts Israel's leadership for their rebellion, obstinate unbelief, and failure to be responsive to the gracious favor of God.

21:28-29. In the first parable (21:28-32) Jesus invites his hearers (i.e., the religious leaders) to consider the different responses of two sons to their father's request to work in the vineyard. Contrary to typical Palestinian family life, the first son directly opposes his father's will by an unqualified refusal to obey (lit., "I do not will . . . "). Eventually, the son changes his mind and obediently goes to work in the vineyard.

21:30-31. With the second son, the response to the father's instructions is just the opposite. Initially, the second son responds positively to the father's will, even assuring his compliance in terms of respect (**I will, sir**). However, in the end his actions do not match his words. The second son fails to follow through on his promise. Jesus then asks the hearers for their assessment of the two sons: **Which of the two did what his father wanted?** They correctly respond **the first**, and thus the stage is set for an unexpected application of the parable to the contemporary situation.

21:32. The religious leaders are represented by the second son, who formerly said "yes" to God's will, but in the end was not responsive to it. This becomes evident by their refusal to believe John who came to show **the way of righteousness**. They **saw** but they **did not repent and believe**. In contrast, **the tax collectors and the prostitutes** recognized his authority as "from heaven," and therefore will enjoy the blessings of the kingdom. This radical reversal of fortunes must have come as both shocking and offensive to a religious establishment that prided itself in its pursuit of piety and strict adherence to the demand of God. But while Israel's leaders remained obstinately unresponsive to the message of John, those deemed as notorious sinners (i.e., tax collectors and prostitutes) responded with faith and repentance. The religious leaders will therefore be supplanted[14] by despised sinners whose only virtue appears to be that they believed John and heeded his call for repentance. In their desperate condition they knew themselves to be in need of God's grace, and they eagerly responded when divine favor was offered. On the other hand, Israel's leaders seemed to rely on their pious claims and legal maneuvering as evidence of God's favor. However, in the end, such can never take the place of genuine faith and a life transformed by the call of God.

F. PARABLE OF THE TENANTS (21:33-46)

33"Listen to another parable: There was a landowner who planted a vineyard. He put a wall around it, dug a winepress in it and built a watchtower. Then he rented the vineyard to some farmers and went away on a journey. 34When the harvest time approached, he sent his servants to the tenants to collect his fruit.

35"The tenants seized his servants; they beat one, killed another, and stoned a third. 36Then he sent other servants to them, more than the first time, and the tenants treated them the same way. 37Last of all, he sent his son to them. 'They will respect my son,' he said.

38"But when the tenants saw the son, they said to each other, 'This is the heir. Come, let's kill him and take his inheritance.' 39So they took him and threw him out of the vineyard and killed him.

40"Therefore, when the owner of the vineyard comes, what will he do to those tenants?"

41"He will bring those wretches to a wretched end," they replied, "and he will rent the vineyard to other tenants, who will give him his share of the crop at harvest time."

42Jesus said to them, "Have you never read in the Scriptures:
"'The stone the builders rejected
has become the capstone[a];
the Lord has done this,

[14]See France, *Matthew*, p. 307.

and it is marvelous in our eyes'[b]?

[43]"Therefore I tell you that the kingdom of God will be taken away from you and given to a people who will produce its fruit. [44]He who falls on this stone will be broken to pieces, but he on whom it falls will be crushed."[c]

[45]When the chief priests and the Pharisees heard Jesus' parables, they knew he was talking about them. [46]They looked for a way to arrest him, but they were afraid of the crowd because the people held that he was a prophet.

[a]*42* Or *cornerstone* [b]*42* Psalm 118:22,23 [c]*44* Some manuscripts do not have verse 44.

The next parable builds on the previous one by portraying Jesus as the "son" who is the culmination ("last of all he sent his son," v. 37) of God's redemptive activity in the midst of his people. The parable highlights Israel's history as one of rebellion and consistent opposition to the will of God. Israel's leaders have aligned themselves with a long history of rebellion and rejection of God's servants. In the end, their rejection of God's Son, who climaxes the sequence of authoritative embassies sent by the Father, results in their rejection and replacement by another "people" (ἔθνει, *ethnei*) who will be fruitful (v. 43).

21:33-34. Jesus' parable of the tenants draws on realistic events in first century Palestinian life.[15] The description of the landowner's preparation and personal investment in his new vineyard (**wall, winepress**, and **watch tower**) clearly indicates a sacrificial investment in the vineyard. When the landowner plants and rents out the vineyard to tenants, he fully expects to benefit from the productivity of the vineyard. Not only is the sequence of events common in everyday life in Palestine; the language is clearly reminiscent of Isaiah 5:1-7 (and possibly Psalm 80). The vineyard is a symbol of God's relationship to Israel, and the wall, winepress, and tower "underline the care and protection God has lavished on his vine-

[15]See the discussions by J.D.M. Derrett, "Fresh Light on the Parable of the Wicked Vinedressers," in *Law in the New Testament* (London: Longman and Todd, 1970), pp. 286-312; and K.R. Snodgrass, *The Parable of the Wicked Tenants* (WUNT 27; Tübingen: Mohr, 1983).

yard, Israel."[16] The departure of the landowner on a journey builds on the tension that often developed between an absentee landowner and the tenants put in charge of a field. The time depicted by the absence of the landowner corresponds to the time after Israel had entered into covenant agreement with God and was left to carry out his will. The **harvest time** depicts a time of accountability, when the tenants are expected to repay that owed the landlord. So at the time of the harvest the landowner sends his servants to collect the proceeds from the vineyard that rightfully belong to him.

21:35-37. The servants sent by the landowner are brutally treated by the tenants: **they beat one, killed another, and stoned a third**. The treatment of the servants recalls the way that Israel responded to prophets that God had sent to the people (cf. 1 Kgs 18:13; 22:24-27; 2 Kgs 6:31; 21:16; 2 Chr 24:19-22; 16:15-16; Neh 9:26; Jer 7:25-26; 37:15; 44:4; cf. also Matt 23:34). Although two groups of servants are sent, they are all treated with impunity. The landowner, **last of all** resolved to send his **son**, being confident that his son will surely not receive the same treatment but would be extended the same respect as he himself. On the one hand, the mission of the son is the same as the servants, to collect fruit for the landowner. However, the superiority of the son is emphasized by the fact that his coming was of a completely different order (ὕστερον, *hysteron*), and with greater expectation: **they will respect my son** (cf. 3:17; 17:5).[17]

21:38-39. The tenants interpret the coming of the son as an opportunity to seize the vineyard as their own, once they have eliminated the rightful heir. Evidently, they perceived the presence of the heir as an indication that the landowner was dead, and thus his son had come to take his rightful possession. They may have assumed that by killing the son nothing stood between them and full ownership of the vineyard. Thus with calloused disregard for the rightful heir they brutally murder the landowner's son and lay claim to the vineyard.

---

[16]Blomberg, *Matthew*, p. 323.

[17]See J.D. Kingsbury, "The Parable of the Wicked Husbandmen and the Secret of Jesus' Divine Sonship in Matthew: Some Literary-Critical Observations," *JBL* 105 (1986), 643-655.

21:40-41. In a manner reminiscent of the trap that Nathan set for David by his story of the ewe lamb (2 Sam 12:1-15), so Jesus' opponents are now forced to face their guilt by responding to a question calculated to be self-indicting. Jesus asks them what the owner of the vineyard should do in response to the actions of the evil tenants. They respond with the suggestion that a just course of action would be to inflict punishment upon the evil tenants and to find new tenants for his vineyard who will produce the seasonal crops. As in 21:31, the response of the religious leaders is self-incriminating and a pronouncement of their own condemnation.

21:42. To drive home the point Jesus cites from Psalm 118, originally a "song of thanksgiving for military victory,"[18] and usually sung by pilgrims in Jesus' day while going to the temple. Originally, the **stone the builders rejected** referred to Israel, but Jesus applies the imagery to himself. He is the "stone" discarded by the builders. The stone imagery becomes very "important in the apologetic of the early church" (see esp. 1 Pet 2:4-8; Acts 4:12).[19] The stone rejected is identified as the **capstone**[20] of the structure, and hence pivotal of the solidity of the entire building. Perhaps Jesus intends to allude to the inevitable downfall of the temple, because of the rejection of such an important foundational stone, i.e., himself. The stone imagery also implies Jesus' vindication by the building of a new temple composed of a new people of God. Such a turn of events will indeed be **marvelous in our eyes**.

21:43. Jesus is emphatic that Israel's leaders have forfeited their privilege of experiencing God's saving presence (=kingdom), and now God's blessings are extended to a new people composed of all ethnic groups, comprising a new, holy nation under the sovereign rule of God (cf. 1 Peter 2:9). It would seem that such language has its fulfillment in the appearance of the church.

---

[18]L.C. Allen, *Psalms 101-50*, Word Biblical Commentary, vol. 21 (Waco, TX: Word Books, 1983), p. 124.

[19]Hagner, *Matthew* 2:622.

[20]As noted by Morris, *Matthew*, p. 543, ". . . we do not have enough knowledge of the way people built in that day to be quite sure which stone it was. It may have been a large stone laid in the foundation at the corner of two walls. In such a place it provided a foundation that could be built on and it also set the position for two walls and therefore for the whole building."

21:44. Although the UBS Greek text enclosed verse 44 within brackets, indicating their view that the verse is "an accretion to the text,"[21] the textual evidence for its inclusion is strong, and therefore the text should probably be accepted as authentic. The text functions as a sober warning of the dire consequences of not taking the stone seriously. With allusions to Isaiah 8:14-15 and Daniel 2:35, Jesus warns that whether we stumble over the stone (Isa 8:14-15) or are crushed by the stone (Dan 2:44) the results are one's destruction, so the hearer ignores the stone at his own peril.

21:45-46. Although Jesus' language is parabolic, the religious leaders caught the force of Jesus' words. Ironically, their response sets in motion the very situation portrayed in the parable. Their intentions are only temporarily thwarted by their fear of the crowd, because, like John, they revered him as a prophet (cf. 16:14; 21:10). If their sinister plot is to come to fruition, they must find a way to discredit him before the crowds. To this end they will eventually turn their attention (22:15-40).

---

[21]See the comments in Metzger's, *Textual Commentary*, p. 58 (cf. Luke 20:18).

MATTHEW 22

G. PARABLE OF THE WEDDING FEAST (22:1-14)

[1]Jesus spoke to them again in parables, saying: [2]"The kingdom of heaven is like a king who prepared a wedding banquet for his son. [3]He sent his servants to those who had been invited to the banquet to tell them to come, but they refused to come.

[4]"Then he sent some more servants and said, 'Tell those who have been invited that I have prepared my dinner: My oxen and fattened cattle have been butchered, and everything is ready. Come to the wedding banquet.'

[5]"But they paid no attention and went off – one to his field, another to his business. [6]The rest seized his servants, mistreated them and killed them. [7]The king was enraged. He sent his army and destroyed those murderers and burned their city.

[8]"Then he said to his servants, 'The wedding banquet is ready, but those I invited did not deserve to come. [9]Go to the street corners and invite to the banquet anyone you find.' [10]So the servants went out into the streets and gathered all the people they could find, both good and bad, and the wedding hall was filled with guests.

[11]"But when the king came in to see the guests, he noticed a man there who was not wearing wedding clothes. [12]'Friend,' he asked, 'how did you get in here without wedding clothes?' The man was speechless.

[13]"Then the king told the attendants, 'Tie him hand and foot, and throw him outside, into the darkness, where there will be weeping and gnashing of teeth.' [14]"For many are invited, but few are chosen."

The parable of the wedding feast continues the emphasis on the exclusion/replacement motif, based upon Israel's refusal to honor the "son" (22:2-3; cf. similarities and differences to Luke 14:15-24). Although Jesus is elsewhere portrayed as a king (2:1-3; 21:5; 25:34), this parable stresses God as king to emphasize that his sovereign intention is that his people pay homage to his "son." By rejecting the king's invitation to honor the "son" they demonstrate that they will not be responsive to God's reign. On the other hand, those who accept the king's invitation acknowledge his authority and demonstrate it by honoring the "son."

22:1-6. Jesus addresses the religious leaders with a third parable, this time comparing the kingdom of God to a royal wedding banquet. A king (=God) is desirous of honoring his son (=Jesus), by means of a wedding feast (=messianic banquet; cf. 8:11; 25:1ff.). Jesus has previously used the figure of a "bridegroom" to depict the messianic times dawning with his ministry (9:15). It was customary to issue two invitations; the first being a general invitation to the feast, while the second brings the message that the feast is now ready.[1] To the second invitation those invited refuse to come. Such a response to a royal invitation constituted "a direct insult to the king's honor."[2] Remarkably, the king exercises great restraint and sends out more servants to implore those who have been invited to come to the feast, for everything has been prepared. But all to no avail. In spite of the royal invitation and the necessity of compliance, those invited are too concerned with their own affairs to honor the king's request. Inexplicably, some of those invited even respond to the invitation with hostility directed at those delivering the invitation. While such a response may seem totally unrealistic, keep in mind that this is a parable, not a realistic depiction of an actual event. As France observes: "If the story verges on the absurd, why not? It is after all, a parable, not a sober historical narrative, and parables are designed to convey lessons, not to be mirrors of real life."[3]

22:7. The king has finally had enough and responds with fierce revenge, resulting in the "destruction of the murderers and the

---

[1]Jeremias, *Parables of Jesus*, p. 68.
[2]Malina and Rohrbaugh, *Social-Science Commentary*, p. 135.
[3]France, *Matthew*, p. 312.

burning of their city." Such language could certainly be interpreted by Matthew's early readers as an allusion to Jerusalem's destruction in A.D. 70.[4] However, the imagery has many OT parallels depicting the downfall of rebellious cities (cf. Judg 1:8; Isa 5:24-25). Therefore, while the language certainly fits the fate of Jerusalem's destruction (esp. the temple), it cannot be determined with certainty that Jesus had Jerusalem specifically in mind by the language of v. 7.

22:8-10. Once again the king sends out his servants with invitations to come to the feast prepared on behalf of his son. This time the invitations are extended indiscriminately, to those occupying the crossroads, city squares, the places where the nonelite of the city would be found.[5] As in the previous parables (see 21:31-32; 41:43) those who failed to respond to God's will are replaced by others who are readily responsive. The result is a wedding hall filled with guests; even if the invitations have attracted all kinds of people, **both good and bad** (cf. 13:47-48). While contemporary Jewish conventions would have assessed such an inclusive practice of table fellowship as ritually polluting, Jesus' parable envisions a social practice not driven by exclusivism or the rejection of people based on social status or cultic purity. Of course, Jesus' welcoming of sinners should not be construed as an endorsement of their sinfulness, as is indicated by the next scene in the parable (vv. 11-14).

22:11-12. The presence at the banquet of a man who lacked the proper wedding clothes serves to indicate that some care and preparation is demanded before one can legitimately partake of the blessings of God. It has been suggested, though with little evidence, that the proper attire for the wedding feast would have been provided by the king to those he invites to the banquet. If such be the case, the king's wrath is stirred because this man had failed to avail himself of the necessary garments suitable for such an occasion. Others suggest that the man's fault is not to be found in his failure to wear a special type of garment, but rather that on such a special occasion the man had failed to change his dirty clothes for clean garments. There is simply not enough evidence to determine with certainty

[4]Although technically the city was not burned, only the temple.

[5]Malina and Rohrbaugh, *Social-Science Commentary*, p. 135.

why the king was so offended by the attire of one of his guests. Whatever the situation, the man was **speechless** when questioned concerning his conduct, thereby acknowledging his misconduct. The scene reminds the hearers that acceptance of the invitation of God to participate in kingdom blessings necessitates a commitment to a life of righteousness and moral reform (cf. 13:20-22).

22:13. The king responds to the offender by ordering his servants to bind him and to cast him outside the banquet hall. For the metaphorical language of **darkness** and **weeping and gnashing of teeth** see 8:12 and 13:42, 50. Needless to say the king takes very seriously the failure of the man to be adequately clothed for such a momentous occasion.

22:14. The closing proverbial saying, (**For many are invited, but few are chosen**) succinctly sums up why this man has been ejected. He is of the class of those who have been invited, but not chosen. In other words, he responded favorably to the gracious invitation, but refused to fully embrace the norms of the kingdom, as indicated by his lack of proper attire. On the other hand, those who are "chosen" (ἐκλεκτοί, *eklektoi*) are those who take seriously their calling and freely adhere to the demands of discipleship. As observed by Blomberg:

> Divine sovereignty and human responsibility are again finely balanced. Neither can be jettisoned at the expense of the other. The man's behavior demonstrates he is not elect. Election does not violate free will nor occur irrespectively of the man's conduct.[6]

H. CONFRONTATIONS WITH THE RELIGIOUS LEADERS (22:15-46)

The series of confrontations that comprise 22:15-46 are introduced by Matthew's observation that, based on Jesus' self-disclosure and warnings to the Jewish leaders (22:15, τότε, *tote*), they conspire to entrap him in debate. However, Jesus knows their "evil intent" (22:18) and demonstrates his authority by reducing the entirety of

[6]Blomberg, *Matthew*, p. 329.

official Judaism to silence (22:46). The reader is reminded of the "authority" theme by the emphasis on the reaction of those who heard: "they were amazed" (22:22; cf. 8:10, 27; 9:33); and "they were astonished at his teaching" (22:23; cf. 7:28; 13:54). Jesus shows himself to be superior by speaking authoritatively of God's jurisdiction (22:17-21), his transcendent power (22:29-30), and the priority of "love" as the greatest commandment (22:34-46). In each instance, Jesus shows that when one takes seriously the role of God in human affairs, dilemmas such as they pose are easily resolved.

1. Paying Taxes to Caesar (22:15-22)

15Then the Pharisees went out and laid plans to trap him in his words. 16They sent their disciples to him along with the Herodians. "Teacher," they said, "we know you are a man of integrity and that you teach the way of God in accordance with the truth. You aren't swayed by men, because you pay no attention to who they are. 17Tell us then, what is your opinion? Is it right to pay taxes to Caesar or not?"

18But Jesus, knowing their evil intent, said, "You hypocrites, why are you trying to trap me? 19Show me the coin used for paying the tax." They brought him a denarius, 20and he asked them, "Whose portrait is this? And whose inscription?"

21"Caesar's," they replied.

Then he said to them, "Give to Caesar what is Caesar's, and to God what is God's."

22When they heard this, they were amazed. So they left him and went away.

22:15-16a. The Pharisaic plan to "trap" (παγιδεύσωσιν, *pagideusōsin*) Jesus in his words was an attempt to discredit him before the crowds by means of public disputation. To that end they send **their disciples**, teamed with the **Herodians**,[7] to pose a question calculated

[7]The precise identity and origin of the group remains problematic. Most likely, as the name implies, they are "Partisans of the Herodian dynasty;" politically siding with the Sadducees as opposed to the Pharisees; see H.W. Hoehner, "Herodian Dynasty," *DJG*, p. 325.

to probe the political-economic implications of Jesus' kingdom-agenda. As noted by Wright, "Jesus' Temple-action is bound to have raised questions like these."[8]

22:16b. Jesus' opponents first use flattery in an effort to provoke a response that could be construed as either undermining Roman authority, or as an endorsement of Roman subjugation. Ironically, their assessment of Jesus as a courageous teacher, who refuses to compromise God's truth to gain popular favor, stands in vivid contrast to their own agenda and nefarious tactics (cf. 21:46). Jesus had a reputation for speaking his mind and not couching his teachings so as to win public acclaim. Therefore, in their mind, Jesus should not be afraid to answer a question having serious political and social implications.

22:17. Their question concerning the payment of taxes raised an extremely sensitive and potentially explosive issue in first century Judaism. First, as noted by Malina and Rohrbaugh, one should not imagine that in antiquity religion, politics and economics were separate institutions, existing in a distinctive realm all their own.[9] In fact, taxation and the political rule of Rome raised serious religious questions, not the least of which was the legitimacy of paying taxes to a foreign power occupying the land that was considered to rightfully belong to Israel. For a fiercely independent people, the vast majority of which were suffering economically, the burden of Roman taxation would have been especially infuriating. It is perhaps significant that the question posed to Jesus pertains to the "lawfulness" of taxation, not to the amount of the tax.[10]

Furthermore, taxation burdens appear to be a major source of social unrest and political agitation among the Palestinian peasantry. Fiensy estimates that "the peasant paid around 12% of his harvest in land taxes, one denarius for everyone in his household over fourteen years old, and a wave offering perhaps equaling one-fortieth of the harvest."[11] If the tax in question specifically referred

---

[8]Wright, *Jesus*, p. 502.

[9]*Social-Science Commentary*, pp. 137-138.

[10]T.E. Schmidt, "Taxes," *DJG*, p. 806.

[11]David A. Fiensy, *The Social History of Palestine in the Herodian Period*, Studies in the Bible and Early Christianity, vol. 20 (Lewiston: Edwin Mellen Press, 1991), p. 103.

to the poll tax, then payment of such a tax was especially burdensome for the poor, since it amounted to a tax on one's body which, like the land, was also viewed as belonging to Rome.[12] No doubt Jesus' opponents felt confident that whichever side of the issue Jesus endorsed they would be successful in undermining his reputation.

22:18-21. Jesus is fully aware of their sinister motives, therefore, addresses them as **hypocrites** (cf. 15:7; ch. 23). The effort to "test" him by means of questioning has been a consistent Pharisaic ploy (cf. 4:1, 3; 16:1; 19:3; 22:35). Jesus unexpectedly calls for them to produce **the coin used for paying the tax**. Certainly the stance of Jesus' opponents was greatly weakened by their own possession of a coin bearing the image of Caesar and the inscription *Tiberius Caesar Augustus, son of divine Augustus.*[13] At any rate, the coin produced was a Roman denarius, most appropriate to illustrate his point. Jesus calls upon his opponents to acknowledge whose image and name were to be found on the Roman coin. Their admission that the coin bore the image and name of Caesar elicits a response from Jesus that undercuts any notion that his kingdom-agenda necessitated either a tax-revolt or a compromise of Yahweh's sovereignty and kingship. The verb translated **give** (ἀπόδοτε, *apodote*) signifies a payment made "in response to an incurred obligation" (Louw-Nida, *Greek Lexicon*, p. 575), hence the payment of the denarius amounts to giving back to Caesar that which already belongs to him. As Bruce observes, "Obedience to God's will is not compromised by letting Caesar have money which bears his name."[14]

---

[12]Ibid., p. 101.

[13]As noted by Malina and Rohrbaugh, *Social-Science Commentary*, p. 137, "If, as is likely, it was the Herodians who had the incriminating coin, they would immediately have set themselves at odds with their collaborators in challenging Jesus: followers of the Pharisees want to avoid all contact with such an idolatrous object." On the nature of the coin see H.StJ. Hart, "The coin of 'Render unto Caesar . . .' (A note on some aspects of Mark 12:13-17; Matt 22:15-22; Luke 20:20-26," in *Jesus and the Politics of His Day*, eds. E. Bammel and C.F.D. Moule (Cambridge: Cambridge University Press, 1985), pp. 241-248.

[14]F.F. Bruce, "Render to Caesar," in *Jesus and the Politics of His Day*, p. 261.

Jesus then enjoins an even deeper obligation: **give to God what is God's**. Jesus' words should not be viewed as suggesting a radical division between the secular and sacred, as if advocating the modern notion of separation of church and state. Instead, Jesus' point is that loyalty to God should remain one's ultimate priority. Simply put, "Caesar is owed what bears his image and name – money. But God is owed what bears God's image and name – our very selves."[15]

22:22. The questioners could not help but be **amazed** with the ease with which Jesus dealt with their question. He had successfully avoided the extremes to which they sought to push him. There was nothing left to do but to leave the scene and let a new group of antagonists take their best shot at him.

2. Marriage in the Afterlife (22:23-33)

[23]That same day the Sadducees, who say there is no resurrection, came to him with a question. [24]"Teacher," they said, "Moses told us that if a man dies without having children, his brother must marry the widow and have children for him. [25]Now there were seven brothers among us. The first one married and died, and since he had no children, he left his wife to his brother. [26]The same thing happened to the second and third brother, right on down to the seventh. [27]Finally, the woman died. [28]Now then, at the resurrection, whose wife will she be of the seven, since all of them were married to her?"

[29]Jesus replied, "You are in error because you do not know the Scriptures or the power of God. [30]At the resurrection people will neither marry nor be given in marriage; they will be like the angels in heaven. [31]But about the resurrection of the dead – have you not read what God said to you, [32]'I am the God of Abraham, the God of Isaac, and the God of Jacob'[a]? He is not the God of the dead but of the living."

---

[15]See Garland, *Reading Matthew*, pp. 223-224; also C.H. Giblin, "'The Things of God' in the Question concerning Tribute to Caesar [Luke 20:25; Mark 12:17; Matt 22:21]," *CBQ* 33 (1971) pp. 522-523.

[33]When the crowds heard this, they were astonished at his teaching.

[a]*32* Exodus 3:6

22:23. The "testing" continues on the **same day** (cf. 13:1), now with the Sadducees attempting to entrap him by posing a question that has no doubt proved vexing to proponents of the resurrection of the dead (esp. the Pharisees). The Sadducees were the aristocratic party, enjoying popularity largely among the wealthy and within high priestly circles.[16] They would certainly have a vested interest in assisting the Pharisees in discrediting Jesus since their security and position would be threatened by any revolutionary overtones suggested by his teachings. Even though they differed radically with the Pharisees on the issue of the resurrection (cf. Acts 23:8; Josephus, *Ant.* 18.16; cf. *War* 2.165), their interrogation of Jesus used that issue in an effort to discredit him and undermine his popularity.

22:24-28. Like the antagonists in the preceding exchange (vv. 15-16), the Sadducees address Jesus as **teacher**. They question Jesus by loosely citing the provision found in Deuteronomy 25:5-6 and Leviticus 38:8 (LXX), which stipulates the obligation of a brother of a man who dies childless to marry his brother's widow in order to provide his deceased brother with legitimate offspring (termed a "levirate marriage"). It is the premise of this injunction that formed the basis of the question posed by the Sadducees. They present a case study, either an actual situation with which they are familiar (note **among us**), or a hypothetical circumstance, perhaps patterned after the story of Sarah in Tobit 3:8-15. Their question involved an unfortunate situation where seven brothers have been married to the same woman, and all have died without any of them providing a rightful heir for the first brother. Since all seven brothers had been legally married to the woman, the Sadducees raise what appears to be an insurmountable problem for those who believe in a literal bodily resurrection: **at the resurrection, whose wife will she be of the seven, since all of them were married to her?**

---

[16]See G.G. Porton, "Sadducees," *ABD* 5:894.

22:29-30. Jesus responds by identifying two fundamental flaws that lie at the root of their misconception: **you do not know the Scriptures or the power of God**). The Sadducees erroneously assume that life in the New Age must be a continuation of our earthly existence, hence heavenly relationships must take the same form as earthly ones. They fail to see that in the afterlife God's power will transform his people into creatures that neither marry nor procreate. Jesus thus envisions a New Age in which God's power has dramatically brought about a new state of affairs where marriage and sex are no longer part of the heavenly order. Jesus illustrates his authoritative pronouncement by comparing the future state of humans with angels, who also do not marry.[17] Hence all family relationships in the life to come will be transcended, and therefore marriage, even in this life, should not be given ultimate priority (see 10:37; 12:46-50; 19:29).

22:31-32. Next, Jesus demonstrates the Sadducean failure to take seriously the implications of Scripture concerning the resurrection. In typical fashion, Jesus chides his opponents with the question, **have you not read . . .** , designed to call attention to their superficial knowledge of Scripture (cf. 12:3, 5; 19:4; 21:15, 42). In this instance Jesus cites from Exodus 3:6 (LXX) where God reveals himself as **the God of Abraham, Isaac, and Jacob** long after the Patriarchs were dead. But why, hundreds of years after their deaths, would God speak in the present tense as being their God if in fact they no longer exist as the Sadducees affirm? The only explanation for the language of Exodus 3:6 is that the patriarchs are very much alive and await the resurrection of the dead. The extreme materialism of the Sadducees has blinded their eyes, both to God's power and to the implications of God's revelation in Scripture.

22:33. While Matthew does not record the reaction of the Sadducees to Jesus' rebuttal, he does observe that the **crowds . . . were astonished at his teaching**. Never before had they heard anyone with such ease and persuasive authority completely expose and refute Sadducean assumptions. It is time for the Pharisees to regroup for a final assault, this time with an "expert in the law" (vv. 34-40).

---

[17]Ironically, the Sadducees also do not believe in the existence of angels (Acts 23:8).

3. The Greatest Commandment (22:34-40)

[34]Hearing that Jesus had silenced the Sadducees, the Pharisees got together. [35]One of them, an expert in the law, tested him with this question: [36]"Teacher, which is the greatest commandment in the Law?"

[37]Jesus replied: "'Love the Lord your God with all your heart and with all your soul and with all your mind.'[a] [38]This is the first and greatest commandment. [39]And the second is like it: 'Love your neighbor as yourself.'[b] [40]All the Law and the Prophets hang on these two commandments."

[a]*37* Deut. 6:5 [b]*39* Lev. 19:18

22:34-36. With the Sadducees defeated, the Pharisees gather together (συνήχθησαν ἐπὶ τὸ αὐτό, *synēchthēsan epi to auto*; cf. Psa 2:2, LXX) to plan their next offensive maneuver. This time instead of sending some of their disciples, they send an **expert in the law** (νομικὸς, *nomikos*)[18] to "test" Jesus. Unlike the Markan account (12:28f), this legal expert is not portrayed as sincere, but like his predecessors questions Jesus in order to find fault so as to accuse him. For the third time Jesus is addressed as **teacher**, and a question is posed having momentous concern within Judaism. The question regarding the relative weight of commandments was perennially debated within rabbinic circles. Among the 613 commandments isolated by rabbinic authorities (365 negative and 248 positive), rabbis differentiated between "light" and "heavy" commandments. However, the distinction was not intended to suggest that some commandments were unimportant or could be neglected. The general principle was, "Be as heedful of a light precept as of a weighty one, for thou knowest not the recompense of reward of each precept" (m. Abot 2:1; see Str-B 1:901-5). Therefore any suggestion in Jesus' response that implied that certain commandments were unimportant would provide the Pharisees with sufficient grounds for Jesus' immediate repudiation.

---

[18]The UBSGNT encloses νομικός within brackets indicating their view that the term originated by a copyist's use of Luke 10:25. But the widespread textual evidence weighs heavily for its inclusion. For discussion see Metzger, *Textual Commentary*, p. 59.

22:37-38. Jesus responds to the question by first citing the *Shema* (Deut 6:5) as the **greatest commandment**; a response that would be widely endorsed within the Pharisaic tradition. Loving the Lord with **all your heart, soul, and mind** simply describes a devotion comprising the whole person, and is not intended to depict a neat triad categorization of the human psyche.

22:39-40. Linked to the first commandment is an equally weighty and binding commandment drawn from Leviticus 19:18: **Love your neighbor as yourself.** Nowhere in Judaism are these commandments linked as having absolute priority among God's commandments. However, even though some Jewish disputants may debate the meaning of **neighbor**, generally, Jesus' high regard for those two commandments as foundational for Jewish piety would not have been regarded as particularly offensive. What might be less favorably received would be the notion that the entirety of the Torah hangs (κρέμαται, *krematai*)[19] from **these two commandments**. Jesus has in effect made the double love command a "hermeneutical filter – virtually synonymous with Hosea 6:6 – that governs the community's entire construal of the law."[20] Those trained for the kingdom no longer ascertain God's will solely through external obedience to legal norms and precepts. Individual commandments and their applications must be sifted through the grid of mercy and love, which remain constant, though applications may vary with different circumstances. Without love, "Obedience to commandments degenerates into mere legalism."[21] Love for God necessarily entails the pursuit of the external welfare of others, regardless of race, class, or economic condition (=neighbor). Love

---

[19]There has been some dispute whether "hang" means that all the commandments can be *deduced* from the double love commandments, or that these two commandments *summarize* all the commandments of God. As Gundry, *Matthew*, p. 450, observes, "Either way, love for God and neighbor must permeate obedience to all the other commandments."

[20]R.B. Hays, *The Moral Vision of the New Testament* (San Francisco: Harper, 1996), p. 101; see also B. Gerhardsson, "The Hermeneutical Program in Matthew 22:37-40," in *Jesus, Greeks, and Christians*, festschrift for W.D. Davies, eds. R. Hamerton-Kelly and R. Scroggs (Leiden: Brill, 1976), pp. 129-150.

[21]Blomberg, *Matthew*, p. 335.

therefore becomes the basis and guiding principle for understanding and applying the law in diverse and complex situations.[22]

4. The Son of David (22:41-46)

[41]While the Pharisees were gathered together, Jesus asked them, [42]"What do you think about the Christ[a]? Whose son is he?"

"The son of David," they replied.

[43]He said to them, "How is it then that David, speaking by the Spirit, calls him 'Lord'? For he says,

[44]"'The Lord said to my Lord:
"Sit at my right hand
until I put your enemies under your feet."'[b]

[45]If then David calls him 'Lord,' how can he be his son?" [46]No one could say a word in reply, and from that day on no one dared to ask him any more questions.

[a]*42* **Or** ***Messiah*** [b]*44* **Psalm 110:1**

22:41-42. The series of controversy scenes is brought to a closure by Jesus taking the offensive and posing a direct question to the Pharisees (cf. Mark 12:35f.) concerning the fundamental nature of the expected Messiah. As Verseput has pointed out, "the question – τίνος υἱός ἐστιν [*tinos huios estin*, **Whose son is he**] – is not one of mere genealogy of the Messiah. Rather, the issue related directly to the character of the messianic figure."[23] The question raises the issue, to whom does the Messiah owe his ultimate nature and filial relationship? Nevertheless, since the Pharisees understand the question to be addressing the lineage of the Messiah, they respond, **The son of David**.

---

[22]Jesus is not suggesting a form of "situational ethics" whereby Christian conduct is determined by what appears to be the most loving thing in a given situation. Rather, as noted by France, *Matthew*, p. 320, the love commandments "direct us to understand and apply the commandments of the law within the context of an obligation to love God and man, an obligation of which the commandments are themselves particular expressions."

[23]D.J. Verseput, "The Son of God Title in Matthew's Gospel," *NTS* 33 (1987), pp. 545-546.

22:43-45. Although Jesus does not challenge their genealogical expectation, the second question inquires *how*, in view of the fact that David by divine inspiration (**by the spirit**) calls him **my Lord**, the Messiah can be understood as *both* David's son and his Lord. The question is not intended to undermine his Davidic roots, but to emphasize the transcendent status of the Messiah. The true nature of the Messiah cannot be understood as merely a kingly figure. He is David's pre-existent Lord, who, as Psalm 110:1 affirms, has been exalted to regal glory by the hand of God. Hence, the suggestive language of Psalm 110 enabled Jesus to stretch the limited messianic hopes popularly associated with Davidic expectations.[24] In addition, Jesus responds indirectly to their authority question (21:23) by showing that it is the Lord (God) who ultimately bestows authority upon the Son (Messiah) by inviting him to sit at his right hand (cf. 28:18-20).

22:46. The Jewish leaders will never perceive the basis of Jesus' authority until they come to understand and accept his transcendent status as David's Lord. Matthew's editorial remark that **no one dared to ask him any more questions** reaffirms Jesus' superior authority and builds suspenseful anticipation concerning the ultimate resolution of Jesus' conflict with the Jewish leaders (26:1f.).

---

[24]For a discussion on the critical role that Psalm 110 had in the proclamation of the early church, see D.M. Hay, *Glory at the Right Hand: Psalm 110 in Early Christian Literature* (SBLMS 18; Nashville: Abingdon, 1973).

MATTHEW 23

I. DENUNCIATION OF THE SCRIBES AND PHARISEES (23:1-39)

Throughout the narrative comprising chapters 21–25 Jesus assumes the role of a prophetic critic, who, like the OT prophets exposed and denounced Israel's religious leaders as corrupt and completely barren of righteousness (cf. Jer 7:14; 26:4-12; Ezek 9:1-10; Dan 9:26). By means of prophetic symbolism (see 21:1-22), and parabolic imagery (see 21:28–22:14), Jesus warns of impending judgment upon an intolerable religious leadership and the temple over which they presided. When his opponents are bested in debate and reduced to silence, Jesus seizes the offensive by exposing and denouncing "root character traits"[1] prevalent among the Jewish leaders (23:1-36), and explicitly spelling out their consequences by pronouncing doom upon the city and its cherished temple (23:37-39; 24:1-33).

Contrary to some[2], it is difficult to see how chapter 23 should be joined to chapters 24 and 25 as part of the fifth and final discourse of Matthew's Gospel. Although the denunciation of Israel's leadership (ch. 23) leads naturally into the judgment themes of chapters 24 and 25, it does appear that because of the change of location and audience (cf. 23:1 and 24:1-3), chapters 23 and 24-25 constitute two distinct discourses[3]. Hence, chapter 23 prepares the reader for Jesus' announcement of impending judgment upon

---

[1]The words of Kingsbury, *Jesus as Story*, pp. 115-127.

[2]Notably Gundry, *Matthew*, p. 453; and Blomberg, *Matthew*, p. 339.

[3]As argued by Hagner, *Matthew* 2:654; Carson, *Matthew*, p. 469; Patte, *Matthew*, pp. 319-320; Terence J. Keegan, "Introductory Formulae for Matthean Discourses," *CBQ* 44 (1982) 415-430.

Jerusalem (ch. 24), by spelling out the internal corruption of Israel's religious leadership.

The language and polemical tone of chapter 23 have been a source of some concern, offending our twentieth century sensibility of religious pluralism, and perhaps lending itself to anti-Semitic attitudes or actions. After all, how can the same Jesus who calls his followers to "love your enemies and pray for those who persecute you" (5:44), at the same time castigate his enemies as "hypocrites," "sons of hell," "blind guides and fools," and a "brood of vipers"? Is not this language vindictive and extremely harsh, and therefore unbecoming of the Jesus who exhorts his disciples to a life of love and forgiveness? In response, it should be noted that Jesus did not intend to indict all Pharisees as hypocritical or guilty of everything mentioned in chapter 23 (cf. Mark 12:28-34)[4]. In opposing the Pharisees and scribes Jesus stands in opposition to a rival religious system that was diametrically opposed and destructive to disciples who are being "trained in the kingdom" (13:52). To some extent Saldarini is correct that chapter 23 intends to "delegitimate rival Jewish leaders" by exposing their lack of personal integrity, and their failure to properly interpret and apply the Jewish law[5]. However, this is not a mere power struggle between competing sects, but a sober warning to the Christian community (note vv. 1-3) to take heed lest the same hypocrisy, pride, externalism, and abuse of authority also result in their rejection.[6]

It should also be pointed out, as noted by Luke Johnson, that polemical conventions of rhetoric in the ancient world differ considerably from the twentieth century[7]. It was not at all uncommon in both Hellenistic and Jewish sources to find similar language as that found in chapter 23 to vilify an opponent or a position being

---

[4]As Hagner, *Matthew* 2:654, notes, "The Pharisees themselves were sensitive to the danger of hypocrisy," hence . . . "many Pharisees would have been in agreement with Jesus' condemnation of hypocrisy."

[5]See A.J. Saldarini, "Delegitimation of Leaders in Matthew 23," *CBQ* 54 (October 1992) 659- 680.

[6]Brought out by D.E. Garland, *The Intention of Matthew 23* (NovTSup 51; Leiden: Brill, 1979), pp. 37-41 and 61-63.

[7]See L.T. Johnson, "The New Testament's Anti-Jewish Slander and Conventions of Ancient Rhetoric," *JBL* 108 (1989), 419-441.

advocated. Johnson observes that, "by the measure of Hellenistic conventions and certainly by the measure of contemporary Jewish polemic, the New Testament's slander against fellow Jews is remarkably mild."[8] Certainly such language offers no endorsement of the modern expression of anti-Semitism. Keeping in mind Jesus' prophetic role and the standard polemical conventions of the first century enables the modern reader to hear the rhetoric of chapter 23 in terms of a precise attack on Israel's religious leaders, whose institutional structure and religious practice presented a formidable rival and challenge to the impact and spread of God's Kingdom.[9]

The discourse neatly divides into three sections: (1) a description of the practices of Israel's leaders and a warning to Jesus' followers (vv. 1-12); (2) a series of woes castigating the religious leaders (vv. 13-36); (3) a lament over the city of Jerusalem (vv. 37-39).

1. Do Not Practice What They Preach (23:1-12)

[1]Then Jesus said to the crowds and to his disciples: [2]"The teachers of the law and the Pharisees sit in Moses' seat. [3]So you must obey them and do everything they tell you. But do not do what they do, for they do not practice what they preach. [4]They tie up heavy loads and put them on men's shoulders, but they themselves are not willing to lift a finger to move them.

[5]"Everything they do is done for men to see: They make their phylacteries[a] wide and the tassels on their garments long; [6]they love the place of honor at banquets and the most important seats in the synagogues; [7]they love to be greeted in the marketplaces and to have men call them 'Rabbi.'

[8]Johnson, "Anti-Jewish Slander," p. 441. It should also be kept in mind that the polemic of the first-century was not between "Christianity" over against "Judaism," as if they were well defined entities (p. 422). Therefore, charging the New Testament writers with anti-Semitism is anachronistic, and fails to see the distinctly Jewish context of the debate between synagogue and church in the first century.

[9]Certainly by the time that Matthew writes his Gospel, whether in the 60s or 80s.

[8]"But you are not to be called 'Rabbi,' for you have only one Master and you are all brothers. [9]And do not call anyone on earth 'father,' for you have one Father, and he is in heaven. [10]Nor are you to be called 'teacher,' for you have one Teacher, the Christ.[b] [11]The greatest among you will be your servant. [12]For whoever exalts himself will be humbled, and whoever humbles himself will be exalted.

[a]*5* That is, boxes containing Scripture verses, worn on forehead and arm
[b]*10* Or *Messiah*

23:1. As in the Sermon on the Mount Jesus addresses both the **crowds and his disciples** (cf. 5:1-2). It has been noted that "the purpose of polemic [in the ancient world] is not so much the rebuttal of an opponent as the edification of one's own school. Polemic was primarily for internal consumption."[10] Hence chapter 23 is intended to provide those hearers (and readers) who are positively disposed toward Jesus a negative model of views and practices that are antithetical to life in the kingdom. Therefore, the chapter "creates a powerful foil for the description of righteous disciples in another sermon – the Sermon on the Mount in chapters 5-7."[11]

23:2-3. Jesus begins his address by first acknowledging that the **teachers of the law** possess a certain authority by virtue of the fact that they **sit in Moses' seat** (v. 2)[12]. It is therefore incumbent upon the disciples to **do everything they tell you** (v. 3a). This text has proved troubling since elsewhere Jesus warns his disciples to beware of their teaching (15:14), and on several occasions opposes their teachings on a variety of subjects (cf., e.g., 12:1-14; 15:2-9; 19:3-9). Is Jesus now giving his endorsement of Pharisaic authority to teach and interpret the Law? Numerous attempts have been made to resolve the tensions between 23:2-3 and the rest of the Gospel[13]. As noted by Powell, virtually all proposals assume that

---

[10]Johnson, "Anti-Jewish Slander," p. 433.

[11]Gardner, *Matthew*, p. 333.

[12]There is some dispute on whether this refers to a literal chair used in the synagogue for those who teach; or if it is intended to symbolically represent a position of authority and clout. Most likely the latter.

[13]For a survey of proposals see M.A. Powell, "Do and Keep What Moses Says (Matthew 23:2-7)," *JBL* 114 (Fall 1995), 424-431.

because the Jewish authorities occupy the "seat of Moses" they have authority to teach and apply the Law. Hence, Jesus' condemnation is suggested by the NIV translation **they do not practice** [ποιεῖτε, *poiete*] **what they preach** [λέγουσιν, *legousin*]. The problem is that "Matthew's Gospel does not portray the Pharisees or other religious leaders as failing to live according their own teaching."[14] In fact, it is their teachings, as expressed in word and deed, that Jesus takes issue with.

Perhaps, as proposed by Powell, Jesus' acknowledgment that the teachers of the Law occupy the "seat of Moses" is not an endorsement of their authority to teach or interpret the Law. It may be a reference to their "social position as people who control accessibility to Torah. They are the ones who possess copies of the Torah and are able to read them [to a largely illiterate people]."[15] It follows that when the disciples hear the Torah as read by the scribes and Pharisees they should heed its words. But it is obvious that their exposition and practice of Torah should not be emulated, since they neither expound the Law correctly, nor live in a manner consistent with the Law's true intent. Only Jesus can speak authoritatively on how the Law is to be understood and put into practice (cf. 5:17-19). Although the religious leaders know the letter of the Law, they have proved themselves to be incompetent as expositors of the Law's meaning and application. As Powell observes,

> When Jesus says that the scribes and Pharisees 'speak'(λέγω) but do not 'do' (ποίεω), the implication is that they 'speak Torah but do not do Torah.' To 'speak Torah' means to cite accurately what the Scriptures say. To 'do Torah' means to demonstrate understanding of Torah through word and deed (5:19). In Matthew's Gospel, Jesus claims that the scribes and Pharisees do cite the Torah accurately but he maintains that their words and their deeds reveal them to be 'blind guides' who do not understand the Torah they cite (15:14; 23:16, 17, 19, 24, 26).[16]

---

[14]Powell, "Do and Keep," p. 423.
[15]Ibid., p. 432.
[16]Ibid.

23:4. The nature of Pharisaic teaching is elucidated in verse four. **They tie up of heavy loads** refers to an exposition of the Law that has become burdensome with the weight of oral and legalistic demands. It refers to a system that assumes that divine favor can be found in the precision of obedience to carefully formulated rules and legalistic injunctions. As Garland observes, they have multiplied "the number of ways in which a man may offend God," but offer no relief for the one struggling under the weight of sin.[17] The reader is reminded of Jesus' promise to give those "who are weary and burdened" rest, because his "yoke is easy and burden light" (11:28-30).

23:5. Jesus is critical of any form of piety that seeks human recognition for religious practice. The Pharisees seem to use every occasion as an opportunity to enhance their reputation for devoutness (see 6:1-19). Specific examples of seeking public recognition can be seen in the wearing of **phylacteries** and **tassels on their garments**. Phylacteries were black leather boxes containing scriptural passages from Exodus or Deuteronomy which were strapped either to the forehead or left arm. Evidently, the practice reflected a literal reading of Exodus 13:9, 16, and Deuteronomy 6:8; 11:18.[18] Tassels referred to the fringes at the four corners of the outer garment.[19] The practice was in literal compliance to the commandments found in Numbers 15:37-39 and Deuteronomy 22:12. There was nothing necessarily ostentatious in wearing tassels, even Jesus may have worn such ornamentation (cf. 9:20; 14:36). However, the Pharisees made their phylacteries extra wide, and their tassels long, so as to flaunt their piety. Such outward displays are not true barometers of the depth of one's religious devotion.

23:6-7. Their love for public recognition extended to any occasion where they might be shown deferential treatment. At **banquets** and in the **synagogues** discriminatory seating was common (cf. James 2:1-4), and one's placement in relationship to the host or leaders made a statement concerning one's social esteem and status (cf. Luke 14:7-11). The Pharisees would be extremely sensitive to

[17]Garland, *Matthew 23*, p. 51.

[18]R.S. Fagen, "Phylacteries," *ABD* 5:368-370.

[19]See J.M. Myers, "Fringe," *IDB* 2:325.

this practice, relishing the privilege of being seated next to the host or master of ceremonies. They also took great delight in being greeted in public places by honorific titles and ceremonial formalities. The honorary title of **Rabbi** (lit., "my great one") would be particularly gratifying to the Pharisee since it conjured up the notion of an outstanding teacher of the Law.[20] But as Jesus demonstrates, they are mere "blind guides" who have no authority to teach God's Law.

23:8. Jesus forbids the use of all honorific titles among his followers (vv. 8-10). The Pharisees used these designations to accent their claim to superiority and worth over others. Jesus' disciples are prohibited from using religious titles so as to avoid any notion of rank or superiority among his followers. The titles of **Rabbi** and **Master** (διδάσκαλος, *didaskalos*, "teacher") belong only to Jesus, who alone has the authority to disclose God's will. It is not that Jesus' followers are forbidden to teach, but that "among his followers there is to be no such system as that among the Jews, with the 'great ones' expounding the law authoritatively and the rank and file permanently occupying an inferior place."[21] Since disciples are all **brothers** there is no hierarchy among Jesus' followers.

23:9. Jesus' prohibition not to **call anyone on earth "father"** must be understood contextually against the common Jewish practice of exalting certain revered rabbinic elders and highly esteemed rabbis of the past, and designating them as "Father" (cf. Mishna, Aboth, "the sayings of the Fathers"). Certainly the prohibition is not intended to forbid the use of "father" in a family unit, or even the metaphorical usage to designate certain spiritual relationships (cf. 1 Cor 4:15; Phil 2:22). But, Jesus does enjoin upon his followers the absolute acknowledgment of God as the one true Father in heaven (cf. 6:9f.)

23:10. A third prohibition forbids the disciples from being called **teacher** (καθηγηταί, *kathēgētai*). The term translated "teacher" occurs only in this verse in the New Testament. It generally means "a guide" or "instructor," but can have the more specific meaning of "tutor." B.W. Winters's examination of the term in

[20]Hayim Lapin, "Rabbi," *ABD* 5:600-602.

[21]As observed by Morris, *Matthew*, p. 576.

P.Oxy.2190 (A.D. 70-90) has demonstrated that καθηγητής (*kathēgētēs*) when used in this papyrus refers to a "private tutor in rhetoric."[22] The term then depicts a "highly personalized relationship," and accords well with v. 8, in that the disciple's relationship with Jesus the Messiah "brooks no intermediary Christian rabbi or schools."[23]

23:11-12. In stark contrast to the Pharisaic quest for public adulation through position and rank, Jesus' followers must pursue a life of humble service. In language paralleling 20:26-27 Jesus highlights *service* as the avenue to *greatness*, and *humility* as the means of ultimate *exaltation*. The values and priorities of the kingdom are diametrically opposed to the pursuit of personal gain and exaltation at the expense of others.

2. Woes Against the Teachers of the Law and Pharisees (23:13-36)

The seven "woes"[24] of 23:13-36 constitute a critical indictment of Israel's religious leaders, (i.e., "the teachers of the law and Pharisees"). While it appears that Jesus directs his address directly to the Jewish leaders, more likely the collection of "woes" functions rhetorically to instruct the original hearers (i.e., the "crowds and disciples," v. 1) by describing the opponents as an "antitype of the disciple."[25] As the first two "woes" indicate, they have proved themselves to be a movement antithetical to the kingdom in their effort to keep others from participating in God's reign, and their zealous effort to win converts to their destructive views (vv. 13-15). In the next two "woes" Jesus exposes the "teachers of the law and Pharisees" as "blind guides," whose fallacious reasoning and fixation with the minutiae of the law lead them to neglect what really matters (vv. 16-24). The next two "woes" demonstrate that Pharisaic purity concerns often result in a hyper-externalism, to the neglect of purity within (vv. 25-28). The seventh and final "woe" climaxes

[22]B.W. Winter, "The Messiah as Tutor: The Meaning of καθηγητής in Matthew 23:10," *TynBul* 42 (1991) 155.

[23]Ibid., p. 157.

[24]On the term "woe" see D.E. Garland, "Blessing and Woe," *DJG*, pp. 77-81.

[25]As observed by Edwards, *Matthew's Story of Jesus*, p. 79.

the series by linking them to a consistent pattern of hostility toward God's messengers. In spite of their claim to honor the prophets, they stand with those who have consistently opposed, persecuted, and even murdered God's spokesmen (vv. 29-36).

The "woes" stand in stark contrast to the "beatitudes" (5:1-12), which describe the way of life when God's reign is taken seriously. In contrast, the "woes" depict a teaching and practice totally antithetical to life in the kingdom. It must be kept in mind that Jesus' caricature of Israel's religious leaders is not intended as an indictment of all Israel, or to imply that all Pharisees were guilty of the vices mentioned. Jesus' denunciation of the Jewish leaders is intended primarily as a sober warning to his followers not to embrace the same patterns of leadership. Hence, rather than focus on the failures of some Pharisees, Jesus' critique should be used as "a resource for self-examination by the church."[26]

13"Woe to you, teachers of the law and Pharisees, you hypocrites! You shut the kingdom of heaven in men's faces. You yourselves do not enter, nor will you let those enter who are trying to.[a]

15"Woe to you, teachers of the law and Pharisees, you hypocrites! You travel over land and sea to win a single convert, and when he becomes one, you make him twice as much a son of hell as you are.

16"Woe to you, blind guides! You say, 'If anyone swears by the temple, it means nothing; but if anyone swears by the gold of the temple, he is bound by his oath.' 17You blind fools! Which is greater: the gold, or the temple that makes the gold sacred? 18You also say, 'If anyone swears by the altar, it means nothing; but if anyone swears by the gift on it, he is bound by his oath.' 19You blind men! Which is greater: the gift, or the altar that makes the gift sacred? 20Therefore, he who swears by the altar swears by it and by everything on it. 21And he who swears by the temple swears by it and by the one who dwells in it. 22And he who swears by heaven swears by God's throne and by the one who sits on it.

23"Woe to you, teachers of the law and Pharisees, you hypocrites! You give a tenth of your spices – mint, dill and cummin.

---

[26]Gardner, *Matthew*, p. 340.

But you have neglected the more important matters of the law – justice, mercy and faithfulness. You should have practiced the latter, without neglecting the former. [24]You blind guides! You strain out a gnat but swallow a camel.

[25]"Woe to you, teachers of the law and Pharisees, you hypocrites! You clean the outside of the cup and dish, but inside they are full of greed and self-indulgence. [26]Blind Pharisee! First clean the inside of the cup and dish, and then the outside also will be clean.

[27]"Woe to you, teachers of the law and Pharisees, you hypocrites! You are like whitewashed tombs, which look beautiful on the outside but on the inside are full of dead men's bones and everything unclean. [28]In the same way, on the outside you appear to people as righteous but on the inside you are full of hypocrisy and wickedness.

[29]"Woe to you, teachers of the law and Pharisees, you hypocrites! You build tombs for the prophets and decorate the graves of the righteous. [30]And you say, 'If we had lived in the days of our forefathers, we would not have taken part with them in shedding the blood of the prophets.' [31]So you testify against yourselves that you are the descendants of those who murdered the prophets. [32]Fill up, then, the measure of the sin of your forefathers!

[33]"You snakes! You brood of vipers! How will you escape being condemned to hell? [34]Therefore I am sending you prophets and wise men and teachers. Some of them you will kill and crucify; others you will flog in your synagogues and pursue from town to town. [35]And so upon you will come all the righteous blood that has been shed on earth, from the blood of righteous Abel to the blood of Zechariah son of Berekiah, whom you murdered between the temple and the altar. [36]I tell you the truth, all this will come upon this generation.

[a]*13* **Some manuscripts** *to. [14]Woe to you, teachers of the law and Pharisees, you hypocrites! You devour widows' houses and for a show make lengthy prayers. Therefore you will be punished more severely.*

23:13-14. The first "woe" accuses the religious leaders of assuming a position that necessarily puts them in opposition to God's will being realized upon the earth (cf. 6:10). While they would assume that their teaching and practice promoted a righteousness in keeping with God's reign, in reality they had established a religious system that only worked to subvert the realization of God's will. Not only do their legalistic tendencies promote attitudes that are counter to the kingdom; they feverishly work to intimidate others so that they also will not enter the kingdom. The imagery of "shutting the door in men's faces" to prohibit participation in the kingdom recalls the counter promise made to Peter that he would be given the "keys of the kingdom of heaven" (16:19). Hence, while God's will is being realized in Jesus' mission, the Jewish leaders have become proponents of a mission and agenda diametrically opposed to God's way of salvation.[27]

23:15. The second "woe" follows naturally the first by highlighting the Pharisaic missionary zeal, in their pursuit of a single convert.[28] However, Jesus pulls no punches in his assessment of the destructive results characterizing the efforts of this rival movement. Their proselyting efforts only result in making the convert **twice as much a son of hell** (on *gehenna* see 5:22), meaning a conversion to Pharisaism only serves to increase the population of hell. These converts even appear to surpass their mentors ("twice as much") in their zeal for Pharisaic teachings and lifestyle. It is inherent within Pharisaic thought, which understands righteousness in terms of the precision and rigorous adherence to minute legalistic demands, to incite a competitive spirit to outdo others in the pursuit of external righteousness (cf. Gal 1:14; Phil 3:6).

23:16-18. In the third "woe," Jesus calls the religious leaders "blind guides" and "blind fools" as evidenced by their casuistic definitions and distinctions regarding the binding nature of various oaths and vows (cf. 5:33-37). The position of the scribes, according to verses 16-18, is that an oath taken by evoking the temple or altar is not binding, whereas one taken by the gold of the temple, or a gift upon its altar is binding. How such distinctions originated, and

---

[27]In the NIV v. 14 is relegated to the footnote because of its absence in the earliest manuscripts, and those witnesses that include it have it in different places: see Metzger, *Textual Commentary*, p. 60.

[28]Although the extent of Pharisaic efforts to make proselytes has been much debated, for a balanced treatment see S. McKnight, *A Light Among the Gentiles: Jewish Missionary Activity in the Second Temple Period* (Philadelphia: Fortress, 1991).

the rationale for deciding what vows are binding and which are not, are usually not stated. Nevertheless, the effect is to trivialize the speaking of truth, since scribal quibbling about the terminology used when making an oath or vow can easily nullify the necessity of following through on one's word. God demands truthfulness from his people, not the manipulation of words in order to escape the fulfillment of one's pledge.

23:19-22. Jesus is critical of the fallacious reasoning that contended that pledges taken based upon certain sacred objects are binding while others are not. By what logic should an oath be considered binding when based upon the "gold in the temple," or a "gift on the altar," but not binding when based upon the temple itself, or the altar upon which the gift is offered? For Jesus there are no "greater" or "lesser" oaths, none more binding than others. Neither can one escape the force of an oath simply because they lack the precise wording as demanded by scribal legislation. Since all oaths are taken in the presence of God, they should be honored, and not sifted through legal maneuvering and arbitrary distinctions.

23:23. The fourth "woe" criticizes the **teachers of the law and Pharisees** for their preoccupation with minutiae to the neglect of what really matters. Tithing was an old custom (cf. Gen 14:17-20), and in the law (see Lev 27:30-33; Deut 14:22-29) one-tenth of specific agricultural products (e.g., grains, wine, oils) along with the firstborn from the herds and flocks were subject to the tithe. Later rabbinic exegesis expanded the tithe to include all agricultural products, including vegetables and herbs, and eventually all forms of income (see Mishna, Maaseroth; cf. Tobit 1:7-8).[29] Mint, dill, and cummin were garden herbs used for seasoning and some medicinal purposes, hence subject to the tithe (see m. Maas 4.5, for the tithing of dill).

Though the mention of these minor herbs may imply that Pharisaic scruples have gone to an extreme, Jesus does not explicitly reject the practice as excessive. Instead, the preoccupation with tithing herbs is deemed of minor importance alongside the **more important matters of the law**, such as **justice, mercy, and faithfulness**. As

[29]J.C. Wilson, "Tithe," *ABD* 6:578-580.

Hagner notes, emphasizing the priority of "justice, mercy, and faithfulness," does have an Old Testament precedent: cf. *justice*, Isa 1:17; Jer 22:3; *mercy*, Hos 6:6; Zech 7:9-10; cf. Mic 6:8; and *faithfulness*, Hab 2:4.[30] Once again, Jesus highlights the core of God's demand for his people (cf. 7:12; 9:13; 22:34-40). While they may continue tithing their herbs, they need to place greater importance on matters that involve character and the treatment of others. As France paraphrases: "Observe your meticulous rules if you like, but don't therefore neglect the things that really matter."[31]

23:24. Jesus further elucidates the principle of the preceding by following up with a humorous anecdote designed to illustrate the absurdity of Pharisaic practice. To illustrate their warped priorities, Jesus imagines a scenario where "gnats" (κώνωπα, *kōnōpa*) are carefully strained from a cup, while "camels" (κάμηλον, *kamēlon*) are gulped down with little thought. While both creatures are regarded as unclean (Lev 11:4; 23), concern for the "gnat" has evidently blinded them to the more obvious pollution of swallowing a camel, the largest beast of Palestine. The hyperbole illustrates the fundamental problem of the Pharisees: they major in the minutiae at the expense of much more important matters.

23:25-26. The fifth and sixth "woes" are critical of the Pharisaic purity codes because they tend to lay greater stress on outward cleanness and purity to the neglect of the internal life (vv. 25-28). Jesus illustrates his point by alluding to early rabbinic disputes over the ritual purity of the inside and outside of cooking and eating utensils.[32] However, Jesus uses the references to "cups and dishes," not to enter the contemporary debate, but as "moral exhortation on the importance of interior purity."[33] While Pharisaic attention to the external was scrupulously observed, often such concern seemed to overshadow the importance of internal cleanness. The result of an overemphasis upon the outside has resulted in corruption within. Therefore, the inside of the vessel (i.e., the Pharisees) is

---

[30]Hagner, *Matthew* 2:670.

[31]France, *Matthew*, p. 328.

[32]For the background of rabbinic debates see J. Neusner, "'First Cleanse the Inside': The Halakhic Background of a Controversy-Saying," *NTS* 22 (1976), 486-495.

[33]*Contra* Neusner; Harrington, *Matthew*, p. 326.

filled with "greed" (ἁρπαγῆς, *harpagēs*) and self-indulgence.[34] Thus, in spite of their external appearance they are polluted within. As Garland observes, "They are scrupulous when it comes to cups but without scruples when it comes to persons."[35] Jesus therefore concludes that internal purity is the determinative factor for purity on the outside. It is only by cleansing the heart that there will be observable conduct that is truly pure because of consistency with the internal state (cf. 5:21-30; 6:1-18; 7:17-18; 12:33-35; 15:7-9).[36]

23:27-28. Jesus continues the thought of the preceding "woes" with a sixth "woe" further illustrating the incongruity between the outward appearance of the Pharisees and their internal state. This time the imagery used to illustrate Pharisaic hypocrisy is the inside and outside of tombs.[37] Since contact with a corpse and graves were considered a source of ritual uncleanness (cf. Num 6:6; 19:16), it was customary, especially at times of festivals, to mark grave sites with whitewash, so that Jewish pilgrims might not accidentally make contact with a grave and thereby become ceremonially unclean (see m. Maas 5.1; m. Shek 1.1; cf. Str-B 1:936-937). The effect of such conspicuous care given graves was only to beautify the outside of that which contained **dead men's bones and everything unclean**. The application makes the same point as in verses 25-26: i.e., the external appearance of the Pharisees only conceals their inner corruption and truly polluted state. Ironically, while they seek to protect the people from the impurity of graves, they themselves are a source of contamination because of their inner corruption. They are hypocritical because their appearance and claim of legal purity are negated by their "lawlessness" (NIV, "wickedness," ἀνομίας, *anomias*), which fails to take seriously the Law's demand of inward purity as expressed in the pursuit of "justice, mercy, and faithfulness." Therefore, their facade of external righteousness, like **whitewashed tombs**, only conceals an inner "lawlessness" that leads to the contamination of all that come into contact with them.

---

[34]See S.Westerholm, *Jesus and Scribal Authority* (ConBNT 10; Lund, Sweden: Gleerup, 1978), pp. 86-87.

[35]Garland, *Reading Matthew*, p. 231.

[36]Gundry, *Matthew*, p. 466.

[37]For Jewish burial practices see Rachel Hachlili, "Burials," *ABD* 1:785-794.

23:29-32. The hypocrisy of Israel's leaders is further illustrated by a final "woe," depicting the inconsistency of their claim to revere and champion the cause of the prophets. The building of tombs and special monuments in honor of leaders and heroes from Israel's past was typical of the first century (see Josephus' references to the tomb of David, *Ant* 16.179-82; 78.108; 20.95; cf. Acts 2:29). While the Pharisees see themselves as supporting the principles represented by the prophets, Jesus' stinging indictment classifies them with those who actually murdered the prophets. Beautifying tombs and constructing monuments to honor the prophets and the righteous are only hollow gestures, since their actions demonstrate that they do not respect their teachings nor emulate their commitment to the will of God. Thus the concluding exhortation to **fill up the measure of the sins of your forefathers**, encourages them to complete what their fathers have started. Jesus therefore understands that the hardened rebellion of the present generation stands in continuity with and brings to a climax the disobedient spirit of their forefathers.

23:33. In language reminiscent of John the Baptist (cf. 3:7) Jesus' indictment of Pharisaic hypocrisy reaches a zenith of verbal vilification by calling his opponents **snakes** and a **brood of vipers**. The reference is intended to underscore their deceitfully harmful tactics that have led to the poisoning of anyone who embraces their destructive teachings. Their description is followed by a rhetorical question implying that there will be no escape from God's judgment to come.

23:34-35. Jesus now brings his invective discourse to a conclusion by directly linking the hostile rebellion of the present generation to a consistent pattern of Jewish rejection of God's messengers. Like God in the past who sent his messengers to Israel, even so now Jesus (note emphatic **I**), sends **prophets, wise men, and teachers** (=disciples) to the present generation. As has been noted previously, they can expect no better treatment than that given God's messengers in previous generations (cf. 5:11-12; 10:40-41). This present generation will prove itself to be in solidarity with the hostility of a previous generation by "killing, crucifying,[38] beating,

---

[38]Although crucifixion was inflicted only by the Romans, its mention here probably intends to link the disciples' experience of taking up their crosses with the literal crucifixion of Jesus.

and driving away" the envoys of God who are sent by one possessing divine power and authority – namely Jesus. Because of their solidarity with their ancestor's evil deeds, they have become guilty of **all the righteous blood that has been shed on earth**, from the first person murdered in the Old Testament to the last. Jesus specifically identifies Abel (Gen 4) as the first righteous man in the Old Testament whose innocent blood was shed by the wicked. A pattern of hostility against the righteous runs throughout the Old Testament history, from the first martyr to the last recorded murder of God's servant, **Zechariah son of Berekiah**. Although there are more than thirty Zechariahs mentioned in the Old Testament, traditionally the Zechariah mentioned by Jesus has been identified with the Zechariah killed in the "courtyard of the Lord's temple" recorded in 2 Chronicles 24:20-21.[39] The obvious difficulty with this view is that the Zechariah of 2 Chronicles 24 is called "Zechariah son of Jehoida the priest" (v. 20). It could be that Berekiah is a second name of Jehoida, or possibly refers to Zechariah's grandfather. Although the prophet Zechariah is specifically identified as the "son of Berekiah" (1:1), there is no martyrdom tradition associated with his death. It may be, as suggested by others, that Jesus' reference to "Zechariah son of Berekiah" refers to a well known figure in his day, whose exact identity is unknown today. Whatever the precise identification, Jesus' point is that the entirety of the Old Testament is bracketed by brutal murders performed by those hardened to the ways of God.

23:36. Jesus then concludes his denunciation by assuring in a most solemn manner (ἀμὴν λέγω ὑμῖν, *amēn legō hymin*, **I tell you the truth**) that **this generation** (i.e., Jesus' contemporary hearers) will witness the horrific acts he has described previously (v. 34). It follows that an entire generation will be held accountable because of the hostility of Israel's leaders directed at the Lord's Anointed (see 24:34).

3 Lament over Jerusalem (23:37-39)

[37]"O Jerusalem, Jerusalem, you who kill the prophets and stone those sent to you, how often I have longed to gather your

[39]For a defense of this view see Hagner, *Matthew* 2:676-677.

children together, as a hen gathers her chicks under her wings, but you were not willing. [38]Look, your house is left to you desolate. [39]For I tell you, you will not see me again until you say, 'Blessed is he who comes in the name of the Lord.'[a]"

[a]*39* Psalm 118:26

23:37. Jesus' strongly worded discourse ends, in the words of Hagner, "with a burst of warm sunshine."[40] Jesus takes no delight in renouncing the failures of Israel's leadership. His lament over Jerusalem spells out his deep disappointment over the city's persistent antagonism and rejection of those commissioned by God, culminating in the rejection of God's own Son. Jerusalem has become known as a city that kills prophets and brutally executes those sent by God. In spite of its history, Jesus has repeatedly made overtures to the city,[41] reaching out to his people to love, protect, and nurture them, like **a hen gathers her chicks under her wings**. The imagery clearly indicates that God intended only his love and grace for Israel, but by their stubborn refusal to be responsive to God's offer in Jesus, they have removed themselves from the favor of God (cf. 8:10-12; 21:43-44).

23:38. Jesus then calls attention (ἰδοὺ, *idou*) to the inevitable destruction of **your house**, meaning either the city, or more specifically the temple. It has been noted that the passive verb ἀφίεται (*aphietai*, "left to you") implies both a physical destruction and a complete abandonment by God.[42] The details of this destruction are spelled out in the discourse to follow (24:4-34).

23:39. With the closing words of verse 39 Jesus indicates that from now on (ἀπ' ἄρτι, *ap' arti*) there will be no more direct appeal for Israel's repentance. The course of events will now move quickly from Jesus' final discourse (chs. 24-25), to his arrest (24:47-56),

---

[40]Ibid., p. 679.

[41]This reference presupposes several encounters with Jerusalem's leaders, which accords with the Gospel of John's account of Jesus' travels to Jerusalem.

[42]As noted by France, *Matthew*, p. 332: "The verb . . . speaks not so much of the physical condition of the temple, as of the fact that *God has departed from it* (cf. Ezek 10:18-19; 11:22- 23)."

trials (26:57–27:26), and his execution (27:27-56). But Jesus does indicate by an until-clause (ἕως ἄν . . . , *heōs an* . . .) that when he is seen again those who greet him will use the same language of adoration and petition as that found in Jesus' entry into Jerusalem (21:9; based on Ps 118:26). This text has led some to see a "glimmer of hope"[43] for Israel, with some even suggesting "a conversion of Israel at the parousia."[44] However, D.C. Allison has made a strong case for interpreting the words "until you say . . ." as a "conditional prophecy" meaning that Israel's deliverance is contingent upon acceptance of the person and work of Jesus. Thus the possibility of salvation is present, but it will only come to those who utter the words **"Blessed is he who comes in the name of the Lord."**[45]

Jesus' characterization of the "teachers of the law and Pharisees" as hypocritical and filled with violence prepares the reader for the ensuing scenes depicting Israel's violence against the Lord's Anointed. Jerusalem has become ripe for destruction, and in the discourse to follow (i.e., 24:4–25:46) the theme of *judgment* prevails.

---

[43]Blomberg, *Matthew*, p. 351.

[44]Gundry, *Matthew*, p. 474.

[45]D.C. Allison, "Matt. 23:39-Luke 13:35b as a Conditional Prophecy," *JSNT* 18 (1983), 75-84; also Garland, *Matthew 23*, pp. 204-209.

MATTHEW 24

J. FIFTH DISCOURSE: JUDGMENT TO COME (24:1–25:46)

Following the diatribe of chapter 23, Jesus' fifth and final discourse[1] spells out the catastrophic events leading to the temple's destruction and the appearance of Jesus as King and eschatological judge. This broad summary of the contents of chapters 24 and 25 is by no means intended to imply that interpreters are in agreement on the general purpose or specific details of Jesus' Olivet discourse. The history of the interpretation of Jesus' discourse (cf. Mark 13:1-37; Luke 21:5-36) is extremely complex, with the literature on the subject immense.[2]

On the one hand those fascinated with the end times have largely ignored any reference to Jerusalem's destruction, and have interpreted the entire discourse as a cryptic outline detailing the course of events leading to the end of time.[3] While such a view may lend itself to bizarre charts and speculations about the timing of the end, such theories fail to take seriously the discourse's literary and historical context. While others have recognized that the discourse speaks about the fall of Jerusalem alongside the "coming of the Son of Man," precisely how the two events relate to one another has not found a consensus. Some are prepared to charge Jesus or the evangelist Matthew with the mistaken notion that the *parousia* was expected to follow immediately Jerusalem's

---

[1]Note the formulaic ending, "when Jesus had finished saying all these things" (cf. 7:28; 11:1; 13:53; 19:1).

[2]For a helpful survey of the literature from 1950 to 1991 see G.R. Beasley-Murray, *Jesus and the Last Days: The Interpretation of the Olivet Discourse* (Peabody, MA: Hendrickson, 1993), pp. 162-349.

[3]E.g., see J.F. Walvoord, "Christ's Olivet Discourse on the Time of the End: Prophesies Fulfilled in the Present Age," *BSac* 128 (1971), 206-214.

destruction.[4] Others attempt to account for both events by distinguishing those sections that refer to the city's destruction (e.g., vv. 4-28), from those texts that refer to end-time events (e.g., vv. 29-31; 36–25:41). However, the way the chapter should be divided remains a matter of dispute.[5]

It has recently been proposed by N.T. Wright that those sections which describe the "coming Son of Man" should not be understood as a literal descent of Jesus on a cloud signaling the "end of the space-time universe."[6] Instead, according to Wright, first century Jewish readers would have understood the "coming of the Son of Man" in terms of Daniel 7:13-14, hence describing a representative of the people of God being vindicated and enthroned, after evil forces have been overcome (in this instance, "the present powers occupying Jerusalem"). Accordingly, Wright interprets the entirety of chapters 24-25 in terms of Jerusalem's destruction, with the "coming Son of Man" references understood in terms of Daniel's "coming to the Ancient of Days" (7:12), not in the sense of a personal return of Jesus. Therefore, the exhortations to "keep watch" because no one knows the day or hour when the Son of Man will come" (vv. 36-44), and the parables of chapter 25 stressing preparedness, responsibility and judgment are all understood in terms of the turbulent times surrounding Jerusalem's destruction.[7]

Wright's thesis has much to commend it. It has always been difficult to understand the disciples' question in 24:3 in terms of Jesus' second coming since, as Wright observed: "they would not yet even thought of his being taken from them, let alone that he might come back . . . ."[8] Furthermore, Wright's reading of the discourse in light of Old Testament prophecy, metaphors, and symbolism is certainly

---

[4]See, e.g., Hagner, *Matthew* 2:711-713.

[5]Cf. the views of Carson, *Matthew*, pp. 488-495; Blomberg, *Matthew*, pp. 351-352; with France, *Matthew*, pp. 333-336; and Garland, *Reading Matthew*, pp. 235-236.

[6]Wright, *Jesus and the Victory of God*, pp. 339-368; although Wright addresses Mark 13 with only an occasional notice of Matthew 24.

[7]Groundwork for his discussion is found in *The New Testament and the People of God* (Philadelphia: Fortress, 1992), pp. 280-338. Wright's treatment of Jewish eschatology is especially helpful, see *Jesus*, pp. 202-220.

[8]Wright, *Jesus*, p. 345.

the right approach for any credible interpretation of the discourse. However, while the discourse would be understood in light of Old Testament imagery, it is also critical to observe the literary and thematic structure of the chapter.[9] It is difficult not to agree with France that verse 36 marks a "deliberate change of subject," from the signs that are to occur within "this generation" (v. 34), to the day the "heaven and earth will pass away" (v. 35), the timing of which no one knows.[10] It would not appear to be too difficult to move from a concrete expression of judgment (i.e., Jerusalem), to scenes depicting the Son of Man coming as eschatological judge. Thus, while the language and imagery of 24:36–25:46 still have Jerusalem's overthrow as its primary background, the collapse of the temple would necessarily conjure up images of the end-times and universal judgment. Hence dividing the discourse based upon the disciple's question in verse three does seem to fit the thematic structure of this twofold focus: vv. 4-35, Jesus answers the disciples' question concerning the temple's destruction; vv. 36–25:46, Jesus answers the disciples' question about Jesus' "coming" (παρουσία, *parousia*) as Israel's King.

In anticipation of the commentary to follow the discourse can be further divided according to the following sections: 24:1-3, Introduction; 24:4-14, Warnings not to be deceived; 24:15-28, The coming tribulation in Judea; 24:29-35, The climactic fall of Jerusalem within this "generation"; 24:36–25:46, Be watchful, alert, and responsible in the interim.

1. Introduction (24:1-3)

1Jesus left the temple and was walking away when his disciples came up to him to call his attention to its buildings. 2"Do you see all these things?" he asked. "I tell you the truth, not one stone here will be left on another; every one will be thrown down."

3As Jesus was sitting on the Mount of Olives, the disciples came to him privately. "Tell us," they said, "when will this

[9]It may be that Wright, *Jesus*, p. 346, dismisses too hastily France's division of the chapter into two halves, vv. 4-35 and 36-51.

[10]France, *Matthew*, p. 347.

happen, and what will be the sign of your coming and of the end of the age?"

24:1. As noted earlier, once in Jerusalem, the locus of Jesus' activity was situated in the shadow of the temple (cf. 21:14-15, 23). However, with the announcement in 23:38 that "your house is left to you desolate," Jesus' departure from the temple graphically symbolizes "the end of its relevance in the purpose of God."[11] In point of fact, Jesus, who is "greater than the temple" (12:6), and who mediates the presence of God (1:23), has replaced the temple as the place "where God mediates salvation to people (cf. 1:21; 26:28; 27:51)."[12] Thus with God's presence withdrawn from the temple it is only ripe for destruction.

24:2. While in the process of departing from the temple, the disciples, evidently awestruck by the enormity and beauty of Herod's architectural accomplishment in the newly constructed temple (on the beauty of Herod's temple, see Josephus *Ant.* 15.11.3; 291-402; *J.W.* 5.5.1-6; 184-226), hope to elicit from Jesus a similar sense of wonder by calling attention to its grandeur. However, the disciples were not at all prepared for Jesus' response. Instead of joining their chorus of adoration and amazement, Jesus announces that the entire edifice will be destroyed. Thus, Jesus verbalizes what his earlier actions symbolized (cf. 21:12-13). His words strike at the heart of Israel's most sacred shrine. While earlier prophetic figures had repudiated the temple cult and announced its downfall (cf. Mic 3:12; Jer 7:12-14; 26:1-19), by Jesus' day an ideology grounded in extreme nationalism had convinced many that the temple was indestructible. It is no wonder that Jesus' claim of the temple's destruction would become widely known and surface in the trial scene (26:61), as well as during his execution (27:40).

24:3. Jesus leaves the temple mount and crosses over to the **Mount of Olives**, a small ridge of hills, running north to south along the Kidron Valley. From this vantage point, some one hundred feet above Jerusalem,[13] Jesus could overlook the temple

---

[11]Ibid., p. 336.

[12]Kingsbury, *Matthew as Story*, p. 30.

[13]W.J. Heard, "Mount of Olives," *ABD* 5:13.

area, and from here he will give his final oracles of judgment upon the city (cf. Ezek 11:23). The discourse comes as a response to the disciples' twofold question: (1) When will the temple and all that it represents (ταῦτα, *tauta*) come to an end? (2) What signs will signal your presence (*parousia*)[14] as eschatological judge, and the end of this present evil age (συντελείας τοῦ αἰῶνος, *synteleias tou aiōnos*)? As noted earlier, it is difficult to understand the second part of the disciples' question in terms of Jesus' personal second coming, since such a scenario could not have been further from their minds. The disciples seem convinced that the temple's destruction signals the inauguration of Jesus' reign over the nations, and the end of this present evil age. Indeed, Israel's national crises always had eschatological overtones attached to them. In response, Jesus first describes events leading up to Jerusalem's destruction (vv. 4-35), followed by a series of "parables" exhorting the preparation and alertness in view of the "coming Son of Man" (24:36–25:46).

2. Warnings Not to Be Deceived (24:4-14)

4Jesus answered: "Watch out that no one deceives you. 5For many will come in my name, claiming, 'I am the Christ,[a]' and will deceive many. 6You will hear of wars and rumors of wars, but see to it that you are not alarmed. Such things must happen, but the end is still to come. 7Nation will rise against nation, and kingdom against kingdom. There will be famines and earthquakes in various places. 8All these are the beginning of birth pains.

9"Then you will be handed over to be persecuted and put to death, and you will be hated by all nations because of me. 10At that time many will turn away from the faith and will betray and hate each other, 11and many false prophets will appear and deceive many people. 12Because of the increase of wickedness, the love of most will grow cold, 13but he who stands firm to the end will be saved. 14And this gospel of the kingdom will be preached

---

[14]The term παρουσία has been defined as "arrival, coming, presence, or visit." Prior to the second century B.C. it was used of visits of kings and emperors to a city. One need not always read the second coming of Jesus into the term.

in the whole world as a testimony to all nations, and then the end will come.

[a]*5* Or *Messiah*; also in verse 23

24:4-5. Jesus' address begins by citing numerous events that anticipate the downfall of Jerusalem but do not herald its imminent end. Jesus' warnings are intended to offset any premature conclusions based upon the deceptive tactics of pseudo-messiahs (cf. v. 27). These false prophets come "in the name" of Jesus and thus lay claim to his messianic office. It is well known that in the years preceding Jerusalem's destruction numerous messianic pretenders appeared with revolutionary aspirations (cf. Acts 5:26-27; see also Josephus, *J.W.* 2.17.8-9; 433- 48; 4.9.3-8; 503-44).[15] Jesus warns his followers not to be deceived by these false messiahs who come promoting themselves by announcing the end of the age.

24:6-8. By means of standard apocalyptic imagery Jesus alerts his followers not to be alarmed either by escalating civil conflicts or by natural disasters, as if they signal that the end is near. Such things **must happen** (δεῖ γὰρ γενέσθαι, *dei gar genesthai*), and therefore fall under the purview of God's sovereign will. It would be easy for false prophets to use the occurrences of famines and earthquakes as signs to promote their misguided eschatology. However, Jesus attempts to calm any apprehension by calling them **the beginning of birth pains** (cf. Isa 26:17; 66:8-9; Jer 22-23; Hos 13:13; Mic 4:9-10). One stream of Jewish thought anticipated an era of distress and extreme suffering (sometimes called the "messianic woes") before the dawn of salvation.[16] Hence, while these signs may signal the "beginning" of the passing of the old age, they are not to be interpreted as signs of the imminent judgment of God. Jesus' disciples must prepare themselves for mission in a world marked by human sinfulness and natural chaos.

24:9. The next paragraph (vv. 9-14) appears to highlight a chronological progression within the period of distress described in

---

[15]Although they may not have made explicit messianic claims their followers certainly regarded them as messianic; see R.H. Horsley and J.S. Hanson, *Bandits, Prophets, and Messiahs: Popular Movements in the Time of Jesus* (New York: Winston Press, 1985), esp. pp. 88-179.

[16]For discussion see Wright, *People of God*, p. 277f.

verses 4-8 (see τότε, *tote*). Thus the period called "the beginning of birth pains" is extended to include persecution at the hand of **all nations**, alongside a worldwide mission to all the nations (v. 14).[17] It is significant that the discourse ends with all the nations being held accountable for their treatment of Jesus' disciples (25:31-46). In the meanwhile, Jesus' disciples are called upon to "disciple the nations," being assured of the abiding presence of Jesus "to the very end of the age" (28:19-20).

In their mission to the nations the disciples can expect outbreaks of persecution that result in their being **handed over** (παραδώσουσιν, *paradōsousin*, cf. similarly Jesus, 17:22; 20:18-29; 26:2; 27:2-3, 18, 26) to extreme suffering and even death. The widespread opposition and hatred of the disciples are caused by their loyalty to Jesus. The reader is reminded of earlier sayings predicting the consequences of allegiance to Jesus (10:17-42; 16:24-26).

24:10-12. The gravity of the persecution described in verse nine leads to a series of negative consequences. First, many will abandon the faith (σκανδαλίζω, *skandalizō*, lit., "be tripped up"), and some will even assist evil forces by "betraying" fellow disciples. With persecution comes a growth of extreme animosity and repudiation within the ranks of Jesus' followers, perhaps stirred by the attempt to escape the wrath of the world. Probably contributing to the general state of anarchy and treasonous activity is the presence of **false prophets** who contrive to **deceive many people**. A general **increase of wickedness** (ἀνομίαν, *anomian*, or "lawlessness") results in a cooling of love for one another. In a situation where lawlessness prevails selfish interests and personal concerns completely overshadow a loving regard for others.[18]

24:13-14. In spite of the hardship they will face, Jesus encourages his followers to **stand firm to the end**, and they **will be saved** (cf. 10:22; Mic 7:7). Although the words of Jesus have in mind enduring the coming crisis as outlined in verses 5-12, certainly endurance in the midst of trials is the way of Jesus in all corresponding circumstances. Jesus promises his followers that faithful

---

[17]See C.L. Holman, *Till Jesus Comes: Origins of Christian Apocalyptic Expectation* (Peabody, MA: Hendrickson, 1996), p. 120.

[18]See the general description of Tacitus, *Histories* 1.2,3.

perseverance will ultimately be vindicated. Meanwhile, it is critical that the disciples continue to proclaim the **gospel of the kingdom** (cf. 4:23; 9:35), throughout the inhabited world (οἰκουμένη, *oikoumenē*) in order that **all nations** might hear the testimony of what God has done in Christ Jesus. Hence, the disciples are not merely to endure the opposition described in verses 9-12; they are to counter such hostility by bearing witness to the presence of God's kingdom.

While earlier the disciples are instructed to go only to Israel (10:5-6), Jesus now envisions a universal mission including all the nations (cf. 28:19). This is in keeping with the prophetic expectations about the involvement of all the nations in God's blessings and judgment.[19] Outreach to the nations must precede the "end," hence Jesus' disciples are encouraged to participate in an active Gentile mission (cf. Rom 11:25-26). Thus, in the interim period, between the universal commission of the disciples (28:18-20), and the *parousia* of Jesus, the church is under an "eschatological necessity"[20] to proclaim the good news of the kingdom throughout the world. It does appear that the early church took seriously its call to mission since by A.D. 70 most of the Mediterranean world had heard the gospel (1 Thess 1:8; Rom 1:5-8; Col 1:6, 23).

3. The Coming Tribulation in Judea (24:15-28)

[15]"So when you see standing in the holy place 'the abomination that causes desolation,'[a] spoken of through the prophet Daniel — let the reader understand — [16]then let those who are in Judea flee to the mountains. [17]Let no one on the roof of his house go down to take anything out of the house. [18]Let no one in the field go back to get his cloak. [19]How dreadful it will be in those days for pregnant women and nursing mothers! [20]Pray that your flight will not take place in winter or on the Sabbath. [21]For then there will be great distress, unequaled from the beginning of the

---

[19]Margaret Davies, *Matthew* (Sheffield: JSOT Press, 1993), p. 167.

[20]The language of J.W. Thompson, "The Gentile Mission as an Eschatological Necessity" *RQ* 14 (1971), 18-27.

world until now – and never to be equaled again. [22]If those days had not been cut short, no one would survive, but for the sake of the elect those days will be shortened. [23]At that time if anyone says to you, 'Look, here is the Christ!' or, 'There he is!' do not believe it. [24]For false Christs and false prophets will appear and perform great signs and miracles to deceive even the elect – if that were possible. [25]See, I have told you ahead of time.

[26]"So if anyone tells you, 'There he is, out in the desert,' do not go out; or, 'Here he is, in the inner rooms,' do not believe it. [27]For as lightning that comes from the east is visible even in the west, so will be the coming of the Son of Man. [28]Wherever there is a carcass, there the vultures will gather.

[a]*15* Daniel 9:27; 11:31; 12:11

Jesus now gives specific instruction to those disciples who will witness the Jewish wars leading to Jerusalem's destruction. It is critical that they not get caught up in the series of events surrounding Jerusalem's punishment. They are to watch for the "sign" that will signal the necessity of flight (v. 15). Haste is to be made. There is not time for delay; flee to the mountains (vv. 16-18). They are to pray that the time for departure does not come when circumstances would hinder a prompt departure or make travel difficult (vv. 19-20). They must not be deceived by messianic pretenders who incite false expectations and hopes by miraculous deeds and claims of a messianic deliverance (vv. 23-26). In short, the disciples are not to be implicated in the coming war; they are to get out and run.

24:15. The appearance of the **abomination that causes desolation** is the sign that signals the necessity of flight. The phrase occurs three times in Daniel (9:26; 11:31; 12:11), and describes a ruler who leads his armed forces against Jerusalem and "desecrates the temple fortress," and "abolishes the daily sacrifice." These references were read in the second century B.C. as indicating Antiochus Epiphanes who in 167 B.C. plundered the temple, ordered the sacrificial system to cease, and polluted the altar of the Lord by turning it into a pagan altar, where unclean sacrifices were offered to pagan deities (see 1 Macc 1:20-24).

Jesus uses the horrifying imagery of Daniel's vision to describe the temple's desecration and ultimate destruction by Roman forces in A.D. 70. It appears that the presence of something detestable (neuter, τὸ βδέλυγμα, *to bdelygma*) so compromised the sanctity of the temple that it must be destroyed. Some have speculated that the presence of Roman soldiers and the planting of their shields in the temple precincts might be the detestable act that will signal the necessity of flight. However, once the Romans had entered the city and planted their shields on holy ground it would have been too late to safely flee the city (see Josephus, *J.W.* 6.6.1, 316). Other attempts to identify some specific event that might be understood as the "desolating sacrilege" can at best be viewed only as guesswork.[21] The most that can be said is that the disciples were to flee when events associated with the Jewish wars (A.D. 66-70) so compromised the sanctity of the temple that its destruction was inevitable.

24:16. The crisis brought on by the repulsive event(s) described in v. 15 necessitates that the inhabitants **in Judea flee to the mountains**. Obviously such a flight makes sense if Jesus' words refer to escaping the dangers of Jerusalem's destruction, and not to his second coming. Traditionally, the hill country with its numerous caves provided a safe refuge from hostile enemies (cf. the flight of Mattathias and his sons from Antiochus, 1 Macc 2:16, 28; see also Gen 19:17). During the Roman siege many people fled to the temple mount hoping for divine protection, only to meet with disaster. Jesus is emphatic – the temple is not a place of refuge, nor should it be defended from invasion. Jesus' followers must abandon the city and run for the hills.[22]

24:17-20. The urgency of a hasty departure is illustrated by emphasizing that neither one resting leisurely on the typically flat Palestinian rooftop, nor the worker in the field has time to secure even basic provisions for their exit. The necessity of flight is too urgent. Jesus expresses sympathy for those in special circumstances

---

[21]For a survey of views see D. Ford, *The Abomination of Desolation in Biblical Eschatology* (Washington, DC: University Press of America, 1979).

[22]According to Eusebius in his *Historia Ecclesiastica* (3.5.3), the Christians fled Jerusalem to Pella, a city on the Transjordanian plateau, located about five miles from the Jordan River. However, it seems difficult to call a descent of 3,000 feet a "flight to the mountains."

(i.e., **pregnant women and nursing mothers**) who will find it especially difficult to travel with haste. They are also to pray that their flight may not take place in the winter because weather conditions might impede a swift flight from danger. Such a scenario "has in view a country in which wadis, which have little or no water in the summer, and even the Jordan itself, became swollen through winter rains, and so make escape difficult or even impossible."[23] Concerning flight **on the Sabbath**, Stanton has observed that the text has been interpreted "in at least six quite different ways."[24] Stanton understands a flight on the sabbath as possibly further provoking the Jews, and thus to avoid further hostility, it should be avoided if at all possible. Others see the text as a "window" into the Matthean community, indicating that observance of the sabbath, including travel prohibitions, would still have been observed by many conservative Jewish Christians. Hence, a flight on the sabbath would be extremely divisive within the Christian community.[25] On the other hand, it has been suggested that a flight from Jerusalem on the sabbath would have been extremely difficult since the gates of the city would have been shut, and it would not be possible to purchase provisions on the sabbath.[26] All proposals have some problematic assumptions that make it difficult to know with certainty why a flight on the sabbath was to be avoided if at all possible.

24:21-22. The reason (γάρ, *gar*) for a hasty departure is now stated in graphic terms (cf. Dan 12:1). The ordeal that they are about to suffer is a **great distress**, unprecedented in its horror, that will never be paralleled in the extent of human suffering and affliction. Although the description of Josephus provides the gory and horrific details of the suffering associated with Jerusalem's destruction (*J.W.* 5.10.1; 420-423; 5.11.3-4; 460-472), the language of verse 21 is probably hyperbolic, using "traditional expressions to denote

---

[23]Beasley-Murray, *Jesus and the Last Days*, pp. 417-418.

[24]See G.N. Stanton, *A Gospel for a New People: Studies in Matthew* (Louisville: Westminster, 1992), p. 193; see the response to Stanton by E.K.C. Wong, "The Matthean Understanding of the Sabbath: A Response to G.N. Stanton," *JSNT* 44 (1991), 2-18.

[25]Hagner, *Matthew* 2:702.

[26]France, *Matthew*, p. 341. However, the securing of provisions seems difficult to square with v. 17.

severe tribulation (cf. Exod 9:18; 10:14; 11:66; Dan 12:1)."[27] The catastrophic nature of the events unfolding has the potential to sweep away all humanity, including the elect, with its destructive force. However, **those days will be shortened** (see 2 Sam 24:16; Isa 45:8) by the sovereign hand of God, who will assure the safety of the elect. Thus, God is in control, in spite of what might appear to be a chaotic catastrophe that threatens even the well being of those who belong to him. "Even the horrors of human warfare come within the providential control of the God to whom 'the elect' belong."[28]

24:23-26. Once again Jesus warns against the allure of messianic pretenders and **false prophets** who attempt to lead astray the **elect.** During a period of crisis people will look to one claimant after another in hope that through him God will deliver his people. Jesus' followers are not to give any credence to the claims that a messianic figure has arisen assuring Israel's deliverance. Even if they perform compelling **signs** (σημεῖα, *sēmeia*) **and miracles** (τέρατα, *terata*) they are not to be believed (cf. Deut 13:1-3). Their purpose is **to deceive** (ὥστε πλανῆσαι, *hōste planēsai*) **the elect**, and evidently their persuasive signs would have succeeded were it not for God's "overriding grace."[29] Because they belong to God, Jesus has forewarned them about the dangers of succumbing to the deceitful tactics of false messiahs and false prophets. Therefore, they must not be caught up in any notion that the presence of the Messiah can be located **in the desert**, or that he is hidden in the **inner rooms** of a house. Whatever claims are made about some secretive knowledge of the Messiah's whereabouts, **do not believe it.**[30]

24:27-28. The presence of the Son of Man will not be a matter of dispute or speculation, because as lightning is visible from the east to the west so will his coming (*parousia*) be. Jesus therefore rebuts any notion of a localized expectation known only to a few. A

[27]So contends Beasley-Murray, *Jesus and the Last Days*, p. 418.

[28]France, *Matthew*, p. 341.

[29]Beasley-Murray, *Jesus and the Last Days*, p. 393.

[30]One stream of Jewish messianic thought evidently believed that at first the presence of the Messiah would only be secretively known (suggested in John 7:27).

second metaphor, the gathering of **vultures** (ἀετοί, *aetoi*, not "eagles")[31] reinforces the first by stressing as surely as the gathering of vultures signifies that a carcass is present, so the presence of the Son of Man will be beyond dispute. There is no need to search out the Messiah as if he were in some obscured location.

4. The Climactic Fall of Jerusalem within "This Generation" (24:29-35)

29"Immediately after the distress of those days
"'the sun will be darkened,
and the moon will not give its light;
the stars will fall from the sky,
and the heavenly bodies will be shaken.'[a]

30"At that time the sign of the Son of Man will appear in the sky, and all the nations of the earth will mourn. They will see the Son of Man coming on the clouds of the sky, with power and great glory. 31And he will send his angels with a loud trumpet call, and they will gather his elect from the four winds, from one end of the heavens to the other.

32"Now learn this lesson from the fig tree: As soon as its twigs get tender and its leaves come out, you know that summer is near. 33Even so, when you see all these things, you know that it[b] is near, right at the door. 34I tell you the truth, this generation[c] will certainly not pass away until all these things have happened. 35Heaven and earth will pass away, but my words will never pass away.

[a]*29* Isaiah 13:10; 34:4 [b]*33* Or *he* [c]*34* Or *race*

24:29. Most often these texts are interpreted in terms of Christ's second coming and the cataclysmic end of the universe. However, verses 29-31 seem clearly connected to verses 4-28 as indicated by

[31]While some, e.g., J.M. Kik, *An Eschatology of Victory* (Nutley, NJ: Presbyterian and Reformed Publishing Co., 1971), pp. 125-126, see the carcass as Jerusalem with the gathering of "eagles" signifying the armies of Rome like eagles swarming Jerusalem. But the imagery seems to reinforce the previous one (i.e., "lightning").

the transitional line, **Immediately** (εὐθέως, *eutheōs*) **after the distress of those days**. The reference to the "distress in those days" seems to assume verses 15-28 as its antecedent. To make the words refer to some form of suffering or tribulation in the indeterminate future, just preceding the *parousia*, clearly ignores the most natural antecedent. Furthermore, the term "immediately" (*eutheōs*) does not lend itself to a long delay between the events described in verses 4-28 and that which is to occur in verses 29-31. This interpretation alleviates the problem of assuming that either Jesus or Matthew thought the *parousia* of Jesus was intimately connected to Jerusalem's destruction.[32] There is no problem if the cosmic symbolism and the "coming Son of Man" terminology are understood not as a description of the "physical collapse of the space-time world," but as "good first-century metaphorical language for two things: the defeat of the enemies of the true people of God, and the vindication of the true people themselves."[33] As such, verses 29-31 function as a climactic description, in vivid Old Testament imagery, of the downfall of Jerusalem.

It is well known that the cosmic portents of verse 29 are drawn from similar language in the Old Testament (cf. Isa 13:9-11; 34:4-5; Ezek 32:7-8; Joel 2:10, 31; 3:15; Amos 8:9).[34] In each instance "this kind of metaphorical language is commonly applied to events of destruction and chaos within the bounds of history and not at the termination of history."[35] Isaiah uses cosmic, universal-type language to describe God's judgment upon Babylon (13:9-10), and Edom (34:4-5). The same language appears in Ezekiel, this time referring to the demise of Egypt (32:7-8). The language abounds in Jewish Intertestamental literature (e.g., As. Mos. 10:1-10; 4 Ezra 5:4-5; 1 Enoch 1:5; 6:2-8; 15:4-16; Jub 4:15; 5:1; T.Reub 5:6-7; 2 Enoch 7:18). In every occurrence the language functions metaphorically,

---

[32]So Hagner, *Matthew* 2:711-713.

[33]See Wright, *Jesus*, pp. 361-365; and France, *Matthew*, pp. 343-346.

[34]See the recent helpful treatment of T.R. Hatina, "The Focus of Mark 13:24-27: The Parousia, or the Destruction of the Temple," *Bulletin for Biblical Research* 6 (1996), esp. 53-59; see also Wright, *Jesus*, pp. 354-360. R.H. Gundry, *Mark* (Grand Rapids: Eerdmans, 1993), p. 745, remarkably interprets the language as "a shower of meteorites" accompanying the *parousia*.

[35]Hatina, "Focus of Mark," p. 55.

highlighting divine judgment against a political entity, and bringing vindication to those who have been suffering under a tyrannical political power. Therefore, it seems best to understand the language of verse 29 not in terms of a literal cosmic upheaval, but rather as a retelling of a well-known story, namely, God will vindicate his people and judge their enemies. However, this time it is the Jerusalem temple that represents all that is opposed to God and the true people of Israel.[36]

24:30. The appearance of the Son of Man **coming on the clouds of the sky, with power and great glory** certainly sounds on the surface to modern readers like a clear reference to the *parousia* of Jesus. However, the language would most likely be understood by a first century reader as an allusion to Daniel 7. In Daniel 7:13 "one like a son of man" stands in contrast to four beasts who emerge from the sea (vv. 3-12). The four beasts represent "four kingdoms" (v. 17) who stand in opposition to Israel, culminating in the little horn of the fourth beast who wages war against the saints and defeats them (v. 21). However, the "one like the son of man" who represents the "saints of the Most High" (vv. 13, 22, 27) finds favor with the Ancient of Days (vv. 22, 26) and is ultimately vindicated by being given authority and dominion over "all the nations" (vv. 13, 27; cf. Matt 25:31). It should be noted that the "coming of the Son of Man" in Daniel 7 is not to earth, but rather a coming before the throne of God where he is vindicated and the "saints of the Most High" are given victory over their enemies. Therefore, the language of Daniel 7 depicting the "coming Son of Man" should not be read as pointing to the *parousia* and God's final judgment. Instead, the background to the "coming Son of Man" terminology hightlights the theme of "vindication through judgment."[37]

Jesus predicts that when **the nations of the earth** see the **sign of the Son of Man . . . in the sky** they will **mourn**. Exactly what the "sign of the Son of Man" is has been the subject of much speculation.[38] Most likely the expression refers to the "coming Son of

---

[36]Wright, *Jesus*, p. 359.

[37]Hatina, "Focus of Mark," p. 59.

[38]The early church identified the "sign" as a sign of the cross that appeared in the sky with Jerusaelm's destruction. For other proposals see *TDNT* 7:236-238.

Man" himself, and therefore should not be interpreted as some outward sign that heralds the arrival of the Son of Man.

It has been suggested by France that the phrase "all the nations of the earth" would be better translated "all the tribes of the land."[39] The reference would therefore depict national grief as a response to the temple's destruction. The "coming Son of Man" should not be understood as a descent from heaven to earth, but rather in terms of Daniel 7:13-14, where the Son of Man is enthroned and given victory over his enemies. Jerusalem's destruction is therefore a powerful sign of God's vindication of his Son.

24:31. The fall of Jerusalem also signals a "turning point in the mission of the church."[40] The prediction of a restoration of the faithful after a prophecy of judgment is a common pattern in the Old Testament.[41] The image of restoration is probably drawn from Old Testament texts like Deuteronomy 30:2-4 and Zechariah 2:6-11. The calling of the elect will be accomplished by means of **his angels** (ἀγγέλους, *angelous*), possibly referring to messengers (cf. Luke 7:24, 27; 9:52; James 2:25; Mark 1:2; Matt 11:10) who gather the elect by means of their Gospel proclamation.[42] The scene need not be depicting an eschatological gathering for the dispensing of eternal reward (cf. 13:41).

24:32-33. Jesus now illustrates the importance of carefully observing the signs that point to the accomplishment of **all these things**. **The fig tree** (cf. 21:18-22) is particularly fitting for illustrating his point, because unlike many Palestinian trees, it loses its leaves in winter, and begins to sprout new leaves in late spring. The presence of the bud is therefore a sure sign **that summer is near**. In like manner, the presence of "all these things" (probably the circumstances described in vv. 15-28) should alert the observer that "it is near" (i.e., Jerusalem's destruction). It is critical that Jesus' followers be discerning and properly read the signs pointing to the imminent fall of the city.

---

[39]See the defense in his *Jesus and the Old Testament* (London: Tyndale, 1971), pp. 236-327.

[40]Garland, *Reading Matthew*, p. 239.

[41]See the discussion in Hatina, "Focus of Mark," pp. 64-66.

[42]Suggested by France, *Jesus and the Old Testament*, p. 208.

24:34. In solemn terms (**I tell you the truth**) Jesus announces that **this generation** (γενεὰ, *geneä*) will see **all these things** come to pass. It is usually argued that "all these things" (πάντα ταῦτα, *panta tauta*) is limited to the events comprising verses 4-28, with verses 29-31 referring to the *parousia*. However, the progression of the discourse from preliminary signs (vv. 4-28), to events after the distress of those days" (v. 29) favors seeing this text as a summary of the entire discourse thus far. Therefore, some comprising the present generation will see the signs culminating in Jerusalem's downfall. Efforts to understand the term "generation" (*geneä*) as anything other than Jesus' contemporaries (e.g., Jewish people in general, humanity, or a generation living in the end-times) is artificial and appears to be based upon suppositions brought to the text (cf. the term in 1:17; 11:16; 12:29, 41, 45; 23:36). Jesus therefore promises that within a generation, Jerusalem's destruction will constitute compelling proof of God's presence in his sovereign reign.

24:35. Although **heaven and earth will pass away**, Jesus' words remain constant, and therefore have permanent value. Jesus stakes his truthfulness and reliability on the fulfillment of his prediciton. What Jesus says about his words echo the words of Yahweh concerning the reliability of his own word (cf. Isa 40:8; 51:6; and Matt 5:18). Jesus will now answer the second part of the disciples' question by turning his attention to *when* the Son of Man will exercise his kingly authority in judgment.

5. The Coming Judgment of the Son of Man (24:36–25:46)

The section comprising 24:36–25:46 contains six parables (24:37-41, 42-44, 45-51; 25:1-13, 14-30, 31-46[43]), with several interlocking themes: (a) the sudden arrival of something or someone that creates a crisis (4:37, 39, 43, 44, 46, 25:6, 19, 31); (b) some mention a time-lag before the return of the key figure (24:48; 25:5, 19); (c) the exhortation to "watch" (24:43, 45; 25:13) and be ready (24:44; 25:10) in light of the unknown time of the return (24:37, 42-44, 50; 25:10); (d) there are clear divisions between good and bad behavior (24:40-41, 45-51; 25:1-13, 14-20, 31-46); and finally, (e) the

[43]The last scene may not technically be a parable; see below.

element of judgment prevails throughout the section (24:39, 46, 51; 25:10-11; 31f.).[44]

Although the entirety of this section has usually been read as warnings and encouragement to preparation in light of the second coming of Jesus' it appears that such an emphasis may only be a secondary focus, foreshadowed by a more imminent crisis facing first century disciples. As Caird observes, "it was a function of prophetic eschatology to present historical crises in light of God's final judgment of history . . ."[45] The parables encourage disciples to live their lives in the interim, between prediction and fulfillment, in a heightened state of alertness in view of the return of Yahweh to Zion. Do not live as if things will continue as they always have (24:38-39), or assume that a delay is a license for irresponsibility (24:45-51; 25:19). Such principles are timeless and speak to the particular crisis facing first century disciples, as well as subsequent generations that live in the interim between the first coming and the final denouement of history.

The Coming Son of Man (24:36-51)

36"No one knows about that day or hour, not even the angels in heaven, nor the Son,[a] but only the Father. 37As it was in the days of Noah, so it will be at the coming of the Son of Man. 38For in the days before the flood, people were eating and drinking, marrying and giving in marriage, up to the day Noah entered the ark; 39and they knew nothing about what would happen until the flood came and took them all away. That is how it will be at the coming of the Son of Man. 40Two men will be in the field; one will be taken and the other left. 41Two women will be grinding with a hand mill; one will be taken and the other left.

42"Therefore keep watch, because you do not know on what day your Lord will come. 43But understand this: If the owner of the house had known at what time of night the thief was coming, he would have kept watch and would not have let his house be broken into. 44So you also must be ready, because the Son of Man will come at an hour when you do not expect him.

44Observations were suggested by Garland, *Reading Matthew*, p. 239.
45Caird, *New Testament Theology*, p. 256.

[45]"Who then is the faithful and wise servant, whom the master has put in charge of the servants in his household to give them their food at the proper time? [46]It will be good for that servant whose master finds him doing so when he returns. [47]I tell you the truth, he will put him in charge of all his possessions. [48]But suppose that servant is wicked and says to himself, 'My master is staying away a long time,' [49]and he then begins to beat his fellow servants and to eat and drink with drunkards. [50]The master of that servant will come on a day when he does not expect him and at an hour he is not aware of. [51]He will cut him to pieces and assign him a place with the hypocrites, where there will be weeping and gnashing of teeth.

[a]*36* **Some manuscripts do not have** ***nor the Son.***

24:36. The language of verse 36 functions to mark a new theme in the discourse. Although Jerusalem's downfall remains in the background, the focus shifts from imminence to living in the interim. Even though Jesus has spoken with certainty that God's judgment is coming upon this generation (vv. 33-34), verse 36 makes it clear that any attempt to calculate the precise timing of God's decisive action is inappropriate. The reason being that such times are knowable only by God, who accomplishes them according to his own sovereign will and purpose. Jesus does not want his followers to become consumed with time-charts or idle speculations concerning the timing of events. Instead they must live their lives in a constant state of vigilance, realizing that the day of the Lord may come at any time. Of course, Jesus' exhortations lend themselves to two levels of meaning: "on one level the destruction of Jerusalem is the End; on another level it points to the end."[46]

It should be noted that the phrase **nor the Son** is missing in the majority of textual witnesses. Its absence is usually accounted for by the "doctrinal difficulty" it presents, most notably a Christology that seems to undermine Jesus' omniscience.[47] However, one must be careful not to read into Matthew's Christology a full-blown

[46]Ibid., p. 256.

[47]See Metzger, *Textual Commentary*, p. 62.

Chalcedonian Christology. Jesus' very real humanity, along with an understanding of the *kenosis* doctrine (i.e., "an emptying of divine prerogative," cf. Phil 2:6-8) completely accounts for the ignorance of Jesus concerning some matters.[48]

Following the thematic statement of verse 36 Jesus now illustrates the unpredictable timing and unexpected nature of the "coming Son of Man" (vv. 37-51). Keep in mind that the phrase "coming of the Son of Man" should be read with Daniel 7 in mind. As Caird observes, "the coming of the Son of Man on the clouds of heaven was never conceived as a primitive form of space travel; it was a symbol for a mighty reversal of fortunes within history and at the national level."[49] The timing of the coming crisis is illustrated by the "days of Noah" (vv. 37-41), the presence of a "thief" (vv. 42-44), and "servants in a household" (vv. 45-51).

24:37-39. First, the **coming of the Son of Man** is likened to the **days of Noah** when his contemporaries were suddenly overwhelmed by a catastrophic flood (see Gen 6:5-24). The flood was an act of divine judgment that caught the people of Noah's day completely unprepared. Life appeared to be going on as usual (**eating, drinking, marrying, and giving in marriage**), when God acted in swift judgment. Only those who took the necessary precautions by heeding the words of the Lord found safety. In the same way that Noah's contemporaries turned a deaf ear to him, so this present generation has rejected Jesus as God's spokesman. And, no doubt, future generations living long removed from the first century, will also be engaging in the normalcy of life when the end comes swiftly.

24:40-41. The "coming Son of Man" will produce a radical division between "one taken" and the "other left." While the toils of everyday life continue (the man working **in the field**, and the women **grinding with a hand mill**), there will come a sudden separation. These verses may have originally been understood as referring to the trauma of arrest and incarceration, thus causing families to be divided. They refer generally to one being taken for "judgment," while another escapes. As Wright observes, "There is no

---

[48]As noted by Hagner, *Matthew*, 2:716.

[49]Caird, *New Testament Theology*, p. 365.

hint, here, of a 'rapture,' a sudden 'supernatural' event which would remove individuals from *terra firma*. Such an idea would look as odd [to a first century reader] . . . as a Cadillac in a camel train."[50]

24:42. In summary fashion, Jesus exhorts his followers to **keep watch** (γρηγορεῖν, *grēgorein*) because the exact timing of these events are unknown. As Morris notes, "If people knew just exactly when the coming would take place, they could delay preparations until just before the time."[51] It is critical that the disciples be ever vigilant so that they might faithfully bear witness to the vindication of the Son.

24:43-44. To further illustrate the unpredictability of the "coming Son of Man," Jesus draws an analogy from a home owner who knows that a thief is going to break into his house. It would certainly not be advantageous for a thief to provide his intended victims with his itinerary detailing the times of his expected arrival. If such information were available, the home owner would have been adequately prepared for his arrival by closely guarding his possessions. But, alas, the thief comes when one least expects it, and therefore a state of constant preparedness is the only solution. In comparing himself to a thief, Jesus is not endorsing such activity, but simply reminding his hearers that, like a thief, the Son of Man comes when least expected. One must therefore be vigilant and ever ready to avoid the risk of being caught up in the consuming judgment of God.

24:45-47. The next parable (vv. 45-51; cf. Luke 12:35-38) stresses the importance of continual faithfulness in spite of the seeming delay of the "coming Son of Man." The **faithful and wise servant** is the one who takes seriously the responsible position given him in the master's absence. In a household of many slaves one is put in charge of the distribution of food at the proper time. In the master's absence one could very easily neglect the appointed duties and serve only personal interests and needs. However, the faithful and wise servant does not concern himself about when the master will return, but in fulfilling the task to which he has been assigned.

---

[50]Wright, *Jesus*, p. 366.

[51]Morris, *Matthew*, p. 615.

This servant, found faithfully discharging his duties, will be delegated even greater responsibility, namely, the trusted position of overseeing all the master's possessions. Faithful service thus opened the door for even greater opportunities to serve.

24:48-51. In contrast to the faithful servant, another servant interprets the absence of the Master as an opportunity to take advantage of others for personal gain. Instead of serving others and obeying his master's instructions, the wicked servant used the opportunity to abuse others and to engage in shameful behavior (**eat and drink with drunkards**). Not knowing the time of the master's return should have motivated faithful service and ethical responsibility, not a lax attitude resulting in riotous living. It appears, as noted by Blomberg, that "the problem in the parable . . . is not that the master was gone too long but that he came back too soon and caught the servant unprepared."[52] Such irresponsible behavior is severely punished by being "cut off" or banished from the community,[53] and ultimately assigned to the fate of the **hypocrites** (on **weeping and gnashing of teeth**, see 8:12; 13:42, 50; 23:13).

---

[52]C. Blomberg, *Interpreting the Parables* (Downers Grove, IL: InterVarsity, 1990), p. 192.

[53]D.J. Harrington, *The Gospel of Matthew*, Sacra Pagina Series, vol.1 (Collegeville, MN: The Liturgical Press, 1991), p. 344; the literal meaning to "cut him in pieces," makes little sense since a literal dismemberment would have left nothing to put with the "hypocrites."

MATTHEW 25

The Ten Virgins (25:1-13)

[1]"At that time the kingdom of heaven will be like ten virgins who took their lamps and went out to meet the bridegroom. [2]Five of them were foolish and five were wise. [3]The foolish ones took their lamps but did not take any oil with them. [4]The wise, however, took oil in jars along with their lamps. [5]The bridegroom was a long time in coming, and they all became drowsy and fell asleep.

[6]"At midnight the cry rang out: 'Here's the bridegroom! Come out to meet him!'

[7]"Then all the virgins woke up and trimmed their lamps. [8]The foolish ones said to the wise, 'Give us some of your oil; our lamps are going out.'

[9]"'No,' they replied, 'there may not be enough for both us and you. Instead, go to those who sell oil and buy some for yourselves.'

[10]"But while they were on their way to buy the oil, the bridegroom arrived. The virgins who were ready went in with him to the wedding banquet. And the door was shut.

[11]"Later the others also came. 'Sir! Sir!' they said. 'Open the door for us!'

[12]"But he replied, 'I tell you the truth, I don't know you.'

[13]"Therefore keep watch, because you do not know the day or the hour.

25:1-4. Jesus continues the theme of the importance of preparedness, this time, however, the problem is not the surprisingly sudden return of the Master, but rather his delay.[1] The imagery

[1]Blomberg, *Interpreting the Parables*, p. 194.

changes from master/servants to bridegroom/virgins. The parable is introduced by likening the kingdom of God not to the virgins, but to what happens during the wedding ceremony.[2] The "virgins" are unmarried young women who attend to the bride and form a procession escorting the bride and groom from the home of the bride's father to the groom's own house.[3] The marriage proceedings would last well into the night, and therefore the bridemaidens needed to be prepared to lead the procession by means of torches that had been soaked with olive oil. While five of the virgins were wise in that they brought sufficient oil in case the bridegroom's arrival was delayed, five others are called "foolish" because they were shortsighted in not anticipating the need for extra oil to replenish their torches.

25:5-7. With the prolonged delay in the arrival of the bridegroom all the virgins fall asleep. They are stirred from their sleep in the middle of the night by the announcement that the groom is coming. With the passing of time their burning torches would have grown dim. All the virgins make haste to rekindle the flame, which necessitates trimming of the burnt parts and reapplying oil so that the flame will burn steadily and with maximum brightness. It is at this point that the difference between the wise and foolish virgins becomes obvious.

25:8-12. The **foolish ones** now realize that their torches are growing dim and will soon be out (σβέννονται, *sbennontai*, the present tense indicates that their torches are getting very dim). They beseech the others to share their oil with them, but there is simply not enough oil to go around. The only recourse is to rush out and purchase more, which would not be easy in the middle of the night. The refusal of the wise virgins to share their resources is not intended as an endorsement of selfishness, but simply an indictment of the foolish women for their lack of preparation.[4]

---

[2]Jeremias, *Parables*, p. 174.

[3]D.J. Harrington, "Polemical Parables in Matthew 24-25," *USQR* 44 (1991), 295, suggests that "The groom had apparently gone there to sign the marriage contract with the bride's father and then to bring the bride to his own house." As Jeremias, *Parables*, p. 173, points out, "the usual reason for delay is that agreement cannot be reached about the presents due to the relatives of the bride."

While the women are away the groom arrives and the procession leaves with the wedding guests to the feast prepared at the groom's house. The symbolism of the "shut door" indicates that only those prepared participate in the festivities, while others are excluded. Even when the **others**, who had evidently secured oil, arrived for the celebration they are refused entry. In fact, the sting of their rejection is underscored with the words, **I don't know you** (cf. 7:23). Of course the words are not intended to imply that the bridegroom was totally unfamiliar with these women (cf. Luke 13:25), but rather they function as "a decisive formula of rejection."[5] It should also be remembered that parables illustrate a spiritual truth and are not intended to be a realistic account of an actual event.

25:13. The lesson to be learned is the necessity of constant vigilance in view of the fact that the time of the Lord's coming cannot be known with any degree of certainty. The only recourse for the coming crisis is an alertness that takes seriously the "coming of God" in judgment. As the next two parables illustrate, spiritual alertness is best expressed "in service for Christ in the world."[6]

Parable of the Talents (25:14-30)

[14]"Again, it will be like a man going on a journey, who called his servants and entrusted his property to them. [15]To one he gave five talents[a] of money, to another two talents, and to another one talent, each according to his ability. Then he went on his journey. [16]The man who had received the five talents went at once and put his money to work and gained five more. [17]So also, the one with the two talents gained two more. [18]But the man who had received the one talent went off, dug a hole in the ground and hid his master's money.

[19]"After a long time the master of those servants returned and settled accounts with them. [20]The man who had received the five talents brought the other five. 'Master,' he said, 'you entrusted me with five talents. See, I have gained five more.'

---

[4]Blomberg, *Interpreting the Parables*, p. 196.

[5]France, *Matthew*, p. 353.

[6]See G.R. Beasley-Murray, *The Coming of God* (Greenwood, SC: Attic Press, 1983), p. 61.

[21]"His master replied, 'Well done, good and faithful servant! You have been faithful with a few things; I will put you in charge of many things. Come and share your master's happiness!'

[22]"The man with the two talents also came. 'Master,' he said, 'you entrusted me with two talents; see, I have gained two more.'

[23]"His master replied, 'Well done, good and faithful servant! You have been faithful with a few things; I will put you in charge of many things. Come and share your master's happiness!'

[24]"Then the man who had received the one talent came. 'Master,' he said, 'I knew that you are a hard man, harvesting where you have not sown and gathering where you have not scattered seed. [25]So I was afraid and went out and hid your talent in the ground. See, here is what belongs to you.'

[26]"His master replied, 'You wicked, lazy servant! So you knew that I harvest where I have not sown and gather where I have not scattered seed? [27]Well then, you should have put my money on deposit with the bankers, so that when I returned I would have received it back with interest.

[28]"'Take the talent from him and give it to the one who has the ten talents. [29]For everyone who has will be given more, and he will have an abundance. Whoever does not have, even what he has will be taken from him. [30]And throw that worthless servant outside, into the darkness, where there will be weeping and gnashing of teeth.'

[a]*15* A talent was worth more than a thousand dollars.

Like the preceding parable (note *gar*, v. 14), this parable is intended to reinforce the necessity of watchfulness in view of the coming judgment (cf. Luke 19:12-27). As with the other crisis-parables, this parable was probably originally understood in terms of Israel's national crisis and not in terms of the end of the world (cf. Luke 19:12, 27). Israel's king is coming, and the kingdom of the Most High has appeared, but it will mean judgment, not a blessing for Israel. In the interim, between promise and fulfillment, faithful servants are expected not to be idle, but to use their allotted "talents" in a productive manner.

25:14-15. In this parable an obviously wealthy man departs on a journey and puts his servants in charge of his possessions (cf.

24:45), defined as a sum of money called "talents" (vv. 15-17; cf. Luke 19:13, "mina," about 600 times less than a "talent"). Even though a "talent" originally was a measure of weight, by the NT era "all the weight units . . . are monetary in nature."[7] Since we cannot be certain what weight was assigned a "talent," or what currency (i.e., gold, silver, copper) the term refers to, it is difficult to be precise concerning the amounts assigned to each servant. Nevertheless, it can be affirmed that the sums entrusted to them were quite substantial, and were proportioned out according to their individual abilities. Hence, one servant received **five talents**, another **two talents**, and a third servant **one talent**. After distributing his resources the man departs on his journey. The focus of the story is upon how each servant discharges his responsibilities during their master's absence.

25:16-18. Although there is no explicit indication that the master told his servants what to do with the money put in their charge, it becomes obvious that he does expect them to use their own initiative to wisely put to use the money assigned them. Two of the servants do just that, and are able to double their original capital. The third servant, who was assigned one talent, opted for the safe course, one with no risk, and buried the money for safekeeping, thereby assuring that when the time came, the money could be recovered. While this may appear to be a prudent move,[8] assuring that at least the money entrusted to him could be returned to his master, this servant will soon learn that his master values productivity over mere preservation.

25:19-23. Eventually, **after a long time**, the master returns for the purpose of "settling accounts" (συναίρω, *synairō*). The language may indicate that the master had certain expectations, and the servants knew their accountability. The two servants that had received the five and two talents respectively, both had doubled their original sum. The master is delighted with their productivity and assures them that their faithfulness **with a few things** will be rewarded by being put **in charge of many things** (cf. 24:47). Hence, the proper use of resources and opportunities results in even greater opportunities to

[7]See M.A. Powell, "Weights and Measures," *ABD* 6:907.

[8]As Jeremias, *Parables*, p. 61, n. 51, notes, "Burying, according to rabbinical law, was regarded as the best security against theft."

use one's abilities. In spite of the different allotments assigned the two servants, the master's commendation is the same. Both servants are invited to share in their master's joy, perhaps by enjoying some of the blessings of his prosperity. The key factor is the necessity of faithful service according to the abilities and opportunities given.

25:24-25. When the master comes to the third servant, who was assigned one talent, rather than joyfully displaying the results of his labor, this servant began to make excuses for his lack of productivity. Apparently, the servant was driven by fear to bury his talent because he thought his master to be a **hard man** (σκληρός, *sklēros,* "severe and demanding"). He further describes his master as one who profits from the labor of others. In other words, he perceives his master as a shrewd businessman who has a knack for turning a profit. Therefore, he imagined that the loss of his master's money in a risky business venture would be severely punished. So by burying the money he could at least assure the return of the amount he had been entrusted.

25:26-27. The master is not impressed with the servant's excuse. He chides the servant as **wicked** and **lazy** (cf. "good and faithful servant," vv. 21, 23). Such an indictment seriously undermines any claim of purity of motives. This servant simply did not have the inclination to use his resources for productive service on behalf of his master. If he totally believed his master was a shrewd businessman, who fully expected to profit from the sum entrusted to his servants, why did he not at least put the money in the bank so that it might accrue interest? Instead, this servant, driven by fear, put it in the ground, with the result that it profited no one. He failed to realize that once he had received the talent he obligated himself to use it wisely.

25:28-30. The failure to use his talent responsibly results in its being taken from him and given to the one having ten talents. This illustrates the principle of verse 29 (cf. 17:12), summarized by Schweizer: "where God's gift has already borne fruit, God gives in superabundance; where it has remained fruitless, it is lost completely. This means that God's gift can never be passively possessed; it is like a muscle: it must be worked and stretched or it withers."[9]

---

[9]Schweizer, *Good News According to Matthew*, p. 472.

Ultimately, the fate of such a **worthless servant** is complete banishment, followed by severe punishment (cf. 8:12; 13:42, 50). This parable, like the previous, calls for a committed resolve to be diligent in service while the master is away.

Judgment of the Son of Man (25:31-46)

31"When the Son of Man comes in his glory, and all the angels with him, he will sit on his throne in heavenly glory. 32All the nations will be gathered before him, and he will separate the people one from another as a shepherd separates the sheep from the goats. 33He will put the sheep on his right and the goats on his left.

34"Then the King will say to those on his right, 'Come, you who are blessed by my Father; take your inheritance, the kingdom prepared for you since the creation of the world. 35For I was hungry and you gave me something to eat, I was thirsty and you gave me something to drink, I was a stranger and you invited me in, 36I needed clothes and you clothed me, I was sick and you looked after me, I was in prison and you came to visit me.'

37"Then the righteous will answer him, 'Lord, when did we see you hungry and feed you, or thirsty and give you something to drink? 38When did we see you a stranger and invite you in, or needing clothes and clothe you? 39When did we see you sick or in prison and go to visit you?'

40"The King will reply, 'I tell you the truth, whatever you did for one of the least of these brothers of mine, you did for me.'

41"Then he will say to those on his left, 'Depart from me, you who are cursed, into the eternal fire prepared for the devil and his angels. 42For I was hungry and you gave me nothing to eat, I was thirsty and you gave me nothing to drink, 43I was a stranger and you did not invite me in, I needed clothes and you did not clothe me, I was sick and in prison and you did not look after me.'

44"They also will answer, 'Lord, when did we see you hungry or thirsty or a stranger or needing clothes or sick or in prison, and did not help you?'

45"He will reply, 'I tell you the truth, whatever you did not do for one of the least of these, you did not do for me.'

46 "Then they will go away to eternal punishment, but the righteous to eternal life."

As noted earlier, it can be disputed whether the climactic scene depicting the judgment of the nations is a parable. It may be, as suggested by several,[10] that it should be regarded as an apocalyptic vision, having much in common with similar material in the OT and later Jewish literature (cf. Joel 3:2-3; 4 Ezra 7:37; 1 Enoch 38, 62). However, while the theme of the judgment of the nations is a typical apocalyptic motif, the prominent role assigned the Son of Man in Jesus' discourse is exceptional. In this instance, it is the Son of Man, not Yahweh, before whom the nations are held accountable.

Several elements in this concluding scene of judgment have posed notoriously difficult exegetical problems for interpreters. A recent history of the interpretation of Matthew 25:31-46 has documented some thirty-two different positions and slants on the meaning and significance of the various sayings found in this the closing section of Jesus' discourse.[11] Three important questions must be addressed if an interpretation is to be given credibility: (a) Who are "the nations" gathered before the Son of Man?; (b) Who are the "least of these brothers of mine"?; and (c) Who are the needy people described as hungry, thirsty, strangers, needing clothes, sick, and in prison? In the comments to follow these and other exegetical issues will be addressed.

25:31-33. The scene opens with the enthroned Son of Man sitting in heavenly glory to execute judgment over all the nations. The imagery is reminiscent of earlier descriptions of the Son of Man coming with his angels (16:27-28), and sitting on his glorious throne (19:28). The scene depicts the consummation of all that Daniel 7:13-14 predicted concerning the ultimate vindication and glorification of the Son of Man, who represents the "saints of the

---

[10] Notably, Stanton, *Gospel for a New People*, pp. 221f.; Hagner, *Matthew* 2:740; Hill, *Matthew*, p. 330, calls it an "eschatological vision"; see also France, *Matthew*, p. 354-355.

[11] See S.W. Gray, *The Least of My Brothers: Matthew 25:31-46: A History of Interpretation* (SBLDS 14; Atlanta: Scholar's Press, 1989).

Most High." Now the enthroned Son of Man exercises his authority and kingly power (v. 34) over all the nations (cf. 24:9, 14, 30). Now there is to be a dramatic reversal of fortunes, where the nations who persecuted and hated the people of God, will now be held accountable for their treatment of the saints of God. Accordingly, **all the nations** does not refer to Christians, or the Christianized nations, but rather to the entirety of the non-Christian world. This seems consistent with the way that the phrase "all the nations" (πάντα τὰ ἔθνη, *panta ta ethnē*) is used in Matthew (cf. 24:9, 14; 28:18-20; see also 13:13; 10:22). Like a Palestinian shepherd who in the evening **separates the sheep from the goats**[12] (cf. Ezek 34:17-19), even so the people comprising the nations will be divided into two groups. Since sheep are more valued than goats they are extended a place of greater comfort and honor ("right hand," cf 20:23; 23:14). The goats on the other hand are herded to a place less favorable. With this brief metaphorical summary, the specifics of judgment are now articulated in verses 34-46.

25:34. The majestic figure earlier described as Son of Man (v. 31) is now identified as **King** (cf. 2:2; 27:37, 42). Since Daniel's "Son of Man" figure was to receive a kingdom (7:14, 27), the depiction of the Son of Man as King indicates that the ultimate vindication and destiny of the Son of Man has been consummated. The scene assumes that the "good news of the kingdom" has been proclaimed throughout the nations (see 24:13), and now Jesus reigns over the nations as their sovereign Judge (cf. Ps 110:1). The reader now learns that the sheep who were separated to the right were representative of those individuals blessed by God to enjoy the consummation of the blessings of the kingdom. To "inherit the kingdom" is to share in the blessings of God's reign. The expression **since the creation of the world**, indicates that such blessings were no mere afterthought, but were always part of God's infinite will. Therefore, their participation (i.e., people from "all the nations") in the kingdom has always been part of God's eternal purpose.

[12]As Jeremias, *Parables*, p. 206, observes, "in the evening the shepherd separates the sheep from the goats since the goats need to be warm at night, for cold harms them, while the sheep prefer open air at night."

25:35-36. The basis for their inclusion in the kingdom is their positive response to six different situations when Jesus was in need: When **hungry** and **thirsty** you were compassionate and gave me food and water. Though friendless and without shelter you extended hospitality. When **I needed clothes** you were responsive to my plight and provided clothes. Even in my sickness you did not turn away in revulsion, but demonstrated your concern by visiting me. When I faced the horror of prison you lifted my spirit by your visit. In short, you provided the basics of human need: food, water, shelter, and companionship.[13]

25:37-39. Then those on the right, now called the **righteous** express surprise at the King's recounting of their treatment of him. They simply cannot recall any circumstances in which they saw the Lord in such dire need and ministered to him. Hence, they inquire *when* such events may have taken place.

25:40. The King responds by pointing to their compassionate regard for **the least of these brothers of mine** as equivalent to deeds of mercy done to him. Most commonly the reference to "brother" has been understood in one of two ways: *generally*, to refer to anyone in need, or more *specifically*, to the plight of Jesus' disciples. Probably the latter is the way that Jesus intended his words to be understood. As Stanton observes, "Matthew's use of both οἱ ἐλάχιστοι [*hoi elachistoi*, "the least," cf. 10:42; 18:6, 10, 14] and οἱ ἀδελφοὶ [*hoi adelphoi*, "brothers," cf. 12:48-50; 28:10] as terms of Christian disciples is firmly established."[14] Furthermore, in Matthew's Gospel there is an emphasis on the solidarity between Jesus and his disciples. Jesus as Immanuel mediates the presence of God with his people (1:23), and he assures them that he will be with them to the end of the age (28:20). Jesus' identification with his disciples is forcefully articulated in 10:40-42: "He who receives you receives me . . ." It seems clear, therefore, that any act of kindness shown to even the most unassuming of Jesus' disciples is service that is rendered to Jesus. It is most remarkable that at least one standard to which the nations will be held accountable involve the manner in which they respond to the plight of Jesus' followers (cf.

[13]Blomberg, *Matthew*, p. 377.
[14]Stanton, *Gospel for a New People*, p. 216.

Acts 22:7). Jesus has in effect applied basic Jewish hopes and expectations of Yahweh's vindication of Israel before the nations, to his own disciples, who form the core of the new Israel (cf. 19:28).

Although this text does not lend itself to a general "humanitarian ethic," since the focus is upon how the nations treat Jesus' disciples, there are plenty of other texts that clearly enjoin an active concern for the needy and the marginalized of society.[15] How we behave toward the world's oppressed and those who are suffering must reflect the benevolent care and teachings of Jesus.

25:41-46. The King then addresses **those on his left** (earlier called "goats," v. 33), and unlike the righteous who are invited to "come" (v. 34), those "on the left" are banished from his presence (cf. 7:23). They are doomed to suffer the "curse" of eternal destruction, formerly reserved only for the **devil and his angels** (v. 41; cf. 18:8; 3:12). The reason they suffer such a fate is their failure to be sensitive to the sufferings and hardship endured by the Lord. Like the perplexity of the "righteous," these people protest the notion that they had ever refused Jesus benevolent care. The King's answer parallels verse 40, except now the neglect of compassion for the **least of these** becomes a basis for their condemnation. Their neglect of Jesus' followers is therefore indicative of their rejection of him. Jesus thus offers comfort to his people, the new Israel, that one day all the nations will be held accountable for their treatment of his lowly disciples. While Israel expected the nations to be judged according to how they have treated Israel (see, e.g., Ps.Sol. 17:23f.; 2 Bar. 72: IQSb 5:23-29; also Ps 2, 18, 104, 110), Jesus will hold the nations accountable for the way they treat Jesus' humble followers who are sent forth to represent him. Therefore this final vision offers "consolation to a persecuted community sent out on a mission fraught with danger in a hostile world."[16] There will ultimately be a great separation, and those who reject the cause of Jesus will be forever banished, while the **righteous** will enjoy a renewed quality of life with Jesus in the eternal kingdom.

---

[15]See the chapter on "Social Justice" in Powell's, *God With Us*, pp. 113-148.

[16]Garland, *Reading Matthew*, p. 244.

MATTHEW 26

VII. THE PASSION AND RESURRECTION OF JESUS 26:1–28:20

Following the discourse (chs. 24-25) the pace of the narrative quickens and leads progressively through the final two days of Jesus' life on earth (26:2). The passion narrative can be divided into three main sections: 26:1-56; 26:57–27:50; and 27:51–28:20. In the first section Jesus actively predicts and accepts the course of events that will culminate in his death. The scenes leading up to Jesus' arrest are given cohesion and progression by Jesus' own words that detail coming events and even set in motion incidents that will lead to his own death. The scenes are punctuated by prophetic announcements concerning the direction of subsequent episodes (see 26:3, 12, 18, 21, 24, 31, 32, 34, 45, 50, 54, 56). By the concentrated emphasis on Jesus' foreknowledge and his resolve to do the Father's will (cf. 26:24, 39, 42, 54, 56), Matthew cast Jesus' passion not as an unfortunate twist of fate, but as a conscious and voluntary self-sacrifice, deliberately undertaken to fulfill the Father's will.

Beginning with 26:57, Matthew's portrayal of Jesus shifts from active predictor and instigator of events to one wherein Jesus assumes a passive role, enduring abuse and humiliation in silence (cf. 26:63; 27:14). In fact, Jesus' silence is broken only by a necessary confession (26:64; 27:11), and prayer (27:46). Although his silence is misunderstood (26:63), and a cause for amazement (27:14), Jesus clearly fulfills the role of God's Suffering Servant, who though "he was oppressed and afflicted, yet he did not open his mouth" (Isa 53:7).

Following the death of Jesus (27:50) God once again assumes an active role in the story (cf. Matt 1-2; 3:16-17; 17:1-5) by dramatically affirming his approval of his obedient Son. Miraculous events, in cosmic proportions, signal God's intervention in nature to stamp his approval on the sacrificial mission of Jesus. In response to the miraculous signs, the earlier mocking taunts of the Jewish leaders (27:38-44) are replaced with Gentile observers confessing him to be "the Son of God" (27:54). Although the Jewish leaders put forth every effort to counter any claim that Jesus has been raised from the dead, in the end God's sovereign will and power prevails. The tomb that had been securely sealed is dramatically opened by the "angel of the Lord," and the human forces guarding its entrance are overwhelmed with fear and become as if dead (28:2-4). The women, however, are commissioned as reliable interpreters of the events, since they have seen the risen Jesus (28:5-10). The Jewish leaders attempt to counter the proclamation of Jesus' resurrection by bribing the guards and concocting a lie to account for the empty tomb (28:11-15). Jesus, however, shows himself alive to his disciples (28:16-17), and commissions them to disciple all the nations by a reliable proclamation of the Good News (28:18-19). In the final climactic scene, God vindicates his Son by endowing him with "all authority," thereby effectively nullifying any claim to authority by the Jewish authorities. Thus, the reader has been led from anxiety during the trial scenes to a point of resolution wherein the fortunes of Matthew's protagonist are reversed and his true character becomes evident. As Matthew tells his story, the identity and mission of Jesus are most clearly revealed and endorsed by God in his passion and resurrection.

It is well known that there are some remarkable correspondences between Matthew's passion narrative (chs. 26-28), and the opening portion of his story (1:1–4:17).[1] The concluding scenes of Matthew's story certainly bring to a climax the opposition to Jesus which builds throughout the story, beginning with Herod's attempt on Jesus' life (2:16-18). It should be noted that early in the story the "chief priests and teachers of the law" (2:4-6) are portrayed as aligned with a political ruler in opposition to Jesus. The reader also observes that the closing section (chs. 26-28) picks up again the emphasis on prophecy and fulfillment in a manner parallel to the

[1]Meier, *Vision of Matthew*, p. 53, calls the infancy narrative "a proleptic passion narrative."

opening chapters (chs. 1-2: cf. 26:56, 59; 27:9-10). The latter chapters also abound with allusions to OT texts (e.g., Ps 22, 69; Zech 11:13; Isa 50-53), and stories (e.g., Gen 22), reminiscent of the emphasis in the infancy narratives. The reappearance of the "angel of the Lord" (28:2), and divine vindication by means of portents (27:51-53; 28:1-4) and dreams (27:19) are features characteristic of both the beginning and end of Matthew's story.

In addition, numerous themes, ideas, and phraseology present in early portions of the story are repeated in the closing chapters: forgiveness of sins (1:21; 9:6; 20:28; 26:28); Christological titles – King of the Jews (2:2; 27:11, 29, 37, 42); Christ (1:1, 16, 18; 2:4; 27:17, 22); shepherd (2:6; 9:36; 25:32; 26:31); Son of God (2:15; 3:17; 4:3, 6; 8:29; 11:27; 14:33; 16:16; 17:5; 21:37-38; 22:2; 24:36; 26:62; 27:40, 43, 54; 28:19). The mocking scenes are thematically related to the temptation narrative (4:1-11), as the mockers echo the role of the Tempter himself (cf. 27:40 and 4:3, 6) in attempting to deflect Jesus from the path of true Sonship.

Finally, the concluding verses (i.e., 28:16-20) recall the themes of (1) a mountain as a place of revelation (4:8-10; 5:1-8:1; 15:29-31; 17:1-5; 26:30; 28:16), (2) the Gospel's universalistic emphasis (1:5-6; 2:1-2; 4:15-16; 8:5-15; 10:5; 15:21-28, 29-39; 27:54; 28:19); and (3) the abiding presence of Jesus (1:25; 18:20; 28:20). With this emphasis in the closing scene it appears that Matthew's story has therefore come full circle with Jesus back in Galilee (cf. 28:16 and 4:12-17). It should be observed that when one reaches the end of Matthew's story, intertextual allusions force the reader to recall the opening scenes. Certainly the concluding command to teach "everything I have commanded you" (28:20) necessitates an ongoing interaction with the total story.[2]

A. THE PLOT TO ARREST AND EXECUTE JESUS (26:1-5)

[1]When Jesus had finished saying all these things, he said to his disciples, [2]"As you know, the Passover is two days away – and the Son of Man will be handed over to be crucified."

---

[2]Dale C. Allison, "Anticipating the Passion: The Literary Reach of Matthew 26:47–27:56," *CBQ* 56 (1994), 703.

[3]Then the chief priests and the elders of the people assembled in the palace of the high priest, whose name was Caiaphas, [4]and they plotted to arrest Jesus in some sly way and kill him. [5]"But not during the Feast," they said, "or there may be a riot among the people."

26:1-2. The narrative block of 26:1–28:20 opens with the familiar transitional formula (i.e., **when Jesus had finished saying all these things**; 7:28, 11:1; 13:53; 19:1) which functions to close the previous section[3] and announce to the reader that a new phase in the story begins. While the passion prediction of verse 2 echoes the previous predictions (cf. 16:21; 17:22-23; 20:17-19), it also marks a shift from the earlier emphasis on geographical location (i.e., Jerusalem, 16:21; 20:18), to an emphasis on the nearness of times (**two days away**), and the circumstances during which events will unfold (i.e., during **the Passover**). It is no accident that Jesus will die during a festival celebrating God's saving power in liberating Israel from slavery in Egypt (see Exod 12). Now the sacrificial death of Jesus brings ultimate salvation with universal significance (cf. 20:28).

26:3-5. Not only does Jesus' prophetic foreknowledge accent his resolution to do the Father's will, his predictive word becomes the primary causal factor moving events to their climax. After Jesus announces the fate of the Son of Man (v. 2), then (τότε, *tote*) the Jewish leaders assemble to plot his demise (συνήχθησαν, *synēchthēsan*, cf. 2:4). As Matera observes, "the adverb 'then' suggests that the plot only takes place because Jesus allows it."[4] Although the Jewish leaders have been portrayed as plotting against Jesus earlier in the story (cf. 12:14; 21:45-46), their portrayal in verses 3-5 indicates that they now have concrete plans to carry out their efforts after **the Feast**. They must, however, resort to deception or trickery (δόλῳ, *dolō*) in order to accomplish their nefarious scheme. Their

[3]The addition of πάντας possibly is intended to signal the completion of all the discourses which Jesus has delivered, see D. Senior, *The Passion Narrative According to Matthew: A Redactional Study* (BETL 39; Louvain, Belgium: Louvain University, 1975), p. 12.

[4]F.J. Matera, *Passion Narratives and Gospel Theologies* (New York: Paulist Press, 1986), p. 88.

efforts are calculated so as to avoid an uproar among the people, who regard Jesus as a prophet (cf. 14:5; 21:11, 46). In the end, Jesus' prediction that he will die during the feast (v. 2) is proven true (27:15f.). "The religious leaders can conspire but God will determine the order of events."[5]

B. ANOINTING IN BETHANY (26:6-13)

[6]While Jesus was in Bethany in the home of a man known as Simon the Leper, [7]a woman came to him with an alabaster jar of very expensive perfume, which she poured on his head as he was reclining at the table.

[8]When the disciples saw this, they were indignant. "Why this waste?" they asked. [9]"This perfume could have been sold at a high price and the money given to the poor."

[10]Aware of this, Jesus said to them, "Why are you bothering this woman? She has done a beautiful thing to me. [11]The poor you will always have with you, but you will not always have me. [12]When she poured this perfume on my body, she did it to prepare me for burial. [13]I tell you the truth, wherever this gospel is preached throughout the world, what she has done will also be told, in memory of her."

26:6. It was typical of Jesus, during the final week, not to spend his nights in Jerusalem (cf. 21:17), but rather with friends in the village of **Bethany**, about two miles east of the city. On this occasion Jesus is **in the home of a man known as Simon the leper**. Nothing more is known about this Simon, and his description as a leper raises unanswered questions: Was Simon actually present during the meal? Is he still a leper? Has he recovered from his leprosy? Did Jesus heal his leprosy? While these questions cannot be answered with certainty, it is significant that Jesus would rather associate with social outcasts than with the religious elite in Jerusalem (cf. 9:10-13).

26:7. In Matthew's passion narrative women play a decisive role in modeling the elements of true discipleship (cf. 27:55-56; 28:1-

---

[5]Ibid.

10).[6] While in the home of Simon, an unnamed woman (cf. John 12:3) takes the initiative to display openly her devotion to Jesus, anointing his head with **very expensive perfume**. While anointing with oil was customarily practiced as an act of hospitality (cf. Ps 23:5; 132:2; 141:5; Luke 7:46), her extravagant sacrifice of very costly ointment goes far beyond the normal practice of hospitality.

26:8-9. Nevertheless, conflicting assessments of her deed follow (vv. 8-13). The disciples interpret the act as wasteful and lacking in discretion concerning the proper use of resources. They are **indignant** (ἠγανάκτησαν, *ēganaktēsan*, cf. 20:24; 21:15) and insist that such valuable ointment **could have been sold** and the proceeds **given to the poor**. While relief of the poor is certainly a noble aspiration, the disciples exhibit little perception concerning the symbolic significance of the woman's extraordinary deed.

26:10-11. Jesus immediately comes to the defense of the woman, challenging their badgering of her (κόπους παρέχετε, *kopous parechete*) and their narrow perspective. Jesus interprets her deed as **a beautiful thing** (lit., "a good work"), hence an acceptable expression of Jewish piety. There will always be opportunities to minister to the poor, but the critical times, associated with Jesus' passion, demand extraordinary action. Jesus is not downplaying responsibility to the poor (see Deut 15:11), but is emphasizing the "urgency of the moment," where "an extravagant manifestation of love is appropriate because Jesus will soon depart."[7]

26:12-13. While the disciples struggle with the reality of Jesus' imminent death, this woman is portrayed as understanding the necessity of the passion and responding accordingly. Whether knowingly or unknowingly her anointing amounts to a "prophetic gesture" underscoring the fate awaiting Jesus.[8] With Jesus' positive appraisal of her deed the reader is led to see that genuine devotion must also embrace the reality of Jesus' death. Consequently, the proclamation of **this gospel throughout the world** will become a memorial of her

---

[6]See Larry Chouinard, "Women in Matthew's Gospel: A Methodological Study," in *Essays on Women in Earliest Christianity*, ed. Carroll D. Osburn (Joplin, MO: College Press, 1993), pp. 425-444.

[7]Matera, *Passion Narratives*, pp. 15, 89.

[8]Possibly Matthew intends the reader to see the anointing as a kingly anointing for his messianic task (cf. 1 Sam 16:13).

insightful act of devotion performed in anticipation of Jesus' death – a memorial far surpassing the Jewish Passover, since this one atoning death is "God's definitive saving deed for all people."[9]

C. JUDAS' BETRAYAL (26:14-16)

[14]Then one of the Twelve – the one called Judas Iscariot – went to the chief priests [15]and asked, "What are you willing to give me if I hand him over to you?" So they counted out for him thirty silver coins. [16]From then on Judas watched for an opportunity to hand him over.

26:14. Although the betrayer has been identified to the reader as early as chapter 10, and Jesus' passion predictions anticipated a betrayal (17:22; 20:18), the actions of Judas begin the process whereby these cryptic references are given meaning. With the religious leaders looking for an opportunity to arrest Jesus (vv. 3-5), they find a willing accomplice in the person of **Judas Iscariot** (see 10:4). The irony is that Judas is **one of the Twelve**, not an outsider or casual bystander, but part of the core group of Jesus' closest followers. In contrast to the extravagant expression of devotion from an anonymous woman (v. 7), Judas' treachery stands out as particularly shocking.

26:15. By going to the **chief priests** Judas aligns himself with those who have repudiated Jesus' identity and mission. It appears from Matthew's account of Judas' request that he was at least partially motivated by financial rewards (**What are you willing to give me . . .** , cf. Mark 14:10-11).[10] His actions stand in stark contrast to the sacrificial deed of the woman in the previous scene (vv. 6-13). The chief priests are no doubt delighted to have one of Jesus' own disciples willing to conspire with them in the execution of their devious plans (cf. Mark 14:11). For his part in the conspiracy they agree to pay him **thirty silver coins** (cf. 27:3-10). Although the

---

[9]Heil, *Death and Resurrection*, p. 27.

[10]Although I agree with Hagner, *Matthew* 2:761, that, "The modest amount and the lack of bargaining on Judas' part suggest that money was not his only or even his primary motive."

exact equivalent amount in modern currency is uncertain, it appears to be the same amount paid for a wounded slave (Exod 21:32), and corresponds to the insulting amount given a prophet that has been rejected by the people (Zech 11:12). Needless to say, it "stands in pathetic contrast to the woman's very expensive ointment (26:7-9)."[11]

26:16. Now the evil forces aligned against Jesus simply await **an opportunity to hand him over** (παραδίδωμι, *paradidōmi*). Although the religious leaders seek an opportune time apart from the Passover feast (v. 5), **Judas** becomes an unwitting agent of the divine intention that Jesus die during a feast commemorating God's great act of salvation on behalf of his people. With the major character groups and themes introduced, the transitional phrase ἀπὸ τότε (*apo tote*) signals to the reader that the climactic events of the story are about to begin.[12]

D. PREPARATION FOR PASSOVER (26:17-19)

[17]On the first day of the Feast of Unleavened Bread, the disciples came to Jesus and asked, "Where do you want us to make preparations for you to eat the Passover?"

[18]He replied, "Go into the city to a certain man and tell him, 'The Teacher says: My appointed time is near. I am going to celebrate the Passover with my disciples at your house.'" [19]So the disciples did as Jesus had directed them and prepared the Passover.

26:17. The **first day of the Feast of Unleavened Bread** refers to the first day of a seven- or eight-day-long Festival associated with Passover observance. After the lambs were slaughtered on 14 Nisan (early on Thursday), and the ritual search for leaven had taken place, Jewish families gathered after sunset (now 15 Nisan)[13] **to eat the Passover** lamb. Between the slaughter of the lambs and the

[11]Heil, *Death and Resurrection*, p. 28.

[12]See D. Senior, "The Passion Narrative in the Gospel of Matthew," in *L'Évangile selon Matthieu: Redaction et Théologie* (BETL 29; Gembloux: Duculot, 1972), pp. 343-357.

[13]See R.H. Stein, "Last Supper," *DJG*, pp. 446-447.

observance of the meal in the evening, **preparations**, about which the disciples inquired, required the securing of a suitable place to gather, the purchase of herbs and wine, and the arrangement of the table for the meal.

26:18-19. Although Jesus' instructions about locating a suitable place for observing the Passover is reminiscent of his earlier instructions for securing a donkey (21:1-3), it is probable that the reference **to a certain man** (cf. Mark 14:12-16) indicates that prior arrangements had been made. The disciples are to inform the man that the **appointed time** has come for the **Teacher** to observe his last Passover with the disciples. Although the significance of the phrase would not have been understood by the story characters, to the reader it communicates "Jesus' conscious fulfillment of a predetermined plan."[14] The disciples are nevertheless obedient to Jesus' authoritative instructions, thus setting the stage for the episode to follow.

E. THE LAST SUPPER (26:20-30)

[20]When evening came, Jesus was reclining at the table with the Twelve. [21]And while they were eating, he said, "I tell you the truth, one of you will betray me."

[22]They were very sad and began to say to him one after the other, "Surely not I, Lord?"

[23]Jesus replied, "The one who has dipped his hand into the bowl with me will betray me. [24]The Son of Man will go just as it is written about him. But woe to that man who betrays the Son of Man! It would be better for him if he had not been born."

[25]Then Judas, the one who would betray him, said, "Surely not I, Rabbi?"

Jesus answered, "Yes, it is you."[a]

[26]While they were eating, Jesus took bread, gave thanks and broke it, and gave it to his disciples, saying, "Take and eat; this is my body."

[27]Then he took the cup, gave thanks and offered it to them, saying, "Drink from it, all of you. [28]This is my blood of the[b]

---

[14]France, *Matthew*, p. 336.

covenant, which is poured out for many for the forgiveness of sins. [29]I tell you, I will not drink of this fruit of the vine from now on until that day when I drink it anew with you in my Father's kingdom."

[30]When they had sung a hymn, they went out to the Mount of Olives.

[a]*25* Or *"You yourself have said it"* [b]*28* Some manuscripts *the new*

Matthew divides the account of the Last Supper into two parts, marked by the twofold reference, "while they were eating" (vv. 20, 26): vv. 20-25, prediction that "while they were eating" one of the twelve would betray him; vv. 26-30, "while they are eating" the Passover, Jesus institutes the Lord's Supper.

26:20-21. After sunset, in Jerusalem (the proper time and place for observing Passover), Jesus gathered with his disciples to observe the Passover (v. 17). Typically, Jewish observers reclined at the meal, around a U-shaped rectangular couch. During the meal Jesus makes a shocking prediction: **one of you will betray me**. Although Jesus is fully aware of the treacherous scheme of Judas, he does nothing to stop him. While Judas' motivations may be self-serving, Jesus is resolved to submit his will to his Father.

26:22. The response of the disciples indicates that they could not imagine anyone of their group committing such a sinister deed. Therefore, instead of looking suspiciously at one another, they become **very sad** (λυπούμενοι σφόδρα, *lypoumenoi sphodra*) and probed their own level of allegiance with a question anticipating a negative response: **Surely not I, Lord?** They simply cannot imagine a scenario where their commitment to Jesus would be so compromised. Their respectful address of Jesus as Lord reinforces their recognition of his authority.

26:23-24. Jesus' reference to his betrayer as **one who has dipped his hand into the bowl** with him is not solely intended as a more precise identification of the betrayer's identity (although compare John's account, "the one to whom I will give . . ."). Rather, the words are intended to intensify the shamelessness of the betrayer's act, by depicting it as a serious breach of intimacy and solidarity usually associated with table-fellowship. Nevertheless, the betrayer's act is in full accord with God's will as expressed in Scripture. As noted by

France, "Here is the paradox of the whole passion story in a nutshell – the events must happen *as it is written*; but this does not excuse the deliberate betrayal."[15] Indeed, the fate of the betrayer is so horrible that it would have been better if he had never been born. Hence, although Judas' actions fulfilled prophetic expectations, Judas is nevertheless accountable for the choices he made.

26:25. Only in Matthew's Gospel does Judas directly question Jesus about his own fidelity. Although the form of his question (**Surely not I, Rabbi**) expresses the same sentiment as that expressed by the other disciples, Judas' inquiry is most likely intended to conceal his sinister motives. Instead of the honorific title "Lord," Judas addresses Jesus with the title "Rabbi," that may show respect for Jesus as a teacher, but does not include an acknowledgment of his authoritative Lordship. Jesus answers the betrayer in a manner (σύ εἶπας, *su eipas*) that places the burden of response upon the questioner (cf. 26:64; 27:11). Therefore, contrary to the negative response Judas may have expected, Jesus, in essence, acknowledges the validity of his question and thereby exposes his duplicity. No doubt Judas left the gathering persuaded that Jesus was on to his deceptive plan.

26:26. While they were eating echoes verse 20 and serves to introduce subsequent events that transpired on into the meal. It is tragic that the observance we know as the Lord's Supper or Communion, intended to celebrate Christian solidarity in the redemptive deed of Christ, has become the source of endless controversy. While space forbids an overview of all the points of controversy, suffice it to say with Blomberg that the "doctrines of transubstantiation (the bread and wine become Christ's actual body and blood) or consubstantiation (Christ is really present 'in, with, and under' the elements) make no sense of Jesus' words in their historical context."[16] Just as the elements associated with Passover were rich in symbolism, so Jesus assigns new meaning to the elements in light of the redemptive deed associated with his death. By partaking of the bread and wine the disciples identify with Christ's unique sacrificial death, and thereby participate in its redemptive significance.

---

[15]Ibid., p. 376.
[16]Blomberg, *Matthew*, p. 390.

However, as Caird rightly points out, the reader should avoid the notion that the Lord's Supper is "mere symbolism" for "many symbols. . . are a means, even the means, of conveying what they represent."[17]

In the traditional Passover celebration the bread was one of three elements to be explained. Therefore, when Jesus **took bread, gave thanks and broke it**[18] his actions would have corresponded to traditional practice. However, his interpretation of the bread ('this is my body") has no parallel in the Passover ritual. Jesus thus connects the breaking and sharing in the bread with his own body about to be sacrificially given up. Perhaps the broken bread is intended to symbolically re-enact the violent nature of his death. Hence, Jesus' actions would prophetically foreshadow his own death. By partaking of the bread the disciple is to be aligned with Jesus' sacrificial mission.

26:27-28. Jesus next takes the cup (presumably the third of four cups drunk during the Passover celebration) and, like the bread, interprets its significance in terms of his sacrificial death. Identification of the wine as the **blood of the covenant** draws upon Exodus 24:8, and recalls the ritual of the pouring out of blood upon the altar to ratify the special relationship and obligations of Israel to Yahweh. But Jeremiah foretold of a "new covenant" wherein the laws of God would be written upon the heart, and sins would be remembered no more (31:31-34). It is apparent that Jesus understood his death as inaugurating the covenant envisioned by Jeremiah. Integral to this new covenant is the offer of **forgiveness of sins** brought about by Jesus' sacrificial death. This explanation of the purpose of Jesus' death has been a dominant theme throughout Matthew's story. His very name (Jesus) was assigned salvific significance by the angel in the birth narrative (1:21). The pivotal factors in Jesus' acts and teachings centered in the spiritual renewal ad restoration of God's people (see 9:6). The language **for many** reminds the reader

---

[17]G.B. Caird, *The Language and Imagery of the Bible* (London: Duckworth, 1980) pp. 101-102.

[18]Bonnie B. Thurston, "'Do This': A Study on the Institution of the Lord's Supper," *RQ* 30 (1988), 207-217, has made a strong case for observing more closely not merely the "elements," but also the symbolic "action" involved in "breaking the bread" and "pouring the wine."

that the Son of Man "did not come to be served, but to serve, and to give his life as a ransom *for many*" (20:28, emphasis added). Furthermore, the language corresponds to Isaiah's depiction of the Suffering Servant who "bore the sin of many, and made intercession for the transgressors" (53:12).

26:29. Jesus does anticipate a reversal to his suffering and death as indicated by his promise of a heightened renewal of table-fellowship after his death. Just as the Passover observance anticipated a renewal of God's favor upon Israel (cf. Isa 25:6-9; 53:13), so the Lords' Supper looks forward to a joyous celebration in the consummated kingdom (cf. 8:10-12; 22:1-14). Jesus thus speaks with confidence of his ultimate victorious triumph.

26:30. The meal concludes with the traditional singing of selections from Psalms 113-118 (the *Hallel*, not identified specifically in the expression ὑμνήσαντες [*hymnēsantes*], **sung a hymn**), which celebrate God's deliverance of his people from Egypt. Jesus then departs to the eastern outskirts of Jerusalem, **to the Mount of Olives**.

F. JESUS PREDICTS THE DISCIPLES' DESERTION AND DENIAL (26:31-35)

[31]Then Jesus told them, "This very night you will all fall away on account of me, for it is written:

"'I will strike the shepherd,
and the sheep of the flock will be scattered.'[a]

[32]But after I have risen, I will go ahead of you into Galilee."

[33]Peter replied, "Even if all fall away on account of you, I never will."

[34]"I tell you the truth," Jesus answered, "this very night, before the rooster crows, you will disown me three times."

[35]But Peter declared, "Even if I have to die with you, I will never disown you." And all the other disciples said the same.

[a]*31* Zech. 13:7

In the series of scenes beginning with Judas' treacherous plot (26:14-16, 20-25), and ending with his suicide (27:3-10), the disciples are portrayed in less than flattering terms. Jesus is, however, not taken by surprise by the course of events to occur throughout the night. He predicts their desertion and Peter's denial "this very night" (vv. 31, 34). Even though they affirm their steadfast loyalty, the events in Gethsemane prove their inability to comprehend the seriousness of the situation (cf. vv. 40-41, 43). Jesus' passive submission to the mob that comes to arrest him results in their desertion and a flight for personal safety (v. 56). When Jesus is taken before the Jewish court, he confesses his identity (v. 64), while Peter before his interrogators fulfills the words of Jesus and denies any allegiance to Jesus three times (vv. 69-75). The series of episodes portraying the failure of the disciples concludes with Judas' suicide, proving that "it would have been better for him not to have been born" (v. 24; 27:3-10). In the end, however, there is hope for the other disciples, as Jesus promises their restoration in Galilee (v. 32; cf. 28:7, 10).

26:31-32. Probably while on the way to the Mount of Olives (cf. Luke 22:39-40), Jesus predicts that Judas will not be the only disciple to compromise his commitment to him. In fact, all the disciples will be "scandalized" by the course of events throughout the night. They will all fail to heed this earlier warning: "Blessed is the man who does not fall away on account of me" (11:6). Since they fail to comprehend that Jesus' mission involves suffering and death, the events about to unfold will result in their cowardly defection. Nevertheless, Jesus' citation of Scripture (Zech 13:7) indicates that even their course of action falls within the sovereign plan of God. Zechariah had foretold of a day when God's appointed leader would be struck down, and the people would be scattered like sheep (cf. 9:36; Ezek 34). The text aptly summarizes what is about to occur with respect to Jesus and his disciples. By changing the original second person imperative ("strike the shepherd") to the first person (**I will strike the shepherd**) Jesus citation indicates that God assumes an active role in the death of the people's shepherd. The fate of the shepherd will have a devastating effect upon the flock. However, Jesus predicts that the scattering of the flock will only be temporary, as he assures the disciples of their eventual regathering in **Galilee**.

26:33-35. Peter, who has often assumed the position of the group's spokesman (cf. 14:28; 15:15; 16:16; 17:4; 18:21; 19:27), is compelled to respond in his customary impetuosity. In effect, Peter contradicts Jesus' prophetic words by affirming that he will be an exception to Jesus' dire prediction. Peter's boast was an attempt to highlight his own personal allegiance, which he claimed would never waver, regardless of the circumstances. However, Jesus is emphatic concerning the nature of Peter's defection. Despite his claim of absolute allegiance, in a few hours he will **disown** (ἀπαρνέομαι, *aparneomai*) his Lord three times. Instead of following Jesus and "denying himself" (16:24) Peter will align himself with Jesus' accusers and deny any connection to Jesus (see 26:69-75). The events will happen **before the rooster crows** (cf Mark 14:30), presumably around 1:30 a.m. Nevertheless, Peter continued to protest, affirming his willingness to die with Jesus. He probably thought the course of events, as predicted by Jesus, to be highly unlikely (cf. 16:22). Peter's presumptuous boast now infects the other disciples, as they too claim uncompromising loyalty.

G. THE GETHSEMANE PRAYER (26:36-46)

36Then Jesus went with his disciples to a place called Geth-
semane, and he said to them, "Sit here while I go over there and
pray." 37He took Peter and the two sons of Zebedee along with
him, and he began to be sorrowful and troubled. 38Then he said to
them, "My soul is overwhelmed with sorrow to the point of death.
Stay here and keep watch with me."

39Going a little farther, he fell with his face to the ground and
prayed, "My Father, if it is possible, may this cup be taken from
me. Yet not as I will, but as you will."

40Then he returned to his disciples and found them sleeping.
"Could you men not keep watch with me for one hour?" he asked
Peter. 41"Watch and pray so that you will not fall into temptation.
The spirit is willing, but the body is weak."

42He went away a second time and prayed, "My Father, if it is
not possible for this cup to be taken away unless I drink it, may
your will be done."

43When he came back, he again found them sleeping, because
their eyes were heavy. 44So he left them and went away once more
and prayed the third time, saying the same thing.

[45]Then he returned to the disciples and said to them, "Are you still sleeping and resting? Look, the hour is near, and the Son of Man is betrayed into the hands of sinners. [46]Rise, let us go! Here comes my betrayer!"

The reader may have difficulty reconciling Jesus' earlier emphatic affirmation of his fate and his resolve to walk the path of suffering and death, with the language of the Gethsemane prayer. Jesus' demeanor has now become "sorrowful and troubled" (vv. 37-38), as he casts himself prostrate upon the ground (v. 39) to plead with his Father for deliverance from the ordeal awaiting him. Such a portrayal may seem incongruent with his earlier resolve. However, as Brown notes, "In the biblical outlook, it is not irreverent to ask God for a change of mind (cf. Exod 32:10-14; 2 Kgs 20:1-6; 2 Sam 15:25-26; 1 Macc 2:56-58)."[19] Jesus is, after all, not a crazed fanatic relishing the prospects of martyrdom. Rather his petition reflects a "prayer of lament, one of the boldest forms of Jewish piety (cf. Ps 31:10; 40:11-13; 42:6, 9-11; 43:1-5; 55:4-8; 116:3-4)."[20] The Gethsemane scene graphically illustrates the dramatic tension between human desires and dread and the divine necessity to submit to suffering and death. Jesus is therefore not a victim of a tragic twist of fate, but a willing sacrifice committed to honor the will of his Father.

26:36. Gethsemane means "oil press" and most likely refers to an olive orchard on the slope of the Mount of Olives.[21] The site was probably frequented by Jesus (cf. John 18:2; Luke 22:39-40) since Judas had no difficulty in finding him. In Gethsemane the intensity of Jesus' resolve to yield to the Father's will stands in vivid contrast to the disciples' failure to appreciate the gravity of the situation.

26:37-38. Like the transfiguration episode (17:1-8), Jesus is accompanied by **Peter and the two sons of Zebedee**. While in the transfiguration scene they are witnesses to Jesus' transcendent glory, now they see his sorrow and dread as he faces the prospects

[19]R.E Brown, *The Death of the Messiah*, 2 vols (Garden City, NY: Doubleday, 1994), 1:127.

[20]Senior, *The Passion of Jesus in the Gospel of Matthew* (Wilmington, DE: Michael Glazier, 1985), p. 78.

[21]J.B. Green, "Gethsemane," *DJG*, p. 265.

of his approaching death. While the three are present for possible human support, Jesus must separate himself from them to engage his Father in prayer. Matthew describes his state of mind as **sorrowful and troubled**, thus highlighting his extreme distress (cf. Ps 22; 42; 43:2-5; 55:2-16). While the text does not say specifically what stirred such emotion, it is no doubt related to the spiritual significance of Jesus' sacrificial mission (i.e., bearing the curse of God as a sin offering). Jesus then expresses his own personal assessment of how serious is the situation: **My soul is overwhelmed with sorrow to the point of death**. The depth of Jesus' anguish is enough to threaten his physical life (cf. Ps 42:5, 11; 43:5; Jonah 4:9). The disciples are therefore enjoined to **[s]tay here and keep watch with me**. They are therefore invited to participate in the gravity of the situation by "watching" with Jesus, and thus exhibiting an alertness to the critical hour approaching. After all, these are the disciples who vowed their undying loyalty only a short time earlier (vv. 33-35).

26:39. Jesus further distances himself from his disciples by **[g]oing a little farther** and prostrating himself upon the ground, in typical reverential posture before the presence of God (cf. Gen 18:2; 19:1; Judg 13:20). Jesus now petitions his Father that **this cup be taken** from him. The request is tempered by the preface, **if it is possible**, and an expressed willingness to comply with God's sovereign will in the matter. The term "cup" in the OT is used metaphorically to symbolize suffering associated with the divine wrath of God (cf. Isa 51:17; Jer 25:15-16; Ezek 23:33; Ps 11:6). Jesus is therefore horrified at the prospects of suffering vicariously God's wrath for the sins of others. Nevertheless, Jesus models the principles of "denying himself" and "thinking the things of God rather than the things of men" (16:23-24). Therefore, priority is given the Father's will over his own (cf. 6:10).

26:40-41. Jesus then returns to where he left the disciples, only to find them **sleeping**, not watching as they were instructed. Jesus singles out Peter for reproof because of his previous boastful claims of steadfast devotion. His claim that he would die with Jesus is somewhat muted by his inability to stay awake for even an hour. All three disciples are encouraged to **watch and pray** in order not to succumb to **temptation** (πειρασμόν, *peirasmon*; cf. 6:13). If the disciples are to avoid being swept up in the catastrophic events about to unfold they must show vigilance and pray that God will spare them. Jesus knows the vulnerability of his disciples as indicated by the spirit/flesh contrast (σάρξ [*sarx*, "flesh"], not σῶμα [*sōma*, "body"]; *contra* NIV). In fact, as noted by Brown, "Jesus himself is in turmoil while praying and facing *peirasmos*," and thus "has experienced the weakness of the flesh . . ."[22] The flesh **is weak** in that it is inclined toward its own needs and earthly concerns. An example would be the disciples' yielding to the flesh by falling asleep. It is important that the disciples learn to give priority to the **spirit**, which is inclined toward the will of God.

26:42. Jesus once again (**a second time**) retreats to seclusion to address his **Father**. This time his words seem to imply a resignation to the fact that the "cup" would not be taken from him (**if it is *not* possible. . . .** , emphasis added, cf. v. 39). Nevertheless, Jesus expresses his absolute commitment to God's will with words that reflect the sentiment of the Lord's Prayer (6:10): **may your will be done**. Jesus thus models what he teaches his disciples about prayer.

26:43-44. When Jesus returns to his disciples, he finds them sleeping again; this time Matthew adds the explanation, **because their eyes were heavy**. They simply found it impossible to overcome the natural tendencies of the flesh. So for a third time, Jesus leaves them and addresses his Father in prayer. Matthew observes that the content of his prayer was the same as his earlier prayer, i.e., an expression of resolve to do the will of his Father.

26:45-46. On the third occasion of returning to his disciples Jesus responds to their sleepiness most likely with a rhetorical question designed to arouse them from sleep (so NIV and NRSV).[23] They are to arise because a critical moment has arrived with the appearance of Judas. The time has come for the decisive hour of fulfillment to commence. Earlier predictions about the fate of the Son of Man are about to become reality with the arrival of Judas to arrest Jesus (cf. 26:24). Jesus is clear that those to whom he will be **betrayed** (παραδίδοται [*paradidotai*], "handed over," cf. 17:22; 20:18; 26:2) are **sinners** who seek their own will. Jesus is fully aware

---

[22]Brown, *Death of the Messiah*, 1:199-200.

[23]Some have suggested that Jesus' words constitute an exhortation to "sleep on now and take your rest"; so Morris, *Matthew*, p. 671.

of the course of events because he has aligned himself with his Father's will. The final words before the arrest, **Rise, let us go! Here comes my betrayer!** demonstrate the transforming power of prayer, as Jesus is now ready to meet his betrayer and face the ordeal before him.

H. THE ARREST OF JESUS (26:47-56)

[47]While he was still speaking, Judas, one of the Twelve, arrived. With him was a large crowd armed with swords and clubs, sent from the chief priests and the elders of the people.
[48]Now the betrayer had arranged a signal with them: "The one I kiss is the man; arrest him." [49]Going at once to Jesus, Judas said, "Greetings, Rabbi!" and kissed him.

[50]Jesus replied, "Friend, do what you came for."[a]

Then the men stepped forward, seized Jesus and arrested him.
[51]With that, one of Jesus' companions reached for his sword, drew it out and struck the servant of the high priest, cutting off his ear.

[52]"Put your sword back in its place," Jesus said to him, "for all who draw the sword will die by the sword. [53]Do you think I cannot call on my Father, and he will at once put at my disposal more than twelve legions of angels? [54]But how then would the Scriptures be fulfilled that say it must happen in this way?"

[55]At that time Jesus said to the crowd, "Am I leading a rebellion, that you have come out with swords and clubs to capture me? Every day I sat in the temple courts teaching, and you did not arrest me. [56]But this has all taken place that the writings of the prophets might be fulfilled." Then all the disciples deserted him and fled.

[a]***50*** **Or** ***"Friend, why have you come?"***

26:47. Even while Jesus speaks, Judas arrives, thus stressing the speed with which Jesus' words are fulfilled. **Judas** is described as **one of the Twelve** highlighting once again the tragedy of Judas' treacherous deed. Earlier Judas had agreed to assist the Jewish leadership in their desire to arrest Jesus at an opportune time, so as not to cause a riot among the people (26:4-5, 14-16). Now Judas leads the arresting party under the cover of darkness, to the place where Jesus can be taken into custody. He has also agreed to provide the arresting party clear identification of Jesus by an agreed upon sign, thus enabling them to distinguish Jesus from the disciples (v. 48).

Judas is accompanied by a **large crowd** armed with **swords and clubs**. It appears that both the Jewish temple police and Roman soldiers joined forces to seize Jesus. They were heavily armed, thoroughly prepared to put down any resistance. The arresting party was backed by representatives of the Sanhedrin, Israel's highest judicial body. Even though Jesus' opponents appear to be in total control, the reader soon realizes that Jesus is in fact orchestrating events according to God's sovereign will.

26:48-49. Judas had earlier prearranged a sign that would enable them to distinguish which one was Jesus. By identifying Jesus with a **kiss**, a customary greeting, Judas hoped to conceal his sinister plans, by appearing as if everything were normal. Judas also greets Jesus with a typical salutation, **greetings** (χαῖρε, *chaire*), followed by the title **Rabbi**, recalling his earlier insincerity during the meal: "surely not I, Rabbi?" (v. 25). Judas evidently played his part well as he lavished Jesus with a particularly affectionate kiss (κατε-φίλησεν, *katephilēsan*). His hypocritical display of affection aptly underscores the depth of his alienation from Jesus.

26:50. Jesus is certainly not fooled by Judas' deceptive tactics, as indicated by his response. Jesus addresses him as **friend** (ἑταῖρε, *hetaire*, cf. 20:13; 22:12), which is probably to be understood ironically, to remind Judas of his longstanding companionship. The words translated **do what you came for** (ἐφ' ὅ πάρει, *eph' ho parei*) are notoriously difficult to translate. They may be understood as a command ("do what you came for," so NIV), a statement (that's what you are here for"),[24] or even a question ("Friend, why have you come?" See NIV footnote). Perhaps the imperative best captures the sense, indicating that Jesus knows Judas' intentions and insists that he get on with his true purpose. Jesus is therefore totally in control and even gives the command that results in his arrest.

[24]For a lengthy discussion of the possibilities see Brown, *Death of the Messiah*, 2:1385-1388.

26:51. In response to Jesus' seizure, one of the disciples, whom John identifies as Peter (John 18:10), drew his sword and with a reckless blow managed to cut off the ear (identified as the "right ear" in Luke 22:50) of a servant of the high priest (whom John identifies as Malchus, 18:10). Only Luke records Jesus' subsequent healing of the man's ear (22:51).

26:52-54. Exactly why Peter had a sword in his possession is unknown, but clearly his violent reaction was totally uncalled for. Jesus was in control and need not be defended by resorting to such extreme measures. Peter is commanded to return his sword to its place, and reminded of the principle that **all who draw the sword will die by the sword**. In other words, violence only generates more violence, so Jesus forbids his followers from resorting to such carnal tactics (cf. 5:39). Furthermore, in this situation Jesus is no helpless victim, since at his disposal are **twelve legions of angels** (=seventy-two thousand). Jesus' submission is therefore not a matter of a lack of power to resist, but a conscious choice to comply with God's will as expressed in Scripture. Hence the fulfillment of Scripture takes priority over the preservation of his life by active resistance. Jesus thus models the principle, "for whoever wants to save his life will lose it, but whoever loses his life for me will find it" (16:25).

26:55-56. Jesus then addresses the crowd and reprimands them for their show of force and the cowardly manner with which they sought his arrest. He sarcastically asks whether they have mistaken him for a leader of a group of bandits (ληστὴν, *lēstēn*, "a robber"), armed and violently predisposed. Earlier Jesus had denounced the Jerusalem temple as a "den of robbers" (ληστῶν, *lēstōn*), because they promoted violence in defense of their nationalism. As noted by Heil, "The confused and misdirected crowds have been sent by real 'robbers' (ληστῶν) to violently capture one who is no 'robber' (ληστὴν)."[25] They had every opportunity throughout the week to arrest Jesus while he taught in the temple precincts. Jesus thus exposes their hypocritical tactics of resorting to treachery and violence under the cover of darkness. They are the enforcers of a hidden agenda, one that seeks to assure that the security and

[25]Heil, *Death and Resurrection*, p. 52.

authority of the religious establishment remains in tact. Nevertheless, the arresting mob are simply fulfilling that formerly predicted in **the writings of the prophets**. Brown observes that the formula introducing the fulfillment citation (**But this has all taken place . . .**) is verbally identical to 1:22, thus forming "an inclusion signaling the comprehensiveness of God's plan stretching from the conception of Jesus by a virgin through the Holy Spirit to his arrest at the hands of sinners 'in that hour.'"[26]

Matthew closes the scene with the flight of the disciples, whose actions fulfill the prediction of Jesus that they will be scattered (26:35). Those who once "left" (ἀφίημι, *aphiēmi*) all to follow Jesus (cf. 4:20, 22; 19:27), now "desert" (the same verb) Jesus and run for their lives. In Matthew's story this is the final contact that Jesus has with his disciples before his death.

I. THE HEARING BEFORE CAIAPHAS (26:57-68)

57Those who had arrested Jesus took him to Caiaphas, the high priest, where the teachers of the law and the elders had assembled. 58But Peter followed him at a distance, right up to the courtyard of the high priest. He entered and sat down with the guards to see the outcome.

59The chief priests and the whole Sanhedrin were looking for false evidence against Jesus so that they could put him to death. 60But they did not find any, though many false witnesses came forward.

Finally two came forward 61and declared, "This fellow said, 'I am able to destroy the temple of God and rebuild it in three days.'"

62Then the high priest stood up and said to Jesus, "Are you not going to answer? What is this testimony that these men are bringing against you?" 63But Jesus remained silent.

The high priest said to him, "I charge you under oath by the living God: Tell us if you are the Christ,[a] the Son of God."

64"Yes, it is as you say," Jesus replied. "But I say to all of you:

---

[26]Brown, *Death of the Messiah*, 1:288.

In the future you will see the Son of Man sitting at the right hand of the Mighty One and coming on the clouds of heaven."

65Then the high priest tore his clothes and said, "He has spoken blasphemy! Why do we need any more witnesses? Look, now you have heard the blasphemy. 66What do you think?"

"He is worthy of death," they answered.

67Then they spit in his face and struck him with their fists. Others slapped him 68and said, "Prophesy to us, Christ. Who hit you?"

[a]*63* Or *Messiah*; also in verse 68

The story now takes a dramatic turn. Thus far in Matthew's passion narrative Jesus has been portrayed as an active agent whose predictive word moved events along. Now with his arrest Jesus assumes a passive role. However, it is clear to the reader that Jesus' passivity before his accusers is a freely adopted passivity. As Root observes, "his destiny does not simply fall on him; he accepts it."[27] In fact, his identity as God's beloved Son and Israel's messianic deliverer is most forcefully seen and understood in terms of his sacrificial mission.

In spite of the voluntary nature of Jesus' sacrifice, Matthew makes it clear that Israel is no less guilty in their efforts to destroy him. In their haste to be rid of Jesus Jewish authorities violated almost every judicial regulation known from the *Mishna*.[28] Of course, the relevance of the Mishnaic law code before A.D. 70 has been much disputed. However, to the extent that the Mishnaic judicial regulations applied in Jesus' day, then the Jewish "trial" exhibited several judicial irregularities: The procedure took place in the evening in violation of *m. Sanh* 4:1. In violation of *m. Sanh* 11:2 the meeting took place in an improper location, i.e., the high priest's house. They should never have begun trial proceedings on the eve of the Passover (*m. Sanh* 4:1). In addition, *m. Sanh* 4:1 prohibits a

[27]Michael Root, "Dying He Lives: Biblical Narrative and the Redemptive Jesus," *Semeia* 30 (1984), 159.

[28]For a survey of the discussion see D. Juel, *Messiah and Temple: The Trial of Jesus in the Gospel of Mark* (SBLDS 31; Missoula, MT: Scholars Press, 1977), pp. 59-64.

trial involving a capital verdict to take place at night. According to *m. Sanh* 7:5 the charge of blasphemy necessarily involved the pronunciation of the divine name (tetragrammaton, YHWH), which does not fit the charge against Jesus. Finally, any verdict in a capital case must wait at least one day (*m. Sanh* 4:1). However, it is hardly surprising, given the extreme animosity characteristic of the Jewish authorities toward Jesus, that strict adherence to legal procedure would not have been a high priority. It might also be questioned whether the proceedings in the home of Caiaphas is a formal trial, or simply a gathering to accumulate sufficient evidence to merit the death penalty. Whatever the legality of the gathering, it is clear that the judicial proceedings against Jesus were extremely prejudicial and predisposed to find him guilty.

26:57. In the night, shortly after the arrest, Jesus is brought to the home of **Caiaphas, the high priest**, the son-in-law of Annas the previous high priest (cf. John 18:13). It appears that leading representatives from the Sanhedrin (composed of seventy-one members), the Jewish supreme court, were present and eager to interrogate the troublemaker from Galilee.

26:58. Although the trial scene remains focused upon Jesus, Matthew has created a "frame" for the episode by references to Peter (v. 58; 69-75). By interweaving the trial scene with the denials of Peter the reader is led to compare the two scenes. Gerhardsson has noted that the two episodes are narrated in roughly the same way.[29] Both scenes involve three charges wherein the protagonist is interrogated and therefore, "the irony of the setting is that . . . both Jesus and Peter are on trial."[30] But whereas Jesus confesses (v. 64), Peter denies his allegiance to Jesus and disclaims all knowledge of him (vv. 70, 72, 74). Not only does the episode confirm Jesus' prediction (26:34), it also functions as a dramatic contrast highlighting the consistency of Jesus' resolve by setting it in opposition to Peter's failure to fulfill his resolution (cf. 26:33, 35). In fact, Peter is portrayed in the role of a spectator who has in effect "changed sides . . . gone over to the enemy's camp" and " in order to save his own skin he howls with the wolf pack" (Gerhardsson, p. 55).

---

[29]B. Gerhardsson, "Confession and Denial Before Men: Observations on Matt. 26:57–27:2," *JSNT* 13 (1981), 46-56.

[30]Ibid., pp. 49-51.

26:59-60. Matthew makes it clear from the beginning that the Jewish authorities are not favorably disposed toward Jesus. The mere fact they arrest Jesus and subject him to a trial before finding incriminating evidence against him is indicative of the level of their animosity toward him. According to Matthew, the authorities were more interested in conviction than they were in the pursuit of truth. They apparently had no scruples concerning the validity of the testimony, only that it was sufficiently weighty to merit the death penalty. Although they had many to give **false evidence**, evidently their testimony did not constitute sufficient legal evidence for condemning Jesus to death.

26:61. At last they have **two witnesses** (cf. Deut 17:6; 19:15) to come forward upon whose testimony they may be able to support a case for capital punishment. Their testimony has some semblance of truth, even though their recollection greatly distorted Jesus' actual words. In fact, Jesus never affirmed that he would personally **destroy the temple and rebuild it in three days**. The witnesses seem to have mixed two distinct statements, one having to do with the temple's inevitable destruction, and the other the raising of his body from the dead (cf. John 2:19-21). Nonetheless, the suggestion that one might actively seek the destruction of the temple could be construed as undermining the sanctity of the holy sanctuary.

26:62. In this light, the high priest pursues a line of questioning designed to force Jesus to either deny that the ever made such a statement (**Are you not going to answer?**), or at least provide an explanation for such a statement (**What is this testimony that these men are bringing against you?**).[31] But Jesus **remained silent**, offering neither a defense nor an explanation of the charges brought against him. Jesus' silence once again recalls the Suffering Servant motif as portrayed in Isaiah (53:7; cf 1 Pet 2:21-23).

26:63. The proceedings take a dramatic turn when the high priest stands and poses the decisive question: **Tell us if you are the Christ, the Son of God**. The question is prefaced by putting Jesus under oath: **I charge you under oath by the living God**. The *Mishna* (*Shebu* 4:3) indicates that if someone is put under oath, using the divine name or attribute, one is bound to respond.

---

[31]See Patte, *Matthew*, p. 373.

However, the reader recalls Jesus' view of such oaths (5:33-37; 23:16-22). Ironically, the language of the high priest echoes the confession of Peter (16:16), who is at the same time outside in the courtyard evoking an "oath" that he does not even know Jesus (v. 72).

26:64. The trial scene now turns on the identity question. The composite expression "the Christ" and the "Son of God" goes to the heart of Matthew's Christology. Given the humble, powerless condition of Jesus, the high priest's inquiry must have been filled with mocking skepticism. Nevertheless, the reader knows that Jesus is indeed Israel's Messiah (11:2-6), and the beloved Son of God (3:17; 17:5). But his messianic status and divine Sonship are most fundamentally observable in his sacrificial mission. However, given the correctness of the titles, Jesus responds affirmatively (**Yes, it is as you say**), though "reluctant and circumlocutory in formation."[32] As Brown observes, "There is truth in what the high priest has said, but he must take responsibility for the way he interprets it and the use he plans to make of it."[33]

Jesus then speaks explicitly about a future reversal of roles. While now they reject his messianic status, one day they will see the Son of Man exalted and endowed with authority (=**sitting at the right hand**, cf Ps 110:1), vindicated by God and triumphant over his enemies (=**coming on the clouds of heaven**, cf. Dan 7:13). The difficult wording of ἀπ' ἄρτι (*ap' arti*, translated **in the future** by the NIV) probably refers to the series of vindicating events associated with Jesus' crucifixion and resurrection. As noted by Senior, "these signs are a foretaste of the Son of Man's triumph over death at the end of the age."[34]

26:65-66. The **high priest** is obviously horrified by such a suggestion. The symbolic tearing of clothes is illustrative of his extreme grief (cf. Gen 37:34; 2 Sam 1:11-12; Lev 10:6; 21:10; 2 Kgs 19:1). The high priest charges Jesus with **blasphemy,** which usually involved the irreverent use of God's name (cf. Lev 34:16; *m. Sanh*

---

[32]Catchpole has convincingly shown that the expression is "affirmative in content and reluctant or circumlocutory in formulation," see David Catchpole, "The Answer of Jesus to Caiaphas (Matt. XXVI. 64)," *NTS* 27 (1970-71), 213-226.

[33]Brown, *Death of the Messiah,* 1:491.

[34]Senior, *Passion of Jesus,* p. 99.

7:5). However, as noted by Brown, the term may mean that "Jesus is being accused of arrogantly claiming for himself what belongs to God and thus insulting God."[35] The high priest is convinced that Jesus has sufficiently incriminated himself, so additional witnesses are no longer needed, only a call for a verdict. It certainly comes as no surprise that the Sanhedrin finally pronounces its sought-after death penalty.

26:67-68. The brutal and humiliating treatment of Jesus by his Jewish accusers is intended to mock his messianic and prophetic claims. Ironically, his tormenters are in the midst of fulfilling Jesus' prophetic words about his brutal treatment in Jerusalem (16:21; 20:17-19). The actions of spitting in his face, beating him, along with their taunting game are all calculated to discredit him and prove his powerlessness in their hands. Yet, the real issue is not a matter of power, but a willing compliance to the Divine will. Likely, Matthew intended his brutal treatment to recall the plight of God's Suffering Servant foretold by Isaiah (cf. 50:6; 53:3, 5).

J. THE DENIAL OF PETER (26:69-75)

69Now Peter was sitting out in the courtyard, and a servant girl came to him. "You also were with Jesus of Galilee," she said.

70But he denied it before them all. "I don't know what you're talking about," he said.

71Then he went out to the gateway, where another girl saw him and said to the people there, "This fellow was with Jesus of Nazareth."

72He denied it again, with an oath: "I don't know the man!"

73After a little while, those standing there went up to Peter and said, "Surely you are one of them, for your accent gives you away."

74Then he began to call down curses on himself and he swore to them, "I don't know the man!"

Immediately a rooster crowed. 75Then Peter remembered the word Jesus had spoken: "Before the rooster crows, you will disown me three times." And he went outside and wept bitterly.

[35]Brown, *Death of the Messiah*, 1:523.

Matthew now returns to the earlier parenthetical remark about Peter following Jesus from a distance, into "the courtyard of the high priest" (v. 58). As noted previously, Matthew has interwoven Jesus' trial with the trial of Peter. The reader is therefore encouraged to interpret them together, noting how their respective points compliment and contrast with each other. In a subtle way Matthew has shown Jesus to be a true prophet by framing the mockery of his prophetic abilities (vv. 67-68) with the fulfillment of his prophetic predictions of his treatment in Jerusalem, followed by the fulfillment of his predictions concerning Peter (26:34).

26:69-70. While Jesus is inside facing the animosity of the Sanhedrin, Peter is outside being confronted by the curious observation of a **servant girl**: **You were with Jesus of Galilee**. Whereas Jesus must respond to the serious inquiry of the high priest concerning his identity (v. 63), Peter faces an innocent observation made by a servant girl concerning his relationship to Jesus. However, it may be, that given the incident that occurred in Gethsemane, Peter may want to avoid any detection. Having heard the young girl's suggestion that he was with Jesus, Peter emphatically denies, **before them all**, having any association with him. He tries to evade the accusation of the woman by pretending not to have any knowledge concerning what the woman is talking about. Therefore, in spite of his earlier boast, "I will never disown you" (v. 35), with even the slightest pressure, Peter is willing to deny any association with Jesus.

26:71-72. Peter then retreats to the **gateway**, probably in hope of escaping further detection. However, he is confronted by **another girl** (cf. Mark 14:69) who emphatically affirms, **This fellow was with Jesus of Nazareth** (see 2:23). Again there is no accusation of any criminal behavior, just that he was a known associate with Jesus. This time Peter reinforces his denial **with an oath**. Ironically, in contrast to Peter, when Jesus is put under an oath he confesses his identity (v. 63). Peter's stance is even more reprehensible since earlier he had expressed his conviction that Jesus is indeed, "the Christ, the Son of the living God" (16:16). But, when he claims, **"I don't know the man,"** he is pathetically correct, since Jesus' identity can only be rightly discerned in terms of his mission to suffer and die.

26:73-74. After a short time elapses (cf. Luke 22:59, "about an hour"), the pressure upon Peter reaches a climactic point (v. 73). This time proof is offered to validate the claim that Peter is one of Jesus' disciples: **Surely you are one of them, for your accent gives you away.** Earlier Jesus was identified as a Galilean, now they are able to link Peter to Galilee because his speech is distinctly Galilean.[36] Peter responds to the charge by evoking a "curse" (καταθεματίζειν, *katathematizein*) and "swearing" (ὀμνύειν, *omnyein*) repeatedly that he does not know the man. Although the object of the first verb form ("curse") is not explicitly stated, it is probable that Peter intended Jesus as the object (contra NIV, **on himself**), in order to further intensify his claim of disassociation from Jesus. Peter has now fallen to the point of aligning himself with those who have completely repudiated Jesus.

26:75. Immediately dramatizes the exact fulfillment of Jesus' words concerning the crowing of a rooster (cf. 26:34). With the crowing of the rooster Peter is made to recall Jesus' words about his threefold denial, alongside his own confident boast that he would never disown him, and would even die with him (26:33, 35). Crushed by the realization of his failure, Peter **went outside and wept bitterly**. Peter's remorse is indicative of his penitent spirit overcome with the enormity of his failure. Ultimately, Peter is restored, along with the other disciples who had fled (see 28:10).

---

[36]See M.O. Wise, "Languages of Palestine," *DJG*, pp. 434-444.

MATTHEW 27

K. TRANSITION TO THE ROMAN AUTHORITIES (27:1-2)

[1]Early in the morning, all the chief priests and the elders of the people came to the decision to put Jesus to death. [2]They bound him, led him away and handed him over to Pilate, the governor.

These verses provide a transition from the Jewish trial to Jesus' appearance before Roman authorities. Like the parenthetical remark about Peter in 26:58, the narration of the Roman trial is momentarily interrupted by the account of Judas' demise (vv. 3-10).

27:1-2. Early in the morning, following the late night proceedings before Caiaphas, the entire Sanhedrin met to ratify the previous night's **decision to put Jesus to death**. It was also important to frame the charges against Jesus in a manner that would impress Roman authorities with the seriousness of the charges against him. Since the Jews did not have the right to execute capital punishment (John 18:31), if their verdict was to be implemented, they must persuade the Roman governor that Jesus deserves to die. Pilate, the Roman governor (A.D. 26-36/37), was notorious for treating Jewish customs with contempt (see Josephus, *J.W.* 2.9.2-3; 169-74; *Ant* 18.3.1).[1] It would therefore not be easy to persuade Pilate to comply with their request for Jesus' execution. The transfer to a Roman authority fulfills Jesus' words that he will be turned "over to Gentiles" (20:29).

L. THE SUICIDE OF JUDAS (27:3-10)

[3]When Judas, who had betrayed him, saw that Jesus was condemned, he was seized with remorse and returned the thirty

---

[1]H.W. Hoehner, "Pontius Pilate," *DJG*, pp. 615-617.

silver coins to the chief priests and the elders. [4]"I have sinned," he said, "for I have betrayed innocent blood."

"What is that to us?" they replied. "That's your responsibility."

[5]So Judas threw the money into the temple and left. Then he went away and hanged himself.

[6]The chief priests picked up the coins and said, "It is against the law to put this into the treasury, since it is blood money." [7]So they decided to use the money to buy the potter's field as a burial place for foreigners. [8]That is why it has been called the Field of Blood to this day. [9]Then what was spoken by Jeremiah the prophet was fulfilled: "They took the thirty silver coins, the price set on him by the people of Israel, [10]and they used them to buy the potter's field, as the Lord commanded me."[a]

[a]*10* See Zech. 11:12,13; Jer. 19:1-13; 32:6-9.

In the interlude between the transfer of Jesus to Pilate and the Roman trial Matthew uses the actions of another disciple as a backdrop highlighting the character of Jesus. Judas becomes a witness to Jesus' innocence with the words, "I have sinned for I have betrayed innocent blood" (v. 4). The theme of "blood" and "innocence" anticipates the next scene wherein Jesus' innocence and Israel's guilt are fundamental to the trial scene before Pilate (see 27:19, 23-25). Even the Jewish leaders are made unwittingly to testify to Jesus' innocence by calling the money paid to Judas "blood money" (v. 6). Matthew once again reminds the reader that although the Jewish leaders act from dishonorable motives their actions serve the larger purposes of God, as indicated by their fulfillment of Scripture (v. 9). In addition, the suicide of Judas brings to fulfillment the words of Jesus: "woe to that man who betrays the Son of Man" (26:24). It is no accident that incidents involving Peter and Judas and their relationship to Jesus are placed side-by-side. As noted by Senior, "Judas' fate is in stark contrast to that of Peter. Both apostles failed their Master, but Peter chose repentance and Judas chose death."[2]

27:3-5. The decision of the Sanhedrin to condemn Jesus to

[2]Senior, *Passion of Jesus*, p. 108.

death evidently produced a "change of mind" (μεταμεληθεὶς, *metamelētheis*) in Judas. The verb form implies that one has taken a different view of something, but does not necessarily entail all that might be conveyed by "repentance" (μετανοεῖν, *metanoiein*). Although Judas experienced **remorse**, it is not clear that Judas' remorse was connected to a genuine regret for his treacherous act. It may be that he never fully foresaw the consequences brought about by his actions. He does, however, attempt to return the **thirty silver coins** paid to him by the chief priests (26:15). His efforts are prefaced with an acknowledgment of his sin and a recognition that his sin was against **innocent blood**. Of course, such a response may be motivated by any number of considerations. Perhaps the description of Paul speaks most appropriately to Judas' situation: "Godly sorrow brings repentance that leads to salvation and leaves no regret, but worldly sorrow brings death" (2 Cor 7:10).

The **chief priests and the elders** are not at all sympathetic to Judas' change of heart. They disclaim any responsibility in the matter (**That's your responsibility**), and thus exhibit a calloused and cavalier attitude toward the whole issue (**What is that to us?**). In frustration, Judas throws the silver coins into the temple (τὸν ναὸν, *ton naon*). Since only the priests could enter the inner sanctuary, exactly where Judas threw the money is uncertain. Suffice it to say that the money had become of no value to Judas and he wanted no part of it. After discarding the money Judas **went away and hanged himself** (cf. 2 Sam 17:23). His tragic end graphically depicts the depth of his despair and his loss of all hope (cf. Peter's response, 26:75).

27:6-8. In spite of their efforts to distance themselves from the sin of Judas, once Judas threw the coins into the sacred precincts, the **chief priests** and elders found themselves implicated by having to dispose of contaminated money (**blood money**; cf. Deut 23:18) that could not be deposited in the temple treasury. They apparently had no scruples about using money from the temple treasury for the shedding of innocent blood, but now are legally concerned about returning the same money to the treasury. Instead, they decide to use the money to purchase **the potter's field as a burial place for foreigners**. Evidently a well known plot of land is purchased to provide a burial place for "Jewish visitors to Jerusalem or proselytes."[3] Hence, unclean money is used to purchase an unclean place. Since the field was purchased with "blood money," Matthew notes that the name **Field of Blood** has become attached to the plot of land, even to Matthew's day. Thus the field stands as an enduring reminder both of Jesus' innocence and the price paid to bring about his death.

27:9-10. In typical fashion, Matthew sees in the series of events the fulfillment of that written by the prophets. However, Matthew's last fulfillment citation poses some difficulties for the modern reader. Although the bulk of Matthew's citation comes from Zechariah 11:3, the passage is attributed to Jeremiah. The terms "potter" and "thirty pieces of silver" seem to be derived from Zechariah 11:12-13, while the phrase "blood of the innocent" may recall Jeremiah 19:1-13, with Jeremiah's purchase of a field mentioned in 32:6-9 being the background for the purchase of a potter's field (Matt 27:10). Therefore, given the language of Matthew's fulfillment citation in verses 9-10 it does appear to be a composite citation, drawing on elements both from Jeremiah and Zechariah. The citation may have been attributed to Jeremiah since he is the better known. Of course, determining the precise source of Matthew's citation is at best only conjectural. The critical issue in the citation from the OT is to make it clear that "even the most difficult aspects of the passion (betrayal of Judas, the refusal of the chief priests and elders to be swayed by innocent blood) lay within God's plan."[4]

M. THE TRIAL BEFORE PILATE (27:11-26)

11Meanwhile Jesus stood before the governor, and the governor asked him, "Are you the king of the Jews?"

"Yes, it is as you say," Jesus replied.

12When he was accused by the chief priests and the elders, he gave no answer. 13Then Pilate asked him, "Don't you hear the

[3]Brown, *The Death of the Messiah*, 1:646; *contra* Hagner, *Matthew*, 2:813 who sees the burial place for "non-Jews who were not allowed to be buried in the same cemetery with Jews."

[4]Brown, *The Death of the Messiah*, 1:652.

testimony they are bringing against you?" [14]But Jesus made no reply, not even to a single charge – to the great amazement of the governor.

[15]Now it was the governor's custom at the Feast to release a prisoner chosen by the crowd. [16]At that time they had a notorious prisoner, called Barabbas. [17]So when the crowd had gathered, Pilate asked them, "Which one do you want me to release to you: Barabbas, or Jesus who is called Christ?" [18]For he knew it was out of envy that they had handed Jesus over to him.

[19]While Pilate was sitting on the judge's seat, his wife sent him this message: "Don't have anything to do with that innocent man, for I have suffered a great deal today in a dream because of him."

[20]But the chief priests and the elders persuaded the crowd to ask for Barabbas and to have Jesus executed.

[21]"Which of the two do you want me to release to you?" asked the governor.

"Barabbas," they answered.

[22]"What shall I do, then, with Jesus who is called Christ?" Pilate asked.

They all answered, "Crucify him!"

[23]"Why? What crime has he committed?" asked Pilate.

But they shouted all the louder, "Crucify him!"

[24]When Pilate saw that he was getting nowhere, but that instead an uproar was starting, he took water and washed his hands in front of the crowd. "I am innocent of this man's blood," he said. "It is your responsibility!"

[25]All the people answered, "Let his blood be on us and on our children!"

[26]Then he released Barabbas to them. But he had Jesus flogged, and handed him over to be crucified.

27:11. Matthew now resumes the narrative line left off in verse 2. Jesus has been delivered to Pilate and now stands before the Roman governor to be interrogated. No doubt Pilate has been briefed by the Jewish authorities, who would have framed their charges in a way to convince Pilate that Jesus poses a threat to the political order of Rome. This explains the nature of Pilate's opening question: **Are you the King of the Jews?** The question indicates that the issue of

Jesus' identity continues to be fundamental for the unfolding of events. Whereas earlier the Sanhedrin probed the religious implications of Jesus' identity (26:63, "are you the Christ, the Son of God?"), the Roman governor is much more concerned with the political implications inherent in the claim to be King. No doubt Pilate's question reflects the form in which the Jewish leaders set forth Jesus' messianic claim. Jesus responds once again with an answer that is both affirmative and yet calls upon the inquirer to be reflective of the sense intended (σύ λέγεις, *su legeis*, cf. 26:25).

27:12-13. Since Jesus had already dealt with the **chief priests and the elders**, he refuses to respond to the charges they bring against him. However, Pilate is amazed by his refusal to defend himself against their charges. Legally, what is Pilate to do with a defendant "who has not pleaded guilty but does not assert innocence or deny the basic charges against him when questioned?"[5] While the legal question may be difficult to decide, theologically, Jesus' silence is intended to be reminiscent of God's Suffering Servant who though "oppressed and afflicted yet he did not open his mouth" (Isa 53:7).

27:14-18. Pilate's **great amazement** with Jesus' refusal to answer their charges may have stimulated his effort to seek the release of Jesus by appealing to his customary practice of releasing one prisoner during the Passover according to popular demand.[6] It appears that Pilate limited the choice to two: **Barabbas**,[7] a notorious prisoner (cf. Mark 15:7, "the insurrectionist who had committed murder in an uprising"), or **Jesus who is called Christ**. Evidently, Pilate was convinced that the **crowd** would opt for the release of Jesus. Pilate knew that the religious leaders had arrested Jesus and wanted him dead because they were envious of his popularity with the crowds (cf. 21:11, 15-16, 46). Pilate's interest in releasing Jesus was probably due, at least in part, to his dislike of being used by the Jewish authorities.

27:19. Another factor contributing to Pilate's desire to release Jesus was the confirmation of Jesus' innocence to Pilate's wife by

---

[5]Ibid., 1:720.

[6]For the widespread practice of prisoner release during festivals see R.L. Merritt, "Jesus Barabbas and the Paschal Pardon," *JBL* 104 (1985), 57-68.

[7]M.J. Wilkens, "Barabbas," *ABD*, 1:607.

means of a dream. Her warning to Pilate while he sat on the **judge's seat** recalls the words of Judas, "I have betrayed innocent blood" (v. 4). Matthew probably intends that her dream be understood as revelatory, much like the dream-motif in the infancy narratives (cf. 1:20; 2:12, 13, 19, 22). As Hagner notes, "Dreams were taken with great seriousness by the Romans . . ."[8]

27:20. In spite of Pilate's inclination to release Jesus he is committed, for political reasons, to accede to the popular view of the crowd. Little did Pilate know, however, that **the chief priests and the elders** were busily persuading the crowd to ask for the release of Barabbas and to call for Jesus' death. This **crowd** is probably composed of residents of Jerusalem and is to be distinguished from the Galilean crowds that hailed him as "Son of David" upon his entrance into Jerusalem (21:9). What arguments the religious leaders may have used to persuade the crowd to call for the release of Barabbas instead of Jesus is not mentioned by Matthew.

27:21-22. When Pilate poses the decisive question concerning which prisoner should be released, the crowd responds as one – **"Barabbas."** Pilate then polls the crowd with respect to the fate of **Jesus who is called Christ**. The reader knows that the crowd has already been persuaded to call for his execution (v. 20). Yet, when they call for his crucifixion, it is shocking that they seek a particularly brutal and horrifying form of Roman punishment. It is obvious that the extreme animosity of the Jewish leaders had thoroughly contaminated and warped their sense of justice.

27:23-24. Pilate's attempt to reason with them by asking, **What crime has he committed?** is only met with louder shouts for his execution. The situation appeared extremely volatile, with the potential of a major **uproar** (θόρυβος, *thorybos*). Pilate's political savvy convinced him that he had better comply with the crowd's demand. But in a last ditch effort to absolve himself of any guilt associated with the execution of an innocent man, Pilate engages in a symbolic cleansing of his hands, while claiming his innocence in the shedding of **this man's blood**. Although there is Jewish precedence for such actions (Deut 21:6-8), there are also "adequate parallels for washing as protective purification in a wide range of Greco-

[8]Hagner, *Matthew*, 2:823.

Roman literature."[9] Therefore, there seems no reason to dispute the historicity of the event. However, Pilate's effort was a hollow gesture, and does not absolve him of complicity in the subsequent events. In spite of the fact that he tells the crowd, **It is your responsibility** (ὑμεῖς ὄψεσθε, *hymeis opsesthe*, lit., "You see to it," cf. 27:4), Pilate cannot escape his responsibility in the matter. In fact, the reality of human sin absolves no one of the tragedy of the cross.

27:25. While Pilate attempts to evade his responsibility, the Jewish crowd enthusiastically asserts, **Let his blood be on us and on our children**. Because they have been persuaded that Jesus is a "blasphemer" who brazenly undermined the traditions of Israel, they are willing to accept responsibility for his death. Their statement reflects "a spontaneous outburst in the frenzy of the moment."[10] The language is reflective of an OT formula wherein accountability is assumed for the taking of life (cf. 2 Sam 1:16; Jer 26:15). Certainly, the language should not be pressed as binding God to curse all subsequent generations of Jews. It may be that God's judgment upon Jerusalem in A.D. 70 should be seen as punishment upon a subsequent generation. Even so, that not every Jew stands under this curse is obvious because the first generation of Christians were largely Jewish. The verse offers no warrant for the modern day expression of anti-Semitism.

27:26. Pilate then acquiesces to the demands of the crowd and releases Barabbas, while Jesus he prepares for execution by first having Jesus **flogged**. As a preliminary to crucifixion, flogging consisted of a whipping with a multiple-thonged whip usually with pieces of bone or metal attached to the end to assure the tearing of the skin. Although performed to hasten death, it was oftentimes fatal in itself (see Josephus, *Ant* 12.5.4; *J.W.* 2.14.19; 306, 308; 5.11.1 etc.). The atmosphere is distinctly Roman since Jews used stoning, not crucifixion, as a means of execution. The Gentile authorities simply fulfill their role in God's redemptive plan as earlier predicted by Jesus (cf. 20:19; 26:2).

---

[9]See Brown, *Death of the Messiah*, 1:834.
[10]Blomberg, *Matthew*, p. 413.

N. MOCKERY AND ABUSE OF JESUS (27:27-31)

27Then the governor's soldiers took Jesus into the Praetorium and gathered the whole company of soldiers around him. 28They stripped him and put a scarlet robe on him, 29and then twisted together a crown of thorns and set it on his head. They put a staff in his right hand and knelt in front of him and mocked him. "Hail, king of the Jews!" they said. 30They spit on him, and took the staff and struck him on the head again and again. 31After they had mocked him, they took off the robe and put his own clothes on him. Then they led him away to crucify him.

In a scene paralleling the abuse endured at the close of the Jewish trial (26:67-68), Jesus also endures abuse and humiliation at the hand of the Romans, as they mock his kingly claim. For the reader the scene is filled with irony because the one they mock as King is truly King, not only of the Jews but also of the Gentiles.[11]

27:27-29. Once Jesus is "handed over" (παρέδωκεν, *paredōken*, v. 26) to be crucified, the Roman soldiers led him to the **Praetorium**, the governor's private residence while in Jerusalem. There they decide to put their prisoner through a humiliating mockery, poking fun at Jesus' claim of kingship. No doubt the activity was also intended to ridicule the Jews and their messianic aspirations. A **whole company** (lit., "cohort," perhaps as may as six hundred soldiers) join in the fiasco. After stripping him of his blood-soaked clothes they dress him in royal attire: a scarlet robe, crown, and a staff (vv. 28-29). Each of the items were intended to ridicule the notion of Jesus' alleged kingship. The robe was the color of royalty, probably worn by upper level Roman officials. The **crown** made from a thorny branch was both humiliating and painful. With a **staff** (κάλαμον, *kalamon*, "reed") functioning as a scepter his wardrobe is complete, and thus the mockery and abuse begins (vv. 29-30).

27:30-31. First they made light of his kingly presence, kneeling before him and addressing him derogatorily, **Hail, king of the Jews**. Then, like the Jewish officials they also spit on him, and then strike him several times in the head with the reed scepter. How

[11]Heil, *Death and Resurrection*, p. 78; see also Patte, *Matthew*, p. 381.

long this activity lasted is unknown. Finally, their fun over, they dress him in his own clothes before proceeding to the place of crucifixion. Usually a prisoner was forced to walk through the streets, carrying the lateral beam of the cross, naked, while being whipped along the way. The clothing of Jesus before they parade him through the streets "may reflect a local concession that the Romans made to the Jewish abhorrence of public nudity."[12] As they now led him to be crucified, little did they know that this seemingly powerless victim was about to reveal his true kingly status in a liberating mission involving his suffering and death.

O. THE CRUCIFIXION (27:32-44)

32As they were going out, they met a man from Cyrene, named Simon, and they forced him to carry the cross. 33They came to a place called Golgotha (which means The Place of the Skull). 34There they offered Jesus wine to drink, mixed with gall; but after tasting it, he refused to drink it. 35When they had crucified him, they divided up his clothes by casting lots.[a] 36And sitting down, they kept watch over him there. 37Above his head they placed the written charge against him: THIS IS JESUS, THE KING OF THE JEWS. 38Two robbers were crucified with him, one on his right and one on his left. 39Those who passed by hurled insults at him, shaking their heads 40and saying, "You who are going to destroy the temple and build it in three days, save yourself! Come down from the cross, if you are the Son of God!"

41In the same way the chief priests, the teachers of the law and the elders mocked him. 42"He saved others," they said, "but he can't save himself! He's the King of Israel! Let him come down now from the cross, and we will believe in him. 43He trusts in God. Let God rescue him now if he wants him, for he said, 'I am the Son of God.'" 44In the same way the robbers who were crucified with him also heaped insults on him.

[a]*35* **A few late manuscripts have** *lots that the word spoken by the prophet might be fulfilled: "They divided my garments among themselves and cast lots for my clothing"* **(Psalm 22:18)**

---

[12]Brown, *Death of the Messiah*, 1:870.

Matthew's narration of the crucifixion is remarkably reserved. All the horrifying and gory details of the physical agony are passed over in virtual silence. After all, Matthew's readers were well acquainted with crucifixion as a form of punishment, hence there was no need to recount the physical suffering associated with the ordeal. Besides, Matthew is more interested in the meaning and significance of the cross than the physical trauma. What may appear as a pathetic defeat as Jesus hangs seemingly powerless, is for Matthew the climactic moment of fulfillment, when Jesus' divine Sonship and true messianic character are revealed. The crucifixion scene abounds with echoes from the OT to remind the reader that what transpires is the working out of God's sovereign will.

27:32-33. The language **as they were going out** may refer either to their departing the Praetorium (v. 27), or to going outside the walls of Jerusalem. On their way to the place of execution they meet a man along the way (cf. Mark 15:21, "passing by on his way in from the country") **from Cyrene** (North Africa), **named Simon** (a common Jewish name), who was probably visiting Jerusalem for the feast. Roman soldiers compel Simon (ἠγγάρευσαν, *ēngareusan*, lit., "Force or press into service")[13] to carry the crossbeam of the cross which would be affixed to the upright stake at the place of execution. Evidently, with the ordeal of the night before, Jesus was physically weakened and unable to carry the heavy beam. The soldier's ordering of Simon to carry the crossbeam was most likely not out of compassion, but fear that Jesus would die before they could execute the governor's sentence. Simon therefore carries the crossbeam to **Golgotha**, a transliteration of an Aramaic term which Matthew translates as **the place of the Skull**. Most likely the place received its name because the site resembled a skull. Traditionally, the site has been located in the vicinity of the modern day Church of the Holy Sepulchre.[14]

27:34. Once they reach the place of execution they offered Jesus **wine to drink mixed with gall** (cf. Mark 15:23, "wine mixed with myrrh"). The concoction as described by Matthew was not intended as a kindly gesture to numb the senses (as possible in Mark), but rather, was made undrinkable by the adding of "gall," and thus was

---

[13]Ibid., 2:914; cf. 5:41.

[14]J.B. Green, "Death of Jesus," *DJG*, p. 150.

intended to further aggravate the situation. Jesus thus tasted the wine and refused to drink it (see Ps 69:21).

27:35-36. Matthew then describes the crucifixion with a single subordinate participle: σταυρώσαντες (*staurōsantes*). Not a word about the nailing to the crossbeam, the form of the cross, or the pain involved when the cross is hoisted to an upright position.[15] Instead, Matthew recounts the confiscation of Jesus' clothes by the soldiers, who then cast lots for them (cf. John 19:23-24). The incident is described in terms unmistakably drawn from the lament of Psalm 22:18 (LXX 22:19): "They divide my garments among them and cast lots for my clothing." This is the first of several allusions to Psalm 22 (cf. v. 46/22:1; v. 39/22:7; v. 43/22:8). Matthew's focus is therefore not so much the ordeal of crucifixion as it is to narrate events that link Jesus' story to the righteous sufferer as depicted in the Psalms. When the soldiers strip Jesus of his clothes, the reader is to see the event in terms of the lament of the righteous sufferer who endures unjust abuse. With Jesus bereft of all dignity and seemingly powerless in their hands, the soldiers take a seat and keep watch to assure that no one attempts to interfere with the execution. Their presence throughout the execution sets the stage for their later confessionary appraisal (v. 54).

27:37. It was not uncommon to affix upon the cross the charges for which a convicted criminal was being executed. In Jesus' case, an inscription was placed **above his head**, which read **THIS IS JESUS, THE KING OF THE JEWS.** Jesus' crime is therefore perceived as a political one, a threat to the established authority of Rome. Of course, the irony is that Jesus is being crucified for being exactly who he is, Israel's King, perceived as such even in his infancy (2:1-2). But a king that passively submits to his enemies was totally incongruent with Israel's messianic hopes.

27:38. In another ironic twist, Jesus had earlier protested that he was being arrested as if he were "leading a rebellion" (lit., as a "bandit" or "robber," 26:55), now he is crucified in the midst of

---

[15]For discussion of the ordeal see E. Bammel, "Crucifixion as a Punishment in Palestine," in *The Trial of Jesus*, festscrift for C.F.D. Moule, ed. E Bammel (London: SCM, 1970), pp. 162-165; M. Hengel, *Crucifixion in the Ancient World and the Full Message of the Cross* (Philadelphia: Fortress, 1977); see also Brown, *Death of the Messiah*, 2:1088-1092.

robbers (λῃσταί, *lēstai*). It is probable that the two crucified with Jesus were not mere thieves, but rather rebels, and like Barabbas were "insurrectionists" who resorted to murder and banditry in their opposition to Rome. With Jesus being mocked as Israel's king, between two rebels, the scene also graphically taunts Jewish political hopes that were centered in the anticipation of a revolutionary king. Yet, for those who have eyes to see, Jesus is actually fulfilling the messianic liberation promised the people of God. His revolutionary activity brings deliverance from the tyranny of sin, the greatest enemy of God's people. As God's Suffering Servant, Jesus fulfills the Isaianic depiction: "he poured out his life unto death and was numbered with the transgressors" (53:12).

27:39. Having identified the place and circumstances of Jesus' execution (vv. 32-38), Matthew now describes the reactions of those who observe his crucifixion (vv. 39-44). Three groups of onlookers are noted ("those who pass by," vv. 38-40; Jewish authorities, vv. 41-43; and the two thieves, v. 44), and all respond with taunts and cruel mockery. It has been pointed out that Matthew's depiction of the crucifixion takes the form of a "testing" comparable to the temptation narrative in 4:1-11.[16] Once again Jesus is enticed to prove his Sonship by exercising his divine power to save his own life (vv. 40, 43; cf. 4:3). The Jewish leaders assume the role of Satan when they challenge his reliance upon God with the remark, "he trusts in God. Let God rescue him if he wants him" (v. 43; cf. 4:5-6). Finally, both Satan and the mockers at the cross promise a reward if Jesus will comply with their suggestion (v. 42 "come down and we will believe": cf. 4:8-9 "all the kingdoms of the world"). However, the suspense of Matthew's story centers in how Jesus' resistance to temptation, which results in his death, in reality exhibits his messianic power and intimacy with God.

27:40. In the first mockery Jesus is taunted by Jews who happen to be passing by. They **hurled insults** (lit., "blasphemed"), and show their contempt by "shaking their heads" (cf. Ps 22:7), and challenging his power to **destroy the temple and build it in three days**.

[16]See B. Gerhardsson, "Gottes sohn als Diener Gottes," *Studia theologica* 27 (1973) 96-103; cf. also his *The Testing of God's Son (Matt 4:1-11 and par)* (ConNT 2; Lund, Sweden: CWK Gleerup, 1966).

They had evidently heard about the charges against him, and thus mock the incongruence of such a claim with his powerless condition. How could one who claims to have the power and authority to destroy and rebuild the temple not be able to even save himself? Hence, they challenge him, **save yourself**; the claim to Sonship depends on demonstrating his power by coming off the cross. Like Satan in the temptation narrative (4:3), the claim of divine Sonship must be validated by the exercise of miraculous powers. But Jesus instead models the principle, "whoever wants to save his life will lose it" (16:25). It is precisely by remaining on the cross that Jesus demonstrates that he is truly God's Son, committed to fulfilling the will of his Father. The mockers truly do blaspheme when they seek to entice God's Son to act contrary to the divine will.

27:41-43. Next, the Jewish leaders, comprised of **chief priests, the teachers of the law, and the elders**, join in the mockery, joking that **he saved others, but he can't save himself**. Of course, the irony of these words will not be missed by Matthew's readers. Indeed, Jesus' mission has brought salvation to others (cf. 1:21; 8:25; 9:21-22; 14:30-31), hence there ought to be no question concerning his power to "save himself." The mockers cannot envision a situation where one would not want "to use the power that is at his disposal to save himself."[17] So the Jewish leaders assume that, while in the past he might have had saving power for the welfare of others, he is presently powerless to save himself. Hence, he could not be God's Son since God would not leave his Son powerless in such a situation. Therefore, any claim to be the **King of Israel**, bringing messianic deliverance to the people of God must be false. They will only believe if he exhibits power by coming down from the cross. Of course, they are assuming the prerogative of dictating how God's will should be manifested. In words based on Psalm 22:9, they assume that if he truly trusted God, God would rescue him from the cross. They do not entertain the possibility that Jesus' Sonship is most powerfully revealed in his sacrificial mission. For Jesus to **come down from the cross** would actually negate any claim to be God's devoted Son. It is his resolve to remain on the cross and to die in conformity to God's will that provides the most convincing evidence that he is truly God's Son (cf. v. 54).

---

[17]Patte, *Matthew*, p. 385.

27:44. The third group of mockers consists of the two bandits being crucified alongside Jesus. Matthew does not record what they said, only that they also **heaped insults on him** (cf. Luke 23:39-43). Once again the Psalmist's depiction graphically captures the horror of the moment: "Dogs have surrounded me; a band of evil men has encircled me, they have pierced my hands and my feet . . . people stare and gloat over me" (22:16-17). Jesus faces his ordeal without a friend, or even a sympathetic voice.

P. THE DEATH OF JESUS (27:45-56)

45From the sixth hour until the ninth hour darkness came over all the land. 46About the ninth hour Jesus cried out in a loud voice, "Eloi, Eloi,[a] lama sabachthani?" – which means, "My God, my God, why have you forsaken me?"[b]

47When some of those standing there heard this, they said, "He's calling Elijah."

48Immediately one of them ran and got a sponge. He filled it with wine vinegar, put it on a stick, and offered it to Jesus to drink. 49The rest said, "Now leave him alone. Let's see if Elijah comes to save him."

50And when Jesus had cried out again in a loud voice, he gave up his spirit.

51At that moment the curtain of the temple was torn in two from top to bottom. The earth shook and the rocks split. 52The tombs broke open and the bodies of many holy people who had died were raised to life. 53They came out of the tombs, and after Jesus' resurrection they went into the holy city and appeared to many people.

54When the centurion and those with him who were guarding Jesus saw the earthquake and all that had happened, they were terrified, and exclaimed, "Surely he was the Son[c] of God!"

55Many women were there, watching from a distance. They had followed Jesus from Galilee to care for his needs. 56Among them were Mary Magdalene, Mary the mother of James and Joses, and the mother of Zebedee's sons.

[a]*46* Some manuscripts *Eli, Eli* [b]*46* Psalm 22:1 [c]*54* Or *a son*

The passion drama now moves to its climactic closure. Thus far Matthew has focused on the cruel mockery and brutal treatment of Jesus by those who surrounded the cross. Now for the first time Jesus breaks his silence with a prayer of lament that he is the object of divine abandonment (v. 46). The taunting of the soldiers continues, this time twisting his prayer into a request for deliverance by Elijah (vv. 47-49). However, they quickly change their assessment when God intervenes with a series of cosmic signs to dramatically display divine approval of his obedient Son. The confession of the soldiers ("surely he was the Son of God," v. 54) provides a powerful contrast to the earlier mocking of Jesus' claim to Sonship (vv. 38-44). Mentioning the women who watched "from a distance" (vv. 55-56) prepares the reader for their pivotal role in the resurrection scene (28:1-10).

27:45. Between the **sixth hour** (noon) and the **ninth hour** (3:00 P.M.), the land was shrouded in **darkness**. The darkness occurs in midday and lasts three hours, and covers **all the land** (probably a local phenomenon rather than worldwide, cf. Exod 10:22). Although attempts have been made to explain the phenomenon naturally (e.g., eclipse, dust storm, etc.), it is most likely that Matthew intended the event to be understood as a supernatural event. God then sends the darkness either to foreshadow judgment to come, or possibly as an expression of great sorrow. If the darkness is intended to recall events associated with the Exodus (Exod 10:22), then Israel stands under the same judgment as Egypt. It may be that the language is drawn from Amos 8:9 where God makes the "sun to go down at noon" and darkens "the earth in broad daylight" as an expression of deep sorrow and mourning. Whatever the background, the mysterious darkness certainly intensifies the dismal and foreboding atmosphere associated with Jesus' death.

27:46. At the end of the three hours of darkness (3:00 P.M.) Jesus suddenly breaks his silence with a **loud voice** (ἀναβοάω [*anaboaō*], only here in the NT; Louw-Nida, *Greek-English Lexicon*, 1:398; "to cry or shout with unusually loud volume"). He petitions his Father with a lament based upon the opening words of Psalm 22:1: **My God, my God, why have you forsaken me?** The words are actually a mixture of Hebrew (eli, eli," cf. Mark 15:34, "eloi, eloi"), and Aramaic (**lama sabachthani**). Jesus may have spoken the Aramaic form ("eloi"), but Matthew deliberately used the Hebrew ("eli"; both terms mean "God")[18] in order to make it clear why the soldiers thought Jesus was calling upon Elijah (v. 47).

Although Matthew translates the Semitic form of the petition for his readers ("my God, my God, why have you forsaken me"), the real difficulty is ascertaining the meaning of Jesus' words. With the gloom of three hours of darkness and his excruciating suffering at the hands of reviling antagonists, Jesus seeks the reason "why" or "for what purpose" (ἱνατί, *hinati*) God has abandoned him.[19] There seems little doubt that Jesus felt forsaken by God, even though we cannot fathom all that it might have meant to the relationship between Jesus and the Father. Yet, his petition does not express hopelessness or utter despair, but a trust in God's ultimate vindication. The prayer highlights his extraordinary sense of intimacy with God ("my God"), and his confidence that God will break through the alienation he now feels. Like the righteous sufferer in Psalm 22, Jesus can confidently say, "In you our fathers put their trust, they trusted and you delivered them. They cried to you and were saved; in you they trusted and were not disappointed" (vv. 4-5).

27:47-49. The soldiers understand his words as a petition for Elijah to come and save him. Once again those who surround the cross assume that only an immediate miraculous deliverance from the cross could validate his claims. Once they assume that he is calling for some sort of miraculous deliverance, one of the soldiers ran to get a **sponge** which they soaked with **wine vinegar** and **offered it to Jesus to drink**. It is difficult to know what to make of their gesture. Was it a friendly gesture designed to keep him alive, at least until they could see if Elijah showed up? Or was it nothing more than another form of mockery echoing the words of Psalm 69:21: "They put gall in my food and gave me vinegar for my

---

[18]The NIV editors have made Matthew's use of Hebrew in this passage somewhat unclear, putting the "eloi" form in the body of the text here, as in Mark, and relegating the "eli" form to the footnote. However, the *UBSGNT* goes with the "eli" form (as reflected by most versions other than the NIV) and considers the "eloi" form in some manuscripts an assimilation from Mark.

[19]See Heil, *Death and Resurrection*, p. 54.

thirst." At least some of the soldiers objected to offering Jesus any relief, but instead insisted that they wait to see if Elijah will come **to save him**.

27:50. While they tauntingly await Elijah's arrival, Jesus once again cries out (κράξας, *kraxas*) and **gave up his spirit**. The words seem to accentuate Jesus' self-sacrifice by noting that of his own accord he freely and sacrificially gave up his life.

27:51. Immediately upon the death of Jesus, Matthew introduces a series of preternatural events which form the climactic scene of his portrayal of Jesus' passion.[20] The events are introduced with the typical *idou*, thus signaling the importance and extraordinary nature of the events (cf. 1:20, 23; 2:1, 9, 13; 3:16-17; 17:3, 5; 28:2).[21] The supernatural events recounted in verses 51-53 are integral to Matthew's characterization of Jesus, as evident by their causal connection (note causal participle, ἰδόντες, *idontes*) to the climactic confession of the soldiers: "Surely he was the Son of God" (v. 54). By juxtaposing Jesus' death with the exhibition of divine power the reader is led to see the events as God's vindication of his Son. As Withrup points out, "since these are all expressed by means of the divine passive, God is the one who really stands behind the confession of faith."[22] The result is that God once again assumes an active role in the story (cf. 3:16-17; 17:5) to dramatically display his approval of his obedient Son.

The tearing of the temple curtain (probably the inner veil, cf. Heb 6:19-20; 9:3; 10:14-20) from the top to bottom could only be performed by God, and signified the end of the exclusionary sacrificial cult associated with the temple. So in one sense Jesus did "destroy the temple" as he removes its *raison d' être*. As such, this sign anticipates the mission to "all the nations" (28:18-20) in which

[20]For what follows I am especially indebted to R.D. Withrup, "The Death of Jesus and the Rising of the Saints: Matthew 27:51-54 in context," in SBLASP (Atlanta: Scholars Press, 1987), pp. 574-585; important also are D. Senior, "The Death of Jesus and the Resurrection of the Holy Ones (Mt. 27:51-53)," *CBQ* 38 (1976), 312-329; David Hill, "Matthew 27:51-53 in the Theology of the Evangelist," *Irish Biblical Studies* 7 (April 1985), 76-87.

[21]As Withrup, "Death of Jesus," p. 579, observes, "it brings the reader synchronically into the story as a direct witness."

[22]Ibid., p. 583.

all people will benefit from the atoning death of one earlier described as "greater than the temple" (12:6).

The motif of "quaking" is loaded with significance in Matthew's story because in the three instances we find the verb σείω (*seiō*; 8:24; 21:10; 27:51), the event is tied to the issue of Jesus' identity. When Jesus stills the σεισμὸς μεγάς (*seismos megas*) on the sea, the disciples raise the identity question, "what kind of man is this . . ." (8:27). Matthew notes that upon Jesus' entry into Jerusalem "the whole city was stirred" (ἐσείσθη, *eseisthē*, 21:10) and immediately inquire concerning the identity: "who is this?" Finally, the shaking of the earth, along with other events associated with Jesus' death, results in the recognition that he is the Son of God (v. 54). As Withrup observes, there is "a progressive revelation in these passages from questioning [8:27], to inadequate confession [21:10], to a fully adequate confession which coincides with God's own view [27:54]."[23] Of course, the "violent earthquake" (28:2) associated with his resurrection is the climactic revelatory disclosure of Jesus' identity (cf. Rom 1:4).

27:52-53. The earthquake sets off a chain reaction wherein **rocks split** and **tombs broke open and the bodies of many holy people who had died were raised to life**. Just as events having cosmic significance accompanied the birth and infancy of Jesus (Matt 1-2), even so, his death is marked by miraculous events signaling God's active presence. Meyers and Strange observe that in first century Judaism the "veneration of the tombs of departed saints was an important element" of Jewish piety."[24] Yet with Jesus' death and resurrection the venerated saints are given life.[25] Their appearance in Jerusalem following Jesus' resurrection vividly dramatizes that Jesus' death brings life, and thus foreshadows the final resurrection (cf. Dan 12:2; Isa 26:19; Ezek 37:7, 12-14).

27:54. The resulting confession (**Surely he was the Son of God!**) is stimulated by God's revelatory participation in the preceding

---

[23]Ibid., p. 581.

[24]See E.M. Meyers and J.F. Strange, *Archaelogy, the Rabbis and Early Chrsitianity* (Nashville: Abingdon, 1981), p. 162.

[25]*Contra* to NIV there is no "and" in verse 53, nor any reason to see a pause between "tombs" and "after"; see J.W. Wenham, "When Were the Saints Raised?" *Journal of Theological Studies* 32 (1981), 150-152.

events (**when the centurion and those with him . . . saw the earthquake and all that had happened . . .**). Much like Peter's confession (16:16), the truth of Jesus' Sonship is revealed by the "Father in heaven" (cf. 11:25-27). Here, however, the confession follows Jesus' suffering and death and is thus climactic to the story since it correctly interprets Jesus' identity in terms of his death. This is further comfirmed by the imperfect verb (ἦν, *ēn*) which makes the testimony concerning Jesus' Sonship extend throughout his entire life and ministry.[26] Thus, despite the apparent failure of his mission the confessionary appraisal of the soldiers constitutes God's full endorsement and approval of Jesus' self-sacrifice (cf. 3:17; 17:5; cf. 16:16).

27:55-56. Also witnessing Jesus' death were **many women . . . watching from a distance**, in marked contrast to the male disciples who had forsaken and fled (26:56). For the first time the reader learns that Jesus' entourage from Galilee included "many women" followers who devoutly served him by caring for his needs. Usually in Matthew's story "women remain nameless or are hidden in the anonymity of the crowd (see 14:21; 15:38),"[27] but of the many women who traveled with Jesus three are specifically named: Mary Magdalene (i.e., from Magdala), Mary the mother of James and Joses (probably the wife of Clopas), and the mother of Zebedee's sons (cf. 20:21-28). The women are mentioned to establish their faithfulness (vv. 55-56, 61), and to anticipate their role as foils contrasting with both the soldiers (28:2-5, 11) and the disciples (28:7-10, 17) in the following scenes.

Q. THE BURIAL OF JESUS (27:57-61)

[57]As evening approached, there came a rich man from Arimathea, named Joseph, who had himself become a disciple of Jesus. [58]Going to Pilate, he asked for Jesus' body, and Pilate ordered that it be given to him. [59]Joseph took the body, wrapped it in a clean linen cloth, [60]and placed it in his own new tomb that he had

[26]As noted by Kingsbury, *Matthew as Story*, p. 90.

[27]See Chouinard, "Women in Matthew's Gospel," pp. 441-442.

cut out of the rock. He rolled a big stone in front of the entrance to the tomb and went away. [61]Mary Magdalene and the other Mary were sitting there opposite the tomb.

It has been suggested that the concluding scenes of Matthew's Gospel exhibit the following structural pattern:[28]

Jesus dead and buried (27:57-61)
  Setting of the guard (27:62-66)
    The empty tomb (28:1-10)
  Report of the guard (28:11-15)
Jesus alive and sovereign (28:16-20)

27:57-58. Sometime between 3:00 P.M. (="ninth hour") and sunset a **rich man from Arimathea** (thought to be located twenty miles NE of Jerusalem), asked Pilate for permission to bury the body of Jesus. While Jewish piety would have been sensitive to leaving the body on the cross after sunset (Deut 21:23), especially on the eve of the Sabbath, Matthew implies that Joseph's interest was primarily motivated by the fact that he had **become a disciple of Jesus** (cf. John 19:38, "a disciple of Jesus, but secretly," and Mark 15:43, "was himself waiting for the kingdom of God"). The reader may be surprised that a rich man is portrayed in such a favorable manner, given what Jesus said earlier about possessing riches (19:23-24). It may be that Joseph's influential status enabled him to prevail upon Pilate in his request for the body of Jesus. Although the Romans usually demanded that the bodies of condemned criminals rot on the cross, it was to Pilate's best interest to grant the request of one so influential. Nevertheless, it did take courage for Joseph to make such a request since he would run the risk of being seen as a sympathizer with a criminal executed for seditious reasons.

27:59-60. Joseph performs a task usually characteristic of one's immediate family or close followers (cf. 14:12) by seeing to it that Jesus had an honorable burial. He wraps the body in **a clean linen cloth** (cf. Mark 15:46; Luke 23:53) indicating his reverence and

---

[28]See France, *Matthew: Evangelist and Teacher*, p. 133; also Garlan *Reading Matthew*, p. 262. For alternative views of structure se *Death of the Messiah*, pp. 1299-1304.

regard for the deceased. He even lays the body in his own family tomb, thus further indicating a love and esteem usually reserved for a family member. Although most family tombs could accommodate several bodies, since Jesus was crucified as a criminal it is doubtful that Jews would have allowed other bodies to be buried in the tomb.[29] The tomb is described as a **new tomb . . . cut out of the rock**. Not only had the tomb never been used, being the tomb of a rich man, it was probably quite ornate and therefore would have been very expensive. The depiction may be intended as an allusion to Isaiah 53:9: "He was assigned a grave with the wicked and with the rich in his burial."

It was customary to seal rockhewn tombs by means of a large rectangular stone rolled in a slot cut in the rock, in order to offer protection from wild animals and grave robbers. Mentioning the size of the stone prepares the reader for the dramatic events to occur in the next chapter (i.e., 28:3f.). As Brown notes, "The reason for mentioning the size of the stone is to increase the miraculous element in the stone's being rolled back when the women visit the tomb on Sunday."[30]

27:61. Matthew closes the section by mentioning the presence of **Mary Magdalene and the other Mary** sitting just opposite the tomb observing the burial proceedings. Their presence at the burial site certainly discredits any notion that a few days later they came to the wrong tomb. It is significant that the women are present at the crucifixion, the burial, and are the first at the tomb on the third day.

R. KEEPING JESUS IN THE TOMB (27:62-66)

[62]The next day, the one after Preparation Day, the chief priests and the Pharisees went to Pilate. [63]"Sir," they said, "we remember that while he was still alive that deceiver said, 'After three days I will rise again.' [64]So give the order for ... to be made secure until the third day. Otherwis... s may

---

...toms see Rachel... ...e Brown, ...94.

...e *Messiah*...

come and steal the body and tell the people that he has been raised from the dead. This last deception will be worse than the first."

[65]"Take a guard," Pilate answered. "Go, make the tomb as secure as you know how." [66]So they went and made the tomb secure by putting a seal on the stone and posting the guard.

27:62-64. Joseph was not the only one to make a request of Pilate concerning the body of Jesus. The day after the crucifixion, i.e., the sabbath (called by Matthew **after Preparation Day**,[31] Pilate is visited by the **chief priests and the Pharisees** requesting that he place a guard at the tomb for a period of three days. They recall Jesus' teaching, either indirectly through his disciples or more likely inferred from his teaching about Jonah and the Son of Man (12:38-40), that a claim was made that he would be resurrected on the third day. Even though the Jewish leadership view Jesus as a **deceiver**, and give no credence to such a prediction, they nevertheless seek Pilate's assistance in securing the tomb in order to prevent the disciples from stealing the body and telling people **he has been raised from the dead**. Ironically, they seem to take more seriously Jesus' predictions about his resurrection than his disciples did. In fact, the disciples exhibit little ability to grasp the importance of Jesus' resurrection predictions, even after they encounter the risen Lord. For the reader, this fact makes absurd the Jewish claim that the disciples, who fled when Jesus was arrested, somehow summoned the courage to embark upon a scheme designed to recover the body of Jesus.

27:65-66. Pilate's response to their request is grammatically ambiguous. It is not clear if the words ἔχετε κουστωδίαν (*echete koustōdian*) mean that Pilate intended to provide them with Roman guards (imperative **Take a guard**), or told them to use their own temple guards (indicative "you have a guard"). If the guards were part of the temple police that would explain their return to the chief priest in 28:14.[32] However, it seems unlikely that Jewish

[31]As Morris, *Matthew*, p. 730, explains, "*The Preparation* was the day when people prepared for the Sabbath, that is, Friday."

[32]View of W.L. Craig, "The Guard at the Tomb," *NTS* 30 (1984), 274.

guards would have feared repercussions from Roman authorities for failing to carry out their responsibilities at the tomb (see 28:14). Most likely, as argued by Brown, Pilate gave the Jewish authorities Roman soldiers and put them under the authority of the Jewish leaders to secure the tomb as best they could.[33] They therefore secured the opening of the tomb by sealing it with a wax substance that if broken would clearly indicate an attempt to remove the stone. With the tomb securely sealed, and human forces guarding its entrance, Matthew has established the setting for the extraordinary events to occur on the third day.

[33]Brown, *Death of the Messiah*, pp. 1295-1296.

MATTHEW 28

S. THE EMPTY TOMB (28:1-7)

[1]After the Sabbath, at dawn on the first day of the week, Mary Magdalene and the other Mary went to look at the tomb.

[2]There was a violent earthquake, for an angel of the Lord came down from heaven and, going to the tomb, rolled back the stone and sat on it. [3]His appearance was like lightning, and his clothes were white as snow. [4]The guards were so afraid of him that they shook and became like dead men.

[5]The angel said to the women, "Do not be afraid, for I know that you are looking for Jesus, who was crucified. [6]He is not here; he has risen, just as he said. Come and see the place where he lay. [7]Then go quickly and tell his disciples: 'He has risen from the dead and is going ahead of you into Galilee. There you will see him.' Now I have told you."

Although the Gospel narratives differ in their depiction of the details surrounding Jesus' resurrection,[1] they are all agreed that early Sunday morning a group of women came to Jesus' tomb and discovered that it was empty. The explanation given them is that Jesus has been raised from the dead. Indeed, they become the first witnesses of the risen Jesus when he appears to them and shows himself alive. It is highly doubtful that Christians would have fabricated a story that depended on the initial testimony of women, since the testimony of women would not be considered highly credible in

[1]For attempts to harmonize the accounts see G.R. Osborne, *The Resurrection Narratives: A Redaction Study* (Grand Rapids: Baker, 1984); Craig Blomberg, *The Hisorical Reliability of the Gospels* (Downers Grove, IL: InterVarsity Press, 1987), pp. 100-110.

a first century Jewish culture (see Josephus, *Ant* 4.219; m. Yebamot 15:1, 8-10; 16:7; Ketubot 1:6-9; Luke 24:10-11). Although no human actually observed Jesus' resurrection from the dead, circumstantial evidence weighs heavily in favor of its historicity.

The details of Matthew's resurrection narrative underscore the role of women as foils, contrasting with both the soldiers (28:2-5, 11), and the disciples (28:7-10, 17). The story of the women at the tomb is interlocked with that of the soldiers by the common motif of "fear" (see vv. 4, 5, 10). Although both the women and the guards when confronted with the same events involving an earthquake, the removal of the stone, and the appearance of the "angel of the Lord" are both gripped with "fear" (vv. 4-5), the women are addressed directly and told not to be afraid (v. 5), while the soldiers' "fear" leaves them as "dead men" (v. 4).[2] Instead of being incapacitated like the solders, the events, coupled with their divine interpretation, move the women to action. Clearly, the women followers of Jesus function as models of discipleship. Exemplary devotion enables them to be present as witnesses of both the crucifixion and resurrection. Discipleship as defined by the action of these women, consists of both recognizing and worshiping Jesus as the crucified and risen Christ, and being obedient to a commission to bear witness to others (see vv. 7, 10). In fact, it is the commission of Jesus given the women to announce his resurrection to the disciples that precipitates the reassembling of the male disciples so they might be commissioned to a worldwide mission (28:16-20).

28:1. Although the expression ὀψὲ σαββάτων (*opse sabbatōn*) can be translated "late on the sabbath," it is difficult to reconcile such a translation with the accompanying line, **on the first day of the week**. It appears that the NIV translation **after the sabbath** provides "the simplest way of dealing with Matthew's double expression . . . ."[3] Therefore, early on Sunday morning Mary Magdalene and presumably Mary the "mother of James and Joses" (cf. 27:56) came "to look at the tomb."[4] Unlike Mark, Matthew does not specify their reason for visiting the tomb (cf. Mark 16:1).

---

[2]See observations of Patte, *Matthew*, pp. 394f.

[3]D. Wenham, "The Resurrection Narratives in Matthew's Gospel," *TynBul* 24 (1973), 26.

[4]Warren Carter, "'To See the Tomb' Matthew's Women at the Tomb,"

28:2-4. Matthew calls attention (ἰδού, *idou*) to an unusual series of events that signal once again (cf. 27:51-54) the Divine presence. A **violent earthquake** is directly related to the **angel of the Lord** coming down from heaven (note *gar*). The appearance of the "angel of the Lord" recalls the infancy narratives (cf. 1:20; 2:4, 13, 19) where the angel also divulges "privileged information about divine activity that is otherwise inaccessible to the characters in the story."[5] The large stone earlier sealed by human authorities (27:66) is now **rolled back** and the angel **sat on it**, thus symbolizing the triumph of God's power over the futile efforts of the Jewish leaders.[6] The description of the angel's appearance recalls the traditional motifs associated with biblical theophanies (cf. Dan 7:9; 10:5-6; Rev 15:6). Ironically, as noted by Hagner, "the ones assigned to guard the dead themselves appear dead while the dead one has been made alive."[7]

28:5-7. The angel speaks only to the women emphasizing that they have no need to fear (note emphatic ὑμεῖς, *hymeis*). Although they seek the crucified Jesus, the angel informs them that he is no longer dead but **has risen, just as he said**. The words function as a refutation to the earlier charge that Jesus is a "deceiver" (27:63), and thus validate the credibility of his earlier predictions (cf. 16:21; 17:23; 20:19; 26:32). Not only does the angel interpret events for the women, he also demands of them certain actions: i.e., **Come and see . . . then go quickly and tell his disciples . . . .** The women who had come to look at the tomb are now invited to behold the empty tomb. The angel's explanation of the absence of the body is intended as good news that must be shared with the disciples. The women thus serve as "reliable intermediaries who are to link the disciples with the reality of Jesus' death, burial, and resurrection"[8] (cf. 26:12; 27:55-56; 28:7).

ExpTim (1996), 205, proposes that the women come to the tomb "to wait expectantly for the resurrection."

[5]Garland, *Reading Matthew*, p. 263.

[6]Heil, *Death and Resurrection*, p. 98.

[7]Hagner, *Matthew*, 2:869.

[8]Heil, *Death and Resurrection*, p. 101.

T. THE APPEARANCE OF JESUS TO THE WOMEN (28:8-10)

[8]So the women hurried away from the tomb, afraid yet filled with joy, and ran to tell his disciples. [9]Suddenly Jesus met them. "Greetings," he said. They came to him, clasped his feet and worshiped him. [10]Then Jesus said to them, "Do not be afraid. Go and tell my brothers to go to Galilee; there they will see me."

28:8. Like Joseph who explicitly obeys the words of the "angel of the Lord" (cf. 1:24-25; 2:14, 21), so these women **hurried** (ταχύ, *tachy*) **from the tomb**, exactly as the angel commanded ("go quickly," ταχὺ πορευθεῖσαι, *tachy poreutheisai*, v. 7). Their emotional state is described as **afraid yet filled with joy** (cf. v. 17). Although their emotions are understandably mixed, they are nevertheless obedient to the angel's instructions. Unlike the guards who in fear "become like dead men" (v. 4), the addition of joy to fear produced in these women reverential awe that must comply with divine instruction.

28:9. While on their way, Jesus suddenly appears to them and thus confirms the reality of his resurrection. Jesus' salutation, **Greetings** (χαίρετε, *chairete*), is met with an act of reverence (**clasped his feet**), resulting in "worship" (προσεκύνησαν, *prosekynēsan*; cf. 2:11; 14:33; 28:9, 17). Certainly, with all that has happened, their worship is intended as much more than a gesture of respect. They have come to see Jesus as deserving adoration usually reserved for God.

28:10. Jesus reiterates the commission given by the angel, with one significant addition, i.e., **my brothers**, indicating the disciples' restored fellowship. The command for them to go to Galilee as "brothers" re-establishes a core relationship that will result in a worldwide commission to disciple the nations (28:18-20). However, if the Great Commission is to become a reality, it will depend upon the disciples believing the testimony of these two women. As noted by Weaver:

> Mary Magdalene and 'the other Mary' have now become the crucial link between the Risen Jesus and his fearful and faltering 'brothers' (28:10). No less is at stake here than the ongoing and worldwide mission to 'make disciples of all the

nations' (28:19-20). This mission is the climax toward which Matthew's entire narrative drives forward. *And this mission – 'to all the nations' and 'until the very consummation of the age' (28:19-20) – rest on the faithfulness of two women once invisible within Matthew's story and once powerless to influence events.*[9]

U. THE BRIBING OF THE GUARDS (28:11-15)

[11]While the women were on their way, some of the guards went into the city and reported to the chief priests everything that had happened. [12]When the chief priests had met with the elders and devised a plan, they gave the soldiers a large sum of money, [13]telling them, "You are to say, 'His disciples came during the night and stole him away while we were asleep.' [14]If this report gets to the governor, we will satisfy him and keep you out of trouble." [15]So the soldiers took the money and did as they were instructed. And this story has been widely circulated among the Jews to this very day.

28:11. In an ironic note, Matthew interrupts the flow of the story to provide the reader one final glimpse of Jesus' opponents. **While the women were on their way** to obey the command of the angel (v. 7) and Jesus (v. 10), to announce (ἀπαγγεῖλαι, *apangeilai*) the resurrection, the guards return to Jerusalem to report (ἀπήγγειλαν, *apēngeilan*) **to the chief priests everything that had happened**. The guards are then given a commission by the chief priests to distort the truth by contending that "his disciples came during the night and stole him away" (v. 13). Thus, in this final scene when the "chief priests and the elders" gather together (πορευομένων δὲ αὐτῶν, *poreuomenōn de autōn*, cf. 2:4; 26:3), the result is a concocted lie to account for the empty tomb. Ironically, the Jewish leaders had earlier requested a posted guard to prevent the disciples from stealing the body and claiming that Jesus has been risen from the dead (27:64). Now they have become perpetrators of the very deception they had hoped to prevent.

---

[9]Dorothy Weaver, "Matthew 28:1-10," *Int* 46 (October 1992), 401-402.

28:12-14. The suggestion that the disciples stole the body while the guards slept is so obviously lacking in credibility it underscores the desperate tactics of unbelief. It is not surprising that it took **a large sum of money** to persuade the guards to agree to such a deceptive, yet ludicrous scheme. Not only were the guards risking serious punishment if Roman authorities discovered they were sleeping while on guard,[10] they also would have extreme difficulty explaining how they knew what happened to the body if they were in fact sleeping. In light of the possible repercussions for sleeping on duty the Jewish authorities promised the guards amnesty if they stick to the story devised by the Jewish council. Hence, while the women are commissioned to announce that Jesus has been raised from the dead (v. 7), the guards are commissioned by means of a bribe to announce that the disciples, under the cover of darkness, stole the body.

28:15. Evidently, the Jewish leaders were successful in their efforts to promote their alternative explanation for the empty tomb since Matthew reports that their **story has been widely circulated among the Jews to this very day**.[11] Thus, to the end, the Jewish leaders are portrayed as deceivers (cf. 27:63) who continue their opposition to Jesus even after God has validated his claim.

V. THE GREAT COMMISSION (28:16-20)

16Then the eleven disciples went to Galilee, to the mountain where Jesus had told them to go. 17When they saw him, they worshiped him; but some doubted. 18Then Jesus came to them and said, "All authority in heaven and on earth has been given to me. 19Therefore go and make disciples of all nations, baptizing them in[a] the name of the Father and of the Son and of the Holy Spirit, 20and teaching them to obey everything I have commanded you. And surely I am with you always, to the very end of the age."

[a]*19* Or *into*; see Acts 8:16; 19:5; Romans 6:3; 1 Cor. 1:13; 10:2 and Gal. 3:27.

---

[10]See discussion in K. Lake and H.J. Cadbury, *The Beginnings of Christianity*, eds. F.J. Foakes Jackson and Kirsopp Lake, 5 vols. (Grand Rapids: Baker, 1979), p. 139; cf. Acts 16:27-28.

[11]Brown, *Death of the Messiah*, p. 1298, calls their deception "a type of antigospel."

As was noted earlier, the final paragraph of Matthew's Gospel (vv. 16-20) brings together several dominant themes that have appeared elsewhere in the story (e.g., Jesus' authority, universal mission, tension between faith and doubt/understanding, mission of the disciples, Jesus as authoritative teacher, and the notion of "God with us").[12] As such, the final scene is not merely the conclusion of the passion narrative (26:1–28:20), but is climactic for the whole Gospel.

28:16-17. Virtually every line of Matthew's description of the setting for the commissioning evokes, by means of retrospection, earlier features of his story. Reference to the **eleven disciples** reminds the reader of the earlier tensions associated with the disciples (cf. 26:30-35), especially recalling Judas' betrayal (cf. "One of the Twelve," 26:14, 20, 47), and anticipating Peter's restoration (cf. 26:69-75). The eleven are in Galilee (cf. 28:7, 10), and thus the story has come full circle (cf. 4:12-16; 2:14-23). Recall also that Galilee was referred to as "Galilee of the Gentiles" (4:15), thus anticipating a worldwide mission to all the nations (v. 19). The eleven gather on a **mountain**, which certainly evokes memories of earlier mountain scenes as a place of revelation and communion with God (cf. 4:8; 5:1-2; 14:23; 15:19; 17:1-2; 24:3; 26:30). Even the response of the disciples when they see the risen Lord (**they worshiped him, but some doubted**), while puzzling to the reader,[13] is in accord with Matthew's portrayal of the disciples. Their response is one of devotion mixed with uncertainty and indecision (ἐδίστασαν, *edistasan*, cf. 14:31), not disbelief or skepticism.[14] The disciples often exhibited a devotion to Jesus while still struggling with a lack of perception and

---

[12]See Bauer, *The Structure of Matthew's Gospel*, pp. 115-128.

[13]See the discussion involving I.P. Ellis, "But Some Doubted," *NTS* 14 (1967-68), 574-580; K. Grayston, "The Translation of Matthew 28:17," *JSNT* 21 (1984), 105-109; K.L. McKay, "The Use of hoi de in Matthew 28:17," *JSNT* 24 (1985), 71-72; P.W. van der Horst, "Once more: The Translation of οἱ δέ in Matthew 28:17," *JSNT* 27 (1986), 27-30. I am persuaded that οἱ δὲ refers to all the disciples, not to "some among the disciples," who experience "a state of uncertainty about what the recent events meant and what might happen next," see Hagner, *Matthew*, 2:885. But even if the reference involves only "some" of the disciples, the fact remains that the commission was given to a group that included those who were hesitant and uncertain.

[14]Hagner, *Matthew*, 2:884-885.

uncertainty about the meaning of events. It is not surprising that with the extraordinary events associated with Jesus' resurrection they still struggle to make sense of it all. Their response, however, is in contrast with the women who also "worship" the risen Jesus (v. 9), but unlike the disciples their worship was not mixed with "doubt" but "fear." Nevertheless, like the women the risen Christ will demand of them action based upon his authoritative disclosure of himself.

28:18. Jesus announces that he **has been given** (ἐδόθη μοι, *edothē moi*, divine passive, i.e., by God), **all authority** "(πᾶσα ἐξ–ουσία, *pasa exousia*) **in heaven and earth** (cf. Dan 7:14). While earlier Jesus claimed that "all things have been committed to me by my Father" (11:27), his reference was to the Father's empowerment of him for his earthly ministry (cf. 9:8). Now Jesus claims a transcendent all-encompassing authority, that like the Son of Man figure in Daniel's vision, possesses "authority, glory, and sovereign power [over] all peoples, nations, and men of every language . . ." (Dan 7:14). The authority extended Jesus signals a critical turning point in God's redemptive scheme, as Jesus becomes "the one through whom all God's authority is mediated."[15] It follows that Jesus' teachings and commands are invested with divine authority and therefore must take precedence in discerning the will of God (cf. 5:17-48).

28:19. The connective οὖν (*oun*, **Therefore**) makes it clear that Jesus' exalted authority noted in verse 18 is foundational for what follows. Grammatically, the imperative verb μαθητεύσατε (*mathēteusate*, "make disciples") is preceded by an aorist participle (πορευθέντες, *poreuthentes*, "go") which shares the imperatival force of the main verb.[16] Hence, the disciples are to **go** (rather than the temporal emphasis, "having gone") **and make disciples**. The object of their mission is to disciple "all the nations" (πάντα τὰ ἔθνη, *panta ta ethnē*). The earlier instructions to go only to the "lost sheep

---

[15]Carson, *Matthew*, p. 593.

[16]D.B. Wallace, *Greek Grammar Beyond the Basics* (Grand Rapids: Zondervan, 1996), p. 645, observes that "there is no good grammatical ground for giving the participle a mere temporal idea. To turn πορευθέντες into an adverbial participle is to turn the Great Commission into the Great Suggestion!"

of Israel" (10:6; cf. 15:24) are now rescinded, replaced by a universal mission to all ethnic groups. However, the commission should not be construed as excluding a mission to Israel, because Israel is now "subordinated and absorbed into the comprehensive reference to the nations."[17]

Two participles follow the main verb (βαπτίζοντες, *baptizontes*, **baptizing**, διδάσκοντες, *didaskontes*, **teaching**) and specify the means by which the "nations" are to be discipled. The former describes the initiation process by which one is brought into a new relationship with **the Father, . . . Son and . . . Holy Spirit**. The prepositional phrase, **in the name** (εἰς τὸ ὄνομα, *eis to onoma*) suggests that the goal of baptism is to transfer the initiate "into a relationship of belonging to the triune God."[18] Therefore baptism marks entry into a new sphere of commitment and allegiance, in which God's will as disclosed in Jesus, is given priority (=kingdom). Although the text is implicitly trinitarian, the singular "name" emphasizes the unity of the triune God. It may be surprising that in spite of Jesus' words to baptize "in the name of the Father, Son, and Holy Spirit," the early church regularly baptized "in the name of Jesus" (e.g., Acts 8:16; 19:5). However, as observed by Albright and Mann: "The mistake of so many writers on the New Testament lies in treating this saying as a liturgical formula (which it later became), and not as a description of what baptism accomplished."[19]

28:20. Critical to the discipling process is ongoing instruction of new disciples in order to ground them in the authoritative teachings of Jesus. As a discipling manual one could hardly do better than the Gospel of Matthew, which conveniently summarizes Jesus' teachings in five major discourses (5:1–7:29; 10:5-42; 13:1-52; 18:1-35; 24:1–25:46). It is the responsibility of the church to lead new believers into an awareness of what life in the kingdom entails. Observe that Jesus does not give his followers the luxury of selecting portions of Jesus' teachings which please them, while neglecting

---

[17]Hagner, *Matthew*, 2:887.

[18]See discussion in G.R. Beasley-Murray, *Baptism in the New Testament* (Grand Rapids: Eerdmans, 1962), pp. 77-92; and Jack Cottrell, *Baptism: A Biblical Study* (Joplin, MO: College Press, 1989), pp. 11-22.

[19]W. F. Albright and C. S Mann, *Matthew*, The Anchor Bible (Garden City, NY: Doubleday, 1971), p. 363.

the rest (cf. 5:19). Life in the kingdom necessitates hearing and doing **everything** that Jesus has commanded. Jesus' teachings are all-encompassing and speak to the total person concerning how to live in a manner pleasing to God.

The Gospel concludes with the One who was introduced to the reader as "Immanuel" (lit., "God with us," 1:23; cf 18:20) promising his abiding presence with his disciples. Jesus' promise to be with his disciples is "not so much a cozy reassurance as a necessary equipment for mission."[20] The risen Lord promises to be with his people **to the very end of the age**, meaning to the end of time and this world. God has thus vindicated his Son, and the story closes with his disciples being assured of the Son's abiding presence, and the anticipation of his presence in eschatological glory (cf. 25:31f.).

[20]France, *Matthew*, p. 416.